# ORGANIZED BUSINESS
# IN FRANCE

"To sum up, one word dominates and illuminates our studies: to 'understand.' Let us not say that the good historian is without passions; at the very least he has the passionate desire to understand—a word, as we well know, beset by difficulties but also full of hope and, above all, of friendship. Even while engaged in action we judge too much. It is so easy to shout, 'To the gallows!' We never understand enough. He who differs with us—a foreigner, a political opponent—is almost always considered evil. Even when battles have become unavoidable one ought to fight them with a little more intelligence of the heart; all the more so when there is still time to avoid them. Once history has abandoned its false pretenses of playing the archangel, it should help us to cure this failing. History is a constant confrontation with the varieties of human conduct, a perpetual meeting with men. Life as well as science has everything to gain when the meeting is fraternal."

Marc Bloch, *Apologie pour l'Histoire ou Métier d'Historien*

# Organized Business
# In France

BY

HENRY W. EHRMANN

PRINCETON, NEW JERSEY

PRINCETON UNIVERSITY PRESS

1957

Publication of this book has been aided by
the Ford Foundation program to support
publication, through university presses, of
works in the humanities and social sciences.

❖

Henry W. Ehrmann is a professor of political science at the University of Colorado.
His earlier works include *French Labor from
Popular Front to Liberation; The Teaching
of the Social Sciences in the United States*,
and numerous articles.

Printed in the United States of America
by Princeton University Press, Princeton, New Jersey

*FOR CLAIRE, MICHAEL, AND PAUL*

*with fond memories of past and high hopes*
*for future common explorations*
*in the Old World and the New*

# FOREWORD

The central aim of Professor Ehrmann's book is to examine and to appraise the activities of employers' associations in France. He is concerned with French business as a private pressure group—as an organized lobby—seeking to acquire and wield political power. In this respect, Professor Ehrmann's book breaks new ground. Many studies have been made of *labor movements* and their political activities in France as well as in other European countries, but to our knowledge this is the first authoritative appraisal of an *employers' movement*. It is based upon lengthy interviews with 130 persons possessing intimate knowledge of the organization and operation of French employers' associations as well as upon an exhaustive analysis of the pertinent documentary materials which are available. Consequently, political scientists will welcome this volume as an important addition to the knowledge of the role of private interest groups in Western societies.

In our judgment, however, the contribution of this book goes far beyond its stated aim. It provides new and penetrating insights into the thinking and character of the many varieties of French businessmen. It sets forth in a clear and authoritative manner many of the fears, hopes, practices and problems of the modern French entrepreneur. It is as much a study of the philosophy and the mentality of various types of French employers as it is an appraisal of the activities of organized business as such. Although the author says that this volume "cannot pretend to offer a satisfactory behavioral analysis of the French businessman or the much needed description of French capitalism in the middle of the 20th century," it is certainly one of the most objective and definitive appraisals of French management that we have today. This volume, therefore, should be of particular interest to students of labor problems, entrepreneurial history and business organization as well as to those whose major concern lies with private pressure groups.

The Inter-University Study of Labor Problems in Economic Development is extremely grateful for the opportunity to include this volume in its group of related studies on management and labor problems in many countries throughout the world. It is a logical companion volume to Val R. Lorwin's, *The French Labor Movement* (Harvard University Press, 1954), which was also a part of the Inter-University program. It likewise provides a significant comparative bench mark for the related studies which are under way in other countries. We thus want to thank Professor Ehrmann for his very significant contribution to the research program of our group.

FREDERICK H. HARBISON
Member, Coordinating Board
Inter-University Study of Labor Problems
in Economic Development*

*Princeton, N.J.*
*July 4, 1957*

* The objective of the Inter-University Study of Labor Problems in Economic Development is to develop a comparative appraisal of the relationships between industrialization, managerial leadership, and the wage-earning groups throughout the world. The research is financed in part by the Ford Foundation. Its coordinating board consists of: Clark Kerr, University of California (Berkeley); Frederick H. Harbison, Princeton University; John T. Dunlop, Harvard University; Charles A. Myers, Massachusetts Institute of Technology.

# PREFACE

Originally I planned this study as a companion volume to my earlier book on the recent history of French labor. It seemed to me that the lasting impact of the mass strikes of 1936 and of the ensuing reform legislation could be understood only if attitudes of management as well as of labor were investigated. What had been, I wanted to find out, the political effects of employers' reactions in an era which had seen the demise of the Third Republic and opened the curtain on the interlude of the Vichy regime? Moreover in the meantime a thunderous encore to the events of 1936 was being played: after the liberation of France a pluralist democracy had enacted, once more, bold structural reforms whose success would depend to a large extent on the climate of industrial relations. Reason enough to study how owners and managers were meeting this new challenge to their authority and the demands of a temporarily strong labor movement, at a moment when there was an almost universal clamor that the country be given at last all the characteristics of a developed industrialized society.

But my inquiry rapidly outgrew its initial purpose, partly because of the turn of events in France, partly because of the enlarged scope which has recently been given in the United States to the study of comparative politics.

Whether political power be defined in terms of influence and control, or in terms of recognized and accepted authority, the concern with the phenomenon of power has constantly broadened our investigations of the political process. When our studies were no longer confined to the interaction between properly constituted organs of government, it was recognized that organized private groups other than political parties influence the decision-making process at many points. While it is more than dubious whether as yet a claim can be made that the "group theory" offers a conceptual framework for the analysis of politics in general,[1] there

[1] On this point see the very interesting critical remarks by a British political scientist, W. J. M. Mackenzie, "Pressure Groups: The 'Conceptual Framework,'" *Political Studies*, III, 1955, pp. 247 ff. He notes that "one must either use the phrase 'pressure-groups' as a handy and intelligible colloquialism, or go a very long way into the history of political theory in the last fifty years."

is agreement that at least in all Western societies a significant amount of power is wielded by interest groups.

To have made their colleagues in other lands aware that the study of group activities is important both for a realistic understanding of the political process and, possibly, for the formulation of desirable policies, has often been described abroad as the single most important contribution American political scientists have furnished of late. The discovery that pressure groups are not an exclusively or primarily American institution (only the term seems to have been exported from these shores) was followed by vigorous and justified demands that an analysis of the role played by groups in different countries be made fruitful for a truly comparative treatment of so important a problem of present-day politics. But here great difficulties arise.

In the United States the anatomy, and of late also the physiology, of individual interest groups have been examined in numerous and often searching scholarly monographs, which have investigated the techniques employed by the groups in their drive for influence, their internal structure, the ideas of their leaders, and the position of their members. But outside this country there existed until very recently no adequate studies of any such groups and of their relation to political process or ideology.[2] To engage in comparisons before data are painstakingly collected, and initial hypotheses formulated and tested, can easily lead to superficiality and may never yield the postulated inclusive theoretical explanation of group activities in the modern state.

When the present volume became, instead of a study in industrial relations (now confined to Chapter IX), an inquiry into the activities of the French business lobby, I could not hope to furnish much beyond a specialized and in some ways preliminary monograph on this influential interest group. The old maxim that a day of synthesis requires years of analysis could have served as sufficient consolation were it not for Marc Bloch's warning that analysis can be used for purposes of synthesis only if it intends from the outset to contribute towards such an ultimate goal.[3] To interrogate the facts must be the first concern of the

[2] See Roy C. Macridis, *The Study of Comparative Government*, Garden City, N.Y., 1955, pp. 46-47.
[3] See his "Toward a Comparative History of European Societies," in Frederic C. Lane and Jelle C. Riemersma, *Enterprise and Secular Change*, Homewood, Ill., 1953, pp. 518-19.

researcher who ventures unto an unknown or neglected field, but the questions he addresses to human beings and to documents can and should be shaped by his familiarity with already investigated phenomena. In this sense my study of organized French business attempts to be at least implicitly comparative. Without hunting for resemblances, but also unconvinced that French society has nothing to offer but "originality," I have formulated many of my questions analogously to those which have proven useful for the examination of group activities in the United States, and more particularly of American business associations. Numerous footnotes record my indebtedness to such studies, although an economy of space and effort made it inadvisable to spin out, at this time, comparisons between France and the United States, or between France and other European countries.

If the task of providing empirical data is inescapable (and to me fascinating rather than exhausting), the aimless collection of facts will in the end leave the quest for understanding unstilled. Aimlessness, however, can be avoided only if a generalized scheme of inquiry is suggested and if the study is set into a halfway adequate framework of a group theory, whether of general validity or confined to the functioning of representative government in present-day France. But is it permissible to advance even the beginning of such a theory on the basis of a monograph which has examined only one, however important, French interest group? Here again, besides regrettably unscientific but indispensable "hunches," a cautious application of the comparative method has pointed the way out of the dilemma. If I have tried to formulate (throughout the book, but especially in Chapters V and X) some tentative hypotheses about the general effect of group activities in the Fourth Republic, I have been able to do so only by leaning heavily on parallel investigations of the American, and lately of the British, political process.

Though in all Western democracies, and probably elsewhere as well, interest groups play a capital role in the development of policy, the impact they make quantitatively and qualitatively ("how much" and "to what ends") depends on the interaction between the groups and other familiar factors which shape public life. We have no exact way of measuring political power. But it can be predicted safely that where pressure groups find between their demands and the final authoritative decision the barrier of well-organized political parties, the influence of groups will be mitigated—at least in a two-party system, where a complete identification of a party with one, even broadly conceived, special interest will hardly ever be possible. On the contrary, in a system that tries to combine parliamentary government with the existence of numerous unstructured clusters hardly deserving the designation as modern political parties, organized interests may reach with ease into the center of decision making. Hence, in post-liberation France the early loss of power by the parties which had emerged from the resistance period strongly disciplined and coalized, led to a proportionate and steady increase of influence for the organized interests until there is today little doubt that the ascendancy of pressure groups is at least equivalent if not superior to that of political parties.

A possible hindrance to the reckless defense of special interests was described by Max Weber, who classified interests as one of the factors bringing—like law, usages, and customs—order into the dynamics of society.[4] But interests assume that function only where their implementation accepts the restraints which commonly shared political and social values will impose. Where, as in France, consensus on such values is largely absent, the lack of integration will communicate itself to all stages of the political process and will, especially through the unbridled activities of pressure groups, impede the emergence of a setting in which simultaneously ascertained interests could further the establishment of an equilibrium. At this point the study of interest groups can add to our insight into the workings and failings of representative government in France, also because such an approach reduces the importance of the more commonly observed but surface symptoms, like cabinet instability, parliamentary mores, or the electoral system.

No claim is made here that the business lobby is in every situation the most influential of French pressure groups, or that all our findings and generalizations are even *mutatis mutandis* valid for the activities of most other groups. Yet in the present political and economic constellation of France organized business, and its efforts to control or influence, well deserve special attention. If

---

[4] See his discussion in *Wirtschaft und Gesellschaft, Grundriss der Sozialoekonomik, III Abteilung*, Tuebingen, 1922, pp. 15 f.

studies of interest groups can throw the political process into a fresh perspective, they must nevertheless guard carefully against neglecting the cultural context in which interests emerge and act.[5] The mentality of the French bourgeois, which had permeated the public life of the Third Republic far beyond the ranks of the bourgeoisie proper, has once more waxed strong. The French employers' movement represents quite naturally in many of its concepts that mentality in so pure a form that an inquiry into its activities will, it is hoped, reveal much about the environment in which also other organizations must make and defend their claims. (However, the reader may be warned at this point: the present volume dealing with the *organizations* of business cannot pretend to offer a satisfactory behavioral analysis of the French businessmen or the much needed description of French capitalism in the middle of the 20th century.)

Because the motive forces and incentives of the employers' movement are characteristic of a broad sector of French opinion, this study turns (in Chapters VI-IX) to the ideologies of organized business, whether expressed in policy statements or in day-to-day practices. That these ideologies are to a large extent expressive of a desire to preserve the existing socio-political setting may be expected from business organizations. But that they occasionally (and of late more so than previously) also express a desire for fundamental change points to conflicts within the movement, to the complicated relationship between the managerial elite and the general employers' organizations, and to the as yet undecided question of what role French organized business will be able to assume in economic development.

Economists have reminded us that such factors as capital accumulation and technological progress are only partial determinants of economic development, and that the thoughts and habits of people and the nature of institutions which bind them together are far more decisive.[6] The thoughts and habits of French management are expressed, frequently perpetuated, and, possibly,

[5] See the methodologically important introductory remarks in Samuel H. Beer, "Pressure Groups and Parties in Great Britain," *American Political Science Review*, L, 1956, pp. 1-3.

[6] See Clark Kerr, Frederick H. Harbison, John T. Dunlop, and Charles A. Myers, "The Labour Problem in Economic Development. A Framework for a Reappraisal," *International Labour Review*, LXXI, 1955, p. 224, and the authors cited there.

fashioned by the dense network of highly structured business organizations. The important part played by the latter in the shaping of rules which affect economic growth, and the special significance which a vigorous growth has for the future of French politics, are another justification for singling out the business lobby among numerous other interest groups equally worthy of inquiry.

When speaking of lobbies and interest groups the temptation to present an angry cartoon, and to indulge in gossipy anecdotes, smacking of scandal and indiscretion, is always and everywhere great. Also in the United States muckraking exposés compete with scholarly studies, since this kind of investigation must turn the light on some dark corners of the political process and since the "de-mystification" which is a legitimate preoccupation of the political scientist often invites facile moralizing. In France the strongly legalistic tradition dominant in the study of politics and economics has until recently made serious observers fairly insensitive to the informal factors in politics; description of pressure group activities was therefore left entirely to the pen of polemicists or slanderers.

When I began research for this study I was therefore handicapped, though not astonished, by the apparent lack of serious documentation and monographic treatment. Actually, as my bibliographic references intend to show, the materials for research are far less scarce than the researchers. The multitudinous publications of the employers' movement and of its organizational ramifications, government publications such as parliamentary debates and the minutes and studies of the Economic Council, memoirs of businessmen and politicians (especially those dealing with the critical Vichy period), and articles by public officials, have yielded a wealth of information, far more than I was able to analyze in this volume. Nonetheless, the novelty of the subject, the necessarily biased presentation of most printed materials, and, not least, the groping way in which I approached this inquiry, made extensive field investigations necessary.

Altogether I have conducted, in France, lengthy interviews with about 130 "informants," not counting a great number of informal conversations on my topic. The majority of the respondents are officials either in the central employers' association or in the most important trade associations, or they are active in specialized and "vanguard" groups of the employers' movement (see Chapter IV). While a considerable number of these pressure group officials are employers or managers in their own right, I also interviewed a number of businessmen who do not hold, or no longer hold, a position in their trade associations but have well-defined attitudes towards the employers' movement. My most important other sources were high civil servants, particularly from those administrations which have frequent contacts with the representatives of organized business; members of both houses of parliament and of the Economic Council; some scholars and writers in the field of political science and economics; and a few trade union officials.

During my early interviews I experimented with the use of a standardized questionnaire seeking answers to questions which have been discussed in regard to American interest groups, and pertaining to the internal structure of the organizations as well as to their participation in the governmental process. But I soon abandoned this approach, when I noticed that the standardization of questions provoked equally standardized answers, and that the high articulateness of the respondents disappeared behind uniform clichés, so that any kind of "quantitative" analysis would have been a sham. From then on my interviews took the form described by sociologists as "circular response":[7] conversations mostly following and sometimes digressing from an outline prepared by me for each interview, and communicated beforehand to my informants only when they requested it. I re-interviewed approximately one-fourth of the respondents, checking on information that I had previously obtained from them or from others. With some of the younger staff members of the central employers' council I held periodic informal conferences about the progress of my work. While I am prepared to argue that for the interviewing of elites this method is most promising everywhere, I have little doubt that no other technique would have yielded comparable results for the specific inquiry I undertook, and given the circumstances under which it was conducted.

[7] See Herbert H. Hyman and Associates, *Interviewing in Social Research*, Chicago, 1954, p. 34. I confess that the kind of interviews I conducted had much in common with the techniques described by a Chinese social scientist and characterized (*ibid.*, p. 1) as "contrary to our rules and experience in modern survey research."

The amount of information offered in these interviews was almost staggering, and at first surprising in view of the often stigmatized secretiveness of the French business community. One of the reasons for such a loosening of tongues was a desire to explain the position of the employers' movement to an American observer, after French employers had been attacked by American industrialists, government officials, and journalists for some of the very attitudes I proposed to investigate. In addition, the deep, permanent conflicts which exist between different sectors of the employers' movement resulted in a proclivity to analyze the overall situation to an outsider, to offer arguments in favor of one's own position, and to criticize the opponent.

But if such motives existed they are far from explaining fully the amount of support given to me by many leading officials of the employers' movement and especially by its *Comité Franc-Dollar*, whose staff members never tired of making available whatever contacts I desired or they considered useful. Such assistance, without which my study could never have been written, was on their part a gesture of hospitality which they extended me as soon as they understood my purpose to be that of a scholarly inquiry. Our meetings were indeed "fraternal," as the great Frenchman Marc Bloch, murdered by the Nazis, wanted all historical studies to be.[8] In the pages of this volume many of the men who talked to me freely and cordially will find critical judgements that will displease them, or evaluations with which some of them will hardly agree. I hope and trust that they will understand the spirit in which such remarks are made, and will not accuse me of having misused their confidence, for which I express once more my gratitude.

In accordance with the wishes of my respondents I have not attributed any of the oral statements made by personalities of the employers' movement, by government officials, or by members of parliament. Where footnote references are lacking, my sources are usually notes recording carefully my interviews and checked for accuracy with many of those interviewed.

No similar concern for discreetness prevents me from acknowledging my indebtedness for advice and for help in establishing useful contacts to a number of French scholars and writers.

[8] In the passage chosen as the motto for this book.

Messrs. Raymond Aron, Maurice Byé, Jean-Jacques Chevalier, Michel Collinet, Maurice Duverger, Jean Gottmann, Georges Lasserre, Jean Meynaud, André Siegfried, and Etienne Weill-Raynal have all shown a gratifying interest in my study in its early stages. My friend M. François Goguel not only assisted me actively during my stay in France, but has since given the entire manuscript a thorough reading. His insight and constructive suggestions have helped me avoid many a pitfall.

In the United States my friend Professor Val Lorwin has given me that full measure of sympathy of which he is capable. In conversations in Paris, Chicago, and the Rocky Mountains we have discussed every aspect of my project; from one version of the manuscript to the next he has constantly advised me on fundamentals, presentation, and style. M. Stanley Hoffmann, formerly of Paris and now at Harvard, has offered invaluable criticism, especially but not only concerning the chapter on Vichy. Professor Gordon Wright of Stanford University and Mr. Philip Williams of Oxford, and temporarily at Columbia University, went over the manuscript most helpfully before it went to press. In June 1955 I was privileged to present something like a synopsis of my book to the Conference on the Comparative Method in the Study of Politics, held at Princeton under the auspices of the Social Science Research Council. I greatly benefited from the observations offered by the members of the Conference. Conversations with its chairman, Professor Gabriel Almond, who in the meantime has also plowed through the final manuscript, have been most useful. Professor Reinhard Bendix of the University of California, and my colleagues Morris E. Garnsey, William Petersen and Clay P. Malick of the University of Colorado, have read different parts of the study and given me their expert advice.

The favorable winds of the Fulbright program brought Mlle. Christiane Rudaux as a graduate student from Paris, Seine, to Boulder, Colorado. Her labors in checking references, preparing tables, and attending to numerous other chores were invaluable, especially when the courage to persevere wore thin.

In Paris the competent staff of the library of the *Fondation Nationale des Sciences Politiques*, in Boulder Mr. Sandoe, Mrs. Binkley, and Miss Jackson, respectively in charge of the Order

Department, the Social Sciences Division, and the Government Documents Division of the University Library, coped efficiently with the demands of an impatient author. Among the secretaries who typed and retyped the manuscript in its various stages the staff of the Institute of Industrial Relations at the University of California (Berkeley) performed particularly valuable services while I was a visiting professor in the Political Science Department.

In this age, when complicated collective research projects and a highly developed division of labor have become the characteristic modes of intellectual as well as industrial production, the individual who still prefers to set up shop by himself has to piece together financial assistance from many sources. That such assistance was given to me unstintingly from several sides is an encouraging sign that the position of the handicraftsman is not altogether forlorn. The University of Colorado has been most liberal in granting paid leaves of absence and sums for research and secretarial help, and altogether in providing the atmosphere in which research and teaching are equally recognized. During one of my leaves I attended a semester's Seminar on Modern France which was held under the chairmanship of the late Professor Edward Mead Earle at the Institute for Advanced Study in Princeton, and where in talks with my French and American colleagues I received the inspiration for many thoughts embodied in this study. Grants from the Social Science Research Council and the Rockefeller Foundation enabled me to spend the academic year 1952-53 in France. When I came back, my drawers full of documentation, but because of other academic obligations with little time to do the sifting and writing, I might never have been able to finish this book without the help offered by the Inter-University Study of Labor Problems in Economic Development, in part financed by the Ford Foundation. One of its directors, Professor Frederick H. Harbison, then at the University of Chicago and now at Princeton, judged that my findings could have relevance to the objectives of the larger project, and generously extended the assistance that was needed to bring my study to completion.

H.W.E.

*Boulder, Colorado*
*New Year's Day, 1957*

# CONTENTS

# PART ONE

Organized Business from Popular Front
to Liberation

# CHAPTER I

# From Matignon to the End of the Third Republic

## *1. "Capitulation before the Enemy"*

"Money can create everything, except men."
Detoeuf, *Propos de O. L. Barenton**

The official birth of a national employers' movement in France dates from the period that followed the country's victory in the First World War. Upon the urging of the government, the employers agreed in 1919 to join together in the *Confédération Générale de la Production Française* (CGPF). Actually the modern and tightly organized movement, of which the present-day *Conseil National du Patronat Français* is the heir, emerged out of the defeat which organized business suffered in the still unforgotten days of June 1936.

When Léon Blum took over the reins of government, as the premier of the Popular Front, more than a million French workers in all parts of the country were on strike, occupying the plants and flatly refusing evacuation. The sit-down strikes had developed while the caretaker government of Albert Sarraut was in office. To its halfhearted appeals for negotiations between management and labor, the employers had opposed a categorical no. Their confederation as well as the most influential trade associations took at first a rigorously legalistic attitude: as long as property rights were being invaded and a single factory remained occupied, all employers were urged to refuse discussion. At the beginning of June, however, reports began to reach the headquarters of the CGPF and its affiliates that employers in a number of plants, large and small, were granting substantial conces-

* The mottos to various sections of this book are all from the writings of Auguste Detoeuf, industrialist, graduate of the Polytechnique, and, until his death, active in the employers' movement. With one exception they are taken from a collection of aphorisms which M. Detoeuf published anonymously in 1938 under the title *Propos de O. L. Barenton, Confiseur, Ancien Elève de l'Ecole Polytechnique*. Posing as the "average" French employer (and a new La Rochefoucauld) the author, with a chuckle, held before his colleagues a mirror of their individual and collective behavior.

sions to the striking workers. The situation had become grave enough to make a sudden change in the attitude of organized business advisable.

One of the first pleas reaching the desk of the socialist premier came from M. Lambert-Ribot, executive secretary of the *Comité des Forges*, the National Association of Steel Industries—for half a century the whipping boy of M. Blum's party. Lambert-Ribot and Blum, both eminent lawyers, had been for long years colleagues as members of the Council of State before they had given up public office, one to enter left-wing politics, the other the service of a trade association. (Typically enough, when Léon Blum as a prisoner of Vichy related the events of 1936 before the Riom court, he still referred to the executive of the *Comité des Forges* as his one-time *"camarade."*)[1]

Using his former connections with Blum, Lambert-Ribot urged the new premier to establish ("without losing a minute," as Blum would say later) contact between the representatives of capital and of labor. The *quid pro quo* Lambert-Ribot suggested was that the evacuation of the plants be obtained by the grant of fairly substantial wage increases. During the night preceding the official presentation of the cabinet to parliament, the premier received four leading personalities of the employers' movement for a preliminary conference. M. Lambert-Ribot was accompanied by René-P. Duchemin, president of the CGPF, by the president of the Chamber of Commerce of Paris, and by the president of the Association of Metal and Engineering Industries (UIMM), an organization which previously had been particularly adamant in refusing all negotiations with the strikers.

In the streets and factories the workers, materially assisted by the socialist and communist city administrations, joined with the population in celebrations of their anticipated victory. In the chambers of the new premier the business leaders protested against the illegality of the sit-down strikes and described the

[1] See *Léon Blum devant la Cour de Riom (Février-mars 1942)*, Paris 1945, pp. 95-99. The account of the Matignon agreement, as given here, is largely drawn from Léon Blum's lucid report; from René P. Duchemin, "L'accord Matignon, Ce que j'ai vu et entendu," *Revue de Paris*, XLIV, 1937, pp. 584-94; from Germain-Martin, "Le Patronat Français, sa situation, son évolution," *ibid.*, pp. 764-84 (implicitly critical of Duchemin); and from Jean Montreuil (Georges Lefranc), *Histoire du Mouvement Ouvrier en France des Origines à nos Jours*, Paris, 1947, pp. 481-86.

state of mind into which the events had thrown their constituents. They appealed to Blum as the wielder of official power, but also to the lawyer and bourgeois he was. The premier readily conceded that the occupations were indeed illegal according to the property conceptions of the *Code Napoléon*. He did not conceal his concern over the sweep of a spontaneous movement, which for the moment nobody seemed able to control. When he stated subsequently his unwillingness to have the factories evacuated by force, none of his interlocutors insisted that any measure be taken which might lead to bloodshed and wholesale destruction of property, perhaps civil war. A hastily convened meeting of the CGPF's Board of Directors authorized those that had served so far as self-appointed spokesmen to enter into negotiations with representatives of the *Confédération Générale du Travail* (CGT) speaking for organized labor. On June 7, in the Matignon Palace, residence of the French premier, the four representatives of management met twice that many union leaders in the presence of four socialist ministers and under-secretaries of the new cabinet. At the end of long hours of negotiations, described by M. Duchemin as "courteous, difficult, and painful," the so-called Matignon Agreement was concluded by the delegates "after," as the official text stated, "arbitration by the prime minister."

The new employers' movement to be re-formed soon after the events of June 1936 was in many ways designed and determined to "draw the lessons from Matignon." What were then the conditions under which the agreement was signed, what was the frame of mind of the men who spoke for organized business during the memorable night at Matignon? How well did they represent the rank and file of French employers?

Among the peasants of the French Midi the year of the storming of the Bastille was remembered for many a generation as *l'annado de la paou*, the year of the great panic. At least for a time, collective fear and insecurity infecting the countryside like a mental contagion triumphed over any joy in the newly won freedom. A similar panic beset the French employers when the victory of the Popular Front at the polls had been followed by the explosion of the sit-down strikes. More than a decade later one of the leaders of the business community would still speak about the period of "mental troubles" which the June days had ushered in for French employers.

Only a few hours before Duchemin and his colleagues met their interlocutors at Matignon, a conservative deputy had inveighed against the employers from the tribune of the Chamber of Deputies in the most acrimonious terms: "Violence and arbitrariness are not sufficient to justify the cowardice of certain employers who have capitulated under threat. . . . The responsibilities which the employers and their organizations bear for the present situation are heavy. . . . Either the workers' demands are justified, then why has one waited so long without giving them satisfaction? Or they are not and hence merely political. In that case how can one excuse the imbecile cowardice of employers who capitulate under threat?" Such words were applauded by the deputies of the right and of the center.[2] At a moment when striking workers were impinging upon the property rights of thousands of employers, the latter were taunted with expressions of contempt by that segment of parliamentarian and public opinion which usually had provided support for business.

The employers' representatives at Matignon felt shocked and ashamed when at the outset the labor leaders brought proof of the low hourly wage rates prevailing in many industries. In their independent accounts of the conference both the president of the CGPF and Léon Blum mentioned how deeply impressed the employers' delegation was by such facts, which now seemed to explain to them for the first time the gravity of the crisis. "How is this possible?" Duchemin asked one of his colleagues. "How could we stand for this? We have neglected our duty when things like this could happen."

Later the CGPF explained that its leadership was quite naturally ignorant of the situation since the peak association of the employers' movement had left the responsibility for wage-hour problems and industrial relations in general to its affiliates, the large federations of trade associations. But this meant that the representatives of business came to Matignon without any serious preparation or documentation, and with little more than hearsay information as to the extent and character of the strikes,

[2] See *Débats Parlementaires, Chambre des Députés*, Session of June 6, 1936, *Journal Officiel* (referred to hereafter as *J.O.*), p. 1319.

while the labor delegation backed its demands by carefully studied and documented facts. Those speaking for labor could point to numerous instances where employers had already granted wage increases which were sometimes substantially greater than the rates under discussion at the conference.

At the moment of Matignon the CGT had reached probably the high point of its unity and cohesion. The reformist and the communist wings of the trade union movement had merged only a few months earlier; new cleavages which appeared shortly thereafter were not yet manifest.[3] Even in the eyes of management the monopoly of the CGT to represent all wage-earners was so complete that nobody thought of inviting to the Matignon conference more moderate trade union organizations, such as the Confederation of Christian Workers (CFTC). The fact that the government was represented at the negotiations solely by socialists entirely in sympathy with labor, if not themselves members of CGT unions, must have brought home to the employers' delegation even more painfully the defeat and humiliation which the recent events held for them. Although those who signed the Matignon agreement in the name of business had at all times held politically aloof, some of their close associates in the employers' movement had, during the right-wing uprisings of February 1934, taken openly a position against the now triumphant republic and had advocated drastic reforms replacing democratic institutions by an authoritarian state. (For details, see below, Chapter II.)

Before long those who had spoken for the trade associations at Matignon were under attack from their own ranks, because their privileged position in business and in the employers' movement made them presumably insensitive to the interest and feelings of the average employer. With the exception of M. Lambert-Ribot, the pressure group official, the members of the delegation headed large-scale enterprises and corporations located in Paris. All four were connected with industries, such as steel, metal, railroads, chemicals, and electricity, which belonged to the protected sector of the economy engaged in a multitude of public contracts

[3] For trade union developments during this period see Val Lorwin, *The French Labor Movement*, Cambridge, Mass., 1955, pp. 67-84, and Henry W. Ehrmann, *French Labor from Popular Front to Liberation*, New York, 1947, pp. 3-35. An English translation of the Matignon agreement is to be found *ibid.*, pp. 284-85.

and sheltered to a considerable extent from the inclemencies of the economic depression.[4]

The enterprises for which M. Duchemin and his colleagues were responsible did not pay the "exceptionally low wages" which set in motion the general wage increase. Although their factories, like others, were occupied by striking workers, those negotiating the agreement were too far removed from the places of work to resent the occupation of the premises with the same sharpness as did most of the patrimonial employers.

A comparison of the Matignon agreement with earlier legislation suggests that, except for the institution of shop stewards, there was not much new in what the employers had conceded. If collective bargaining was to be initiated and the freedom of association to be guaranteed, a law concerning collective bargaining agreements had been on the statute book since the aftermath of the war; the freedom to organize in trade unions had been granted by the law on associations of 1884, which had also given the decisive impulse to the organization of business.

Yet the statistics of the Ministry of Labor on the number of collective agreements actually concluded indicate that, except for a short period after the war, the practice of bargaining never extended very far. As soon as the depression set in, collective bargaining lapsed almost completely. While some of the trade associations, primarily those in which large concerns were represented, favored "in principle" practices of collective bargaining, their advice was ignored by the entire business community.[5] In answer to an official inquiry, the influential UIMM

[4] M. Duchemin was president of the Etablissements Kuhlmann, the most important French chemical trust. It participated in a great number of chemical and related firms. He also was a regent of the Bank of France and director of other banking and industrial establishments. Before becoming president of the CGPF, M. Duchemin had headed the trade associations of the chemical industry. See his *Quelques Souvenirs du Syndicat général des Produits Chimiques et de l'Union des Industries Chimiques, 1910-29*, Paris, 1942. For the extended industrial and financial connections of all four members of the employers' delegation, see R. Mennevée, "Les Elections du Mai 1936 et le Ministère Léon Blum," *Les Documents Politiques*, 1936, pp. 403 ff.

[5] For a succinct description of such developments, see Michel Collinet, *L'Ouvrier Français. Esprit du Syndicalisme*, Paris, 1951, pp. 62-63; Pierre Laroque, *Les rapports entre patrons et ouvriers*, Paris, 1938, pp. 319 ff.; and Edouard Dolléans, *Histoire du Travail*, Paris, 1943, pp. 257 ff. Both Dolléans and Laroque point to a certain divergency of managerial opinion in regard to collective bargaining. Favorably inclined toward the conclusion of collective agreements was, for instance, the

expressed in the early thirties the opinion that collective agreements had been a failure in almost every branch. Under then-prevailing conditions, with a divided and ineffective labor movement, the association considered the entire institution as worthless.[6]

At the annual meetings of the CGPF, its executive secretary spoke frequently of bargaining as a "danger." At the same time he criticized sharply most of the pending bills concerned with social legislation, such as proposals for minimum wage rates, paid vacations, and arbitration of labor conflicts. The opposition of organized business was one of the factors that led regularly to the defeat of such bills, sometimes in the Chamber of Deputies, always in the Senate. At the height of the depression the CGPF went on record deploring certain features of the social security system; unemployment assistance was blamed for abetting the lazy. In 1935 the employers' movement criticized the forty-eight-hour week: "While in an economic depression overtime is less frequent, it is all the more needed in special cases."[7] During the years preceding the victory of the Popular Front, almost every issue of the labor and socialist dailies reported on the dismissal of trade union members from their jobs. The law of 1884 had become ineffective as a guarantor of the right to join a labor union. It was known that frequently an employers' association imposed a heavy fine on those of its members who had hired an active trade union organizer.[8] For many years the CGPF and the principal trade associations ignored even the reformist wing of the labor movement to the extent of failing to acknowledge occasional letters which the CGT addressed to them.

For an employers' movement which held such views till the

---

one-time vice-president of the CGPF and president of the Coal Mining Association, Henri de Peyerimhoff. See his interesting article "Le Programme Patronal," *Revue des Vivants*, II, 1928, p. 819.

[6] See Conseil National Economique, *Les Conventions Collectives de Travail*, Paris, 1934, p. 212. The quasi-official historian of the employers' movement, Etienne Villey (*L'Organisation Professionnelle des Employeurs dans l'Industrie Française*, Paris, 1923, pp. 333 ff.), concluded as early as 1923 that because of the workers' mentality collective bargaining was impractical.

[7] See the annual reports, Confédération Générale de la Production Française, *Assemblée Générale*, esp. 1930, p. 8; 1931, p. 17; 1934, p. 16; 1935, pp. 16, 18; and also François Goguel, *La Politique des Partis sous la Troisième République*, Paris, 1946, pp. 90-91.

[8] See Laroque, *op.cit.* (n. 1-5), p. 135.

eve of the mass strikes, the Matignon settlement amounted to nothing less than a capitulation before the enemy. Léon Jouhaux, the leader of the CGT, correctly called it the greatest victory in the history of French labor. Although soon afterwards organized business tried to shift to the government the responsibility for what had happened,[9] it was still true that the employers' delegation had pledged to guarantee the freedom to organize and the right to bargain collectively. It had granted at least a *de facto* monopoly of labor representation to the CGT. It had admitted implicitly the concept of a minimum wage, and had opened the gates to further wage-hour legislation, which was to include vacations with pay and a forty-hour week. A decade later one of the younger leaders of management still spoke gravely about causes and consequences of the June events: "In 1936, capitalism signed a peace of compromise with labor. Actually it emerged defeated from fifty years of struggle because it had been unable to voluntarily seek an equilibrium between the social forces. Ever since then it has been out of breath."[10]

For the employers, their defeat in the premier's chamber climaxed the deep and lasting impression left by the sit-down strikes.[11] The entirely spontaneous origin of the strike, though grudgingly admitted by the trade associations, was obvious to all who had been in close contact with the events, hence to many employers. In their eyes the fact that their workers had joined the movement on their own initiative was actually a graver insult and a more serious threat to their authority than if the strikes had been the result of political maneuvers instigated by outsiders. It is true that a political movement, the Popular Front, had enhanced the self-confidence of the workers. But its program

[9] See the collection of documents published by Mennevée, *op.cit.* (n. 1-4), pp. 383-401.

[10] Delemer, president of the *Jeunes Patrons*, in a meeting held on June 23, 1945; quoted from J. Lasserre, "Où va le Patronat Français?" *Cahiers Notre Jeunesse*, July-August 1946, p. 44.

[11] The impact of the strike movement on the employers has been described by Collinet, *op.cit.* (n. 1-5); Montreuil, *op.cit.* (n. 1-1); and Simone Weil, *La Condition Ouvrière*, Paris, 1951, pp. 161-74 (this part of Mlle. Weil's work was first published as an eye-witness report in June 1936). The novel by Maurice Lime, *Les Belles Journées*, Paris, 1949, gives a particularly vivid and psychologically interesting account. Also valuable is the commentary coming from a writer in sympathy with the fascist leagues but full of admiration for the strikers of 1936, Jean-Pierre Maxence, *Histoire de Dix Ans, 1927-1937*, Paris, 1939, pp. 346-58.

had paid little attention to social reforms; its vaguely outlined strategy had not foreseen the use of the strike weapon, which seemed completely blunted during the depression.

To the extent that the strikes were politically motivated, they were directed in the first place against the individual employer and his political attitude rather than against the economic function of management as such. The Popular Front had mobilized the masses after the attempted fascist coup of February 1934; the demand for the dissolution of the patriotic leagues had probably had a stronger appeal than any other part of the program for republican action. The workers resented deeply the actual or surmised affiliation of many employers with the right-wing leagues, and the financial support given by certain business groups to these movements. Employers, who for whatsoever reason were unpopular, were easily branded as "fascist" even when their political sympathies were merely to the right of center. There was a general, and on the whole correct, feeling that management was not moved by any effective loyalty towards the republican regime and that a large part of the bourgeoisie was "by instinct" hostile to democracy.[12]

Once the victory at the polls had been theirs, the workers considered themselves the rightful executors of a "republican mission." Certainly, the explosion of the strikes and the accompanying aggressiveness on the part of the workers were in part caused by tensions that had built up during the years of depression and economic hardship. But the employers also considered the strikes as a political affront addressed to them, a settling of accounts which the workers did not feel quite safe to entrust either to "their" government or to the trade unions, before the strikes which were still weak in most privately owned firms.

In France, as elsewhere, ordinary strikes had become an accepted, though still resented, form of social anger; but the sit-down strike, then a completely novel form of labor conflict in France, added considerably to the humiliation of the employers. A factory emptied by a strike is still controlled by the boss; in a plant filled with strikers the employer has lost his place. His very position is disputed, which is more than the momentary divesting

[12] See Bernard Sérampuy (François Goguel), "Le comportement du Patronat Français," *Esprit*, VI, 1938, p. 660.

of profits. For the workers the strikes were a vehicle of long-missed self-expression. Their self-respect, which had been badly mauled during the preceding years, was won back over-night. In the occupied plants they found an exhilarating feeling of belonging to a new community.

The employers, often voluntarily sequestered in their offices, were isolated and lonely. Also for many of them the past years first of monetary instability and then of depression had left unpleasant memories. Absorbed by a constant fight for a share in an always limited and now still-narrowing market, beset by credit difficulties, cynical about domestic policies, disturbed about international developments, many employers knew nothing about the living conditions and the mentality of their own workers. To them the strikes came with the furor of an unexpected earthquake.

When the boss of a struck plant wanted to leave the premises, he had to wait in line with his employees in order to obtain a pass from the minutely organized strike committee. The workers, while seldom lacking the customary politeness, enjoyed thoroughly and visibly this symbolic collapse of the hierarchy in the shop. An engineer, vice-president of a Parisian employers' association, described his visits to the members of his organization "camping" as it were in their own plants: "In these factories where they knew every corner, . . . the psychological levers of command which normally existed between them and their workers were suddenly disengaged. Their men no longer thought of obeying them, nor did the employers think of giving orders. The employers, who spent night and day on their posts, which had been once those of authority, had the feeling of living in an unreal atmosphere; not in a nightmare, but in a dream or in a play by Pirandello."[13] The workers never tried to take over the management of any firm, but protected and polished the machines, which they would show proudly to their visiting families. This seemed to prove that the strikers did not intend to attack the institution of private property and merely wished to obtain more human living conditions within the framework of the existing

[13] Jean Coutrot, "Les leçons de Juin 1936," *L'Humanisme économique*, 1936, pp. 15ff. On the interesting personality of the writer see below, Chapter II.

society.[14] With the exception of occasional carnival-like farces, when the workers burned top-hatted straw men representing the *Comité des Forges*, there was hardly a disorderly act observed in any of the thousands of occupied plants.

For many employers this atmosphere only added to their humiliation and was a disturbing portent of things to come. The first sit-down strike had occurred in a factory whose owner, harassed by economic difficulties, had almost voluntarily surrendered his property to the workers. If now, after the strikes had destroyed managerial authority, the burden of the new social legislation were seriously to aggravate the plight of industry, what would stand in the way of drastic socialization measures, which the CGT had demanded? The momentary self-restraint of the workers appeared to many employers to promise only a respite before another storm that would destroy altogether the rights and privileges of ownership.

During the Matignon negotiations the representatives of the CGPF never insisted on a forceful eviction of the strikers from the plants. But individual employers frequently appealed to the police stations and sometimes to the prefects for help against the strikers, only to be told that no instructions for any such action had been given. In general, it seems to have been true that the lasting psychological impact which the strikes left on management increased in inverse proportion to the size of the enterprise. For a moment panic and fear of the future struck the directors of large corporations and the patrimonial owners alike. But when it became evident that the triumph of the Popular Front was but ephemeral, big business had little difficulty in finding its bearings. Many an owner of a family business, however, never overcame the shock of having felt his personal status attacked by the June events.

During the strikes a young intellectual, who during the depression had spent some time in the factories and had been almost crushed by that experience, extolled the moral encouragement that would come to the workers from the sit-down strikes. Speaking about the employers she added: "I believe that it is also good

---

[14] This was admitted later by Claude C. Gignoux, the new president of the CGPF, *La France en guerre*, Paris, 1940, p. 130.

for them, for the salvation of their soul, to have been compelled, once in their life, to submit to force and to experience humiliation. I am happy about it for them." The same writer, reflecting a few years later on the reasons for her country's defeat, admitted the disastrous effect of the events which she had greeted earlier with so much naïve joy: "For the youth of the bourgeoisie the shock of 1936 penetrated to irreparable depths. Nobody had done them harm. But they had been afraid, they had been humiliated by those they regarded as their inferiors, in their eyes an unpardonable crime."[15]

The feeling of isolation for the employers was increased by public reaction to the Matignon agreement. Before 1936 they had counted on the general approval of a bourgeoisie which wished to be master in its own house and was more interested in conserving than in building for the future. When Matignon was greeted by a fairly general applause as the beginning of a "new era in industrial relations," a shift in public sentiment seemed to have taken place. As again in 1944, the business community faced at best general indifference if not opprobrium for having caused a grave social crisis.

Simultaneously, the employers felt often betrayed by their own associations. Many employers, though belonging to a variety of local, regional, or national trade associations, were ignorant of the fact that statutorily the CGPF was empowered to act for the vast majority of French business enterprise as it had done at Matignon. In the multiple negotiations which were to start immediately in order to implement the agreement on collective bargaining, many of the same handicaps under which Duchemin and his colleagues had labored hampered those who represented management. The cruelest description of the employers' situation was sketched by the president of a smaller trade association. He pictured the employers' delegations as having almost no documentation at their disposal, as being often unaware of what the new agreements would mean for their membership. "They lack organization and orderly representation; they speak topsy-turvy and contradict each other because of opposite personal interests. Old of age, they face young and energetic opponents."[16]

[15] See Weil, op.cit. (n. I-11), p. 158, and L'Enracinement, Paris, 1949, p. 113.
[16] Colonel P. Brenot, Deux Ans d'Activité du Comité de Prévoyance et d'Action Sociale, Paris, n.d., pp. 27 ff.

Under the impact of extraordinary events the employers' organization had shown its defects, the deceptively impressive façade of the CGPF had crumbled. It became obvious that, in spite of a multitude of organizations, entire sections of business were actually lacking any unity of action. One of the best organized of the industrial federations, that of the textile industry, left the peak association immediately after Matignon in wrath over the agreements. Centrifugal tendencies of other powerful trade associations away from the CGPF seemed difficult to halt. If a unified representation of management were to disintegrate at the very time organized labor was reaching unprecedented membership and unity, the grave defeat already suffered might well turn into catastrophe. Since, moreover, the newly enacted social and economic legislation called in many instances for the government to consult the qualified representatives of capital and labor, there was no time to lose.

Faced by such a crisis, organized business engaged in a thorough overhauling of its structure, its personnel, and its ideologies.

## 2. The Employers' Movement before 1936

Before the business organizations were put to the trying tests which the crisis of 1936 imposed, their structural defects and their brittleness went largely unnoticed. The critics of the movement seemed to agree with its architects that the CGPF had long reached the point where it could legitimately speak for the entire business community. As early as 1929, M. Duchemin had boasted that "the 'bloc' of the French employers' movement is from now on an accomplished fact, a living and actual reality. . . ." And in the opinion of a usually clear-sighted writer, in sympathy with the democratic labor movement, "the individualism [of the employers] gave way to powerful employers' associations soon after the first World War."[17]

Only a few months before Matignon the general secretary of the CGPF had pointed to the fact that the number of primary

[17] See Duchemin, *Organisation syndicale patronale en France*, Paris, 1940, pp. 11-12, but also Pierre Frédérix, *Etat des Forces en France*, Paris, 1935, pp. 88-89, and Collinet, *op.cit.* (n. 1-5), p. 142. More realistic appraisals of the true strength of the CGPF were not entirely lacking. See, for example, Pierre Laroque, "Les Syndicats Patronaux," *Homme Nouveau*, 1, December 1934, no pagination; a short commentary, but among the most thoughtful on the employers' movement.

trade associations in the country had increased from 1,500 in 1919 to more than 4,000. He confidently described the Confederation as "coordinating and multiplying" the efforts of its affiliates, the employers as being animated by a "boundless energy." It is true that, in concluding, the speaker implicitly admitted continuing deficiencies when he pleaded for increased activities of the primary organizations, "the living cells of the total organism." Upon their regular and more and more active functioning, upon their faithfulness to the notion of employers' "discipline . . . depends the circulation of just ideas, the efficiency of common action. More indispensable than anything else is their spirit of solidarity. . . ."[18]

Now it is undoubtedly true that, in spite of its subsequently revealed weaknesses, the founding of the CGPF in 1919 was a significant, if only partially successful, effort at bringing order into the chaos which was characteristic of the employers' movement before the First World War. The new confederation gave promise of drawing together organizations which for almost a century had grown profusely and confusedly.[19]

In France as elsewhere employers' associations had been the result of a variety of defense reactions. This, however, is not to say that French business organized at first merely as a counterweight to the trade-union movement. The first trade associations were formed early in the 19th century during the Napoleonic regime at a period when the individualistic Le Chapelier law was still enforced with full vigor against all attempts at organizing labor.[20] The desire to protect industry and trade, here

[18] See the report on the activities of the CGPF in 1935, op.cit. (n. 1-7).

[19] For good accounts of the early history of the employers' movement, see Villey, op.cit. (n. 1-6), pp. 1-21, and passim; "Employers' Organizations in France," *International Labour Review*, XVI, 1927, pp. 50-55; and International Labour Office, *Freedom of Association* (Studies and Reports, Series A, Industrial Relations, No. 29), Vol. II, pp. 86 ff. Particularly vivid and interesting is Pierre Bézard-Falgas, *Les syndicats patronaux de l'industrie métallurgique en France*, Paris, 1922. The introductory parts of the study, pp. 1-132, deal with the employers' movement in general.

[20] For a critical discussion of the differences in growth and legislative tolerance of the organizations of management and labor, see Montreuil, op.cit. (n. 1-1), pp. 426-27, and Joseph Paul-Boncour, *Le Fédéralisme Economique*, Paris, 1900, pp. 64-69. It appears as if the Le Chapelier law, often discussed as the legislative incorporation of unmitigated individualism, was more than anything else an enactment born out of the desire to remedy a specific situation. See Maurice Bouvier-Ajam, "Le Corporatisme en France," *Archives de Philosophie du droit et de sociolo-*

against legislation or administrative measures, there against foreign or domestic competition, had provided the incentive to seek defense in organization long before the emergence of the labor movement.

Since protection was sought against a variety of obstacles and opponents, business organizations were marked from the very beginning by altogether empirical forms and policies. Such traits were reinforced by the influence of a continuing restrictive legislation which permitted associations to grow in spite of the law, rather than under its systematizing encouragement. Only when the legislative acts of 1884, 1901, and 1920 gradually removed earlier hindrances, were more systematic efforts made to cover all fields of industry and commerce with employers' organizations. The parliamentary debates preceding the liberalization of the association laws revealed a desire to extend the benefits of organization to the small enterprises, since it was assumed that large concerns would find the proper way of self-defense even without formal organization.[21] For that reason, trade associations were established where the prerequisites of extensive organization were hardly existent, and paper organizations abounded at many levels. Frequently their activities were restricted to an annual banquet, giving to a representative of the government an occasion to pin a medal on the chest of a meritorious board member.

Before the CGPF saw the light of day, four other attempts had been made to draw business and employers' associations together in a single national organization. The earliest of those attempts dated back to 1859 when the "National Union of Commerce and Industry" was established in spite of legislation declaring all associations of capital or labor criminal. But in fact neither the union nor its successors were more than façades, and not even impressive ones at that.

---

*gie juridique*, VIII, 1938, pp. 162-63. An interesting account of the legislative history of the law and the text of its main provisions is to be found in Joseph H. Kaiser, *Die Repräsentation organisierter Interessen*, Berlin, 1956, pp. 32-33.

[21] For a discussion of the reform legislation of 1884 and the debates revealing the intentions of a number of deputies, see Bézard-Falgas, *op.cit.* (n. 1-19), pp. 7-78. Only the law of 1920 conveyed to the trade associations full legal personality, which facilitated by the same token the activities of cartels and similar organizations.

Nevertheless, all of those earlier experiments left their mark on the more elaborate structures that emerged later. From the outset, French business organizations were designed to represent their constituents in their twofold capacity of businessmen and employers. At the national as well as at the lower levels, and at variance from arrangements in most other countries, the functions of trade associations and of employers' associations were merged. It was hoped that, when defended simultaneously, economic and social interests would reinforce each other and provide more density and depth to the defense than specialized organizations could afford. This was deemed particularly important because of the known fragility of most of the existing organizations.

Before the First World War, associations or federations which proved particularly ineffective were those that tried to organize the masses of small and medium-sized enterprises. The few well-established trade associations, recruiting their membership principally among large concerns, considered it unnecessary, perhaps even detrimental, to coordinate their activities with those of organizations aiming at a broad representation of all industrial and commercial enterprises. Whatever coordination of employers' organizations existed before 1919 was provided almost exclusively by the personal efforts of a small group of industrialists and trade association officials, prominent among them those connected with either the *Comité des Forges* or the closely affiliated UIMM. These organizations had recognized early the advantages to be derived from a highly qualified professional staff. In the person of M. Pinot the steel interests had found a systematic organizer. Neither an industrialist nor an engineer but the respected laureate of the Ecole Normale, preparing in general for a teaching career, M. Pinot was the prototype of a modern pressure group official as he would become common in the French employers' movement only decades later.

Through the UIMM the Steel Association was able to attach to its wagon a broad agglomeration of other interests, notably mining and a variety of metal-processing and engineering industries. In a self-portrayal drawn in 1951 the UIMM could boast quite correctly that, prior to the First World War, it had played to a considerable extent the role of a general employers' confederation.[22] During that period it explicitly opposed the idea of an all-embracing employers' organization. The pretext for its hostility was that, once such a general federation was established, the employers would no longer be able to denounce the CGT as being interprofessional and hence "illegal." The true reason was admitted later by M. Pinot: what had been repulsive to him was the thought that industries, such as mining, the metal trades, and engineering, would have to bow to the combined wishes of stone quarry owners, the leather industry, precision instrument makers, innkeepers, and brewers.[23]

The experiences of the First World War prompted both the leaders of the employers' movement and the government officials concerned with industrial and economic problems to seek a higher degree of integration for the trade associations. During the hostilities the government had, through its control of the markets, insisted that organized business perfect its organization. Like the system created in Germany by the industrialist Walther Rathenau, the French consortiums provided the link between the individual concerns in the major branches of industry; these consortiums, which wielded considerable power, were often identical with existing or rapidly emerging trade associations.[24]

At the end of the war the arduous but promising task of reconstruction raised the perspective of rapid industrial development. At such a moment it seemed inadvisable to let the employers relapse into their individualistic reluctance to organize. In an official document the Ministry of Commerce described the task it wished to see assigned to organized business as "carrying out general programs which would permit the development of national wealth through the intensification of production, the increase of our trade, and the progress of our economic expansion and of our influence abroad."[25]

[22] See Union des Industries Métallurgiques et Minières, de la Construction Mécanique, Electrique et Métallique, *Brochure publiée à l'Occasion du Cinquantenaire de l'UIMM*, Paris, 1951, pp. 19-20.

[23] See André François-Poncet, *La Vie et l'Oeuvre de Robert Pinot*, Paris, 1927, pp. 259-60.

[24] On the consortiums see ILO, *op.cit.* (n. 1-19), pp. 104-05, and, with many interesting details, especially on the close connection between the employers' organizations and the consortiums, Robert Pinot, *Le Comité des Forges de France au service de la Nation*, Paris, 1919, passim.

[25] Quoted from M. Brelet, *La Crise de la Métallurgie. La Politique Economique et Sociale du Comité des Forges*, Paris, 1923, p. 175.

It is frequently said, and by employers with shamefaced apologies, that the CGPF was brought to life by the initiative of a member of the government, the minister of commerce, M. Clémentel. This, however, could hardly be regarded by the business community as "outside interference." Before and after his ministerial career Senator Clémentel was not only the chairman of the powerful Committee of Commerce of the upper house, but also the president of an influential interest group in the field of foreign trade; he came fairly close to the prototype of the politician who first as a deputy and then as a senator represented all but openly the interests of organized business in parliament.[26]

From beyond the border the example of existing employers' peak associations in other European countries such as Germany, Great Britain, Switzerland, and Belgium indicated the course of desirable action. In the United States too, war-time experiences made the government seek, through the United States Chamber of Commerce and the National Association of Manufacturers a more active collaboration of organized business. The temporarily increased strength of the French labor movement bolstered the CGT's claim to provide unified representation of the wage earners on a variety of advisory bodies, both national and international. This made it all the more imperative to create a similarly unified employers' movement.

But however necessary it was to create an organization able to speak and act for the entire business community, this alone would have been insufficient. The employers' movement could fulfill the functions assigned to it only if the trade associations to be affiliated with the new confederation were strengthened and made more representative. Strenuous efforts were thus undertaken to rearrange them in more logical fashion.

If illusions about the actual strength of the post-war employers' movement were to arise later, this was principally due to the elaborate organizational framework of the new confederation, the CGPF. Its very comprehensiveness gave promise of permanence; the high degree of an internal division of labor for which its structure seemed to be designed gave every indication

---

[26] For some of the attitudes and activities of M. Clémentel as senator, see Villey, *op.cit.* (n. 1-6), pp. 144, 169, and his interesting book on what is now known as the alcohol lobby: Etienne Clémentel, *Un Drame Economique*, Paris, 1914.

that there existed a great frequency of interaction within organized business as a whole. Hence the prerequisites for a truly representative and effective organization appeared to have been created.[27]

The trade associations affiliated with the CGPF were organized into large groups, of which there were twenty-one in 1919 and twenty-seven at the time of Matignon. With one exception, all of these groups were arranged so as to represent the major branches of economic activities.[28] While a large amount of autonomy was left to the groups, the by-laws of the CGPF prescribed that each of them was to hold every year a convention and should designate from its midst the delegates to the General Assembly of the Confederation. The annual gatherings of the CGPF became rapidly a forum for the dissemination of information among the affiliates and provided the setting for the widely heralded addresses by the organization's president.

Each group elected its own board of directors; its president served ex officio on the General Council of the Confederation. The General Council in turn elected annually, and after the General Assembly of the CGPF, the Executive Committee of the Confederation, consisting of a president and eight additional officers. At first it had been suggested that, in order to emphasize to the utmost the loose confederate structure of the organization, the presidency should rotate among the presidents of the groups. But this would have had the inconvenience of entrusting the presidency at least occasionally to the representatives of those economic interests which the best-organized affiliates considered as secondary. As it turned out, only two men presided over the destinies of the CGPF between 1919 and 1936, both the spokesmen of powerful groups, Messrs. Darcy and Duchemin. The

[27] For these criteria see David B. Truman, *The Governmental Process,* New York, 1951, pp. 112-13. Throughout this study I have drawn heavily on Professor Truman's enlightening work for concepts and criteria.

[28] By 1929 the following groups were established: food and drink processing, commerce in food and drink; public works and building trades; quarries, ceramics, glass, lime, and cement; hides and leather; textiles; clothing industries; chemical industries; mining, iron and steel works; metallurgical products; maritime and river transport; aeronautics; cycles and automobiles; precision instruments; book trades; art and luxury trades; finance; travelling and tourist industries; railway transport; insurance; foreign trade; wood (industry and commerce); internal navigation; colonial enterprises; and (the only group not organized along lines of trade) the federation of regional associations.

former, who represented in the councils of the CGPF the mining interests, was also a board member of large banks and had been before and during the war a leading figure in the UIMM. The business connections of his successor have already been described.

From the outside the edifice of the CGPF seemed to be imposing enough to justify its loudly voiced claim of representing French business interests as a whole.[29] Its powers appeared sufficient to "coordinate," as its by-laws promised, "the efforts of all employers' and trade associations." At the national level, the new confederation was able to eliminate or discipline other employers' organizations, some of them survivors from an earlier period. When they were not completely ignored, they were invited to sign declarations of common policy with the CGPF. With other, more significant economic pressure groups, such as the National Association of Economic Expansion, the Union of Economic Interests, or the Committee of Economic and Tariff Action, the CGPF entered into a close working contact, often facilitated by common directing boards.[30] On the lower echelons of the organization the CGPF and its affiliates sought to discourage businessmen from joining associations which refused membership in the official employers' movement.

During the twenties and early thirties delusions of strength were further encouraged by the fact that the labor movement had lost its unity of pre-war days, divided as it was between a reformist and a communist wing. While the government had difficulties deciding which labor organization deserved to be considered as "most representative," the CGPF and its affiliates were designated as the proper representatives of business whenever the government sought authoritative advice. The same exalted place was given to the CGPF among the delegates to the International Labour Office or to the numerous international conferences of the post-war period.

[29] See for instance a remark made in a speech by the first president of the CGPF, M. Darcy: "We are the national production, we are the workers who manufacture and sell; in other words, we are the nation with the exception of a small minority of laggards who do not count." Quoted in Georges Wallon, *Les Associations Régionales Interprofessionnelles*, Paris, 1924, p. 19.

[30] See, for a manifesto signed by an interesting assortment of such organizations, Duchemin, *op.cit.* (n. I-17), pp. 313-28.

Whether directly consulted or not, the CGPF made its voice heard in regard to all major legislative projects affecting economic or social life. Tax and tariff questions came under the purview of special committees established by the Confederation. When monetary and economic troubles befell the country in 1925, the organization publicized its suggestions for an early salvation, criticizing the measures suggested by the *Cartel des Gauches*, and supporting the course steered by Poincaré. Speaking on these and similar occasions seemingly with "one voice," the CGPF gave continuously the impression of an all but monolithic organization.

In reality the employers' movement, as it existed before 1936, never convinced the masses of French businessmen that there were advantages in organization. The same problems, it is true, have beset employers' organizations in other countries. Not only in France have manufacturers considered the activities of trade associations as a possible infringement on cherished independence; almost everywhere it has proven difficult to enlist the support of retailers for any kind of sustained common action.

But in France the bourgeois mentality which had developed most strongly during the *belle époque* of the nineteenth century had survived well-nigh unchanged. The mores of the business community were not altered by the elaborate structure of an employers' confederation and its sub-divisions.[31] Even the better-organized trade associations and their national federations were often, in their consultations with the public authorities, unable to provide the most elementary data.[32] The files of most organizations were completely empty of statistics. Distrust of the competitor resulted in extreme reluctance to communicate to the trade associations any information concerning output, production methods, or other business details.

Everywhere conflicts of interest can be expected to be most pronounced in organizations, such as the normal trade associations, which seek to unite competitors belonging to the same branch of industrial or commercial activity; a reluctance to

[31] An excellent description of the handicaps which the bourgeois mentality put in the way of the growth of French business organizations is given by C. J. Gignoux, *L'Industrie Française*, Paris, 1952, pp. 106-07, 117-19. For general difficulties see also "Employers' Organizations in France," *op.cit.* (n. 1-19), p. 53.

[32] For a telling example see Duchemin, *op.cit.* (n. 1-4), pp. 142-43.

organize will often result from such conflicts. But a higher degree of cohesion will normally obtain in organizations which
bring together all employers of a given locality or region, since
here more unified interests may emerge and be mobilized in opposition to labor or other competing groups. The French trade
union movement has traditionally emphasized organization
around the local labor federations, known as *Bourses du Travail*,
and their associations at the level of the department (the unit of
governmental administration) or of larger regions. On the employers' side, however, the departmental or regional association
played a less than secondary role, although the CGPF had added
in 1923 to the existing groups, organized along trade lines, the
regional associations as a distinct group. The fact that at all
times a rather mediocre personnel was in charge of their activities
was another indication that regional associations were tolerated
as an anomaly rather than accepted as forming the backbone of
a solid employers' movement.[33]

For all these reasons impressive membership figures published
from time to time by the CGPF or its affiliates, and conveying
the impression that the majority of French business enterprises
belonged to its units, were in no way significant or indicative of
actual strength or cohesion. More realistic estimates admitted
that altogether not more than 15 to 20 percent of the French employers could be counted as "dues-paying" members of their
respective organizations. In terms of employed labor force and of
capital investment, the majority of industrial interests might
have been represented in the councils of the CGPF, since the
large firms were organized to a far higher degree than the
medium-sized or small concerns.[34] Yet, as a yardstick of effectiveness such data were fairly meaningless. They rather served to
strengthen illusions from which the defeat suffered in June 1936
provided a rude awakening.

Nevertheless, it would not be correct to conclude that between
1919 and 1936 the CGPF was an artificially created myth

[33] About the activities of such geographical units as the Chambers of Commerce,
see below, Chapter IV.

[34] Some interesting critical figures are provided by Jean Bareth, *Le Syndicalisme
Patronal*, Paris, 1943, as quoted by Montreuil, *op.cit.* (n. 1-1), p. 430; more complete,
but taking the officially communicated data at their face value, Maurice Bouvier-
Ajam, *La Doctrine Corporative*, Paris, 1943, pp. 183 ff., 217-21.

parading a non-existing movement before public opinion and in consultations with the authorities. The employers' movement did in fact exist, but only as an expression of the policies followed by those trade associations or their national federations which either had already been strong before the war or had grown to importance during the hostilities.

It is generally true that, when constituent units exist prior to the creation of a federal body, the interests which the former represent are not easily or speedily absorbed by the latter. The federation can take over only those functions which its affiliates can be induced to abandon.[35] In the case of the CGPF hardly any such relinquishment took place. This meant that, the by-laws of the new confederation and some of its formal organizational arrangements notwithstanding, the employers' movement was effectively governed and directed by the representatives of certain important industries, as before 1919. The steel industry through the *Comité des Forges*, the mining concerns represented by the almost equally powerful *Comité des Houillères*, railroading, the chemical and the electrical industries, and the insurance companies furnished the informal directorate of the post-war employers' movement. The spokesmen for these interests met frequently and reached their decisions mostly without voting and without any serious dissent. The corporations over which they presided were characterized by a great number of interlocking directorates, so that in many cases transactions of CGPF business became indistinguishable from the regular board meetings of the major industrial concerns. Except for the insurance companies, only industry was represented in this "inner circle," with commerce and, in fact if not in form, even banking conspicuously absent.[36] The same industries undertook to finance the entire employers' movement; but where their interests were not directly involved they were far from lavish with their subsidies. Since in general even those large corporations whose plants were located

[35] See Truman, *op.cit.* (n. 1-27), p. 120.
[36] Banking was represented by M. François Lehideux, cabinet minister under Vichy, who was considered by the major banking interests as an outsider. That the business of the Confederation was transacted outside official channels by a small group of influential leaders of industry was told to me not by hostile outsiders, but by the very men who had belonged to the inner circle; they spoke about their earlier activities with much nostalgia.

in the provinces were managed from Paris, decision making in the employers' movement originated almost entirely in the capital.

Especially in view of the general apathy of the employers toward their organizations, this directorate and the staff attached to it formed a self-perpetuating active minority which found it easy to concentrate in their hands whatever authority there was. As before the war, much of the staff work was carried out by the UIMM, which formally "lent" to the CGPF its large industrial relations staff. During the war and its aftermath, the unity of the UIMM had been threatened when the engineering industries had become restive under what they considered the tyranny of the *Comité des Forges*. The conflict had however been resolved shortly with the steel interests triumphant,[37] and thereafter the UIMM continued to assume many of the functions of a general employers' movement. Occasionally such a situation attracted the wrath of the outsider. As early as 1922 an abbot, active in the Catholic social movement, spoke of the CGPF contemptuously as merely legalizing by its monthly board meetings the policies and decisions of the *Comité des Forges*. Implied was the criticism that the *Comité* and the UIMM did not act as a truly federal organization of business, but imposed on the totality of the employers the sole viewpoint of the steel industry.[38]

From yet another side the identification of the general employers' movement with a relatively narrow sector of highly organized business interests appeared to be complete. The significance and the historical development of the French cartels, the *comptoirs* and *ententes*. will be dealt with in greater detail below (see Chapter VIII). Here it is sufficient to state that, in spite of their juridical status and formal independence, cartels and trade associations were closely affiliated. In the words of its official historian, the employers' movement provided the back-

---

[37] For a succinct history of the *Comité des Forges* during that period, see *Le Monde des Affaires en France de 1830 à nos Jours*, Paris, 1952. On the interesting conflict between the steel and the metal trade industries, see Brelet, *op.cit.* (n. 1-25), pp. 98 ff., and Henry Coville, *Le Syndicat des Industries Mécaniques. Cent ans d'action syndicale, 1840-1940*, Paris, n.d., pp. 11-15.

[38] See Brelet, *op.cit.* (n. 1-25), p. 173. The criticism of the *Comité des Forges* was widespread: the socialist deputy Barthe had specialized in substantiated attacks directed from the tribune of parliament against the *Comité*; see *J.O. Débats, Chambre des Députés*, January 25, 1919, pp. 204-14. The columns of the right-wing *Action Française* were not less hostile to the organized steel interests.

bone of the *comptoirs* during the twenties.[39] This is tantamount to admitting that very often the employers' associations were little more than a fairly transparent screen for the cartels.

Between the wars French industry and commerce developed in a twofold direction: a considerable concentration into larger concerns, employing an increasing share of the working force, was accompanied, at least after 1931, by a simultaneous increase in the number of small-scale enterprises.[40] The large enterprises, especially those living to a considerable extent on government orders (usually referred to as the *secteur abrité*), were generally inclined to submit to the disciplines of cartel agreements. But to invite the "dust" of small shop- and storekeepers to participate in the cartels and *comptoirs* was generally considered inadvisable. Under such conditions those activities of organized business that called for planning, energy, and discipline took place in the *comptoirs* and cartels, while the employers' associations as such, in spite of their outwardly complete structure, led in many cases a shadowy existence. This, however, meant that the CGPF and its affiliates no longer functioned, as had been planned, as organizations of employers, but at best as coordinating centers for certain industrial producers.[41] If a minority had learned to show discipline in economic matters, all questions of social policy and industrial relations were viewed with time-honored lackadaisical individualism.

Under such conditions the CGPF and its affiliates could not evoke from French employers feelings of loyalty or solidarity. The great majority felt, on the whole correctly, that their own organizations kept them out of the center of association activities. Since the leadership of the employers' movement was identified with big business, the distrust with which most employers regarded their organizations was reinforced by a sometimes anachronistic hostility toward bigness.

[39] Villey, *op.cit.* (n. 1-6), pp. 162-66. An excellent description of the interlocking connections between cartels and employers' organizations is to be found in Firmin Bassonier, "Les Accords Matignon," in Institut d'Etudes Corporatives et Sociales, *Les étapes de la législation corporative en France*, Paris, 1944, pp. 7 ff.

[40] For figures, suffering from even greater uncertainties than other French statistics, see "De la France d'avant-guerre à la France d'aujourd'hui," *Revue d'Economie Politique*, LIII, January-February 1939 (cited hereafter as *France d'avant-guerre*), pp. 168-72; 221-24.

[41] Very illuminating in regard to this point is Laroque, *op.cit.* (n. 1-5), pp. 32-35.

The "trusts," the "two hundred families" controlling them, and a dozen *"grand commis"* running the CGPF in their name were, in the eyes of many owners of small industrial or commercial firms, just as evil as the propaganda of the Popular Front pictured them. However, such partial identity of views did not induce the small businessmen to espouse the cause of a political movement that had the backing of the labor unions.

M. Gignoux, who was to assume the presidency of the CGPF after Matignon, sought to exculpate his predecessors by pointing out that it was not their fault if the leadership of the employers' movement had fallen to the sole representatives of big business: "It is not true that organically [*sic!*] the Confederation has been manipulated by a minority which ruled autocratically over the destinies of the entire French economy. The truth is that, with the exception of a few carefully organized national federations, the entire French economy was disinterested in its own defense. Every Frenchman is individualistic and the French employer as much if not more so than anybody. While the trade associations were numerous, their activity was small, their means of action insignificant, their documentation scarce."[42]

Given such a situation it might be doubted whether the economic philosophy developed by the leadership of the organization was not merely expressing the ideology of that very leadership. The point has sometimes been made that the ideas formulated by M. Duchemin and some of his close associates were more coherent than any creed which the French employers' movement has ever been able to agree on before or since. The fact remains that there is little proof of an actual consensus about the beliefs expounded by the confederation's president in his annual addresses, always applauded and never discussed.[43]

What the CGPF called its formal commitment to the "defense of a sane doctrine of liberty" was a professed economic liberalism, strongly conditioned by a belief in the beneficial effects of

[42] Claude-J. Gignoux, *Patrons soyez des Patrons*, Paris, 1937, p. 8. More severe for the pre-Matignon CGPF was a Catholic writer, Gaston Lecordier, "Le mouvement patronal," *Chronique Sociale Française*, LVIII, January-February 1949, pp. 67-84.

[43] The following account is largely based on the writings and the yearly speeches of the CGPF president contained in Duchemin, *op.cit.* (n. 1-17), and on an article by de Peyerimhoff, "Les formules modernes d'organisation économique," *Revue des Deux Mondes*, IC, March 15, 1929, pp. 439-50.

industrial cartelization. Much of Duchemin's thinking was concerned with the relationship between government and economic life. The state should be run in an orderly manner, yet as cheaply as possible, so that more savings could be accumulated and more investments remained available to business. Calls for the greatest possible "discipline" were not issued to the government alone: consumers and producers alike should forswear the old Gallic tradition of insubordination and licentiousness.

To the degree the employers were able to give a shining example of such discipline, they could regain their position as an elite in society. The call for the emergence of elites was a favorite theme of the presidential addresses. M. Duchemin recognized that, in a system of universal suffrage, the employers would never succeed in bringing about by themselves what he considered the needed regeneration of the country. Yet, typical of the chemical engineer he was by training, he assigned to the employers the role of a central crystal around which all valid forces of contemporary French society would group themselves sooner or later in perfect symmetry. At this point, as elsewhere, the CGPF undertook to prove, as all successful pressure groups must do, the complete identity between the defense of its own special goals and that of the general welfare. "We no longer ought to limit our efforts to the immediate defense and protection of our industries," the first president of the CGPF had declared. "We have the duty to lead the country back to a sane realism and to awaken public opinion. To the extent that public opinion becomes vocal and active it will be able to give the government the strength it needs to perform its mission."[44]

The approach of the economic crisis, first abroad and later in France, offered an opportunity to clarify further the thinking of the organization. According to the CGPF's leadership the depression did not prove the failure of economic liberalism; such factors as credit inflation, heavy private and public expenditures, moral depravity, and lack of human intelligence had permitted the tampering with the ever valid laws of classical economics. If only those laws were left unmolested, nothing would stand in the way of an automatic absorption of the crisis and of its secondary symptoms. It was considered to be business's foremost

[44] See Frédérix, op.cit. (n. 1-17), p. 113.

task to combat what M. Duchemin would call a "collective neurasthenia" of fear. Government was summoned to interfere with economic activities even less than during prosperous times.

It is true that on the issue of tariff protection and export-import quotas the principles advanced by the CGPF lost much of their coherence. Divergencies arose between some of the influential affiliates of the organization and had to be openly acknowledged by M. Duchemin. During preceding years, the employers expected the government to protect the already high-priced French products by frequently renegotiated tariff agreements which often included the most-favored-nation clause. After 1931 the CGPF demanded, over the protest of certain export industries, that the emergency clause of the previous agreements be used for the establishment of quotas and for the abandonment of the most-favored-nation clause. Such measures were described as only provisional and truly preparing for a new "larger system of free trade."

Where foreign countries had sought a way out of the depression by an increased amount of government intervention, they were sharply criticized, the New Deal not less than Dr. Schacht or the Italian and Portuguese corporations. When also in France corporative remedies for the crisis were recommended, the CGPF and among others the Steel Association protested loudly in the name of liberalism. Corporativism was described as tantamount to a return to the medieval guild system and its tyrannies.[45]

Yet while "guild practices" were rejected, freely entered cartel agreements were given unstinted praise at all times. Already in 1927 M. Duchemin had invited his colleagues in somewhat vague terms to "reach an understanding so as to avoid unnecessary and hazardous competition and to distribute among them . . . the different elements of production." A year later he exhorted the "producers of the same branches" to organize "in common" the activities of their factories. At the height of the depression he expressed the belief that the cartels were eminently useful and that, wherever they could be formed, they were apt to let "order

---

[45] Note the exceptionally vehement tone in which M. Duchemin used to denounce corporatism in one of his early addresses, generally most moderate in tone. *Op.cit.* (n. 1-17), pp. 200-02. In a similar vein Marcel Tardy and E. Bonnefous, in *Le Corporatisme*, Paris, 1935, published as a supplement to the *Bulletin Quotidien*, sponsored by the *Comité des Forges*.

and discipline rule, where anarchy and confusion had reigned
before." Here again the government was asked not to interfere.
Except for willful abuses, which could be checked by the provisions of the criminal code, there should be no regulation of the
self-chosen activities of the cartels. Cartels extending beyond the
national borders and comprising the major European powers
were recommended as a remedy for the disruption of trade and
as the trail blazers for a full-fledged European customs union,
administered by business.

In his yearly addresses M. Duchemin never tired of highlight-
ing, in the tone of moral and intellectual superiority in which he
excelled, the many contradictions he discovered in the attitudes
and outlook of his fellow Frenchmen. To the leaders of the CGPF
it did not occur that simultaneously to espouse economic liberalism and believe in the benefits of a powerful cartel system might
have exposed them to the reproach of being similarly inconsist-
ent. To the query whether cartel agreements would not interfere
with the "classical laws" of laissez faire, they would have retorted without flinching that, because of the very nature of their
interests, producers would never disturb the workings of the
economic mechanism. In their eyes liberty was safeguarded as
long as the government refrained from controlling business and
business agreements.

The doctrine presented by the leadership of the CGPF did not
alone suffer from its internal contradictions. It had little meaning for the actual practices of the major trade associations forming the backbone of the employers' movement, and was ignored
by the majority of French businessmen. Therefore it is not
astonishing that this self-styled "neo-liberalism" did not survive
the shock suffered in 1936. Different forms of a corporative philosophy, artificially suppressed while M. Duchemin held the reins,
swept aside the Manchesterian credo that had become hollow
long ago.

After an existence of more than fifteen years, the CGPF had
proven unable to fulfill most of the functions which the government had assigned to it at the end of the First World War.
Where it wanted to act as a spokesman for the employers in
general, it was not really considered or respected as such—and
from within the business community it was so considered and

respected less than from without. Where it was expected to develop constructive action in the field of economics or industrial relations, it lacked realistic theory as well as the means of action. In the contemptuous words of a businessman who had been active in the employers' movement: "The [pre-Matignon] CGPF was never anything but a sort of central information agency, preaching to the employers the advantages of unity, tendering advice to the public authorities if the government happened to ask for such advice, from time to time admonishing its constituents—but with so feeble and uncertain a voice that it was never heard far away."[46]

### 3. Reorganization and Reorientation

"The decision one takes is of little importance:
What matters is to live up to it."
          Detoeuf, *Propos de O. L. Barenton*

The transformation of the French employers' movement took place in two phases: a few weeks after the Matignon agreement the name, the by-laws, and the structure of the CGPF were changed. In October 1936 M. Duchemin resigned his function as president of the confederation and opened thereby the way for a significant turnover in the leadership of many business organizations. The withdrawal of M. Duchemin from the presidency was clearly a resignation under pressure. The farewell speech which the former president made before the newly formed General Council hardly concealed the fact that he considered himself the victim of a palace revolution.[47] He acknowledged that not only was he saddled with the heavy responsibilities incurred by the signing of the Matignon agreement, but also that there existed between him and many members of the new Council fundamental differences as to tactics and doctrine. Under those circumstances M. Duchemin feared that his usefulness as an arbiter between conflicting interests was dangerously impaired.

Activated by the crisis of 1936, the vast majority of employers had turned almost angrily against their former leaders.[48] The

---

[46] Jean Mersch (one-time president of the *Jeune Patron*, which formed an integral part of the CGPF), "Le Syndicalisme Patronal depuis les hostilités," *Le Droit Social*, IV, 1941, p. 68.

[47] See Duchemin, *op.cit.* (n. 1-17), pp. 272-76.

[48] In the words of an official of one of the minor trade associations, the former masters of the CGPF had been the "overlords of big industry" and were animated

previous officials of their organizations were suddenly recognized as what they always had been: representatives of certain corporate interests who could maintain themselves as spokesmen for the entire business community only as long as their position was not challenged. Within a few months after Matignon, all those who had signed the agreement in the name of management had been dropped from their erstwhile positions, with the significant exception of M. Lambert-Ribot. A pressure group official himself, he was closer to the personalities who were now becoming prominent in the employers' movement.

Claude J. Gignoux, who assumed the presidency of the transformed CGPF, was the prototype of the new leadership. He was characterized by a political opponent as "one of those people who are strangers among the employers and strangers to industry, but who either by partisanship or because of doctrinal fanaticism sometimes bring to the defense of employers' interest more acrimony than the employers themselves."[49] What Léon Blum failed to acknowledge was that the "employers themselves" entrusted M. Gignoux with his new position. In a situation in which they felt that the authority of management, and perhaps even the institution of private property, were threatened, they preferred to see their interests in the hands of somebody who was not himself identified with any of the possibly conflicting subgroups of business and who would therefore rise more easily to the defense of the employers as a class.

M. Gignoux's past career also seemed to promise success in the political arena, where management was to seek, first, protection against further assaults and, later possibly, revenge for the defeat it had suffered. As a conservative deputy of the Loire Department after the war, M. Gignoux had served in Laval's first cabinet as a member of the premier's brain trust in economic affairs. Beaten in subsequent elections, the former graduate of the Paris Law School, who had at one time taught economics in provincial universities, turned to pressure group journalism. Until 1936 he edited with great ability and tact the daily *Journée Industrielle*, which during its long history was subsidized by a

by a "caste spirit," by "egoism and arrogance. . . ." See Pierre Nicolle, *Cinquante Mois d'Armistice*, Paris, 1947, Vol. I, p. 8.

[49] See Léon Blum, *op.cit.* (n. 1-1), p. 133.

variety of industrial interests and was not as exclusively identified with heavy industry like *Le Temps* or the *Bulletin Quotidien*.[50] Numerous books showed M. Gignoux to be a writer of some distinction and with a passion for history. Whatever his opportunism, it was obvious that he had recognized more realistically than the past president of the CGPF the transformation which the capitalistic system had undergone since the days of laissez faire. But only after the demise of the Third Republic would he openly express the corporatist beliefs that must have been his long before.[51]

With him M. Gignoux brought to posts of responsibility in the CGPF a host of people of similar background, though seldom similarly gifted. Younger in age than the previous staff, more energetic, authoritarian rather than paternalistic, most of these *homines novi* were trained in engineering or public relations rather than in business. Within the major national trade associations and industrial federations changes in personnel were less frequent or less drastic, for the simple reason that many of them had already before 1936 employed the services of *"agents,"* or pressure group officials.[52]

The changes in the by-laws and in the structure of the CGPF all indicated the desire of creating the broadest possible representation of business.[53] The name of the Confederation was modified to read *Patronat* rather than *Production* (the initials remaining

---

[50] Most of the biographical data were taken from A. Hamon, *Les Maîtres de la France*, Paris, 1935-36, Vol. II, pp. 122-23. While generally informative, the statements by this left-wing author should be used with caution. He errs, for instance, when he describes the *Journée Industrielle* as entirely controlled by the *Comité des Forges*. More reliable on this point is Brelet, *op.cit.* (n. 1-25), p. 127.

[51] Prominent among Gignoux's early writings is his *L'Après-Guerre et la Politique Commerciale*, Paris, 1924. Since then his books have ranged over a great number of economic and historical topics. In 1943 M. Gignoux spoke (in his preface to Jacques Basset, *Travail et Propriété. Actualité Révolutionnaire de la Tour du Pin*, Paris, 1943, pp. v, vi) about the "bastard regime, honorably qualified as liberalism, under which we lived before the war . . . a non-authentic liberalism."

[52] Lucien Romier, Gignoux's predecessor as editor of the *Journée Industrielle*, gave this definition: "One calls *'agents'* of the industrial and financial aristocracy all those who owe their place [in this aristocracy] to some other virtues than a package of shares negotiable in the stock exchange." See *L'Opinion*, December 22, 1922. Quoted here from Brelet, *op.cit* (n. 1-25), p. 101.

[53] The by-laws of the Confederation, first drastically changed in August 1936, were again revamped in 1938. For their texts and some comments comparing the structure of the old CGPF and the new, see Duchemin, *op.cit.* (n. 1-17), pp. 265-71, 288-309.

unchanged), not alone because the former name did not give sufficient recognition to commerce. By stressing the employers' function of businessmen, the new designation was to symbolize the increased role which the reorganized Confederation wished to play in the field of industrial relations rather than merely in the defense of economic interests.

In order to make room for large and small firms, for industry and commerce alike, the membership of the new General Council was substantially increased. Big business interests were to be diluted in the Council, which was vested with new functions. The "groups" continued to form the constituent elements of the Confederation but were redesigned to represent industry and trade of the same branch in order to merge, whenever possible, their respective interests.

Very strenuous efforts were made to give to the small and medium-sized firms a prominent place at all levels of the employers' movement. From that milieu had come the most violent complaints about the Matignon agreement. Fearful of the consequences of the new social legislation, small businessmen felt sold short and often continued to believe in the existence of a "plot between the 200 families and the Marxist government." Now that the events had frightened this group out of its traditional indifference and inarticulateness, it was important to overcome its diffidence towards employers' organizations.

France has remained a country where an aureole surrounds everything that is small. When the employers' movement found it necessary to transfer at least part of its activities to the political field, it was advantageous to give the largest possible place and voice to the representatives of small enterprises, all the more since within the Popular Front coalition the radical-socialist party had a clientele of petty bourgeois elements. Addressing a meeting of the CGPF, the new president of the organization asked the delegates of big business "to withdraw from the control of the important trade associations and to leave a predominant influence to the owners of small and medium-sized enterprises, to whom big business will continue to provide advice and whole-hearted assistance."[54] For the first time there appeared on the

[54] See *Revue Générale des Industries Radio-Eléctriques*, 1936, as quoted in *La Tribune des Fonctionnaires*, 28 November 1936. For efforts undertaken by the

roster of the Confederation the name of M. Gingembre, who was to play a considerable role in the "small business" movement of the future.

On the lower levels the employers' movement was redesigned in order to match the corresponding organization of the CGT. It was understood that the desirable cohesion of the movement could be obtained only if the primary single-trade associations and the local or regional inter-trade organizations were to be solidly built. Previous inequalities, where some federations could rely on strong associations while others remained mere façades, had to be eliminated. "Employers, be employers," urged M. Gignoux, "rally around your associations. . . . There must be no more isolation."[55]

At the top the Executive of the Confederation was completely redesigned. All major business interests were represented, yet the Board remained manageable in size so as to play an effective role in decision making. To an increasing extent, the Executive was no longer composed of the presidents of federations and of groups, usually active businessmen, but of the ranking members of the professional staff of the associations. At the same time the presidency of the Confederation was greatly strengthened by the new by-laws, which tried to strike a balance between freedom and discipline when they stipulated: "The largest autonomy is left to all constituent organizations. However, the organizations constituting the CGPF pledge to submit to the president of the CGPF, prior to any definitive decisions on their part, all those questions which involve a principle of important consequence for the economic life in its entirety. . . ."

A new "Social Service" was given particular prominence under the direction of the energetic, if autocratic, Baron Petiet, who now served as a deputy general for industrial relations in addition to his function as executive of the important trade association for the automotive industry. The Confederation urged its member organizations to turn for advice to this new service, so that all important questions of social policy could be properly coordinated.

---

UIMM to give more room to the representatives of small business, see UIMM, *op.cit.* (n. 1-22), p. 45.

[55] See Gignoux, *op.cit.* (n. 1-42), p. 45.

The new Confederation was most successful in preventing any broadening of the gains which labor had obtained in the summer of 1936. It refused adamantly to enter into any new national agreement or even to negotiate with its counterpart, the CGT. Since the hostility of its constituents to Matignon had been among the most important motives for the changes in organization and leadership, the CGPF flatly turned down requests by the government to facilitate the working of the new social legislation through a new and more elaborate understanding with labor. Gignoux declared that his organization was unwilling to obligate once more all of French management by its signature and to give to the CGT, where now the communists were in ascendancy, a new claim to the monopoly of labor representation.[56] There were no longer, it is true, millions of strikers occupying thousands of plants in all of France. The refusal of the employers' organizations left the government no choice but to introduce new legislation concerned with arbitration and conciliation of labor conflicts. When this legislation yielded on the whole unsatisfactory results, the employers' movement was prone to reproach the government for too much interference in industrial relations.[57]

Because of their reluctance to meet organized labor on a national level, the employers' federations refused to conclude collective agreements with the corresponding national trade union federations. Where occasionally one of the national trade associations was inclined to enter into such an agreement, the resistance coming from primary trade associations and the warnings from the CGPF always prevented nation-wide collective bargaining. At the same time, a number of local or regional employers' associations seem to have dissolved their organizations after 1936 so as to avoid signing the collective agreements which were required under the new legislation. Local trade associations had sometimes to be reminded by the courts that it was their duty to communicate to their members the terms of an arbitration

[56] See Claude-J. Gignoux, "Le Statut Moderne du travail," *Revue Politique et Parlementaire*, CLXXIV, 1938, pp. 201-14, and, for a general comment on the employers' attitude towards the proposed statute, Georges Lefranc, *Les Expériences Syndicales en France de 1939 à 1950*, Paris, 1950, pp. 244-45.

[57] See Lorwin, *op.cit.* (n. 1-3), pp. 76-79, and Ehrmann, *op.cit.* (n. 1-3), pp. 47-49.

award.[58] "I am not sure," remarked one progressive industrialist, "that bad faith is to be found only on the side of the workers. . . . We are still very much at the beginning of an era of good faith . . . also on the employers' side there are too many cases of trickery. It is true that the labor press generalizes such cases out of proportion."[59]

The new CGPF concentrated all means of action at its disposal against a bill concerned with hiring and firing of workers and particularly with making the use of public employment exchanges compulsory. The CGT had urged such an enactment when its affiliated unions complained only a few months after the Matignon agreement that systematic lay-offs of trade union members were taking place in many plants. The CGPF and its affiliates decided that this was an issue on which the near totality of employers could be aroused, since the proposed law involved the right of the employer to choose his workers. By giving wide publicity to the messages which Gignoux addressed to the government, by a number of public meetings held in Paris as well as in the provinces, by employers' delegations pleading with the authorities on the departmental level, enough direct and indirect pressure was brought upon parliament, and especially upon the Senate, to prevent the adoption of the law.[60]

In spite of all this, the internal cohesion and discipline of the employers' movement remained unsatisfactory. Many of the objectives which the new CGPF strove to achieve were never attained.

There have been in the history of organized business in France at least four new departures: one initiated by the formation of the first General Confederation in 1919, the one brought about

[58] For details, see Lecordier, *op.cit.* (n. 1-42), pp. 76-79. For a warning addressed to an employer syndicate and describing a fairly typical situation, see the decision of the *Cour Supérieur d'Arbitrage* of March 29, 1939, published in *Le Droit Social*, II, 1939, p. 293. A general criticism of the new collective bargaining agreements, especially as applied to small enterprises, was formulated by a spokesman for the employers, Alban de Canisy, "Le Contrat Collectif," *Revue des Deux Mondes*, CVI, October 15, 1936, pp. 887-98. See also, as one example of many, the almost irate discussion on collective bargaining in the General Assembly of the Textile Union of December 1937, *Bulletin Mensuel de l'Union des Syndicats patronaux des Industries Textiles de France*, IXXX, 1937, pp. 463-64.

[59] Auguste Detoeuf, in Paul Planus, *Patrons et Ouviers en Suède*, Paris, 1938, p. 11.

[60] See, also for the following, the excellent account given in Noël Regis, "L'Autorité Patronale est-elle menacée ?" *Esprit*, VI, 1938, pp. 556-77.

by the crisis of 1936, another sponsored by the legislation of Vichy, and finally the emergence of the present-day National Council during the early days of the Fourth Republic. Each of these fresh starts was heralded as overcoming the weaknesses which the movement had shown in the preceding phase, and as guaranteeing the emergence of a movement truly equipped to fulfill its tasks. But so far, at the end of each period, it had to be admitted that once more the organization had fallen short of its goal and had not proven equal to needs.

In spite of arduous efforts M. Gignoux was unable to bring back to the fold of the general employers' movement the important textile industry, which, next to the steel industry, could boast the densest network of well-organized trade associations. The extreme individualism prevalent in an industry still largely imbued with traditions of stern paternalism made the integration of the industry into a general employers' movement difficult from the start. The progressive cartelization of French industry alienated the textile industries further from their brethren. With the exception of the wool industry, where the trends toward a corporative organization had been notorious, the various textile industries resisted over-all cartelization and resented such developments when they took place elsewhere among organized business.[61] The loss of so large a sector of economic activities impaired the prestige of the CGPF and represented a serious defect for a movement that pretended to have achieved completeness of representation and membership discipline.

The attempts made to mobilize the small and medium-sized enterprises for the employers' movement met with varying, but on the whole unsatisfactory, success. Except for handicraft establishments, the Popular Front legislation did not actually lead to the anticipated elimination of smaller business firms. If it had any effect at all on the business structure, the new legislation resulted rather in a widespread subcontracting from the larger

[61] A convincing picture of a typical family enterprise in the textile business of northern France is drawn in André Maurois's novel *Bernard Quesnay*, Paris, 1928. The extremely authoritarian attitude characteristic of many employers in the North after 1936 was described by Blum, *op.cit.* (n. 1-1), p. 187. Early differences between the CGPF and the textile industry were reflected in President Duchemin's annual addresses; see *op.cit.* (n. 1-17), pp. 132, 201, and passim. For the attitudes of the textile industry towards cartel agreements, see Marc Aucuy, "Structure industrielle," *France d'avant-guerre, op.cit.* (n. 1-40), pp. 185-86.

to the smaller enterprises, presumably because the new work-hour and shop steward legislation was applied less strictly in the smaller firms.[62]

Nevertheless, the consequences of the social reforms and the new status of labor had an important impact on the mentality of these businessmen. The resentment over the sit-down strikes was frequently aggravated by the unionization of labor even in small enterprises. The bureaucratization of economic life, which so far had often spared the smaller firms, was now rapidly engulfing them. The inflationary spiral of wages and prices which the Popular Front experiment set loose anew resulted in credit and market difficulties with which the small businessmen were poorly equipped to cope. There was evidence that quite frequently small firms were reluctant to accept new orders if this involved more red tape or protracted negotiations with labor exchanges or trade unions.[63]

Many of the owners of modest enterprises complained that the difficulties which they had to face day after day resulted in so much overwork that they felt more isolated than ever and had no time to spare for activities in their own associations, although the employers' movement made efforts to assist them. There was, however, more than a lack of time which prevented the small and medium-sized firms from giving active support to their organizations. The solidarity of interest, created temporarily by dramatic defeat, gave way soon to the Gallic inclination to be happy over the neighbor's misfortune. Seldom did economic difficulties lead to greater discipline. In most cases hardship resulted in strengthening egotism, and the trade associations were resented as always helping out—the competitor.[64]

[62] See *ibid.*, pp. 259-60.

[63] For typical complaints see *ibid.*, p. 193, and Weil, *op.cit.* (n. 1-11), pp. 188-90. M. Detoeuf, director of a major electrical concern, admitted (*ibid.*) that the extreme bitterness of the businessmen, whose conversation Mlle. Weil had overheard, and their reluctance to take on new orders, "reflected a very widespread state of mind." Elsewhere M. Detoeuf denied that the employers engaged in anything like a sabotage of production. See his "Sabotage Ouvrier? Sabotage Patronal?" *Nouveaux Cahiers*, No. 13, November 1, 1937, pp. 11-12.

[64] See the very cogent characterization of his colleagues by an active businessman, J. Barnaud, "L'Industriel," *ibid.*, No. 2, April 1, 1937, pp. 11-12. A remarkable analysis of the different types of employers and their behavior pattern during the period here discussed is provided by Bernard Serampuy, *op.cit.* (n. 1-12), pp. 657-67. In another analysis the same writer (F. Goguel) concluded, "The individualism of French management adapted itself to the new condition without really disappearing." *Op.cit.* (n. 1-7), p. 102.

Moreover, the attempted modernization of the CGPF and of its affiliates necessarily involved a greater need for information from the membership on business conditions, production plans, and sales. The CGPF had organized a special service for the mediation of possible conflicts between member organizations; the compromise solutions it would suggest were to involve sacrifices for some of the interests concerned. But very often such advice or the request for information was resented by the majority of businessmen as "dictatorial" interference by "outsiders," be they even officials of their own associations. The same officials who complained, often bitterly, about the unchanged mentality of their constituents lacked the courage to discuss openly the difficulties they encountered. Since outside of the major branches of industry employers' organizations were still staffed with rather mediocre personnel, these were often insufficiently assertive. Men who very frequently had acceded to their position in the employers' movement after failure in business or the professions did not have the necessary authority to educate their membership effectively.

The headquarters of many organizations consisted as before of unattractive one-room offices where an overworked secretary tried to cope with piles of dust-gathering files. The attitude of many a local organization toward the Paris headquarters of its federal association remained reserved if not outright hostile, and many of the national associations felt no more warmth toward the CGPF. Frequently the minutes of even the more active organizations recorded the lack of a quorum for the election of officers. Under such conditions the treasuries of most organizations which relied on membership dues remained meager. As before 1936, the peak association and the most important national federations lived by the contributions of the big concerns, which thereby could once more assert their preponderance.[65]

[65] The description here given corresponds to the (on the whole unfavorable) balance sheet drawn after the war by Auguste Detoeuf, *Passé, Présent, Avenir de L'Organisation Professionnelle Française*, Paris, 1946, esp. pp. 14-15. But also the ex-president of the CGPF, Gignoux, reflecting during the Vichy period on his failures and successes in the employers' movement, was hardly sanguine. See his *L'Economie Française entre les Deux Guerres, 1919-1939*, Paris, 1942, pp. 278-81. Similar conclusions for the 1936-39 period were reached by the historical survey of the well-informed article XX, "Le Conseil National du Patronat Français," *Le Droit Social*, IX, 1946, p. 206, and by Gérard Dehove, "Le sens et la portée de quelques expériences récentes en matière de relations industrielles et de réformes de l'entreprise," *ibid.*, X, 1947, p. 387.

The failure of a twenty-four-hour general strike announced by the CGT in November 1938 as a protest action against decree-laws constituted in many ways a victory for management. But it turned out that this day of "revenge for Matignon" also defeated many of the organizational efforts of the employers' movement. Because the threat from organized labor had receded and because the government had passed from socialist into more friendly hands, businessmen considered it safe to relax employers' discipline even more. The officers of the CGPF and of some trade associations pointed out that, just because outside pressure had diminished, the time had come to turn the employers' movement from mere defense towards more constructive purposes. There was, however, little inclination to follow such advice. Warnings against wholesale dismissals of union members in the shops remained similarly unheeded.[66]

Ironically, but naturally enough, the leadership which the movement had sought out in the hours of its greatest danger was falling rapidly into discredit among the rank and file of French employers. Now Gignoux was considered as an outsider and a neophyte, since he had never been in business. His philosophical bent and the literary elegance he displayed in his communiqués to the press and in open letters to the government were regarded with suspicion.[67]

\*      \*      \*

The shock of 1936 had brought in its wake a desire to reassess the basic tenets of a business philosophy. In an address before an employers' gathering, Gignoux once declared that in France one could never "rally opinion around mere questions of in-

[66] The mentality of the employers after the general strike of 1938 was vividly, if somewhat dejectedly, described by the participants of a round table discussion, most of them employers. See Barnaud, "Après la grève générale," *Nouveaux Cahiers*, No. 36, December 15, 1938, pp. 1-2; G. Lamiraud, "Après la grève générale," *ibid.*, No. 37, January 1-15, 1939, pp. 4-8; E. Raynaud, "La Collaboration patronale et ouvrière," *ibid.*, No. 39, February 15, 1939, p. 2. The members of the round table admitted that the majority of their colleagues considered with skepticism and mockery all reform proposals for the improvement of industrial relations.

[67] For interesting details of such criticism of the CGPF leadership by most employers, see Serampuy, *op.cit.* (n. 1-12), pp. 658 ff. On the weakening of employers' discipline as soon as the immediate danger was over, see also A. Detoeuf, *Construction du Syndicalisme*, Paris, 1939, pp. 33-34.

terest," and the account of the meeting noted at this point, "lively applause."[68]

But given the confusion and division of opinion among businessmen, the official employers' organizations were hardly the proper vehicles for elaborating doctrines that would prove satisfactory as an explanation of past experiences and useful as a guide for future behavior. The French labor movement has had, since its inception, a tradition of harboring in its midst numerous factions and wings, mirroring different political and trade union philosophies. Now there emerged also in the employers' movement a number of groups which were often sharply divided in general orientation and proposed tactics. Consensus seemed to exist only in regard to the belief that the kind of economic liberalism which the old CGPF had preached was hopelessly outdated. Inasmuch as these groups tried to determine the place of business in society and to find the ideological basis for a hitherto unknown degree of employers' discipline, all of them were tinged with a philosophy of corporatism. But there was little agreement on the course of action to be developed from such analysis.

Politically most outspoken was the *Comité de Prévoyance et d'Action Sociale* formed very shortly after the June events. The president of the Committee, M. Germain-Martin, had been a right-wing politician who had served as finance minister in various conservative post-war cabinets. Earlier he had been one of M. Gignoux's teachers at the University of Paris. On the permanent staff of the Committee (in its own description an "elite general staff") hardly an employer was to be found, but instead that agglomeration of retired officers, journalists, and public relations experts that had always found its way into the leadership of authoritarian organizations in France.

To the CGPF the Committee proposed a division of labor: since its by-laws and general character prevented the Confederation from engaging in outright political action, the Committee offered to conduct an energetic campaign to win the sympathies of the general public for the badly discredited cause of business, and to mobilize public opinion against the "enemy," organized

[68] See *Compte Rendu de l'Assemblée Générale du Comité Central de l'Organisation Professionnelle*, Paris, 1939, p. 32.

labor, which in the Committee's propaganda was rapidly confounded with communism.

The *Comité de Prévoyance* went about its self-assigned mission with the seriousness of a military campaign. It promised that its activities would be "like all great maneuvers . . . both the school and image of war."[69] Its weapons, "needed as any army needs weapons," were a weekly publication, a series of posters and handbills, regular news services, and a number of pamphlets. Brushing aside as old-fashioned the more factual and fairly restrained information services which the *Comité des Forges* had maintained in its respected *Bulletin Quotidien*,[70] the new Committee proposed to swamp employers and, when possible, the public at large with openly partisan and polemic materials. The new social legislation and all trade union activities were denounced as expressions of red totalitarianism and as an attack upon the institutions of free enterprise. In some of the meetings organized under its auspices, the spokesmen for the Committee openly encouraged the employers to cease all activity, i.e. to strike, if additional legislation were to interfere with their freedom of choice in hiring and firing. Wherever feasible, company unions should be formed.

The relations between the Committee and the CGPF remained cordial at all times; a number of trade association officials served on the Committee's Board of Directors. Gignoux praised repeatedly what he called the "parallel" action of the Committee; the Committee, however, criticized the official employers' organization for still speaking the more diplomatic language of big business. Since Germain-Martin and his staff wished to appeal frequently to the owners of small and medium-sized firms over the heads of their organizations, the Committee accepted as members only individual employers, not trade associations. Posing as "anti-political," like most political movements of this kind, the Committee recommended itself as a rallying point for all

[69] Most informative for the doctrines, activities, and methods of the Committee is Brenot, *op.cit.* (n. 1-16), composed of reports by the Committee's president and by its executive director. See also the pamphlet *Aux Patrons Français*, Paris, 1939, published by the Committee; its periodical *l'Elan Social*; and the writings by Germain-Martin, esp. *Les dangers économiques et sociaux du contrôle d'embauchage*, Paris, 1937, and "Le Patronat français, sa situation, son évolution," *La Revue de Paris*, XLIV, April 15, 1937, esp. pp. 781-83.

[70] Published by the *Société d'Etudes et d'Information Economiques*. For details see Bézard-Falgas, *op.cit.* (n. 1-19), pp. 379-85.

those who, coming from different political camps, had grown tired of the prevailing atmosphere.

In terms of business organization, Germain-Martin advocated that all those employing more than one worker be compelled to join the association of their trade. Even more imbued with corporative ideas was the firebrand of the Committee, Jules Verger, a former worker who was then head of his own electrical equipment firm. He boasted about having fought off singlehanded attempts by the labor unions to establish a closed shop at the Paris World's Fair of 1937. His anti-union activities were praised by Gignoux and General Weygand for having opened a new era of class collaboration.[71] Under the Vichy regime, Jules Verger was for a time entrusted with trying out his corporative schemes on a larger scale.

The Committee's admiration for foreign authoritarian and presumably corporative regimes was outspoken enough. Nazi and fascist youth organizations were praised as setting a desirable example for France. During the Munich crisis the Committee accused the communists of conspiring for war, and M. Germain-Martin became the most outspoken advocate of appeasement in the general business press.[72]

How much influence the Committee had among employers is difficult to determine. The language and imagery it used were known to please owners of small shops and factories who were deeply worried over their dreaded loss of authority. Yet the frankly political overtones of the Committee's propaganda were repugnant to many an employer who reacted to the dramatic ups and downs of the pre-war years with utter distrust of all political and civic matters. While an atmosphere of pre-fascism was settling over France, the masses of businessmen preferred to remain politically incognito.[73]

[71] See Verger's self-portrayal, not excelling in modesty, in Jules Verger, *Ses Ouvriers, sa maîtrise . . . une famille*, Paris, 1937; and see Jules Verger, *L'exposition a-t-elle été sabotée? Par qui? Comment? Pourquoi?* Paris, 1937, a publication sponsored by the *Comité de Prévoyance*.

[72] See his article in *Le Capital*, September 27, 1938, quoted by Charles Micaud in *The French Right and Nazi Germany, 1933-1939*, Durham, N.C., 1943, p. 84. See *ibid.*, p. 125, for similar though more moderate statements by the *Bulletin Quotidien*, warning in 1936 against provoking Nazi Germany and playing thereby the game of Stalinist Russia.

[73] On the general climate which prevailed then, see Jacques Madaule, "Préfascisme Français," *Esprit*, VII, 1938-39, pp. 327 ff.

Like most of the groups that emerged in the employers' movement during the years between Matignon and the war, the *Comité de Prévoyance* had its major significance as the harbinger of things to come. The creed of the Committee and its apostles played its role under the Vichy regime. More important, the demagogic and political appeal addressed by the Committee to small businessmen was emulated by certain sectors of the employers' movement in the Fourth Republic.

Where the *Comité de Prévoyance* indulged in the use of almost plebeian propaganda methods, another business group espoused the aristocratic ways of a philosophical society as they had flourished in the France of earlier days. The group, which became identified with its journal, *Nouveaux Cahiers*, launched in the spring of 1937, had been drawn together shortly after the antirepublican riots of 1934. Troubled by the deepening split which divided the French body politic, and by the dangerous accumulation of social resentment, a few industrialists had established contacts with like-minded associates from the professions and the upper bureaucracy, with intellectuals and non-communist trade union leaders. Most of the businessmen were connected with large concerns in the electrical industry, some with banking. By training, temperament, and position they were managers rather than employers. Best known among them were Messrs. Detoeuf, Isambert, de Tarde, and Barnaud. A few trade association officials such as Henry Davezac had joined with them.

In public and private meetings and in the columns of its remarkable periodical, the group developed views which ranged over a wide area but were principally concerned with problems of industrial relations and economic organization. The group pleaded with French employers to consider, for practical reasons as well as for reasons of principle, the existence of strong labor unions as a good rather than as an evil.[74] Traditional paternalism was criticized for its desire to "help" the worker where he "should

[74] See "Pourquoi les Nouveaux Cahiers?" *Noveaux Cahiers*, No. 1, March 15, 1937, p. 2. For the history of the group see also the note by Guillaume de Tarde, "Sur les Nouveaux Cahiers," *ibid.*, No. 20, March 1, 1938, p. 13, and the interesting testimony given by Barnaud before an investigation committee of the National Assembly in 1947 in Assemblée Nationale, Première Legislature, Session de 1947, *Rapport fait au nom de la Commission chargée d'enquêter sur Les Evénéments survenus en France de 1933 à 1945*, Annexe, Dépositions, Vol. VIII, pp. 2291-92 (cited hereafter as *Evénéments survenus . . .*).

help himself through his organization." An acknowledged fascination with the pattern of industrial relations in Sweden served to clarify the differences that existed between France and other democracies, and led to the formulation of a tentative program of action. Since the stratification of French society would hardly permit any cultural proximity between the employer and his workers, conflicting interests should be compromised on the level of the labor unions and the corresponding employers' associations. Detoeuf, director of Alsthom and in many respects the leader of the group, recommended compulsory affiliation of workers and employers alike with their respective organizations. In a country like Sweden voluntary organization could guarantee desirable and orderly social relations. But in France the perennial anarchy, particularly pronounced on the employers' side, could be transformed into order and mutual good faith only if capital and labor were compelled to organize. Such views differed from those of the full-fledged corporatists inasmuch as Detoeuf acknowledged that class conflicts were genuine and could not be artificially resolved by either corporations or the state. But his suggestions as to how the conflicting interests of employers and workers could be compromised "at the industry level" remained vague and confused.[75]

Admittedly none of the members of the group had any faith left in the benefits of economic liberalism, "killed not by the wish of men nor by the deliberate action of governments, but by an unavoidable internal evolution."[76] Most of the industrialists sponsoring the *Nouveaux Cahiers* were closely connected with French and international cartel activities. To them more orderly industrial relations, based on the mutual respect of the partners

[75] See Detoeuf, *op.cit.* (n. 1-59), pp. 12-15. For the thinking of Detoeuf and of the group on questions of industrial relations and economic organization, the entire collection of *Nouveaux Cahiers* is useful. Most interesting are the contribution (and ensuing discussion) by M. Moré, "Sur le Syndicalisme," *ibid.*, No. 24, May 1, 1938; A. Detoeuf, "Le Rôle social du Patron," *ibid.*, No. 26, June 1, 1938; A. Ariès, "Sur la Construction du Syndicalisme," *ibid.*, No. 39, February 15, 1939; and H. Denis, "L'Organisation professionnelle," *ibid.*, No. 43, April 15, 1939, pp. 2-6. The most comprehensive, though a scattered, statement of A. Detoeuf's general views is to be found in his volume of aphorisms, *Propos de O. L. Barenton, Confiseur*, Paris, new ed., 1950.

[76] A. Detoeuf, "La fin du libéralisme," *Bulletin du Centre Polytechnique d'Etudes Economiques*, May-August 1936; quoted here from Robert Langele, *La Mission économique et sociale du Patronat Français*, Paris, 1942, p. 11.

and of their respective interests, were the complement of a high degree of economic organization. After the First World War, de Tarde, one of the founders of the group, had formulated a proposal to settle the problems of reparations and post-war reconstruction by cartel-like agreements among the continental industries. Such suggestions were largely identical with the ideas put forward by the German Rathenau, but in contradiction to concepts defended at the time by Anglo-American interests.[77]

At the approach of another war, these industrialists believed that events had vindicated much of their thinking. Satisfactory international relations could be established even between republican France and nazi Germany, if the pattern of cartel agreements was to be followed, for "although cartels bring together people who detest each other, they are nevertheless operative when they are well designed and as long as they offer advantages to their members." While most of the group's members favored the Munich agreement, they did not indulge, like the *Comité de Prévoyance*, in a vulgar adulation of totalitarianism, but instead frequently criticized nazi Germany in the sharpest terms.[78] In terms of political philosophy, *Nouveaux Cahiers* remained devoted to a broad, personalistic humanism, although many of its articles hardly concealed the impatience of its authors with the contradictions and indecisions of French domestic and foreign politics.[79] After the liberation, when the political role which the group might have played was investigated, such impatience became suspect as an expression of distrust in republican institutions; the ideas which *Nouveaux Cahiers* had put forward in the field of foreign policies were criticized for being akin to the concepts of Hitler's New Order.

Between the outbreak of the war and the defeat in 1940 the group advocated the political and economic unification of the

[77] For a note submitted to Poincaré in 1922 and signed by Guillaume de Tarde, François-Poncet, and J. Benoit, see Alfred de Tarde and Robert de Jouvenel, *La Politique d'aujourd'hui*, Paris, n.d., p. 146.

[78] For the attitude of the group toward Munich and Nazi Germany, see *Nouveaux Cahiers*, No. 32, October 1-15, 1938, p. 16; and Detoeuf, "Le Nouveau Danger," *ibid.*, No. 35, December 1, 1938, pp. 2 ff. M. Pierre Laroque, one of the civil servants collaborating with the group, was one of the few to criticize the Munich agreement.

[79] Very significant is the short contribution by a writer who is still playing a leading role in the employers' movement, Henry Davezac, "Choisir," *ibid.*, No. 33, November 1, 1938, pp. 5-6.

continent as the only valid war aim of the democracies. Industry agreements on a European scale should pave the way for a general European federation. Such proposals developed by the business-men in the group were enthusiastically endorsed by the trade union leaders who had joined them.[80]

The intellectual contribution which the *Nouveaux Cahiers* made to the discussion of the major problems besetting a troubled country was quite remarkable. Theirs was the first endeavor ever made to assess the functions of business in society and, by considering a wide range of questions, to sharpen the sense of civic responsibility among the business community. But the in-fluence which this frankly elitist group had on employers and on the leadership of the employers' movement was severely limited. Immediately after the Matignon agreement, at a time when the old leadership of the CGPF was discredited and confused, it had seemed for a moment possible that men like Detoeuf and his associates would step into the vacuum and assume control of the general employers' movement.[81] They were, however, actively and effectively opposed by a characteristic alliance: stubbornly authori-tarian big business leaders, such as the car manufacturer Louis Renault, who were hostile to any voluntary reforms in the field of industrial relations, were joined by those who looked askance at the cartel-mindedness and the managerial orientation of the *Nouveaux Cahiers* group.

Another organization, the *Comité Central de l'Organisation Professionnelle* (CCOP), set itself up as a clearinghouse for corporatist thinking and for practical experimentation with corporatist solutions. Though directly affiliated with the CGPF, it was organized as an independent association with a leadership of its own.[82] Prominent among its promoters were patrimonial employers rather than managers, most of them controlling

[80] See Detoeuf, "Buts de guerre?" *Nouveaux Cahiers*, No. 52, December 1, 1939; and the subsequent issues of the journal.

[81] This information, gathered by me during conversations with prominent former members of the group, is confirmed by some, contradicted by others. It is inter-esting enough to speculate on what the development of the French employers' movement and perhaps over-all industrial relations would have been if the "palace revolution" of 1936 had given the control of the CGPF into the hands of the *Nouveaux Cahiers* group.

[82] See, for a description of the various projected activities of the CCOP, Con-fédération Générale du Patronat Français, *Annuaire*, Paris, 1939, pp. 415 ff.

medium-sized firms, usually in the light industries. The group made a conscious effort to bring together businessmen who long since had advocated or practiced various forms of corporatist organization, and younger employers who, dissatisfied as they were with the ideological emptiness and the purely defensive character of the official employers' movement, were seeking to modernize traditional corporatism.

In France as elsewhere corporatism made strange bedfellows and presented itself in manifold, sometimes contradictory, forms. Admittedly authoritarian were such men as Eugène Mathon and Pierre Lucius, who combined the wielding of a passionate and polemical pen with careers of active businessmen in the wool and leather industries. In their respective trades, which had been in distress since the early twenties, they had created market research and sales organizations and had enforced a fairly effective system of quotas for production and sales.[83] In their writings they professed unqualified adherence to the counter-revolutionary creed of a La Tour du Pin or de Mun. The individualistic Le Chapelier law was considered as one of the worst errors of revolutionary rationalism, which had to be overcome by a new "community" concept.[84]

The institutional setting for the new social order was to be created by compulsory organizations of capital and labor holding regulatory powers in matters of economic and social legislation. The economic sphere was reserved entirely to the decisions of the employers' associations, while collaboration between the employers and the labor organizations was admitted in the field of industrial relations, extending to the determination as to whether a

---

[83] On the *Comité de la Laine* see Paul Despature, *L'Industrie Lainière*, Paris, 1935, pp. 124-50; on the organization of the leather industry, Pierre Lucius, *Une Grande Industrie dans la Tourmente*, Paris, 1935.

[84] The most significant work by Mathon, summarizing the ideas expounded in his numerous speeches, is *La Corporation, Base de l'Organisation économique*, Paris, 1923 and 1934. For a highly sympathetic evaluation of his work see Henry-Louis Dubly, *Vers un ordre économique et social. Eugène Mathon. 1860-1935*, Paris, 1946. For the much more extreme Lucius see especially his *Faillite du Capitalisme* (with a preface by Mathon), Paris, 1932, and his *Rénovation du Capitalisme*, Paris, 1933. For an excellent description of corporatist tendencies among French employers, see Matthew H. Elbow, *French Corporative Theory, 1789-1948*, New York, 1953, esp. pp. 132 ff., and Bouvier-Ajam, *op.cit.* (n. 1-20), esp. pp. 170 ff.

strike was justified or not. According to their own testimony these men felt just as antagonistic to the classical forms of capitalism as to the labor movement. Praising those who had fought and died in February 1934 for the fascist leagues, Lucius called them the martyrs of the "national revolution . . . hostile to the great anonymous and irresponsible capitalism which governs France, and to materialistic and internationalistic Marxism."[85]

Political supporters of the businessmen who favored corporatism in its most traditionalist forms submitted a bill to the Chamber of Deputies in 1937 amalgamating the various proposals that had been made for a new economic organization, outlawing strikes, and condemning national confederations of either capital or labor.[86] The legislation was abortive until the Vichy régime, born of defeat, launched its halfhearted corporatist experiment.

In the "classical" country of individualism and rationalism, the search for a new "community" extended far beyond the acolytes of La Tour du Pin. It found an expression also in the writings of such frankly anti-authoritarian groups as *Esprit*, which before the war was not without influence among younger businessmen. The columns of its journal warned, however, against a corporatism that would not first have cleansed itself entirely of the "spirit and techniques of contemporary capitalism."[87]

The CCOP tried to steer a middle course between such extremes. The state was urged to turn over many of its functions to well-organized employers' associations. The existing cartel agreements were considered as the desirable model for what a satisfactory and complete "vocational organization" could achieve. While some of the actual cartel practices were considered abusive, the CCOP gave unstinted praise to the cartels as an idea and an organizational pattern. Once it were possible for the employers' associations to obtain, as did many of the cartels, more complete information from their constituents on business condi-

---

[85] Pierre Lucius, *Révolutions au XXᵉ siècle. Perspective de restauration d'un ordre social français*, Paris, 1934, pp. 263-64.

[86] See *J.O. Débats, Chambre des Députés. Annexe*, January 1937, pp. 49 ff.

[87] Emmanuel Mounier in *Esprit*, quoted from François Perroux, *Capitalisme et Communauté de Travail*, Paris, 1938, p. 161. The work by Professor Perroux is one of the most serious attempts at elaborating a modern corporatist doctrine. See also the more critical work by G. Pirou, *Essais sur le Corporatisme*, Paris, 1938, esp. pp. 65, 97 ff., on the corporatism of business leaders; and Paul Vignaux, "Corporatism in Europe," *Review of Politics*, IV, 1942, pp. 194-205, 303-14.

tions and to enforce greater discipline, they could extend regulatory powers to many fields.[88]

Like the *Nouveaux Cahiers*, the spokesmen for the CCOP denounced paternalism in all its forms. But on the question of how the desired collaboration between employers and workers could be organized, the group remained as vague as Detoeuf, probably because it was unable to reconcile the various points of view within its membership. Occasionally the CCOP would recommend that its member employers regularize relations with unions affiliated with either the CGT or the CFTC, while the more conservative corporatists would openly encourage the formation of "independent" company unions.

The extreme confusion into which the period of "mental troubles" following Matignon had plunged many reform-minded employers found its way into all kinds of experimentation on the plant level. Ill considered and romantic as they were many of these ventures ended in complete disruption of labor-management relations.[89] The debates and publications of the CCOP highlighted many of the motives underlying the general reform thinking of business during the interlude between Matignon and the war. The attractiveness of economic liberalism and of rationalism was not entirely denied. But it was argued that the danger of anarchy made a partial abandonment of liberty advisable; the despair over the disjunction of society led to frequently sentimental appeals for unity within and among classes. In most of its forms corporatism recommended itself as a solution to the dilemma of having to choose between continuing disorder and totalitarian dictatorship.

Within the CCOP there developed, first as a study center, then as an autonomous organization, the *Jeune Patron* group. It grew out of the desire to make a more intensive appeal to the younger generation of employers at a time when the political movements

---

[88] For a short history of the CCOP and an exposé of its doctrines, see Mersch, *op.cit.* (n. 1-46), pp. 68-69, with speeches by Gignoux and by Maurice Olivier, president of the CCOP.

[89] As an example see the picture drawn by Ramon Fernandez in his powerful novel *Les Violents*, Paris, 1935. For a description (in a Jesuit magazine) of a more successful experiment in a new kind of industrial relations at the plant level, see XX, "Le Journal d'un Patron," *Etudes*, ccxxxvii, November 5 and 20, 1938, esp. pp. 332-46.

of the right and left were wooing the young.[90] Of the several movements here described, the *Jeune Patron* was the only one to survive war and occupation. Its principles and activities will therefore be described more fully below (see Chapter IV).

## 4. The End of the Republic

The outbreak of hostilities in 1939 and the months of the "phony war" which followed had little effect on the outward structure of the employers' movement. When M. Gignoux was called into the army, the presidency of the CGPF was taken over by Baron Petiet, who for having been a businessman himself enjoyed greater prestige among his colleagues than Gignoux, all the more as his views were known to be authoritarian and sharply anti-unionist. To almost equal prominence rose a man of similar, perhaps even more determined, outlook: M. Aymé Bernard, who before the war had given his particular attention to the development of regional associations.

In general, the military mobilization measures affected particularly the "opinion groups" and those sectors of the employers' movement in which younger men, activated by the events of 1936, had made attempts to obtain a wider representation of smaller business interests. Hence the CGPF and its principal affiliates recovered quite naturally the character they had before the days of the Popular Front. During the first months of the war a personality such as M. Gingembre resigned from all functions he had held in the employers' movement, since he felt that in the councils of organized business the "trusts" and especially heavy industry were once more predominant. His own and similar reactions by the great mass of employers would explain why, a few months later, after the capitulation of France, the dissolution of the CGPF was accepted without any criticism.

Legislation adopted in 1938 had entrusted the trade associations with important functions in a war economy. But if the legislator had wished to see a systematic organization take the place of the improvisation characteristic of the First World War,

[90] The beginnings of the *Jeune Patron* movement are told in *Une Etape*, Paris, 1945, pp. 5-7, and Jean Martin, "Le Mouvement Jeune Patron," *Hommes et Mondes*, VI, October 1951, pp. 71-73. A socialist, Vincent Auriol, the first president of the Fourth Republic, gave later a sympathetic evaluation of the movement in his *Hier . . . Demain*, Paris, 1945, Vol. II, pp. 106-07.

it was found that, when war was declared in 1939, very few of the necessary administrative regulations had been issued. The relations between government and business remained for many months uncertain and confused. The optimistic assumption that a material superiority of the Allies would insure an easy victory over Germany accounted in part for the failure to set the war-time machinery into motion.[91]

There is no room here to discuss the responsibilities which the business community shared with others in the dismal lack of industrial and military preparedness. After the war, witnesses in no way suspected of systematic hostility towards industry testified to the lack of morale and initiative prevalent among all too many employers. Before an audience of Catholic employers a building contractor admitted that business attitudes during the first months of the war gave no reason for pride: ". . . disorder, lack of discipline, insufficient imagination, egotistic drives, and generalized attempts to get away with as much as possible." The minister of armaments, M. Raoul Dautry, painted an even darker picture.[92] Here a man who had spent most of his life as a manager of large private and public corporations, and who had since his student days at the *Ecole Polytechnique* associated with business leaders, described a manifest lack of patriotism on the part of many industrialists. The administration had rudely to prod some of the largest concerns into intensified war production. In part M. Dautry ascribed such torpor to an exaggerated taxing of war profits. But in his opinion there were political reasons as well which prevented many industrialists from having "the same heart and ardor as in 1914." (There is some testimony to the effect that, for reasons of contrast, M. Dautry might have embellished the past record and exaggerated the degree of support which business gave to the war effort at the beginning of the First World War.)[93]

[91] For an excellent description of war-time economic organization and the attempted incorporation of the trade associations into the machinery of government, see Jean-Guy Mérigot, *Essai sur les Comités d'Organisation Professionnelle*, Paris, 1943, pp. 57 ff. For the legislation, esp. articles 48 and 49 of the law of July 11, 1938, see *J.O.*, July 13, 1938, p. 8336.

[92] See George Cazin in *Cahiers de la CFP, Patrons' 46*, p. 36, and Dautry in *Evénements survenus . . .* , *op.cit.* (n. 1-74), Vol. VII, pp. 1950-93.

[93] See the invidious remarks in Beau de Loménie, *Les responsabilités des dynasties bourgeoises*, Vol. III, Paris, 1954, pp. 72 ff.

The unsatisfactory state of labor-management relations undoubtedly contributed to the mediocrity of production.[94] Shortly after having assumed office, M. Dautry wished to bring together the representatives of business and of labor so as to improve industrial relations in the factories. But the fear of subscribing to a "new Matignon" was still unallayed on the employers' side, so that all appearances of a new meeting between the two confederations had to be avoided. M. Jouhaux and M. Lambert-Ribot did not meet in the name of the CGT and the CGPF, but as the delegates of French labor and management to the International Labour Organization. The agreement resulting from this meeting at the Hotel Majestic indulged in a number of high-sounding generalities, promising the "confident collaboration of government, employers, middle-management, foremen, and workers." M. Dautry seems also to have hoped that by a special pledge class strife could be wiped out. The two sides solemnly declared that there was "no room either today or tomorrow for the pursuit of selfish interests or of class struggle."

Only during the last week of May 1940, when the battle of France was already lost, could the organizations of capital and of labor be brought to sign another common declaration which, by jacobinic language, tried to make up for the lack of labor-management collaboration during the preceding years and months.[95]

Notwithstanding official pledges, the actual climate of industrial relations had remained extremely unsatisfactory. Not only the labor press but also the columns of *Nouveaux Cahiers* recorded with grave concern instances of an increasing hostility between management and labor.[96] In an official meeting of the CGPF, its vice-president chided the CGT and the Majestic

---

[94] I have given in *op.cit.* (n. 1-3) a full account of labor-management relations during the first months of the war. What follows in the text is in part only a shortened version of Chapters X to XII of my earlier book.

[95] For the full text of the Majestic agreement and of the declaration of May 26, 1940, see *ibid.*, pp. 197-98, 231. On the history of both agreements see also Lefranc, *op.cit.* (n. 1-56), pp. 28-29.

[96] See Georges Lefranc, "Inquiétudes Ouvrières," *Nouveaux Cahiers*, No. 57, April 1940, p. 3; Pierre Sauvage, "Où en-est le problème des délégués?" *ibid.*, pp. 11-12; and Pineau, "Entre Patrons et Ouvriers," *ibid.*, p. 6. See also René Belin, who, within the CGT, had been the protagonist of labor-management collaboration, in *Syndicats*, April 4, 1940.

agreement.[97] French employers, he said, were able to organize assistance for mobilized workers and provide for industrial hygiene without meeting with the representatives of labor. As long as the statutes of the CGT continued to ask for the abolition of private property and of the wage system, the speaker declared amidst applause, he would regard the war-time conversion of the trade unions as purely temporary. The former sins of the CGT, such as the strikes of 1910 and 1917, the Popular Front, and the general strike of 1938, would never be forgotten. The speaker then turned to the war-time shop-steward legislation which, in order to forestall the possible election of communists, had given to the established trade unions, by then cleansed of all communists, the right of nominating shop stewards. The CGPF criticized this law and its nomination procedures, since the shop stewards would not be responsible to their colleagues but would depend on "influences from without" and on "irresponsible clubs"— which terms were obviously used to designate the labor unions.

There were, especially in the industrial North, notable exceptions to an atmosphere of systematic hostility. Contacts between management and labor unions which had existed there since 1936 were intensified and regularized after the Majestic agreement. A permanent committee of coordination was set up in Lille and in other important industrial centers to provide for the adjustment of grievances, since the war-time suspension of arbitration procedures had left a gap. Speaking in the name of the CCOP and also as an active businessman in both the steel and textile industries of the North, M. Olivier addressed an open letter to René Belin, the deputy secretary of the CGT, and for some time singled out by a number of employers as a desirable replacement for Jouhaux. In his letter Olivier made a number of suggestions for management-labor cooperation, proposals which were tinged with corporative concepts entirely acceptable to Belin.[98]

In general, however, French employers were afraid that, in a full-fledged war economy and in spite of the weakness of the union movement, their own status might be further diminished. Their wrath frequently turned against the government, which they held responsible for such loss of prestige and for the war.

[97] See *Bulletin Quotidien*, 5 April 1940, pp. 12 ff.
[98] See *Syndicats*, 18 April 1940.

At the same time, a sometimes justified fear of communist influence among their workers and of possible sabotage by the outlawed communist cadres was growing. Employers were unable to know how many of their workers belonged to an underground cell. Cases of actual sabotage became known and were tried on the eve of the German invasion.[99]

Wherever the employer turned there was uncertainty, anxiety, and danger. Here were indeed the "political reasons" to which a Dautry had ascribed the lack of patriotism among many industrialists. Here were also the reasons why most French businessmen accepted the demise of the republic coming in the wake of defeat with equanimity, and sometimes with glee.

[99] The situation is well described by Lefranc, *op.cit.* (n. 1-56), pp. 31-33.

# CHAPTER II

# Organized Business under Vichy

## *1. Businessmen and the Vichy Government*

> "France is the only country that has a school for philoso-
> pher-engineers: she derives pride from it; whether also
> strength, I don't know. . . . The error of Napoleon and of
> the entire nineteenth century was to believe that science
> leads to action: that is not at all true; science leads
> straight to nihilism or at least to indifference. . . ."
>
> Detoeuf, *Propos de O. L. Barenton*

"In general the *haute bourgeoisie* and the nobility gave their wholehearted support to the regime which had resulted from the defeat. In doing so they renounced the role of societal leadership for which they believed themselves to be foreordained."[1] Such a judgment, reached some ten years after the event, by an author who belonged to the classes he criticized, appears to be a sober statement of fact. Since the present-day employers' movement owes much, both in strength and in weakness, to the experience of the Vichy years, it is necessary to determine in greater detail what kind of support the *haute bourgeoisie* furnished to the regime and why the support was given.

The disintegration of French society during the last years of the republic, its "uprootedness,"[2] accounted for much in the rapid collapse of June 1940. While in Germany a similar uprootedness had produced aggressiveness, in France lethargy and inertia were the symptoms of the malady that had befallen the country. The new authoritarian regime seemed to hold out promise that the slumber of irresponsibility might be prolonged indefinitely. Now corporatism, at once officially enthroned, revealed its full senti-mental content as a solution to the longing for community and as a means of escaping the burden of individual decision. One of the ardent advocates of corporatism, whom the new government put in charge of an ambitious Institute of Corporative Studies, con-

[1] Marquis d'Argenson, *Pétain et le Pétinisme (Essai de Psychologie)*, Paris, 1953, p. 95.
[2] Simone Weil, *op.cit.* (n. 1-15), p. 49.

cluded an elaboration of the new economic doctrine with an emphatic: "The Marshal calls to us: 'He who loves me, follows me!' We love him. Let us follow him."[3] The official iconolatry of Vichy had understood to the fullest one of the perversities of modern dictatorship: the leader compels love and adulation and yet requires that the love be voluntary.[4]

Sentimental reasons and moral confusion alone offer an insufficient explanation of the fact that a majority of business leaders of all categories identified themselves with the Vichy regime and embraced corporatism. In the eyes of most employers all governments since the First World War, with the sole exception of Poincaré's, had badly sinned against the interests of the country. They had, in the words of an influential trade association, misjudged "fundamental economic and financial laws and were all guilty of demagoguery, incompetence, and greediness for power."[5] If during the strikes of 1936 the workers had often been moved by a desire to chastise the employers for their lukewarm republican sympathies, the day of ultimate revenge for the defeat at Matignon had now come with the defeat of the republic. The critics of democracy felt vindicated by the inability of the defunct regime to stand the test of battle.

Charles Maurras spoke about the emergence of the Pétain rule as a "divine surprise." Only a small number of businessmen had found the anti-republican hysteria of the *Action Française* to their liking. But to many others the "surprise" consisted in seeing broader avenues to official power and influence opened before them. In France fashionable and unending discussions about "changing elites" are frequently little more than a pretext for manifestations of sheer snobbery and a screen for feuds between competing cliques. The unfolding story of the Vichy regime also reveals that the presumed emergence of a new elite amounted to little more than a partial displacement of personalities. To most industrialists the "national revolution" recommended itself,

[3] See Maurice Bouvier-Ajam in C. J. Gignoux et al., *Le Corporatisme Français*, Le Mans, n.d., p. 26. After the fall of the Vichy regime the author found solace in Stalinism.

[4] For examples see the appendix to the work by d'Argenson, *op.cit.* (n. II-1), pp. 169-79. For profound comments on the relationship between the modern dictator and his followers, see Alain, *Politique*, Paris, 1952, p. 31.

[5] Syndicat des Fabricants de soieries et de tissus de Lyon, *Compte-Rendu des Travaux, Années 1939-1940*, Lyons, 1942, p. 34.

not by an affinity to the theories and practices of nazism, but by
the promise of bringing to the fore and freeing from parliamentary
influence an officialdom more favorable to their own economic
concepts.

After the armistice many prominent businessmen and government officials believed that their stature as the nation's elite was
to be measured by their ability to keep a cool head in the midst
of national disaster. "Business as usual" became a positive moral
value, permitting the convenient merger of individual and national interests. Even those who might have been cynical about
the implications of the official corporatist philosophy prided
themselves upon their "realism." The presence of the Germans
on French soil and their control of the country's resources were
part of that reality which had to be accepted without a whimper.
To safeguard the "economic substance" of the nation furnished
the justification for collaborating with the conqueror.[6]

"It is more unfortunate for a country to lose its physical
strength than to choose the wrong camp," concluded Jean Bichelonne, one of Pétain's ministers, who until today has remained
an idol of many French business leaders. The longer the war
lasted, the more feverish became the illusions that France could
yet emerge as the arbiter between the contending forces. But if
she were to play that role, it was believed necessary to keep the
powder dry and production rolling.

Pétain's belief that the defeat and its consequences were the
deserved punishment for past dissoluteness was widely acclaimed
by the business community. By promising discipline and order
the new regime reassured the bourgeoisie. If Vichy were able to
eliminate the threat that had arisen to employers' prestige from
the existence of a free labor movement, businessmen were willing
to play their role as producers and, if need be, accept for themselves a more disciplined behavior. In the words of a cruel but
perceptive description of the employers' mentality after the

---

[6] It is not within the scope of this study to give a detailed account of the economic collaboration of French businessmen with the Germans. An interesting
general view of political and economic collaboration is provided in the final report
of Dr. Michel, chief of the German *Militärverwaltung* authorities, although there
may be some doubts about the authenticity of the report. For its full text see
*La France intérieure,* No. 50, November 15, 1946, pp. 4-13, and No. 51, December
15, 1946, pp. 3-19. For many details see also the collection of articles by Raymond
Aron, *De l'armistice à l'insurrection nationale,* Paris, 1945.

armistice: "That Germany might requisition all factories, what was more natural? The victor has all the rights, and what would we have done if we had been in his place? But no, how could one imagine that a lazy France, a France in sympathy with communism, could have triumphed over as well-constructed a war-machine as that of Germany? How could France have won without a leader, without even wanting a leader? A leader—that was the dream of every employer. A smart-looking leader in uniform, a true Frenchman who loved neither the British nor the Germans and who would restore political order. . . ."[7]

In the opinion of many industrialists, not only republican institutions had failed. Business itself, by clinging to an outmoded economic liberalism corresponding neither to reality nor to the interests of French industry, had compromised and weakened its cause. The Marshal's announcement that he had come to "deliver us from lies" appeared to have opened the way to a frank reorganization of business along the lines of a corporatist economy.

The members of the motley group who wanted to become the spokesmen for business under the new conditions never understood that even the most needed reforms introduced under the control of the occupying authorities could not succeed. Besides much cleverly adorned opportunism, there had been at the beginning of the Vichy rule some active and sincere faith in the possibilities of far-reaching reforms. But such faith as had existed was bound to dry out before long. The regime itself, veering uneasily between total submission to the conqueror and erratic resistance to his demands, became rapidly much too weak to provide the order and discipline for which the employers had craved.

What remained was the concern for saving one's own firm rather than the nation's "economic substance." The regime which had started by denouncing the "crass materialism" of the republic was soon reduced to defending nothing but material interests.[8]

[7] See the novel by Henriette Psichari, *Usines 42*, Paris, 1946, p. 190.

[8] An excellent picture of the prevailing mood is drawn in another novel: Jean Dutourd, *Au bon beurre*, Paris 1952. Even years afterwards influential industrialists looked at their decision to carry on business during the occupation with an exalted sense of historical responsibility which hid from them altogether the possibly less than idealistic motives of their action. As an example of this widespread mentality, see how Jean Prouvost, owner of important textile concerns in the North, spoke to his collaborators about the period of occupation in *Peignage Amédée Prouvost & Cie.*, Roubaix, 1951.

After having called for a greater sense of responsibility it gave rise, as its supporters admitted, to the worst manifestations of irresponsible action inside and outside the government. Inasmuch as Pétain's propagandists continued to extol the idealistic motivations of the armistice regime, they frequently outdid all earlier "hypocrisy" which the Marshal had attacked with senile anger.

The near-anarchy characteristic of the Vichy rule, the clash of feuding personalities and of contradictory policies, were particularly pronounced in all matters pertaining to economic organization and industrial relations.[9] The only enduring trait of legislation and practice in those fields was to favor that amalgamation of high civil servants and business magnates which had already been under way before the war. The administration of scarcity which the armistice regime had to undertake greatly furthered the close working contact between the two groups.

A similar mentality strengthened an affinity produced by a common social and educational background. The more the economic crisis of the 1930's had revealed the inability of parliamentary government to cope with long-range problems, the more the bureaucracy had felt the same scorn for weak governments and for shifting electoral majorities as the critics of the republic in high business circles.[10] The inspectors of finance in particular had long played the role of a talented camarilla, supervising if not actually running many sectors of the administration and of economic life according to their own concepts and undisturbed by the wishes of the electorate. Before the war the Inspectorate

[9] Much of this impression is conveyed by the memoirs of writers close to the regime during much or all of the Vichy interregnum, such as Henri du Moulin de Labarthète, *Le Temps des Illusions*, Geneva, 1946; Yves Bouthillier, *Le Drame de Vichy*, Paris, 1950; and Nicolle, *op.cit.* (n. 1-48). Du Moulin, a member of Pétain's personal staff and formerly an *inspecteur des finances*, was by family and marriage affiliated with big business interests. Bouthillier, one-time Vichy minister of finance, had an almost identical background. It must of course at all times be considered that these accounts published after the war are colored by their authors' special pleading and their desire to present themselves and some of their associates in the best possible light to an audience presumed to be hostile to the Vichy regime. Yet they all contain valuable materials. The work by Nicolle, who had been an official in a minor employers' organization before the war, and who obviously was subsidized after the defeat by Pierre Laval, is often unreliable. Nevertheless, it remains highly interesting because of the account it gives of many people "behind the scenes" in Vichy.

[10] For an excellent, though in its generalizations perhaps too cruel, analysis, see Louis R. Franck, "The Forces of Collaboration," *Foreign Affairs*, XXI, 1942-43, esp. pp. 44-46.

had been described by one of its members as providing "a little of that cohesion and discipline of which Germany gives us the example."[11] In the councils of the French puppet regime the inspectors of finance rose to unprecedented prominence, foremost among them those who earlier had felt slighted by the republican regime in their promotion and those who by birth or marriage were most closely affiliated with industry and banking.

Another group of officials similarly impressed its outlook on the economic policies of Vichy: that of the *ingénieurs d'Etat*. While most of the inspectors of finance were graduates of the exclusive *Ecole libre des Sciences Politiques*, the state engineers had received their rigorous training in the *Ecole des Mines* or in the *Ecole Polytechnique*, the "X" in the parlance of the initiated. All three of these institutions had also been the nurseries of the French business elite. When Raoul Dautry had taken over the Ministry of Armaments in 1939 many of the state engineers assumed high administrative functions, granting favors, as their minister would later admit, to their business friends, and preferably to the most anti-republican elements among them. As soon as the battle for France had begun in earnest, most of the state engineers considered the capitulation unavoidable. And when the unavoidable had happened, they stayed in office. Their own brand of realism, not dissimilar from that of the business community, was soon regarded as particularly becoming a graduate of the celebrated "X." The strength and permanence of such traditions was perhaps best illustrated by the undisputed fact that, of all institutions of higher learning, the student body of the "X" furnished the least members to the resistance movement;[12] instead many among them volunteered for labor service in Germany.

It has correctly been noted that the Vichy rule amounted actually to three or four regimes which succeeded each other and each of which brought to the foreground a different personnel and a different set of political beliefs.[13] Untouched by such changes, the

[11] See François Piétri, *Le Financier*, Paris, 1931, p. 87.

[12] See Jean Guéhenno, *Journal des Années Noires (1940-1944)*, Paris, 1947, p. 313. The report by the German occupation authorities, *op.cit.* (n. 11-6), came to similar conclusions. For Dautry's statement, see above n. 1-92.

[13] This is the thesis defended in the remarkable book by Robert Aron, *Histoire de Vichy*, Paris, 1954.

continuous and progressive fusion of officialdom and business took place behind a stage on which at various times widely divergent policies were acted out.

For a time at least, the Marshal's personal animosities and preferences asserted themselves by a condemnation of the forces whom he would scorn as "agents of class warfare" and by the adornment of traditionalist symbols. The national confederations of both capital and labor were done away with by decree; together with the CGT and the CGPF, the mining and the steel associations—the *Comité des Houillères* and the *Comité des Forges*—were dissolved as representing in popular imagery the evil forces of national disunity.[14] When the "old guard" of the employers' movement, principally those who had been its leaders before 1936, appeared in Vichy, they were treated rather rudely by Pétain and Laval. They were told that their usefulness was considered to be at an end, since in the eyes of the public they were too closely identified with the rule of the "trusts," and also because they had been too conciliatory to the governments of the republic and above all to the Popular Front. In fact, the peak associations of the labor and the employers' movement had already grown so weak before the capitulation that their legal disbanding seemed to make little difference.

The void supposedly created by the banning of the two confederations was to be filled by corporatist institutions. With its characteristic concern for symbolic decorum, the government decided that class collaboration would best be manifested by entrusting the administration of industry and of labor to the same minister. Several industrialists and other candidates—among them C. J. Gignoux, the post-1936 president of the CGPF, then still a prisoner of the Germans—were considered for the office but rejected in favor of René Belin, a former assistant secretary of the CGT. Politically acceptable because of his staunch anticommunist stand and as the mainstay of appeasement policies in the trade union movement, Belin had been close for some time to a number of employers, particularly of the *Nouveaux Cahiers* group. His philosophy corresponded to that of the progressive

14 The dissolutions were pronounced in application of the law of August 16, 1940 (to be discussed subsequently), by decree of November 19, 1940, *Journal Officiel de l'Etat Français* (hereafter referred to as *J.O.E.F.*), November 12, p. 5653.

wing of the corporatists; it was hoped that his ambition would be matched by organizational talents.[15] But from the first the industrial sections of the ministry were put under the control of experienced businessmen, most of whom rose to prominence and cabinet rank during later phases of the regime.

As minister of state Lucien Romier became Pétain's advisor on matters pertaining to the solemnly announced new economic and social order. Though never a businessman himself, Romier had served the cause of organized business for many decades as a publicist and a popularizer. He had been Gignoux's predecessor as the editor of the business daily the *Journée Industrielle*, and later became an editor of *Le Figaro* and a frequent contributor to *Le Temps*, which Jean Jaurès had once called "the bourgeoisie made into a newspaper." In the 1920's and during the early 1930's Romier had taken a prominent part in one of the rare attempts made by French industrialists to play an outright political role.

*Le Redressement Français* had been founded and was financed by Ernest Mercier. Tycoon of the electrical industry and a leading personality in the old CGPF, Mercier had been for a time the disburser of funds to many of the right-wing movements and fascist leagues.[16] He had prevailed on other prominent business leaders to serve on the board of the *Redressement;* Romier became the principal spokesman of the group, which as early as 1928 issued openly authoritarian appeals to the business community and to the public. Since the republic had proven incapable of preserving the national patrimony, it should be replaced by a regime run according to the principles, if not by the men, that had long been tested in the administration of industrial enterprise. Somewhat mystical elite concepts and a more concrete technocratic philosophy pervaded all of the movement's propaganda. At the approach of the Stavisky crisis in 1934, Mercier and Romier called for the "necessary punishment" of parliament and described Marshal Pétain as a close sym-

[15] For the circumstances leading to Belin's appointment see Nicolle, *op.cit.* (n. 1-48), Vol. I, pp. 27 ff., and Lefranc, *Expériences, op.cit.* (n. 1-56), pp. 40 ff. Nicolle is hostile to Belin while Lefranc seeks to defend his every move.

[16] On the relationship between business groups and the fascist riots of 1934, see the well-documented study, by Georges Michon, *Les Puissances d'argent et l'émeute du 6 février*, Paris, 1934, pp. 6 ff. and passim.

pathizer of the *Redressement*. They greeted with delight the Doumergue cabinet, which promised constitutional reforms and in which for the first time the names of Pétain and of Laval were to appear together.

Although the ministry soon disappointed the high hopes for drastic political changes, Mercier and some of his associates decided in 1935 to withdraw their support from the *Redressement Français* which thereupon had to dissolve.[17] Such developments seem to have reflected a split in the foreign policy orientation of French business. While a large sector accommodated itself in the camp of appeasement, Mercier was afraid that the movement he had wanted authoritarian and anti-communist might become a tool of German subversion. He also felt, and the emergence of the Popular Front movement gave reason to ponder, that if he had wanted to experiment with the active participation of business in politics, the *Redressement* had not been rewarding. In 1940 the elevation of Lucien Romier to officialdom was considered, as were so many other aspects of Vichy rule, as a belated revenge for ideas and schemes that had been frustrated earlier.[18]

At Pétain's table and in the numerous committees set up to consider how the blueprints of the corporatists could be transposed into reality, many personalities congregated who had been active in the employers' movement. Others were to play a similar role in the future. Gignoux, though not considered the proper choice for the Ministry of Industrial Production and Labor, was invited to become a ranking member of Vichy's National Council, which had the task of preparing the new (and abortive) constitution for the *Etat Français*. Another member of the same council was a then little-known owner of a family business, M. Antoine Pinay, whose political star was to rise yet higher in the Fourth Republic.

---

[17] On the history of the *Redressement Français* and its connections with the employers' movement, see R. Mennevée, "Le Redressement Français," *Les Documents Politiques, Diplomatiques et Financiers*, xv, April 1934, pp. 176-78, and "Un important Evénement politico-oligarchique: La Dissolution du Redressement Français," *ibid.*, xvi, December 1935, pp. 549-53. For Lucien Romier's ideas when he was one of the foremost spokesmen for the movement, see his *Le Redressement Français. Idées très simples pour les Français*, Paris, 1928.

[18] On Romier's role, see Aron, *op.cit.* (n. 11-13), pp. 379-80. The author ignores, however, the part Romier had played in the *Redressement*.

A self-made employer like Jules Verger, who before the war had sparked the *Comité de Prévoyance*, recommended himself to the Marshal by his rabid anti-labor feelings, and by his crude corporative beliefs which in their confusion matched those of the chief of state.[19] Verger was easily the most fascist-minded among the businessmen in Pétain's entourage. He later became involved in Doriot's *Légion des Volontaires*, upon whose pro-nazi activities the more conservative industrialists would frown. But Pétain also sought counsel from men unequivocally representing the "trusts" which the chief of state denounced in his official messages. Here the managers of concerns in the electrical and electro-chemical industries prevailed, since their directors had been more interested than others in social and economic experimentation. Among them seem to have been Messrs. Detoeuf and Davezac, who had promoted the *Nouveaux Cahiers*, and M. Perrin, who was to assume the leadership in one of the "vanguard groups" of the employers' movement in the Fourth Republic. But the steel and metal industries were also represented: Léon Daum, one of the mainstays of the officially dissolved steel association, and Jacques Lente seem to have shared the Marshal's confidence. At present Daum is the French member of the Coal and Steel Community, Lente still the president of a most influential trade association.

Pierre Laguionie, controlling extensive department store interests and today prominent in the employers' peak association, was joined by Jean Mersch, then president of the *Jeune Patron* group, and by many of the other businessmen here mentioned in a "Committee on Vocational Organization." It was to advise the government on the economic and social reorganization of the country along corporatist lines.[20] But the Committee, like similar creations, soon bogged down in the intrigues and controversies characteristic of the authoritarian state without authority, which the armistice regime turned out to be. Some of the in-

[19] For Pétain's vague concepts as revealed in the conversation with one of his close confidants, see du Moulin de la Labarthète, *op.cit.* (n. 11-9), pp. 159-65. Less vague was an article signed, though perhaps not written, by Maréchal Pétain, "La Politique Sociale de l'Avenir," *Revue des Deux Mondes*, cx, September 15, 1940, pp. 113-17. In that article, as far as I can tell never commented upon by the historians of the Vichy regime, Pétain explained that the main ideas of Nazi social thought and the "authentic" French tradition were one and the same.

[20] For a membership list of this committee, see Lefranc, *op.cit.* (n. 1-56), pp. 50-52.

dustrialists, who had flocked to the chambers of the new regime in the expectation that they might be permitted to test their own long-cherished brands of corporative organization, admitted their disappointment and generally tried to avoid compromising themselves further. Others, who had come to establish useful business connections or to share in political influence, soon understood that the access to power lay elsewhere than in the entourage of the "venerable patriarch," or in formless advisory committees.

Organized business found its most effective expression through the Committees of Organization, to be discussed subsequently, and through a group of men serving at various times as ministers in Vichy cabinets or holding high office in certain administrations. While it is true that the group rose to prominence when Admiral Darlan took over the reins in February 1941, some of its members were installed in the Ministry of Industrial Production and Labor as soon as it was established in the summer of 1940, just as most of them survived the comeback of Laval to power.

Their very survival through all phases of the unsteady "French State" gave these men unusual weight in decision making. Their participation in a musical chairs game by which they exchanged positions of influence among themselves was apt to multiply their power. First as directors in Belin's ministry, where they participated in the setting up of the Organization Committees; as managers of some of these Committees; as ministers in charge of Franco-German economic relations; as secretaries of state for industrial production after such functions had been taken away from the former labor leader Belin; as delegate-general for national equipment; as minister of the interior—during the four years of the regime always the same names were to appear: those of Jacques Barnaud, M. Bardet, Jean Bichelonne, François Lehideux, Pierre Pucheu, Gabriel Leroy-Ladurie, and some others of lesser significance.

There were, as one would expect, differences in temperament among these men; their social origins were not identical. Some of them had worked together closely since before the war; for others their acquaintance was quite recent. Nevertheless, their careers before and after the armistice, their talents, their general outlook on the role of business in society and in politics, their appraisal of the international situation and of the role of France, indeed their predilections and animosities bore enough similarities to outweigh such differences as existed. In many respects their mentality resembled that of a larger, albeit less vocal, group on which these men had to lean for the execution of their policies: the high civil servants, who most of the time served them well.

Before he entered private banking Barnaud had been an inspector of finance, and as such a member of the staff of several conservative ministers during the Third Republic. In the far-flung affairs of the Worms Bank he established business connections with many of those who were to become his associates in the Vichy ministries. Both Barnaud and Bardet, the latter the manager of an important machine tool company, had actively participated in launching *Nouveaux Cahiers*. François Lehideux had for a time been the director of the Renault works; he was the son-in-law of Louis Renault, who immediately after the armistice ran headlong into economic collaboration with the Germans. In the councils of the CGPF Lehideux had once represented the banking interests.

Neither Pucheu nor Bichelonne was born into a family of great wealth; their careers were typical of those brilliant students who are discovered early by the business elite as hopeful material for assimilation. While most of the other members of the group were graduates of the "X," Pucheu had prepared for a teaching career at the *Ecole Normale* as had before him such officials of the *Comité des Forges* as Robert Pinot and François Poncet. Like them, Pucheu rose rapidly in the exacting organization serving the steel interests. Still young, he became one of the architects of the European steel cartel of the 1920's and managed the export services of the *Comptoir Sidérurgique*, the sales organization of the steel association.

After the uprising of 1934 Pucheu participated actively first in the ultra-nationalist league of de la Rocque, later in Doriot's fascist PPF. So as not to embarrass the steel association he left his post in the employers' movement, and assumed instead the management of an important industrial concern, also part of the Worms "empire." Typically enough, he grew soon impatient with the inefficiency and corruptibility of the political groups he had joined. But as an individual he continued to develop before various audiences his blueprints for a "new economy" where discipline of producers and workers was to be guaranteed by a hierarchy of corporative organizations—and by an energetic police.

Once in power, and especially after assuming, as minister of the interior, control of the police, he soon transformed everything he touched. He frightened his own colleagues in the Ministry by the ruthlessness which he used to introduce a French brand of totalitarianism. In his dealings with the Germans he sought to profit from the connections he had established before the war and counted on the support not only of French heavy industry but also of the German industrialists and generals who, behind the broad back of Göring, had established their niche in the nazi system. General Weygand considered Pucheu one of the "principal agents of Berlin"; he is probably described more correctly as having believed with a perverse fanaticism in the virtues of a Continental "new order" in which the common interests of European business would eventually prevail over the stratagems of political amateurs. He coldly assumed responsibility for the shooting of communist hostages by the Gestapo. His subsequent attempt to use business contacts in the United States to win the favor of the Allies did not save him from the Free French firing squad.[21]

The same disregard for the human element, coupled with an urge for solutions of mathematical precision, characterized a man like Jean Bichelonne, from the beginning of the regime one of the masterminds of its economic organization, and later its most influential administrator in many fields of business and industry. By his final examinations he had established himself as the most brilliant graduate of the *Ecole Polytechnique* in more than a generation. Belonging to the exclusive corps of state engineers, he had like so many others exchanged public service for private business shortly before the war and entered the steel industry. In Dautry's Ministry of Armament he was among those officials who soon spoke openly in favor of capitulation. Some of his contemporaries admired his vast technical intelligence to the

[21] For Pierre Pucheu's career and concepts, see his autobiography, *Ma Vie*, Paris, 1949, written during his imprisonment in Africa; Jacques Madaule, *Histoire de France*, Paris, 1945, Vol. II, p. 418; and du Moulin de Labarthète, *op.cit.* (n. II-9), pp. 339, 352-60. An almost painfully balanced evaluation of his ministerial career is provided by Aron, *op.cit.* (n. II-13), pp. 386-89.

extent of comparing him in all earnestness to Napoleon or to Colbert. Less enthusiastic observers expressed doubts whether this scientific prodigy would not have needed another "twenty years merely to reach the age of political puberty."[22]

His religious trust in the virtues of economic organization was the counterpart of his low estimate of human creativeness and decency. In his opinion neither employers nor workers, when left to their own devices, would ever be able to overcome waste, routinism, and short-sighted egoism. Since to him knowledge and reasoning power were all that mattered, Bichelonne concluded that the workers' emancipation would result from their understanding of economic intricacies. But such understanding would be provided by placing industry into the framework of a flawless economic organization, through which the elite could express its views.

The more weight Bichelonne carried in the councils of the regime—and for a time he became an increasingly close confidant of Laval—the more he let himself be driven into playing the role of a singlehanded "hero of collaboration." "There will be plenty of volunteers for cabinet posts after the war," he remarked, "but nobody would want to do what I am doing now—except idiots and cowards who would let go of everything." To preserve to the greatest possible extent the French economic patrimony was to him the most important rationalization of his behavior. In the evaluation of the *Militärverwaltung* he was a "rightful and patriotic Frenchman . . . who recognized with even less mental reservations than others that French interests could be defended only in the framework of a new Europe created by the collaboration between France and Germany." Where Pucheu had turned over French hostages to their nazi executioners, Bichelonne signed without hesitation the ordinances sending thousands of French youths to labor service in Germany. When leaving with Pétain and Laval for Sigmaringen, he still expressed publicly his belief in the early and ultimate "European victory of Germany."[23]

[22] Du Moulin de Labarthète, *op.cit.* (n. ii-9), p. 348. Most of the material on Jean Bichelonne's career and concepts was obtained from a memorandum prepared by one of his close collaborators. Of interest as an evaluation of the "phenomenon" Bichelonne, see also Bouthillier, *op.cit.* (n. ii-9), p. 271, and Aron, *op.cit.* (n. ii-13), pp. 496-98.

[23] See Nicolle, *op.cit.* (n. i-48), Vol. ii, pp. 461-62, and the report of the *Militär-*

The lasting significance of Bichelonne for the employers' movement lies partly in the legacy of the Organization Committees which to an extent were his creation. But more significant is probably the boundless admiration for his talents and ideas to be found even today among many industrialists and leaders of organized business. To a great number of his colleagues who have survived him, Bichelonne has remained, though perhaps not the "hero of collaboration," the apostle and high priest of a still-revered creed: that of *organisation professionnelle*, of "vocational organization."[24]

The point has been made here that the men whose careers, outlook, and activities have been described formed a fairly well-defined and closely knit group. But were they more than a clique? Did they belong, as was whispered in war-time Vichy, Washington, and Paris and has been loudly asserted since, to a widespread conspiracy, to a secret society to which the name of "Synarchy" has been attached? The question is of some importance for the historian of the French employers' movement. Since many associates of those who were the prime movers in the alleged conspiracy are now prominent in business organizations, and since undeniably many of the concepts supposedly developed by the secret society are still in vogue, one could conclude that the Synarchy has survived, assuming it ever existed.

According to the most imaginative accounts, drawing on documentary evidence of dubious character, the organization could be traced back to a secret "Martinist" sect founded in the last century by a graduate of the "X." In the 1920's this graduate's technocratic ideas are supposed to have been emulated by a number of more recent disciples of the *Polytechnique*. One person in particular, Jean Coutrot, and one firm, the Worms Bank, are described as having facilitated extensive ramifications of the

---

*verwaltung, op.cit.* (n. 11-6), No. 51, p. 6. There is little reason to believe in the veracity of the legend spread in present-day France that Bichelonne, after his transfer to Germany, was the victim of a "medical murder" by the nazis.

[24] The activities of men like Bichelonne and Pucheu and of the group connected with them show that it is extremely difficult to draw a line between the "conservatives" and "fascists" within the regime. That distinction forms the main thesis of an otherwise able book by Paul Farmer, *Vichy: Political Dilemma*, New York, 1955, but is clearly inapplicable here.

society on the national and even on the international level.[25] It is quite true that most of the men here mentioned have been connected with the Bank or its diversified affiliates.[26] It is also a fact that for years Coutrot had developed a tireless propaganda in favor of extreme technocratic ideas among various groups of the employers' movement. He was for a time the guiding light of the National Committee of French Organization (CNOF), to which a number of leading businessmen belong today (for details, see Chapter VIII). Together with other polytechnicians he founded a study group called *X-Crise* which gained the support of the older industrial elite. The group provided a forum for interesting discussions, among others for a fairly sensational report Ernest Mercier gave when he had severed his connections with the semi-fascist *Redressement Français* and recommended, upon his return from a trip to the Soviet Union, economic and military collaboration between France and Russia.[27] Later Coutrot took an interest in the activities of the CCOP and contributed an article to the *Nouveaux Cahiers*, though he probably never belonged to the inner circle of the latter. Most

[25] For the most elaborate treatment devoted to the Synarchy and reproducing many of the documents which, at one time or another, have been circulated concerning this subject, see D. J. David, "Le Mouvement Synarchique d'Empire (M.S.E.) et le Pacte synarchique révolutionnaire (P.S.R.) liant les Affiliés Français," *La France Intérieure*, No. 29, February 15, 1945, pp. 3-11 and *id.*, No. 30, March 15, 1945, pp. 9-16. This enormous account, which seems to mix truths, exaggerations, and falsehoods, deserves more critical examination than can be provided here. In a similar vein are the articles by Pierre Hervé about the Synarchy in the (communist) *Action*, October 5, 12, 19, 26, and November 2, 9, 16, 1945. Du Moulin de Labarthète, *op.cit.* (n. II-9), has given (pp. 330-68) another comprehensive and interesting picture which is considered by some to be well informed, by others to be superficial and reckless. The work by Nicolle, *op.cit.* (n. I-48), is filled from the beginning to the end with documents concerning the Synarchy and with bitter complaints about its activities in the administrations of the Vichy government. See esp. Vol. I, pp. 511-32. Much indirect material on the Synarchy can also be gathered in the testimonies of Barnaud (presumably one of the leaders of the Synarchy) and of Dautry in *Evénements survenus . . . , op.cit.* (n. I-74), passim. It is true that these hearings provide mostly negative evidence inasmuch as the witnesses tried to convince the committee that the Synarchy never existed.

[26] When there were complaints that Darlan was bringing into his cabinet the entire Worms Bank clique, the admiral replied: "That's still better than the choir boys who have been around here. No generals, no students of theology, but young people, shrewd and *who will get along with the fritz* [Germans] *and will cook you a good soup.*" Du Moulin de Labarthète, *op.cit.* (n. II-9) p. 347 (emphasis supplied). For the history of the Bank see *Le Monde des Affaires, op.cit.* (n. I-37), p. 704.

[27] See the highly interesting *URSS. Réflexions par Ernest Mercier*, Paris 1936. For details on Detoeuf's and Mercier's trip to the Soviet Union and on their industrial connections, see Hamon, *op.cit.* (n. I-50), Vol. I, Paris, 1935-36, p. 284.

of his writings were devoted to the scientific organization of production, frequently mixing technical discussions with far-flung philosophical considerations.[28] Described by some as un-balanced to the point of near madness, he also had his admirers—usually the same as Bichelonne. After Coutrot's sudden death at the beginning of the war, he was made posthumously the "true founder of the sect," and all organizations with which he had been in contact were suddenly recognized as having been mani-festations of the Synarchy.

When it became apparent that economic affairs at Vichy had come under the control of men who had often belonged to the same organizations, were graduates of the same *Ecole Poly-technique*, and had known each other for a long time through close business affiliations, no further proof of conspiracy seemed necessary. From the outset contradictory statements abounded. In Paris, under the auspices of the arch-fascist Marcel Déat, the movement was accused of secretly undermining the Marshal's anti-trust policies, and of stalling for the sake of Anglo-American interests economic collaboration with the Germans. Simulta-neously Allied propaganda considered a rather broadly defined "Worms clique" as the core of Franco-Nazi collaboration.[29] Actually the Worms Bank, because it was partly Jewish-con-trolled, underwent some of the treatment generally meted out to "non-Aryan" enterprises. As to the supposed anti-trust policies, they were most effectively defeated by the Organization Commit-tees flourishing with official blessing.

After the liberation none of the judicial inquiries were able, much as they tried, to obtain evidence that the activities of the circle were part of a concerted plot. As soon as definite allegations

[28] For the mentality and activity of Jean Coutrot see his *Planning, Préparation du travail dans l'entreprise,* Paris, 1939, with an interesting, somewhat critical preface by Raoul Dautry, and his "Offensive d'hiver sur le front intérieur," *Nouveaux Cahiers,* IV, January 1, 1940, pp. 5-6. (M. Barnaud was therefore curi-ously wrong when he testified that Coutrot had never written for the *Nouveaux Cahiers.*) A passionate defense plea of not guilty for Coutrot was entered by his widow in a letter to the editors of the magazine which had published the most damaging material about the Synarchy and Coutrot's role. See *La France Intérieure,* No. 34, July 15, 1945, pp. 16-19.

[29] See William L. Langer, *Our Vichy Gamble,* New York, 1947, esp. pp. 168-69, 201, and the U.S. government reports cited therein. When Louis R. Franck, *op.cit.* (n. 11-10), p. 47, identifies the entire *Nouveaux Cahiers* movement with the Worms group and its collaborationist tendencies, he is certainly unjust.

seemed to have been brought by some, they could be demolished by others as exaggerated, superficial, sometimes even as outright fantastic. It is not a novel fact that in France the members of an organization, the "ins," take the discreet aspects of their affiliation extremely seriously (this includes the French Free-masonry), and that correspondingly the "outs" consider history in terms of plots and of conspiracies. Such traditions lent addi-tional strength to the widespread belief in a mythical conspira-tional Synarchy.[30]

In reality, the relationship of the men who won undeniably great influence in the administration of economic life under the armistice regime was less romantic. What existed was tantamount to an "objective" plot: not deliberate scheming, but a common mentality; not identical goals, but similar objectives, suggested by analogous experiences and by their agreement on what the situation held for their country. Their philosophy, if philosophy there was, had been described long before the war as "industrial-ism," a belief that politics ought to be subordinated to the point of view of the producer.[31] While such a creed contained elements of an ideology also to be found in the thinking of the German Rathenau, and of the American technocrats, the legacy of the physiocrats and of St. Simon gave it a distinct French character cultivated by the education which many of the French industrial managers received at the *Ecole Polytechnique*.[32]

Impatient with the inefficiency of political institutions and the slow pace of economic progress in France, men trained in logic and mathematics believed that they could find the correct formula for the solution of vexing problems. Cynical about everything except the belief in their own ability, abstract to the point of moral nihilism, they were frequently so amateurish in

[30] That the Synarchy, conceived as a secret conspiracy, was a myth, is also the conclusion reached by Aron, *op.cit.* (n. II-13), pp. 381 ff., and by Farmer, *op.cit.* (n. II-24), p. 265. Ironically enough, one of the most level-headed evaluations of the Synarchy, regarding it as a "very open circle of young technicians of business," is contained in the report by the German military administrator, *op.cit.* (n. II-6), No. 51, pp. 5-6.

[31] See the interesting work by Albert Thibaudet, *Les Idées politiques de la France,* Paris, 1932, pp. 62-80.

[32] There exists no better discussion of the strength and weaknesses of the educa-tion at the "X" than that by its slightly facetious alumnus Auguste Detoeuf, *Propos, op.cit.* (n. I-75), pp. 193-201.

their economic reasoning that they would have failed even if they had operated under more auspicious circumstances than under German occupation and in the midst of a world war. More fundamental yet were their political errors. As one observer who had watched these men for many years remarked: "Political experience is not gained in the board meetings of corporations. It calls for strong roots in the country, for the limelight of open action, for biting criticism, and for the blow of fresh air that never fills the sails of the oligarchies and synarchies, nor penetrates chapels or office buildings."[33]

Understood as a mentality rather than as a conspiracy the Synarchy existed and flourished under Vichy. In that sense it also has survived the collapse of the regime. The belief in the inherent virtues of institutional arrangements that insure discipline of economic behavior continues to be particularly strong among the business executives who have assumed positions of leadership in the employers' movement. Sometimes their contempt for the politics of democracy, though less frank, is hardly less pronounced than that harbored by the "synarchs" of Vichy.

## 2. The Organization Committees

"Common sense and logic: a leader.
Common sense without logic: an employee.
Logic without common sense: a catastrophe. Hence the failure of
   many graduates of the *Polytechnique*."
                                  Detoeuf, *Propos de O. L. Barenton*

Those who after the liberation sought to defend the institution of the Organization Committees have pointed to the complete chaos into which the economy of the country had fallen in the summer of 1940. Unemployment was rampant in both zones, but in occupied France the economic standstill had a particularly threatening portent. The occupation authorities started a campaign trying to convince the workers that their employers were at fault if the machines were not turning. There was talk that German commissars would take over the direction of factories; posters promised the workers that, since their employers and in many cases all the technical personnel had fled, the occupation

[33] Du Moulin de Labarthète, *op.cit.*, (n. II-9), p. 368.

authorities would care for them. Lack of raw materials hampered even those firms which were prepared to resume production.[34]

Under these conditions the law of August 16, 1940, "concerning the provisional organization of industrial production," was born,[35] designed presumably above all to encourage the return of the employers to their posts and to permit the resumption of production at the earliest possible moment. It seems to be true that at first the German authorities were highly displeased with the law since they would have preferred to deal with French industry piecemeal rather than with a structured planned economy copied in many respects from their own.

Yet in addition to these motives, which cannot be impugned for lack of patriotism, the drafters of the law were obeying other impulses, quite clearly revealed in the report preceding the publication of the text and in the first directives for its application. The pseudo-liberalism of pre-war days, the "abuses of individualism," and the lack of discipline were made responsible for the technical backwardness of French industry and for an insufficiently developed market. As a beginning of thorough change the law sought to make *tabula rasa* by announcing the forthcoming dissolution of all associations of labor and capital which might be an obstacle to the functioning of the newly instituted organization.

The lack of statistical and general economic information had particularly been felt during the war. The inability of most trade associations to fulfill the functions which the earlier law on the organization of the nation in war-time had assigned to them had become obvious. It was assumed that under the even more difficult post-armistice conditions an entirely new organization would be needed to undertake what article 2 of the law considered as indispensable measures: inventories of all production facilities, of available raw materials and manpower; the establishment of manufacturing programs; the organization of the purchase and distribution of raw materials; the development of standards for production, quality, and competition; price fixing; and, finally,

[34] A vivid description of this situation, tending to make the institution of the Organization Committees appear mainly as an act of patriotism, is given by Barnaud in *Evénements survenus . . .* , *op.cit.* (n. 1-74), Vol. iii, pp. 2294 ff.; similarly, Bouthillier, *op.cit.* (n. ii-9), p. 273.

[35] *J.O.E.F.*, August 18, 1940, pp. 4731-33.

over-all measures designed to lead to a "better functioning of any particular branch of industry in the common interest of enterprises and their employees."

The new *Comités d'Organisation* (CO) to which these tasks were entrusted were admittedly both authoritarian and para-corporative. For this mixture the introductory report apologized simultaneously in two directions: for not achieving "industrial democracy," and for not having turned over the government of industry to the industrialists themselves. On paper, neither was done. In fact, the second solution prevailed. According to the statute the nomination of the Committee members was made by the minister who could, however, choose them from among men proposed by the trade associations. All decisions of the Committee were to become valid only after the approval by the minister or the commissar whom the government would appoint to serve with each committee. Trade associations and all other employers' organizations were submitted to the strictest supervision by the CO.

Undoubtedly the superior and freshly experienced efficiency of the German system was uppermost in the minds of the men who drafted the law. But they also believed that some previous French developments pointed in the right direction. The consortiums of the First World War, the activities of the influential trade associations, and the experiences made in the cartelized sectors of industry all seemed to demonstrate the advantages of organizing the incipient self-government of industry. By investing the CO with broad powers, so that they were apt to interfere effectively at every level of economic life, and by associating in their operation interest groups and government, the law hoped to insure both flexibility and efficiency. It was assumed that one would thereby avoid the alternate evils of totalitarian planning and of a predominance of self-seeking special interests.

The solution presented in 1940 acknowledged its empiricism as well as its voluntarily provisional character. Because of the important role played in the new organization by the state, the law was far from satisfying the corporative theorists who abounded in the entourage of Pétain. It was announced that another law introducing a complete framework of economic and social reorganization was being studied and would soon replace the emergency statute. Political circumstances prevented this: the law of 1940 was soon attacked from so many quarters that its sponsors preferred not to tamper with it, for fear it would never be replaced by anything else.[36]

When it was enacted, the law reflected well the outlook of the men who took a major part in its drafting. Besides Belin, the trade union leader whose development has been described, a number of civil servants and businessmen participated. Pierre Laroque, a member of the Council of State, had devoted much past effort to a study of industrial relations in France and had reached as early as 1934 the conclusion that neither its mentality nor its organization equipped the employers' movement to represent management in a modern economy.[37] Laroque seems to have been responsible for strengthening in the law those features that sought to insure the tutelage of the state over the trade associations.

Henri Lafond, another member of Belin's staff and alumnus of the "X," had served for a while in government service before he accepted executive positions in a number of mining companies, principally those with holdings in the colonies. By outlook and business connections he was closely connected with the men who were considered members of the Synarchy. However, Laval's personal animosity against him led to Lafond's ouster from his official post in 1942. For having severed his connection with the regime early enough, Lafond was able to assume after the liberation leading functions in the new employers' movement; but he has remained a convinced advocate of most of the principles once embodied in the CO.

The other two men who fashioned the law, Bichelonne and Barnaud, remained intimately connected with its working. As time went on, Bichelonne impressed more and more the seal of his personality on the activities of the CO. Indeed during the

[36] This is the explanation given by Belin; it is largely supported by Lefranc, *Les Expériences, op.cit.* (n. 1-56), who makes the best possible case for Belin's activities as a member of Pétain's government. For the circumstances surrounding the drafting of the law and for the names of those who participated in it, see also Aron, *op.cit.* (n. 1-13), pp. 244-45.

[37] See his *op.cit.* (n. 1-17 and 1-5). Laroque later joined the Free French movement and became the director of the social security system in the Fourth Republic.

lifetime of the Vichy regime, perhaps for posterity, the law of August 1940 was known, praised, or cursed, as the case may be, as the *loi Bichelonne*.

*    *    *

From the very first the members of the Committees were leading businessmen who often held functions in their trade associations. This led early to an almost complete fusion between Committees and trade associations. "The CO were in fact nothing but the trade association in another form," was the considered judgment of a contemporary observer, echoed by many others outside and inside the employers' movement.[38] Since the CO were clearly based on the leadership principle, the decisions of a Committee's president alone mattered; the Committee members, if they cared at all, were at best endorsing the decisions reached by the president.

But since the presidents were active businessmen, and heads of large-scale enterprises at that, they frequently delegated their functions to full-time executives solely concerned with the administration of CO affairs. These directors were usually selected from among the salaried officials of the trade associations. So far the process by which employers' organizations would entrust the running of their affairs to a professional staff, rather than to a slow-grinding committee of businessmen, had been irregular in pace. Only the most important trade associations had been able to attract truly competent men and to overcome the distrust of the employers against a personnel with a background different from their own.

The new functions which the CO offered to able administrators speeded up a development which had been initiated by the *Comité des Forges* before the First World War. Wherever the trade association had an able administrator, he would take over the directorship of the corresponding CO. In other cases where traditions and meager financial means had prevented younger men from rising in the hierarchy of the employers' organizations,

---

[38] See Mérigot, *op.cit.* (n. 1-91), p. 336. Similarly, Syndicat des Fabricants de Soieries, etc., *op.cit.* (n. II-5), p. 49, and Henry Davezac, "L'Organization Professionnelle," in *Organisation Professionnelle, Les Documents Jeunes Patrons,* Paris 1947, p. 21. The present discussion relies for factual data heavily on the balanced and richly documented monograph by Mérigot. Its frank criticism of the CO is all the more remarkable as it was published during the Vichy regime.

a new, competent personnel would easily be recruited for well-paid posts that yielded considerable influence. The criteria of selection were bitterly criticized by an old-style employer: "Not the person who knows best has been chosen but he who knows best how to apply the general concepts of the *Ecole Polytechnique*."[39]

In this and other respects the "palace revolution" within the employers' movement, which had started after Matignon but was after 1936 confined mostly to the peak organization, was now reaching the level of all trade associations. The modernization of the employers' movement, which before the war had once more faltered because of a lack of discipline and the ensuing dearth of funds, was now making progress. The CO had the right to issue orders and to levy a tax on all businessmen.[40]

Since activities of the trade association were indistinguishable from those of the CO, the former profited from the powers and the finances accruing to the Committees. At times well-organized industrial associations, such as the sales agency of the steel industry, would collect the dues for the CO from their members. Differently from the conditions under which many employers' organizations had operated in the past, the CO ruled over the "scarcity economy" of the armistice regime from luxurious buildings with ample personnel and modern equipment. After the liberation the former staff of the CO formed a valuable reservoir for recruitment by the trade associations. Through the Vichy experience their members had become accustomed to see their affairs administered by competent professionals—and to pay for such services.[41]

---

[39] Eugène Schueller, *La Révolution de l'économie*, Paris, 1941, p. 130.

[40] The estimates of the funds which the CO raised in form of compulsory dues vary. After a little over two years of activities the CO were believed to have obtained about two billion francs. See Mérigot, *op.cit.* (n. 1-91), p. 548. But already at that time other estimates were as high as four billion. And the CO continued to function well into 1944.

[41] A comparison of the presidents, directors, and responsible staff members of the main CO, as contained in the *Répertoires des Comités d'Organisation, mis à jour fin Septembre 1941*, with the corresponding positions in the trade associations as they emerged after the liberation reveals that most of the important positions (and many of the minor ones) are in the same hands. No percentages of continuity and change are offered here, since it is not believed that a quantitative analysis would be of significance. What seems to be significant is that such identity is far more frequent between the personnel of the CO and the post-war organization than between the CO and the trade associations that were affiliated with the pre-war CGPF. Hence the turnover took place under Vichy.

Another amalgamation took place simultaneously. Just as the trade associations had before the war become in fact closely affiliated with the cartels, cartel organizations and CO all but merged in many cases. In a few instances the CO ordered the dissolution of cartels which under the new conditions had lost their value for organizing the market. Far more frequently the CO used their powers to transform what had at least theoretically been a voluntary agreement among producers into a compulsory organization intolerant of outsiders. Many cartels were given the function of sub-allocating raw materials, and for this and other tasks were invested with means of control which in the past they had never been able to exercise to the fullest. Where formerly many cartels had often been mere sales agreements, the CO first encouraged and then frequently enforced an extension of their activities to the fields of standardization, specialization, and the setting of production, as well as sales quotas. Some of the most successful CO, such as that of the foundry industry, offered an example of a complete fusion of functions and personnel between the Committee, the trade association, and the cartel organization. The CO, ably directed by Pierre Ricard, one of the foremost personalities in the post-war employers' movement, undertook what is generally considered a pioneering effort in the domains of productivity and market research.

It was natural that, because of the very extensiveness of their functions, at least the larger CO were presided over by big business leaders, since they alone were considered to possess the necessary vision, competence, and authority to determine the destinies of an entire branch of industry. Only a very few of them, such as M. Detoeuf, considered it necessary to sever their business connections when assuming their new position. The directors and other staff members to which they entrusted the actual administration of CO (and thereby often of cartel affairs) served as their "agents" to the same extent as a pressure group official defends the interests of his constituents.

For the owners of smaller enterprises the activities of the CO were far too time-consuming. Where they were invited to serve as Committee members, so as to make the CO more representative, their role seems to have been largely nominal. Later many of the businessmen in this category resigned their posts on the Committees to which they had been appointed at the beginning of the regime. Sensing that the CO had become more and more discredited in the milieu to which they belonged, they did not wish to compromise themselves further. At one time Bichelonne, as minister of industrial production, attached to his cabinet M. Gingembre, asking him to devise measures that would insure a more effective representation of small business in the CO. M. Gingembre, who already after Matignon had become the "professional" defender of small and medium-sized firms, was singularly unsuccessful in his efforts at democratizing the CO. But by his activities he acquired a reputation as paladin of small business and a popularity which waxed strong once the Vichy regime, and with it the CO, had perished.

Eventually most CO were completely controlled by what their critics called the "trusts." In such branches as the textile industries the heads of large family enterprises had initially controlled the CO. But, feeling uncomfortable in surroundings that became more and more those of corporate enterprises, they too often resigned their posts, leaving the field entirely to the managerial group.

Even in Pétain's immediate entourage the development which the CO had taken was sharply criticized. Those hostile to the CO succeeded in having the Marshal denounce them over the radio: "The power of the trusts is trying to assert itself once more by utilizing for their particular ends the institution which had been designed to correct the errors of capitalism." One of Pétain's closest confidants wrote later that the CO by "giving too large a representation to big business reproduced all too often in their microcosm, on a reduced scale, the physiognomy of the directing boards of the most important corporations. Their pre-corporative taxes were too heavy and arbitrary. . . ."[42] At Paris a financial paper expressed openly what was whispered in many circles: "The nomination of the executives has been a terrible disappointment for the country. Within a few weeks, the leaders of the mining industry and of banking, after having precipitated the country successively into revolution, war, and defeat, have recovered the mask of the CO. . . . Under the title of the Com-

[42] See Pétain, Broadcast to the French Nation, *J.O.E.F.*, August 14, 1941, pp. 3394 ff., and du Moulin de Labarthète, *op.cit.* (n. 11-9), p. 360.

mittee of the Steel Industry, the *Comité des Forges* was entrusted
with bringing into the steel industry initiative and boldness. The
*Comité des Houillères*, dressed up as the Committee of Solid
Mineral Combustibles, is supposed to introduce progress in the
mines. The French aluminum industry, under the disguise of the
CO for Aluminum and Magnesium, is called upon to dissolve
the monopoly which it had instituted for its own profit. The
masquerade has taken incredible proportions. The *Comité des
Forges*, for instance, has given rise to not less than four CO. . . .
This installation of the trusts under the guise of a revolutionary
formula has led to the results which were to be expected: a policy
of conservatism and of sterility leaving free range to the satisfaction of special interests."[43]

Today many members of the high French bureaucracy, who
even in retrospect are not entirely inimical to the economic organization inaugurated by the Vichy regime, criticize it mostly for
having given too large a place to the representatives of business.[44]

The law of 1940 had stipulated in its article 5 that the CO
would function under the close scrutiny of the public authorities.
While the commissioners installed by the government had the
right to veto the decisions taken by the CO, they in fact let almost
all rulings become final. Thereafter violators could be penalized
by sanctions that ranged from heavy fines to the closing of a
refractory enterprise. It is true that the commissioners, assigned
to a CO, often participated in preparing general as well as detailed regulations so that no opposition could be expected from
them. Yet the daily contact between the representatives of
government and of business seemed to hold little promise that
the public interest would emerge unscathed. The commissioners
were largely drawn from the Inspectorate of Finance and the
various categories of state engineers. The managerial business
group in control of the CO often had an identical educational
and often a similar family background.

If already before the war these qualified technicians had
shifted from public to private employment, the conditions under
which the CO operated made the line between the two categories

[43] *Journal de la Bourse*, December 6, 1941, quoted in Mérigot, *op.cit.* (n. 1-91),
pp. 541-42.
[44] See Charles Brindillac, "Les hauts fonctionnaires," *Esprit*, XXI, 1953, p. 875.
I have heard similar opinions expressed by many high civil servants.

so fine as almost to disappear. Not infrequently an official would first serve as public commissioner with the same CO which then induced him, often by offering him a higher salary, to serve on the managerial staff of the Committee. In the words of an irate industrialist, the civil servants considered the corporative organization as a "new and vaster Ministry of Armament, capable of employing thousands of bureaucrats, where everybody would find his place for eternity, during all future peaces and all future wars."[45]

In its triumph over the theoretical schemes of the corporatists, the system of industrial organization as developed during the Vichy years came actually very close to the forms which the Italian dictatorship had adopted for its war economy; both were characterized by the close integration of bureaucracy and the economic "oligarchies."[46] The CO gave perfect expression to what has aptly been called the "pluralism" of the Vichy regime.[47] They were the channels through which business, one of the several groups making up the power structure of that regime, could assert itself without feeling the need for specifically political institutions such as a totalitarian party.

The administrative control of the CO was organized from another side through the intricate machinery which the law of September 10, 1940, had set up for the allocation of industrial raw materials.[48] That statute had evidently been enacted upon the urging of the German authorities, who wished to gear the French economy more directly to the needs of their war machine. German officials supervised various levels of the distribution

---

[45] Eugène Schueller, *op.cit.* (n. II-39), p. 132.

[46] The description of the Italian system given shortly before the war by Louis Rosenstock-Franck, "Le Corporatisme Italien" *Archives de Philosophie, du Droit et de Sociologie Juridique*, VIII, No. 3-4, 1938, pp. 127-58, reads especially in its conclusions, like an analysis of the functioning of the CO. For an excellent discussion of Italian corporatism in retrospect, see also Stuart Hughes, *The United States and Italy*, Cambridge, Mass., 1953, pp. 69-98. The situation prevailing in the Third Reich was largely different because of the predominant role of the nazi party. However, there were great similarities between the industrial organization of defeated France and the concepts which Walther Rathenau and some associates tried vainly to put into practice after Germany's defeat in the First World War. See the interesting article by Fritz Redlich, "German Economic Planning for War and Peace," *Review of Politics*, VI, 1944, pp. 315-335.

[47] See Stanley Hoffmann, "Aspects du Régime de Vichy," *Revue Française de Science Politique*, VI, 1956, pp. 44-69.

[48] Law of September 10, 1940, *J.O.E.F.*, September 12, 1940, pp. 4970-71.

apparatus, headed by the indefatigable and unfortunate Biche-lonne. Also, between the abundantly staffed agencies of distribution and the CO the overlapping of personnel was frequent. Sometimes the same men headed a "section" of the distribution board and the corresponding CO. Since by law all persons employed in the administration of raw materials became public officials, the CO presidents who assumed such functions obtained civil service status. Hence not only did there occur another fusion of private and public interests, but the CO also became of necessity the agents of the distribution machinery, especially for the sub-allocation of raw materials. Where conflicts arose, usually the distribution authorities prevailed since their demands had the backing of the Germans. But this only discredited the CO further; whatever initial intentions might have prompted their creation, in the end they were bound to become the indirect adjuncts of the invader. In the summary judgment of one observer: "The work of the CO has been smashed at the top by the supremacy of the distribution authorities; at the bottom it has been steadily narrowed down by a lack of social courage."[49]

Those who had sponsored the law of August 1940 had also hoped that the CO would open an era of increased technological advancement. But it turned out that restrictive practices, for which organized business had frequently been indicted in the past, instead of being abandoned, had now been given official sanction. As a general rule the allocation of raw materials was made on the basis of production and sales figures for 1938. Although such rigidity sought its excuse in general economic conditions, it often expressed merely an unwillingness to disturb an established situation in the market and led to a freezing of production and productivity.[50] In that respect the CO were unable to change the business mores which the new institution had set out to combat.

As might have been expected, the reactions of employers towards the CO varied greatly according to the size and the char-

---

[49] Henry Laufenburger in his preface to Mérigot, op.cit. (n. 1-91), p. vi. In a similar vein is Detoeuf, who is generally sympathetic to the activities of the CO, in op.cit. (n. 1-65), p. 20.

[50] "If a hundred years ago there had been a CO of the mail coaches it is unlikely that there would ever have been railroads," wrote M. Bellet in the *Journal de la Bourse,* December 27, 1941; quoted in Mérigot, op.cit. (n. 1-91), p. 539.

acter of their firms. The satisfaction which directors and managers of large concerns derived from the institution and from the role they played in it stemmed principally from the increase in prestige they experienced. To a large extent the CO embodied what they hoped would be a lasting vindication of their politico-economic concepts: the leaders of industry would assert themselves as the nation's elite through the kind of "industrial self-government" which the CO had instituted and which would eventually lead to the rule of the managers in the political field as well. The emphasis which the work in the CO placed on technical and administrative skills was welcome to men whose training in economics and business matters had been notoriously weak.

On the other hand the owners of small and medium-sized firms felt once more frustrated and oppressed by a new and far heavier bureaucracy. The number of CO had risen from 91 in the spring of 1941 to 234 three years later; many had overlapping functions; all produced numerous questionnaires containing often hundreds of questions. Small business felt treated in the offices of the CO with rude contempt. The "lilliputian Caesarism" of the CO was all the more resented, as businessmen who had never paid dues to a trade association were now compelled to contribute heavily to an institution they distrusted.[51] When several thousands of marginal enterprises were closed down by the authorities, this was attributed, rightly or wrongly, to the action of the CO.[52]

The longer the war lasted, the more employers justified or at least rationalized their hostility towards the CO with patriotic motives. Since the information requested by the CO was useful to the occupation authorities and would facilitate their plundering of the French economy, why not withhold or falsify data French businessmen were traditionally reluctant to part with? Henceforth resistance to the directives emanating from the CO

[51] It is true that the director of the CO of Commercial Establishments estimated that in spite of existing legal sanctions more than 200,000 shopkeepers managed to ignore their respective Committees. At the liberation at least 80,000 still owed their dues and had to be amnestied for their failure to pay.

[52] The question is controversial. Mérigot, op.cit. (n. 1-91), attributes the closing of firms to the initiative of the CO. Gilles Martinet in his essay "Le Révolutionnarisme, maladie sénile du capitalisme" in La Crise Française, Paris, 1945, states (p. 102) that such actions were undertaken upon orders of the occupation authorities "and not upon the initiative of the Organization Committees." Because of the CO's general policy of respecting all established situations, the latter assertion may well be justified.

became the employers' contribution to the *résistance*. Very often the wrath of these businessmen over the tyranny of the CO found its expression in a diminishing enthusiasm for the "National Revolution." In 1940 both the modern and the backward sector of business had lent their united support to the armistice regime. As time went on, the latter became disgruntled, though most of the time quite passively. The managerial group continued, with some notable exceptions, its identification with a government that had turned over to them the running of the economy—under the enemy's heel.

Because of the conditions under which the CO had to operate, the net result of the entire experiment was at best ambiguous. In contrast to the inflation of bureaucratic organization provoked by the CO, industrial production contracted in most fields.[53] The broad planning functions which the law of 1940 had assigned to the CO were entirely neglected, and here the presence of the Germans did not explain everything. The Vichy regime never had a unified economic policy, but was also in that field torn between conflicting needs and concepts, often identified with the various cliques within the government.[54] Where the CO proceeded with more specialized tasks their results varied with different sectors of the economy. They contributed to the further modernization of firms that were already efficient, but hardly succeeded in penetrating to those that were archaic. The authoritarian policy of the CO, reasoning in terms of quantity and of the hierarchy of needs, failed to influence the habits of firms which lived by the individualism of producers and consumers alike and which during

[53] The index of industrial production during the Vichy years shows the following development (1939 = 100):

| May 1941 | 72 |
| May 1942 | 61 |
| May 1943 | 55 |
| May 1944 | 44 |

Significantly, the extraction of iron ore was maintained at a level of 97, that of steel production at 87 (both until the spring of 1943). The building industry maintained a rather high level; the chemical and textile industries were substantially reduced. See Ministère des Finances et des Affaires Economiques, Institut National de la Statistique et des Etudes Economiques, *Mouvement Economique en France de 1938-1948 (mis à jour pour 1949)*, Paris, 1950, p. 64.

[54] On the absence of an economic policy under Vichy, see the remarks by a high official of the Finance Ministry, Paul Delouvrier, *Politique Economique de la France*, Paris, 1952, Cours de l'Institut d'Etudes Politiques, 1951-52, pp. 189-203. Interesting on this point also is Mérigot, *op.cit.* (n. 1-91), pp. 552-54.

the occupation and its aftermath survived by their retreat to
the black market.[55] For these reasons the CO could but widen
the gap between what is modern and what is obsolete in the
French economic structure and sharpen, at least in the long
run, the mutual animosities of businessmen belonging to the
different sectors.

The most lasting effects of the CO are to be found probably
much less in their direct impact on the French economy than in
the transformations they wrought on organized business. They
streamlined anew the structure of the employers' movement; to
some trade associations they gave the funds and the personnel
which enabled them to emerge for the first time from a mere
paper organization into a functioning body; for others, already
powerful before the war, they greatly increased the means of
action. In many cases they established among employers the
beginnings of an elementary discipline of dues paying and a somewhat greater willingness to furnish statistical information to the
trade associations. To that extent the CO succeeded where earlier
efforts, based solely on persuasion, had failed.

At their apex the CO insured the continuity of an employers'
peak association in spite of the decree that had dissolved the
little-lamented CGPF. Whereas the labor confederations remained banned until the end of the Vichy regime, a Joint Inter-
trade Information Center of the CO (*Centre d'Information
Interprofessionnelle*) was established in 1941 upon the initiative
of Pierre Pucheu. Legally the Center was considered the successor
to the CGPF, absorbing all of the documentation and much of
the personnel of the CCOP, the core of corporative organization
within the old confederation. Established as an organ of liaison
between the CO it fulfilled for the closely affiliated trade associations the role of coordinating the various branches of the
employers' movement, furnishing them as the CGPF had done
general economic, financial, and legal information. The Center's
various sections corresponded to the services of the dissolved
Confederation with the difference that also on that level the
new body was far more affluent than its predecessor. For years
the Center was presided over by another prominent member of

[55] See the very pertinent remarks on the Vichy economy in Ministère des Finances,
*op.cit.* (n. II-53), p. 75.

the Worms group, M. Bardet; on its board the ten most important CO were represented by their presidents, most of them also presidents of major trade associations. By publishing a bulletin and by setting up a School of Higher Education, concerned with theoretical and practical problems of economic organization, the Center provided the focus for all efforts at perfecting further the organizations of business.

## 3. Employers and the Labor Charter

The legislation which established the CO had been the result of a hastily improvised compromise; subsequent events shaped it into a fairly consistent pattern of "government by business." The Labor Charter, though promised for as early as the summer of 1940, saw the light of day only fifteen months later. Throughout its painful gestation it became evident that the conflict between contradictory social philosophies at Pétain's "court" was so great as to make any valid compromise impossible. The text of the Charter itself and of its amendments swarmed with inconsistencies.[56] The mutual hostility of those in charge of its implementation made entire sections of the Charter inoperative.

The circumstances surrounding the publication of the law were grotesque enough, especially for a regime that justified its existence by accusing democracy of disorder. For all its instability the republic had never experienced a situation where different ministers of the same cabinet would steal from the government printing office the galley proofs of a statute or supervise personally its printing so as to assure that the "right" version would be published; where a head of government would be prevented from making the speech he intended to deliver upon the promulgation of the law; where the secretary of labor would sign only the text but not the official report introducing a fundamental piece of labor legislation.[57]

[56] For the text see *J.O.E.F.*, October 26, 1941, pp. 4650 ff. For a general and fully documented discussion of the Labor Charter, see Lefranc, *op.cit.* (n. 1-56), pp. 43-91. See also Elbow, *op.cit.* (n. 1-84), pp. 182-186, and Shepard B. Clough, "The House that Pétain Built," *Political Science Quarterly*, LIX, 1944, pp. 30 ff.

[57] Two only slightly different versions of these events are given by two writers of fundamentally opposite views in Nicolle, *op.cit.* (n. 1-48), pp. 340-41, and Lefranc, *op.cit.* (n. 1-56), pp. 52-53.

In his grandiloquent way Pétain had declared that the "aim which I pursue in publishing this Charter is to suppress the class struggle." The introductory report to the law minimized the obstacles that might stand in the way of such noble objectives: "Experience has shown that wherever men of good will get together for a loyal and frank explanation, oppositions dissolve first into mutual esteem, then into friendship." Such sentimental misreading of industrial relations in France was characteristic of the convinced corporatists, who could count on Pétain's sympathies but on little support elsewhere.

Among them were a number of intellectuals and an impetuous military man, Colonel Cèbe, the Marshal's personal adviser and friend. The only prominent figure to join the group was C. J. Gignoux. From his writings and his activities during the Vichy interlude, one gains the impression that his belated embracement of the corporative cause amounted to an act of repentance for having served too long the "trusts" and their masters.[58] Only a few employers shared the beliefs of the traditionalist corporatists, who wished to see the concepts of Le Mun and La Tour du Pin triumph in twentieth century France. Men like Jules Verger and Pierre Lucius were considered as outsiders by their own peers.[59] The flirtation of some managers of large-scale enterprise, such as Perrin, with this school of thought was of short duration.

The disciples of extreme corporatism were dissatisfied with many stipulations of the Labor Charter but even more with the implementation of the statute. While the prohibition of strikes and lockouts and the establishment of "professional families" were to their liking, they criticized the fact that trade unions and employers' associations were permitted to survive on the local, regional, and even the national level. They feared that as long as these organizations were not dissolved the mixed workers' and

[58] For Gignoux's corporatist thinking see above (n. 11-3) and especially his *La Tour du Pin*, Le Mans, 1943, where he describes, p. 6, the father of French traditionalist corporative thought as the "axis of the . . . betrayed [*sic*] National Revolution."

[59] For their pre-war activities and writings see above, Chapter I, esp. at n. 71, 84, and 85. For their disappointed comments on the Vichy legislation see especially Jules Verger, *Dans le Cadre de la Révolution Nationale. L'Education Professionnelle vers l'Ordre Social Nouveau*, (n.p., n.d.), and Pierre Lucius, *Je suis partout*, October 22, 1943, quoted in Lefranc, *op.cit.* (n. 1-56), p. 79.

employers' committees, the cells of classical corporatism, would never acquire sufficient strength to effect the merger of the economic and the social domain. But such a fusion, at all times vaguely defined, was the core of "radical" corporative thinking.

The spokesmen for business inside and outside the government were opposed to the very principle of the proposed merger between economic and social questions. They had successfully insisted that the Labor Charter explicitly recognize all economic questions to be within the domain of the CO, "until otherwise decided." Once again the provisional was perpetuated, and the attributes of the CO were never impinged upon by the Labor Charter. Since industry found little fault with the workings of the well-established CO, it was unwilling to see the Committees share their powers with any of the institutions that were to be created in application of the Labor Charter. The approach of business to the question of corporative organization was essentially empirical, spurning the theories of the apostles of corporatism and solely concerned with the employers' preponderance in the chain commanding economic decisions. At least in this respect the views of organized business were very similar to those taken by their brethren in fascist Italy and nazi Germany. In France businessmen and the trade unionists who supported first Belin and then his successor, Lagardelle, were united in their common resistance to nebulous "mixed" organization. Their motivation, it is true, was different. While the labor leaders hoped to insure the survival of their muzzled organizations, business simply believed that, given the general political situation, there was little need for "suppressing the class struggle" by an elaborate network of suspect labor-management committees.

The employers who opposed bold corporative innovations counted on the continuing weakness of the labor movement, manifest long before the republic had fallen. The split between communists and anti-communists, and the split between those who had followed Belin into his venture at Vichy and those who were opposed to it, were not conducive to any revitalization of the trade unions. Moreover, the Vichy legislation even without further implementation of the Labor Charter had done enough to insure the predominance of capital over labor. The simultaneous disappearance of the peak associations on both sides had given only for a moment the appearance of an equalization of force. Through the CO and through the general access to official-dom, business and its organizations had won far more than the advantages to be derived from outlawing a painfully surviving trade union movement. The employers also knew that social peace was not really threatened as long as the regime would assert itself as a police state and as long as the workers were aware that insubordination might result in deportation to Germany.[60]

A full-fledged corporatism would have led to the dissolution of employers' organizations and trade unions alike. This, in the opinion of most business leaders, was too high a price to pay at the moment when the trade associations acquired unprecedented strength through their connections with the CO, and when nothing was to be feared from the labor movement. For these reasons the corporatists lost out, deprived as they were of all sup-port by organized business. Their influence diminished even in the entourage of the Marshal, until finally the Institute for Corporative and Social Studies, solemnly consecrated at the beginning of the regime, was asked to cease all activities.[61]

The only institutions of the Labor Charter which most employ-ers considered valid were the social committees to be established under the law of 1941 in all firms employing more than 100 workers. Those committees concerned themselves with such welfare matters as factory canteens, cooperative stores, industrial hygiene, and health care—questions which took on particular importance during the war. The workers' delegates on the commit-tees were usually selected by the employer. Even in those plants where elections took place, the trade unions were prevented from playing any significant role.

Frequent circulars and directives from the Labor Ministry warned against allowing the social committees to become vehicles of an "outdated paternalism." But in general both employers and workers, equally unwilling to consider this creation of the

[60] A writer such as Lefranc, who usually takes the defense of the Vichy legisla-tion, believes that many employers held such opinions; see *op.cit.* (n. 1-56), passim. See also the convincing if cruel description in the novel by Psichari, *op.cit.* (n. 11-7), pp. 295 ff.
[61] For an interesting account of the "decline of corporatism" under Vichy, see Maurice Bouvier-Ajam, *Traité d'économie politique et d'histoire des doctrines économiques*, Paris, 1952, pp. 242-48.

Labor Charter as the ground floor of an ambitious corporative structure, were entirely satisfied with letting the committees concern themselves with an improvement of material conditions and nothing else. It is difficult to determine whether the committees had any influence on the climate of industrial relations. Where the relationship between employers and workers was satisfactory and especially where a common understanding was reached on the best ways for outwitting the occupation authorities, the collaboration between labor and management in the social committees seems to have strengthened mutual sympathy. In certain concerns the employer utilized the committees for sharing with his workers the difficulties he experienced in the running of the firm. Some experiments leading to a more developed form of labor-management cooperation had their origin in the common hardships of the war years.[62]

Far more frequently the workers regarded the social committees of the Charter as just another device for enforcing unilaterally an ever stricter discipline. When the German defeat drew closer and the defenses on which many businessmen had relied began to crumble, fears were expressed that by their intransigence the employers would prepare another day of reckoning. "The Charter has been sabotaged from all sides," noted a writer who had always been an enemy of labor. "Fearful of any control by the workers, big business is committing one stupidity after the other and is inviting the revolution into which they will drag all employers."[63]

## 4. Employers and the Resistance Movement

"The greatest courage is not the military courage which has public opinion with it: it is the civic courage which dares to go against it."

Detoeuf, *Propos de O. L. Barenton*

Though at the beginning almost the entire business community was willing to lend the Vichy regime its support, such general approval of principles and policies did not last long.

[62] Retrospectively the UIMM, speaking for the steel and metal industries, lauded the social committees as the only valid institution created by the Labor Charter. See its *op.cit.* (n. 1-22), pp. 51-52. The Charter itself was criticized in the same brochure as a violation of the freedom of association.

[63] See Nicolle, *op.cit.* (n. 1-48), Vol. 1, pp. 428-29.

When Laval addressed a gathering of sixty selected businessmen in Paris in the summer of 1942, he concluded already at that time that most of them expected or even wanted an American victory.[64] In that respect employers seem to have followed closely the general trend of opinion: a shrewd observer remarked afterwards that a Gallup poll in war-time France would probably have shown 95 percent of the population "Pétainist" after the armistice, 50 percent until the Allied landings in North Africa, and still 30 percent on D-Day.[65]

Nevertheless, there existed, especially among the workers at the time of the liberation, the belief that as a class the employers had a worse patriotic record than other Frenchmen, that they had collaborated to the fullest extent with the enemy and his Vichy satellites. Such an estimate was not based solely on some flagrant cases of economic collaboration. The conspicuous absence of employers from the resistance movement, inside and outside the country, was considered as proof that, as a group claiming elite status in society, business had failed the country.

To be sure, some employers did not shrink from acts of individual resistance, defying the orders of the Vichy government or of the occupation authorities. Some outright sabotage was committed with at least the connivance of industrialists. Names of businessmen were not altogether absent from the lists of deportees in nazi prison camps. The action program of the National Council of Resistance acknowledged that the protest strikes which had flared up in many parts of the country on Armstice Day 1943 had often been organized in common by workers and employers. But such acts as were committed were the deeds of individuals, in no way representative of the milieu to which they belonged. Indeed their courage was regarded by many of their colleagues as inopportune rather than admirable. "They were accused of nonconformism, always a grave reproach in those circles."[66]

No part of the employers' movement ever took a stand which could have been regarded as an encouragement to the manifold force that were or became hostile to Vichy. While at least part of organized labor was pushed by the events into an early oppo-

[64] *Ibid.*, p. 465.

[65] See Jean Galtier-Boissière, *Mon Journal depuis la Libération*, Paris, 1945, p. 38.

[66] Marquis d'Argenson, *op.cit.* (n. II-1), p. 92.

sition to the regime, organized business saw its influence enhanced by the Vichy legislation and by its administrative practices. Some sectors of the employers' movement, it is true, were less integrated with the armistice regime than others. Organizations which were more particularly concerned with social policy, such as the UIMM and the *Union Textile* assisted their member associations and firms in developing welfare policies for their workers. In doing so, employers' associations sometimes succeeded in delaying or even preventing workers' deportations to Germany.[67]

After the liberation the employers' movement complained bitterly that the true motives of the business community were constantly misrepresented and its patriotism falsely impugned. Its spokesmen failed to understand that, seen against the background of the CO and of the Labor Charter, even such collective measures as were undertaken by the employers' movement were at best understood as manifestations of a benevolent paternalism, not as acts by which the employers as a class had asserted their leadership and courage.[68]

Among the hundreds of underground organizations active during the period of occupation, the *Organisation Civile et Militaire*, known as the OCM, included relatively the largest number of employers, managers, and members of the high bureaucracy close to business.[69] Originally an amalgamation of anti-Vichy officers and professional men, the group was particularly strong in Paris and the industrial regions of the North; already in 1942 it had a membership of several thousands. While businessmen formed a small minority, some of them belonged to the group's leadership—for example, Maxime Blocq-Mascart, scion of an

[67] A description of such activities is to be found in UIMM, *op.cit.* (n. 1-22), pp. 48-51.

[68] The conclusion that no organized group of employers participated in the resistance movement and that their contributions to the resistance was altogether very small has been reached by most authors; see, e.g., Henri Michel, "Comment s'est formée la Pensée de la Résistance," in H. Michel and B. Mirkine-Guetzewitch, *Les Idées Politiques et Sociales de la Résistance*, Paris, 1954, pp. 33-34. In the same sense, Pierre Laroque, *Les grands Problèmes sociaux contemporains. Problèmes de Structure Sociale*, Paris, 1950-51, p. 345, and Renée Petit, "Etudes sur la Réorganisation syndicale en France depuis la Libération," *Droit Social*, IX, 1946, p. 74.

[69] For the history and composition of the OCM, see Henri Michel, *Histoire de la Résistance*, Paris, 1950, pp. 29-30; Michel and Mirkine-Guetzewitch, *op.cit.* (n. II-68), p. 275; and Martinet, *op.cit.* (n. II-52), p. 68.

old banking family and himself a banker; Aimé Lepercq, one-time director of the Skoda works and closely connected with the Schneider trust; and Pierre Lefaucheux, engineer and industrialist, who after the liberation was to become the first director of the nationalized Renault works. Blocq-Mascart represented the group in the National Council of Resistance. The only other businessman on the Council was Joseph Laniel, textile industrialist and a deputy in both the Third and the Fourth Republic.

The OCM was successful in winning the support of a number of younger businessmen and of university graduates interested in a business career. It also developed a number of "cells" in some high administrations, such as the Inspectorate of Finance and the Joint Intertrade Information Center, the agency which co-ordinated the activities of the CO. At one point the OCM, recruiting mostly elements of the upper bourgeoisie, established an alliance with the predominantly socialist underground movement of *Libération-Nord*. The OCM also worked in loose contact with the *Union des Cadres Industriels*, created much later when the maquis operation had reached its greatest density and when industrialists were asked to help defray the rapidly increasing costs incurred in organizing active resistance against deportation measures.[70]

The OCM was among the first resistance groups to study in detail desirable post-war reforms; its members rejected the idea of a return to the institutions and the conditions of the Third Republic. While it cannot be determined with certainty whether the employers who participated in the movement shared all or most of the opinions formulated in the underground publications of the OCM, it is known that Blocq-Mascart and Lefaucheux played an outstanding role in elaborating the doctrine and the program of the group. In view of their background it may be assumed that they expressed, in the project of a constitution and in the studies published in the *Cahiers* of the OCM, the general views of many of the businessmen who had joined the group.[71]

[70] For a vivid description of the part which some industrialists played in this form of resistance movement, see Pierre Audiot, *Paris pendant la Guerre*, Paris, 1946, pp. 222-23.

[71] For the views of the group see Maxime Blocq-Mascart, *Chroniques de la Résistance*, Paris, 1945; and Michel and Mirkine-Guetzewitch, *op.cit.* (n. 11-68), pp. 275-78, 366-70, 386-87. For various articles published in the underground press and

The intellectual leaders of the OCM probably considered themselves as socialists, though they were opposed to "state socialism," as devotees of a planned economy, though they preferred planning by "contractual agreement" to direct governmental intervention. Their concept of private property recognized the priority of social and community interests. Burnhamites without knowing it, they were preoccupied with the role of the manager in the modern corporation.[72] Themselves members of the managerial group, they concluded that economic power, after its separation from property title, was based on the successful runing of modern business enterprise. In turn, the success of the manager and his claim to prestige in firm and society were a function of his devotion to the cause of technical progress. The group accused corporatism of a tendency to restrict production at a time when the most vigorous development of the country's technology was required. The extensive retooling of industry and the acceleration of technical progress were considered indispensable to insure France's position as a strong nation in the post-war world, even if collective security were to become a reality.

The group tried to differentiate its ideas from those of the technocrats, stressing that it preached the cause of productivity as a means for human emancipation, not as an end in itself. Hence the economic measures it proposed were supplemented by demands for drastic reforms of the educational system and for changes in population policies. Although the group was free from communist influence, its publication expressed boundless admiration for the Soviet Union, which at that time also a de Gaulle would address as *"la chère et grande Russie."* Russia was praised by the group for its rate of economic growth and for

the preamble to the draft of a new constitution, see also the interesting article by Pierre Lefaucheux, written presumably before the liberation but published only afterwards, "Passage au Socialisme," *Les Cahiers Politiques*, March 1945, pp. 37-53; April 1945, pp. 37-48; and Martinet, *op.cit.* (n. 11-52), pp. 68-78. The last-named source gives, together with ample quotations from OCM publications, a Marxist-inspired critique of the group's view.

[72] Some French authors have always maintained that Burnham's thesis was nothing but an American adaptation of the book by the Italian Bruno R[izzi], *La Bureaucratisation du Monde*, Paris, 1934. Similarities between the theses of the two authors, both formerly marxists, are quite striking. But to accuse Mr. Burnham of plagiarism is unnecessary because obvious objective developments may have suggested themselves independently to the two authors.

the dynamics of its society; it was hailed as the most important future ally of France.

In regard to economic organization the OCM advocated contractual agreements between producers and public authorities. Its proposals tried to combine certain features of the CO legislation, and earlier suggestions for an industrial democracy as they had been developed by the pre-war labor movement. As a form of self-government of industry, the CO were regarded as a desirable form of organization, although the OCM avoided referring to them explicitly as they had become unpopular. Nevertheless, the group believed that the CO could be useful in bringing about the needed production discipline tempered by the necessary amount of individual initiative and responsibility. What had to be changed was the policy rather than the institution: economic expansion instead of restriction, flexibility rather than rigidity of the production plans. Unlike the Vichy CO, the reformed committees would rely on representatives of workers and technical cadres on all levels of decision-making and enforcement. But while there was to be democratization from the top, inside the plant the authority of the employer should not be challenged by either trade unions or plant committees. In this respect the group's thinking differed from suggestions made by the underground labor movement.

What role the state would have to play in supervising economic activities remained characteristically uncertain. Government should not hold too predominant a place; the beneficial effects of nationalization *per se* were not rated too highly. But the writers recognized that, to judge from the experience of the CO, one could hardly expect the "general interest" to emerge automatically. Hence proposals were made for a general administrative reform designed to bring about a greater independence for the civil servants who were to represent the government in the framework of the economic organization. A new institution, the "economic prefects," would wield sufficient power to correct decisions which could affect the general interest unfavorably.

There was a definite congruity of views between these businessmen, who had joined the resistance movement in spite of the general disapproval of their class, and the business group enjoying power and prestige under Vichy. They shared a lack of confidence in the automatism of a free market economy, contempt for the traditional ways of the individualistic French businessman, a belief in the important role of the technical elite. Lefaucheux, one of the leaders of the OCM and in many ways closer to socialist beliefs than the others, was quite logical when he objected strenuously to the idea that all those who had served Vichy should be eliminated from the tasks of reconstruction. As long as they had not committed crimes against *la patrie*, they should be invited to help in laying the groundwork of the new republic, obviously without being asked to renege all of their past beliefs.[73]

Here as in many other fields the Vichy regime has used and abused both ideas and men. The divisions and memories that have survived as legacy of the National Revolution have made it difficult to assess correctly which lessons ought to be drawn from the defeat in 1940 and from the experiences of the "corporative state."[74] That errors in economic policy had been a factor in the military collapse of the republic was generally conceded. But who was responsible for such errors was already controversial during the Vichy period. Aggravated by the futile exercises in penitence prescribed by Pétain, economic disorder has also turned into moral disorder. For it has become impossible to diagnose the ills without being identified with one of the two sides in the unending debate about the merits or the disgrace of the Vichy experience. Since there is basic disagreement about the meaning of that experience, the discussion has been fruitless from the start. But are the greatest national catastrophes not those from which nothing is learned?

The modern employers' movement owes much, in many cases all, to the impulses it received during the Vichy interregnum. It is therefore not astonishing that the war years have left their impact on many leaders of organized business—a traumatic impact, as it were.

[73] See Lefaucheux, *op.cit.* (n. II-71), April 1945, p. 47.

[74] For an excellent analysis of the legacy of Vichy, see Dorothy M. Pickles, *France between the Republics*, London, 1946, pp. 24-26 and passim. Among employers, discussions about the right and the wrong attitude during the war years continue, at least in private conversations, with a great deal of aggressiveness.

# PART TWO

Structure and Activities of Present-Day
Business Organizations

# CHAPTER III

# The CNPF and the Industrial Trade Associations

## *1. Uneasy Beginnings*

The liberation and the months of "dictatorship by consent" which followed opened a difficult era for employers and for organized business. The government no less than the man in the street was convinced that the employers' record during the most difficult hours of the country had been at best undistinguished, in many cases despicable. When de Gaulle, shortly after his return to France, received a motley group of employers who had come to pay their respects, he greeted them with a harsh "I haven't seen any of you gentlemen in London," adding contemptuously, "Well, after all, you are not in jail."[1]

The all but complete absence of the employers from the entourage of de Gaulle and from the Consultative Assembly in Algiers meant, if nothing else, a lack of contact with the new regime. A man like Blocq-Mascart incurred early the displeasure of de Gaulle and his closest advisers. He had suggested that the provisional government issue immediately a provisional constitution promising subsequent revisions to be enacted by an elected body or a plebiscite. After de Gaulle had turned down this proposal as dangerous and illegal,[2] most of the other suggestions which the OCM had elaborated during the resistance were eyed with suspicion as the concepts of an ambitious and possibly anti-democratic technocracy.

The progressive liberation of the territory brought in its wake spectacular expropriations, not only of industrialists who were accused of open collaboration with the enemy, such as

[1] Years after the event prominent personalities in the employers' movement would still refer with scorn to this episode from which they derived a deep-seated resentment against General de Gaulle. The best general discussion of the era is provided by John E. Sawyer, "The Reestablishment of the Republic in France: The de Gaulle Era, 1944-45," *Political Science Quarterly*, LXII, 1947, pp. 354-67, and Pickles, *op.cit.* (n. II-74), pp. 109 ff.

[2] See Gordon Wright, *The Reshaping of French Democracy*, New York, 1948, p. 52.

Berliet and Renault. Other concerns had their capital sequestered without any immediate decision as to ultimate ownership. Several thousand employers were for shorter or longer periods eliminated from the management of their firms, which were either temporarily closed or run, haphazardly enough, by workers or vigilantes.[3] Within weeks most of these employers recovered their property, sometimes without recourse to courts or administrative decisions. But the experience of having come close to expropriation had once more harmed the employers' self-esteem and was resented even by those who had remained undisturbed.

Public opinion polls revealed that industrialists and storekeepers were considered as having suffered little under the German occupation, with only the farmers yet better off. Given the general mood of the country in post-liberation days, such a judgment did not enhance the prestige of the bourgeoisie, especially since it was generally believed that the working class had been hit hardest during the war years.[4]

That portion of the press and those political parties which had been the consistent supporters of business in the past were in eclipse; individual journalists found it compromising to comment favorably on the role which employers had played during the occupation. Instead there developed in the newspapers and in the government-controlled radio a steadily harassing and at times violent campaign against the "trusts." De Gaulle and the labor press joined in denouncing their evilness in terms no less harsh than those Pétain had used to condemn them. The employers not only were attacked for the lack of patriotism they had shown during the war, but were also accused of still reaping illegal profits on the black market and of being lukewarm to the tasks of reconstruction.

Many businessmen retorted that, as long as such a campaign continued unchecked, they could not be expected to work with

[3] See George Lasserre, *Socialiser dans la Liberté, Vocation de l'Europe*, Paris, 1949, p. 152. According to J. Galtier-Boissière, *Histoire de la Guerre, 1939-1945*, Vol. v, Paris, 1948, p. 391, the fact that there were only temporary imprisonments and no trials of industrialists who had collaborated with the Germans was due to an agreement between de Gaulle and the communists.

[4] See *Sondages*, vii, February 1945, p. 8.

enthusiasm. In one of the trade association journals the head of the provisional government was beseeched "to order [*sic*!] that the French employers be given back their dignity and their freedom in a rejuvenated and reformed employers' movement."[5] By the end of 1945 numerous businessmen were preparing to emigrate from the country, since the days of Coblenz an unusual reaction on the part of the French elites.[6] If the hostility that surrounded business had been merely the result of communist propaganda, the employers might have been able to pass off the campaign as a political maneuver. But in fact a communist minister of industrial production implemented the party line of the moment by trying to woo the employers and to assure them of sympathetic understanding.[7] For the moment he only aggravated their humiliation.

The general ostracism which the business community felt directed against it had been prepared by the thinking of many non-communist resistance groups. At a time when the representatives of big business swarmed the councils of the Vichy government and the CO, expecting to reaffirm thereby their leading positions in society, many of the regime's foes concluded that the bourgeoisie had irretrievably lost its role as an elite.

In post-liberation France it was widely believed that reproaches such as François Goguel had addressed to the ruling classes of the Third Republic were fully justified. Writing in German captivity he had accused the bourgeoisie of having falsely claimed to hold a monopoly of the basic philosophy on which the French community rested. To him the ideas defended by the bourgeoisie were in fact little else than "patriotic sentiments mixed with the prejudices of economic liberalism, all

[5] Jean Constant, "Le Climat moral de l'Industrie," published in the August-September 1945 issue of the *Bulletin Mensuel du Syndicat Général des Industries Mécaniques*, and reprinted in the author's *Economie 45 ou l'Economie mal dirigée*, Paris, 1946, pp. 52-55. For a similar and very complete contemporary picture of the employers' mentality and their place in society during the period, see Ives Comar, "Réactions Patronales devant les faits actuels," *Cahiers de la CPF*, *Patrons '46*, Paris, 1946, pp. 16-19.

[6] See Louis Charvet, then executive secretary of the National Steel Association, in *Le Figaro*, December 29, 1945; see also *ibid.*, December 27, 1945 (quoted in Lucien Laurat and Marcelle Pommera, *Le Drame économique et monétaire français, depuis la Libération*, Paris, 1953, pp. 130-33).

[7] Marcel Paul, *Le Figaro*, February 19, 1946 (quoted in Lasserre, "Où va le Patronat Français," *op.cit.* [n. 1-10], p. 45).

cleverly dosed so as not to compromise the interests of the propertied class." But, he concluded, "those clever maneuvers are things of the past. . . . The development which the Third Republic underwent during the last decades of its existence has made the bankruptcy of the bourgeois value system unavoidable. Vichy has only consummated its fate. No one will resurrect the system of bourgeois ideas."[8] At about the same time Léon Blum concluded in his German prison cell: "For more than a century everything that has happened in France suggests that the bourgeoisie has been using up its sap."[9]

The moderate elements in the resistance movement had hoped that the middle classes would understand the historical justification for the transfer of power and that they would assist the "new popular elites" with their skills and their experience. At the time of the battle of the bulge, a widely heralded article sounded the "alert to the bourgeoisie." It appealed to the middle classes to abandon an attitude which could only be interpreted as their estrangement from the cause of liberation and of liberty. The coolness they had shown towards the resistance movement had been bad enough a manifestation of the ancestral bourgeois distrust of the *sans-culotte*. If now the upper bourgeoisie refused the part it could play in the reconstruction, it would commit a "national crime."[10]

Such strong words remained unheeded. After the first postwar elections seemed to have resulted in the nearly complete eviction of the traditional representatives of the middle classes from political life, a spokesman for organized business declared that the employers had no reason to depart from their self-chosen resignation. As long as they encountered general hostility and were excluded from public life, they would patiently wait for

[8] François Goguel, *op.cit.* (n. 1-7), Vol. II, pp. 342-43. For a similar indictment of the bourgeoisie, accusing it for never having been a true elite, see Georges Bernanos, "La Trahison du démocrate chrétien," a posthumous article, *Combat*, March 7, 1950.

[9] Léon Blum, *For All Mankind*, London, 1946, p. 71. Blum added on pp. 81-82 that the only way in which the employers could hope to preserve their authority was by helping to bring about a new prosperity.

[10] Jean-Bernard Derosne, "Alerte à la Bourgeoisie," *Carrefour*, December 9, 1944. This article, written by a journalist friendly to the milieu which he addressed, seems to have been used fairly widely during the 1945 election campaign by the MRP.

a change in the political climate and for a greater objectivity in governmental policy.[11]

Georges Sorel, frequently contemptuous of the French bourgeoisie even at the moment of its greatest influence during the Third Republic, had expected that a grave crisis might invigorate the defenders of capitalism and help them to find "the warlike qualities they once excelled in."[12] No such reaction could be observed in the critical post-war days. One of the prominent leaders of the employers' movement acknowledged later that his class had been unwilling and incapable of offering even verbal resistance to measures that threatened its economic status. To M. Lacour-Gayet, who was a fervent devotee of economic liberalism, such paralysis resulted from an exaggerated concern for security.[13] Other observers have remarked that such discreetness as they showed enabled the employers to retreat to various forms of "bourgeois anarchism": tax evasion, withholding of statistical data, black marketeering, and sundry manifestations of civic disobedience.[14]

Legislative enactments by the provisional government and the Constituent Assemblies gave additional strength to the employers' belief that they were treated as pariahs. In the summer of 1944 a decree had abolished the Labor Charter and thereby given back to labor its full organizational freedom. The trade union confederations, both CGT and CFTC, had re-formed as underground organizations after their dissolution in 1940. They had had their martyrs in the *maquis* and the German concentration camps, and their representatives in Algiers. But the same ordinance which reinstated the labor movement to legality provided that all employers' organizations could be dissolved if their personnel did not give sufficient guarantees of patriotism. The government appointed special committees to "reconstitute"

[11] See the interview of Pierre Fournier, temporary chairman of the provisional employers' delegation, published in *Temps Présent*, December 7, 1945. The attitude of the employers' movement during that period is described in a similar vein by XXX, "Le Conseil National du Patronat Français," *Le Droit Social*, IX, 1946, p. 206.

[12] See Georges Sorel, *Réflexions sur la Violence*, 11th edn., Paris, 1950, p. 120.

[13] Jacques Lacour-Gayet, in André Armengaud et al., *Vingt ans de Capitalisme d'Etat*, Paris, 1951, p. 10.

[14] See the very sharp but pertinent observations by Alfred Sauvy, "La Situation Economique," *Le Droit Social*, XI, 1948, p. 363. His characterization of employers' attitudes was acknowledged as correct by a number of industrialists.

trade associations and their affiliates at the national and departmental levels. In a few cases such measures led to an actual dissolution or purge. While the labor confederations recovered their assets, no mention was made of the funds that had belonged to the employers' organizations before their formal disbanding by the Vichy government.[15]

The nationalizations touched many of those sectors of the economy which had given to the employers' movement of the past most valuable support. The trade associations of the mining industry and insurance business, especially, had borne a substantial share of the funds on which the employers' movement had lived. The nationalizations in these fields aimed deliberately at depriving organized business of the possibility of subsidizing, as of old, the press and other information media. The new legislation on banking and credit, and the fundamental policies of the Monnet plan, foreshadowed a further decrease of business influence. In the domain of industrial relations the first ordinance on plant committees had already infringed on employers' prerogatives. The discussion of the law in the labor press made it evident that the new institution might be strengthened and enlarged so as to alter drastically labor-management relations in the private sector of industry.[16]

A decree proposing criminal sanctions against "illegal profits" singled out business but left undisturbed the profits made by other groups of the population, especially the farmers. When in 1946 parliament authorized an investigation of possible "sabotage" of economic recovery by business, the indignation of the employers threatening a regular "production strike" was finally violent enough to stop the proceedings.[17]

[15] See the basic ordinance of July 27, 1944, *J.O.*, August 30, 1944, pp. 776-77, and the decrees instituting "purge committees," e.g. of November 24 and 26, 1944, *J.O.*, November 29, 1944, p. 1547; for decrees dissolving employers' organizations see, for instance, one of December 2, 1944, *J.O.*, December 5, pp. 1677-78, and others during the same month. Later new provisions for further purging were made; see the law of February 25, 1946, *J.O.*, February 26, 1946, p. 1663. For a good study of the legal situation of employers' organization during the post-liberation period, see Petit, *op.cit.* (n. II-68), esp. pp. 74-76.

[16] For a full discussion of the employers' attitude towards the problems of nationalization, organization of credit, the Monnet plan, and plant committees, see below, Chapters VI, VII, and IX.

[17] For the indignation of the employers about the legislation concerning illegal profits, see Constant, *op.cit.* (n. III-5), pp. 17-21. On the attitude concerning an

The estrangement and apathy of the middle classes were all the more dangerous as, in spite of the nationalization and other reforms, the general physiognomy of French economic life was unchanged; private enterprise remained its basis and, as it were, its primary cell.[18] Generally speaking, the boards of directors of all large firms consisted of the same men, and almost always of the representatives of the same social groups, as before the war. Hence it was all the more necessary to normalize as soon as possible the relations between state and business.

The very few concrete plans that had been formulated before the liberation concerning the organization of the private sector of the economy had all assumed that eventually the generally unpopular CO would have to be disbanded. Even if the expected scarcity of raw materials and commodities necessitated the temporary maintenance of a planned economy, the institutions of Vichy would have to be transformed in spirit and structure, especially by eliminating what the resistance press had called the "oligarchy of big business leaders" from the control of the CO.[19]

Legislation, largely inspired by such views, was promptly enacted under the socialist minister of production, Robert Lacoste. While the Central Allocation Board for Raw Materials was "provisionally maintained" as previously organized, the CO were transformed into "Industrial Offices." Like their predecessors, the Offices were in charge of over-all economic planning and control of production. They also inherited from the CO the powers of enforcement, including the right to require statistical information and to levy contributions from all industrial and commercial firms. The predominance of the representatives of big business and its organizations was to be broken by replacing the former directors and presidents of the CO by commissioners, who were civil servants and frequently the directors of the corre-

order of April 1946, authorizing an investigation by a "citizens' committee" of black market practices, see Conseil National du Patronat Français, *Assemblée Générale*, June 1946, unpaged.

[18] See on this point the interesting discussion by G. Libeaux, "Réflexions sur le syndicalisme patronal," *Politique*, XXI, 1947, p. 716.

[19] See André Hauriou, *Vers une Doctrine de la Résistance. Le Socialisme Humaniste*, n.p., 1944, p. 103, and the suggestions for a reform of the CO formulated during the underground period by the OCM and discussed above, Chapter II.

sponding branches in the various technical ministries.[20] The representatives of trade associations were relegated to consultative committees, formed to assist each Office, and composed of an equal number of workers' and employers' representatives.

For being either too little like the CO or too much like them, the Industrial Offices were received unfavorably by both business and labor. In spite of the wording of the law, many of the larger Offices were controlled by the same personnel that had presided over the destinies of the CO. As late as April 1945 this was presumably the case for three-fifths of all Offices.[21] Even where the trade associations had lost their grip, the commissioners whom the government had put in charge were frequently the same who had played a subdued supervisory role during Vichy. They were little prone to formulate and impose policies incurring the displeasure of the industrialists with whom they had worked for so long. Where newly selected commissioners tried to assert independent policies, they would provoke the enmity of two categories of business leaders: those who had been the mainstay of the previous organization and those who, principally representing the small and medium-sized firms, had been dissatisfied with the CO already under Vichy. The Offices would now be criticized from many sides for wielding just as heavy a bureaucratic hand as their predecessors, for involving the struggling business firms in red tape just as confusing as before, and for exacting financial contributions which were more oppressive than ever.[22] In the past many businessmen had considered it their "patriotic duty" to lie to the CO when furnishing the required statistics; the atmosphere prevailing after the liberation was not particularly conducive to reestablishing veracity.[23]

[20] See the ordinances of June 22, 1944, *J.O.*, August 5, 1944, pp. 670-71, and those of October 7, 1944, *J.O.*, October 8, 1944, pp. 891-92.

[21] See Bouthillier, *op.cit.* (n. II-9), p. 274, quoting from the communist *Action* of April 1, 1945.

[22] For a violent attack on the institution of the Industrial Offices by a spokesman for the National Association of Engineering and Metal Industries, see Constant, *op.cit.* (n. III-5), pp. 29-34. It is true that Constant had been at all times critical of the CO. For a forthright defense of the Offices as offering all guarantees of democratic controls, see Henry du Verdier, "Des Comités d'Organization aux Offices Professionnels," *Les Cahiers Politiques*, No. 14, 1945, pp. 64-71.

[23] See André Heilbronner, "L'Eclipse de l'Organisation Professionnelle," *Droit Social*, IX, 1946, p. 314.

The attacks coming from the left and especially from the communists and the communist-controlled labor movement criticized not only the insufficient purge of Vichy personnel but also the very idea of giving to the representatives of business any official status in the economic organization. Even if the role of businessmen was diminished, the institution was still out of line with the desires of the resistance movement, which had wanted to eliminate the upper bourgeoisie from the levers of economic and administrative power. Finally the communists, in a deliberate demagogic appeal, pilloried the Offices for upholding the much-maligned *dirigisme*, a system of planned economy.[24]

When Léon Blum returned from captivity in the spring of 1945, he noted that instead of a will to sacrifice and renovate he found only "a tired, nonchalant, and lazy convalescence which is the proper breeding ground for all infections."[25] A progressive industrialist such as Auguste Detoeuf agreed in his analysis with the socialist Blum, and prescribed long years of austerity and sacrifices in the interest of technological progress as the only way to lasting recovery. Like Blum, Detoeuf had to acknowledge that such policies seemed to have little appeal and that his own fellow industrialists showed no inclination to heed such advice.[26]

The almost universal cry for a "liberation of the economy" following all too closely the liberation of the country was in part a reaction to the privations which a majority of Frenchmen had suffered during the war years. The provisional government maintained authoritarian policies in the fields of raw material allocation and price and wage fixing, but was unable either to control inflation or to prevent the spreading of the black market. The coexistence of the two markets permitted the reaping of abnormal profits at the many points where the legal and the illegal circuits touched each other. To the consumer, hard hit

[24] For a full statement of the communist griefs against the Offices, calling for their complete suppression as early as September 1945, see Benoît Frachon's report to the National Committee of the CGT, reproduced in his *La Bataille de la Production*, Paris, 1946, pp. 175-77.

[25] The impressions of Blum after his return from captivity were described in a series of articles which he published in June 1945 in *Le Populaire* under the title "Le cycle infernal."

[26] Auguste Detoeuf, "Le Problème du travail français," *Revue de Paris*, LII, 1945, pp. 37 ff. This is one of the first comprehensive statements, though far from typical, by a French employer after the liberation. See also Detoeuf's article in *Le Figaro*, July 1, 1945.

by such conditions, all institutions which strove to regulate the legal sector of the economy appeared not only as the residue of a detested past, but also as the sole cause of continuing scarcity. The period of occupation had developed the patience and ingenuity of the French people and of many businessmen, but also their lack of discipline and their leniency towards deceit. Since the liberation their patience had worn thin, but their insubordination remained strong and turned against all economic regulation.[27]

The provisional government, far from providing guidance to public opinion, pursued an unsure course and enforced its economic policies in the most fragmentary manner. After Pleven had won out over Mendès-France in May 1945, the staff of the Ministry of Finance (and to a lesser extent that of the Ministry of National Economy) could successfully resume its tradition of seeking the confidence of capital and of industry. If at the same time other departments, such as the Ministry of Food and the Ministry of Industrial Production, wished to take drastic measures against the same business groups, this could only increase the confusion, and lead to vacillating policies towards the employers.[28]

Opposition to the still-surviving Industrial Offices gave a common expression to the wrath of the victimized consumer and the individualistic producer. When the communists decided to espouse the consumers' cause, they found themselves in a position in which they upheld in fact the demands of business, small and large alike. In general, the period of greatest communist strength coincided with a tacit and sometimes open agreement between trade unions and employers to derive the greatest possible advantages from an inflationary economy by insisting

[27] For an excellent description of the economic situation of the period and its socio-psychological implications, see *Le Mouvement Economique, op.cit.* (n. II-53), pp. 25, 82; Gabriel Le Bras, "Note sur la sociologie et la psychologie de la France," *Bulletin International des Sciences Sociales,* I, 1950, p. 25; and Alfred Sauvy, *Le Pouvoir el l'opinion,* Paris, 1949, pp. 70-71.

[28] See on these points Sawyer, *op.cit.* (n. III-1), p. 360, who reaches the probably somewhat too sweeping conclusion: "Thus, the old ruling classes, at the times they themselves were looking for cover, found in de Gaulle an ally." It is, of course, true that de Gaulle personally made the decision for Pleven and against Mendès-France. In a similar vein, with more details dealing with many aspects of the entire period, see Emile Giraud, "Le Gouvernement du Général de Gaulle. Un Echec relatif," *Revue Politique et Parlementaire,* cvc, 1948, esp. pp. 286-89 and passim.

on simultaneous wage and price raises.[29] In the pursuance of such policies it was logical to strike down an institution which left in the hands of government an instrument for economic intervention.

The law of April 26, 1946 abolished the Industrial Offices over the signature of a communist minister of production. So general was the desire to do away with an institution which had at least attempted to control an economy in reconstruction that the Constituent Assembly passed the statute without discussion.[30] Only later were voices heard from many quarters that here a "liberation" had come too early: it had been Karl Marx, speaking about French affairs, who once commented on the role which stupidity plays in all revolutions and how such stupidity is always exploited—by the rascals.

Obviously the mere elimination of the Industrial Offices did not create plenty. For years to come scarce materials had to be allocated by the government. In order to decentralize procedures, the Ministry of National Economy surrendered the sub-allocation, i.e. the distribution of materials among industrial firms, to such employers' organizations as the trade associations and the Chambers of Commerce. Local associations or local sections of national trade associations were put in charge of supplying the medium-size and small firms; the "most representative" national trade associations would service the large enterprises. Where the national associations were considered sufficiently representative of an entire branch of industry, they could be entrusted with sub-allocating materials to all concerns, large and small.

Hence at the same moment when the employers' movement was freed of all governmental supervision, it had to assume important and quasi-official functions. In order to assist them in their new tasks the government decided on channelling to the

[29] For fuller discussion, especially of the so-called Palais-Royal agreement, see below, Chapter IX.

[30] See the law of April 26, 1946, *J.O.*, April 28, pp. 3534-36. For good contemporary evaluations of the law see P. Simonet and Liet-Vaulx, "La loi du 26 avril portant dissolution d'organismes professionnels et organisation de la repartition des produits industriels," *Droit Social*, IX, 1946, pp. 262-69, and Heilbronner, *op.cit.* (n. III-23), pp. 314-16. Later Heilbronner noted correctly that, seen from a distance, the law had by no means put an end to state-approved representation of interests; see André Heilbronner, "Le Pouvoir Professionnel," in Conseil d'Etat, *Etudes et Documents*, Paris, 1952, esp. pp. 51-52.

trade associations archives, statistics, and other information which the CO had assembled over the years. The self-government of industry had once more received an important boost by the legislator. But was the employers' movement, still recovering from the hazards of the post-liberation period, fully enough structured to assume its role? If nothing else, the need for determining the "most representative" organization in each branch called for a national organization with sufficient authority and standing.

\* \* \*

The new employers' confederation which was formed during the first half of 1946 represented the fusion of many efforts and trends that had emerged in the employers' movement since the liberation.

As early as August 1944, General de Gaulle had appointed an informal Committee of Employers' Representation without consulting any of the personalities who had been active in the employers' movement. The Committee's chairman, Pierre Fournier, a grain merchant who before the war had been on the staff of the Paris Chamber of Commerce, was little known and even less respected in the movement. He owed his mission principally to personal relations with de Gaulle, who at that time cared little whether his choice was approved by the business community. Various government ordinances created similar employers' committees for the Paris region and in the provinces. Their composition was haphazard everywhere; in general the authorities sought out those notables of the business world whose record under the occupation had been unblemished and who had not compromised themselves by too close a collaboration with the unpopular CO. By the application of such strict and noble standards, these committees excluded automatically all influential and truly representative leaders of the employers' movement.[31]

[31] For the decree of November 26, 1944, instituting the National Committee of Reconstitution, etc., see *J.O.*, November 29, p. 1547. All through December of the same year, the *J.O.* lists several decrees instituting similar committees on the department level.—In addition to statements by the principal *dramatis personae* this account of the pre-history of the CNPF is drawn from Petit, *op.cit.* (n. II-68), p. 76; XXX, "Le Conseil National," *op.cit.* (n. III-11), pp. 206 ff; and Lecordier, *op.cit.* (n. I-42), pp. 73-76.

At about the same time as de Gaulle nominated his committee, the socialist minister of industrial production called in even more informally another group of businessmen, who soon became more active than their less experienced colleagues around Fournier. When Lacoste's predecessor, Bichelonne, had followed Pétain to Germany, he had turned over to M. Pierre Ricard funds earmarked by the Vichy government for workers whom the advance of the Allied troops had put out of work. Under the Vichy regime Ricard had served simultaneously as the director of two of the more successful CO and as executive of the foundry trade association. During the phony war both he and Lacoste had served on Dautry's staff in the Ministry of Armament. Now the former trade union and resistance leader Lacoste and the CO official Ricard found little difficulty in establishing a satisfactory working relationship, which in part was based on similar views about the need for economic planning in a difficult period of reconstruction. From these contacts there emerged committees designed to assist industries in resuming production, but which also proved an excellent vehicle for bringing a number of ranking business leaders, among them Marcel Boussac, the "cotton cloth king," to the antechambers of Lacoste and of other ministers. Slowly but actively Ricard, and with him Henry Davezac, laid the groundwork for a new employers' confederation. Like Ricard, Davezac had originally been a civil servant who long before the war had become the executive of one of the most highly developed trade associations. Organizing the broad field of electrical engineering industries, it was intimately connected with a well-functioning cartel. Admirer and close collaborator of Auguste Detoeuf, Davezac had been during the war the executive of the CO over which Detoeuf presided, and had solidly cemented the operations of the CO, the trade association, and the cartel.

It is no accident that personalities like Ricard and Davezac were undaunted in their energetic efforts at rebuilding the employers' movement and that their energy left the imprint of their outlook on the structures which were to emerge. Surrounded by general hostility, patrimonial employers, whether controlling large or small firms, felt personally hurt and retreated sullenly into social and political inactivity, fearful as they were of further invasions of private property. But the "adoptive children of capitalism," the managers and highly qualified professional advocates of business interests, knew well that, even after the transfer of property title to public corporations, there would still be use for their abilities.[32] Their greater insight into political and economic developments may also have convinced them that in reality power had not really shifted as drastically as it appeared to the superficial observer. Not feeling defeated as did the majority of their colleagues, they showed no signs of defeatism, but went about preparing a comeback for the employers' movement by the means they judged most appropriate for the movement. The groundwork they laid for a new and unified employers' movement had to reckon with developments which were then shaping the organizations of business.

The economic organization of the armistice regime had greatly strengthened the position of the national trade associations and of the federations which in many cases grouped the associations in a larger branch of activities. The difficulties that arose for all business after the liberation made contacts between the trade associations and the ministries in the capital mandatory. The employers' organizations which did not have their seat in Paris were compelled to appoint special representatives to defend their interests with the administration. A great amount of further centralization ensued, and there was an increased need for forceful and yet flexible staff members. Where the Vichy period had not brought new and energetic men to leading positions in the trade associations, they now assumed office. A number of the older officials did not have enough stamina to persevere under the morally and materially difficult conditions of the post-liberation period. They were soon replaced by executives who were willing and able to face up to the tasks that awaited them as trade association officials. A number of them were men who had been purged from the civil service because of their all-too-compromising activities during the occupation. The leadership of some of the most influential federations and national trade associations, paying little heed to the government-appointed committees, acknowledged the need for a new representative employers' confederation. But from many sides it was once more stressed that the pre-war organization

[32] For a brilliant commentary on this category of businessmen, see Pierre Dieterlen, *Au delà du Capitalisme*, Paris, 1946, pp. 359-63.

had not proven its worth and that for new problems a new solution would have to be sought.[33]

As long as business was ostracized, the large trade associations, controlled as they were by big business, went quietly about the defense of their interests. Other employers' groups, however, found it possible to launch upon a more spectacular career. M. Gingembre, after only a brief interlude of silence which was deemed opportune because of his close collaboration with the Vichy minister Bichelonne, organized with ardor and noise the Confederation of Small and Medium-Sized Enterprises (CGPME). The organization was set up as early as October 1944, and claimed a few months later the adherence of 700 employers' associations. Gingembre clearly exploited the unpopularity of big business, but also the fear of small industrialists and shopkeepers who saw a wave of communism and state control engulfing them. In a situation where small businessmen felt helplessly isolated, only M. Gingembre's confederation offered solace and attracted many thousands of distraught businessmen. Moreover, in the employers' movement as a whole, the weight of small units had undoubtedly increased after some of the monopolized industries had been nationalized, and when others were threatened by further legislation which would at least modify the traditional characteristics of private enterprise.

When the question of a unified employers' representation could no longer be eluded, M. Gingembre made it known that his constituents were unwilling to accept another authoritarian, distant, and undemocratic confederation. The small businessmen had suffered too much from an employers' movement "identified with the 200 families." Even if a new peak association were to present itself as a "young and pretty child" with a new "make-up," his organization would remain skeptical as long as the council would draw its support from big business. In an article published at the time the first General Assembly of the new employers' confederation convened, M. Gingembre threatened that the CGPME reserved the right to withdraw from it at any

[33] As an example see Constant, *op.cit.* (n. III-5), p. 67, in an article first published in a trade association journal in November 1945 and endorsing wholeheartedly the propositions which one of the non-communist leaders of the CGT had suggested for a reorganization of the employers' movement.

time in order to "challenge the power of the trusts and to keep open the breach which the nationalization of credit had made in the wall of money power."[34]

During the same period also, the *Jeune Patron* movement had begun to stir. Though appealing to the same clientele as the CGPME, the *Jeune Patron* (JP) abhorred the shrill campaigns and the exclusively defensive character of the Confederation. Like its predecessor the CCOP, the JP was deeply imbued with a corporative philosophy which had found its partial vindication in the Vichy organizations. It had, however, steered clear of compromise with the regime, partly because it distrusted the technocratic bent that had been prevalent in the CO, partly because its members, mostly practicing Catholics, were opposed to nazism on religious grounds. Employers belonging to the group were known, at least to their own workers, for acts of solidarity, less blemished by paternalism than the attitude of other industrialists. Moreover, the movement had ceased all publications during the last years of the occupation so as not to incur the blame of having expounded their convictions with the approval of the enemy.

After the liberation a closely knit group such as the JP was able to find again its identity with greater ease than others. The group soon came forward with a public declaration stating the "rights and duties" of French employers and acknowledging that in the past businessmen and their organizations had committed grievous mistakes.[35] While the JP recognized the need for a new employers' confederation, it also insisted on guarantees of democratic representation and on a thoroughly reformed structure.

Just as the JP itself accepted as members individual employers only, not organizations, proposals were made from several sides that the new employers' movement abandon, wholly or in part, its traditional structure. Unlike the labor movement, it was argued, business organizations had never mobilized human beings, but incorporated economic units. Where the trade unions fought a human risk, exploitation, employers' organizations re-

---

[34] See Léon Gingembre, *La Tribune Economique*, December 21, 1945. For a full discussion of the CGPME and its leadership, see below, Chapter IV.

[35] See the Declaration of the Rights and Duties of the Employers, in Doctrine Jeune Patron, *Une Etape*, Paris, 1945. For a fuller discussion see below, Chapter IV.

acted by defending property rights. Did not the precarious situation created for the private sector by the post-war legislation call for a more personalist solution, for an organization of capitalists rather than of capital, an organization also in which the managers of private and perhaps of public corporations would find a more sensible place?[36]

During most of 1945 the groups formed to cooperate with the various ministries, the principal federations and the newer organizations, such as JP and CGPME met in a loose "Committee of Liaison and Study," where they compared their divergent opinions and attempted to compromise the interests which each had in building a new employers' confederation. How far the hostility surrounding them had intimidated many business leaders to the point of humility can be measured by the fact that, during the negotiations, recommendations were heard to omit from the name of the peak association any reference to *patronat* (employers).

Time was pressing from many sides. With the expected disappearance of the Industrial Offices it could also be expected that the discipline which the CO had introduced would be vanishing rapidly. As before the war the organizations would have to rely on voluntary dues-paying instead of receiving tax-like levies. The apostles of "vocational organization" dreaded the prospect that the progress made during the war years would be lost and that the employers' movement would return, under adverse political and economic conditions, to its pre-war status of impotence, and often chaos. The economic and technical functions of the trade associations, which in their opinion many CO had assumed so successfully, needed to be developed and generalized. Hence the national trade associations, the backbone of the employers' movement, should not become what they had been so frequently before the war: façades without authority, and

---

[36] See the rather confused discussion, formulated before the creation of the new CNPF, in Pragma, Publications de l'Institut de Science Economique Appliquée, *La Participation des salariés aux responsabilités de l'entrepreneur*, Paris, 1947. There is an excellent discussion of the general principles involved in Paul Durand, "Le régime juridique des syndicats patronaux," *Le Droit Social*, IX, 1946, pp. 372-76; and for a suggestion coming from the secretary general of the National Steel Association, who at that time was also prominently active in the MRP party, see Louis Charvet, "Mirages et perspectives de l'Organisation Professionnelle," *Politique*, XXI, 1947, pp. 104-23.

organizations lacking in constructive action. The moment public institutions were no longer serving as the cast by which such associations could be held together and made effective, cartel agreements should come once more into the foreground, perfected and provided with the disciplinary power previously wielded by the state.

In the past, rivalries between organizations had often prevented an effective structuring of industrial federations. Without a peak association arbitrating such conflicts, only a few well-organized trade associations could attend to the tasks that awaited them. But, if the employers' movement lost strength at a moment when other economic groups in society such as labor and agriculture were commanding increasing power, the danger was acute that the private sector of the economy would lose further ground and the *fonction patronale*, the private employers, be altogether without a hearing.

In the face of such a danger, those who since the liberation had spoken with uncertain voices for different groups of business felt enough urgency to bring the organizations and movements they represented together in a "Constituent Assembly," which convened in December 1945. By then opinions had crystallized into two major trends: there were those who believed that the situation warranted the creation of a powerful organism, well equipped not only to represent employers' interests at all levels of governmental operations, but also to enforce disciplined behavior among its constituents; others preferred a rather loose coordinating body voluntarily refraining from centralized action and from assembling a numerous staff.

For the moment, the second school won out, and the advocates of a more effective peak association decided not to press their proposals. At the summit of the organization, representatives of the small and medium-sized enterprises, of the regional inter-trade associations, and of such "vanguard" groups as the JP occupied an important place. In view of the antipathy which big business continued to encounter, it was necessary to have the full support of the smaller firms for the new organization. Moreover, the communists, still in ascendancy and preparing for the referendum on the Constitution, were just then developing an active propaganda to win the sympathies of small businessmen.

Their "General Confederation of Commerce and Industry" was making some headway with the most opportunist, or the most frightened, elements who were seeking to insure themselves against the possibility of communist rule. In such a situation the "light cavalry" which M. Gingembre had assembled in his confederation seemed indispensable. Since also some of the industrial federations such as the Textile Union disagreed on important points with the ideas entertained by their colleagues in heavy industry, the interests which had dominated the employers' movement in the past appeared to be in eclipse.

It took another six months before those designated in December 1945 were ready to report that an agreement had been reached on the by-laws of the new organization, christened *Conseil National du Patronat Français* (CNPF). In the meantime the newly formed CNPF had sought formal recognition by the government and had finally been received, one month after de Gaulle's resignation, by the new premier, the socialist Félix Gouin. The declaration which the employers submitted on that occasion had been written, according to his own claims, from beginning to end by M. Ricard. It read indeed like the charter of the new employers' movement, then in its formative stage.[37]

The new confederation boasted of representing all business activities and of giving a clearly predominant place to the small and medium-sized enterprises. While the employers complained that they had not been consulted in the post-liberation period and could therefore not assume responsibilities for legislation and administrative rulings, their language was moderate throughout. For the future, full collaboration by an employers' movement "conscious of its rights and duties" was promised. The coexistence of a private and a public sector of the economy, and thereby at least implicitly the nationalizations that had been enacted previously, were considered as an established fact. Business merely sought guarantees against future nationalizations and against the granting of unilateral privileges to nationalized enterprise. Private business, the government was assured, would adapt itself to the needs of a planned economy—an obvious reference to the Monnet plan, which was being elaborated at the

[37] For the full text of the declaration, see XXX, "Le Conseil National," *op.cit.* (n. III-11), pp. 207-08.

time. In the interests of some of its members the confederation asked that the government pay special attention to the needs of the luxury and export industries and that at least small firms be immediately and completely exempted from all controls. In general, the shackles of the war-time economy should fall soon, since business could do all that needed to be done, "strengthened by the discipline of its large organizations, which form the irreplaceable relays between the state and the enterprises."

Along with this credo in the benefits of business organization, the declaration assured the government of the new confederation's progressive outlook on social policy. Employers had complete understanding for the aspirations of the working class on both moral and material grounds. More specifically, the CNPF pledged its willingness to apply the first ordinance on plant committees in both letter and spirit. As long as the employers' authority was safeguarded, they were entirely willing to give to the workers a greater share in the "life" of the enterprise. In concluding, the employers' confederation declared its readiness to confront its views in "full objectivity" with the "large organizations of workers and of middle management."

The press gave only a limited play to the declaration and to the news that a reformed employers' organization had emerged. The general public, and many employers with it, took first notice of the new CNPF when, during the first referendum on the Constitution for the Fourth Republic, posters signed by the Employers' Council appeared all over France. Unlike the CGT, which campaigned ardently for the approval of the Constitution, the CNPF in characteristic moderation merely admonished all citizens to do their duty and to cast their ballot. Obviously, the employers hoped that the hint would be understood and that their posters would help block the unpalatable constitutional draft.

When the first General Assembly of the CNPF convened in June 1946, the first Constitution had already been rejected by the electorate. But inside and outside parliament hostility against business continued to manifest itself; the next elections would return the communists as the strongest party. Under such conditions the CNPF adopted its new by-laws and selected the leadership to guide it through the stormy years ahead.

## 2. The New Federal Structure and Its Functioning

The new employers' confederation, which saw the light at about the same time as the Constitution of the Fourth Republic, was in many ways a new creation. The most decisive changes, however, were due less to differences in structure and by-laws than to the transformations which the affiliated organizations had experienced since before the war.

In its official yearbook the CNPF points with particular pride to the features by which it claims to be distinct from its predecessor: there is no longer a predominance of the large over the small and medium-sized firms, of the capital over the provinces, of industry over commerce.[38] While in all these respects the structure of the confederation has indeed been altered, only a closer scrutiny of the workings of the new organization can reveal whether these are truly the most important changes.

As before, the employers' peak association accepts for membership only associations, not individual firms. Since, moreover, with only a few exceptions, secondary and not primary employers' associations join the Council, the enterprises are separated from it by at least two, if not more, levels of organization. In its own description the CNPF comprises today:

"On the vertical plane:

"The confederations, federations, or unions . . . grouping all employers of a given industry or a branch of trade, beginning with the individual employers and reaching from the local and national trade associations to the confederation, federation, or national union; . . .

"On the horizontal plane:

". . . the General Confederation of Small and Medium-Sized Enterprises, which . . . groups the organizations representing the small and medium-sized industrial and commercial enterprises;

". . . the Federation of Regional Associations, which . . . is composed of the local employers' groups."[39]

In reality the network of organizations is more complex than this listing suggests, the intricacy being generally the consequence of historical developments. In France as elsewhere a wavelike

[38] See Annuaire Général du Patronat Français, 1955, Paris, 1955, p. 10.
[39] Ibid., p. 7.

pattern existing between business and labor organizations has often led on the part of the employers to an imitation of trade union developments. In addition, employers' organizations of the past have left their traces where other organizations have superimposed their newer structures.

The previously explained fact that in France the functions of trade associations, dealing with market conditions, and those of employers' organizations, dealing with industrial relations, are merged, complicates matters further. At the lower level of the primary organization the merger is complete, though the different functions are sometimes handled by different staff members. At the higher levels a more marked specialization might take place. Generally speaking the "vertical" organizations will attend to the defense of economic interests, the "horizontal" groups will be mainly preoccupied with social or industrial relations problems. But such classification breaks down frequently, as in the case of M. Gingembre's confederation: though "horizontal," it is mostly interested in fighting economic issues. And while such organizations as the UIMM and the Textile Union handle principally industrial relations matters, they are "vertical" in the sense that their affiliates belong to one branch, however broad, of industrial activities.

In order to illustrate the complexities and the completeness of the modern employers' movement, Table I (see Appendix) pictures the organizational connections involving, at various levels, a small (fictitious) concern manufacturing metallic boxes in Bordeaux. The primary organization, the local trade association, represents the firm's total interests as a producer and as an employer. In principle the primary organization will rely for information and action involving the common trade interests of all producers in this particular branch of industry on the vertically arranged organizations, and for all questions involving industrial relations on the horizontal hierarchy. But this relationship is blurred because actually most important advice and support in matters affecting the employer-employee relationship will come from the UIMM, to which horizontal and vertical organizations belong. In addition, the special interests of the smaller industrial firms are articulated by their connection with the Association of the Small and Medium-Sized Industry and through it with the CGPME. Moreover, according to the inclination of its owner, the firm taken here as an example might also have sought direct affiliation with such organizations as the *Jeune Patron* or the *Centre Français du Patronat Chrétien.*

Had the example chosen been that of a commercial firm, the picture would not have been essentially different, except that the firm would be affiliated with the central employers' confederation through yet another organ, the National Council of Commerce.

For the apex of the entire structure, the CNPF, two opposite dangers had to be avoided, dangers which are generally present in the formative stage of any new federative organization, but which were particularly acute in the French post-war situation. The still-continuing threat to private enterprise and the not-yet-broken advance of the communists, who seemed to be moving closer to the centers of political and economic power, suggested that the employers' movement needed to be equipped for swift and centralized action. A loosely drawn structure, devoid of the power of decision making, might fail to produce the authoritative leadership and the prestige for which all employers craved. But an organism openly concentrating power and authority in the hands of a small self-perpetuating minority would have provoked discord and perhaps revolt on the part of the member organizations. In a period characterized by an all-pervading democratic frenzy, employers' interests needed the justification of all-inclusiveness providing the democratic legitimacy of the large number.[40]

The balanced solution which was adopted was almost unavoidable. Outwardly the new organization appeared as a loose, democratic, and decentralized federation, creating or strengthening intermediate organizations between the firms and the confederation so as to give to divergent interests the possibility of expression and articulation before they were to be integrated at the top. But at the same time the council structure did not pre-

[40] On the significance of the "democratic mold" for pressure groups of almost any kind in modern society, see Truman, *op.cit.* (n. 1-27), pp. 129-39. For the particular problems facing business organizations, see Alfred S. Cleveland, *Some Political Aspects of Organized Industry*, unpublished Ph.D. thesis, 1946, Harvard University, p. 39.

vent a closely knit group in its midst from developing authority and energetic defense of the employers' cause.

Article 2 of the by-laws defining the "object" of the CNPF describes the powers of the employers' confederation with extreme care. It is to:

"a. Insure the liaison and the permanent coordination between each of the constituent groups, the latter retaining their individuality, their autonomy, and their own means of cooperation within the framework of the general policy discussed and accepted jointly.

"b. Insure the general representation of heads of enterprises in negotiations with the government, or organizations of producers and wage or salary earners, on all economic or social questions with regard to *which its members have agreed. Each union, federation, or group would therefore be bound only by the policy of the Council insofar as its representatives have not previously expressed an opinion to the contrary.* [Emphasis supplied.]

"c. Propose to its member groups those common actions that can improve the conditions of economic and social life of the country, and organize and defend the employers status [*fonction patronale*]."

This provision had been hotly debated during the framing of the new constitution, and therefore had not been adopted lightly. For M. Gingembre's organization, as well as for other employers' organizations, the granting of the "veto" right was an essential condition for adherence to the CNPF. The by-laws of the pre-war CGPF, while also speaking about "great autonomy," had nevertheless insisted that the member organizations "observe the decisions of the CGPF regarding employers' discipline" and had asked that all matters involving questions of general interest be submitted to the president's approval. Now the situation seemed to be reversed: by its veto every member organization was supposedly able to dissociate itself from any, even the most important, action of the confederation. But the true difference between the pre-war and the post-war by-laws of the employers' peak association consists in the fact that the CGPF was never able to enforce the discipline to which it wished to submit its members, while the CNPF, in spite of the broadly framed rights of its affiliates, can most of the time command a far greater respect for its decisions than its predecessor.

The organ symbolizing outstandingly the desired "democratic mold" of the CNPF is its General Assembly. Because of the values and attitudes which prevailed when the by-laws of the new organization were adopted, the General Assembly was enumerated first among the federal organs, while in the different by-laws which the CGPF had known before the war, the Assembly ran a poor third.

The composition of the General Assembly is broad enough to give representation to all elements of the employers' movement. (For an organizational chart of the CNPF, see Appendix, Table II.) Out of 500 seats, the industrial federations and the large trade associations are entitled to 275, the commercial organizations to 75 delegates. The regional intra-trade organizations send to the Assembly another 75 delegates, and the General Confederation of Small and Medium-Sized Enterprises an equal number. The over-all distribution of votes makes it certain that within the General Assembly the few federations which represent large-scale enterprise, and which are usually best organized, can never obtain a majority of votes. Their weight can always be offset by associations representing predominantly small firms, in such fields as jewelry, embroidery, ceramics or glass, dry cleaning and drug stores. Those organizations joining with the delegates for the CGPME and the regional associations could easily insure to small-scale enterprise a large majority of representation.

The federations and trade associations are autonomous in the choice of their delegates. Whether they have to consult the primary or secondary organizations, which are their constituents, depends on their own by-laws, but in general the individual employers have no say in the choice of delegates. According to the official list of delegates to the General Assembly, most organizations are represented by their presidents, who usually are active businessmen in the Paris region.

Yet the official delegates do not necessarily attend the meetings. According to the rules of procedure, they may designate as proxy either an employer belonging to the same organization, or members of the professional staff of their association. If businessmen were actually chosen to attend the meetings, the General Assembly might recover the "grass-roots" character which it was intended to have. But far more frequently the ranking members of the professional staff represent the delegates, so that the meetings are often attended by a majority of "bureaucrats" of the employers' movement.

According to the by-laws, the powers and functions of the General Assembly are considerable. It is supposed to pronounce itself on the report dealing with the general activities of the organization and outlining its future course of action. It approves the budget and decides on the admission and expulsion of members. Every second year it elects the members of the Board of Directors. A complicated election procedure seemingly insures that also in these elections the votes of the delegates of small business cannot be submerged by those of the large industrial federations.

In reality, the role of the General Assembly in decision making is insignificant. For a short time after the formation of the CNPF the meetings of the Assembly were the scene of rather vivid discussions, where the small businessmen gave expression to their desire for a good measure of anarchy and clashed with the representatives of large corporations calling for unpopular disciplines in the name of "government by business."[41]

In such earlier days the CNPF also made use of another "democratic" device, that of a "referendum" on a rather loosely worded question concerned with further liberalization of the economy and the distribution of raw materials by the trade associations. Actually, the "referendum" was restricted to the members of the General Assembly, and of those present less than half voted. Since then no such experiment has been repeated. A general consultation of the membership, as it is occasionally practiced by the NAM and more frequently by the United States Chamber of Commerce, is totally unknown.

At present, controversies are no longer aired in the General Assembly. The meetings, held biennially, are devoted to the

[41] On these earlier discussions, see Conseil National du Patronat Français, *Assemblée Générale*, June 1946 (mimeographed, unpaged), and CNPF, *Bulletin du Conseil National du Patronat Français* (referred to hereafter as *Bulletin*), I, No. 11, January 1948, pp. 9-10.

delivery of a presidential address and the endorsement by the audience of lengthy and mostly technical reports prepared by the CNPF's staff committees. The budget and occasional modifications of the by-laws proposed by the Executive are regularly approved without criticism. The election of the Board of Directors is a pure formality; its membership is renewed regularly. Such changes in the personnel of the Board as have occurred have originated with the affiliated organizations replacing, for reasons of their own, their representatives on the Board.

According to the sarcastic comments of some leading personalities in the employers' movement, the General Assembly has ceased to fulfill any useful function and is nothing but a waste of time. Similar gatherings of American business groups have equally little weight in decision making. But such an institution as the annual Congress of American Industry, organized by the NAM, still has the important task of "spreading the word, rather than determining it."[42] Since the Congress is used as a vehicle of public relations, it is natural that members and non-members alike can attend. Propaganda materials displayed during the meetings illustrate the general views of management while far less attention is paid to concrete action proposals.

Quite differently, the General Assembly of the CNPF is closed to all except the official delegates. Neither observers nor press are admitted. As a means of "spreading the word," the meetings have only limited value, since practically all of the material presented is published shortly afterwards in the CNPF's bulletin. Moreover, since the audience is composed of affiliates, and sometimes even employees, of trade associations, the policies of the organization can be expounded more effectively elsewhere than in these large gatherings. The work in which the delegates are involved brings them in constant contact with the CNPF or its sub-divisions. Even if the delegates disapprove of the policies and procedures of the peak association, they obviously do not consider the biennial meetings the proper arena for voicing their opposition. If these meetings fulfill any function of "internal propaganda," it is that of providing a certain amount of galvanization, a one-day, more or less solemn, interruption of the hum-

42 See Truman, op.cit. (n. 1-27), p. 197.

drum daily activities to which most of the delegates are sub-jected. For that reason it is necessary to exclude all outsiders, since otherwise there would be little pride and fascination in belonging to the supreme body of the employers' peak association.

What is vastly more important is to present the meetings of the General Assembly to public opinion at large as the proof that the employers' movement is run in democratic fashion. The closest parallel might be found in the elaborate efforts of Ameri-can corporations to give to their stockholders' meetings an aspect of large attendance and active "member participation." The press conferences which the president of the CNPF holds at the close of each General Assembly are ringing affirmations of the representative character of the organization and of its internal cohesion and unity. Without the formal ratification by the Gen-eral Assembly, the policies followed by the CNPF could be attacked with greater apparent justification as the handiwork of a small active minority within the organization.

The Board of Directors (*Comité Directeur*) has in many ways the characteristics of a standing committee of the General As-sembly, convening regularly eleven times a year. Most of the Board members are also members of the General Assembly; the structure of the Board is generally the same as that of the Assem-bly: the seats are divided among representatives of the industrial and commercial trade associations, of the regional associations, and of the PME—the small and medium-sized enterprises. But since the number of Board members may not be larger than one-fourth of the number of delegates to the Assembly, the designa-tion must obviously be more selective.

By their origin, their position in industry or commerce, their role in the employers' movement, the Board members are an extremely varied group. A majority of them (about 90 of the total of 120) are "presidents" of trade associations and there-fore, as has been explained, generally active businessmen. The not negligible minority of about 30 are ranking staff members of the associations; a few of the latter have, also, managerial positions in industry. Most of the members list their business address as Paris—99 as against only 21 coming from the prov-inces. The positions of those who are active heads of enterprises vary from one branch to another. In the most important activities the managers are more numerous than the patrimonial owners. The latter predominate, as would be expected, in branches representing the luxury goods industry and commercial establishments, but also in the textile and leather industries.

Most noteworthy is the fact that very few of the country's outstanding businessmen are members of the CNPF's Board of Directors, at least if one excludes those who are also serving on the next higher level of the Council's hierarchy. As compared with the pre-war CGPF—and especially with the Confederation as it existed before Matignon—the number of leading industrialists and bankers among the Board members has sharply diminished. Today their names are rather to be found among the French delegation to the International Chamber of Commerce or as presidents of some of the CNPF's ranking committees.[43] On the other hand both the presidents and the staff members who have reached in their associations a sufficiently high position to be selected for the Council's Board are a more alert, younger, and better-trained group than before the war. Here the changes brought about by the economic policies of the Vichy regime, and especially through the CO, have been most marked.

In general, also, the role of the Board of Directors in policy formation and decision making is far from significant. It has steadily declined over the years with the growing centralization of the organization. Its meetings serve to inform the Board members on the past activities and on plans for the immediate future, as formulated by the Executive. According to some officials, divergent views among the affiliates of the CNPF are actually compromised in the meetings of the Board of Directors. But in the words of a disgruntled Board member: "The dish is brought in all cooked; it has been prepared elsewhere."

Lately the steady decrease in the Board's activities and in its prestige has been almost openly recognized. According to article 12 of the by-laws, a group of persons could be attached to the Board "in view of their competence in economic, social, and business matters." In the past some of the best brains of the employers' movement served in this capacity, and among them

[43] For further discussion of the committee structure, see below. For the membership of the French Committee of the International Chamber of Commerce, see *Annuaire, etc., op.cit.* (n. III-38), pp. 754-55.

men, such as the representative of the JP movement, who would not always endorse without discussion the decisions which were laid before the Board. This group has now been whittled down to numerical and general insignificance.

Moving in the opposite direction, the Executive Committee (*Bureau*) has seen its membership raised twice and counts at present twenty-eight members. While the Executive Committee and its president are elected annually by the Board of Directors, the election amounts in general to but another formality: the proposed slate is always approved with quasi-unanimity. Under such conditions the turnover of members of the Executive has been practically nil; except for the addition of new seats and for elimination by death, the membership has remained almost identical for over a decade. The only significant resignation was that of M. Gingembre, founder and leader of the CGPME, who withdrew as early as 1947 but was replaced by another representative of his organization.[44]

Now even a body of twenty-eight members is too large to provide the homogeneous leadership which the CNPF has known during most of its existence. To single out those who within the Executive are playing the foremost role in policy shaping and decision making is not too difficult. It is more complicated to determine which outside personalities these key figures of the CNPF might rely on for advice and support.

From the very beginning the organization has given an exalted position to its president. His election takes place by special ballot, separated from the balloting for other members of the Executive. The present and so far only incumbent of the post, M. Georges Villiers, has seen to it that his office and personality are afforded the necessary adornments to heighten further his dignity and authority. His picture appears as frontispiece in the imposing directory of the employers' movement, and is to be found in many offices of the CNPF's affiliates. His executive secretary bears the proud title of *chef de cabinet* so that the president of the CNPF might enjoy the same paraphernalia as a premier of the French Republic. The weekly meetings of the Executive in the sumptuous headquarters of the CNPF are made

[44] For the developing relationship between the CGPME and the CNPF, see below, Chapter IV.

to resemble as much as possible those of the French cabinets—
except that this cabinet's survival is never threatened by a fickle
parliament.

Villiers' first contacts with the employers' movement date back
to the troubled days of 1936; after the sit-down strikes the
young Lyonnais industrialist, who was known among his workers
as an authoritarian boss, was made president of the local section
of the metal-trades association and one of the vice-presidents of
the Chamber of Commerce. Like his father and grandfather before
him, he had graduated from the School of Mines in St. Etienne,
a good provincial technical school which does not do much for
the general education of its students. Georges Villiers did not
immediately enter the family business, a metal-working factory
of modest dimension, but which had secured considerable afflu-
ence to its owners. He became first the employee and soon the
director of a competing firm of similar character. Today both
concerns are merged in a company which employs a total of 700
workers. Moreover, M. Villiers and members of his immediate
family are now also managers or board members of other concerns of some importance in the same general field.

In 1941 when Edouard Herriot, the great old man of the
radical-socialist party, was dismissed as mayor of Lyons, Villiers
was appointed by the Vichy government to replace him. He remained mayor for the better part of two years.[45]   Differences
with the government brought about his resignation. In June
1944, during the vanishing days of the nazi occupation, he was
arrested by the Gestapo for participating in the underground
movement, condemned to death, but later transferred to Dachau
and work in the salt mines, where, according to the testimony
of some ardent syndicalists who were his fellow inmates, he gave
an example of fortitude and solidarity.

When in the winter of 1945-46 Pierre Ricard decided that a
new central employers' organization needed to be formed, but
that he himself should rather play the role of the gray eminence,

[45] It seems impossible to obtain a clear picture of M. Villiers' activities
during the Vichy years. Different sources differ even in regard to his years of
office as mayor, the date of his arrest, etc. It is not suggested that M. Villiers has
to hide anything, but that, possibly because of the changed political atmosphere,
he no longer wishes to boast of his resistance record, which at the time earned
him two military decorations.

he found in Villiers, allegedly after some others had declined the offer, a person admirably fitted to fill the needs of the moment.[46] Here was a man with an authentic resistance record, a victim of the nazis. That he was almost totally unknown in the employers' movement of Paris was only welcome. Businessmen from the provinces could feel assured that they would not be entirely dominated as in the past by the interests of the capital. Villiers' position in industry was particularly satisfactory to the temper of the period, since he was neither an exponent of big business like Duchemin, nor a pressure group official like Gignoux, but an authentic patrimonial employer. On the other hand his personality, his discreetness and finesse, were a guarantee that he would never descend to the level of small business demagoguery practiced by M. Gingembre. Today M. Villiers' critics admit that his personal stature within the employers' movement has constantly grown, and that the admiration for him is sometimes accompanied by true affection, rarely felt by French businessmen for anybody outside their family. The considerable increase in prestige and influence which the employers have known since 1946 is often attributed to him personally, though the outside observer would conclude that the general trend towards economic and social conservatism in the Fourth Republic has played a more decisive role.

It is admitted that intellectually the president of the CNPF is inferior to many of his associates. When he strays from prepared reports he will easily strike emotional chords which do him honor as an amateur devotee of music and the Oriental arts, but do not indicate any familiarity with complicated economic problems or doctrines. If "charismatic leadership" has come to denote authority which cannot be explained rationally, M. Villiers is a charismatic leader.

At the beginning of his career as CNPF president, he professed skepticism as to the future of economic liberalism: "We will try," he then said in an interview, "to make the employers of good will understand that any return to an excessive liberalism is impossible, and that they must accept the necessary

---

[46] In the judgement of one of the old-time staff members of the CNPF: "Ricard has invented Villiers."

disciplines in the framework of organized business."[47] Some years later he declared that he would no longer formulate his thoughts in such a manner. Indeed some of the worst tactical mistakes he committed were due to his fascination with attempts at propagandizing the shallowest concepts of "free enterprise."

When in 1951-52 a move developed to unseat M. Villiers, he astonished those who had regarded him as the pawn of others by his resilience and his ability to use in his favor what remained of the "democratic mold" of the employers' movement. His opponents, a number of big business spokesmen, had come to the conclusion that, because of the change in general conditions, M. Villiers' usefulness had come to an end and that he should be replaced by a man whose shortcomings, if any, were less apparent. But by touring the country, by appealing to individual members of the Board of Directors, and by using his contacts with the trade associations, M. Villiers was able to build the support he needed to survive as president. It is true that in his campaign for reelection he made much of his personal ability to hold together and integrate conflicting trends and interests within the Council—a strong argument with members of business organizations whose cohesion is frequently threatened.

Among the six vice-presidents of Executive, M. Pierre Ricard occupied from the beginning the most prominent place, commensurate not only to his talents but also to the efforts he had spent in bringing the CNPF to life.[48] However, neither his career nor his beliefs and personality inspired sufficient confidence among the great mass of French patrimonial employers; hence he was disqualified to play the role of the "great unifier" which Villiers has assumed. Like Jean Bichelonne, Ricard was the laureate of his graduating class at the *Polytechnique*, and he admitted that he was sometimes haunted by the possibility that his talents matched those of the unfortunate "Colbert of Vichy." His critics maintained that it was indeed M. Ricard's ambition to become one day minister of production in a regenerated France;

[47] See *Témoignage Chrétien*, April 22, 1946.
[48] After this was written M. Ricard died at the age of 57. Because of the prominent role he played in the employers' movement during the period this study is mostly concerned with, the passages devoted to his career and activities have not been altered. For the time being he has not been replaced, inasmuch as his functions in the CNPF have been divided among several persons.

presumably the political color of the regime would have been of less importance to him than the extent of the powers wielded by the Ministry. After additional studies at the famed National School of Mines in Paris, Ricard served for fifteen years in the Ministry of Commerce. In 1938 he left the public service, which to him, as to many of his fellow graduates, was little more than the prologue to a business career. He became the manager of an important foundry concern which is closely connected with the famed Mar-Mich-Pont combine in the steel industry.[49]

From there M. Ricard's connections spread rapidly both during and after the war, so that at the time of his death he was manager or board member of more than a dozen corporations in far-flung fields, including concerns in the steel and metal industry, a paper mill, a rubber factory, and a contractor's firm; he also was one of the directors of the nationalized Crédit Lyonnais. The considerable personal fortune which M. Ricard had been able to accumulate during his career enabled him to buy himself into the ownership of a number of firms. For him, as so often in France, the dividing line between the adoptive and the legitimate children of capitalism, between the managerial and the patrimonial employers, had become blurred, and the change in legal position had its psychological consequences as well.

In Burnham's analysis the managers are apt to shed many of their bourgeois concepts and their concern for status, since their status is not inherited. It appears that in France the patrimonial businessmen, members of a closely knit class, are tenacious and stubborn enough to mold into their own patterns of thinking the minds of those whom they admit from the outside. To many a French managerial employer his functions in the enterprise are just as personalized and status-bearing as to the owner of a family firm.[50] The strength of bourgeois traditions is sufficiently

[49] For details see *Le Monde des Affaires en France, op.cit.* (n. 1-37), pp. 114-16. For a detailed and interesting portrait of M. Ricard and his business connections, see *Entreprise*, I, No. 2, 1953, pp. 1-3.

[50] By far the best analysis of the mentality of the traditional French business-man is given by David Landes, "French Business and the Businessman: A Social and Cultural Analysis," Edward M. Earle, ed., *Modern France: Problems of the Third and Fourth Republics*, Princeton, 1951, pp. 334-53. Burnham's thesis is of course contained in his *Managerial Revolution*, New York, 1945. Peter F. Drucker, *The New Society. The Anatomy of the Industrial Order*, New York, 1949-50, gives closer attention than Burnham to the peculiarities of the European situation. While

great to amalgamate the managers and even those who come from positions in government service, such as M. Ricard and some prominent figures of the present-day employers' movement. Such differences in mentality as continue to exist are often more verbal than reflected in actual behavior. In France true opposition exists rather between the heads of large and efficient business units, whether managerial or patrimonial, and those of the smaller obsolete enterprises.

In his self-image, it is true, M. Ricard remained a technician rather than an employer, an administrator at least as much as the defender of a patrimony. Among the members of the CNPF Executive he was probably the most outspoken champion of both productivity and "industrial organization," which to him meant essentially productivity through cartels.[51] To him the term *dirigisme*, standing for government intervention in economic life, held less terror than to most of his colleagues. His bluntly expressed resentment was often directed less against the labor movement than against the myriad of small businessmen. At the time when the CNPF had found in Antoine Pinay its temporary shield, Ricard had little sympathy for the premier, who to him symbolized the narrowness of a small businessman turned politician. After the bitter struggle over the ratification of the Schuman plan, during which M. Ricard kept cautiously on the sidelines, he obtained one of the most coveted posts in the entire employers' movement: he was made the executive of the National Steel Association, the former *Comité des Forges*.

Two other vice-presidents of the CNPF, Marcel Meunier and Emmanuel Mayolle, have belonged from the beginning to the inner group of the Executive. M. Meunier's career is fairly typical of those French employers who have reached their executive positions in industry only after much struggle. Not born to wealth and with no education beyond the secondary level, their slow upward climb has made them often more rigid

---

he is correct in stressing (p. 350) that on the whole the European industrialists have followed the pattern of the French *propriétaire*, he too insists, in my opinion, too much on the difference between patrimonial employers and managers.

[51] Since M. Ricard wrote little, the clearest exposés of his beliefs used to be his speeches in the Economic Council, from which he resigned in 1953. See, e.g., his remarks, not uncritical of other employers' opinions, in a debate in the *Bulletin du Conseil Economique*, July 11, 1948, pp. 1034-36.

and more rigorous in their outlook on industrial relations than either the employers of "divine right," who feel secure enough in their inherited positions, or the modern managers, who know that they owe their place to training or connections.[52] M. Meunier owns a telephone equipment factory employing about 300 workers and is also the director of a much larger firm manufacturing elevators. For years he has played a foremost role in the employers' organization of the metal trades and especially in the UIMM. As president of the CNPF's Committee on Industrial Relations, he not only impresses his own social philosophy on many Council activities but, together with his chief collaborators, provides the traditional amalgamation of services between the general employers' confederation and the UIMM, just as M. Ricard personified the connection between the steel interests and the CNPF.[53]

Without his position in the trade associations Emmanuel Mayolle would always have remained the "average French businessman" he still looks and acts. He runs a family enterprise in the soap and perfume industry and has become over the years the director of a few other relatively modest firms in related fields. Before the war the trade associations of the soap industry and the industrial federation over which M. Mayolle presided were typical of the employers' organizations without funds and without staff. This changed radically when they were absorbed into the influential Vichy CO for Industrial Fats and Oils, of which Mayolle became the director. Through his activities he established an intimate contact with the organizations of the chemical industries, and when the CNPF was founded he represented in its midst more or less openly the chemical interests, at least until

[52] Until recently it has been difficult to obtain data on the social and educational background of French industrialists. See the complaint in an interesting thesis by Louis-Marie Ferré, *Les classes sociales dans la France contemporaine*, Paris, 1934, commenting on the meager results of an earlier inquiry resented by businessmen as being too "intimate." Since the war the situation in this respect has improved. Most of the biographical data included in this study was volunteered by the CNPF. The work *Le Monde des Affaires, op.cit.* (n. 1-37), from which additional information on business connections was gathered, is published by persons close to the business community, while previously information of this kind could be found only in decidedly left-wing publications. Finally the magazine *Entreprise*, published since 1953 by a firm equally friendly to management, almost specializes in presenting carefully selected biographical details about business leaders.

[53] For details about the views of M. Meunier on industrial relations and the work of his committee, see below, Chapter IX.

other spokesmen for these industries were appointed to the Executive.

The other vice-presidents, not belonging to what is often called the "quadrumvirate" of Messrs. Villiers, Ricard, Mayolle, and Meunier, take a far less active part in the work of the peak association. Until his death in 1956, Edouard Bertaux was a businessman of great wealth who owned a family concern in the wholesale meat industry. As president and vice-president of several employers' organizations of the food industry and connected commerical establishments, he represented in the CNPF those well-organized interests.

Bernard d'Halluin was added much later to the group of vice-presidents when, after the death of his predecessor, he moved to the top position in the influential Textile Union. Descendant of an old family of wool manufacturers in the north of France, he had to give up plans of becoming a professor of philosophy and took over the family concern after his older brother was killed during the First World War. His social philosophy is deeply impregnated by the faith of a modern-minded practicing catholic; the regional trade associations of which he still has charge have been intensely active in fields of low-cost housing, technical training, and apprenticeship.[54]

The small business interests are represented among the vice-presidents by Paul Pisson, owner of a small piano factory, who seems to have stepped out of a Balzac novel into the strange surroundings of a modern pressure group. Among his more impetuous colleagues in the CGPME he is suspected of being nothing more than a prisoner of the "trusts" which the small business interests had organized to fight. Nevertheless, M. Pisson has been able to remain simultaneously at the helm of the small business confederation and of the CNPF for more than ten years.

In addition to the president and the vice-presidents there are twenty-one members on the Executive. Chosen from the most important branches of industry and commerce, these men also have a remarkable diversity of backgrounds: large and small business, patrimonial employers as well as managers, businessmen as well as trade association officials, but with one exception all

---

[54] For a sympathetic portrait of M. d'Halluin, see *Entreprise*, 1, No. 6, June 15, 1953, p. 23.

Parisians. It is generally admitted that, also on the level of the Executive, the active participation of members is most unequal and that only a few of them can be considered as belonging to the inner group which determines the tactics and long-range policies of the organization. To single out the latter is sometimes hazardous since, on various occasions, members of the Executive use their formal status to become active as long as certain questions involving the interests which they represent are being decided. Once such issues are settled, they relapse into their former passive role and relative indifference.

But a number of Executive members have been at all times close to the center of decision making. M. Henri Lafond represents more than anybody else the large financial interests and the most highly concentrated industries. His earlier career in government and business has already been described.[55] When he entered the CNPF, Lafond was president or board member of several of the country's largest corporations, in varied fields such as heavy industry, the electrical, petroleum, and chemical industries, shipbuilding, banking, and private railroading. His relations with the executives of the national enterprises in both industry and banking are particularly cordial.

In spite of his big business background, M. Lafond is convinced that the political advantages of an all-embracing unified employers' representation far outweigh the inconveniences, which others complain of when considerations for the employers' rank and file hamper constructive action by the Council. M. Lafond, whose lucidity and cynicism are admired and resented by his friends and enemies alike, admittedly believes that, whenever decisive action is necessary or even when a "doctrine" needs to be formulated, the small inner group of the CNPF will never in fact be hampered by "outsiders," however high their official position in the employers' movement may be.

Another forceful member of that inner group was André Métral, president of the Trade Association of Engineering Industries, who led the metal-processing interests into opposing, side by side with the steel industry, the ratification of the Schuman Plan.[56]

[55] See above, Chapter II.
[56] For details see below, Chapter VIII, and Henry W. Ehrmann, "The French

A graduate of the "X" and the School of Mines, M. Métral had a distinguished teaching career at various graduate technical schools and held an important chair in engineering at the *Conservatoire National des Arts et Métiers*. His publications, predominantly in the field of aerodynamics, number by the hundreds; the range of his honorary positions in France and abroad is staggering. Already before the war he became the manager of a number of aeronautical engineering firms and of one of the outstanding machine tool concerns in the country. Residing in North Africa at the moment of the American invasion, he was partially instrumental in negotiating the truce, and served in the Free French forces after that. M. Métral's rapid rise in the employers' movement seemed to match his considerable ambitions, when criminal proceedings started against him for allegedly fraudulent war damage claims put at least a temporary end to his career.

One of the most prominent businessmen on the CNPF's Executive is M. Pierre Laguionie, who took over a prosperous family concern in the retail business and then rose to the headship of *Le Printemps*, one of the country's largest department stores, with numerous branches in the provinces and several establishments of the dime store type. Since before the war M. Laguionie has also been a prominent member of the French delegation to the International Chamber of Commerce, the body on which traditionally the outstanding business interests of the country are represented.

At present the chemical industry is principally represented in the leadership of the CNPF by Robert André and Maurice Brulfer, the presidents respectively of the Union of Petroleum Industries and the Union of Chemical Industries, both solidly organized federations of numerous trade associations in their field. M. André, a doctor of law, is the son of the celebrated inventor-industrialist who was the founder of the mother company for Esso-Standard of France. Robert André is its present president and a board member of the *Compagnie Française des Pétroles*, the most important holding company for a great variety of French oil interests abroad. Prominent in the Vichy CO for the chemical industry, Maurice Brulfer is today the manager of the *Société Progil*, one of the most modern concerns in the chemical industry, with an extremely diversified production and widespread participations connecting it with the giants of the chemical industry such as Kuhlman, Pechiney, and several colonial enterprises. Both André and Brulfer are known as active lobbyists in parliament and with the administration.[57] The link between the CNPF and colonial interests in general is effectively established by M. Paul Bernard. Another alumnus of the "X," he hails from a family which for generations had diversified business connections in the colonies, and especially in Indochina. M. Bernard himself manages a number of financing and holding companies which control still today major industrial and transportation concerns in the major overseas possessions of France. He also presides over several of the trade associations for colonial enterprises in Indochina and elsewhere.[58]

The career of Henry Davezac, executive of the trade association for the electrical equipment industry, has been described previously. Though one of the most fervent devotees of complete and efficient business organization, M. Davezac had for a time disassociated himself and the industries he represents almost completely from the CNPF. He had criticized as dangerous the political activities in which the Council had become entangled and condemned its bowing to the wishes of the steel industry in the fight over the ratification of the Schuman plan. He felt that the employers' movement would become vulnerable to attacks from the outside if it permitted itself to be distracted from its foremost constructive tasks of organizing economic performance. To assure M. Davezac a place on the Executive and to give him access to its inner circle seemed the only way of bringing a highly respected trade association back to the fold. It remains to be seen whether M. Davezac, and some of the other newer members of the Executive who feel as he does, will be able to affect decidedly the tactics of the peak association.

It is quite characteristic that several of the businessmen who belong to the top decision-making group won election to the

[57] For details on the business connections and activities of Messrs. André and Brulfer, see *Le Monde des Affaires*, *op.cit.* (n. 1-37), pp. 212-14, 192.

[58] On M. Paul Bernard's far-flung connections, see *ibid.*, pp. 348, 502 ff.

Executive only in 1953, when six new seats were created in order to "insure a wider representation of the different branches of business," as was officially explained.[59] At that time all new seats went without apologies to representatives of large-scale industry and of banking. When the Executive was first formed in 1946, the tribute paid to the temper of the time had resulted in giving foremost representation to the less concentrated industries and principally to those where small and medium-sized firms predominate. This had a twofold consequence: since too many important interests were unrepresented on the Executive, Villiers and his close associates would often altogether disregard CNPF channels and consult trade associations or business leaders of their choice before making weighty policy decisions; since on the other hand the steel industry and the related metal trades were represented on the Executive by some of their outstanding spokesmen, the old pattern of an employers' movement dominated by the *Comité des Forges* seemed to emerge once more. The additions to the Executive, piously endorsed by the General Assembly, gave formal status to other important industrial and financial interests, thereby establishing a better balance between the different sectors of big business. But by the same move the more peripheral members of the Executive, and especially those representing small business, were pushed further away from the center of decision making.

Moreover, policy formation in the CNPF is not confined to its Executive. The presidents of the so-called "study committees" of the Council carry considerable weight in elaborating policies and strategy. Where its predecessor, the CGPF, attempted to dispatch its work through five large and shapeless committees, the CNPF has sub-divided three major committees into not less than thirty-two sub-committees, all of them with an appointed president and a *rapporteur* in charge of staff work. In more than one way the authority and the working methods of these committees resemble those of the French parliament; this in turn facilitates frequent and fruitful liaison between organized business and the National Assembly.

The three principal committees, entrusted respectively with domestic economics, international economics, and industrial rela-

[59] See *Bulletin*, VII, No. 93, February 5, 1953, p. 1.

tions, are presided over by the three most prominent vice-presidents of the CNPF. Also a few of the most important subcommittees are headed by other influential members of the Executive. The simultaneous assigning to members of a variety of offices and functions is obviously intended to increase the authority and prestige of the CNPF's inner group.[60] But the majority of the committee presidents are selected from prominent personalities of the business world who are thereby connected with policy formation of the CNPF without a formal election.

The Committee on Price Policies is in the hands of the able director of Marcel Boussac's combine in the cotton cloth industry, owning factories which employ more than 10,000 workers. Two executives of the Pechiney trust, controlling 80 percent of the French aluminum production and a sizable sector of the chemical industry, are in charge of the Committees on International Cartels and on Private Enterprise. Two former members of the bureaucracy, now directors of large shipbuilding, shipping, and paper concerns, preside over the CNPF Committees on the Monnet Plan, on Productivity, and on Trade Liberalization. The committees dealing with questions of foreign trade and overseas investment are handled by highly respected businessmen who by themselves or through their families have majority interests in a wide range of fields, such as shipping, banking, heavy industry, perfume, dairy products, and colonial enterprises. The president of the Committee on Trade Agreements is the director of one of the largest foundry concerns, tax problems are handled by the director of a large liquor distillery, transportation questions by the president of the most important company of inland waterways transport. Especially in view of the intricate horizontal and vertical inter-connections prevalent in many sectors of French business life, it is likely that in some way or another many, perhaps most, of the outstanding firms of the country are represented in one or several of the CNPF committees. Only committees devoted to the study of more theoretical questions, such as those on the Legal Status of Enterprise and on Plant Committees, are entrusted to the heads of smaller concerns.

---

[60] For an analogous situation obtaining in the NAM, see Cleveland, *op.cit.* (n. III-40), p. 228.

Forming a bridge between the business community and the employers' movement, the operations of the CNPF committees fulfill a variety of functions. To an extent they establish transmission belts between the Council and its affiliates. Membership in the committees is open to anyone chosen by his trade association as a delegate. Those assigned to the various committees will feel sufficiently identified with the reports submitted to the General Assembly so that their organizations will hardly voice opposition to the decisions reached on the basis of the reports.

At the same time the work of the committees permits meshing the business interests represented on them with the staff activities of the CNPF. While M. Villiers and his associates will confer with the committees' presidents on questions of over-all policy, the preparation of reports and the gathering of the frequently extensive documentation are the task of the *rapporteurs* or general secretaries. With a few exceptions these are all regular staff members of the CNPF. The committees have therefore become an indispensable vehicle for accrediting and publicizing the work which the staff of the peak association performs and which is given here the seal of approval by some of the country's outstanding business leaders.

Any attempt to determine the process of policy formation in the employers' peak association should not overlook the fact that, in spite of an enlarged Executive and notwithstanding the web of committee activities, the leaders of the CNPF still engage in frequent consultations with businessmen who do not have any formal status whatsoever in the organization. A fairly good impression as to who these unofficial advisers are can be gained from the large delegation which the CNPF sent to the First International Conference of Manufacturers in New York, sponsored in 1951 by the NAM. Among the members of the delegation, pressure group officials were joined by the executives of many leading corporations.[61] During a trip through the United States, during the conference, and later when its members exchanged and evaluated their impressions, the French delegation achieved a cohesion and unity of views which was far from artificial.

[61] For the list of the members of the French delegation, and some of their business connections, see *Proceedings of the First International Conference of Manufacturers*, New York, 1951, pp. 13-15.

It is sometimes noted by less-than-friendly observers that the absence of many truly prominent industrialists and businessmen from leading positions in the CNPF reflects a lack of esteem of the business community for the Council and does not speak well for its representative character. Such an evaluation, while partly justified, fails to take into account that the active minority which has taken hold of the peak association has bestowed legitimacy upon itself not only through the organizational antennas and contact points it has built, but also through the increasing homogeneity and cohesion it has achieved. It is true that many of those who today control the CNPF are the adjuncts[62] of the great captains of industry, rather than those captains themselves who were prominent in the pre-war employers' confederation. But by and large the professional leaders of the present-day Council, its staff and the businessmen serving on its boards and committees, are representative of an important stratum of business life. They are impregnated with the mentality of the modern corporation official, convinced of the virtue of discipline and the need for efficient organization. There are many problems, and some of them of considerable weight, on which these men differ. Yet homogeneity in outlook has so far always prevailed, and their able and aggressive leadership has asserted itself, to the point where the Council, originally conceived as a loose confederation, functions with a great deal of structured direction and predictability.

\* \* \*

So far the point has been made that during the first decade of its existence the employers' peak association has built a valid organization which relies for its functioning on a homogeneous leadership and on the active support of the corporate sector of business life. But to what extent did the CNPF fulfill the tasks which its by-laws had assigned to it, namely coordinating all elements and groups of an employers' movement, where, numerically speaking, non-corporate and small business units prevail? How far has it been able to formulate and to propose to its affiliates those "common actions" which the movement as a whole was pledged to undertake?

[62] The French term *commis*, often used in this context, is, to be sure, more pejorative.

From the start the CNPF has endeavored to gain the recognition of its affiliates by rendering services which, useful at first, might later become indispensable. Once the Council had proven its worth, it might then be able to evoke enough loyalty so that its constituents would accept the proposals for common action.

At first the CNPF was seriously hampered by the resolve of member organizations to keep the staff of the confederation's headquarters small. Over the years the staff has steadily grown to number today a total of about 120 employees, including clerical and non-professional help. While this is far larger than the personnel of the CGPF, the Council's predecessor, the most significant difference is to be found once more in the nature and quality of the professional staff rather than in its numerical strength. Among several dozen highly qualified and well-trained people there are graduates of the best law schools in the country, of the Institute of Political Sciences, or of the *Ecole Normale* in Paris; some are holders of high academic degrees, others have passed examinations which opened to them top positions in the civil service. A few staff members have been held over from the pre-war employers' organizations; but most are younger men recruited from a group which before the war and before the relative decline in civil servants' pay would have sought employment in the administration. Today the most gifted of the staff members consider their work for the employers' movement, be it in the CNPF or in the affiliated trade associations, only as a stepping-stone to still more lucrative positions in private business.

As in similar organizations in the United States the paid staff plays a fairly considerable, if discreet, role in shaping policies and in formulating over-all objectives.[63] Probably the staff of the CNPF is somewhat less independent than its equivalent in American manufacturers' associations because of the close interest which the CNPF's "inner group" takes in the organization's affairs. Yet in conjunction with these members of the Executive the staff members' influence is growing. Their familiarity with the day-by-day operations of the Council, the contribution they furnish to the work of the important study committees, and also the authority which most of them command because of their ability and training make them indispensable for rendering the

[63] See on this point Truman, *op.cit.* (n. 1-27), pp. 144-45.

peak association useful to its constituent organizations and to businessmen in general.

From the outset, efforts to "sell" the CNPF to its membership had to reckon with the suspicion with which most businessmen would regard any evidence of showy salesmanship. While it is said that all members of the NAM receive with every morning's mail a tubful of materials from the organization, the only regular publication issued by the CNPF is its monthly bulletin, printed in not more than 20,000 copies. The *Bulletin*, it is true, has grown in size and quality since its extremely humble beginnings and is now a well-presented, though not particularly attractive, monthly magazine of between sixty and eighty pages. Besides giving accounts of meetings within the organization and its national or international affiliates, the *Bulletin* publishes fairly regularly a leading article explaining the employers' position on some well-defined problem. The editorial is signed by the president, but presumably discussed between him and his closest associates. The major part of each issue of the *Bulletin* is devoted to factual and often statistical data about national and international economic developments, and to information on tax, trade, and colonial problems. Of greatest interest are the issues publishing semi-annually the lengthy reports which in theory are submitted to the General Assembly for its approval, for these reports reflect the current thinking of the organization on a wide range of economic and social problems. But its academic and somewhat forbidding character makes the *Bulletin* little suited to establish an effective liaison among the membership, let alone to create a community of thought. It serves even less as a suitable means for explaining and propagandizing the employers' point of view to outsiders.[64] Hence the CNPF and organized business in general have still only limited official means of published expression.

Other services installed by the peak association prove undoubtedly of greater practical value to its member organizations and the business firms affiliated with them. A competent industrial relations staff (*Service Social*) digests social legislation, lends occasional help in collective bargaining, and is generally open for

[64] M. Villiers' frequent appeals to utilize the *Bulletin* for "spreading the word" among all businessmen have met with little success. For a discussion of the media which the CNPF utilizes for explaining itself to the outside, see below, Chapter V.

consultation. But as before the war, it draws for its resources in personnel and documentation largely on the much larger staff of the UIMM. In another field a fairly recent creation, the *Comité Franc-Dollar*, has proven extremely useful for the export industries. The Committee, which is encouraged and partly financed by the French government, is staffed and housed by the CNPF. It seeks to facilitate Franco-American trade by a great variety of consultative and promotional activities on both sides of the ocean.[65]

Different from the "study committees," whose role is confined to the formulation of general policies, the CNPF's "Service of Legislative Studies" is an operating agency. Its openly acknowledged function is to appraise members of parliament of the point of view which the Council has taken in regard to pending or proposed bills and to go on record with a warning or an encouragement. While a bill is traveling through the different phases of the legislative process, the CNPF's Service keeps a close watch on all possibilities for bringing its influence to bear. If an opportunity arises, the Service will gladly lend a helping hand in drafting entire bills for deputies and senators, and especially for those among them who are members of parliamentary committees. That part of the CNPF's lobbying which is visible might not be the most significant portion of such activities, but as far as it goes it is located in the Legislative Service.[66]

At this point, however, there arise serious limitations on the Council's effectiveness. In its relation with the various branches of government, the CNPF and its services make no attempt to prevent interventions by special interests that are represented within the organization. The principal trade associations engage in temporary or permanent lobbying activities of their own without much interference by the peak association. Wherever possible the Council seeks to facilitate and coordinate such activities by its member organizations, keeping thereby a certain amount of control over the official contacts of its affiliates. In the frequent cases where conflicting interests clash, it might attempt to use good offices and persuasion to make those policies prevail on

[65] On the activities of the Committee, see *Annuaire* . . . , etc. *op.cit.* (n. III-38), pp. 748 ff., and *Bulletin*, No. 129, March 1955, pp. 71-72.
[66] For a full discussion of the CNPF's lobbying activities, see below, Chapter V.

which its Executive or its committees have agreed. More often than not, serious divergences will prove that the CNPF's prestige is not strong enough for it to impose its views; it will simply bow out and maintain its own cohesion by giving to its affiliates a free hand in defending their mutually contradictory interests. But this means that wherever differences exist the CNPF has to be content with defending the lowest common denominator of business interests, or face the risk of not being able to enforce its policy recommendations. During the immediate post-war years, when the very institution of private property and with it the *fonction patronale* seemed threatened, enough apparently common interests could be gathered to establish a fairly solid front, cemented by fear.[67] But since the political climate has become more favorable to the employers, questions have been raised from within the movement as to whether the price paid for all-inclusiveness is not too high and whether truly constructive action will not be impeded to the point of leading ultimately to weakness rather than to strength. Even among the leaders of the CNPF, there are those who believe that in the present situation the pre-war organization had undeniable advantages over the unwieldy Council. The frequent opposition of industrial and commercial interests in France is deemed particularly harmful, the place given in the organization to the small enterprise exaggerated and paralyzing.

Pierre Benaerts, the executive of the National Council of Commerce, stated once with unaccustomed bluntness what has been repeated since then frequently: "Let us recognize sincerely . . . what the main line of trade association policy has been for years. Whether in regard to taxation, to legislation, or to the various obstacles put in the way of free initiative, we have done our utmost, for the benefit of the laggards, to delay the march of progress and to bar innovations." What sense was there, Benaerts added, in producing with the speed of a modern locomotive as long as distribution was handled the wheelbarrow way?[68]

[67] See on this point R. M. MacIver, *The Web of Government*, New York, 1947, p. 415: "The sense of the common overrides the differences within the group but it does not abolish them. . . . Often the appreciation of the common is intensified by the threat to it, real or imagined, from the hostile difference of another group."

[68] Pierre Benaerts, "Un quart d'heure d'autocritique," *Bulletin*, VII, February 5,

When cartel practices are discussed, it will have to be considered to what extent such criticism is entirely candid or consistent.[69] But whether or not they engage in convenient rationalizations, the members of the active minority who are running the CNPF without being particularly tolerant of the views of small business still maintain that the negative influence of the marginal firms is fairly constantly felt. By their opposition to any action beyond the mere defense of fundamental employers' interests, such firms and their associations presumably prevent the Council from taking a stand on many issues; by their passive resistance they invite the inactivity of the CNPF and of many of its sub-divisions. If the marginal sectors of the economy are generally acting as a drag on the economic and social development of a country in need of modernization, such an effect is therefore repeated and intensified on the level of the employers' movement.[70]

In one of his speeches to the General Assembly, President Villiers admitted that in spite of its efforts to prove its usefulness the CNPF was often little known or even ignored by the mass of French employers, since the peak association was "acting through the industrial federation and the regional associations."[71] He could have added that many of the member organizations have more ample financial means and, relative to the number of their constituents, a far larger staff. The sheer number of trade associations and other employers' organizations appears staggering. From the approximate data given in Table III (see Appendix), one gathers the impression that in commerce and industry combined there exist close to 5,000 regional and more than 800 national trade associations. They are bound together in over 200 national federations or, in other cases, in almost the same number of "groups."

---

1953, p. 55. The speaker is quite typical of the pressure group official who looks with a certain amount of contempt on his clientele. Yet since such officials are the employees of the businessmen whose behavior they criticize, their effectiveness is understandably limited.

[69] See below, Chapter VIII.

[70] Details illustrating this statement will be discussed below when the attitude of the employers' movement to important economic and social issues is analyzed. See esp. Chapters VI, VII, and VIII.

[71] See *Bulletin*, vii, No. 103, July 20, 1953, p. 3. This speech gives a well-balanced and fairly accurate picture of the activities of the CNPF.

Officially it is claimed that through this network covering all of metropolitan France and many of the colonies the employers' movement represents 900,000 firms, employing a labor force of more than 6,000,000. More critical observers estimate that, even in 1948-49 when the employers' movement had reached its organizational height, the firms that had joined never represented more than 50 to 60 percent of the total employed labor force. In terms of invested capital, however, the percentage of the affiliated firms might now reach approximately 90 percent.

The dues by which the impressive organizational pyramid of the employers' movement and its many thousands of staff members live are usually calculated on the basis of the turnover of the affiliated firms; only where such a calculation would be misleading is the contribution determined proportionately to the wages paid out by the firms. The CNPF exists presumably solely on that share of their income which the secondary (or sometimes tertiary) organizations—the industrial and commercial federations—turn over to the peak association. From openly voiced complaints one gathers that there are great disparities in the regularity of these contributions, undoubtedly reflecting considerable differences in the treasuries of the trade associations. (According to some the steel, chemical, oil, engineering, and textile industries bear some 80 percent of the CNPF's operating costs.)

The activities of the "vertical" employers' organizations are as different as their resources. While by now all, including even the small regional associations of stationery stores and similar trades, have their professional staff, there are even on the level of national organizations wide discrepancies between the majority of associations responsible for a branch of commercial activities and, for example, the association of the producers of special steels. Housed in sumptuous and modernly equipped offices, many of the industrial associations can boast of extensive services and of a documentation which proves that in some fields it has been possible to overcome the reluctance of French businessmen to part with elementary information. But there are other, and more numerous, associations whose publications and services are proof of continuing indigence. At the level of the federations the same differences are reproduced.

The most active and most efficient of these organizations

perform many of the "positive" functions of a modern employers' movement. They develop to a considerable extent the customs and usages in such matters as form contracts, unfair competition, and standardization.[72] Quite a few have set up elaborate research facilities which, whether they are technical or commercial in nature, prove of great value to many of the member firms. Productivity drives and occasionally full-fledged production programs are promoted by some of the best-organized trade associations; at that point, however, their activities imperceptibly shade over into, or openly merge with, the operations of cartels.[73]

In the social and industrial relations field, primary or secondary associations will prove equally valuable. Assistance is rendered for collective bargaining at various levels. In some regions, especially in the industrial North, the employers' organizations have developed remarkably fruitful programs in such fields as workers' housing, apprenticeship and in-service training, industrial hygiene, and the like. In all such matters the CNPF can only give advice through either its committees or its own staff, and such advice as is given is couched in generalities. The employers' confederation is too far removed from the needs and conditions of the various business activities to be of true usefulness. Performance must be left to the industrial or regional associations, which, if they are successful, see their prestige accrued and possibly not only with the constituent firms but also with the communities in which they operate.

This, however, frequently has a centrifugal result as far as the peak association is concerned. The well-developed sectors of the employers' movement are moving ahead, not without encountering the distrust or envy of other trade associations. The paralyzing effect produced by the "laggards" becomes more noticeable the more one approaches the higher echelons of the movement.

*    *    *

Some have argued that, since there are obvious difficulties in the way of constructive action, the peak association should at least have justified the renewed claim of the business community

---

[72] This aspect of the activities of the employers' associations is stressed with interesting details in François Perroux, *Cours d'économie politique*, Paris, 1939, 2nd ed., Vol. I, pp. 508-09.

[73] For details see below, Chapters VII and VIII.

for elite status by developing a coherent philosophy. Its failure to do so in a society which still lives, or pretends to live, on broad and general ideas is in fact a serious handicap. To an extent the CNPF suffers here from the general mood that has settled over the country. The biological exhaustion, caused by the human losses in the two wars, is undoubtedly aggravated by a morose fascination with the magnitude of the losses. Great tidal waves of hope and enthusiasm have been followed so often by disappointment that by now most Frenchmen, and especially many of the younger Frenchmen, believe in the predestined failure of any idea or effort. Perhaps because such recent movements as the Popular Front and the Resistance had aroused particular hopes for economic and social rejuvenation, the present lethargy results in pronounced skepticism towards all social movements.[74] Indeed the employers' organizations would probably be less respected if the labor movement were not affected by a similar crisis due, at least in part, to similar causes. It will be discussed[75] how among the managers of modern corporate enterprise the influence of the fiery "physico-politics" of Saint Simon has not yet spent itself. But the mass of French employers, where they are not sheer cynics with a notorious lack of civic education, might be considered the faithful, if seldom conscious, disciples of the curious philosopher-essayist Alain.[76] To the French bourgeois, strongly imbued with peasant traditions, his most important residual power still lies in the measure of his ability to resist authority and to deny the quest for reformatory action, whether such quests come from the administration, from parliament, or from an organized social group. Freedom becomes indistinguishable from insubordination; the individual who thinks against society is truly virtuous; his opposition is directed not only against the monster state but against any elite that might attempt to mold the individual and to make claims upon him. For the businessman such glorification of the self-centered individual also means

[74] It is, for instance, generally admitted that at present it would be impossible to launch a periodical resembling the pre-war *Nouveaux Cahiers*. (See above, Chapter I.)

[75] See below, Chapters VII and X.

[76] The essence of the political writings of Alain (pseudonym for Emile Chartier) is now available in a convenient collection (presented by Michel Alexandre), *op.cit.* (n. II-4). A somewhat sweeping but interesting analysis of French individualism and its present impact is to be found in Gabriel LeBras, *op.cit.* (n. III-27), pp. 20 ff.

secretiveness in the conduct of his affairs and distrust or contempt for his competitor. In the words of Detoeuf, critic of his own class and of his colleagues in the employers' movement: "France remains the country of generous ideas and a narrow economy, of the love for liberty and the absence of collective spirit, of a large intellectual life and of small material interests. Everybody believes himself the center of the country."[77]

Actually the narrowness of the economy will regularly lead the businessman to "betray" the precepts of a sincere individualist such as Alain. All governmental interference might be considered unsound, except those measures that protect his own special interests, preserve his "acquired rights," and shelter him from competition. In this acceptance, perhaps expectancy, of protection, the managerial group which occupies positions of leadership in the CNPF and the rank and file of patrimonial employers are of one mind. But such a mentality, even if widespread, is still ill suited to provide the foundation for a doctrine of the employers' movement.

During the first year of his presidency M. Villiers could defend the lack of any expressed common beliefs by pointing, with a *primum vivere deindere philosophari*, to the need of first insuring the survival of private enterprise.[78] But after the emergency had passed, the efforts undertaken to formulate a "positive" policy made it clear that the ideological difficulties are just as great as the other obstacles to constructive action.

Also before the war the spokesmen for organized business were critical of existing political institutions; yet the *haute bourgeoisie* identified itself as a matter of course with the nation and with the defense of its patrimony, in metropolitan France as well as in the colonies. That such an attitude was shaken during the first post-war years, when the permanent elimination of the bourgeoisie from power was a publicly proclaimed goal, could be expected. But although the bourgeoisie has since returned to its former positions in society, bourgeois anarchism that believes

[77] See Detoeuf, Preface to Planus, *op.cit* (n. 1-59), p. 4.
[78] See the interesting discussion between M. Villiers and A. Sauvy, "La Penseé Patronale se dérobe-t-elle," *Nouvelles Economiques*, June 13 and 27 and August 15, 1947. Though less hostile than M. Sauvy, the observations of M. Libeaux, executive of a minor trade association, *op.cit.* (n. 111-18), pp. 717-23, arrive at some of the same critical conclusions.

itself freed from civic responsibilities has not significantly receded.[79]

Most of the studies which the CNPF wishes to present as its "positive contribution" to the solution of urgent problems are actually little more than attempts to whitewash the business community of all guilt in acknowledged shortcomings in the country's economic structure. If broader reform proposals are made, they are almost always accompanied by an expression of doubt whether within the framework of the existing political institutions anything valid could be achieved.[80]

Plagued by limitations which the character of his organization entails, M. Villiers has sought refuge in proclaiming the CNPF as the wise defender of the general interest. As similar advocates have done before, the CNPF wishes to convince its audience that the special interests it defends are reconcilable and indeed identical with the interests of the nation.[81] Just because the CNPF represents in reality not one class but congeries of classes, it is assumed that the special interests in its midst will easily cancel out their possible noxiousness to the public and permit somewhat miraculously the emergence of the general interest. In the final resort the absence of too clearly defined an economic (or political) doctrine becomes a virtue, because any identification of the CNPF with such a doctrine would destroy the myth which seeks to accredit the employers' association as the shield of an overriding public interest.

It is not accidental that one of the constructive plans which M. Villiers has cherished personally, and about which he has spoken for years before an indifferent audience at the meetings of the General Assembly, has made very slow progress. The

[79] Here again the sharpest criticism has come from M. Alfred Sauvy in two of his chronicles on the social situation in *Droit Social*, xiv, December 1951, p. 665, and xv, March 1952, p. 157. At the time he suggested that perhaps when business would have recuperated all its former power, this "divorce between the bourgeoisie and the state" would come to an end. Such expectations have hardly materialized.

[80] See as one example among many the remarks by M. Villiers in connection with a report the CNPF had prepared on the problem of the disparity between French and world prices, *Bulletin*, No. 122, August 1954, pp. 2, 13.

[81] See the very pertinent remarks on the problem of the defense of special and general interests in present-day France in Beau de Loménie, "Les puissances d'argent," in *La Nef*, viii, April-May 1951, pp. 130-32; Henry Peyret, "Les groupements professionnels et le parlement," *ibid.*, p. 117; and Léo Hamon, "Gouvernement et intérêts particuliers," *Esprit*, xxi, June 1953, pp. 842-43, 848. For fuller discussion, see also below, Chapter V.

Employers' Center of Research and Study, finally founded in 1953, has established a series of courses to which active business-men might turn for a mixed curriculum offering advanced train-ing in business management and over-all orientation of more or less inspirational character. The Center also proposes to establish a link between the business community and "other milieus of the national collectivity, especially the university," a link which in France is nearly non-existent.[82] While it is too early to appraise the Center's work and its effectiveness, it has been hampered from the outset by the lack of a common ground and of a philosophy, however pragmatic.

One must therefore conclude that, for all its impressive organi-zational achievements, the present-day CNPF has been unable to rise above the defense of frequently fragmented special inter-ests. With only a few and generally insignificant employers' associations outside the Council, unity in sheer organizational terms has been achieved more fully than ever before.[83] But most of the time it has remained a unity for unity's sake. The "common actions" which the CNPF promised are little more than those of an efficiently functioning pressure group. They are seldom backed by a common purpose involving constructive action. It might be doubted whether business organizations can, because of their very nature and composition, ever play the role of a positive and assertive elite.[84] It remains, however, a fact that, precisely be-cause in French society business occupies a far less respected place than in other industrial civilizations, the CNPF had en-tered the claim of building an integrated force and of creating a new image of the business community. In that it has failed.

[82] For a description of the Center's objectives, see *Annuaire, op.cit.* (n. III-38), pp. 764 *bis*; and on its progress, *Bulletin*, No. 129, February 2, 1955, pp. 5-6.

[83] For a list of employers' organizations not presently associated with the CNPF, see *Annuaire, op.cit.* (n. III-38), pp. 771-82. The president of the pre-war Confedera-tion states flatly, that the present-day employers' movement "presents an organic unity that is more seeming than real." See Gignoux, *op.cit.* (n. I-31), p. 166.

[84] Robert Michels, *Political Sociology*, Minneapolis, 1949, p. 120, makes the point that only seldom will businessmen's organizations have enough homogeneity to function as an elite. But Michels wrote at a time when the "unorganized" economic elites—the "bourgeois dynasties"—still held an undisputed role in society. Similarly Simone Weil, who is today admired by some personalities in the em-ployers' movement, remarked in *L'Enracinement, op.cit.* (n. I-14), p. 31, that, differently from the labor movement, the employers' movement should never try to elaborate a doctrine, or even an idea, but should content itself with defending separate interests separately.

The CNPF won prestige for its part in foiling the attacks to which private business was exposed after the war. But after that was won, neither its own constituents nor outsiders have found much in the employers' movement that would command their undivided respect. Hence the CNPF, the sole spokesman of all business, frequently speaks, in spite of appearances, with as uncertain a voice as its predecessors.

# CHAPTER IV

# Other Inter-professional Groups

## 1. The Council of Commerce and the Regional Federations

At its founding in 1919 the CGPF was almost exclusively an organization of industry: among its twenty-one groups only one was reserved to "Finance and Commerce," and it was headed by a banker. Since then a constant, though not always successful, effort has been made to represent in the central employers' organization an economic activity which in 1938 furnished fourteen and in 1949 sixteen percent of the national income. Also after Matignon the employers movement remained weak among commercial establishments, except for a few branches, among them the association of department stores. Here too the years of Vichy taught at least a small group of persons active in the employers' movement that great advantages could be derived from better coordination. The executive of the general CO of Commerce had been Pierre Benaerts, holder of a high academic degree, who had been active in the federation of the food trade and the CGPF since the early 1930's. When the CO was dissolved, the framework of a general commercial organization remained, and already in 1945 a coordinating council of all commercial federations began to function. Indeed, under multiple pressures from without and accustomed by the Vichy experience to a modicum of discipline, commercial firms continued to join their organizations, and more trade associations than ever before began to develop at every level.

If private enterprise in general had to face public opprobrium after the liberation, the animosity against commercial activities at every stage was even more outspoken. Most profits from trade were considered illicit, wholesale concerns regarded as wasteful intermediaries, retailers accused of reaping advantages from general scarcity. Years later M. Benaerts admitted that the French distribution system was still under heavier fire than almost any other institution.[1]

[1] See Benaerts, op.cit. (n. iii-68), p. 54.

A rapid increase in the number of commercial firms after the war not only created problems of high cost for the consumer; it was resented also by the older establishments. The intrusion of undesirable elements was feared, and it was expected that the turnover for many of the smallest units would dwindle threateningly once the abnormal windfalls of the post-war situation had disappeared. When the scarcity of consumer goods and the inflationary price rise induced public and private industrial concerns to open factory canteens (previously far less numerous in France than elsewhere) and stores for their workers, animosity between commerce and industry was bound to increase.

For all these reasons it seemed imperative to create a well-articulated employers' movement in all branches of commercial activities and to integrate it with the general employers' council which was then in its formative stage. Yet this had to be done in a way which would dispel, in the words of M. Benaerts, "the old suspicions of commerce against any employers' organization where the industrialists are preponderant."[2] Today the National Council of Commerce (CNC) is described as an "autonomous organ of action and representation of commercial interests within the framework of the CNPF." It furnishes four members to the latter's Executive and a corresponding number to the Board of Directors and the General Assembly. The CNC itself is built in the image of the parent organization, holding its General Assemblies in connection with the gatherings of the CNPF. It has its own "Study Committees" duplicating in a number of fields those of the CNPF, but at the common headquarters coordination is easily obtained through the close and daily cooperation between the paid staffs of both organizations.

The CNC boasts that about 160 national commercial organizations are affiliated with it, a number of them grouped in elaborately structured federations or confederations.[3] Officials of the CNC admit that many of its regional and local organizations exist only on paper or are identical with sections adhering directly

[2] For an account of the beginnings of the reformed employers' movement in commerce see *Bulletin*, I, No. 2, December 15, 1946, pp. 7-8, and *ibid.*, VI, No. 78, February 1952, p. 41.

[3] For a complete list of the commercial federations and their various affiliations, see *Repertoire des Federations Professionnelles affiliées au Conseil National du Commerce*, Paris, 1952.

to M. Gingembre's confederation. The decisive question, however, seems rather to be how many of the country's commercial
employers have been converted by the CNC and its affiliates to
accept organizational disciplines to which they had been adverse
in the past.

Statistics concerning the total number of commercial establishments are known to be particularly unreliable. According to the
CNC there are about 916,000 such firms in metropolitan France,
more than half of them dispensing foods or beverages; the National Institute of Statistics counts 1.1 million, the Commission
of National Accounts 1.3 million.[4] (See also Appendix, Table
IV.) Such different estimates are only in part due to different
nomenclatures; elaborate statistical presentation hardly conceals
a polemical intent of either defending or attacking commerce.
The same uncertainty prevails in regard to the number of new
distribution points that have opened since the war. A rather
superficial comparison of registered firms arrives at an increase
of 400,000 units; the trade associations arrive at an increase
of only 116,000; the Committee of the Ministry of Finance
maintains that between 1938 and 1949, 300,000 new firms
opened their doors. According to the same data and during
the same period the proportion of those gainfully employed
in commercial establishments increased from 49 to 54 per thousand of the total population (which compares with only 46 per
thousand in present-day England and Western Germany). Contrary to trends observed elsewhere, in France a marked regression
of concentration in the commercial field has occurred. While in
1931, 109 firms employed more than 500 people, in 1936 only
98, and in 1952 not more than 60, firms were counted in that
category of large-scale establishments. (For some comparisons,
see Appendix, Table IV.)

The lilliputian size of many firms is illustrated by the fact
that there is (according to the Commission of National Accounts)

---

[4] For the various sets of figures see "La Distribution Commerciale," *France
Documents* (a publication sponsored by the employers' movement), Nouvelle Série,
No. 70, November 1952, esp. pp. 4-6; Institut National de la Statistique et des
Etudes Economiques, *Bulletin mensuel de Statistique,* Supplement April-June
1952, pp. 40 ff., and *Rapports du Service des Etudes Economiques et Financières
du Ministère des Finances sur les Comptes Nationaux Provisoires de la Nation des
Années 1951 et 1952 et sur le Budget Economique de l'Année 1953,* Paris, 1953,
referred to hereafter as *Mendès-France report 1953,* pp. 65-68.

only 0.74 salaried employee per firm, while in the United States the corresponding figure amounts to 5.8. Trade association statistics show that there exist in France one retail establishment per 62 people, presumably the highest ratio in any country, while in Germany there is only one per 102 and in the United States one per 91. To an extent these figures reflect merely the demographic structure of a country with only ten cities of more than 240,000 inhabitants. On the other end of the scale there are 10,000 towns with a population of less than 200 and 27,000 with less than 5,000. Such low density is at least one of the factors that have permitted the survival of the small provincial bourgeoisie composed of shopkeepers and of the owners of minuscule transportation enterprises.[5]

The CNC claims that some 700,000 commercial enterprises employing 1.2 million people are affiliated with it. But it is safe to assume that this figure is grossly inflated, for if true it would indicate that all firms employing only a single employee and about half of the firms without any employee are members of the trade association movement.[6] Such pretended strength can hardly be reconciled with the constant laments that the treasuries of the organization are depleted. M. Benaerts, who takes an intellectual's delight in giving to his addresses historical and allegorical embellishments, spoke once with great details of the new mendicant order—the employers' associations.[7] The CNC lives in fact mostly on alms offered by the CNPF.

The General Assemblies of the organization hear repeated and substantiated complaints that the membership hardly responds to the action undertaken in its name. On more than one occasion the officials of the employers' movement have attacked the mores of the small shopkeepers and particularly of the newcomers among them; they have criticized their tax evasion and general

[5] See Charles Morazé, *La France Bourgeoise*, Paris, 1946, p. 192. The author's figures have been partly corrected and arranged according to the results of the 1954 census; see Ambassade de France, *Service de Presse et d'Information*, No. 18, January 1955, New York, p. 3.

[6] In *France Documents*, *op.cit.* (n. IV-4), p. 7, the total number of salaried personnel employed by commercial firms is given as 1,120,000; in the *Mendès-France Report 1953*, *op.cit.* (n. IV-4), p. 66, as 960,000—a perfect example of the confusion arising out of polemical statistics.

[7] See Pierre Benaerts, *Un Nouvel Ordre mendiant*, an address made before the General Assembly of the CNC, held in January 1952 (mimeographed).

lawlessness, but also their false liberalism which constantly appeals to the government or to their own associations for protection, but which will otherwise ignore the same organizations. Such sharp self-criticism, seldom heard in other sectors of the employers' movement, is an expression of the fact that there exists in the commercial field an unusually wide gap between the leaders of organized business and their clientele. The active members of the CNC Executive are predominantly connected with large-scale commercial enterprises, usually wholesale establishments. In many commercial associations the same type of modern pressure group official has become active who is to be found in the industrial federations. The important federation of the clothing trade is represented on the Executive by Raymond M. Boisdé, a lawyer and engineer by training, who like his colleague M. Benaerts has spent most of his professional life as an employee of economic defense organizations. In 1951 he entered parliament to become two years later an under-secretary of commerce in Laniel's cabinet, the first time since the days of Vichy that the official of a business organization had achieved such political prominence.

M. Boisdé organizes from time to time a rather showy congress, proudly called the States General of Commerce. These conventions, arranged in close cooperation with the CNC and also the CNPF, are designed to attract wider attention to the problems faced by French trade; they therefore serve in part designs of improving public relations, an approach from which other sectors of the employers' movement prefer to shy away.[8]

The officials of the CNC and of its foremost affiliates are making serious efforts to develop methods by which the efficiency of the French distribution system would be increased and its costs reduced. The "Center of Commercial Studies," founded in 1947 and affiliated with the employers' movement, issues a number of publications and tries to spread the knowledge of advanced commercial techniques. An International Council of Commercial Employers which the French have initiated is engaged in analogous attempts to learn from foreign experiences. But the leaders

[8] For an interesting account of the States General organized in 1948 see "Les Etats Généraux du Commerce," *France Documents, Nouvelle Série*, No. 25, pp. 1-25. For some of M. Boisdé's thinking and writing see below, Chapter V.

of the movement are not very sanguine about the results of their efforts and the responses they are able to elicit from the great masses of French shopkeepers, 90 percent of whom declare to the tax collector yearly sales of less than ten million francs ($29,000).

In 1954 the president of the CNC announced in deliberately vague terms that the structure of the CNC might have to be overhauled for more effective action; but he also complained that commercial interests were underrepresented on the Board of Directors of the CNPF.[9] When one considers that simultaneously the complaints of industrial leaders about the deadweight of the commercial sector grow louder, it appears that the solidarity of commercial and industrial interests which the CNPF was anxious to establish is once more, as in the pre-war employers' movement, showing the effects of serious strain. Such conflicts might worsen the more the modern and the backward segment of the economy grow apart.

\*     \*     \*

When the CNPF was formed, deliberate efforts were made to overcome the traditional weakness of the regional associations grouping employers on a geographical basis. As late as 1948 M. Villiers expressed the great interest of the employers' movement in expanding the regional organizations as an instrument of inter-professional solidarity and of "social equilibrium." But the president of the CNPF had to acknowledge that, as of old, employers were more interested in the work of the vertically organized trade associations of a given branch and regarded as burdensome the existing duality of organizations.[10] Since then the regional organizations have hardly overcome such handicaps, and the industrial federations, most of them with Paris headquarters, remain the backbone of the employers' movement.

There exist today approximately 100 of such regional organizations, as a rule coextensive with the administration units of the French departments. In the exclusively rural regions horizontal federations may cover several departments; the industrial departments on the other hand have several such associations.

[9] See *Bulletin*, No. 122, August 1954, p. 83.
[10] *Ibid.*, III, No. 23, December 1, 1948, p. 1.

Local differences are so great that it is difficult to generalize about the activities of the associations; most frequently the owners of middle-sized establishments take an interest in their work since the representatives of large concerns feel more at home in the national federations and since the small businessmen are attracted by the more frankly political appeals of the CGPME. Employers in the greatly varied metal and engineering industries of the provinces usually pay most attention to the regional organizations; elsewhere the yet more individualistically inclined owners of textile firms dominate the life of the associations. Even the headquarters of the stronger regional federations are seldom as impressive as those of the national trade associations or their federations. Among the regional officials there are a fairly large number of former Vichy officials, some of them prefects or sub-prefects who were purged from public service after the liberation.

In the northern departments association activities are well developed: a "Center of Social Information" coordinates numerous employers' activities in fields such as workers' housing, training, and welfare. Elsewhere an unimpressive periodical publication proffers tax and general business information which the members could probably easily gather from other sources inside or outside the employers' movement. Matters of industrial hygiene and accident prevention are discussed in periodic meetings that are often poorly attended. Probably the regional associations would be less anemic if they could assist their members in collective bargaining; but where agreements are negotiated on the departmental level, the industrial federations usually provide the needed services and they become signatories to the contract.[11]

The associations may become more active when a labor conflict affects simultaneously several industries of a region. In their contacts with the public authorities, such as the prefects or mayors, the regional organizations develop normal pressure group activities. But here they are limited by the degree of political centralization, which frequently renders ineffective or unnecessary all interventions outside the nation's capital.

[11] For details see below, Chapter IX, and Lorwin, *op.cit.* (n. 1-3), pp. 190-97.

Nationally the regional associations are bound together in a federation of their own; on its Executive and its Council serve usually the same men who are the regional delegates to the CNPF's Board of Directors. With the sole exception of the representatives from the North, none of these regional delegates plays an outstanding role in the employers' movement. Every month all the presidents of regional federations are conveyed to a meeting at the Paris headquarters. These gatherings and a thick weekly bulletin, commenting on a variety of economic and social problems and on pending legislation, are vehicles for filling the provincial delegates with the organizational zeal which has always lagged outside of Paris.

The effectiveness of these efforts depends of course on the vigor which these delegates are able to impart to their clientele in the departments. It seems to be generally agreed that the periodic visitations to provisional organizations by leading personalities of the CNPF or of the major industrial federations are more instrumental than the work of the regional associations in creating a climate in which the general policies of organized business might be carried out. Also on this level the energy and authority of a centralized leadership group has proven more successful than an elaborate organizational framework, grown out of a traditional desire for completeness and symmetry which has often led to weakness rather than to strength of the employers' movement. Given the limited enthusiasm which most French businessmen show for their own organizations, the simultaneous functioning of a horizontal and vertical pyramid was too much to expect. As in the past the regional associations seemed to be condemned to play a secondary role until the Poujade movement shook some of them out of their passivity.

## 2. The Chambers of Commerce

It has already been noted that with the emergence and the consolidation of the CNPF, practically all other inter-professional organizations of business have lost whatever little importance they might still have possessed before the war. Some of the survivors, such as the *Association Nationale d'Expansion Economique* and the *Comité d'Action Economique et Douanière*, have had in the past a considerable audience when they spoke in the name of the business community on either long-range or detailed points of economic policy.[12] Today the CNPF has no difficulty in controlling her older sisters, which duplicate but do not harm the activities of the peak association. The Executive Boards of the Association and Committee are studded with personalities prominent in the CNPF. The reason for their continued existence is obviously the conservative reluctance of firms which have subsidized these organizations for many years, to give up what has become a worthless endeavor and thereby to admit "defeat."

The only business organizations outside of the CNPF to have preserved some limited autonomy are the Chambers of Commerce. When the trade associations and the modern employers' movement were freed from the shackles of restrictive legislation, they found in the old-established Chambers of Commerce a possible competitor for an identical clientele. Authorized in their present form under the First Empire, they had survived all political vicissitudes of the century until their role as representatives of the commercial and industrial interests was firmly established. From their beginnings the Chambers of Commerce had a semi-official character which was solemnized by the charter afforded them by the law of April 9, 1898, essentially still valid today.[13]

Like similar organizations in other countries, the French Chambers of Commerce have since performed a number of technical and administrative services for their members and for businessmen in general. The larger ones and especially the Chamber of Commerce of Paris own and administer sections of the stock exchange, testing services for such wares as diamonds and firearms, warehouses, and port facilities. More than a dozen business schools where primary school pupils learn trades and others where graduates of the primary schools can obtain in-service

[12] On the pre-war activities of these organizations, see Shepard B. Clough, *France, A History of National Economics, 1789-1939*, New York, 1939, pp. 293-95.
[13] For a good analysis of the development and the role of the Chambers, see the highly perceptive essay by E. Pendleton Herring, "Chambres de Commerce in France: Their Legal Status and Political Significance," *American Political Science Review*, xxv, August 1931, pp. 689-99; Brèthe de la Gressaye, *Le syndicalisme, l'organisation professionnelle et l'Etat*, Paris, 1930, pp. 290-93; *Le Monde des Affaires, op.cit.* (n. 1-37), pp. 392-93, 516; and the short but pertinent remarks by David Thomson, *Democracy in France, The Third and Fourth Republics*, New York, 2nd edn., 1952. A general impression of the activities and personnel of the Chambers can be gained from *Annuaire, op.cit.* (n. 11-38), pp. 843-55.

training in a variety of sales and other commercial techniques are built, equipped, and run by the Paris Chamber, which is respected throughout the country. Located in a sumptuous building, provided with a competent staff and an excellent library, the Chamber of Paris has retained its luster and dignity.[14] The Marseilles Chamber has played a predominant role in extending and modernizing the harbor and airfield facilities of that Mediterranean city.

While for such specialized activities the domain of the Chambers was clearly marked out, conflicts between them and the employers' movement could easily have arisen where the Chambers, according to the statute of 1898, were called upon to present their views to the government as to appropriate means of promoting industrial and commercial prosperity and to advise the administration on all questions referred to them. Writing in 1931, Pendleton Herring discussed the possibility that the Chambers would ultimately become agencies to which the government would devolve some of its functions in the complex field of economic regulations.[15] At the time he wrote, the CGPF had been in existence for more than a decade, and yet neither the employers' peak association nor the trade associations seemed well enough organized to inform government or legislator of the general business point of view. Hence the idea that the Chambers of Commerce might provide a means whereby business would participate in the governmental process. Since then neither have the Chambers and the employers' movement merged nor has one absorbed the other. But the coordination of activities which has been achieved gave clear predominance to the employers' associations over the Chambers of Commerce.

By their constitution, by their membership, by the character of their financial means, and by their legally stipulated relationship to the public authorities, the Chambers were little suited to play the role of fully developed pressure groups in a modern state. Were it not for the comfortable niches in nineteenth century style which present-day France still offers to the nostalgic, they might have lost all of their status. As semi-official bodies

---

[14] According to the Chamber of Paris its library with 200,000 volumes and 2,000 foreign periodicals is the largest specialized library of its kind in Europe.

[15] See Herring, *op.cit.* (n. IV-13), pp. 691, 699.

the Chambers draw their income from certain taxes, and from state subsidies which make the Chambers fairly affluent but too dependent on the government to have all the desirable freedom to maneuver. The Minister of Commerce has a veto right over all of their decisions, the prefects or sub-prefects may attend their meetings.

Also the voting and membership rules are alien to the concepts which determine the activities of a freely organized interest group. Every employer is qualified to vote for the small group of those who serve a (renewable) six-year term as "members" of the Chambers; each of the 164 Chambers in France and Algeria has 21 members, and in Paris 40 members represent the business interests of the capital and the Seine Department. Only a small minority, until recently less than 7 percent of the businessmen qualified to vote, ever cast a ballot, and those who voted belonged mostly to the wealthiest or at least to the most firmly established businesses, with a clear predominance of the patrimonial employers, since no salaried executive has the right to vote.[16] Membership in the Chambers had become something of an honor, similar to that bestowed by a decoration, and in general this honor went to the notables of each business community, seldom to either the very small businessmen or the managers of a modern concern. This long-established pattern was upset for the first time when in 1955 followers of Pierre Poujade gained membership in many Chambers throughout the country and even in Paris, after thousands of shopkeepers obeyed the directives of their new-found leader and, by casting their ballot for the first time, had no difficulty in crowding out their quieter and more affable colleagues. While these elections sent up storm signals indicating the extent of many businessmen's wrath about the tax legislation, it remains to be seen whether the new elements which have entered them will seriously and lastingly affect the Chambers' activities. By seeking and finding political outlets for his movement, the shopkeepers' messiah of Saint-Céré seemed to admit that the Chambers of Commerce offer severely limited possibilities for demagoguery or even maneuver.

[16] The figure given in the text seems to be more realistic than that of 20 to 30 percent mentioned in the otherwise informative articles on the present status of the Chambers in *Le Figaro*, February 25 and March 1, 1955.

Under Vichy the Chambers had been assigned an ill-defined task of serving as liaison between the CO and regional interests. At the time of liberation it appeared for a moment as if the Chambers might rise to new prominence. Yet if that occasion was a test of their vitality, the test was not met. After the Free French had established themselves in North Africa, the Chambers of Commerce in Algiers and elsewhere took over a variety of functions as long as the more formal branches of local government were disorganized. Because of its suspicion against other business organizations, the Provisional Government attempted, after its return to Paris, to put the Chambers of Commerce on an equal footing with the employers' movement. They were to act as auxiliaries to the Industrial Offices and by the law of April 1946 were admitted to serve, like the trade associations, as agencies for sub-allocating rationed raw materials.[17]

But as soon as the trade associations had regained their status and after the national peak association had been formed, the earlier division of labor between the Chambers on the one hand and the CNPF and its affiliates on the other prevailed once more. In this as in so many other fields, the Fourth Republic found out that it was unable to change traditions that had been established in the Third.

The Chambers of Commerce continue to engage in a great number of ornamental activities ranging from receptions for distinguished visitors, banquets, and organization of trade fairs, to providing flowers for the graves of their lamented members; their publications often convey the quaintness of Flaubertian scenes. Local differences are frequently determined by the temperament of the Chambers' presidents. At all of their meetings local and regional Chambers adopt a number of *voeux*, expressions of wishes which are published monthly in the handsome bulletin of the nation-wide Assembly of Chamber Presidents. The *voeux*, as well as occasional letters to a particular administration, alternate between sweeping general propositions and detailed requests for relief for a distressed group of businessmen. Though they are given wide distribution among the ministries concerned and among the deputies, there is hardly ever a follow-up by a personal audience, nor is other pressure brought; lobbying

[17] See above, Chapter III.

is left to the employers' movement at its various levels. If there were no other reasons, an almost complete lack of staff would explain such inertia. Even the Assembly of Presidents, in which each of the twenty economic regions of the country is represented, has neither a secretariat nor an official address.

Since 1946 the mutual inter-penetration of the employers' movement and of the Chambers of Commerce has made further progress and is systematically promoted by M. Villiers in the interest of a unified representation of all economic interests. The most energetic presidents of local or regional Chambers usually also are active in trade associations or serve on one of the directing boards of the CNPF. Until M. Poujade disturbed established traditions the trade associations fully controlled the membership in the Chambers by nominating the candidates for the elections. At the very least, candidates could hardly hope to be successful without the endorsement of their trade association. Because of its proximity to the CNPF, the respected Paris Chamber engages even less in political and pressure group activities than some of the provincial Chambers, which might make their voices heard when the regional organizations of the general employers' movement are weak.

Of those serving on the Paris Chamber's Executive a majority also occupy positions on the Board of Directors or in the Assembly of the CNPF. Wherever representatives of the Chambers meet with their colleagues from the CNPF on private or public boards or committees, they always vote in unison with the spokesmen for the employers' movement. The coordination between the somewhat old-fashioned Chambers and the more modern expression of organized business left little to be desired until the surprise elections of 1955.

Only once in recent years has such pre-established harmony been slightly disturbed. When the promoters of the Schuman plan in the administration, and especially in the Monnet Plan Office, had grounds to fear that the ratification of the treaty might be defeated in parliament by the violent campaign unleashed against the plan by the National Steel Association and the CNPF, they turned to the Chambers of Commerce in order to mobilize business interests in favor of the plan. They calculated, on the whole correctly, that the metal-processing industries should rejoice in the prospect of lower prices for steel and were prevented by their trade associations from voicing their opinion. Actually under well-organized prodding, the membership of those Chambers and regions where such interests prevailed expressed some mildly favorable views on the issue of ratification, while the trade associations continued to bombard parliament with expressions of unmitigated hostility. The fact that in the end the treaty was ratified by an unexpected majority may have had something to do with the stand the Chambers of Commerce had taken. How much they counted with the deputies is impossible to say, since a variety of factors were involved in the decision.[18]

### 3. The Confederation of Small and Medium-Sized Enterprises

"Of all timorous people those are most dangerous who are afraid of not appearing bold enough."
Detoeuf, *Propos de O. L. Barenton*

Of all the segments of the French employers' movement, none is a more personal creation than the CGPME. First as president of a modest trade association, after 1936 as small business representative in the reorganized CGPF, under Vichy as a one-man anti-trust division in the cabinet of Bichelonne, M. Gingembre has had ample training in the art of organizing firms that are small in size and large in number.

Slightly younger than most of the leaders in the employers' movement, Léon Gingembre comes from a respected though not prominent bourgeois family. After studies of law and political science at the University of Paris, he contemplated a university career, but instead became a practicing attorney working for a number of years for the Paris Chamber of Commerce. In 1934 he took over the family business, a safety-pin factory of modest dimensions which he still runs. The strikes of 1936 impressed the young industrialist deeply; his ambitions drove him to seek an active role in the employers' movement, which was then in turmoil. He became what he himself calls a "maniac" of small business organization, preaching its cause even in the prisoner-of-

---

[18] For details see below, Chapter VIII, and Ehrmann, *op.cit.* (n. III-56), passim.

war compounds in Germany, until he was freed at the request of the Vichy government. His activities and methods have alienated him from his milieu and family: an older brother, a graduate of the "X," is director and board member of a number of large corporations belonging to the world of the "trusts" against which Léon Gingembre inveighs with all the vehemence at his disposal.

When after the war M. Gingembre set out to organize the confederation which is often identified with his name and person, he successfully avoided an organizational dilemma.[19] It was not advisable to create new primary organizations to present the interests of small business. After many decades of slow growth, the existing employers' associations, both vertical and horizontal, were too deeply imbedded in traditions to make another complicated framework desirable; the history of the labor movement had shown the weakening effects of competing *syndicats*. On the other hand, from his experiences in the CGPF, Gingembre had come to mistrust any arrangement by which the small firms were merely assured of representation in the councils of the employers' peak association; even a generous share of seats on the executive and in committees seemed no guarantee of effective defense as long as there existed no autonomous organization of the smaller enterprises.

The *Confédération Générale des Petites et Moyennes Entreprises* was created as such an autonomous organization. Among the existing primary trade associations and the regional organizations, those of their members who qualify as small and medium-sized industrial and commercial firms adhere to the Confederation. (See Appendix, Tables I and II for illustration.) The Confederation claims that at present slightly over 3,000 primary organizations are affiliated with either its industrial or its commercial union and with its intra-trade regional council.[20]

---

[19] For the beginnings of the CGPME, see above, Chapter III. For an interesting parallel showing many similarities between the problems of small business organizations in France and the United States, see Oliver Garceau, "Can Little Business Organize?" *Public Opinion Quarterly*, 11, Summer 1938, pp. 469-73.

[20] The organization of the CGPME and its underlying ideas are best described (probably by M. Gingembre himself) in the anonymous article "Confédération Générale des Petites et Moyennes Entreprises," *France Documents*, Nouvelle Série, No. 15, January 1948, pp. 1-19. On pp. 20-25 this publication contains something like the listing of organizations which the *Annuaire, op.cit.* (n. III-38), provides for the CNPF. The indications about the number of affiliated organizations vary but fluctuate around 3,000.

From its beginnings the CGPME has been particularly successful in winning the adherence of the area horizontal associations. Through its flexible organization, and by inviting the local and regional bodies to play more than the secondary role to which they are restricted in the general employers' movement, the Confederation has seen to it that the representatives of small business constitute in many cases, especially as far as commercial interests are concerned, the only existing area association; in many others they are its most active elements. Since there is no division of membership at the base of the organizational pyramid, the controversial question as to which are the "small and medium-sized" enterprises needs no precise answer. In the summary classification of the CGPME, small enterprises are those employing a personnel of not more than 50; middle-sized the firms which employ between 50 and 300. Attempting to describe his clientele in a slightly more sophisticated fashion, M. Gingembre had defined the "PME" as all enterprises of whatever juridical form (1) which are financed by the personal capital of the owner or of his family, (2) whose risks are assumed entirely by the owner, and (3) in which the employer has direct contacts with his personnel. According to M. Gingembre's probably vastly exaggerated estimate, coming somewhat out of nowhere, the shares of these firms in total industrial production and in the volume of distribution amount respectively to 50 and 95 percent. The CGPME claims to group through its affiliated unions a membership of about 100,000 industrial and 700,000 commercial firms, employing about 48 percent of the total labor force in industry and commerce. This would mean that a large majority of all existing "PME" would have found a way to organize. But these and similar statements cannot be checked because the notions of membership and of affiliation are conveniently obscured by the chosen form of organization.[21]

Precisely because the CNPF had granted in its by-laws ample representation to the small and medium-sized enterprises on all of its formal organs, a man like M. Gingembre, extremely sensi-

[21] At other times the CGPME changes its claims and maintains that among the 800,000 firms it calls its members, 250,000 are manufacturers. At any rate it must be kept in mind that the 800,000 firms presumably in the CGPME are part of the 900,000 firms which the CNPF counts among its affiliates (see above, Chapter III). Outsiders maintain that all of these figures are greatly exaggerated.

tive as he is to questions of power and influence, recognized the urgency of making the activities of the CGPME sufficiently distinct from those of the general employers' movement. The leader of the CGPME knew that in order to maintain his organization's identity and to prove its continuing usefulness to the undisciplined legions of the small businessmen, the Confederation would have to assume a fundamentally different role from that of the CNPF. Almost from its inception, the CGPME has become a political organization, the purest type of a pressure group among all business organizations.[22] Its mostly shrill voice speaks in the name of the small businessman frequently without consulting him and always without obligating him. If business leaders complain, as they will often do, about the reckless demagoguery of M. Gingembre, when they compare the activities of his confederation with the more restrained and supposedly more constructive attitudes of the other employers' organizations, they misjudge the character of the CGPME. It is not merely a branch of the general employers' movement, specializing in problems of the small firm, but a group *sui generis*, openly playing its part in the arena of politics, while the political pressure applied by other business organizations seeks more discreet forms of influence.

The most remarkable aspect of the relationship between the CGPME and the CNPF is the fact that the latter has been unable to challenge M. Gingembre's monopoly as the paladin of the small business interests or to restrain his political activities, which frequently prove embarrassing to the more dignified employers' movement. After the liberation, when the business interests were in hiding, they considered the forces which M. Gingembre had mobilized without losing time as a welcome "light cavalry," able to clear the terrain and provide cover wherever necessary. But after the thorough transformation of the political situation, why does the CNPF still give to the CGPME as large a representation as it does on all levels of its organization? Why is there no serious attempt made to check the vagaries of its delegate general? Why does the general employers'

[22] This is also the conclusion reached in the excellent study by Georges E. Lavau, "Note sur un 'Pressure Group' Français. La Confédération Générale des Petites et Moyennes Entreprises," *Revue Française de Science Politique*, v, 1955, pp. 370-83.

confederation rather try to minimize the differences that exist between its policy and that of small business?

The internal structure of the CGPME accounts for part of this situation. According to the by-laws of the Confederation, the position of the delegate general is yet stronger than that of the CNPF's president. While all other officers of the organization are elected indirectly in elaborate stages by the affiliates of the Confederation, the delegate general is designated each year in plebiscitarian fashion by acclamation after he has addressed the General Assembly in one of his customary speeches, which are both terse and inflammatory. As an *ex-officio* member of all of the Confederation's directing boards the delegate general, once he is reconfirmed in his position, exercises the broadest of powers. With his acute sense for the significance of symbolism, M. Gingembre has given wide distribution to an organization chart which dramatizes to the utmost the independence of the Confederation's *Fuehrer*. The other officers of the organization and of its affiliates are all active businessmen—modest merchants or manufacturers. They have neither the time nor the temperament to provide effective leadership. Even when they have misgivings about their delegate's tireless activities, they still let him speak in their name. Hence M. Gingembre is able to raise everywhere the standard of the small business world and to accumulate "in the interest of effective coordination" an ever-increasing number of assignments. Once more his opponents miss the point when they accuse him of superficiality and legerdemain in the performance of his far too numerous tasks. It is precisely his political function to be everywhere, to multiply himself, and to sound off—what he says is of far less and frequently of no significance.

Of even greater importance, however, is the fact that the CGPME is able to exploit to the fullest feelings it did not have to create. The respect which the country reserves for everything "small" has opened the way to a "demagoguery of the *petit*"[23] (which is not entirely peculiar to France). Just as for Anatole France's immortal peddler, Crainquebille, the shop of a fruit dealer is a "trust," elsewhere "anybody whose business is bigger

[23] The expression was coined by the former president of the CGPF; see Gignoux, *op.cit.* (n. 1-31), pp. 14-15.

than your business is big business."[24] The difference between France and countries of similar structure is rather to be found in the extent to which this "demagoguery" has remained institutionalized in the political and administrative process. Because of the ostracism which big business had incurred, the Fourth Republic, in spite of its plans for modernization, continued and frequently strengthened such traditions. The Gingembre confederation has become shield and symbol of the Gingembre France, "busily engaged in 'skimming the cream' of the French social product, the whole idyllic, old-fashioned France of little shops and small factories."[25]

Statistical data reveal how numerous the little shops and small factories have remained. (See Appendix, Table IV.) Also, in the field of industry, concentration seems to have been stopped altogether. Although industrial production had increased 26 percent in 1952 over 1931, the number of firms employing a labor force of more than 500 had diminished from 1,134 to 985.[26]

While M. Gingembre effectively transforms the awe in which his clientele is held into a position of political strength, he gives equally effective expression to the feelings of helplessness and frustration which are widespread among individual businessmen. The propaganda of the organization reveals a distinct paranoid trait: attacks directed from many sides against the integrity of small business must be combatted, maneuvers be unveiled, calumnies exposed, and plots exploded.

[24] That differences in the prestige of the small businessmen nevertheless exist in France and the United States is well illustrated by the excellent remarks in John K. Galbraith, *American Capitalism. The Concept of Countervailing Power*, Boston, 1952, p. 29. The very way in which one talks in this country about the "small but successful businessman" seems to indicate that smallness is considered a handicap that can be overcome rather than as in France a virtue that must be universally admired.

[25] Herbert Luethy, *France Against Herself*, New York, 1955, p. 301. Mr. Luethy has made a description of the deadweight exercised by the "Gingembre France" one of the central themes of his highly perceptive book. The collection of essays, published by the Association Française de Science Politique, *Partis Politiques et Classes Sociales en France*, Paris, 1955, contains ample documentation, esp. pp. 69 ff. and p. 77, that all parties attempt to ensure the support of the small businessmen and the small farmers.

[26] For these figures see J. M. Jeanneney, *Forces et Faiblesses de l'Economie Française, 1945-1956*, Paris, 1956, p. 259. If the figures given by Professor Jeanneney and those presented by the National Institute of Statistics (see Appendix, Table IV) were entirely comparable, they would indicate that between 1950 and 1952 deconcentration continued.

By constantly using such language, M. Gingembre strikes chords which are certain to find resonance among many small businessmen.[27] In their eyes the world around them has been hostile for a long time. Competitors, customers, purveyors, personnel, and tax collector have all joined in a conspiracy to deprive them of the hard-won fruits of their labor. All means are permitted if they help in warding off the dangers that threaten from many sides. The cynicism and anarchism of the small businessmen feed on the reality as they perceive it: others have made fortunes through illicit maneuvers, others have used political push to win where they have lost. By appealing to such confused feelings and by promising successful defense without exacting any collective effort, the Gingembre confederation has acquired a stature which is respected by organized business and by politicians alike.

In order to make its action as efficacious as possible, the CGPME has at all times sought to form broad coalitions with other forces and organizations. Already in 1936 M. Gingembre had promoted a Central Committee of the Middle Classes. After the war his Confederation entered into a National Committee of Liaison and Action of the Middle Classes. With M. Gingembre as one of its vice-presidents, the Committee speaks in the name of artisans, intellectuals, and various professional groups. An "Economic Front" was formed upon the initiative of the indefatigable delegate of the CGPME in the fall of 1949 to coordinate opposition to the budget which the Bidault government prepared at the time; the "Economic Front" brought together all employers' associations, the most militant middle-class organizations, and important agricultural interest groups. Since the election of 1951, it has extended its activity into parliament through the Study and Action Group for Private Enterprise, of which M. Gingembre is the secretary and which has enlisted the majority of deputies.[28]

But in every alliance it concludes, the CGPME is anxious to safeguard its full freedom. Like Stalin and for identical reasons, Léon Gingembre will only tolerate "parallel actions" and not more: "The CGPME wants to be represented only by itself; it

[27] For the following see the excellent description of the small businessmen's mentality in Weil, op.cit. (n. 1-15), pp. 191-92.

[28] For details on the activities of these groups see below, Chapter V.

does not let anybody speak in its name. From all organizations to which it belongs the Confederation admits neither influence nor arbitration and considers them merely as means of liaison and of information through which it will be able to arrive at its own position."[29]

In its methods and means of expression the CGPME is free of the restrictions which hamper an organization such as the CNPF. Afraid that a backing by the "200 families" will be the kiss of death even for the soundest of policies, the employers' peak association refrains from opening its meetings to a wider audience, from expressing its views except in carefully restrained communiqués, from publicizing its dealings with administration and politicians. The CGPME wishes to be heard and seen everywhere since it can boast that hardly anybody, least of all the communist CGT, dares to attack it publicly.

The Confederation controls two newspapers, both presented in the make-up of the sensation-hungry boulevard press.[30] The widely publicized debates of its annual General Assembly are supplemented whenever it is deemed useful by special gatherings of its affiliated unions. If the situation is particularly propitious, the Confederation organizes noisy States General of the small and medium-sized enterprises formulating the claims which the organization wishes to lay before parliament and public opinion. During the first post-war years, M. Gingembre held several mass meetings in Paris where, according to his claims, seventy to eighty thousand small businessmen shouted their indignation against the government.

During the elections, whether national or local, the CGPME does not hesitate to intervene openly. Its operations, termed a "depoliticization" of the vote, consist in obtaining from the candidates a written promise to support the action program of the Confederation, whereupon the CGPME will invite its followers to vote for the candidates so pledged, whatever their party affiliation. When reporting on his lobbying activities, M.

[29] *La Confédération Générale des Petites et Moyennes Entreprises* (mimeographed, November 15, 1951), p. 2.

[30] *La Volonté du Commerce et de l'Industrie* (monthly), printed in various regional editions, presumably in 80,000 copies and *Les Informations Industrielles et Commerciales* (weekly), in a 30,000 edition; and for internal circulation a printed bulletin, *Les Informations Confédérales.*

Gingembre relates in detail which material he has used to "bombard" the deputies, which bills have been deposited at his request, on which ministries he and "middle-class" delegations conducted by him have descended. He "denounces," he "regrets," and frequently utters hardly veiled threats. Whenever legislation or administrative regulations are passed which the Confederation considers satisfactory, it claims full credit for them just as it boasts of having brought about the downfall of governments of which it disapproves.[31] The public gatherings of the CGPME are always attended by a number of deputies and other politicians. At the traditional final banquet of the General Assembly, ranking cabinet ministers, and on one occasion even a premier, must defend themselves in good-humored speeches against the insults heaped against the government during the preceding meetings. But to incur the hostility of small business is considered by most of the shaky French cabinets too great a liability to be borne.

The deliberate and advertised interference with governmental policies reached a climax during the lifetime of the Pinay cabinet in 1952. The premier had acknowledged frequently that he himself belonged to the "milieu PME" and that he could be counted upon as a faithful supporter of that milieu's interests. Hence the Confederation greeted the government at first as if it had invented it; but as soon as some of M. Pinay's policies incurred its displeasure, it took even more liberties with this government than with any of its predecessors. It warned the premier against "plots" hatched by the administration and especially by the despised finance inspectors; it distinguished between acceptable and evil cabinet members; it protested sharply against some of its bills and chastised its budget proposals.[32]

The Confederation is somewhat miscast in the quieter role of a participant in public administration. Yet in practically all of the numerous tri-partite advisory boards which exist in the fields of economic and social affairs, a number of the seats reserved to business go to representatives of small and medium-sized firms,

---

[31] For a lengthy list of such activities and the self-advertisement that was given to them in the publications of the CGPME during an eighteen-month period, see Lavau, op.cit. (n. IV-22), pp. 374 ff.

[32] See Etats-Généraux des PME, Aix-les-Bains, June 21/23, 1952, Les Informations Confédérales, No. 164-66, July 15, 1952, p. 4112, and the article by Léon Gingembre, "Rappelez-vous, M. Pinay," Les Informations Industrielles et Commerciales, November 21, 1952.

and the CGPME holds an unbroken monopoly for designating them. The contribution which these delegates make to the work of such agencies might be of small value. But to the Confederation its participation gives an aura of representativeness which further increases its political weight.

The program of the CGPME, frequently ill defined and frequently contradictory where defined, differs little from the natural preoccupation of small business everywhere. Requests for an increase of state-backed credit facilities and for a share of small business in the investment program of the Monnet and Marshall plans alternate with denunciations of all forms of *dirigisme*. A balanced budget is considered a necessity, but any tax increase is rejected. While the "power of the trusts" is still under attack, the CGPME has rejected, along with all other business organizations, even the mildest proposals for an anti-trust legislation. M. Gingembre criticizes the existing social security system as wasteful but requests that its benefits be extended to the retired businessmen. In a curious *quid pro quo* he prodded the Pinay government into enacting sliding wage scale legislation, which previously had been the long-sought objective of the labor movement.[33]

It is generally agreed that the organization probably passed the peak of its influence based on mass support some time in 1947, and that its political weight has considerably diminished since the fall of the Pinay cabinet. M. Gingembre attributes the decline, which he admits, mainly to the exclusion of the PME and of their organizations from the scene of international business dealings. According to him French and American big business interests have conspired with their governments to exclude the CGPME from the activities and consultations of the ECA and OEEC. Unable to wangle an official invitation for a trip to the United States, Gingembre wrote an intentionally insolent public letter to the head of the ECA Mission in Paris accusing the United States of bestowing its favors solely on basic industries, since it feared the competition of the French processing industries. Knowing in advance that M. Villiers would have to take exception to such attacks, the delegate general of the CGPME

---

[33] For details on some of the attitudes and policies of the CGPME see below, Chapters VI-IX.

stated that his organization had given to the CNPF no mandate and was "as such" not even a member of the peak association, with which the American authorities were dealing.

In Europe none of the slowly emerging agencies of economic integration has been willing to concede to the PME the degree of representation that was so over-generously granted to them during the infant years of the Fourth Republic. That fact alone explains why M. Gingembre has not wavered in his hostility to the Coal and Steel Community, even after the steel interests had apparently accepted the *fait accompli* of the pool. By sparking an International Union of Small and Medium-Sized Enterprises, M. Gingembre hoped to find a surrogate for the missing international connections of his organization. But little recognition and even less power has accrued to the Union.

There are also other, and for M. Gingembre's ambitions graver, handicaps in the way of a continued and expanding effectiveness for his organization. If the CNPF and the trade associations are frequently and disastrously hampered by the deadweight of small business, it turns out that conversely the CGPME, and especially its impetuous delegate general, are the captives of the general employers' movement. Were it not for the more moderate elements in the Confederation, M. Gingembre would have broken off long ago all relations with the CNPF and have restricted the contacts of the PME with the employers' movement to the primary organizations. M. Gingembre has declared that since the common communist danger has receded, no tie ought to exist between two organizations which recruit their members in a different social milieu. He has insinuated that the CNPF is living in sin with the arch-enemies of small business—the high bureaucracy and other "technocrats." All this has not prevented dozens of small business representatives from taking their place on the various boards of the CNPF just as they, and M. Gingembre with them, are regularly casting their votes in the Economic Council and other advisory bodies alongside those of the CNPF. Of the hundreds of issues coming before these committees there has been an insignificant number on which large and small business were divided. It proved more difficult to maintain independence and to prevent identification with other business interests than ringing declarations of principle had promised.

As long as the CGPME remains identified with the general employers' movement, it obviously cannot transcend the bounds of legality. M. Gingembre, it is true, has threatened repeatedly to launch a tax strike, to instruct his clients not to surrender any information to the authorities, to bring about the closing of all shops; he likes to talk about the "spirit of revolt which would blow away unbearable regimentation." But those dire warnings have no morrow, as long as the CGPME must avoid the open advocacy of a recourse to violence.

The dilemma became evident, and soon dramatic, when there arose in Pierre Poujade's *Union de défense des commerçants et artisans* a competitor appealing with the same slogans to the same audience. Since Poujade's Union was a grass roots movement, free of all affiliation with other organizations, it could launch, in earnest and without consideration for legality, the campaigns which a Gingembre had only brandished.[84] Small wonder that the two organizations and their fiery leaders were soon at odds! For Poujade the CGPME had betrayed its membership and had already lost most of its following. Gingembre denounced the *Union de défense* for engaging in demagoguery and for using the platform of small business interests as a means for launching a political movement, fascist in nature, and at first communist-sponsored. He decried the disunity which his rival had sown in the never very solid ranks of small business. All of a sudden M. Gingembre discovered the evils that arise from mixing politics with the sober objectives of a "corporative" organization, from submerging the requests of discontented shopkeepers in a broad front embracing farmers and other middle-class elements. While Poujade treated the deputies of the National Assembly with contempt and ridiculed the entire parliamentary system, the delegate general of the PME admonished his readers to recognize the benefits to be derived from the changes in the

[84] The Poujade movement need not be discussed here, since it is in fact not a business organization. The literature on its significance is already large. Among the best studies are Jean Touchard, "Bibliographie et Chronologie du Poujadisme," *Revue Française de Science Politique*, VI, 1956, pp. 18-43 (containing *inter alia* interesting references to the relationship between the Poujade and the Gingembre movement), and Stanley Hoffmann, *Le mouvement Poujade*, Paris, 1956.

tax laws which government and parliament had conceded. If M. Gingembre wanted to demonstrate thereby that the ways of legality still held promise, he forgot that the concessions which he advertised had been made under the almost physical threats which his robust competitor from Saint-Céré had organized in the lobbies of parliament and in the mass arena of the Vélodrome d'Hiver.[35]

Together with many others, M. Gingembre mistakenly assumed that the Poujade movement would soon collapse under its own contradictions. The elections of 1956 proved a rude awakening from such illusions, though they also established clearly the political character of this organized revolt, which thereby seemingly left the domain of the CGPME. But the phenomenon Poujade, whatever the future of his movement might be, will haunt the leadership of the CGPME for a long time. It remains to be seen whether the Confederation can survive without considerable loss of prestige and effectiveness a trial which has uncovered its own basic duplicity of purpose: can it go on straddling the position of an employers' association, devoted to the corporative defense of special interests, and that of a political movement, organized on principles only slightly less authoritarian than those of Poujade?

The Homeric battle between "Pierrot and Léon" has its comical aspects, thoroughly enjoyed by many an onlooker. It also provides an object lesson for all pressure groups—there are boundary lines which their activities cannot transgress without risk, either to themselves or to the society in which they operate.

## 4. The "Opinion" or Vanguard Groups

It has been explained why the official employers' movement has in fact abandoned the task of developing anything but the most rudimentary business philosophy.[36] Such an assignment has fallen to small groups of businessmen, some of them closely integrated, others only loosely connected with the general movement; sometimes but not always desirous of obtaining a share in the

---

[35] For the highly revealing criticism of the Poujade movement by Gingembre, see his articles in *La Volonté du Commerce et de l'Industrie*, January, May, July, September, 1955.

[36] See above, Chapter III.

control of the larger organizations; invariably seeking to expound a fairly elaborate set of beliefs and to win for them the broadest possible support.

All of the "opinion" groups that have emerged since the war had to face a number of problems besetting everywhere the minorities which arise within larger interest groups.[37] How can a well-defined program be developed without letting the "elite" degenerate into a "sect"? Should purity of principle occasionally be sacrificed to effectiveness? What should be the relationship between the group and the larger organization; is double affiliation or outright competition preferable? Should the group seek the maximum of potential strength or should it be content with serving as a lighthouse providing guidance from afar?

*The Centre des Jeunes Patrons (CJP)*. The beginnings of this group have been described earlier.[38] Its desire to continue as in the past as a movement of young employers has proven since the war a great handicap for the recruitment of the CJP. The mood of those who have grown to manhood since the liberation is little propitious for a group which makes heavy demands on idealism and self-devotion; a self-centered practicality, coolness towards all myths, often outright cynicism are the characteristic reactions of French and European youth to the past nightmarish years of nazism. The CJP admits that it recruits relatively few members among the truly young employers and that it has become difficult to keep the membership figure at the peak of 2,500 which was reached soon after the war.

The CJP had therefore to waive strict age limits, so that at least the core of the membership is still the same as before the war or during the occupation. But those who were the sons of employers or were junior partners in the family business have by now assumed major responsibility for their firms. Their change in status as well as their advance in age seems to have cooled the reformatory zeal of some; by dragging their feet they often prevent the movement from advancing. On the other hand certain of the ideas advanced by the pre-war JP, especially in the field of industrial relations, have by now been espoused by

[37] For parallel developments in the United States see Truman, *op.cit.* (n. 1-27), p. 170.
[38] See above, Chapters I and III.

broader segments of the employers' movement; hence the "vanguard" seems at times to be lagging behind the main formations.

Quite apart from the temper of its older members, the present composition of the group is indicative of a failure to reach announced objectives. It had been stated that ideally employers should join the CJP between the age of twenty-five and thirty-five, assume leadership functions in the group when between thirty-five and forty-five, and afterwards leave the CJP to "occupy leading positions in the CNPF, the important trade associations and federations."[39] Not having obtained such positions within the general employers' movement, many members have stayed within the CJP so as not to lose a forum for their activities. M. Villiers himself has occasionally expressed the opinion that members of the CJP should be found in responsible positions throughout the employers' movement. But with a few exceptions this has not come about. While the CJP continues to be organizationally tied to the CNPF, such a relationship has also its negative aspects. When the employers' peak association is under attack for reactionary attitudes or for procrastination, its spokesmen will point to the fact that it has in its midst such a progressive group as the CJP. Instead of being permitted to act as a leaven in the CNPF, the most responsible elements in the CJP have often the impression that they serve as a fig leaf. While *Jeune Patron* has assumed the leadership of the CNPF-sponsored Employers' Center of Research and Study,[40] its participation in the decision-making process of the Employers' Council has become perfunctory at best.

The CJP has been even less successful in the self-assigned task of "penetrating" the confederation of M. Gingembre. Although economically and sociologically speaking the two organizations appeal to the same audience, differences in outlook and methods have been so great that the CGPME and the CJP are hardly on speaking terms. Consequently the masses of owners of small and medium-sized firms are not in the least touched by the mentality which the CJP has tried to propagate.

Today most of the CJP's membership consists of patrimonial

[39] *Jeune Patron*, ii, November 1948 (reporting on the debates of a congress celebrating the tenth anniversary of the movement), p. 36.
[40] See above, Chapter III.

employers responsible for enterprises employing a personnel between 50 and 500. The organization has hardly any contact with large industrial concerns, while the management of a number of large commercial firms, especially in the food trade, furnish some of its most active members. The owners of truly small firms usually pay little attention to the CJP. They not only lack the time for activities such as the CJP proposes, but their outlook is also generally hostile to the constructive program of the movement.

The CJP estimates that its members employ a total of about 200,000 wage earners in about sixty cities or towns. Regionally the membership is mostly concentrated in the north and east of the country while but little support is provided by the middle-sized enterprises of the south or west. An Executive Council of thirty members, the Executive Council's president, and a very small professional staff provide the active leadership of the organization. The nonbureaucratic character of the movement is striking, especially when its gatherings and methods of work are compared with other sectors of the employers' movement. There are discussions from the floor, lively controversies, and a frequent turnover in the membership of the Executive Council. Only the president of the Executive Council is generally reelected for several years, so that for the last few years M. Guy Raclet has occupied the position. Born in 1917, head of a medium-sized concern manufacturing camping materials, graduate of the *Ecole des Hautes Etudes Commerciales*, the most distinguished among the country's business schools, M. Raclet is entirely representative of CJP membership. A majority of his colleagues on the Executive Council also manage old-established family enterprises; and most of them have a better education than the rank and file of French employers, usually in engineering, the law, or business science.

In the best fashion of French philosophical societies, the Executive Council "retreats" once a year to formulate a program of currently proposed activities and to elaborate the *"doctrine Jeune Patron,"* the more fundamental philosophy of the group. As a result lengthy studies or shorter "notes of application" are sent out to the membership, which presumably discusses these materials in its regional or local meetings. The numerous publications of the CJP—pamphlets, brochures, and above all its monthly journal, *Jeune Patron*—seek to address a wider audience than the CJP membership proper.

By the excellence of presentation, judicious and yet lively style, objectivity in reprinting or digesting writings from a wide array of fields and authors, the publications of the CJP are easily superior to all other materials issued by the employers' movement. Quite apart from the social and economic philosophy which they express, they provide a wealth of statistical and factual data rarely to be found in any other periodical literature in France. Equally remarkable for France, and indicative of the untraditional approach which the Center takes in regard to many questions, is the fact that these publications are said to be self-supporting, due to the unusual amount of modern advertising which they carry.

The movement claims to represent above all a state of mind, to be primarily interested in spreading what it calls the "mentality *Jeune Patron*," so that its actual strength cannot be measured by the mere counting of its members. It is quite true that press and radio give the CJP far more attention than the size of its membership would warrant. Its public gatherings attract a fairly wide and varied audience; they serve as a platform for what has become rare in present-day France—the exchange of ideas among distinguished men from different camps and of opposite allegiance. At least for a time it was believed that the Center might crystallize efforts waged from several quarters to overcome the economic and social stagnation that had befallen the country so soon after the liberation. But what does the movement's creed consist in, and what are the chances of translating its creed into action?[41]

As late as 1948 the founder of the JP, Jean Mersch, could claim without being contradicted that the true ancestors of the movement were La Tour du Pin and Albert de Mun, its "grand-

---

[41] The following analysis is based on publications issued by the CJP. Among the many revealing pages of its journal, those which record the annual conventions (usually the September-October issues) are especially of interest. Among the pamphlets published in two series, one called *Doctrine Jeune Patron*, the other *Documents Jeune Patron*, the following are most interesting: *Une Etape*, 1946; *Orientations Economiques*, 1950; *L'Entreprise Moderne*, 1951; *Vers une nouvelle Etape*, 1951, etc.

fathers" men like Gignoux, Lobstein, and Olivier. Now, all of the writers or businessmen he mentioned belong to the school of conservative and traditionalist Catholic corporatists.[42] It is no accident that more than a few of the Catholic employers and intellectuals who had assisted Vichy officials in their efforts to develop a corporatist doctrine are now collaborating with the CJP. Though the movement disclaims any official religious ties, it attracts hardly any non-Catholics, who are fairly numerous among French business leaders.

It would, however, be unjust to see in the beliefs of the CJP nothing more than a re-edition of anti-republican nineteenth century doctrines or a re-enactment of Vichy illusions. Though the CJP is even after the experience of the CO convinced that, "ideally," vocational organization (*organisation professionnelle*) holds all imaginable virtues, its leadership admits that the practices of many trade associations and of their affiliated *cartels* run counter to the over-all objectives of the *Jeune Patron*. Hence M. Raclet has repeatedly acknowledged that "vocational organization" was but a means, not an end, and that, misused by a "class-conscious" employers' movement, it could aggravate the evils it was designed to remedy. Especially during the last years the Center's outlook has been deeply influenced by critics like Mendès-France or Sauvy, who attribute the manifestations of economic and social maladjustment to the insufficient development of the country's human and material resources. While the CNPF in the name of French business denies all responsibilities for an unsatisfactory rate of economic growth and seeks the culprit elsewhere, the *Centre des Jeunes Patrons* readily accepts the reproach that frequently the attitudes of manufacturers and merchants alike hamper economic development. To "increase the standard of living of Frenchmen" has become of late a leitmotif of the CJP. But once the notion of a dynamic economy is accepted, solutions must be found that are fundamentally different from the stagnant corporative system of the Catholic traditionalists.

Yet in spite of sincere attempts to reexamine earlier notions in the light of experience, the economic vistas of the movement have remained blurred, partly because of its inability to cut

[42] For a discussion of their doctrine, see above, Chapters I and II.

itself loose completely from the strands that went into the making of its philosophy. If the CJP announces that the economy based on the *locatio operis* of the civil law should be transformed into an "economy of association," it fails to clarify whether these desired and ill-defined changes should take place on the level of the plant or on that of the national economy.[43] Its criteria of how to judge the dangers or desirability of economic concentration and of competition have remained hazy. All too often the Center's publications exhibit specimens of the national weakness that seek to satisfy the hunger for clarity by a well-polished formula which on closer scrutiny dissolves into a worthless platitude.

The general philosophy of the movement in matters of social policy and industrial relations is equally well-meaning and equally vague. The "mixed committees" which the CJP proposed for all enterprises shortly after the liberation were similar to the Social Committees of the Vichy regime, cleansed of some authoritarian features but still designed to "abolish" class antagonism by institutional gadgets. In 1946, however, the CJP was not less opposed than the CNPF to the new law on plant committees which made only cautious steps toward "codetermination." A few years later the CJP published, together with other "vanguard" groups of the employers' movement, a declaration pledging its membership to take concrete measures for an improvement of the industrial climate through a frank adoption of human relations techniques.[44]

For the CJP the human personality is the unifying concept which underlies its economic and social philosophy and motivates its proposals for action: "Man as creator and as intelligence; man with his hierarchically ordained needs demanding satisfaction; man fit to enter a group with rights and responsibilities; capable of accepting responsibilities and exercising authority; capable of fulfilling a common task in order to live and to help the life of others. . . ."[45]

[43] For a more detailed discussion of the proposals for the reform of enterprise, see below, Chapter VII.

[44] For a discussion of the declaration and other questions of social policy, see below, Chapter IX.

[45] Jean Queneau, "Réflexions sur la Doctrine Jeune Patron," *Jeune Patron*, VII, January 1953, p. 18. This article was introduced by the editor as expressing elements of the movement's authentic doctrine.

The very breadth of this personalism to which the sanction of natural law is attached seems to account in part for the vagueness of the movement's doctrine and for the pompousness and lyricism that frequently characterize its literature. The acknowledged inability to translate generous thoughts into concrete and generally effective reformatory action derives from a constant preoccupation of the reformers with their own moral satisfaction. Describing the motivation of his hero, an industrialist who was prompted by the events of 1936 to inaugurate ill-conceived reforms in his plant, Ramond Fernandez, correctly characterized this side of the "JP mentality": "Fundamentally Robert was only thinking about himself. He would sacrifice everything to the nobility of his attitude. What he called a 'principle' was the permission to hope against hope with a good conscience."[46]

The CJP is well aware of much that is weak in its position. It knows that in many respects it moves within the French traditions of social utopia. Its ever-renewed efforts to give directives on how the agreed program should be put into practice are designed to prove to its devotees and to the outside world that the Center has its "feet on the ground." But even when the positions of the CJP are commendably "modern" and productivity-minded, their artificial concreteness makes these directives appear like the messages of a sect speaking to its faithful.

The president of the CJP Executive Council, who before he visited the United States compared his movement to the Junior Chambers of Commerce, now likens it to the Committee on Economic Development, with the CNPF assigned to the role of the National Association of Manufacturers. Actually this analogy points to the weakness of the *Jeune Patron*. For all the devotion and the sincerity of many of its followers, for all the respect it has earned outside the employers' movement, the CJP lacks the weight which the business practicality of its members has given to the CED in the United States. In spite of promising beginnings it appears that the CJP will fall short of its self-conceived goal of rejuvenating the employers' movement.

*The Confédération Française des Professions (CFP).* The group of Catholic employers—the Confederation also goes under

[46] Fernandez, *op.cit.* (n. 1-89), p. 119.

the more suggestive name of *Centre Français du Patronat Chrétien*—dates in its present form back to 1926. At least in its early days conceived of as a counterpart to the confederation of Catholic trade unions, the CFTC, the confederation of Catholic employers grew slowly until, in 1935, it claimed a membership of 12,000, recruited predominantly among small businessmen and also among professional men such as lawyers, doctors, and accountants.[47] Joseph Zamianski, who was to remain the Confederation's president for a quarter of a century, was administrator of a number of smaller corporations, but also a university graduate in the fields of literature and the law.

Contrary to those of the *Action Catholique*, the Confederation's activities are not taken to be the responsibility of the Catholic hierarchy. The CFP has stressed at all times that it wants to establish its identity as a social, not a religious, movement, and that only one member of the Catholic hierarchy serves on its Board of Directors, and at that in an exclusively advisory capacity.[48]

Nonetheless, the CFP assumed early the role of an authorized apostle of the social doctrine contained in the papal encyclicals and, before the war, developed in its publications and in a training institute for employers the ideological foundations for a reorganization of the economy along corporative lines. When the Vichy legislation undertook to build the house for which the Catholic employers' movement had furnished the blueprints, the CFP, though not dissolved like other employers' confederations, refrained from playing an active part in efforts whose value it considered vitiated by the occupation.

Since the war the CPF has never reached the membership figures it claimed before. It has now at most five to six thousand firms on its rolls, three-fourths of which are commercial estab-

[47] For the early history of the Catholic employers' movement, see the friendly account by Pierre Henry, *Etude sur le mouvement patronal catholique français*, Paris, 1936, brought up to date in the jubilee article, "Vingt-cinq ans d'action patronale," *Professions*, January 27, 1951. See also, the reflections of the CFP's first president, Joseph Zamianski, *L'Avenir de l'entreprise. Un patronat qui s'engage*, Paris, 1948.

[48] However, the *Jeune Patron* was founded by employers who previously had belonged to the Catholic *Centre Français du Patronat Chrétien* and who wished, in the interest of broader recruitment, to shake off too close a relationship with the church. The Catholic confederation still considers the JP as its own "youth movement."

lishments, usually smaller than the firms affiliated with the *Jeune Patron*. But contrary to the latter, the Confederation counts among its leaders at least three representatives of large corporations who presumably support the CFP financially: a Baron Reille, administrator of a large steel and metallurgical concern which is also an omnium-gatherum of financial participations in various industries; the director of the Suchard chocolate company; and the director of a fairly large pharmaceutical concern.

The membership of the CFP's Board of Directors is similar to that of the *Jeune Patron*'s Executive Council except for a difference in age. It is also true that some of the officers of the CFP occupy fairly important positions in the trade association movement, while the *Jeune Patron* has difficulties in penetrating the higher ranks of the hierarchy. The CFP's current president, M. Bernard Jousset, an engineer and director of a small factory in the Paris suburbs, presides with much moderation over the standing committee of the CNPF concerned with the "legal status" of firms.

In spite of its larger membership, the Confederation's own organization, especially in the provinces, is far less active than that of the *Jeune Patron*. It comes to life mostly for its annual conventions, which attract public interest because they are often used by the church as a forum for expounding its social doctrine. With the characteristic multiplication of analogous efforts typical of the present-day French employers' movement, the CFP has its own study committees, a weekly newspaper, and a monthly magazine.[49] Such problems as unemployment, productivity, collective bargaining, workers' housing, and the rationalization of commercial distribution have come under its purview. Though no longer as outspokenly corporatist as before the war, the Confederation still preaches the gospel of the *organisation professionnelle* and seeks in vaguely described mixed social committees the antidote to class struggle and communism. It has at times criticized French employers for being lukewarm towards collective bargaining and has recommended premiums as means to interest workers in higher output.[50] As one of the cosigners of the

---

[49] *Professions* and *Documents et Commentaires*, respectively.
[50] See *Positions du Patronat Chrétien*, Paris, n.d., (1950?).

declaration which was published by the "vanguard" groups of the employers' movement in 1952, the CFP was found to be more cautious than the other organizations in regard to implementing the promises which the declaration had made.

Faithful to the lessons of the movement's saint, Léon Harmel, who experimented at the turn of the century in his spinning mill with profit-sharing plans and a labor-management committee,[51] the CFP has studied means to reform the system of capitalist enterprise. The present president of the organization admits viewing the question of reform with greater caution than his predecessors, though he has developed in his own factory a widely advertised system of "suppressing the proletarian condition" by giving the workers "access to capital."[52] But when the so-called Lasserre report recommending more fundamental reforms of the enterprise was submitted to the Economic Council, the Catholic confederation denounced it as "socialistic" with the same fervor as the official representatives of the CNPF.[53] The leaders of the movement confess that the various statements by which the popes first criticized certain forms of capitalist property, and then expressed strong reservations against the idea of codetermination, need to be clarified before the CFP will feel free to make further constructive suggestions.[54]

The differences which exist between the more conservative Catholic confederation and the more dynamic CJP are those of language, formulation, and temper, much less of general outlook. The organizations have similar difficulties in recruiting and permeating the general employers' movement with a new mentality. Both promise, in almost identical terms, to be practical and pragmatic. But neither of them has at present the following, the means, or the philosophy that would open the way to effective social change.

[51] For Harmel's concepts and activities, see Léon Harmel, *Lettre d'un Industriel sur le conseil d'usine du Val-des-Bois*, n.p., 1894, and his *La Démocratie dans l'usine*, n.p., 1907.

[52] Bernard Jousset, *L'accession des Travailleurs au Capital*, n.p., n.d., and his *Un Résumé du Système Jousset—La Suppression de la Condition Prolétarienne et la Stabilisation du Cycle Economique par les Sociétés Ouvrières de Placement*, Paris, 1948.

[53] For details see below, Chapter VII.

[54] The dilemma is rather clearly expressed in Charles Harmel, "Un Programme économique et social du Patronat Chrétien," *Documents et Commentaires*, No. 93, Nouvelle Série, No. 1, December 1952, pp. 57-63.

*The Association des Cadres Dirigeants de l'Industrie (ACADI).* The document by which ACADI announced in September 1945 its founding and its guiding principles reflected well that troubled period.[55] At a time when it was uncertain how far the young republic would go in transforming the traditional economic structure, but also when the marching wing of the working class indulged in daily orgies of patriotism, the sponsors of ACADI had no hesitations in joining in the communist campaign for the "battle of production." The manifesto claimed that the executives of industry, whom ACADI sought to organize, would have to fulfill their vital functions *"whatever might be the economic system"* (emphasis in the original).

There may have been in this credo elements of opportunism offering collaboration to the new rulers of the country. But after the progress of nationalization had been stopped, ACADI still sought to amalgamate into its ranks the managers of private and public enterprise. Years before the CNPF was prepared to make its official peace with the nationalized sector and its administrators,[56] ACADI encouraged frequent exchanges of opinion between private and nationalized industries and published objective studies on achievements and difficulties of the nationalized concerns. In the organization's bulletin high civil servants, instead of being vilified as they are in most of the employers' press, are often referred to as *nos camarades*. The great number of graduates of the "X" among the membership gives to ACADI the character of a confraternity, but one at least as open as past "synarchies."

Based on the principle of coopting new members, ACADI has obtained a homogeneity which it considers indispensable for playing its self-assigned role. All existing organizations of capital and labor, ACADI argues, have their *raison d'être* in the economic position of their members and are therefore by their very nature condemned to a defensive outlook. By acting on a different plane, by speaking not for economic interests, but for a status—that of the industrial managers, ACADI believes in its ability to make a special contribution.

[55] See *Principes et Position d'une Association des Cadres Dirigeants de l'Industrie pour le Progrès Social et Economique*, Paris, September 1945.
[56] For details see below, Chapter VIII.

Since the "cadres of industry" are situated at the junction point of the economic and human factors and are not personally interested in profit, they are, in the opinion of ACADI, ordained to serve the sole cause of economic and social progress. Curiously enough, when this "order of the managers" found itself painted in Burnham's colors, it did not like the portrait and denied much of the validity of the author's hypotheses. At least in part, the group wished thereby to differentiate itself from the "technocrats," who especially since the experience of the Vichy CO have had a bad reputation in France. By defining the technocrats (and their Burnhamite effigy) as being merely interested in a narrowly conceived technical progress and neglectful of the human and civic responsibilities which ACADI wants to emphasize, the group defended itself in advance against any possible identification with an undesirable species.[57]

In line with its principles of organization, ACADI has kept its membership small: in 1953 its yearbook listed 300 regular members fulfilling the statutory condition of "exercising or having exercised an executive position in an industrial enterprise of either the national or the private sector." There are in addition 75 associate members, such as bankers and high civil servants who are in sympathy with the objectives of the group and move in the circles to which the regular members belong.

Practically all of the nationalized enterprises are represented on ACADI's roster, most of them by several of their ranking administrative or technical personnel, and some by such men as the late Pierre Lefaucheux (*Renault*) and Gabriel Dessus (*Electricité de France*), who through their work and their publications have become the recognized spokesmen of the public sector. Similarly the list of executives of private concerns who have joined ACADI reads like a "Who's Who" of big business. But some characteristic omissions indicate that their position alone is not decisive. Preference is given to those who are expected to share the mentality of the managerial rather than of the traditional patrimonial employer. Particularly numerous are those

[57] See the review article about Burnham's book by the Association's general secretary, de Longevialle, "L'Ere des Organisateurs'." *Bulletin de l'Association des Cadres Dirigeants de l'Industrie* (abbreviated hereafter to *Bulletin Acadi*), No. 6, May 1947, pp. 16-19.

industrialists who have shifted from public to private employment.

The industries represented most heavily are iron and steel, chemical, electro-chemical, and electrical equipment concerns, and the private mining companies. A number of leading personalities of the employers' movement, such as Messrs. Davezac, Ricard, and Lafond, are among the members or the sympathetic supporters of the group. M. Charvet, Ricard's predecessor in the post of an executive of the National Steel Association, has written editorials for the group's bulletin. One of ACADI's vice-presidents is prominent in the Trade Association of Fine and Special Steels, which also ranks high in the councils of the *Comité des Forges*. Other spokesmen of the employers' movement look at the group's activities with some scorn and consider its members apostates of the cause of free enterprise. The attitudes taken towards the ACADI are frequently so outspoken that they provide something like a test for separating the "traditionalists" from the modern-minded leaders of the employers' movement.

The active promoter of the organization, and since 1950 its president, is René Perrin, director of the Ugine electro-chemical combine, which employs in its 24 plants about 10,000 persons, of whom 600 are engineers. By interlocking directorates the Ugine is closely affiliated with one of the other giants in the field, the Pechiney group, which furnishes several of the presidents for the CNPF study groups.[58]

A graduate of both the *Polytechnique* and the National School of Mines, M. Perrin has had a rapid rise in private industry, holding also executive positions in an important steel concern and a paper mill. Immediately after the armistice he was one of Pétain's closest advisers and for a time participated actively in the planning of Vichy's corporative state.[59] Since the war M. Perrin, who hitherto had contributed only widely noted technical articles to specialized journals, has followed in the literary footsteps of the late August Detoeuf. In a number of articles he has taken the French employers to task for their lack of discipline

[58] Together Ugine and Pechiney control the entire French aluminum industry. For their far-flung industrial and business connections, see *Le Monde des Affaires*, etc., *op.cit.* (n. 1-37), pp. 118-19.

[59] See above, Chapter II.

and interest in civic activities and for their insufficiently developed concern for economic and social progress.[60]

More so than even the other vanguard groups of the employers' movement, ACADI has adopted deliberately the style of a traditional French "philosophical society." It has hardly any staff or office space. Its only publication is an outwardly unpretentious monthly bulletin with a limited circulation.

Since its beginnings the group has conducted what might be called a top-level public relations program. For its dinners it invites as speakers prominent politicians or high-ranking administrative personnel. But generally only those are afforded an opportunity to address the group whom ACADI considers as being in sympathy with its general aims.

Mendès-France was invited to develop before a sympathetic audience his ideas about a necessary tax reform in the summer of 1953 not long after his first effort to secure approval for his policies from parliament had been defeated by a coalition in which the employers' movement had played a prominent role. Premier Pinay, on the other hand, who had been given the wholehearted endorsement of the CNPF and the CGPME, was submitted earlier by ACADI to a critical interrogation which was conspicuously lacking in the proverbial French politeness.[61]

Major forthcoming legislative bills are scrutinized by various committees which ACADI has formed. The published and unpublished studies of the group find their way to the desks of responsible administrators with whom many of ACADI's members share a common background and have frequent dealings.[62] For these reasons most of the articles published in the Association's *Bulletin* are of a technical nature. Questions of public finance and private credit, of accountancy and of workers' remuneration, the functioning of the plant committees and of the

[60] See, e.g., R. Perrin. "Notre sort est entre nos mains," *Bulletin Acadi*, No. 17, June 1948, pp. 3-8, and his "Quelques considerations sur les problèmes économiques et sociaux français," *ibid.*, No. 74, November 1953, pp. 349-69.

[61] See *ibid.*, No. 80, May 1954, pp. 155-60, for the debate with Mendès-France; *ibid.*, No. 68, April 1953, pp. 145-54, for that with Pinay.

[62] A general review of the Association's activities is given annually during the General Assembly by the secretary general, M. de Longevialle. His reports are usually published in the March issues of the *Bulletin*. Of particular interest for some of the notions of ACADI is the report contained in *ibid.*, No. 78, March 1954, pp. 78-103.

social security system, the organization of private and nationalized concerns, but also larger problems such as monetary reforms, cartel legislation, and European economic integration are frequently discussed in factually written articles which take their place with the best in French economic literature of today. In line with the group's principal tenets, most of the studies advocate solutions which would achieve increased productivity in a climate of lessened social tension. A constant concern with fighting established routines is discernible even in the most technical articles. Because of the composition of its membership, ACADI is able to sustain a campaign against the inordinate number of commercial establishments and their outdated methods. But also small manufacturers are taken to task for their inefficiency; in the opinion of ACADI their claim to be financially unable to modernize is frequently unwarranted.

Though the group deplores the slow rate of economic growth, it is not willing to improve the situation by opening the gates to a competitive free-for-all. While ACADI acknowledges that French cartel practices frequently facilitate the survival of marginal enterprises and may therefore contribute to the high cost of production, the group is more outspoken than any other sector of the employers' movement in its praise of "useful" cartel agreements. It has criticized most vigorously even the feeblest legislative attempts at controlling cartels, just as it launched a vitriolic attack against the Schuman plan because of its anti-trust and anti-cartel provisions.[63] In the discussion of these problems the philosophy of the group becomes quite apparent: much as it wishes to see the mores of the business community transformed, "government by business" should be given the widest possible range and its sphere should be kept free of legislative and political interference. Admittedly a French version of the NRA codes is the blueprint for economic organization which many of the industrialists in ACADI want to design.

In other matters, especially where it detects a static and merely

[63] For details see below, Chapter VIII. The most significant articles which ACADI published on these subjects are R. Morizot, "Les Ententes Economiques," *ibid.*, No. 45, February 1951, pp. 41-53; R. Morizot, "La politique de concurrence et l'exemple américain," *ibid.*, No. 66, February 1953, pp. 43-51; R. Perrin, "A propos du décret sur les ententes," *ibid.*, No. 72, September 1952, pp. 273-75; and "Plan Schuman," *ibid.*, No. 45, February 1951, pp. 54-75.

negative attitude towards reform proposals, the group differs sharply from policies recommended by the CNPF and its Social Committee. It deplored the rejection by the employers' movement of the comprehensive report on enterprise reform submitted to the Economic Council.[64] ACADI seeks an improvement of industrial relations through, above all, economic expansion and attaches less importance to the complicated schemes of profit sharing which the other vanguard groups have put into the foreground of their thinking. While the general employers' movement, and even the CJP, were critical of the expanded plant committee legislation of 1946, ACADI has for years persisted in its efforts to see the institution used as a means for a continuing dialogue between organized labor and management.[65] After the declaration of the four employers' organizations had been issued in 1952, ACADI actively urged its implementation and a further generalization of the policies announced therein.

But many ACADI members will acknowledge that, as managers of large enterprises, they are frequently too far removed from the plants to insure the translation of generous proposals into measures apt to bring about an actual change in the social climate.

*The UCE.ACT and Other Minor Groups.* "We must liberate enterprise from its capitalistic structure, for the latter is unjust when it is not accepted [by the workers]. No forthright conscience, and a Christian conscience less than any other, can tolerate the continued existence of what it has understood to be unjust."[66] This admonition by one of the founders of the UCE.ACT expresses well the basic philosophy of the association and the motivation of its members.

Alexandre Dubois' thinking was shaped equally by his personal experiences as an industrialist and by his close connections with

[64] See "Le Rapport Lasserre au Conseil Economique," *ibid.*, No. 51, October 1951, pp. 357-64; and also an earlier article by Louis Charvet, "Réforme et évolution de l'entreprise," *ibid.*, No. 2, January 1947, pp. 1-6.

[65] See, e.g., *ibid.*, No. 48 (May-June 1951), an entire issue devoted to a publication of reports presented at a study meeting on the question, organized by ACADI.

[66] Alexandre Dubois, *Structures Nouvelles dans l'Entreprise*, 2nd edn., Paris, 1946, p. 71 (prefaced by a Dominican priest). For other writings by the same author, see *Vers la Communauté d'Entreprise*, Paris, 1943, published by the Centre des Jeunes Patrons, and "Vers une Structure Nouvelle de l'Entreprise," *Economie et Humanisme*, III, 1944, pp. 431-79.

the Dominican order. As president-engineer of a small corporation manufacturing cutlery steel in an isolated valley of the French Alps, he has waged a long but eventually successful up-hill fight for making his concern highly productive. At the same time he has organized the participation of his personnel, consisting of two to three hundred workers, in the profits as well as in the conduct of the enterprise.[67] His concept of an association of producers replacing capitalist enterprise was largely inspired by such writers as Hyacinthe Dubreuil and François Perroux, who because of their criticism of laissez-faire capitalism were considered the ideological path-breakers for some of the reforms which the Vichy regime attempted.[68]

Dubois as well as Lucien de Broucker, another leader of the UCE.ACT, originally had high praise for the Social Committees of the Labor Charter and for the Charter itself.[69] But the failure of the regime to improve industrial relations convinced them of the futility of all benevolent paternalism.

While the *Union des Chefs d'Entreprise. Action pour des Structures Humaines*, founded in 1945,[70] is by far the smallest of the four "vanguard" groups, it prides itself on being insistently practical and on not tolerating mere verbosity. Its fifty ( ! ) members, all owners or managers of small or middle-sized concerns, are under an obligation to introduce into their firms measures which transform the structure of their enterprise, or to renounce their membership. Insisting on practicality rather than on mere theory, the group has nevertheless developed a doctrine which is interesting enough and which makes in many ways an original contribution.[71]

[67] For a description of the conditions under which his firm is run, see Dubois, "Une Etape," *Bulletin Acadi*, No. 47, April 1951, pp. 136-47.

[68] See especially F. Perroux, *op.cit.* (n. 1-87), and Hyacinthe Dubreuil, *A chacun sa chance. L'organisation du travail fondée sur la liberté*, Paris, 1935.

[69] See Lucien de Broucker, *La Communauté et son Chef*, Paris, 1943, pp. 59 ff., and Dubois, *Vers la Communauté*, etc., *op.cit.* (n. iv-66), pp. 15 f. It would be wrong not to stress that the thinking of these industrialists has changed considerably since they expressed themselves in these writings.

[70] Originally the organization was called *Union des Chefs d'Entreprise pour l'Association du Capital et du Travail*. The change of name (though not of initials) was prompted by the desire to differentiate the group from the proposals for an *association capital-travail* which de Gaulle's RPF wanted to promote. For details on the RPF's proposals, see below, Chapter VIII.

[71] What follows is largely based on the exposition of principles and policies of the organization contained in UCE.ACT, *Structures Humaines dans l'Entre-*

The notion that private enterprise is based on property rights is altogether repudiated. The property concept of the *Code Napoléon*, which gives to the owner the right of absolute command and discretion, vitiates in the opinion of the group any reform of modern industrial enterprise. (The American reader must be reminded here that such ideas are much more "revolutionary" in France than in the United States, since in fact the common law concept of property has lent itself to a more dynamic interpretation than the rigid notions of the *Code*.)

The essential reform consists in a diffusion, though not a dissolution, of the role of the entrepreneur through the establishment of a truly constitutional system in the plant, linking the investors, managers, and personnel. The organization of the enterprise is to be based on a contract of association which for the workers should be entered into by the trade unions represented in the firm. By putting the plant community on a contractual basis, the UCE.ACT believes that it can effectively combat the mutual distrust of management and labor and therefore attain one of its major goals. The group points to the fact that in the firms of its members a great variety of arrangements prevail, and that often minorities of workers, usually those affiliated with the CGT, are left free not to enter into an association contract. Presumably such minorities are likely to join later once the material and moral advantages to be derived from the "community" have become convincing.

What is readily overlooked is the fact that what may seem possible in a few pilot enterprises of modest dimensions is hardly practicable on a larger scale. Hence also the efforts of this organization have a utopian quality when they are suggested as solutions of problems which are national in scope, such as an improvement of industrial relations.

The leaders of the group do not deny that even the boldest reform of enterprise will have a limited effect without corresponding changes in the economic system. The Vichy experience

---

*prise et dans l'Economie*, Neuilly s/Seine, n.d. There is some similarity between the concepts of the group and those expounded by Peter Drucker, especially in his *op.cit.* (n. III-50). Mr. Drucker's thinking is generally received with great sympathy by all the vanguard groups of the French employers' movement. See for instance the presentation of his "Philosophie réaliste de la société industrielle moderne," in *Bulletin Acadi*, No. 66, February 1953, pp. 37-42.

is understood as having demonstrated that business organization per se has little virtue since it might merely produce increased collective egoism. While a more disciplined behavior of business is deemed desirable, the UCE.ACT knows that the question of "discipline for what?" remains to be answered. The group has favored a large cooperative sector in the economy, seeking inspiration in the Scandinavian, Canadian, and British examples, but it acknowledges that legislation will have little effect where a change of mentality is needed. Its suggestions for the establishment of an "Economic Authority" have remained vague since admittedly the Authority's composition and functions pose "delicate problems."

Whatever significance the group has today consists in the moral ascendancy of its leaders who, in a generally stagnant employers' movement, have the courage to seek out new solutions and to act according to their convictions. Actually the "Declaration of the Four" was largely due to the initiative of Alexandre Dubois, who is not only an active member of all four vanguard groups but also the founder-president of a trade association.

Besides the four groups discussed so far, which have all maintained their identity for at least a decade and sometimes much longer, there exist a number of other business organizations, more or less ephemeral or at least periodically shifting the emphasis of their activities, all of them children of the lively sectarian traditions which French social movements have known for many a day. Some of these groups and committees may be classified as "one purpose" organizations, bent on propagandizing a particular technique among the employers' movement or businessmen in general. To this category belong the old-established *Comité National de l'Organisation Française* (CNOF), a management counseling and training service, interested of late in all questions affecting productivity, and the *Comité d'Action pour le Développement de l'Intéressement du Personnel et de la Productivité des Entreprises* (better known as CADIPPE), which proposes to employers and trade union leaders that they study, in common, profit-sharing schemes which might lead to an increase of productivity. Similar objectives are pursued by yet other bureaus and groups which have all developed a different approach to solving the problem of low output and unsatisfactory industrial relations.[72]

A more deliberate mixture of technical suggestions and management philosophy goes into the making of the *Comité pour l'Amélioration des Relations Humaines dans l'Economie* (CARHEC). It owes its inspiration to Henri Migeon, director of the *Télémécanique* concern, and to Louis Salleron, professor at the *Institut Catholique de Paris*, who under Vichy specialized in agricultural corporatism, and who has now become the prime mover of a number of fringe organizations of the employers' movement. In part CARHEC represents an attempt to spread the ideas which have found their practical application in M. Migeon's firm among a broader group of industrialists. Its spokesmen do not conceal their anxiety that too exclusive an emphasis on productivity will, in the social climate of present-day France, easily lead to "inhuman" attitudes.[73]

Other organizations have made the jump from the advocacy of a new business philosophy to a call for political action. A *Comité d'Etude des Groupes d'Action Régionale* and now its outgrowth, the *Centre d'Etudes Politiques et Civiques* (CEPEC), want to develop among businessmen civic action and a sense of responsibility which would enable them to play the role of the nation's foremost elite. Besides M. Salleron the Count Baruzy, head of a prosperous metallurgical concern, and M. Georges-René Laederich, respected textile industrialist in the Vosges, support these organizations, which criticize the lobbying activities of the CNPF and the trade associations as undignified. The constructive activities on which these groups insist place in the foreground the importance of the provinces over the capital, and the cult of human relations rather than respect for trade unions. There is a good dose of authoritarian impatience in the program

[72] Some of these organizations and their activities will be discussed below together with the problems of productivity and enterprise reform; see Chapters VII and VIII. On CADIPPE see the reports in *Jeune Patron*, vii, No. 65, May 1953, pp. 39-40, and *Bulletin Acadi*, No. 78, March 1954, pp. 81-82.

[73] For a lecture by Henri Migeon explaining the principles of action of CARHEC, see his "Relations Humaines et Economie" (offprint of *Travail et Méthodes*), No. 50, February 1952; interesting also is Louis Salleron, "Principe et substance des relations humaines (offprint of *Industrie*), September 1952. For a short account of CARHEC's proposed activities, see *Bulletin Acadi*, No. 59, June 1952, pp. 236-38. On the significance of the *Télémécanique* experience, see below, Chapter VIII.

of the groups; their frankly elitist mentality was highlighted when they sought and obtained the blessings of a man like General Weygand, who before the war had sponsored as anti-republican an employers' organization as the *Comité de Pré-voyance.*[74]

All of the opinion groups, old and new, promise to furnish what the CNPF and the major trade associations have been unable to provide: positive action and an affirmative doctrine. Although these groups are known to be at least implicitly critical of the general employers' movement, their existence is generally welcome to the CNPF and its affiliates, since it seemingly attests to the democratic character of business organizations. Such cohesion as exists within the CNPF has so far never been threatened by the activities of its "vanguards," unable to dispute the bureaucratic control which is firmly established in most sectors of the employers' movement. For all its ideological weakness, the strength of the CNPF consists in the comprehensiveness of its framework and its claim to represent the entire business community. The more the Fourth Republic has taken on some of the features of a corporative state, the more necessary it has become to present to parliament, administration, and public opinion a unified employers' organization.[75] In general, the vanguard movements are quite prepared to acknowledge the value of such a claim.

Here lies the ultimate reason for the congenital weakness of these groups. With insignificant exceptions, all of them are deeply imbued with a belief in the need for solid organizations, able to impose strict and far-reaching disciplines. Most of them acknowledge the parentage of Catholic traditionalism, though some can claim to have modified earlier concepts. All of them are inimical to liberalism, though only a few are prepared to recommend a return to authoritarian policies, whether of the

[74] For a clear statement of M. Baruzy's criticism of the employers' movement and of his proposals, see his "Action patronale," *La Presse Métallurgique,* April 21, 1953, and his "Aspect d'ensemble de la Question Sociale" (mimeographed), November 1952. For some of the ideas of the CEPEC see the interesting series *Les Cahiers du C\*E\*P\*E\*C,* and especially the speech by Georges-René Laederich entitled "Les Origines, le Programme et les Buts du C.E.P.E.C." and one by Général Weygand, "Appel aux Elites Françaises," both contained in No. 4 of the *Cahiers,* 1955.

[75] For a full discussion of this point, see Chapter V.

Vichy or another variety. They believe in the benefits of cartels, but cartels are indissolubly linked with the existing employers' movement. The groups insist, to be sure, on a fresher outlook in many fields, on a transformation of the mores of businessmen and of business organizations alike, on dynamic rather than restrictive practices, on more constructive purposes, and on less lobbying. But unless, as in 1936, a grave crisis shakes the passive confidence which insures to its present leadership the control of the employers' movement, the opinion groups will continue to lack the strength to alter, from within or from without, the course of the CNPF.

# CHAPTER V

# Organized Business and Politics

## *1. The Employers and Public Opinion*

"Many people say: 'I don't care about public opinion.' The
fact that one says it shows that one cares."
                        Detoeuf, *Propos de O. L. Barenton*

"If the large business concerns were to show clearly the role
which they are playing in the economic life of the nation, the
burden which they have to carry, the way in which they make
use of their profits, then the atmosphere of suspicion which surrounds them might at least in part be dispelled." And the
*Bulletin* of the CNPF from which this statement is quoted goes
on to regret that the French business community has so much
less faith than its American counterpart in the benefits of public
relations.[1] In France it is not less true than in the United States
that "group leaders, whatever else they may neglect, cannot
afford to be ignorant of widely-held attitudes bearing upon the
standing and objectives of their organizations."[2] But convinced
that public opinion feels antagonistic towards it, French organized business despairs of altering existing attitudes by an open
and frontal attack.

If French business has never fully made the transition from
the "old lobby" of the wirepullers and socialites to the "new
lobby" of organizations speaking and acting in the open,[3] this
may in part have been caused by the events of the First World
War and its aftermath. During the hostilities various trade
associations, and especially the *Comité des Forges*, had been
associated closely with the government's efforts to mobilize the
country's resources and to make appeals to the patriotism of its
citizens. But as soon as the war was over and the lid of censor-

[1] "Les 'Public Relations,'" *Bulletin*, v, No. 68, June 20-July 5, 1951, pp. 16-17.
Note that there is no French term for "public relations."

[2] Truman, *op.cit.* (n. 1-27), p. 213.

[3] The terminology is that of Pendleton Herring, *Group Representation before
Congress*, Baltimore, 1929, esp. pp. 30-52. For an application of such distinctions to
the tactics of American business organizations, providing implicitly an interesting
contrast with the French picture, see S. H. Walker and Paul Sklark, "Business
Finds Its Voice," *Harper's*, CLXXXI, 1937-38, pp. 113 ff., 317 ff., and 428 ff.

ship blown off, bitter complaints were voiced inside and outside of parliament against the policies pursued by the steel interests.

The term "economic Malthusianism" seems to have been coined first to criticize the *Comité des Forges* for having tolerated, if not actively encouraged, an insufficient development of industrial capacities during the crucial pre-war years.[4] (Ever since then those business policies have been blamed as "Malthusianism" which have a proclivity to limit production and to spread work as well as profits.) After 1918 it was said that even during the war the special interests of the steel industry prevailed over the needs for effective production and low-cost arms, and that a collusion between the *Comité* and the military had prevented the bombing of the Briey region to save the French steel works which had fallen into German hands during the first weeks of the war.[5] Robert Pinot, the executive of the steel association, undertook valiant efforts to clear his own record and that of the main interests he represented, especially those of the Schneider and Wendel concerns. A parliamentary investigation led nowhere, and in the end several officials of the *Comité des Forges* were awarded military decorations for their alleged merits. Yet in the words of M. François Poncet, Pinot's biographer and eulogist, the whole affair left a lasting impact on the relations between industry and the public. "Public opinion remained distrustful of industry in general and of the steel industry in particular. People suspected that there existed a privileged group acting to the detriment of the majority. Industry remained shaken and hesitant. . . . Having been denounced to the vindictiveness of the masses, it could not overcome feelings of insecurity and uneasiness. Politics, which ought to have been its auxiliary, was increasingly regarded by industry as an enemy...."[6]

Many years later, whenever the president of the CGPF, M.

---

[4] On the socialist campaign directed against the steel industry see the debates in the Chamber of Deputies, especially of January 31, 1919, *J.O. Débats Chambre*, February 1, pp. 344 ff.; A. François-Poncet, *op.cit.* (n. 1-23), pp. 241-55; and R. Pinot, *op.cit.* (n. 1-24), pp. 23, 60, and passim. Industry could complain with some justification that even Loucheur, himself an industrialist and Minister of Armaments and later of Reconstruction, had been lukewarm in his defense of the steel association.

[5] The interesting discussion in Richard D. Challener, *The French Theory of the Nation in Arms, 1866-1939*, New York, 1953, pp. 128 ff., shows that the errors of industry were those of the military and political leadership of the nation alike.

[6] François-Poncet, *op.cit.* (n. 1-23), p. 254.

Duchemin, broached in his yearly addresses the subject of desirable political reforms, he would regularly refrain from answering the questions he had raised himself, since he did not wish to enter, as he put it, into "political controversies."[7] Neither the experiences which some industrialists had made when they launched the *Redressement Français*, nor the compromising activities of the Vichy CO and the "Synarchy," seemed to indicate that business had anything to gain from openly parading its views before the public eye.[8]

After the Second World War the apparently complete, though only temporary, disassociation of political and economic power gave new reasons to the business community to seek protection in withdrawal rather than in frank explanation. If already in the past French businessmen had been less stimulated by an identification with national goals and ideas than their colleagues in other lands,[9] the post-war situation undoubtedly drove them into outright opposition to the community surrounding them. Almost all efforts to mold public opinion in favor of the business community were suspended.

But in part the acute crisis offered only an excuse to indulge in attitudes for which French businessmen had a long-standing predilection. An industrialist suggested shortly after the liberation that the French employers have "always attached an excessively high price to secrecy. This is undoubtedly the inheritance of a peasantry exploited incessantly for centuries by an insatiable fisc. The passion, indeed the mania, of secrecy is incidentally not an attitude exclusively characteristic of the employers; it corrupts all groups. The moment a minimum of private property permits one to hide from others one's life, acts, and resources, the Frenchman covers himself with secrecy. Walls are typical for us. The Frenchman is not a chess player, but a card player; he chooses games where one hides."[10]

For businessmen the roots of this passion for anonymity go

---

[7] See Duchemin, *op.cit.* (n. 1-17), p. 252.

[8] See above, Chapter II.

[9] A point made by John E. Sawyer, "The Entrepreneur and the Social Order—France and the United States," in William Miller, ed., *Men in Business*, Cambridge, Mass., 1952, p. 16. The author's contention that such identification of the business group has *never* existed in France appears somewhat too sweeping.

[10] Auguste Detoeuf, "Les Comités d'Entreprise," *Le Figaro*, May 15, 1945.

still deeper. Since many of them have been unable to rid themselves of the pre- or anti-capitalist feelings in their own heritage, they lack the assurance and conviction to defend their position and their objectives before a skeptical audience. For a country where literary incarnations still command wide popular appeal, it is significant that in the French novel there seems to be not a single example of an outstanding entrepreneurial pioneer; where they appear at all, they are slightly ridiculed rather than pictured as heroes.[11] During the first decade of this century French industrialists were taken to task by a syndicalist labor leader for failing to command by their performance the respect and prestige which had been the reward of their American colleagues.[12]

It has been explained earlier why the present-day employers' movement is prevented by its structure and membership from developing even the elements of a unified business doctrine. In addition, any desire to formulate a "message" is dampened by the belief that the soundest idea will be discredited if it is put forward as forming part of the employers' creed. A student of the American NAM has stated that the framing of issues and the development of popular support for them occupies an increasing share of the organization's activities.[13] No similar conclusion is warranted for the CNPF, which has preferred not to revive the large Committee of Propaganda, formed by its predecessor after 1936.

Here Robert Brady's controversial thesis about the relationship between the political process in a democracy and the activities of business organizations shows its limitations when applied to the French situation. "Monopoly-oriented business," Professor Brady states, "which attempts to evade effective democratic restraints can dominate government only through control over the thinking processes of the mass of the people who dwell at the base of the social pyramid."[14] That there is in fact considerable domination of government by the French business interests

---

[11] See Georges Gojat, *Le Patron dans le Roman Français (1830-1950)*, unpublished MS of the Centre d'Etudes Economiques, Ecole Pratique des Hautes Etudes, Paris, 1952, p. 28.

[12] Victor Griffuelhes, "L'infériorité des capitalistes français," *Le Mouvement Socialiste*, XXVIII, 1910, pp. 329-32.

[13] See Cleveland, *op.cit.* (n. III-40), pp. 323 ff.

[14] Robert Brady, *Business as a System of Power*, New York, 1943, p. 320.

will be shown in more detail, but such domination as exists does not depend on thought control. It is true that Brady argues in terms of a modern "business civilization," and that one might doubt whether even contemporary France can be so classified.

If in the United States an original hostility against large-scale enterprise has been considerably modified, over the last decades, by a careful public relations campaign carried on by the large corporations and by some trade associations, in France antagonistic feelings have never been overcome. One of the CNPF's leaders is probably justified in his belief that it would be unthinkable to engage in France in the kind of propaganda which the American army spread when it informed GI's about the high profits made during the war by certain major corporations. Instead of arousing pride in the vitality of the national economy, in France such news would cause general wrath.[15] The NAM wants to create confidence that high profits insure an efficient and healthy industrial system.[16] French employers feel that they should minimize their profits not only in their tax declarations but also before the bar of public opinion. Such reserves will naturally accredit widely held beliefs in the enormity of business profits, even though the estimates may be exaggerated. A business community which is convinced that its appeals will never be able to overcome a basic hostility will easily freeze in a "public-be-damned" attitude, all the more as employers are congenitally convinced that only those live happily who live in concealment.[17]

Of late pleas to overcome unwarranted discreetness and aloofness have been made in publications which are friendly to industry. France should no longer, as one writer puts it, remain the country of "counter-publicity."[18] Its businessmen should not only open their books but also make the sacrifice of some leisure

[15] See Pierre Ricard in his discussion of the impressions he gathered during a trip to the United States, *Bulletin*, April 15, 1952; supplement, p. 5.

[16] See Cleveland, *op.cit.* (n. III-40), p. 343.

[17] These aspects are stressed in an interesting comparison between the mentality of French and that of American employers by a writer close to the CNPF, Louis Salleron, "Patronat français et Patronat américain," *Fédération*, IX, No. 89, June 1952, pp. 428-33.

[18] For several quotations from the French press, see *Le Monde des Affaires, op.cit.* (n. I-37), p. 10. One of the newspapers complaining about the attitude of businessmen is *L'Aurore*, which is owned by the industrialist M. Boussac.

time and seek civic if not political activities which would offer them an opportunity to explain themselves to their fellow citizens.[19] While a certain trend in that direction is discernible, especially in the vanguard groups, the great mass of businessmen and their associations remain mute and seek the defense of their interests by other, more occult means.

It is quite true that in the Fourth Republic the employers have been deprived of general important media of communication which they controlled before the war. Previously *Le Temps* was owned by the steel and mine associations and was, at least between 1933 and the outbreak of the war, the internationally respected common mouthpiece of the *Quai d'Orsay* and heavy industry. The *Bulletin Quotidien*, openly sponsored by the steel association, furnished daily a wealth of material on economic social, and even political matters to newspapers, journalists, and politicians. In its days the *Bulletin* ranked above all other services provided by business organizations the world over. Its vigorous editorial policies defended less the special interests of the steel industry than those of big business in general. Another daily newspaper, the *Journal des Débats*, was to an extent the private domain of the Wendel steel trust. The *Journée Industrielle*, backed successively or simultaneously by the mining and railroading interests, the chemical, electrical, sugar, and wool industries, was an all but official publication of the CGPF. Other newspapers such as *L'Information* and *Le Capital* represented the banking and insurance interests in general, counting among their frequent collaborators a number of ranking politicians.[20]

The nationalizations and the reorganization of the press after the liberation left the employers' movement without a major newspaper and without much support in the press of respected standing. Some publications, such as the *Bulletin Quotidien*, disappeared altogether. The plant of *Le Temps* was taken over by *Le Monde*, a remarkably independent newspaper frequently

[19] For a criticism of the general employers' attitude and an urgent plea to engage in political and civic activities, see Louis Salleron, "Le Patronat a-t-il un rôle politique?" *Le Mois Textile*, No. 59, November 1952, pp. 1-5. This article published in one of the more interesting trade association journals seems to have been well received, but did not provoke the general discussion it was designed to bring forth.

[20] For a description of business support to the pre-war press, see A. Hamon, *op.cit.* (n. 1-50), Vol. II, pp. 125, 137.

publishing articles which are violently resented by business circles for their criticism of "economic Malthusianism" and of pressure group activities. *Le Figaro* is now owned by the wool and other textile interests. But since it earns its own way, it is also run in an independent fashion, seldom acting as the spokesman of business and certainly not of heavy industry, which so far has kept out of any major journalistic venture. *L'Aurore*, a newspaper with mass appeal, is controlled by the Boussac cotton combine. After having absorbed an ever-increasing number of newspapers that had seen the light immediately after the liberation, it can now be counted upon to uphold the policies of every conservative government. But also *L'Aurore* prefers not to act openly as an interpreter of the views held by organized business. From radio stations the employers' movement feels almost systematically excluded. The spectacular failure of a journalistic venture, backed by a number of large industrial concerns, such as Michelin, Citroen, Les Tréfileries du Havre, and others, showed that also in 1955-56 the difficulties had not subsided. *Le Temps de Paris*, a daily wishing to resume the traditions of the pre-war *Le Temps*, had to cease publication after a short and unglorious career which added nothing to the prestige of business.

That the terse and often technical communiqués of the CNPF, usually carried by the press in small print, are not impressing public opinion is generally recognized. None of the official publications of the CNPF or of the trade associations reaches a larger public than that of a rather restricted segment of their membership; neither content, nor tone, nor presentation is designed for a wider appeal. Only *L'Usine Nouvelle*, speaking mostly for steel and connected interests, commands a somewhat wider attention, though it has not reached the distribution of its predecessor, *L'Usine*. Typically enough the only effective propaganda magazine, speaking in the name of French organized business, appears—in English. The attractive bulletin, *France Actuelle*, published by the CNPF's *Comité Franc-Dollar*, seems to have done exceptionally well in its endeavor to combat unfavorable American opinions about the French business world. But this enterprise, which was undertaken upon the urging of American advisers, is viewed with unconcealed distrust, and in some cases contempt, by some of the leaders of the organization.

Other personalities in the employers' movement who regret the absence of an effective public relations program criticize the existing dearth of publications media. But they too have been unable to prevent the prevailing dispersion of efforts and funds. Especially during the first troubled post-liberation years, business granted subsidies to mediocrities in the fields of journalism and public relations; since then many of these adjuncts have carried on their ventures without ever reaching a wide audience, but not without seriously compromising by their lack of talent or by a shady past the gospel they are paid to preach.

One of the more ambitious undertakings, backed with enthusiasm by M. Villiers, but frowned upon by some of his colleagues, is the *Association de la Libre Entreprise*.[21] Headed by a former official of the Michelin rubber concern, which before the war was prominently connected with para-fascist movements (but refrained during the armistice from all collaboration with the Germans), the abundantly staffed *Association* is a propaganda outfit specializing in the fight against *dirigisme* and all forms of government activities. Popular pamphlets using cartoons and pictorial graphs explain the financial burden which the modern state imposes on the consumer; learned articles analyze the Inca society as an abhorrent example of economic stagnation brought about by public control. The *Association*, which prides itself on having learned much from American public relations methods, claims to have circulated some of its pamphlets in more than 300,000 copies; other, more confidential materials are distributed among selected business leaders. Occasionally the *Association* offers its materials for free reprint by newspapers.

Another publication, acknowledgedly financed by the petroleum and steel industries, specializes in furnishing editorial materials to the press; a weekly bulletin of *France Documents* contains columns on domestic and international affairs, contributed respectively (though not signed) by Pierre Gaxotte and Pierre-Etienne Flandin, both known during the Third Republic for the strong support they gave to policies of appeasement. In vitriolic language these writers criticize the world around them; their anti-communism does not prevent them from being just as

[21] For the praise and description of *Libre Entreprise* by M. Villiers, see "La Libre Entreprise," *France Documents*, No. 22, August 1948, pp. 1 ff.

hostile as the Soviet Union to the idea of European economic integration. As a monthly, *France Documents* furnishes useful and carefully slanted information designed like the weekly bulletin primarily for heads of enterprises. Its special issues give a detailed picture of particular industries, of employers' organizations, of administrative agencies, and of colonial problems.

Also very close to the CNPF is *La Nouvelle Revue de l'Economie Contemporaine*, whose committee of patronage includes a number of ranking personalities of the employers' movement together with some former labor leaders who served in Pétain's cabinets. Its director is Achille Dauphin-Meunier, who from an advocate of Léon Blum's New Deal turned arch-collaborationist under Vichy and found himself in prison at the liberation. The journal provides a vehicle for more or less official expressions of opinion by leaders of the employers' movement; but it also publishes articles by politicians, scholars, and journalists who uphold here regularly the point of view of organized business. Comparable in presentation and characteristics to the former *Bulletin Quotidien* is now the *Bulletin S.E.D.E.I.S.*, a bi-monthly newsletter, publishing fairly extensive studies and an economic chronicle. Especially since a respected writer, Bertrand de Jouvenel, has assumed its editorship the *Bulletin* (produced in the offices of the CNPF) recommends itself to the fairly restricted circle of its subscribers by its moderate tone and the generally high quality of its information.

A *Comité d'Etudes pour le Redressement économique et financier* issues brochures of little distinction on a number of politico-economic questions, frequently written by members of parliament known to be reliable defenders of business interests.[22] A newspaper, published by the same committee, shows how close this group is to circles which in the Third Republic amalgamated the conservative wing of the radical party, the Freemasonry, and some of the processing industries. At times the publication,

---

[22] Of the brochures several are authored by Senator Marcel Pellenc, whose role as a defender of business interests will be described below; see, e.g., his *L'Assainissement des Finances Publiques. Le Bilan de Six ans d'Erreurs. Sommes-nous défendus dans les Airs?* One of the pamphlets is prefaced by Robert Lacoste, socialist deputy and minister; another one, prefaced by a radical-party politician, is critical of the policies of the *Comptoir des Produits Sidérurgiques*, expressing certain divergences within the industry.

which is said to pay its contributors handsomely, seems to be little more than a "hospitality center" for politicians whose vote or intervention is being solicited. A yet less respectable journalistic enterprise which the CNPF has financed has been made into a means of supporting some non-communist trade union papers.[23]

It is whispered or known that a number of other publications live on subsidies from the employers' movement but defend its point of view only *sub rosa*. After the liberation when industry was anxious to secure some allies, it established contacts with a wide array of social and political movements, usually little suspected of being in any way affiliated with the employers' movement. As usual in France, subventions once granted continue to flow. As a result business even in a completely changed situation still supports these media instead of presenting its position with frankness and from a platform that is commensurate with its regained strength.

In general, the employers' movement continues to trust only those who are on its official or unofficial payroll. Whether this diffidence is another heritage of peasant and small businessmen's traditions, or whether it is a traumatic after-effect of the liberation period, is difficult to decide. Yet it leads easily to outright paranoid behavior which has made the employers' movement occasionally the laughing stock of the informed public,[24] and results even more frequently in a rather negative selection of those whom business organizations use as their "agents." Hence an all-pervading mentality rather than any moral depravity induces personally impeccable and honest business leaders to seek and maintain contacts with the riff-raff every society pro-

---

[23] For a discussion of this affair, equally painful to the employers' movement and the CGT–*Force Ouvrière*, see Roger Lapeyre, "Un spécimen de la France moderne: M. Georges Villiers du gang des périphériens," *La Révolution Prolétarienne*, XXI, No. 359, 1952, pp. 17-65 to 23-71; Gérard Dehove, "Le mouvement ouvrier et la législation sociale" in *Revue d'Economie Politique*, LXII, 1952, p. 577; and *ibid.*, LXIII, 1953, pp. 761, 768.

[24] The CNPF has duplicated with a costly magazine *Essor* a highly successful independent magazine devoted to business matters, *L'Entreprise.*—It has refused to answer a questionnaire which a respected scholarly journal addressed to it, because it "distrusts" the journal's editorial policy.—When a French journalist reported in a magazine of wide circulation, subsidized by the textile industry, on the estimates by Washington economists of French business profits, the magazine reached the newsstands with the figure solidly blacked out by printers' ink; see Raymond Cartier, "Les Américains aux Patrons Français: Vous favorisez le communisme," *Paris Match*, July 21, 1951.

duces. Such dealings, frequently criticized from within the employers' movement but nevertheless continued,[25] fill business leaders with contempt for "democratic" politics. To the outside world the employers' movement appears in the worst possible light when it becomes known by what means the CNPF and the trade associations seek to build support. Eventually no voices are heard except those of the panegyrist whose honesty is suspected, and of the systematic defamer whose information is faulty. But this amounts to a telling defeat for all efforts aimed at winning a favorable audience for the business community.

In terms of content, organized business has failed to develop any broader political program, designed to arouse or even crystallize public opinion. M. Villiers likes to allude in many of his speeches to the necessity of proceeding with drastic constitutional changes. The weakness of the executive branch of government is considered by the employers' movement as an excuse for not submitting a more coherent reform program: without an effective amendment of the constitution of 1946, the argument or rather the rationalization for the absence of any such program runs, nothing valid or lasting can be achieved. There exists, presumably in the files of M. Villiers' office, an elaborate constitutional draft proposing *inter alia* to strengthen the powers of the upper house and to give more stability and independence to the executive. But for fear of antagonizing elements inside and outside the employers' movement who might disagree with this particular set of proposed constitutional amendments, the CNPF keeps its draft strictly confidential. Other spokesmen for organized business are known to believe that an electoral reform rather than more drastic constitutional changes is all that is needed. (But in December 1955 Edgar Faure found the opportunistic and opportune support of business when he dissolved the National Assembly in order to forestall the electoral reform which Mendès-France tried to obtain.)

Just because organized business has so far been unable to mobilize support for its objectives in the country, it became particularly important to gain direct access to the point of polit-

[25] Gignoux, *op.cit.* (n. 1-95), pp. 85-86, complained retrospectively about the unnecessary clandestineness of many of the pre-war political dealings which made business suspect even where it had nothing to hide. When speaking privately, many of the present-day business leaders voice a similar criticism.

ical decision making. The failure to arouse understanding and sympathy in the broad daylight of public relations campaigns forms a striking contrast to the ascendancy of the business lobby in the Fourth Republic. Such contrast necessarily had its impact on the preferences and the methods of those who were seeking to recuperate for capitalist enterprise the influence it had temporarily lost after the war.

Since the discreet methods of the "old lobby" proved to be so much more successful than the newer approach recommended in the name of democracy, was there not an encouragement to concentrate the best efforts once more on politicians and administrators?

## 2. Elections, Parties, and the Legislative Process

"Politics—the nightmare of industry; the dream of the industrialist."

Detoeuf, *Propos de O. L. Barenton*

It has been observed acutely, though perhaps with some exaggeration, that in France "parliament is qualified to deal only with those matters which already belonged to the domain of government during the 19th century. It has not become similarly qualified for most of the matters in which the state has started to take an interest in the 20th century."[26] To the extent to which this is true, such limitations of parliamentary effectiveness must shape the tactics of most pressure groups and especially of the business lobby. Hence its most intensive and fruitful efforts are presently directed to the high bureaucracy in a number of important ministries.

Nevertheless, the National Assembly retains its importance for the business lobby as the maker and unmaker of governments. The threat to overthrow a cabinet will often suffice to prevent legislation which is deemed onerous, or preclude the ratification of undesirable treaties. This negative effect of parliamentary action is frequently all that matters, since to defeat competing claims is for organized business generally more decisive than to

[26] François Goguel, "La déficience du système parlementaire," *Esprit*, XXI, 1953, p. 854. Similarly, the judgement of a high civil servant, Paul Delouvrier, *op.cit.* (n. II-54), p. 22: "Parliament intervenes less than is generally believed in matters of economic policy."

secure new laws for which there is little need as long as business can count on a sympathetic administration.

Furthermore, the National Assembly (and to a lesser degree the Council of the Republic) are important to the employers' movement as a means to gauge and, if possible, to fashion the political mood of the country so that existing animosities against the business community are diminished. Parliament thus becomes one of the channels by which the CNPF and its affiliates are willing to undertake the task of appealing to public opinion, whereas the direct approach through various information media of a public relations program is rarely sought. Hence today the employers' movement is as preoccupied as it was during the Third Republic with the composition of the elective bodies and consequently with the elections themselves. An election which sends an increased number of conservative deputies to parliament is still considered a victory for business, whether or not the laws which the new Assembly might enact prove of value. With the goals unchanged, many of the lobbying tactics of earlier days have been revived and merely adapted to somewhat changed conditions.

Under the liberal Empire and during the first decades of the Third Republic, a fairly large number of prominent bankers and industrialists entered parliament and became cabinet members. Thereafter, partly by design and partly because of other pre-occupations, these notables gradually disappeared from the political arena and voluntarily made room for *homines novi*, often of modest origin, and seldom businessmen.[27] For a time after this change had occurred, the deputies and senators who proved satisfactory to the business community were invited to join the boards of industrial and banking concerns; the lawyers among them such as Waldeck-Rousseau, Millerand, and Poin-caré were entrusted by large firms with the pleading of rewarding law suits. Yet later those who were to defend industry and banking in parliament usually steered clear of all open business connections.

During the long armistice between the two world wars, busi-ness extended its influence into parliament mainly through three

[27] On the early developments see Beau de Loménie, *op.cit.* (n. I-93), Vol. I, passim, and Vol. III, pp. 24-25.

channels: the so-called *Comité Mascuraud*, the *Union des Intérêts Economiques*, and the *Alliance Démocratique*.

The first, officially called the *Comité Républicain du Commerce et de l'Industrie*, had seen its best days before 1914. Managed by Senator Mascuraud, who was also a highly placed Freemason and a Parisian jeweler by trade, the Committee distributed funds primarily to politicians just left of center and acted as a broker between business and the radicals during the period when that party dominated the destinies of the republic. While the Committee was at least in part financed by big business, it assisted mostly those deputies who were known as the defenders of the revered small economic interests. The Committee's importance declined[28] when there arose in the *Union des Intérêts Economiques* a better-organized group which was more intimately connected with the employers' movement. The Union had been founded only shortly before the war by about thirty trade associations for the explicit purpose of facilitating the elections of candidates who were sympathetic to the outlook of business. It scored its first success when the "blue-horizon" elections of 1919, not unlike the khaki elections in Great Britain, resulted in a conservative victory at a time when the expected economic spoils of military victory were to be reaped. An extremely vague program had been drafted by the Union in preparation for the 1919 elections; it contained broad principles of economic liberalism, protests against any form of government control of business, requests for an "egalitarian" tax system (to wit, the rejection of a progressive income tax), opposition to the right of parliament to propose expenditures, and demands that the trade associations and other employers' organizations should be consulted on all legislation of interest to them. At a period when the labor movement was undergoing the radicalizing influences of the post-war crisis and the Russian revolution, the program spoke in favor of an undefined "union of capital and labor."[29] The

[28] On the *Comité Mascuraud* and its diminishing importance see Sérampuy, *op.cit.* (n. 1-12), p. 658; also Beau de Loménie, *op.cit.* (n. 1-93), Vol. III, p. 221. Today the still-surviving Committee is chaired by a radical-socialist deputy from Lyon, M. Jules-Julien.

[29] For the text of the Union's program and a short description of its activities, see René Rémond, *La Droite en France de 1815 à nos jours*, Paris, 1954, pp. 289, 192 f. An excellent analysis of the Union's role using the findings of the parliamentary investigation is contained in James K. Pollock, *Money and Politics Abroad*, New York, 1932, pp. 305 ff.

funds which the Union distributed from then on at election time seem to have been considerable; they came predominantly from the large insurance firms, the mining and railroad companies, the building trades, and the alcohol distillers and distributors. It was generally believed that more than half of the deputies, and a large number of unsuccessful candidates, obtained the Union's support for at least part of their campaign expenses and utilized posters, pamphlets, and other campaign materials which it put at their disposal.

A certain amount of light was shed on the operations of the Union when after the elections of 1924 a parliamentary investigation was started to determine the role of organized business in influencing elections and deputies. In the midst of public apathy, a few brave speeches were made from the tribune of the Chamber denouncing "the flood of immorality and low materialism" which the Union had let loose by spending "hundreds of millions." The investigation did not go very far after Ernest Billiet, disburser of the Union's funds and senator from Paris, blatantly refused to testify before the parliamentary committee. It was hurriedly called off when it became known that a member of Herriot's cabinet had drawn subsidies from the Union though running on the platform of a "leftist" radical-socialist.

Like interest groups everywhere, both the Union and the older *Comité Mascuraud* attuned their activities to the functioning of the political institutions upon which they desired to act. Looseness of organization and almost complete lack of party discipline have always characterized conservative French politics, operating as it was through "alliances" and shapeless committees.[30] But the outlines of the radical party were equally hazy so as to make it subject to determined outside pressures. When the Union took over much of the clientele of the *Comité Mascuraud*, it found it possible to enlist also the sympathies of radicals in the Chamber and especially in the Senate. Although officially the Union was committed to fight the *Cartel des Gauches*, formed of radicals and of socialists, as an "anti-national coalition," it actually attempted its division by coddling certain radicals and by concentrating attacks on their partners to the left.[31]

---

[30] For a fuller discussion of this point, see Rémond, *op.cit.* (n. v-29), p. 250.
[31] See Beau de Loménie, *op.cit.* (n. I-93), Vol. III, p. 441.

The third group connected with business interests, the *Alliance Démocratique*, was in form not an agency designed to influence politicians but itself a political party whose leadership and members were closely affiliated with business and its organizations. After the first post-war elections, the Alliance abandoned its earlier occasional shifts between the moderate left and the moderate right and joined firmly with other conservative forces. From then on the newly formed CGPF and the big business interests which dominated the employers' peak association considered the Alliance as their own political arm.[32] For all that, the Alliance did not acquire the internal cohesion unknown to all French "parties" of the right and center. Actually its dissentions and leadership conflicts came to reflect different trends which prevailed among business circles during the inter-war period. Pierre-Etienne Flandin considered most of the time deflationary policies the only cure for the economic crisis; at the approach of the war he became a leader in the appeasement camp. Paul Reynaud tried to convince his party and parliament of the necessity for a well-manipulated devaluation and criticized the Munich agreements as folly. The one became a minister in a Vichy cabinet, the other an inmate of a Vichy prison.[33]

To an extent the divergences between Flandin and Reynaud seem to have survived in the antagonism between the two outstanding businessmen-politicians of the Fourth Republic: Pinay had been a member of Vichy's National Council, and Laniel served on the clandestine National Council of Resistance; both now belong to the same conservative "party" and both are close to different wings of the general employers' movement.[34]

\* \* \*

When the Fourth Republic was born, the employers' move-

[32] For a short and extremely convincing description of the relations between the business world and the *Alliance Démocratique* see E. Beau de Loménie, "La politique et les Affaires," in *Le Monde des Affaires*, *op.cit.* (n. 1-37), pp. 563-65; see also the same author's lengthier remarks in his *op.cit.* (n. 1-93), Vol. III, pp. 234 ff. and passim. It is true that for him the significance of the Alliance has become something like an obsession and leads him to neglect occasionally other political formations and factors, such as the *Fédération Républicaine*, which had also strong business ties, especially with the steel interests.

[33] On the opposition between Reynaud and other elements of the Alliance, see Goguel, *op.cit.* (n. 1-7), Vol. II, pp. 28 ff.

[34] On the interesting parallel between Flandin-Pinay on the one, and Reynaud-Laniel on the other hand, see Rémond, *op.cit.* (n. v-29), p. 225.

ment had not alone lost most of its leadership and organizational identity, its prestige, and its press; in addition its support in parliament had dwindled to almost nothing. In the Constitutional referendum of October 1945, less than 4 percent of the electorate approved of recommendations which had been made by the conservatives. The parties with which the business community had maintained particularly friendly relations were no more. Because of their activities under Vichy some of their leaders seemed forever disqualified for a political role. There was almost general agreement that the Senate, the upper house of parliament, which had proven a stalwart defender of business, would not be revived; at best its former powers would be seriously clipped. "After 130 years during which success and reverses, defeat and revenge had alternated, the history of the political Right seemed to reach its end in 1945 in a disaster unprecedented in both its dimensions and its apparently definitive character."[35]

Precisely because the crisis into which events had thrown the employers' movement was so unprecedentedly deep, it was decided soon after the CNPF had been founded that it was important to create political sympathy by the same means which the *Union des Intérêts Economiques* had used. Because it was as yet unknown in which form or shape political parties would emerge under the new conditions, and whether any of them could be counted upon to speak for business, no electoral program was advanced by the employers' movement and no particular group of politicians singled out for assistance. Obviously such tactics, designed to buy support without setting the price or defining what was expected from the recipients, required even more complete anonymity and perhaps secrecy than had shrouded similar dealings before the war. The greater centralization which the employers' movement had achieved through the CNPF also afforded an opportunity to channel financial subsidies through a single agency rather than to distribute them through a variety of sources.

The organization which the employers' movement created in 1946 to offer assistance to candidates for political office was denounced in parliament years later as an "enterprise of corruption" and the "buyer of conscience." The role it was playing in

[35] *Ibid.*, p. 230.

politics, the speaker concluded, indicated that "something was rotten in the affairs of France and the republic was threatened."[36] It is true that these incriminations came from the communist benches. But the facts they brought to light were largely drawn from documentary evidence; little, if anything, was said in denial of what had long been common knowledge. The debates clearly conveyed the impression that deputies from almost all parties were mostly interested in cutting short the discussion about the role which business subsidies play in present-day politics. This time the demands for a parliamentary investigation were defeated from the outset; attempts were made to have the accusations deleted from the record. That many of the allegations remain in the realm of speculation, that no judgment is possible as to how effective the corrupting influence of the subsidies might be[37]—such uncertainty, inviting political mythology, is unavoidable as long as French legislation does not require any disclosure of campaign or political expenses.

The enterprise set up by the CNPF goes under the unassuming name of the *Centre d'Etudes administratives et économiques*. From its Paris location it is usually referred to as the *"rue de Penthièvre,"* which by now has acquired a symbolic, and sinister, significance as earlier had the *"rue de Madrid,"* where the headquarters of the *Comité des Forges* are located. The Center seems to subsidize a number of the generally insignificant publications in which the CNPF has an interest. Far more important is the financial assistance which the Center has offered since 1946 to needy candidates at election time. When the obviously authentic letter of a disappointed deputy was read from the tribune of the National Assembly, its edifying details attested to the crude working methods of the disbursers. After the 1951 elections, a list of 160 deputies believed to have been assisted by the *"rue de*

---

[36] For parliamentary debates on the "Boutemy affair" and the dealings of the *"rue de Penthièvre"* discussed below, see *J.O. Débats Assemblée*, November 25, 1948, pp. 7195-96; *ibid.*, January 23, 1953, pp. 228-30; *ibid.*, February 18, 1953, pp. 1065-68. See also the daily newspapers commenting on these debates and esp. *Le Monde*, January 13, 1953, discussing "Le Patronat et le pouvoir."

[37] A close and critical observer, Delouvrier, maintains (without substantiation) that in regard to their impregnability to corrupting influences the parliaments of the Fourth Republic have a better record than their predecessors; see his "L'Etat envahi," in Cinquantenaire des Semaines Sociales, *Crise du Pouvoir et Crise du Civisme*, Lyons, 1954, p. 77.

*Penthièvre*" was circulated in parliament, and that list was held
to be far from complete. The averment that every candidate of
the radical-socialist party was able to obtain half a million francs
for the asking, and twice that sum when he had been a cabinet
minister, has never been disproved or even denied. At the 1951
election also a number of candidates of de Gaulle's RPF, known
to be in financial difficulties, were allegedly supported in similar
fashion. To some observers this is the most plausible explanation
for the fact that the RPF began disintegrating as soon as the
employers' movement decided on supporting the Pinay government, which had been blackballed by de Gaulle.

The role which Ernest Billiet played in the *Union des Intérêts
Economiques* of the Third Republic is now held by André
Boutemy. Boutemy, who before the war was a subaltern civil
servant in the Ministry of Finance, climbed under Vichy the
ladder of the administrative hierarchy with vertiginous speed.
Having served under Pucheu and Laval as a responsible police
official whose mission it was to keep tab on all potential and
actual opposition movements, he became prefect in several departments and was appointed in the summer of 1944 a super-
prefect for the region of Lyons, with the express approval of the
German authorities.[38] Those who accuse him of direct responsibility in the slaughtering of resistance fighters, and those who
bring testimony that he has earned the gratitude of some intended
victims of militia and nazi terror, are probably equally correct;
during the declining phase of the Vichy regime that was the
attitude of many of its more subtle officials who sought to survive
the present and yet to insure their future.

After the liberation the rehabilitation of M. Boutemy was in
many ways not more than a typical instance of the "national
reconciliation," restoring political virtuousness to many who in
1944 were branded as "Vichyite traitors." Acquitted by the
criminal courts, he had nevertheless been cashiered from public
office and was told as late as 1948 by the Council of State that,
whatever his good deeds might have been, "he had associated
himself in the exercise of his functions in an intimate and active

[38] This is confirmed by an entry in Nicolle's diary, *op.cit.* (n. 1-48), Vol. II,
p. 430, more candid than other comments since it was made years before
M. Boutemy's return to the political scene.

fashion with the policies of the [Vichy] government. . . ."[39] But the Pinay government first permitted him to "resign" from official functions he no longer held, and then cleared his record by appointing him an "honorary prefect." Besides Boutemy, other fairly prominent Vichy officials grace the staff of the *"rue de Penthièvre,"* all on the payroll of the employers' movement.

Like his predecessor, Senator Billiet, Boutemy must have decided that he could defend his clients' interest better from within the parliament than from without: in May 1952 he was elected a senator from Seine-et-Marne, a predominantly rural constituency. His new senatorial functions did not prevent him from exercising in the lobby of the Palais Bourbon, the lower house, the functions he had assigned to himself after the elections of 1951 had given to the conservative groups a pivotal position. Especially on days when a premier-designate sought to obtain his investiture, Boutemy's presence, and perhaps his advice, were often sufficient to remind deputies of the political debts which they had incurred at the previous elections.

But the senator and the forces behind him overplayed their hands when, early in 1953, Premier René Mayer was prevailed upon to accept Boutemy into his cabinet as Minister of—Public Health. (Unproven but plausible allegations had it that the chemical industry, whose trade association had always been close to the *"rue de Penthièvre,"* attributed a particular importance to that cabinet post, since Boutemy's predecessor had gone uncomfortably far in preparing for a European "pool" of pharmaceutical products.) Boutemy's elevation to cabinet rank set loose a storm which showed many deputies to be indignant about the imbroglio of political and pressure group affairs. Defended halfheartedly by the premier, and energetically only by a deputy who is generally considered to be one of the most faithful spokesmen of industry in parliament, Boutemy had to resign his cabinet post but retained his seat in the Senate.

Within the employers' movement this interlude provoked a rather serious leadership crisis. Villiers had backed Boutemy to the last since, according to the president of the CNPF, who had

[39] See F. Lebon, *Recueil des arrêts du Conseil d'Etat*, March 5, 1948, p. 115. Boutemy's career is described with some inaccuracies in Ronald Matthews, *The Death of the French Republic*, London, 1954, pp. 18-19.

once been deported by the nazis, the former Vichy police official had successfully demonstrated that business could buy its way back to the influence it had lost after 1944. But Joseph Laniel, deputy and textile manufacturer, who carries much weight in the councils of the *Union des Industries Textiles*, was reported to have indignantly refused to become a member of a cabinet which counted Boutemy among its ministers. Other leaders of the employers' movement saw their belief confirmed that the CNPF would court disaster if it did not keep away from this kind of political activity. They are convinced that, if a new Popular Front were to form, it would draw strength from scandals such as now the very name of the *"rue de Penthièvre"* suggests. Villiers' attitude has somewhat impugned his saintliness, which formed part of his charisma, but it is in fact quite typical of many a business leader's outlook on politics. They are convinced that politics, "being what it is," is best managed by people whom they would probably hesitate to employ in their own firms.

Since then a compromise seems to have been reached within the CNPF between conflicting views. Senator Boutemy's agency has not been dissolved but has narrowed, at least for a time, the range of its activities. What role it played during the elections of 1956 is controversial and remains to be determined.

\* \* \*

For the tactics of the business lobby the emergence of large and disciplined parties after the liberation was among the most important transformations of the political structure. Where political parties are little more than a "network of personal relations,"[40] interest groups have other, and generally easier, means of access than when they have to deal with disciplined and well-structured party organizations. Memories of the ways in which pressure groups had operated in the Third Republic motivated majorities in both Constituent Assemblies to adopt proportional representation. By an abandonment of the *scrutin d'arrondissement*, it was hoped to free the deputy from too parochial an

[40] The term was coined by E. Pendleton Herring, *The Politics of Democracy*, New York, 1940, p. 204. A very complete and interesting comparative discussion of the relationship between the structures of parties and pressure groups is to be found in Kaiser, *op.cit.* (n. 1-21), pp. 232 ff.

outlook and to shield him better than before from the pressure of special interests which in a small constituency had frequently been able to control marginal votes.[41]

Additional factors promoted the interest in strong party organization. The size and the discipline of the communist following persuaded the rest of the electorate to seek protection behind party formations of similar consistency. The general drift away from individualism towards organization in all spheres of national life also favored disciplined politics over the individual practices of the pre-war period. Finally the numerous political novices who stood for election in post-war France often lacked the personal following of their predecessors in the *Chambre des Députés* and needed therefore the support of national parties.[42]

From the very beginning neither the "new look" in party life nor the electoral reform banned the action of interest groups from the parliamentary scene. If the importance of parish-pump politics and of local notoriety had diminished, there was increased need for support from regional or national organizations. The far larger constituencies multiplied election costs and, when the party treasuries remained meager, created a financial problem for many candidates, which explains in part their reliance on such agencies as the *"rue de Penthièvre."* For the parties of the left a strong attachment to such interest groups as the labor unions, but at first also the General Confederation of Agriculture, was a foregone conclusion. The MRP relied on the network of the equally well-organized Catholic groups.

In its dealings with the parties of the Fourth Republic, the tactics of the employers' movement naturally changed with the mutations on the political scene. During the period of *tripartisme*, when communists, socialists, and the MRP shared governmental responsibility, organized business declared officially that it would "keep out of politics," which for pressure groups everywhere merely means to avoid complete and open identifica-

---

[41] For a vivid though highly colored description of how the "manipulators of money" would, in the Third Republic, succeed in corrupting the politicians in the countryside, see Alain (E. Chartier), *Eléments d'une doctrine radicale*, Paris, 1925, p. 42.

[42] On all these factors and on their cumulative effect, see the excellent discussion in Philip Williams, *Politics in Post-War France*, London, New York, 1954, pp. 308-26, 346 ff.

tion with any one political party or faction. But just as earlier the business organizations had differentiated the radicals from the socialists within the *Cartel des Gauches*, they now courted the non-communist partners of the government coalition as the lesser evil.[43]

To gain at least a foothold in the SFIO and the MRP seemed all the more necessary as long as the future of the parties farther to the right was altogether uncertain. Still, the strongly disciplined character of both the socialists and the MRP presented a different problem than the loose pre-war organization of the radicals. Methods other than the traditional ones of winning influence had to be tried. At least one prominent official of the employers' movement, Louis Charvet, then the executive of the National Steel Association (and today still one of its vice-presidents), became a member of the MRP's Executive Committee. In numerous writings published during 1945 he espoused ideas of labor-management codetermination, though he remained at all times within accepted concepts of a progressive social Catholicism.[44] In the provinces, where the MRP *militants* formed at first a fair cross-section of the various social categories, a number of businessmen, some of them active in their trade associations, joined the ranks of the party, at least until the party lost part of its following to the right.

A bridge to the socialist party was established by the close working contact which some prominent leaders of the employers' movement, such as M. Ricard, had enjoyed after the liberation with the socialist minister of industrial production and former trade union official, M. Lacoste.[45] A certain affinity of views, if nothing else, existed between a number of socialist leaders interested in the technical problems of a planned economy, and the trade association officials with a pronounced propensity for managerial concepts.

[43] The relations between organized business and the communist labor unions were, however, quite cordial as long as the communists were at their peak of strength. For some details, see below, Chapter IX.

[44] See in addition to Louis Charvet, *op.cit.* (n. iii-36), his "L'évolution de l'entreprise," *La Vie Intellectuelle*, xiii, March 1945, pp. 52-75; April 1945, pp. 90-99; May 1945, pp. 77-93; and "Cogestion de l'Entreprise," xxxii, Semaines Sociales de France, *Compte Rendu in Extenso*, Paris, 1945, pp. 161-78.

[45] See above, Chapter III. In 1956 Lacoste became minister residing in Algeria.

Obviously the more natural sympathies of the employers' movement went to parties farther to the right, which in the elections of 1945 and 1946 had obtained only a meager one-fourth of the votes. The relationship between the radicals and organized business became rapidly more cordial than before the war. The party's opposition to the new constitution and to the nationalizations had transformed it for a time into a truly conservative force.[46] The *Rassemblement des gauches républicaines* (RGR), into which the old radical-socialist party merged, accepted for membership that wing of the *Alliance Démocratique* which had always been particularly close to important business interests. Most attractive for operations of a pressure group was the fact that the radicals remained faithful to their traditions of loose organization. Contacts, frequently intensified through financial dealings, could therefore be established with individual radical deputies or senators.

On the extreme right the *Parti Républicain de la Liberté* attempted to create a solid front, based on a fundamental opposition to the state of affairs as it had emerged from the liberation. Certain big business circles strongly supported the party, which soon failed in its endeavor to give cohesion to the conservative forces in the country. As early as the elections of 1946 its following dwindled, to the benefits of other old or new conservative groups.[47]

When *tripartisme* had come to an end in the spring of 1947, the communist threat was not yet eliminated. During the uneasy months that followed, the CNPF moved close to outright, if still discreet, support of General de Gaulle, whose newly-founded RPF soared in the municipal elections of that period. The business leaders had not forgotten the general's sneering attitude towards them on his return from London. They still had a low esteem of his judgment in economic matters. Yet Villiers and most of the other CNPF leaders were then convinced that only

[46] Excellent on the shifting of the radical party to the right is Rémond, *op.cit.* (n. v-29), pp. 233-34; and now, likening the "radicalism of the right" to a "true French Tammany Hall," Association Française de Science Politique, *op.cit.* (n. IV-25), p. 237. See *ibid.* for the relationship between the radicals and interest groups.

[47] For the early history of conservative groupings in the Fourth Republic, see Paul Marabuto, *Les Partis Politiques et les Mouvements Sociaux sous la IVe République,* esp. pp. 56-62. For later developments the book by Williams, *op.cit.* n. v-42), is indispensable.

the strong hand and the prestige of de Gaulle would be able to stop the spread of communism. Villiers himself entered into negotiations with de Gaulle and attempted to constitute a "shadow cabinet" for the general under the premiership of Paul Reynaud.[48]

But the attitude of the employers' movement changed again, when after the failure of the mass strike the danger of a communist coup receded. The party discipline enforced by fear gradually diminished; the governmental majorities became once more precarious and "unprincipled." And while the return to the practices of the Third Republic was far from complete, the employers' movement and other interest groups could fall back on tactics to which they had been accustomed in earlier days.

The RPF had outlived its usefulness for the employers' movement before the party ever contested a national election. The high amount of discipline which de Gaulle sought to enforce on his followers threatened to screen candidates and deputies from the demands of interest groups. Personality clashes between the authoritarian leader of the party and the spokesmen of the employers' movement were unavoidable as soon as business had regained its self-confidence. When in 1949 the RPF came forward with a scheme for the reform of capitalist enterprise through "capital-labor associations," the employers' movement immediately took issue with this aspect of the party's program and philosophy. Knowing that these proposals, designed to satisfy the working-class elements among de Gaulle's following, would easily antagonize the bulk of the party's supporters, who were of bourgeois origin, the CNPF used successfully the issue of the capital-labor associations for the disintegration of the RPF.

The animosity of de Gaulle against the activities of the business lobby during the 1951 election campaign was vivid enough before he found himself deserted by an increasingly large number of deputies who had been elected on RPF lists. Immediately after the election the general accused the employers' organizations of being just as "politicized" as labor.[49] But whether or not

---

[48] On this point see R. Matthews, op.cit. (n. v-39), p. 240. Notes taken by Mr. Matthews in 1947 and which he was kind enough to communicate to me indicate that M. Villiers was as intent on bringing about such a government as he was dilettante about it.

[49] See Le Monde, June 24-25, 1951. De Gaulle must have felt very strongly

Boutemy's funds accelerated the downfall of de Gaulle's party, a trend away from such a crisis organization as the RPF towards the more customary forms of French conservative politics was bound to occur once the immediate danger had passed. The CNPF and its agents could do no more than hasten the development.

Since then the employers' movement has found on the right-hand benches of both houses of parliament once more a situation that resembles, with some significant changes, the pre-war picture of party life. Individualism is again the outstanding characteristic of the conservative groups, splintered into antagonistic personal and local coteries. Especially the two parties which have inherited many seats from the defunct RPF, the Independents and the ARS, furnish classical examples of being agglomerations of "notables" rather than modern party organizations. Just because of the all-pervading refractory individualism, it is impossible to count every deputy and senator of the right among the staunch and reliable supports of business interests. On the occasion of many important showdown votes, the business lobby found that its suggestions were not heeded by many conservative members.

Yet the primary objectives of the business lobby in parliament have been achieved. Most of the parties accessible to the employers' movement were once more loosely enough organized to permit an application of the permeating tactics through which business can hope to reap the greatest advantages.

In addition, especially after the elections of 1951, both houses gave an adequate expression to the fact that the general political temper of the country had once more become conservative. The center of political gravity had shifted more to the right than at any other time since the beginning of the Third Republic.[50] This was due in part to the evolution of the radical party as a reliable conservative force, at least prior to the emergence of Mendès-France as an active political factor, and in part to the existence of a still-strong communist party excluding the representatives of one-fifth of the electorate from any except obstructionist participation in parliamentary life.

---

about the point, since he made his remark in a press conference during which he was entirely non-committal on all other matters. For the attitude of the employers' movement towards de Gaulle's proposals for enterprise reform, see also below, Chapter VII.

[50] See Rémond, op.cit (n. v-29), pp. 231 ff., for an elaboration of this point.

Against such a general background of party developments the present-day operations of the business lobby in parliament must be understood.

*      *      *

Everywhere the particularities of the legislative process determine the methods of the pressure groups. The French deputy is, if he takes his work seriously, harassed and overworked with insufficient secretarial help and no technical staff whatsoever to assist him in legislative drafting. Yet private member bills are still numerous, though few of them become law; to make matters worse the parliamentary committees insist on redrafting many of the public bills submitted by the cabinet. Currently only a small minority of deputies have any training in business, economics, or engineering.[51] Under such conditions wealthy interest groups such as the business lobby can be of true assistance to the individual deputy, by furnishing him with the documentation he has neither the time nor the means to obtain otherwise. At one point the trade association of the cotton industry was reported to have offered complete secretarial services to "indigenous" members of parliament. Various business organizations, among others the Legislative Service of the CNPF, sometimes oblige by transmitting to the deputies a ready-made bill, drafted in their offices.[52]

However, the most important target for those who wish to influence the legislative process is still the powerful standing committees, since no bill, private or public, may be debated in the Assembly before it has been discussed and reported upon by a committee. That the committees lend themselves particularly well to the intervention by special interests has been an often-heard complaint. Since the early days of the Third Republic the mem-

---

[51] See Goguel, op.cit. (n. v-26), p. 855, for a discussion of the professional composition of the National Assembly after the elections of 1951, and now the very complete data in Association Française de Science Politique, op.cit. (n. IV-25), pp. 291-328. The study by Georges Galichon, "Aspects de la Procédure Législative en France," Revue Française de Science Politique, IV, 1954, gives, especially on p. 809, an excellent insight into the working methods of the deputies.

[52] For details on the functioning of the Legislative Service of the CNPF, see above Chapter III. Arthur F. Bentley, The Process of Government, 2nd edn., Bloomington, Ind., 1949, p. 432, described almost half a century ago the situation quite accurately: ". . . a purely voluntary organization may be formed, may work out legislation, and may hand it over completed to the legislature for mere ratification."

bers of the most important standing committees were not selected for their competence but from among the deputies who, for political or personal reasons, wished to be closely affiliated with the work undertaken by the committee. Until today each committee attracts members whose constituents are particularly interested in the subject treated by it.[53] This in turn gives to the pressure groups the desired leverage to influence the members of the committee, and especially its *rapporteurs* and chairmen, often literally besieged at the time of committee meetings. Hence majorities for or against proposed legislation form long before a bill is coming up for a plenary debate and is voted upon. As early as the Third Republic a professor of constitutional law who was also a conservative deputy concluded that the action of pressure groups on the standing committees begot within the womb of the legislative process "the embryo of an empirical organization of economic interests."[54]

How the oldest of business organizations, the *Comité des Forges*, utilized the possibilities which such a corporative set-up offered was classically described by the biographer of M. Pinot, the executive of the steel association: "As soon as a public or private member bill is printed and distributed he [Pinot] gets hold of it and studies it. If necessary he communicates the text to the members of the association, invites their reactions, organizes an inquiry among them, and in collaboration with them arrives at a decision. He writes a memorandum which lays down in general and in detail the position of the *Comité des Forges* or of the UIMM and assembles the figures and arguments that are best suited to sustain that position. . . . . Then he approaches the standing committee to which the bill has been referred; he contacts its president, the *rapporteur*, and those of the committee members who are apt to understand him; he submits his documents to them; he draws their attention to those points which he

[53] For a number of examples of how seats on the committees are distributed at present, see Williams, *op.cit.* (n. v-42), p. 240, fn. 19. This was the main criticism of the committees which Léon Blum expressed as early as 1919; see his *La Réforme Gouvernementale* (first published anonymously after the First World War), Paris, 1936, pp. 188-98.

[54] Joseph-Barthélemy, *Essai sur le travail parlementaire et le système des commissions*, Paris, 1934, p. 152. The book is still a classic treatment of the question. See *ibid.*, pp. 146 ff., for a lengthy description of the interaction between various economic interest groups and the principal parliamentary committees.

considers important; he seeks to convince or impress them. If necessary he brings before them a delegation of the interested trade associations. When the bill is up for discussion before the house, he sees to it that parliament is informed of the amendments which incorporate his point of view. . . ." Always to have acted in such a way that the committee members would never consider the advocate of special interests their adversary was to M. Pinot the most plausible explanation of his success.[55]

Nothing has changed to invalidate this description of the *démarches* which pressure group officials undertake in parliament. The committee system has rather been strengthened in the Fourth Republic. The number of committees was increased either by adding new ones or by forming sub-committees. The Committee of Industrial Production, especially, has created sub-divisions which are concerned with so small an economic sector that most of their members are known to be the quasi-professional defenders of the interests involved. Here the vastly improved organization of the trade associations is proving its value. Where before 1914 only M. Pinot was prepared to furnish the committees with valuable documentation, now every industry feeds facts and figures to the committee members, who in general seem to accept material coming from private sources with greater confidence than they extend to government documents. In this way many committees have truly become the "institutional façade for the operation of pressure groups."[56] When a lone deputy suggested once that three of the committees, three which had shown themselves all too subservient to the directives of the trade associations, be abolished through merger, the proposal was rejected almost without discussion by a majority of three-fourths of the Assembly.[57]

The reliance of all parliamentary committees on high administrative personnel gives to the interest groups another means of access. A civil servant is attached to every committee and guides its work, especially when a committee undertakes the revamping of a public bill. This practice has frequently been criticized as a

[55] François-Poncet, *op.cit.* (n. 1-23), pp. 164, 188.
[56] Williams, *op.cit.* (n. v-42), p. 240. For an excellent description and criticism of the present-day functioning of the committees see *ibid.*, pp. 234, 251, and François Goguel, *France under the Fourth Republic*, Ithaca, 1952, pp. 166-69.
[57] *J.O. Débats Assemblée*, March 27, 1952, pp. 1502-03.

violation of the separation of powers and has actually led in many instances to a preeminence of the bureaucracy in committee activities.[58] Since the war the existence of hostile cliques within the administration has added to the confusion. Antagonism has developed with particular sharpness over questions of economic policies and has been projected into the work of the parliamentary committees. Different committees reflect today often the opposite views of members of the bureaucracy, especially since civil servants on detached service with the committees are almost completely removed from ministerial control. The resulting further dilution of political responsibility turns to the advantage of pressure group politics. The business lobby is in a particularly favorable position to exploit this situation because of its excellent relations with the high administration. Keeping fully informed about existing alignments and controversies, the trade associations are able in their dealings with the committees to play successfully on known rivalries and ambitions.

If the committees offer the best terrain for the interest groups, they are not the only channels through which influence is brought to bear. There have been occasions, such as the debates on the Franco-Italian Customs Union or the ratification of the Schuman plan, when all deputies and senators have been flooded with documentation issued by the trade associations. These legitimate practices have sometimes been accompanied by tactics which the deputies resented as forms of intimidation. A time-tested method in which the various sectors of organized business seem to specialize is to fill the lobbies, the offices, and during the debates and votes the galleries of the Assembly with massive delegations. Their number and demeanor are sufficiently impressive to make the deputies feel that they are deliberating under threat.

During the Third Republic a deputy had described how the organized interests were constantly hovering over the deputies who had a role in shaping proposed legislation. He had stressed that the silent demeanor of the delegations watching from the galleries was particularly oppressive. For every deputy knew that such silence was only temporary. Immediately after a

[58] Maurice Reclus in *Le Temps*, August 17, 1932, quoted from Joseph-Barthélemy, *op.cit.* (n. v-54), p. 173. For the present situation see Goguel, *op.cit* (n. v-26), pp. 856-57.

vote had been taken, publications of the trade associations would loudly praise or blame the deputy. Where a powerful association with a large membership raised its voice, it could easily determine the chances for reelection.[59]

More recently a moderate deputy, M. Henri Teitgen of the MRP, found it necessary to express from the tribune of the Assembly his indignation about the ways in which the truckers' lobby had attempted to prevent a proposed tax revision: "During our recent session quite a few among us have received vehement complaints by voters who are likely to be affected by the taxes under discussion. Sometimes these protests have taken the form of veritable threats. As long as efforts of that kind are only individual, it is up to each of us to give the answers we believe appropriate according to the concepts we have of our mandate and our dignity. But there was something else and worse. People were arrogant enough to bring collective pressure to bear on this Assembly and that pressure was brought into this very house. In the galleries of the Assembly there appeared more or less qualified representatives of special interests who sometimes had, with greater speed than even our parliamentary press, the latest information about the attitude of the government. They then sent through the personnel of the Assembly, while we were in session and in the midst of discussion, the result of their deliberations, in other words their injunctions, to certain members of the Assembly. Such procedures appear to me absolutely intolerable. . . . We are the representatives of the general interest and have to be concerned with special interests only in order to arbitrate conflicts. . . . There are dialogues a regime cannot tolerate unless it is ready to sign its own death warrant, and there are those among us who do not want to sign the death warrant of the Republic. No special interest or group, whatever its membership, whatever its power be it based on money or on anything else—no group, even if it defends a just cause, can talk to the Republic and to its national parliament on an equal footing. And let nobody fool you. Let nobody tell you that these are not really pressures but merely ruses and logrolling propositions. If

[59] Georges Izard, "Le Parlement et les Professions," *Europe Nouvelle*, xx, 1937, p. 738, an important though short article, one of the first to describe realistically the influence of economic interest groups on the political process.

the latter are less brutal than outright pressures, they are even more insulting, or at any rate just as unacceptable."[60]

Though M. Teitgen's speech was widely applauded and his warnings were endorsed by the speaker of the Assembly, it did little to change the methods of the interest groups. As if to compound the insult of which the speaker had complained, the executive of the truckers' association decided to run for parliament at the following election and became a deputy in 1951.

For all the energies which the interest groups display to impress the lawmakers, the importance of parliament in the legislative process continues to diminish, especially in the field of economics. By comparison the function of the National Assembly of making governments and of keeping them in power until it has a change of mind is now politically the most significant of its attributes, particularly since the life span of the cabinets has once more become short. As would be expected, the pressure groups operate therefore in the lobbies of parliament with increased vigor during the period when the fate of a cabinet is at stake. It is no accident that complaints about their activities have of late been voiced mostly during a ministerial crisis or during the electrically charged period preceding such a crisis. Two weeks before his resignation Premier Mayer, who once had been himself in the service of a trade association, accused the National Assembly of having become a "corporative chamber," giving free reign to organized interests.[61] His colleague Reynaud, the former leader of the *Alliance Démocratique*, warned, before he failed to obtain the investiture, that the "economic congregations" were paralyzing the state from within the national parliament.[62] The next day an MRP deputy suggested that one would only have to apply existing regulations to expel "certain interest groups . . . from our lobbies and our offices."[63] Still during the same cabinet crisis Mendès-France, before being defeated in his first bid for the premiership, stated that during the twenty-five years of his career as a deputy he had never experienced in the lobbies of the

---

[60] See *J.O. Débats Assemblée*, January 4, 1950, p. 26. It is true that in this instance not the truckers but the government remained victorious, if only by four votes and only by invoking the question of confidence; see *ibid.*, January 3, p. 13.

[61] See *Le Monde*, May 10-11, 1953.

[62] See *J.O. Débats Assemblée*, May 27, 1953, p. 2850.

[63] *Ibid.*, May 28, 1953, pp. 2859-60.

Assembly a similar "cloudburst of would-be officials and informers, of confidence peddlers and rumor-mongers."[64]

It is extremely difficult to determine with any degree of certainty which part specific pressure groups, like the business lobby, are playing in any such situation. During a cabinet crisis parties, groups, and individual deputies are submitted to a variety of composite influences so that it is generally impossible to ascertain the origin of the pressures that are brought. In addition the habit of many cabinets of retiring without being defeated by a formal vote makes it impossible to test the alignments of deputies and parties known to follow frequently the directives of organized interests.

In the Third Republic a number of situations arose where it was known or surmised that pressure groups had been instrumental in shortening or prolonging the life of governments or were responsible for the composition of a cabinet. According to close observers, the intense activity of some groups, and among them organized business, during the frequent cabinet crises of the recent past has had equal effects.[65] There exists here an obvious contradiction between the pronouncements and the actions of the employers' movement. The president of the CNPF and some other spokesmen for business never tire of inveighing against governmental instability; they accredit further the widely held belief that no valid reform of any kind is possible without first insuring a greater stability of government. But they, along with other pressure groups, frequently contribute to the demise of governments, to the prolongation of ministerial crises, and hence generally to the dissolution of power.

Only in one case, that of *"p'tit Monsieur Pinay,"* the business lobby identified itself openly and not very wisely with a particular government.[66] Neither the CNPF nor M. Gingembre's

---

[64] *Ibid.*, June 5, 1953, p. 2962.

[65] For a short but interesting discussion of the intervention by interest groups leading to the fall of governments under the Third Republic, see A. Soulier, *L'Instabilité Ministérielle sous la Troisième République 1871-1938*, Paris, 1939, pp. 378-82. For the present see the testimony of a reliable observer, Delouvrier, *op.cit.* (n. v-37), pp. 86-87, asserting that the pressure groups are extremely active at the times of ministerial crises. This is, however, denied by other observers.

[66] See, e.g., the speech by President Villiers at the General Assembly of the CNPF in June 1952, *Bulletin*, VI, No. 84, 1952, p. 2, and *ibid.*, VI, No. 82, 1952,

particularly pronounced enthusiasm were able to save Pinay from his downfall; in fact the question whether to support him or not had become a controversy within organized business even before he fell. Since that experience the business lobby has despaired of expressing a unified attitude towards any government. All cabinets, including that of M. Mendès-France, have had their friends and their foes among the business community. Some policies and some personalities have been criticized more than others; some special interests have been more rabid than others in their demands for the "rolling of heads." But the governments have been judged more by their acts than by their announced program or personnel.

*　　　*　　　*

Which, then, are the business organizations that take a particularly active interest in the work and the votes of parliament?

Through its Legislative Service the CNPF is well equipped to furnish useful information to all deputies and parliamentary committees. The peak association arranges for meetings and hearings; members of its Executive and especially President Villiers have frequent conferences with deputies and senators. Because of the relatively dignified character of its open interventions and because of the fact that it claims to speak for all of French business, the CNPF commands a certain respect in parliament. Its structure and nature, however, limit its effectiveness so much that the main lobbying activities of the peak association are carried on somewhat less than openly, which explains in part the operations of the *"rue de Penthièvre"* and why it generally concentrates its attention on the high civil servants rather than on members of parliament.

Since the CNPF is by its by-laws prevented from engaging in any action on which its affiliates are not unanimous, it must actually leave most questions to the individual trade associations or other employers' organizations. If the CNPF is sometimes described as "a state within a state," it must not be forgotten that it frequently suffers from the same weakness which afflicts

---

p. 3. Also M. Fougerolle, then president of the Paris Chamber of Commerce, expressed himself enthusiastically about the Pinay "experiment." Some business leaders compared Pinay to Poincaré.

the French government. Because of the variety of interests it represents, because it cannot afford to antagonize the associations from which it draws its main financial support, and because it fears losing cohesion and prestige, the CNPF will hesitate to take any forthright action in parliament. Hence the central organization of organized business is condemned to the same kind of immobilism which proves harmful to the political process.

Its identification with big business interests is a further handicap to the CNPF's success in parliament. Electorally speaking, big business is everywhere insignificant. In France the pronounced unpopularity of the "trusts" and the "two hundred families" turns all ties with large enterprise into a liability. On the one major issue on which the CNPF took a strong stand in both houses of parliament, it not only suffered defeat but had to admit after the vote that its opponents won by a surprisingly large majority in the National Assembly.

In the fight over the ratification of the Schuman plan, the CNPF believed that it could intervene openly since the treaty was opposed by the prominent trade associations in the steel, chemical, and engineering industries, and also by such organizations as the CGPME and ACADI, usually antagonistic to each other.[67] During the parliamentary debates conservative deputies and senators drew heavily on materials which the employers' movement had distributed to all members of parliament. In fact they repeated each other to such an extent that it was possible to gauge from the debates which arguments and documentary evidence the CNPF and the steel association considered particularly effective in discrediting the treaty. Those in favor of the Schuman plan were able to make much of the fact that big business interests were fighting the treaty and that their colleagues, who had been swayed by the pressures of the business lobby, were opening the way for a "Europe organized by the *Comité des Forges*." Its defeat taught the CNPF that its open intervention on the parliamentary scene was harmful to its objectives.

It is perhaps generally true that the large representative

[67] For a detailed account of the legislative battle around the Schuman plan, see Ehrmann, *op.cit.* (n. iii-56), giving (p. 455) complete references to the debates in both houses.

organizations, such as the CNPF, the Chambers of Commerce, or the General Confederation of Agriculture, are less suited for frank and intensive pressure group activities than the more specialized "corporative" groups.[68] The latter are free from the restraints which their quasi-official character and their unwieldy membership impose on the representative organizations. Their tactics are uninhibited and more frankly political than those which the CNPF and some of the large federations of trade associations dare to employ. Since in addition they have frequently ample financial means, they are the most effective of the "economic feudalities" denounced inside and outside of parliament as besieging the French state.

Most effective access to members of parliament has been won by the trade associations which combine a numerous clientele with an energetic leadership and an efficient organization commensurate with their goals. Since the dispersion of organized parties, many deputies once more owe their election to a relatively small number of marginal votes. Under such circumstances it might be political suicide to incur the hostility of a well-organized interest group commanding electoral support.

One of the most powerful lobbies in post-war France is the trucking industry, organized in the *Fédération Nationale des Transports Routiers*.[69] Because of the low population density the truckers represent an important economic activity employing an estimated 240,000 persons. Alongside a few large firms a mass of small enterprises own two or three, seldom more than ten, vehicles. The voting strength represented by the owners of these artisan-like enterprises is spread fairly evenly over the entire country. The Federation had no difficulties in winning members when, after the war, the distribution of fuel was entrusted to the trade associations. Its energetic president, M. Litalien, once a trucker himself ("a man *sans culture*, but with large views," his closest collaborators would say of him), had like so many others risen to prominence in the trade through the Organization Committee of Vichy days.

[68] This useful distinction is made by Delouvrier, *op.cit.* (n. v-37), p. 78.

[69] For the activities of the organization, see the interesting remarks in Bernard Jarrier, "L'Etat investi par les intérêts," *Esprit*, XXI, 1953, esp. p. 886, and George Rotvand, "Les Cent Hommes qui de Paris mènent la France," *Réalités*, No. 65, June 1951, p. 140.

After having defended for years the interests of his constituents in the lobbies (and sometimes from the visitors' galleries) of parliament, Litalien ran for election in 1951—like his senatorial colleague, Boutemy, on a "farmers' party" list. In the self-description French deputies furnish traditionally to the so-called *"Recueil Barodet,"* the pressure group official turned statesman spoke out for a "politics of public welfare and national recovery," and of himself (in a grammatically involved sentence) as "the man who on a national scale has fought since 1949 with fierce energy the battle of taxes and of fuels which threatened the circulation of motor vehicles."[70]

The Federation, which has also been ably led since M. Litalien's death in 1952, has been successful in obtaining sizable tax privileges for truckers and in preventing for a long time higher taxes on motor fuel. Large indirect subsidies are flowing from the public treasury into the trucking industry because of its effective fight against the coordination of rail and road transport: the truckers compete with the national railroads on profitable lines, but cannot be induced to take over where transportation by rail is uneconomical. At a time when housing remains the most pressing social problem of the country, parliament has been prodded into subsidizing the construction of super-highways.[71]

The Federation has multiplied its effectiveness by establishing alliances with other groups and thereby creating that wider audience of "fellow travelers" many business groups lack. Its own regional organizations extend downward to local associations which group altogether not more than 30,000 members. But the Federation also forms the core of the *Union Routière*, a vast agglomeration bringing together all organizations whose membership is interested in road transportation—car manufacturers, filling stations, repair shops, gas refineries, innkeepers, and touring clubs. Hence when the Union makes demands on legislator or government, it raises its voice in the name of the "first industry

[70] See *Recueil des textes authentiques des programmes et engagements électoraux des députés proclamés élus à la suite des élections générales du 17 juin 1951*, Paris, 1952, p. 374.

[71] For the point of view of the Federation see Georges Litalien, "Le Problème des Transports Routiers," *Revue Politique et Parlementaire*, ccIII, February 1951, pp. 174-81. For criticism of the Federation's propaganda and its effect see Sauvy, *op.cit.* (n. III-14), xIV, 1951, pp. 665-66.

of France," claiming to employ more than a million people.[72]
With the aid of allied interests the truckers' federation has frequently organized monster banquets attended by hundreds of
deputies from almost all parties and presided over by the minister
of works and transports, whether he be a socialist or a conservative.[73] So far no government has seen fit to answer the well-
synchronized propaganda of the Federation and the Union,
which has brought much confusion into the discussion of such
questions as the tax and price structure of gasoline and of public
and private transportation.

Another pressure group commanding easy access to parliament
is the alcohol lobby. Special legislation, born partly of emergency
measures during the First World War, has bestowed steadily
enlarged privileges on the distilleries, and to a lesser extent on
the growers of sugarbeets, wine, and fruit. The losses to the
public treasury are enormous: the government-controlled *Régie*
makes cash payments to the growers and distilleries, buys their
products at prices which permit the survival of the marginal
producer and insure a large profit to the efficient. The government stocks the unused surplus and eventually bears a large
share of the social costs of alcoholism.[74]

A broad coalition of well-organized interests has imposed such
sacrifices on the community. The National Union of Distillers of
Alcohol is an affiliate of the CNPF, and groups all trade associations of distillers, organized according to the product they are
processing. The sugarbeet growers and the distillers from sugarbeets form a coherent block, many growers owning shares in the
foremost distilleries. Numbering by themselves probably not
more than 150,000, the sugarbeet growers are associated in the

[72] See *Le Monde*, May 12, 1953.

[73] As one example among many, see the declaration by the Union's president,
M. Gallienne, to *Le Monde* (weekly edition), July 24 to 30, 1953. Quite typical
is the violence with which that declaration reacted against a slight criticism of the
gasoline interests by Premier Laniel, himself a businessman.

[74] For an excellent study of the alcohol lobby, see Georges Malignac, "Le Statut
de l'alcool," *Esprit*, xxi, 1953, pp. 903-08. Actually the protection of the distillers
reaches back even further than the article indicates. See, e.g., the doctoral thesis
by Roger Galtier de Laroque, *Le Privilège des Bouilleurs de Cru*, Toulouse, 1902,
commenting on a law of 1902 and yet earlier legislation granting such privileges.
The author reaches the conclusion that the privileged position of the alcohol interests is to the best of the country. His arguments are identical with those still
employed today.

Confederation of Agricultural Producers and in the Distillers' Union with the far more numerous wine growers; frequently they also claim to speak in the name of the wheat farmers since the beet growers have accredited the legend that wheat output increases by an intermittent cultivation of sugarbeets. In 1952 the Distillers' Union launched one of the rare public relations enterprises of French business: it founded the French Institute of Alcohol explicitly devoted to "studies and publicity concerning the uses of alcohol."[75]

Hardly any deputy can afford to remain indifferent towards such a vast alliance of industrial and agricultural interests. All legislation concerning alcohol is scrutinized by the parliamentary "Committee on Beverages." The state-owned *Régie* relies for the framing of most of the administrative regulations on the advice of the Superior Council of Alcohols, on which a majority of seats is reserved for the trade associations and other interest groups. Before the 1951 elections the Council's president was a socialist deputy who was also the chairman of the Assembly's Finance Committee. Jean Jaurès, the socialist leader, once spoke bitterly about the "bistrocracy" and its hold on the country. Half a century later a prominent member of his own party would become an essential cog in the wheels of pressure politics set turning by that same bistrocracy.

Also conspicuously active in the lobbies of parliament are the two trade associations in which the shipbuilding industry and the firms equipping vessels are organized. René Fould and the brothers Labbé, who speak in the name of the two organizations, are prominent industrialists and members of the CNPF's Board of Directors. Robert Labbé is also one of the co-owners of the Worms firm, much talked of as the seat of the "Synarchy" under the armistice regime. Both he and his brother were prominent in Vichy's Organization Committees.[76]

These industries, living largely on government orders, have been able to obtain more than a fair share of outright grants and subsidies which not only shield them from foreign competition but have permitted costly practices: in the atomic age sailing

[75] See *Annuaire, op.cit.* (n. III-38), p. 205.
[76] For details on the shipbuilding lobby, see Jarrier, *op.cit.* (n. v-69), pp. 890-91.

ships have been built and outfitted; identical vessels are ordered simultaneously from two shipyards at a price determined by the high costs of the inefficient firm. But the deputies from constituencies where the shipyards are located are usually prevailed upon to sponsor the enabling legislation: a socialist deputy from Marseilles has done much to provide the crutches for which industry asked.[77]

The interests of the department stores are successfully defended in parliament by a special "Coordination Committee." The Boussac combine develops tireless efforts on behalf of the cotton industry. Enterprises in the field of publicity have found able defenders of their interests in the *Palais Bourbon*.

Since small business does not have to fear public opprobrium and since it represents considerable voting strength,[78] it operates openly, and at times noisily, within the parliamentary chambers. Although the Standing Order of the National Assembly prohibits the "constitution within the Assembly of so-called defense groups of special, local, or economic interests," it has always been easy to circumvent that provision by establishing "study groups" which bring together deputies and representatives of interest groups. In the National Assembly elected in 1951, M. Gingembre formed with his customary energy a Study and Action Group for Private Enterprise. The group had its origin in the "Economic Front" to which the CGPME had earlier invited all major economic interest groups, including the CNPF and the General Confederation of Agriculture.[79] After the elections all candidates who had obtained the endorsement of the Economic Front for having pledged the support of "free enterprise" were invited to join the parliamentary intergroup. More than 300 deputies became its members: the majority of the RPF deputies, practically all those elected on the farmers', independent, and radical party lists, more than one-third of the MRP, and four socialist deputies. The deputies belonging to the group, whose secretariat was as a matter of course entrusted to M. Gingembre, met in the building

[77] Similarly a socialist deputy from the North was very active in warning against the Steel and Coal Community. Later he bowed to party discipline and voted for ratification.

[78] It has been calculated that the shopkeepers' vote alone amounts to two and a half million; see *Manchester Guardian*, May 20, 1950.

[79] For details see above, Chapter IV.

of the Assembly, usually with representatives of the various economic defense organizations united in the *Front Economique*.[80]

Opinions were divided as to how effective the work of this group has actually been. For a time after the 1951 election it considered every major piece of economic or social legislation; its executive committee, composed of only six deputies and an equal number of pressure group officials, met frequently to consider matters of common interest. But it had no means to compel the deputies to abide by its decisions. The CNPF, considering the group to be mostly a vehicle for M. Gingembre's organization, and knowing that the employers' peak association had better-controlled and more discreet channels of influence in parliament and administration, soon took a line of somewhat "aristocratic" detachment from the vagaries of the Economic Front. If the intergroup had any influence it was that of opposing an eternal "no" to all proposals of legislative reform. As soon as the Poujade movement entered the political scene, the group lost the cohesion it might have had at one time: not only the rebellious shopkeepers but also the deputies were more impressed with the demonstrations Poujade was able to organize than with Gingembre's *démarches* in parliament.

\* \* \*

Already during the last decades of the Third Republic few prominent businessmen sought elective office, and that trend has continued in the Fourth. In the National Assembly elected in 1951, seventy-seven deputies (or 14.2 percent of the total) declared themselves as "businessmen" in the broadest sense of the word.[81] Only very few of them, such as the ex-premier, Joseph Laniel, are men of considerable wealth and standing in the business community. When Laniel was first elected deputy in 1932, he succeeded in the Chamber of Deputies his father, owner of a successful family business in the textile industry, who had been a member of parliament for almost forty years. Joseph Laniel,

---

[80] See the report in *Le Monde*, July 22-23, 1951.

[81] See Goguel, *op.cit.* (n. v-26), p. 855; and Association Française de Science Politique, *op.cit.* (n. IV-25), pp. 318-21. Jean Galtier-Boissière, "Scandales de la IVe," *Crapouillot*, No. 27, 1955, publishes (pp. 33-40) a list of the business connections of deputies and senators. For reasons mentioned earlier in the text such a listing though interesting is politically not as revealing as the author believes it to be. Moreover, the information contained in *Crapouillot* is no longer as reliable as it used to be before the war.

the only industrialist on the National Council of Resistance, was returned to parliament after the liberation and has been reelected regularly since then as an "independent." He remains the honorary president of his trade association and is by marriage a relative of M. Fougerolle, for many years the president of the Paris Chamber of Commerce.

Among the senators Jean Maroger, already a member of the upper house in the Third Republic, is one of the truly prominent industrialists in parliament. He is the director of a chemical concern, producing fertilizers, and a board member of the Pechiney company. As president of the *Tréfileries et Laminoires du Havre*, Senator Maroger controls one of the largest metal-processing concerns in the country, with plants in many regions and interlocking business connections with steel mills and aluminum factories.[82] When the senator, as *rapporteur* for the Council of the Republic's Finance Committee, advised against the ratification of the Schuman plan, he defended the point of view of organized business, though clothing it at one point in the seemingly nationalist issue of the Saar question.

But in general the businessmen elected to the National Assembly or the Council of the Republic neither are prominent business leaders nor have more than a natural individual affinity for the point of view of organized business. Instead two kinds of elected representatives have been relied upon to defend the trade associations and the employers' movement from within parliament: some pressure group officials have sought election; some other deputies and senators have been found to be particularly amenable to the suggestions coming from business organizations.

That some of the businessmen sitting today in either house of parliament have also been active in their trade associations is not necessarily significant. Because of the complete network of trade associations covering the country, a businessman outgoing enough to enter politics is likely also to take an interest in the affairs of his association. This alone does not make him into an ardent defender of special interests, were it only for the perfunctory

---

[82] M. Lafond, who has been described above, Chapter III, as one of the most influential members of the CNPF's inner group, is, or was, a board member of the *Tréfileries*.

character of the position which many active businessmen, as distinguished from pressure group officials, hold in their trade associations.

A case in point is M. Antoine Pinay. Undoubtedly his position and policies before and after his premiership were conditioned by the fact that he was regarded as the prototype of an average French businessman, "little industrialist of the provinces, mayor of a small town." (He would try, his admirers announced, to "impregnate parliament and state with the habits of wisdom and organization in which he has excelled during his career as a small employer and a great administrator.")[83] But that he has served as president of some trade associations seems to have been without much importance, though being scrupulous he resigned his functions as soon as he became a cabinet minister.

Quite different is the case of those members of parliament who are officials in the employers' movement. Here the assumption is warranted that by running for an elected office they seek to better defend the special interests of which they have the charge. The cases of Senator Boutemy and of the late Georges Litalien have been heralded widely as undiluted and therefore somewhat compromising forms of pressure politics in parliament.

Another executive of a trade association elected to parliament in 1951 and reelected since is M. Raymond Boisdé, connected with the National Federation of the Clothing Industry. Paralleling M. Gingembre's efforts, M. Boisdé attempted to rally deputies across party lines in 1949-50 in a manifesto against the "tyranny of taxes and totalitarian statism."[84] Having entered parliament as one of de Gaulle's followers, he became one of the main architects of the *Groupe d'Action Républicaine et Sociale*, which in 1952 split de Gaulle's party wide open. More than anything else Boisdé's prominent connection with it made for the group's close connection with urban business interests. In parliament M. Boisdé obtained a seat in the most important of the

[83] See *Antoine Pinay, cet honnête homme*, Bourg, 1953, pp. 15 f. (Quoted here from Association Française de Science Politique, *op.cit.* (n. IV-25), p. 273.

[84] See *Défense du Public*, December 15, 1949–January 1, 1950. Raymond Boisdé contributes fairly frequent guest editorials to such newspapers as *Le Monde* and *Le Figaro* and is the author of a number of books on a wide range of political and economic problems; see, for instance, his *Idées Forces et Idées Fausses*, Paris, 1948. For M. Boisdé's position in the employers' movement, see above, Chapter IV.

committees concerned with economic questions—that of Industrial Production and that of Finance. As an under-secretary in the Laniel government he vowed to transform the Ministry of Commerce into a true "Ministry of the Consumers." Since then he has strenuously publicized an economic system which he likes to term a "new social economy," and which is to be based on far-reaching agreements between the government and the trade associations, a contractual reedition of the Organization Committees.[85]

To determine which deputies and senators belong to the group of those who are considered spokesmen for organized business, although they do not have any official connection with its organizations, is obviously less easy. Here the field is wide open for conjecture if not mere rumor. But members of the two houses frequently mentioned in this connection are so definitely identified with the business lobby that the latter's strategy cannot be adequately described without a brief characterization of their role.[86]

M. Pierre André, an "independent" deputy from Meurthe-et-Moselle, France's most important steel-producing center, is generally classified as the staunch supporter of heavy industry, although the trade associations disclaim any direct connection with him. This intransigently nationalist son of Lorraine seeks to prove his independence by couching the point of view of industry, which he always defends, into his own sometimes singularly naïve terms. During the debate on the Schuman plan, for instance, André warned that the Coal and Steel Community would pin a "static and lethargic" France to a "dynamic" Germany. Yet during the same debate one of his own party colleagues acknowledged, tongue in cheek, that André had "defended from the tribune of the Assembly the legitimate interests of an important sector of our industry."[87] After having been for years simultane-

---

[85] See *Le Monde*, May 8, 1954.

[86] Several deputies belonging to this group were not reelected in January 1956 and are therefore not mentioned here.

[87] The National Steel Association was sufficiently aware that it was being identified in the eyes of the public with M. André to apologize once to Robert Schuman for a tactless attack which the deputy had directed against him. It is likely that all pressure groups find their advantage in having their position defended by deputies who themselves may not always realize that they are the mouthpiece of organized interests.

ously a member of the Assembly's Committees on National Defense and on Labor and Social Security, M. André advanced to the still more important Finance Committee.

In the Council of the Republic the business lobby can count on so many sympathizers that it operates at times even more openly than in the National Assembly. Together with other conservative forces organized business has urged a restoration of the prerogatives which the upper house had held in the Third Republic and which the new constitution so painfully restricted. Though the admirers of the old Senate obtained partial satisfaction by the constitutional amendment of 1954, it is not yet clear whether and to what extent the increase in the Council's powers will affect the tactics of the interest groups.

In previous years the business organizations were content with seeing their point of view expressed in senatorial speeches and reports without insisting that their friends among the senators introduce bold modifications of the bills voted by the lower house. In addition to the industrialist-senator Maroger, whose position has been described, two senators have been particularly reliable exponents of the business point of view: Messrs. Armengaud and Pellenc. Both of them, singly and together, have occupied strategic positions on those committees and sub-committees of the upper house which control finances, defense expenditures, and the management of nationalized enterprises. In committee reports, in speeches from the Council's rostrum, and in publications which appear over their names, both senators castigate the nationalizations and administrative waste. In a book, authored by the two senators and by the most outspoken Manchesterian liberals among the leaders of the employers' movement, Pellenc described it as his mission to "change the orientation of the lower house."[88]

Senator Armengaud, who led the fight against the Schuman plan in the Council of the Republic, has continued to criticize the Coal and Steel Community in a widely respected journal.[89] In the same article the author agreed with the criticism which certain sectors of big business harbor against the plethora of in-

[88] See Armengaud et al., *op.cit.* (n. III-13), p. 232.

[89] See André Armengaud "L'Intégration Economique Européenne et la Communauté du Charbon et de l'Acier," *Politique Etrangère*, XVIII, 1953, pp. 345-66.

efficient small firms. What appears to be the brave espousal of an unpopular cause might also be explained by the fact that Senator Armengaud does not owe his seat to any election but to an endorsement by the associations of Frenchmen living abroad, a curiosity of the new constitution.

Since Senator Pellenc is a member of the radical group in the Council, his reports are distributed by the *Comité d'Etudes pour le Redressement Economique et Financier.*[90] The senator, who has collected diplomas in the field of law, engineering, and medicine during a colorful partly administrative, partly political career, is given to mixing demagogical and violent tirades with figures and data whose accuracy is often doubted.

Pellenc, and to a lesser degree Armengaud, seem to have discredited themselves so much that once Premier René Mayer left the government bench and stalked out of the Council chambers while Pellenc was speaking. For this deliberate affront against one of their colleagues the premier earned the applause of numerous senators.[91] It is also true that Pellenc's violent recriminations against the nationalized sector of the economy are no longer in step with the thinking of the most influential leaders of the employers' movement.[92]

Altogether the deputies and senators whom the business lobby has chosen as spokesmen prove frequently a liability. As in the case of ventures into the public relations field, the employers' movement can be blamed for a negative selection which some of the movement's own leaders regret. Such a choice, which in the end must defeat the intended purposes, results once more from a profound distrust of even the most friendly elements as long as they are unwilling to forego their independence of thought and action. There seems, moreover, to exist in the minds of many businessmen a particular ambivalence: their contempt for the politician and his function is intermixed with a secret passion for playing themselves a role on the political stage, or at least in its wings. The outcome of such amateurish endeavors is often disastrous for government and frustrating for the business interests.

[90] See above, this chapter, for an account of the Committee's activities and especially note 22 for several of Senator Pellenc's writings.

[91] See *J.O. Débats Conseil de la République*, February 4, 1953, p. 512.

[92] For details see below, Chapter VIII.

The most ambitious effort to associate interest groups with the legislative process was made by the Constitutional provision establishing the Economic Council as one of the organs of the new republic. The drafters of the Constitution and of the subsequent law "on the composition and functioning of the Economic Council" expressed hopes that by providing a forum of expression for organized interests they would succeed in canalizing and airing lobbying activities.[93] Differently from its predecessor, the National Economic Council, which was in the end entirely dominated by the high civil service,[94] the Economic Council of the Fourth Republic relies for most of its membership on designation by the "most representative" organizations in the various fields of economic and social activities.

According to the law a variety of representative trade associations and employer organizations were to cooperate in the designation of the employers' delegates to the Council. In practice the CNPF and the Assembly of Presidents of the Chambers of Commerce agree easily on the choice of their business representatives. The secretariat of the "Heads of Enterprise Group" in the Council is handled by one of the more prominent staff members of the CNPF. In deference to the statutory requirement that small and middle-sized firms be given a "clearly defined and proportionate representation," six members of the employers' group are chosen from among those who speak for the CGPME in the councils of the CNPF.

Traditionally the attitude of French employers towards bodies like the Economic Council had been cool; in the post-World War I period, labor not capital had taken the initiative for functional representation. But in 1946 business greeted the establishment of the Council with satisfaction and was content even with the rather meager representation private industry and commerce were allotted: not more than 24 representatives out of a total membership of over 160.

[93] For the legislative texts, see the Laws of October 27, 1946, *J.O.*, October 28, 1946, pp. 9177-78, and of March 20, 1951, *J.O.*, March 24, 1951, pp. 2979-80. For a succinct but careful general description of the organization and the functioning of the Council, see International Labour Office, *Labour-Management Cooperation in France*, Geneva 1950, pp. 42-50.

[94] On the pre-war Council, see the excellent and very critical evaluation by André Ferrat, *La République à refaire*, Paris, 1945, p. 193.

During the first few years of the Council's life the employers' delegation took a very active part in its plenary meetings and the work of its numerous sub-committees. At a time when the CNPF felt isolated and without means of communication, the Council debates offered an opportunity to be heard. Since it is the Council's role to examine bills and international treaties of economic or social interest and to give its opinion on all national economic plans, on official economic forecasts, and on the evaluation of the national revenue, there seemed to exist here an opportunity to expound something like an employers' doctrine on the major issues of the period. Accordingly at that time the prominent personalities of the CNPF, with the exception of Villiers, were Council members and spoke frequently in the debates as did the president of the Chamber of Commerce of Paris and the delegate general of the CGPME.

In subsequent years, however, the attitude of the employers' group towards the work of the Economic Council changed rather drastically. Partly this was due to a general disappointment with the effectiveness of the Council, partly it was a consequence of the changed position of the employers' movement in society and political life.

The reasons for the obvious failure of the Council to influence the work of either the legislature or the executive cannot be discussed here.[95] From the outset much muddled thinking about the exact role of the Council impaired its effectiveness. But more generally experience in France as well as in other countries seems to suggest that in a modern democracy functional representation will never produce the satisfactory results that are frequently expected from it. A realistic appraisal of the Council's work has led many members of the employers' delegation to the conclusion that the results were too meager in proportion to the energy spent. "It is a waste of time," is a frequently heard complaint; and men like Ricard, Lafond, and Fougerolle were replaced on the Council by less eminent personalities.

More important, however, is the fact that the French employers' movement now feels that it no longer needs any such

[95] On this point see Dorothy Pickles, *French Politics*, London, 1953, pp. 229-30, and Harry Seligson, "An Evaluation of the Economic Council of France," *Western Political Quarterly*, VII, 1954, pp. 36-50. Excellent also is Williams, *op.cit.* (n. v-42), pp. 297-300.

sounding board as the Council, and that the Council's work often proves embarrassing. While the Council has been unable to shape legislation or administrative action, the employers' movement knows that it has won once more direct and effective access to parliament and to government bureaus. But besides being more effective, lobbying activities are also more discreet. Hence those who promoted the Council as a means by which classical pressure politics could be forced into the open have failed spectacularly. The behavior of the employers' delegation in the Council is often deliberately restrained, and by the same token far from candid. Since the CNPF knows that it can make its point of view prevail elsewhere, there seems to be little point in taking a strong position on any particular question in an assembly where its votes can be counted and paraded before public opinion as the official attitude of business.

Of late the customary tactics of the employers' delegation in the Council has been either to abstain when the votes are cast or to conceal its position by procedural subterfuges.[96] On other occasions the group has refrained entirely from participating in an important debate and neglected to explain its final vote.

An additional reason for the employers' reluctance to use the Council for a frank exposition of their attitudes is the desire to maintain cohesion and unanimity within their delegation. Since the group comprises heads of enterprises from industry and commerce, from large concerns and small firms, the delegates and the interests they represent must differ on many a question under discussion. During the plenary debates, and presumably even more in the standing and *ad hoc* committees of the Council, such divergencies came occasionally to the surface. But at the moment of the vote, and in spite of the efforts made by some other Council members to play up existing differences, the employers' delegation votes usually *en bloc*.[97]

[96] In the debate on the Schuman plan the employers' delegation expressed its fundamental opposition to the majority report, which recommended ratification, but then abstained from voting in order not to affect adversely "public opinion abroad." See *Bulletin du Conseil Economique*, November 30, 1951, p. 189.

[97] Separate investigations have found this to be invariably true except occasionally on minor isues; see Harry Seligson, *The Economic Council of the Fourth French Republic* (unpublished Ph.D. thesis, University of Colorado), 1953, esp. pp. 196-210, and Edward G. Lewis, "The Operation of the French Economic Council," *American Political Science Review*, XLIX, 1955, pp. 166-72. Interesting

Especially if one considers that M. Gingembre, whose fundamental opposition to many of the policies of the CNPF is known, continues to be a member of the employers' delegation to the Economic Council,[98] such unanimity as prevails seems artificial. But just because the Council is construed as a collection of natural enemies, most of the groups represented, and the employers with them, find it important to present a united front. This by itself makes for a political structuring of the deliberations and resolutions and is not particularly conducive to the work of an expert body such as the original promoters of the Council had hoped to create.

On certain questions the employers' delegation is faced by a true dilemma. When for instance the Council was asked to give advice on the desirable distribution of public investments among the various sectors of the economy, the employers' delegation suggested that parliament decide on the desirable priorities.[99] It is obvious that if such advice were followed, the Council would cut itself off from one of the important functions entrusted to it, and it would thereby further diminish its already mediocre prestige. But it is equally obvious why the employers' group wants to transfer the decision from the Economic Council to the National Assembly. There organized business can make controversial suggestions without publicity and hence without endangering the cohesion of an organization as sprawling as the CNPF!

There had also been expectations that as a meeting ground for the representatives of many interests, the Council would further the harmony among classes and groups. But such hopes too have come to naught. The employers' delegation is known to avoid carefully and almost studiedly all contacts with labor representatives without differentiating between the non-communist unions and the CGT. At least in the prevailing economic and social

---

comments on the apparent unanimity of the group vote in the Council are offered by one of the Council's members, Maurice Byé, "Le Présent et l'Avenir du Conseil Economique," *Politique*, v, 1948, pp. 592-610.

[98] It is no accident that M. Gingembre still considers the work of the Council as extremely valuable and therefore actively participates in it. Such feelings reflect the isolation of his organization and of small business in general from the activities of the CNPF and the principal trade associations.

[99] See *Bulletin du Conseil Economique*, December 16, 1952, p. 437.

climate the role of the Economic Council can hardly be significant.

## 3. Organized Business and the Administration

"Before 1914 France lived on the disinterestedness of 500 great civil servants. There are less than 100 left. Poverty, lack of consideration, and even more the impossibility of accomplishing a great task have dispersed them."

Detoeuf, *Propos de O. L. Barenton*

"Practically, the functioning of the State," Lucien Romier remarked more than a quarter of a century ago, "depends on the administration. On it also depend the life and death of the laws voted by parliament. . . ."[100] The administration of a statute, be it by a formal decree or by a mere circular letter, is under any governmental system an extension of the legislative process and can give a new sense or no sense to any law. In the Fourth Republic the practice of delegated legislation has not in the least been checked by article 13 of the Constitution, forbidding the National Assembly to shed its legislative powers. Under another name the decree-law procedure has increased rather than diminished in intensity and importance, making thereby the administrative bureaus the fountainhead of legislation which in fact is primary.[101]

Since M. Romier wrote, the role of government in economic life has substantially increased and so have the functions and powers of the bureaucracy. In a system where nationalized enterprises are upstream from the most important economic activities of the private sector, where credit and many investments are tightly controlled by the authorities, where export and convertibility restrictions continue, where government price-fixing prevails for many agricultural and some other products, and where wages move between points determined by official rulings, the most important decisions on the changing distribution of

[100] Lucien Romier, *Explication de notre Temps*, Paris, 1925, pp. 230-31. It will be remembered that M. Romier was closely associated with certain anti-democratic efforts of big business circles during the thirties, and played a prominent part in the Vichy cabinets.

[101] The comments by Otto Kirchheimer, "Decree Powers and Constitutional Law in France under the Third Republic," *American Political Science Review*, xxxiv, 1940, pp. 1104-23, are in substance still applicable to the present situation.

wealth are made on the administrative level. Since the bureaucracy formulates and weighs the interests of the state against conflicting demands from within and without the government, interest groups in France as well as elsewhere are continuously concerned with the minutiae of administrative rulings.[102] Moreover, the cooperation between administration and organized interests is often indispensable to transform abstract or rigid laws into workable operations.[103]

The points at which the employers' movement has won access to the administrative process are almost as numerous as the administrative decisions themselves and defy therefore description or even enumeration. Most valuable in this respect are, and on this both sides agree, the informal contacts which are continuously maintained between about 200 ranking personalities of the employers' movement and a slightly larger number of high civil servants or their immediate assistants. Most of the trade association officials involved in this kind of collaboration represent large, rather than small, enterprises, and held high positions in Vichy's Organization Committees.

Of course such informal contacts are neither new nor unique in present-day France. The executive secretary of the pre-war CGPF promised that the organization would continually "ask the government to safeguard the interests of industry and commerce . . . by the necessary administrative measures."[104] As for the parliamentary activities of a pressure group official, the biographer of M. Pinot has also furnished an excellent description of the "post-legislative" phase: "After the passage of a law M. Pinot does not cease his efforts, since the legislator likes more and more to leave the application of the principles he has formulated to administrative regulation. Hence Pinot intervenes with the administration and the Council of State. While they are writ-

---

[102] In Great Britain, for instance, a similar relationship between interest groups and civil servants prevails; see Beer, *op.cit.* (n. Pref.-5), esp. pp. 6 ff. Excellent, and with many examples also, is Kaiser, *op.cit.* (n. 1-21), p. 267 ff. explaining the importance which bureaucracy holds for the pressure groups: ". . . all defense of interests tends towards the point of gravity of governmental powers."

[103] Professor Perroux, *Cours d'Economie politique*, 2nd edn., 1939, Tome I, p. 508, stresses correctly the function of the employers' organizations in providing "flexibility" to the legislative enactments.

[104] See Frédérix, *op.cit.* (n. 1-17), p. 92.

ing the text of a ruling or an ordinance, they are often more than happy to profit from M. Pinot's profound knowledge of the subject without giving up their freedom of judgment. Finally, when the law and ordinance are published, he has them printed and distributed with commentaries and explications which inform the membership [of the *Comité des Forges*] of the nature of the new law and the duties and rights it involves."[105]

Here too the picture has remained essentially the same. The most successful trade association officials boast that they obtain easily, and frequently after one short conference, administrative ordinances which are "tailored to fit" the needs of their industries. The density of employers' organizations often leads to such a multiplication of interventions by interest groups that the day-by-day activities of government officials are seriously disrupted. Rumor mongering and influence peddling by the pressure group officials create an atmosphere which makes it difficult for the administrators to think and act with calm detachment.[106]

More institutionalized than the informal contacts is the collaboration between administration and interest groups in numerous advisory board and committees. In all modern nations advisory committees fulfill so many functions that it is difficult to generalize about them.[107] Committees are created because the prevailing mores demand as a measure of "fairness" that individuals and groups likely to be affected by governmental action be heard beforehand. Other committees set out to incorporate the technical knowledge of the represented group into the administrative decision. Yet others are means of testing the reaction of the interests to which the rulings will apply and possibly of shaping the rules according to the reaction.

In France committees through which the government obtained advice from business actually antedate the revolution. Colbert had created a Council of Commerce where "deputies" from business centers, in fact wealthy businessmen, were sitting side by

---

[105] See François-Poncet, *op.cit.* (n. 1-23), pp. 164-65.

[106] See Delouvrier, *op.cit.* (n. v-37), p. 83. The author not only is a high administrator in the Ministry of Finance, but also had the opportunity of watching interest group activities from various ministerial cabinets, especially those of M. René Mayer.

[107] See, also for the following, the excellent analysis of advisory committees in Truman, *op.cit.* (n. 1-27), pp. 457 ff.

side with public officials. Under the chairmanship of Colbert's son-in-law that Council voiced loud protests against undue interference by government in economic questions or against *dirigisme*, as the descendants of the "deputies" would have phrased it.[108]

Today there is an almost incredible proliferation of advisory committees in all domains of economic and social policy. There are the Councils of Credit, of Accountancy, of Transports, of Prices, of Commerce, of Productivity, of Utilization of Energy, of Collective Bargaining Agreements, of the Labor Force, of Social Security, of Industrial Hygiene, and others. Consultative committees are attached to different divisions of such ministries as Industry and Commerce, Finance, Labor, Armed Forces, and Reconstruction, and to the Commissariat for the Plan. Others operate on the regional or departmental level.[109]

One consequence of this abundance of advisory committees is a further dilution of ministerial responsibility. Objections and advice emanating from the committees add weight to the administrator's objection to a decision which his minister might propose. The cabinet in turn may burden with the responsibility for inaction the committees, which since the time of Colbert have proposed but never executed.[110]

For the representatives of small business the participation in advisory committees is usually their only means of expressing their views to the administration. Not infrequently their membership affords the ministry an opportunity to pin the decoration of the Legion of Honor on the lapel of small manufacturers or shopkeepers. The spokesmen of big business will contribute to the files of the committee the serious documentation furnished to them by the CNPF or the important trade associations. In many cases the research activities carried on by various sectors of the employers' movement are geared to the work of the advisory committees.

[108] On this and a number of other early committees see Gignoux, *op.cit.* (n. I-31), pp. 52, 60.

[109] See CNPF, *Annuaire, op.cit.* (n. III-38), pp. 832-40, and International Labour Office, *op.cit.* (n. V-93), esp. the tables on pp. 91-93. In the 1930's a critical study counted more than 200 consultative committees; see Gilbert Dauphin, *L'Administration consultative centrale*, Paris, 1932.

[110] On the relationship between the "government by committee" and administrative efficiency, see Marcel Abraham, "Le Ministre et ses services," *La Nef*, VIII, April-May, 1951, esp. p. 103.

Where in the opinion of prominent trade association officials committees and boards have lost their usefulness because they are too large, organized business will treat them with the same aloofness which it shows towards the Economic Council. This will especially be true when cordial informal relations exist between the administration and big business outside of the committee. A case in point is the National Council of Credit, established by the first Constituent Assembly in the course of its seemingly sweeping reforms of the banking and credit system. According to its permanent secretary the periodic and non-public meetings of the National Council have been quite fruitful, since they have given to the representatives of capital and labor, of consumers, and of other groups at least a glimpse of the intricacies of public finance and the problems involved in a budget. But in the opinion of the foremost banking expert of the CNPF, the Council does not "educate" anybody and might well be dispensed with. He and M. Villiers, it is true, have constant access to the director of the Bank of France, who is still as before the nationalization the undisputed master of credit policies.[111]

Of acknowledged value to both sides are the contacts which are maintained between business and the so-called technical offices (*directions techniques*). These offices exist within the various ministries which exercise what is generally called the *tutelle* (tutelage) over a given branch of the private sector of the economy. Most of them are located in the Ministry of Industry,[112] but there are also some in that of Public Works and Transports and yet other administrations. Wherever such offices exist they have frequent and direct contacts with the trade associations in their field. In the words of the director of the Office of Engineering and Electrical Industries: "I am in touch with seven or eight persons; through them I reach 29,000 firms which employ a total of more than one million people." The persons

[111] On the operations of the Credit Council, see the article by its executive secretary, Pierre Besse, "Le Conseil National du Crédit," *La Revue Economique*, 1951, pp. 578-90. For an almost scornful warning addressed to the government of M. Edgar Faure by the director of the Bank of France, see *Le Monde*, March 2-3, 1952. By family connections and friendships the director of the Bank, M. Baumgartner, is closely connected with prominent private banking circles.

[112] The Ministry is changing its name frequently: at times it is also called Ministry of Industrial Production, of Industry and Commerce, or of Industry and Energy.

he had in mind are the executives of well-organized trade associations, such as Davezac, Métral, and the Baron Petiet, who also play a role of the first order in the councils of the CNPF.

Another very harmonious relationship between a *direction* and its industry existed in the field of steel production, until the High Authority of the Coal and Steel Community assumed most of the functions previously held by the Ministry of Industry. When in 1947 private industry regained its freedom from governmental controls, the steel industry was given a special status: production plans, distribution of raw materials, allocation of orders, investments, and foreign trade were to be approved by the Ministry. For the implementation of its policy the Ministry turned officially to the National Steel Association and the closely connected marketing organization, the *Comptoir*.[113] The two organizations together have a staff of about 750 employees, the *direction* at the Ministry not more than a dozen. In the opinion of an irate representative of the industrial consumers of steel, the ministerial office was "an organ without powers and without means of action."[114] In fact the business organizations made the policies instead of implementing them, and the office, which maintained especially good relations with M. Ricard of the CNPF, withheld only seldom the seal of official approval from the decisions reached in the *rue de Madrid*.

This routinized relationship between ministries and business dates back to the period of the First World War and was strengthened greatly by the experiences of the Second. After the Vichy institutions and their successors, the Industrial Offices, had been dissolved, the various *directions* and the corresponding trade associations took over many of the functions of the CO and their governmental commissioners, among others those of collecting and evaluating trade statistics. What has developed in parliament around the major committees is to be found on the administrative level in the interaction between the public and private bureaucrats in the *directions* and the trade associations respectively—the core of a corporative organization

[113] See *J.O.*, July 4, 1947, p. 6234. The decree was signed by the socialist Robert Lacoste.

[114] See Association des Utilisateurs de Produits Sidérurgiques, *Bulletin d'information*, No. 1, July 1951, p. 2. About the origin and the character of the Association, see Ehrmann, *op.cit.* (n. III-56), pp. 473-74.

within the framework of the democratic state. An administrative solidarity between the offices and the business organizations has waxed so strong that both sides complain when other administrations interfere with the bilateral relationship. No lines of command should be tolerated, a prominent industrialist holds, which are "ruinous for the authority of the *direction technique*, natural tutor [of industry]."[115]

It would not be correct to assume that the high administrators in charge of the *directions* or in other posts important for the shaping of economic policies are always ready to endorse the suggestions made to them by the trade associations. When they are caught between pressures transmitted to them by their ministers and the demands from organized business, they may feel little inclination to become the martyrs of either side. They will assert what appears to them subjectively an affirmation of their independence. But the position they take and the decision they eventually reach is determined by a more subtle affinity created by the personal and social relationship between the public administrator and the business executive or pressure group official.[116]

* * *

It is generally admitted that presently the civil servants belonging to the so-called *grands corps*, namely to the Inspectorate of Finance, the Council of State, and the Court of Accounts, have not lost any of their traditional predominance in those domains of public administration which are concerned with economic matters.[117] In 1952 these three groups, numbering about 500 members, filled at least forty all-important positions in various fields of economic control; many others belonging to the younger generation aspired to positions of equal significance, often earn-

[115] A debate on the relationship between administration and industry, organized by ACADI in 1952, furnished interesting comments on the problems here discussed. See R. Morizot, industrialist and executive of the trade association for special steels, "A propos des Rapports entre Fonctionnaires et Industriels," *Bulletin Acadi*, No. 60, 1952, p. 266, and J. Durand, a high government official, "A propos des Rapports entre Fonctionnaires et Industriels," *ibid.*, No. 56, 1952, p. 116.

[116] For lack of space, only the relations with the national administration are discussed here. There also exist both routine and other relations between the employers' associations and the authorities on the regional and local level, especially with the prefectures in each department.

[117] See the excellent study by Charles Brindillac, *op.cit.* (n. 11-44). The discussion which follows here owes much to M. Brindillac's lucid analysis.

ing their stripes in the *cabinets* of a minister. About forty-five members of the same *corps* are in charge of public enterprises, commanding more particularly the banking and credit system of the nation. The nationalized industries proper are in general the domain of the slightly less closed *corps* of technicians recruited among the honor graduates of the "X" and the National School of Mines; they also prevail in the Technical Offices of the various ministries.

It is too early to evaluate what impact the far-reaching postwar reforms for the training of the bureaucracy will have on the mentality of the high administrators. The changes in rules of admission and in the curriculum for the new School of Administration and the former School of Political Science were explicitly designed to alter the social composition of the high administrative strata and to reduce the closeness of these groups. Easy generalizations about the influence which such apparent democratization will have on the mentality of the high bureaucracy are unwarranted.[118] At any rate those who hold at present the posts of command and are in contact with the representatives of organized business had their training under the old system and have generally not even been exposed to serious competition from the new recruits.

From Peyerimhoff, one of the leaders of the defunct private mining industry and of the pre-war CGPF, the saying is reported: "We are all *fonctionnaires*."[119] Then and now one of the traits common to *fonctionnaires* of the public and private interests is a disdain for parliamentary incompetence and political blundering, although both administrators and pressure groups may have contributed to the disorders they lament. The spuriousness of a Senator Pellenc, however close he may be to the employers' movement, is ridiculed not less by certain business leaders than by the bureaucracy. At a time when the CNPF endorsed officially the policies of a Pinay, the opposition against some of

---

[118] For a vivid description of the proposed reforms and the pre-war situation motivating the reforms, see Herman Finer, "The French Higher Civil Service," *Public Personnel Review*, IX, 1948, pp. 167-77. The conclusions on the effects of the reforms reached in the interesting study by T. B. Bottomore, "Higher Civil Servants in France," in *Transactions of the Second World Congress of Sociology*, II, London, 1954, p. 143 ff., are admittedly tentative. Where they attempt to be more than that, they are not convincing.

[119] Quoted approvingly by Dolléans, *op.cit.* (n. 1-7), p. 238.

his mild trust-busting activities and his projects of tax amnesties not only came from the bureaus of the Ministry of Finance, but was also surreptitiously supported by influential trade association officials.

Business leaders compare the talents of the top administrators with the incompetence observed in the political sphere. They sincerely and profoundly admire the knowledge, training, intelligence, judgment, and the literary style of many civil servants.[120] Frequently, it is true, such admiration is one for their own past; the corporation president may have been a member of the bureaucracy before entering private industry.

The notions which both groups hold regarding the role of government in economics are also fairly similar. In their public utterances some big business leaders may still denounce as *dirigisme* all interference of government in the private sector of industry. In reality, however, they do not object to the *tutelle*, implying both control and protection, by civil servants for whom they have respect. Some have traced the concepts shared by business and bureaucracy to an enduring influence of Saint-Simon and the Saint-Simonians. It is true that some of their doctrines are still preached, or at least discreetly revered, in the schools which train leaders in both business and administration. The first disciples of the Count de Saint-Simon had been students at the *Polytechnique*, and until today the beliefs of the Saint-Simonians are called the "pantheism of the polytechnicians."[121] The French railroad and the banking system, at present in many ways the basis of the nationalized sector, owe much to the venturesome energy of Saint-Simonians. But also the *Comité des Forges* was first devised by Léon Talabot, steeped in the same traditions.

Today, however, neither the members of the bureaucracy nor the businessmen have anything like a well-defined economic creed spelling out the regulatory role of the government; their *dirigisme* is mostly empirical. It is based on the experiences of the last fifty years, which have shown that in France free enterprise, left

---

[120] For an expression of such admiration see G. Desbrière, "A propos des Rapports entre Fonctionnaires et Industriels (suite)" *Bulletin Acadi*, No. 58, May 1952, pp. 168-69.

[121] By C. Bouglé, as quoted by Gignoux, *op.cit.* (n. 1-31), p. 91. An American author, Harold Larrabee, in his article on "Saint-Simon and the Saint-Simonians," *Encyclopaedia of the Social Sciences*, Vol. XIII, New York, 1934, p. 510, calls Ford, Rathenau, and Loucheur "unconscious Saint-Simonians."

alone, has lacked the dynamism, the insight, and the organization to do what had to be done.[122]

The feelings of the bureaucracy towards organized business are not free from ambivalence. The civil servants admittedly need the practicality and the experiences of the business world, especially as long as in their own training an almost exclusive emphasis was placed on rhetoric, mathematics, law, and economic theory of the nineteenth century. But they will criticize quite openly those practices of the trade associations and the cartels that lead to "economic Malthusianism." As long as such practices continue to protect the marginal firms, irrespective of costs, the civil servants hold that big business is hypocritical if it complains about the political demagoguery favoring the "little men." They regret and sometimes ridicule the overcautious attitude of industry towards problems of investment and modernization. They castigate what they consider the employers' slovenliness towards housing and other social problems, and are aware of the need for protecting unorganized interests, especially those of the consumer. They blame many of the difficulties that stand in the way of European economic integration on the reluctance of French business to face the competition of a wider market. Especially the younger administrators who have already reached high positions show an increasing amount of impatience with the ingrained habits of the business community.[123]

To the extent that such a divergency of views between the *haute bourgeoisie* in administration and that in business exists, it would become politically significant only if it were regularly reflected in decisions made by the bureaucracy and running counter to the demands of special interests. Actually, however, the general circumstances surrounding the high civil servant in present-day France will often either obliterate the differences between his mentality and that of the business leaders, or render

[122] Interesting on the attitude of both civil servants and industrialists towards *dirigisme* are Brindillac, *op.cit.* (n. II-44), p. 875, and Durand, *op.cit.* (n. v-114), pp. 115-16.

[123] See an industrialist's complaint about the younger civil servants' impatience in Desbrière, *op.cit.* (n. v-120), p. 171. Generally speaking, in the interviews I conducted some of the most substantiated though measured criticism of the employers' position came from high administrators in frequent contact with business leaders and pressure group officials.

them meaningless because they do not in fact influence the adjustment of competing claims. Such a gap between discernment and determination can often be attributed to the shifts in employment from public service to private business, occurring far more frequently than in the past.

Differently from the situation in the United States, such changes usually take place in peace-time France in one direction alone—the civil servants leave the administration, while only a national emergency would induce the businessman to accept a post with the government. Already before the war the number of former *fonctionnaires* who were employed by private corporations had steadily increased. Many among them, it is true, always had belonged to the capitalist milieu created by *"convivium* and *connubium."*[124] By accepting private employment they merely returned to the group from which they came after having enjoyed, partly at the expense of the state, the still highly regarded training and experience afforded by public service.

Since 1946 such switches have, for a variety of reasons, become much more general. Undoubtedly the insufficiency of civil servant's salaries in an inflationary situation was in some cases an important factor. Where previously the members of the upper bourgeoisie could afford a somewhat austere monthly pay, the shrinking of many private fortunes rendered the situation more precarious. Yet monetary necessities or allurements alone do not explain many of the instances where private employment is finally preferred to an anticipated long and distinguished public career.

The prime motivation for seeking a place in the upper administrative hierarchy in France had frequently been the satisfaction derived from status, authority, and power. Frenchmen speak without any irony about their public servants as *"mandarins"* (just as it seems to be a common trait of the French and of the Chinese to classify their citizens according to the rank obtained in rigorous examinations). An inspector of finance, for instance, may disdain the considerably higher emoluments of a private banker, as long as he occupies a position from which he can influence the credit flow in an entire sector of the economy.

---

[124] This term is employed as a characterization of the French ruling group by Laroque, *op.cit.* (n. II-68), p. 92.

But should he feel that political interference is all too frequent, that administrative responsibilities have been diluted so as to diminish his own radius of action, that he is no longer able to determine the priorities for which he has opted, then he may abandon his public position. While it is not always easy to distinguish between a subtle rationalizing and actual motivation, many a former government official has given the "crisis of the regime" as the reason for his resignation. In private industry he hopes to find a more gratifying field for the exercise of his talents. The aureole and the status which previously glorified public service seem to wear off.[125]

On the other side, the employers' movement is now able to offer positions which seem to combine the advantages of private employment with the prospect of wielding more influence than as the executive of a business firm. Before the war, only a few well-organized trade associations had been able to secure the services of well-paid and qualified staff members. The Vichy era and the greater willingness of business to organize have significantly increased the number of promising positions in the employers' movement.

The administrative background of some prominent CNPF leaders has been discussed.[126] Numerous other personalities in the employers' movement have been civil servants also. The delegate general of the trade association for the cotton industry is a former inspector of finance, presiding now over a newly formed CNPF committee, set up to study reforms of the economic structure. The chairman of the CNPF Committee on the Liberalization of Trade was previously the director of commercial agreements in the Ministry of Finance. The ranking staff member in charge of Franco-American relations is a civil servant on detached assignment who has recently become the general *rapporteur* of the important CNPF Committee on International Economic Relations. Frequently the administrator who has been in charge of controlling an economic activity becomes the executive of the trade association in the same field: the director

---

[125] See the motto for section 3 of this chapter. For an interesting recent comparison between the salaries of higher civil servants and industrial managers, see Jeanneney, *op.cit.* (n. IV-26), pp. 194-97.

[126] See above, Chapter III.

of the governmental Alcohol Division became president of the distillers' association; staff members of the technical offices frequently accept jobs in the trade associations with which they had long been in contact.

Reliable and sufficient data on the transfer from public to private employment are not available.[127] Information on the finance inspectors, i.e. on the uppermost elite, indicates that of the 240 living inspectors, 70, or a little less than 30 percent, have resigned or taken permanent leave for private employment. Approximately two-thirds of these 70 have entered a large industrial or banking concern.[128] In this respect at least, the candidates for the National School of Administration, though coming from a socially less closed group than their elders, seem to continue, and perhaps to reinforce, existing traditions: 60 percent of the entering class declared that they prepared for the higher civil service only in order to get positions in private business subsequently.[129]

The impact which such shifts must have on the dialogue between the public servant and the advocate of business interests has been perceptively described by an observer who has an intimate knowledge of the milieu: "For the elite making up the *grands corps* of the state, the administration is nothing but the antechamber to a business position. The engineer is called upon to direct the enterprise which he controlled yesterday and where his former subordinate will control him tomorrow. . . . Strange collusion. The same *camarades* find each other all along a career which conducts them from the benches of their schools to the administrative services and then to the Board of Directors of corporations. The same *camaraderie* presides over their mutual relations, a *camaraderie* which does not preclude a certain hierarchization. The representative of the state outranks the business leader, and the latter will come to see the civil servant when they meet. But there is a contradiction between the position of the man

[127] The bi-monthly magazine *Entreprise*, specializing in a description of the relationship between the public and the private sector of the economy, published in every issue and especially in its column "*La Vie qui va*" news items about shifts between the two groups.

[128] These data are given by Brindillac, *op.cit.* (n. II-44), p. 867, without indication of source.

[129] See Pierre Lelong, *Politique et Fonction Publique*, thesis, Paris, 1952, quoted in Bottomore, *op.cit.* (n. v-118), p. 148.

who has 'arrived' and has won real authority and success, on the one hand, and the hierarchy of functions, on the other. It is human that the actual worth of a position is more important than mere hierarchy. . . . Between eminent minds accustomed simultaneously to the disciplines of administration and of industry no great divergences of views are to be expected. The advocate of private interests knows in what tone he ought to talk to the advocate of a state which he himself has served previously; what one should say and what not, better still what one should think and what not. He is conscious of serving the interests of his firm without doing a disservice to those of the state. He reasons quite naturally on the level of his enterprise, and since he is convinced of the justification of his cause he is apt to merge it with that of the state. He has always known the desk in front of which he talks. . . . He hardly notices that he is no longer on the same side of that desk. . . . Why did he change places? . . . Such changes are so frequent that he does not even ask himself the question. . . . In conformity with the pre-established harmony of the career of a high civil servant, his metamorphosis has nothing unusual in his eyes. The *corps* to which he has gained entrance by his rank in the examination has pre-destined him to his present position just as it pre-destined his *camarade* to whom he now talks and whom he calls by his first name to become the representative of the state. It never comes to his mind that he earns part of his salary just because the two of them call each other by the first name. One must assume that big business finds all this rewarding. But what about the state?"[130]

Other observers have noticed that it is frequently possible to estimate, merely by talking to him, how long ago a pressure group official or industrialist left public service. At first the newly adopted son of private capitalism may still scoff at many of the ideas of his new colleagues or constituents, and feel closer to his former associates in government. But most likely, it will not be long before his new milieu will have assimilated him.[131] And will there not be a similar "gradualness" of views of those civil servants to whom the idea of leaving their jobs has not yet

[130] Dieterlen, *op.cit.* (n. III-32), pp. 359-60.
[131] For a singularly frank description by M. Pierre Ricard of his own "metamorphosis," see *Bulletin du Conseil Economique*, February 11, 1948, p. 118.

occurred and of those who, for a variety of reasons, are already considering a change in employment?[132]

Characteristically enough, the views of the high bureaucracy and those of business leaders on the proper organization and the functions of a modern employers' movement are almost identical. Both groups wish to see that solidly organized trade associations in the major branches of economic activity assure the flow of information and control in either direction. Efficient organization calls for competent and honest leadership which seeks to obtain voluntary discipline by the quality of the services it provides. An employers' movement of such nature would have enough moral authority to enforce decisions which might be distasteful to the laggards, but would be salutary for the over-all interests of the industry or the economy as a whole.[133]

That such views leave a great many decisive questions unanswered may be felt; it is hardly ever acknowledged. At what point will the claims of the unorganized interests or of the organized minority interests be recognized by administrative decision? Will not the desired strength of the trade associations, representing special interests, make it eventually impossible to arbitrate between them and broader, overriding considerations? Will not the accord between public and private officials in regard to business organizations result in a confusion of functions which might prove disastrous for the democratic process?

At times it is recognized that there exist here the foundations for a technocracy operating within an indifferent political system. But even those who cannot fail to see the political dangers of such a prospect seem to prefer it to the existing disorder.[134]

## 4. Summary

Apprehensive of the considerable and often resented power of business interests in pre-war politics, the Fourth Republic enacted

---

[132] Another group of men holding "transitory" views consists of directors of some of the nationalized enterprises. For more details see below, Chapter VII.

[133] Such concepts are developed with some forcefulness by M. Morizot, *op.cit.* (n. v-115), pp. 270-71. There are analogous remarks in Brindillac's analysis of the *fonctionnaire*'s outlook.

[134] See, e.g., the conclusion reached by Peyret, *op.cit.* (n. iii-81), pp. 117-18. His otherwise very critical (and realistic) analysis of pressure group activities ends on a note of hope in the results of collaboration between progressive businessmen and administrators. See also below, Chapter X.

nationalizations of industry and some other control measures partly in order to narrow the basis from which organized business had operated in the past and had exercised its influence over parties, press, and public opinion. By demolishing what before the war was known as the conjunction of banking, insurance, and the stock exchange with certain heavy industries, and by altering the entire mechanism of public finance and of currency manipulation, the government hoped to free itself from the enveloping maneuvers of the business lobby. The experiences of the last decade have shown that such measures as were taken undoubtedly had their effect on the tactics of organized business, but did not and probably could not relieve the pressure of the interest groups on the governmental process.[135]

What distinguishes French pressure groups, and the business lobby with them, from similar groups in other democracies is not their "operational code," the ways in which they seek to win and to maintain access to the various organs of government. On that level, and only with some significant exceptions, the similarities are as great as one would expect. Very considerable differences, however, some of them alarming for the future of democratic institutions in France, exist in regard to the effects of group activities. But such differences result rather from the general economic and political milieu in which the groups operate.

The employers' movement, just like other interest groups everywhere, is seldom able to recognize, let alone strive for, those social and economic needs which may be in contradiction to specific short-run desires of its membership. (Not even to see the long-run interests of their own constituents has been described as an important feature of the mentality of most pressure groups.)[136] Terminology and rationalizations notwithstanding, most of the political activities carried on by the CNPF and its affiliates are principally defensive.

It has been observed that American trade associations are concerned with government action not so much because they wish to promote constructively their own interests as because they

---

[135] This point is stressed by François Goguel, *Le Régime Politique Français*, Paris, 1955, p. 108.

[136] See the short but interesting discussion of that "mentality" in Albert Lauterbach, *Man, Motives, and Money—Psychological Frontiers of Economics*, Ithaca, 1954, pp. 80-82.

desire to see the activities of their economic and political rivals controlled, and because they wish to forestall measures which might operate to the disadvantage of their members.[137] The same holds true for the French trade associations.

But already here the insufficient economic development of the country conditions group behavior. It has been calculated that in 1953 the needs of the population had increased by about 78 percent since 1913, while gross national income during the same period had grown by only 32 percent.[138]

Such an excess of needs over resources leads not only to a vast complex of social frustration obsessing most classes and groups of the population, but also to the ferocious determination of all economic defense organizations to hold on to that share of the national income which their constituents have obtained.

Since, nonetheless, frustration continues, all interest groups blame the government, its wastefulness and inefficiency, as the source of their discontent; but they also inveigh stridently against each other. It has often been observed that capital and labor, or at least their organizations, face each other in France like two hostile nations, "each having its great men, its slogans, its newspapers, its books, and soon its own syntax and its own language."[139]

Since the war the phenomenon has become far more widespread. In the words of a report by the ACADI group: "Every faction of the social organism has the, often justified, feeling of not being understood by the others. No group has a monopoly of this obsessional fever which sometimes is diagnosed solely among the working class. Actually farmers, civil servants, professional people, shopkeepers, intellectuals, and, we have seen it, employers are suffering just as much from it."[140]

The fear of every actual or presumed competitor leads to a freezing of existing relationships, to an immobilism necessarily harmful to economic and social progress. Such a situation could

---

[137] See Herring, op.cit. (n. v-3), p. 101.

[138] See the admittedly bold but interesting calculation of these indexes in Sauvy, op.cit. (n. III-14), pp. 331-32. The question of economic expansion and pressure group activities will be discussed more fully in the subsequent chapters.

[139] Daniel Halévy, Décadence de la Liberté, Paris, 1931, p. 89.

[140] De Longevialle, "Rapport sur l'Activité de l'Association en 1953," Bulletin Acadi, No. 78, March 1954, pp. 86-87.

be relieved only if there were a government vigorous enough to exercise its function as an arbiter among competing claims and to mobilize public opinion behind the solution it proposes.

But the government lacks the stability and strength to fulfill that role. Shifting coalitions and the ensuing shifting of purposes make it impossible for any government to explain its actions to the groups operating in the antechambers of politics and to the public at large. Unable to persuade or compel public and other groups to accept the priorities which are necessary, the government is forced by the organized interests into decisions which are seldom its own. "To the extent," Mendès-France has commented, "that conscious and reasoned policy calls for choices, it cannot help but dissatisfy at first a fraction of the country. If one does not want to irritate anybody, one is condemned to a total immobilism."[141]

During the last few years loud and substantiated complaints have been voiced about the disastrous effect of pressure group activities. René Mayer has warned the convention of his radical party not to exult over the decline of organized labor, as long as the coalition of labor confederations has merely been replaced by a coalition of business and agricultural organizations.[142] The first president of the Fourth Republic has spoken about the "assault of the corporative or technocratic economic feudalities"; the royal pretender has denounced the organized strength of the steel industry, the beetgrowers, and the alcohol distillers.[143] But it is not enough to conclude that political power is "infested" by organized interests. The main threat consists in a dissolution of power, an anarchy that becomes general though the administrative machinery may clatter on.[144]

When the Third Republic was born, Gustave Flaubert rejoiced because finally "the provisional, normal, and true condition for

[141] See "La Réforme constitutionnelle suffira-t-elle ?" *Le Monde*, April 10, 1953.

[142] See *L'Information Radical Socialiste*, VII, No. 247, October 1952, p. 5. He called "CNPF + CGA + CGV + PME" as unsatisfactory a formula as "FO + CFTC + CGC − CGT."

[143] See *Le Monde*, June 30, 1953; and for a quotation from the Bulletin of the Comte de Paris, *ibid.*, July 27, 1951.

[144] This is the conclusion reached by G. E. Lavau, "La dissociation du pouvoir," *Esprit*, XXI, 1953, p. 830, and by most of the contributors to this excellent special issue of the magazine *Esprit* on the relationship between economic and political power, frequently quoted in this chapter.

everything has become a constitutional reality." Since then, the operations of French governments have retained much of their provisional character; but at the same time the vast majority of the community has come to hold the government responsible for the prosperity of the country. Neither parliament nor administration is equipped for the tasks of social and economic engineering it is called upon to undertake, or at least to coordinate. A state that interferes in most aspects of economic life and yet proves weaker than the coalitions of organized interests surrounding it will be constantly in a precarious position.[145] The political and administrative disorder thus created reduces the government to an agency for the expedition of current matters, while the pressure groups are able to transfer and transmit their conflicts to the machinery of government itself. The immobilism of the pressure groups is soon matched by an analogous immobilism of the political organs. The employers' movement has moved into the foreground of all interest group activities almost by default. Business has reemerged as a new-old elite in present-day France after most of the forces which during the war were considered as likely claimants to leadership and elite status had failed. Its position may still not compare with the prestige which the business community enjoys in the United States. But relative to other forces in their own country, the organizations defending private enterprise wield considerable influence, especially because of their closeness to that remaining seat of decision making, the high bureaucracy.

In a situation coming close to that of a power vacuum in a modern state, the natural temptation of a well-organized interest group might induce it to move forward to model political power according to its concepts and in its own image. This is not to say that organized business is ready or able to step into the vacuum if and when it becomes complete. But given the present situation and the relative weight of organized business in both the present and foreseeable future, it becomes imperative to examine more closely its economic and social concepts. To that analysis the remainder of this study will be devoted.

[145] Pertinent on this point is Raymond Aron, *Les Conséquences Sociales de la Guerre* (Cours, Institut d'Etudes Politiques), Paris, 1946-47, Fasc. 5, p. 17.

The chapters describing attitudes of organized business in the field of economic policies will, selective as they must be, deal consecutively with the following spheres: the intersection of public and private decision making (Chapter VI); the internal organization of the firm and the impact which enterprise reform has had on the outlook of private business (Chapter VII); French business in the market place, whether national or international (Chapter VIII). A separate chapter (IX) will analyze, again without claim to completeness, those attitudes and practices which reflect the views of the employers' movement in the broad realm of industrial relations.

(It will be noted that the perspectives of organized business on colonial policies in general and on the North African situation in particular are not included here, just as the present chapter has not dealt with the role which the employers' movement is playing in the "colonial lobby." Such an omission, while intentional, does not indicate that organized business is indifferent to the decline of the French empire. The contrary is true to such an extent that for reasons of space alone I had to forego a discussion of the extremely intricate problems here involved. The field is wide open for future investigation.)

# PART THREE
Attitudes and Policies of Organized Business

# CHAPTER VI

# Economic Issues: I

## *1. Statistics and Economic "Stock-Taking"*

"A country whose industrialists do not furnish statistics
is a country without an industrial mentality."

Detoeuf, *Propos de O. L. Barenton*

The participation of businessmen and of their organizations in
the gathering of statistical data furnishes a lively case study of
the struggle between the needs of a modern business civilization
and the bourgeois virtues of the French manufacturers and
merchants.

How the production index was established in the early 1920's
by an energetic civil servant who travelled around in his own car
and at his own expense begging for indispensable information is
an episode of economic history still awaiting the satirical treatment it deserves.[1] For about fifteen years that index continued
to be published, based here on material contributed by a well-
organized trade association willing to cooperate with the authorities, and there on a trickle of incidental information. It was for
instance impossible to obtain any details on the production of
rubber tires though there existed only five large factories in the
field. The number of cars produced had to be gauged from the
car licenses delivered by the police. By 1938 the index, though
looking deceptively complete, had become so unreliable that the
ministry decided to abandon its publication.

Shortly thereafter a new law tried to compel heads of enterprises to furnish such basic data as the volume of produced goods,
number of employees, and working hours. While the law was
praised by those business leaders who advocated effective organization and the abandonment of secretive practices, one of the

---

[1] The development of industrial statistics is retraced by one of its former
directors, Alfred Sauvy, "Les réformes statistiques utiles à l'évaluation du Revenu
National," in Conseil Economique, *Etudes et Travaux, Etude sur le Revenu
National*, Paris, 1951, pp. 144 ff. Writing as an official of the Vichy administration,
M. Sauvy had earlier described the same facts in a different light; see his contribution to *l'Organisation de la Production Industrielle. Collection Droit Social*, No. 7,
1941, pp. 19-20.

influential trade associations had seen to it that at the last moment all enforcement provisions were deleted from the statute.[2]
The decree laws enacted after Munich opened the way to a more
efficient handling of the problem; but immediately the question
arose whether it did not amount to creating a corporative system
if the understaffed administrative bureaus entrusted the trade
associations with the necessary powers to enforce the surrender
of statistical data.

The Vichy regime resolved such scruples by making it the foremost duty of the Organization Committees to establish and
continue a comprehensive economic census, backed by drastic
sanctions and delving into business details hitherto carefully
hidden from the outside world (and often from the owner's son).
It is generally admitted that the statistics gathered during that
troubled period of French history still form an indispensable
basis for present-day economic calculations.[3]

But just how reliable a basis was established then is justly
controversial. Undoubtedly the force of law seemed to have
achieved in many cases what attempted persuasion had been
unable to obtain. To the extent to which the Vichy legislation
contributed to the scaffolding of a more thoroughly organized
modern employers' movement, it created organizations which
considered it their duty to draw from their constituents as much
statistical information as possible.

On the other hand the statistics obtained through the Organization Committees suffered from the circumstances surrounding all
Vichy institutions. Since the enemy could be expected to use the
information for his own ends, it became an act of patriotism to be
as secretive as before, only under a new disguise: to lie outright
where in the past the firms had simply withheld information.
Years after the liberation the question of industrial statistics still
envenomed discussions between the employers and their antago-
nists. In the Economic Council a CGT delegate accused industry
of withholding basic statistical information now when the govern-

---

[2] For a much too optimistic evaluation of the pre-war legislation by a leader of
the CCOP, an employers' group which has been described earlier, see Monestier,
"Pour réaliser l'Organisation Professionnelle," *Nouveaux Cahiers*, III, No. 44,
May 1, 1939. In characteristic exaggeration this writer concluded that thereafter
business secrecy was to vanish.

[3] Interesting on that point is Ministère des Finances, etc., *op.cit.* (n. II-53), p. 57.

ment of the republic was asking for it, while the same data had been given to the occupation authorities. The CNPF retorted that the reluctance of its members could be explained by the fact that they had made false statements under the German occupation and were now compelled to revise all of their references.[4]

On the whole, different sectors of the employers' movement have since the war developed widely varying attitudes towards the general problem of economic stock-taking. In many trades the willingness of industrial and commercial firms to provide the authorities or their own trade associations with detailed data has lapsed again. The traditional reserve of the businessmen has slowed down the progress towards a greater transparency of business transactions and trends. In its publications the CNPF strives to offer as much reliable statistical information as it is able to obtain. But it lacks the authority that would be necessary to fill the existing gaps.

There are a number of trade associations which have established and steadily improved their statistical surveys and services, foremost among them that of the electrical equipment industries. Already before the war its executive, M. Davezac, had made the collection and publication of statistics the pivot of association activities. Today he claims that of the 2,000 concerns affiliated with the organization 85 percent, including many small firms, regularly furnish answers to questionnaires which cover an extremely wide field. But also many other trade associations have come to believe that their efficiency and prestige depend on their ability to extract from an often unwilling membership basic business information. There are fields such as those of the manufacture of rubber tires and industrial rubber, entire industries such as wool, where no data existed before the war and where now the trade associations collaborate closely with the government to insure a flow of valuable information. Also the steel industry and its organizations have made remarkable progress in establishing statistics including comparative cost studies. Elsewhere difficulties have arisen from the fact that even well-organized trade associations operate sometimes in too narrow a sector to make their data sufficiently meaningful. The leaders of trade associations, eager to improve statistical information, avow frankly, at

[4] See *Bulletin du Conseil Economique*, December 21, 1950, pp. 331, 336.

least in private conversations, how much they admire the excellence of American statistics and deplore the mentality which explains the insufficiency of their own data.[5] A group such as the *Jeune Patron* conducts a constant campaign among its membership for the improvement of statistical "morals."

In 1951 another law on "duties, coordination, and secrecy in statistical matters" attempted once more to make the surrender of certain statistical information compulsory and established moderate fines for non-observance. According to the law, trade associations and other employers' organizations can be entrusted by the government with the task of collecting the data; in that case they have to communicate only global figures and a list of the firms from which information has been obtained.[6] In fact the CNPF spared no effort to bring into being administrative ordinances insuring that the application of the law—deferred for more than two years—would not violate the needed anonymity of all firms offering information.[7]

But in industries such as wood, textile fabrics, leather goods, glass, and paper, where trade association statistics are either nonexistent or unreliable, the problem is still the same as in pre-war days: where the employers' organizations are incapable of providing the needed data, there is no possibility of enforcing the law. The insufficiently staffed ministry considers it useless to seek information from those industries where no "statistical habits" have been created. It is generally admitted that many years will have to pass before sufficiently complete basic data can be compiled to permit the establishment of a reliable national economic budget.[8]

[5] For a typical statement see Syndicat des Fabricants de Soieries, *op.cit.* (n. 11-5), Année 1951, p. 20: "Modern economic life, however much one may regret its trends (sic!), demands that statistical information be perfected, and, we must admit it, in that domain our industry has much to do. . . ."

[6] See the law of June 7, 1951, *J.O.*, June 8, pp. 6013-14.

[7] On these matters see *Bulletin*, XII, No. 81, May 5, 1952, p. 5; No. 84, July 20–August 5, 1952, p. 15; No. 122, August 1954, p. 82. Of late the newly established CNPF Committee on Professional and Economic Organization has made some energetic appeals for better business statistics; see *ibid.*, No. 129, February 1955, p. 15.

[8] For this and the foregoing see the highly interesting discussions, Service des études économique et financières du Ministère de Finance, *Rapport sur les comptes provisoires de la nation de l'année 1953 et sur le budget économique de l'année 1954*, hereafter referred to as *Mendès-France Report 1954*, esp. pp. 176, 190, 211-14, 219 f. Senator Armengaud, whose position has been discussed above (Chapter

Almost without exception the employers' movement is opposed to the very concept of an economic budget and to all methods concerned with collecting and evaluating the necessary information. After the work on the economic budget undertaken by the government had made progress and had come up for appraisal in the Economic Council, M. Meunier, vice-president of the CNPF, first voted in a sub-committee for the acceptance of the report with certain amendments. But because of violent protests voiced by the representatives of small business, M. Meunier had to declare in the plenary meeting that the employers' delegation would now have to reject the report since it "called for more reserves than originally formulated." When the so-called Mendès-France report incorporated the findings of the economic budget in a larger summary of "national accounts," the employers' delegation was almost the only group in the Economic Council not to approve of it, because it did not want to "sanction" the figures it contained.[9]

The CNPF was admittedly afraid that any kind of an economic budget might facilitate the intervention of the government in economic matters, or might also "explode" certain contradictions of over-all economic and financial policies.[10] But what the CNPF feared even more was to become in the eyes of its affiliates an auxiliary of the public authorities in their attempt to collect information which many a French businessman is still unwilling to surrender. When the employers' spokesmen voiced concern lest the obtained statistics could be used against the business community, and when they declared that most firms had neither the time nor the means to gather the desired data, they expressed the feelings of many of their constituents.

The "Malthusian" attitude of the businessmen towards economic forecasts is also illustrated by the results of a periodical inquiry which the National Institute of Statistics conducts among

---

V), showed himself particularly skeptical about the possibility of obtaining complete and reliable statistical information from industry.

[9] For the various discussions see *Bulletin du Conseil Economique*, December 21, 1950, p. 336; December 23, 1952, pp. 461-64, and May 13, 1953, pp. 173, 177. Actually a number of ranking CNPF officials had served as members of the Commission of National Accounts.

[10] On this aspect of the opposition to the economic budget in general, see Pierre Mendès-France and Gabriel Ardant, *Economics and Action*, Paris 1955, pp. 131-32.

a carefully selected panel of industrial firms. When asked to make prognoses concerning business conditions in the period immediately ahead, most employers underestimate the possibilities of their firms, large or small, and the ability of the market to absorb their products.

On another level, the lack of transparency of economic life takes on more general significance. Just because there is so little reliable information available on the distribution of national income, on the actual size of profits and of costs, on the degree of industrial concentration, every class and category has sufficient reasons, good or bad as the case may be, for envy and suspicion.

By their exaggerated concern for secrecy, many employers unwittingly contribute to the hostility of which they complain. Mutual distrust in turn will further the freezing of acquired positions and result in the rigidities which plague so many sectors of the French economy. And out of frustration and uncertainties are born the "myths" which are periodically shaking the foundations of society only to leave behind them renewed disappointment and aggravated resentment.

## 2. Economic Planning

"France is statist, a little by weakness, much by necessity."
Detoeuf, Preface to Paul Planus, *Patrons
et Ouvriers en Suède*

When the Provisional Government entrusted to M. Jean Monnet the task of preparing the "Plan of Modernization and Equipment," it accepted the alternative with which the commissariat for the plan prefaced its own action: "Modernization or decadence." In the post-liberation period the efforts centering around the Commissariat expressed the earnest desire for vigorous transformation and an almost spiritual faith that the sacrifices of war and occupation need not be excuses for exhaustion and laziness but could prove stimuli for progress.[11]

[11] The best authoritative materials on the plan are the periodic reports of the Commissariat, especially its first: Commissariat Général du Plan de Modernisation et d'Equipement, *Rapport Général sur le premier plan de modernisation et d'équipement*, Paris, 1947; and its final report: *Cinq ans d'exécution du Plan de modernisation et d'équipement de l'Union Française*, Paris, 1952. For the most interesting discussion of the major technical problems involved, see J. R. Rabier et al., "Le

But if Monnet and his collaborators were undoubtedly moved by faith in the virtues of economic planning, there was on their part no dogmatic commitment to any particular method of planning; they were obviously desirous of establishing first of all a flexible institutional setting to which neither the "liberals" nor the "interventionists" could easily object.[12] Modernization to them was not as much a condition of things as a state of mind which they wished to propagate widely. Hence Monnet appealed during the very first months of his activity to "practical men" representing on the working committees of the Commissariat most of the economic interests in the nation, whether organized or not.

Since the employers' movement was still in a state of flux when the Commissariat started to operate, and also because M. Monnet was unwilling to give to the trade associations any official status, the numerous business representatives on the Modernization Committees were invited individually rather than as spokesmen for their organizations.[13] However, when in November 1946 a full-dress meeting of the (consultative) council for the plan was convened to discuss the general report on the first plan, M. Ricard and M. Gingembre were invited to represent respectively the newly founded CNPF and the CGPME. In a speech which did not lack dramatic suspense, M. Ricard assured the Commissariat of the enthusiastic if carefully worded support of organized business.[14]

In the words of the first vice-president of the CNPF, who had done much to create the organization, the Plan of Modernization and Equipment corresponded to the general preoccupations of the new peak association. Also for Ricard the plan was an "act

Plan Monnet," *Collection Droit Social*, No. xxxvi, 1950. A good survey is contained in Pierre Uri (chief economist of the Monnet Office), "France: Reconstruction and Development," in Howard S. Ellis, ed., *The Economics of Freedom*, New York, 1950, pp. 269-74.

[12] The same point has been made in regard to M. Monnet's later creation, the Schuman plan, by Horst Mendershausen, "First Tests of the Schuman Plan," *Review of Economics and Statistics*, xxxv, 1953, p. 271.

[13] Interesting materials on the relationship between the employers' movement and the Commissariat are given in William H. Harbold, *The Monnet Plan: The French Experiment in National Economic Planning* (unpublished Ph.D. thesis), Harvard University, 1953.

[14] See *Bulletin*, No. 2, December 15, 1946, pp. 10-14. See *ibid.*, pp. 14-15, for M. Monnet's letter submitting the first plan to the CNPF.

of faith" to which he personally was ready to subscribe "in all sincerity and with complete loyalty."

By granting the profit motive an important place in the French economy, by speaking out for a better-balanced public budget and greater administrative efficiency, by assuring the organizations of business of constant consultation, M. Monnet had in advance eliminated the objections of the employers. This the vice-president of the CNPF recognized, though he had to admit that the majority of French businessmen might as yet see in the plan nothing but another experiment in *dirigisme*. While acknowledging that he was for the time being speaking mostly for himself and "for his friends forming the team at the helm of the CNPF," he pledged that the new leaders of the employers' movement would endeavor to spread their own concepts among their constituents and make them into disciplined and active supporters of the planning enterprise.

Today M. Ricard's speech remains a highly interesting testimony to the orientation which he and his associates intended to give to the employers' movement at that time. Neither the traditions of a Colbert and a Saint-Simon, alive in the general outlook of the plans, nor the intimate collaboration between government and business were strange to a Ricard, who had been, as he specifically reminded his audience, a *fonctionnaire* for seventeen years and who had behind him the recent experience as the director of an influential Organization Committee.

In line with the pledged collaboration the CNPF recommended to its principal member federations the adaptation of their production programs to the plan. As long as the General Assemblies of the CNPF remained the forum of lively discussions among the delegates, exchanges of controversial views on the merits of the Commissariat usually held the foreground with M. Ricard defending the plan as "serious, intellectually honest, objective, and impartial."[15]

Most of the press close to business circles reported favorably on the objectives and methods of the commissariat. The ACADI group gave to the plan its most enthusiastic support; in an ad-

[15] For discussion within the CNPF, see esp. *ibid.*, No. 3, February 1947, pp. 12-13; for the directives of the peak association to its affiliates, see Harbold, *op.cit.* (n. VI-13), p. 128.

dress before members of parliament the group's president, M. Perrin, discussed constructively the broad aspects of a planned reconstruction of the economy.[16] The executive of the National Steel Association, M. Charvet, expressed himself more guardedly but still in fundamental agreement with the objectives of a plan and especially with the idea of creating an office in charge of developing long-range economic policies.[17]

The industry representatives on the various working committees of the plan took from the very first an attitude of only cautious approval. They invariably would show concern whether there would be a sufficient market for the increased production called for by the plan. They would hedge whenever the plan recommended structural reforms such as the merger of enterprises and the elimination of the most unproductive firms. When after the demise of the Industrial Offices the law had designated the trade associations as agents for the sub-allocation of rationed raw materials, most of the employers' organizations undertook that assignment in the spirit of economic Malthusianism on which the Monnet plan had declared war. In order to avoid reproaches from their membership, the trade associations simply allocated the raw materials on the basis of the needs that had existed—in 1938. Such a static method obviously eluded all responsibility for eliminating the unfit and favoring the productive firms.[18]

On the whole, however, the impetus in favor of modernization and reequipment was during the first years of the plan still strong enough to balance retardatory behavior. In some instances the staff of the Commissariat was able to play one industry group against the other: when for fear of over-production the Wendel group of the steel industry refused to install a continuous strip mill, the companies located in the north of the country and grouped in the USINOR combine eagerly availed themselves of the opportunity to outdistance the production of their competitors. This led later to similar modernizations and a reorganization

[16] See the interesting press review in *Bulletin ACADI*, No. 2, January 1947, pp. 19-28, and, for M. Perrin's speech, *ibid.*, No. 6, May 1947, pp. 1-6. At that period also *France Documents*, which has been described above as the mouthpiece of prominent industrial federations, joined the chorus of friendly voices; see its special issue on the plan, No. 5, March 1947.

[17] See Louis Charvet, "La Reconstruction et le Plan," *Politique*, xx, May-June 1946, pp. 445-60.

[18] See on this point Lasserre, *op.cit.* (n. III-3), p. 118.

of the eastern companies into the SOLLAC and the SIDELOR combines.[19]

But little by little the opposition of business to the Monnet plan became more resolute and more outspoken. The continuous, if unevenly paced, inflation was not only detrimental to the objectives of the plan; it also bolstered the penchant of the business group towards insubordination and routinism.[20]

When it turned out that the investment program of the Monnet plan obviously entailed sacrifices, parliament and the organized interests influential with the deputies became increasingly reluctant to lend their support. It now became evident that the policies of the Monnet Plan Office had been merely the concern of an elite and had roused very little interest in public opinion at large.[21]

As so often, M. Gingembre personified the attitudes of the average small businessman. At the first meeting of the Planning Council in 1946 he too had approved of the plan. But in the years that followed he expressed the feelings of his followers when he denounced the work of the Commissariat as an enterprise of a technocracy without interest to the masses of businessmen.

In their meetings and associations the employers began to speak cynically about grandiose schemes of modernization which were meaningless in terms of their daily experiences and of the seemingly insurmountable obstacles which they had to meet in operating their firms. If faith had been, in the language common to M. Monnet and M. Ricard, indispensable to the success of the plan, that faith had already crumbled.

Also the personal relations between industry and the commissariat deteriorated under the stress of administrative and economic disorder. In the conflict between the Ministry of Finance and the Ministry of National Economy, the Commissariat usually sided

[19] For highly interesting details on the present status of the steel industry in various regions, see *Le Monde des Affaires, op.cit.* (n. I-37), pp. 121-30.

[20] Very illuminating on the impact of inflation on the Monnet plan are Pickles, *op.cit.* (n. v-59), pp. 68-69, and Uri, *op.cit.* (n. VI-11), pp. 247 ff. For the reaction of businessmen to the inflation, see below, this chapter.

[21] In April 1948 a public opinion poll revealed that only 22 percent of those questioned knew that the plan was in effect; 34 percent had never heard about it. When asked to classify certain specifically named tasks facing the government in order of urgency, 21 percent of those who had heard about the Monnet plan relegated it to the bottom. See *Sondages*, November 15, 1948.

with the advocates of continuing controls against the more liberal Finance Ministry, mainly because of the danger which every inflationary pressure presented to their enterprise, and also because of the Christian-socialist outlook of many of Monnet's younger staff members. If that displeased many spokesmen for business, the administrative independence of the "planners" became even more bothersome, especially after the business lobby had regained its former ascendancy over parliamentary committees and the traditional administrative bureaus. While also the Commissariat had some finance inspectors on its staff, it remained the only agency of economic administration to avoid control by the *grands corps* with which big business was on a particularly cordial footing.

During most of the first plan's running time the CNPF as such abstained from formulating a clear position towards the issues involved. In typical fashion leading personalities in the CNPF would comment afterwards that "not all has been bad, not all has been good in the plan." M. Migeon, active in some of the employers' movement vanguard groups and widely respected for the achievements of his firm, the *Télémécanique*, was far more positive and declared publicly that "the direct and especially the indirect benefits of the Monnet plan have been considerable."[22] But on the whole the employers' peak association left it to the major trade associations to continue individual collaboration with the Commissariat while others were permitted to attack violently an undertaking supported by their colleagues.

The fact that the steel industry obtained the largest single share (16 percent) of any investments allocated by the Modernization Plan to the private sector of the economy formed a natural basis of continuing understanding between the National Steel Association and the Commissariat: between 1947 and 1951 almost one-third of the total investments in the steel industry came from various public funds.[23] When, shortly before the outbreak of the Korean War, parliament sought to curtail modernization credits, those trade associations whose industries had particularly profited

---

[22] See his address in CIERP, *Productivité mais . . .* , Paris, 1952, p. 133.

[23] See Commissariat Général du Plan, *Cinq ans d'exécution*, etc., *op.cit.* (n. VI-11), pp. 67-69, 320-21, and the *Mendès-France Report 1953*, *op.cit.* (n. IV-4), p. 50 ff. For details on the collaboration between the Steel Association and the Commissariat see Harbold, *op.cit.* (n. VI-13), pp. 48 ff.

from the plan, such as steel, electrical equipment, shipbuilding, and petroleum, proved valuable allies of the Monnet Office in its eventually successful efforts to have the credits restored. It seems that at the time also the services of the CNPF lent their support and influence to achieve that result.

At the same time other affiliates of the CNPF, and not only the representatives of small business, started a vituperative campaign against the Monnet plan. It was claimed that the nationalized sector had been unduly favored and that the private sector of industry had hardly profited at all from either Monnet or Marshall plan funds. While this was in itself a vast exaggeration,[24] such arguments also neglected the fact that the first Modernization Plan had given deliberate emphasis to basic industries, whether public or private, and that many private industries outside the scope of the first plan had indirectly benefited through increased orders from the expansion of capacity in the basic sectors.

The most energetic spokesman for the critics became M. Métral, who had been placed at the helm of the Association of Engineering and Metal-Processing Industries (and on the Executive of the CNPF) shortly before the fight against the ratification of the Schuman plan treaty began in earnest. In his speeches and articles M. Métral lashed out against *dirigisme* in general but also played cleverly on the fears of those French businessmen who instinctively dread a "socialism" at home supported by dollar subsidies.[25] Yet it turned out that the attacks which were presented as a principled opposition to state intervention were to a large extent merely preparing the terrain for obtaining a larger share of public investment credits for the metal trades and other secondary industries.

[24] While between 1947 and 1951, nationalized industries obtained from public funds investment credits in the amount of 1,016 billion francs, the private sector drew from the same sources 810 billion. Thirty-six percent of the total investments in private industries were derived from government subsidies. Though this proportion was substantially higher for the nationalized sector, it must not be forgotten that the latter does not have access to certain modes of financing which are available to private concerns.

[25] As examples see the speech by M. Métral, reproduced in *Bulletin*, No. 80, April 5, 1952, pp. 10-11; his article "Investissements et exportations," *Nouvelle Revue d'Economie Contemporaine*, No. 35, November 1952, pp. 12-14; and, with a frankness bordering on brutality, his article "La coupe est pleine," *Les Industries Mécaniques*, No. 78, November 1951, pp. 1-8.

The pressures to switch the emphasis of the second Modernization Plan towards the manufacturing industries were largely successful. This time the Commissariat itself favored substantial production increases of between 60 and 70 percent in building activities, in the engineering, electrical, textile, and other secondary industries. Such increases were incorporated into the overall goal of the plan to raise the national product between 1953 and 1957 by one-fourth. Investments from public funds are to account for about half of the total investments and to benefit the private sector to a considerable extent.[26]

As soon as the work in preparation for the second Modernization Plan had begun, the CNPF study committee on the plan reported regularly on the progress made.[27] Industry representatives participated once more actively in the meetings of the working groups at the Commissariat. It is true that the more solemn mood which had prevailed at the elaboration of the first plan was now superseded by practical and sometimes hard bargaining concerned with the distribution of investment credits. But in return the employers' movement was willing to defend the plan, as it was evolved in numerous meetings between the representatives of interest groups and the administration, against efforts made by parliament to tinker with the technicalities and over-all objectives of the plan. In significant terms the CNPF committee remarked: ". . . [We] believe that the second plan is the result of labors by experts of administration and of industry. Their report explains objectively the problems faced by the French economy and proposes lines of action which should be followed during the four years of the plan's running time. The efficiency of such action depends on a continuity which must be maintained in spite of possible changes of political orientation."[28] Such language was

[26] For the text of the second plan see *J.O. Documents parlementaires. Annexes aux procès-verbaux des scéances*, Annexe No. 8555 à la Scéance du 1 Juin 1954, pp. 899-939, and the interesting reports by the Economic Council and its committees in *J.O. Avis et Rapports du Conseil Economique*, August 3, 1954, pp. 650-728. For a critical appraisal see Alfred Sauvy, "La Situation Economique," *Droit Social*, XVII, 1954, pp. 395-97.

[27] The Committee's chairman is M. René Norguet, a productivity-conscious engineer with an honorable record in the resistance movement who has become the director of a shipbuilding concern after long years of government service.

[28] See *Bulletin*, No. 129, February 1955, p. 35; for other CNPF reports commenting favorably on the progress of the second plan, see *ibid.*, No. 103, July 20, 1953, pp. 13-14; No. 114, February 5, 1954, pp. 27-28; No. 122, August 1954, pp.

all the more remarkable because the CNPF seemed thereby to subscribe also to those parts of the second plan which acknowledged that its goals could not be reached without determined reforms of the country's economic structure. Among the evils to be overcome the plan mentioned, besides a general lack of elasticity and the immobility of the labor force, the existence of too great a number of obsolete industrial and commercial firms.

How actively the leadership of the CNPF will strive to enlist the support of its affiliates for the policies advocated by the plan remains to be seen. When the plan had come up for consideration in the Economic Council, the employers' group voted unanimously against a motion endorsing it; characteristically enough they avoided a public commitment to which especially the representatives of small business were unwilling to subscribe.[29] But such an attitude does not augur well for the forcefulness of the CNPF in convincing its membership of the need for establishing the priorities which the plan envisages.

Altogether the vagaries of French politics have transformed considerably the original impulse for planning and modernization. Unlike the first plan, which was designed for action, the second, formally accepted long after its running time had started, is in many respects not much more than an instrumentality for economic forecasts, comparable to the reports of the Council of Economic Advisers in the United States. In addition various cabinets and ministries have come forward with their own "plans," mostly designed to allocate investments from public funds for shorter periods. Inasmuch as they are all concerned with increases of production and productivity, they could be considered a tribute to M. Monnet's fundamental concept. But they have also brought back to the field of economic policies the jumbled and often wasteful approach which characterized the pre-war period.[30]

---

16-17. For an equally sympathetic view on the plan in a publication close to the steel industry see *L'Usine Nouvelle*, VIII, No. 48, November 27, 1952, p. 3.

[29] See *Bulletin du Conseil Economique*, July 9, 1954, pp. 398-420. These discussions showed the employers delegation singularly devoid of candidness, especially in view of the attitude taken by the CNPF Committee before and after these debates in the Economic Council.

[30] A good general view on the various plans and funds is given in *Bulletin*, No. 117, March 20, 1954, pp. 13-15, and *ibid.*, No. 130, March 1955, pp. 31-35. Very critical is Jean Constant (formerly active in the employers' movement), "Les Plans Louvel et Edgar Faure," *Le Monde*, March 10, 1955.

In such a situation the employers' movement is able to collaborate empirically with the administration in policies which are the reverse of economic liberalism without having openly to abandon traditional hostility to governmental intervention in business. "One can say," two well-informed observers have concluded, "that all economic policy is located on two planes: on a plane of declarations where principles are affirmed; and on a plane of daily action where the only search is for means of implementing exceptions to the affirmed principles."[31]

While this criticism was primarily addressed to governmental policies, it is equally applicable to the behavior of organized business. The president of the CNPF lends personal and enthusiastic support to *La Libre Entreprise*, which denounces practically all governmental activities as pernicious. Its propaganda against *dirigisme* describes bureaucratic wastefulness, social costs of production, nationalizations, and investment policies as fitting into a compound picture of paralyzing tyranny.[32] At the same time members of the CNPF Executive and staff sympathetically view economic planning policies which are characteristic of a rather advanced stage of *dirigisme*.

M. Fabre, who for a long time was the ranking staff member in charge of economic questions in the CNPF, developed before a trade union audience moderate and realistic views about the role of government and administration in the economy.[33] The factual *Bulletin* of the CNPF frequently acknowledges the benefits which private industry derives from investments out of public funds, while a magazine subsidized by the same organization is permitted to criticize the investment policies as dangerous to free enterprise.[34]

---

[31] Paul Delouvrier and Roger Nathan, *Politique économique de la France*, Cours à l'Université de Paris, 1953-54, Fasc. III, p. 22. M. Delouvrier's position has been described earlier; M. Nathan has changed from a high administrative post to prominent business positions and the chairmanship of the CNPF Committee on Trade Liberalization.

[32] For details see above, Chapter V.

[33] See Robert Fabre, "Rôle de l'Etat, des Administrations Economiques et des Professions dans la Vie Economique," Supplement to the *Bulletin*, III, No. 28, February 15, 1949, pp. 1-7.

[34] Cf., e.g., the account on public investments in *Bulletin*, No. 116, March 5, 1954, pp. 7-9, with the article by Féraud, "La liaison des Plans Monnet et Marshall," *La Nouvelle Revue de l'Economie Contemporaine*, quoted in Laurat et al., *op.cit.* (n. III-6), p. 259.

The clue to such patent contradictions is partly to be found in the divergent interests of the movement's affiliates. To develop among the members of the business community more realistic insights into the role of governmental action in economic life would require a long-term "educational" campaign which neither the CNPF nor the principal trade associations feel able or authorized to undertake. Since also cabinet instability prevents the government from enlightening the public, the French businessman is generally left without knowledge of the economic and financial conditions under which he operates.

Particularly in those regions which are least affected by economic and social progress, the lowest common denominator for the ill-defined interests of a large part of the urban business community and of the rural population is a common hostility to *dirigisme*.[35] That hostility is frequently kindled by the propaganda of the employers' movement, or at least by the absence of any advice which would run counter to current beliefs.

Another, and perhaps the foremost, reason for prevailing uncertainties resides in the fact that the issue at stake is not really one between free and planned economy. The true controversy centers around the question as to who should be in charge of the planning, the administration or organized business? Will the *dirigisme* be directed by an independent bureaucracy or by the accredited representatives of industrial "self-government"? Since the schemes for economic planning in post-war France contain elements of both solutions, the employers' movement continues to be ambivalent towards them.

## 3. Investment, Price, and Monetary Policies

When compared with other countries of western and northwestern Europe, France lags, in spite of her rapid post-war recovery, in per capita industrial output, in per capita consumption of such basic commodities as steel, cement, and energy, and in the increase of employment in the engineering and chemical industries. In terms of average per capita income, the United Kingdom and most of the smaller northwest European countries

[35] On this point see the pertinent observations by Goguel, *op.cit.* (n. v-56), p. 145.

now exceed France, once the richest country in Europe, by one-fifth or more. Also Germany is rapidly overtaking France in this respect.[36]

If French statistics, taking usually the year 1938 as a reference, present a more encouraging picture, it must not be forgotten that on the eve of the Second World War industrial and agricultural production hardly exceeded the level of 1914.[37] The relatively rapid and in many fields massive recovery which set in after 1946 was not able to overcome simultaneously the war losses and the economic slowdown from which France had suffered in the 1930's.

At present, the economic health of the country is being scrutinized more than ever before by foreign and French observers. The collapse in 1940, the political strains which the resurrected republic began to show almost immediately, the importance which cold war strategies bestowed on France and her empire have led inside and outside the country to unending discussions about the merits and errors of the economic policies pursued since the war. From the beginning, French businessmen have been in the center of these discussions. Accusations against them have come from such strange bedfellows as French communists and American business executives, from conservative politicians and liberal intellectuals in France, from United States and from United Nations reports.

Attacked from many sides for their failure to espouse resolutely the cause of economic and technical progress and to introduce overdue changes of business structure, the employers, individually and through their organizations, have retorted with indictments of government and the political system, of competing interests, and of outside influences whether emanating from Moscow or

[36] For these data see the periodic reports of the U.N. Economic Commission for Europe esp. *Economic Survey of Europe Since the War*, Geneva, 1953, hereafter referred to as *U.N. Report 1953*, pp. 78-81, and *Economic Survey of Europe in 1954*, Geneva, 1955, hereafter referred to as *U.N. Report 1954*, esp. pp. 174 ff, and the important charts in Ingvar Svennilson, *Growth and Stagnation in the European Economy*, Geneva, 1954, esp. pp. 204-13. For a French survey of the fields in which France is badly lagging behind other European countries, see "Le grand sommeil de l'Economie Française," *Réalités*, No. 92, September 1953, pp. 56-59.

[37] The best survey of the stagnation of the French economy between the two World Wars is provided by Charles Bettelheim, *Bilan de l'Economie Française, 1919-1946*, Paris, 1947.

Washington. Some of the partisan discussions have attempted to saddle businessmen with responsibilities which were not theirs or which they have inherited from preceding generations. In their refutations the official spokesmen for business when discussing price, investment, and monetary policies have painted a black-and-white picture of their own and have tried to disculpate completely their constituents.

Also the debates on the reasons for the "slumber of the French economy" are envenomed by the fact that in the words of the Commission of National Accounts, "of all developed nations, France is undoubtedly the least informed about its economy."[38] Such obscurity, the report states, does not increase the freedom of action for the individual enterprise. On the one hand the empirical and haphazard regulatory interventions about which business complains, and, on the other the overcautious view of marketing possibilities which business usually takes are based on the lack of reliable information about present status and future alternatives of the economy. Under such conditions, "the only freedom that remains is that of error, waste, and panic, apart from the hypothesis of lucky accidents."[39]

In such a complicated field as that of monetary, price, and investment policies, not only the lack of information but also the admittedly deficient economic education of the average French businessman and even of many business leaders proves an additional handicap.[40]

It is beyond the scope of this study to discuss the reasons for the gap in French economic theory and instruction, still largely subservient to the law schools. With the sole exception of the *Ecole des Hautes Etudes Commerciales*, most of the institutions preparing for the higher echelons of a business career offered to

[38] See *Mendès-France Report 1953, op.cit.* (n. IV-4), p. 11.

[39] The notorious insufficiency of economic information has led some of the keenest observers of the French economy—among them Albert Sauvy, Pierre Mendès-France, Paul Delouvrier, and many finance inspectors to an opposite exaggeration: they sometimes express the opinion that a greater amount of economic information and education is all that is needed to transform the country. The will to act would still be necessary even after more insight had been won.

[40] See especially Mendès-France, "Equilibre Economique et Progrès social," *La Nef*, Nouvelle Serie, June 1953, speaking (p. 239) about the "economic ignorance extending to the elites." For interesting suggestions as to how to overcome the lag in theory and instruction, see M. Allais, "Les chances actuelles de la pensée économique française," *Le Monde*, August 9, 1953.

their students, at least prior to the war, an altogether insufficient training in economics.[41] The vast majority of businessmen, especially those entering a family business, quit school after their secondary education, which for all its general excellence does not provide even a basic knowledge of the economic process.

Since the war, various reforms of higher education have attempted to remedy that situation. The impact of the Harvard Business School and similar American institutions has undoubtedly made itself felt. Yet many businessmen, and among them corporation executives and interest group officials, still think little of giving more room to economics in the curricula of the foremost educational institutions. They argue that the technical knowledge acquired in such schools as the School of Mines and the *Ecole Centrale*, or the precise mathematical or legal training in which the law schools, the "X," and the pre-war *Ecole des Sciences Politiques* specialized, are all that is needed before the business executive acquires practical experience in the firm. Frequently training in economics proper is considered not only as "bookish," but also as providing a false perspective for the running of an individual enterprise. Hence what outside observers and critical businessmen alike sometimes characterize as signs of an "intellectual laziness" among French employers results often from an inability to understand basic economic problems, let alone the intricacies of that bizarre mixture of tradition and innovation which the French economy presents.

*          *          *

To say that for some time the French people as a whole have been permeated by an inflationist mentality is hardly exaggerated. Not that the consumer likes the rise in prices which reduces his purchasing power. Not that the businessman particularly enjoys a situation which deprives him of the possibility of exact cost calculation and of comparisons among his suppliers. But in situations which call for prolonged sacrifices, no individual or group which can help it is willing to avoid further inflation by such sacrifices. With the few exceptions of entirely unprotected categories of citizens, "the French people have had forty years in

[41] For a survey of the institutions of higher learning training the business elite, see *Le Monde des Affaires etc.*, *op.cit.* (n. I-37), pp. 566-74.

which to learn how private advantage can be maximized (or disadvantages minimized) in inflationary conditions."[42]

The basis for the long-lasting and progressive inflation was laid before and during the First World War when the French government, with the full assent of industry, relied less on taxes and far more on loans than other democracies for the financing of armaments. After the war the floating debt was steadily increased, once more with the applause of business, though it sharply criticized at the same time the growing budgetary deficits.[43] Since then, even when deflationary trends have prevailed for a time as before 1936 and during the occupation, they have not succeeded in bringing about stability. Whenever the wage earners were eliminated from political influence, wage adjustments tended to be delayed until the finally unavoidable increase was likely to be substantial and brought about a fresh rise in prices.

While between 1914 and 1939 the annual depreciation of the franc amounted to an average of eight percent, the depreciation between 1939 and 1948 rose to a yearly average of forty percent and was resumed after the outbreak of the Korean war. The most striking feature of post-war developments remained the alternation between periods of industrial expansion and rising prices and periods of price stability, during which industrial production increased negligibly. Obviously the French economy has been less able than other countries of Western Europe to combine full employment and rapid economic expansion with monetary stability.[44]

The trade associations have been unwilling to acknowledge that inflation is not only the cause but also the consequence of economic disorder. They have accredited the beliefs of most

[42] *U.N. Report 1953, op.cit.* (n. VI-36), p. 79. Excellent on the generalized inflationist "mentality" Mendès-France, *op.cit.* (n. VI-40), pp. 210-12 and, not without reproaches addressed to his fellow-employers, Michel Flichy, "Réflexions sur la monnaie et l'économie conduisant à la politique," *Jeune Patron,* VIII, January 1955, pp. 15, 17.

[43] On the role which the spokesmen for business played in the debate on the financing of the First World War and on its consequences, see Beau de Loménie, *op.cit.* (n. I-93), Vol. III, esp. pp. 26, 156, 232-33. But also Gignoux, whose outlook is far more friendly to business than that of Beau de Loménie, is equally critical; see his *op.cit.* (n. I-31), p. 128.

[44] *U.N. Report 1953, op.cit.* (n. VI-36), pp. 78, 128. For many details on the post-war inflation, see also Uri, *op.cit.* (n. VI-11), pp. 247 ff.

French businessmen that instability of governmental policies and the costliness of public administration are solely responsible for monetary instability and high prices. Undoubtedly monetary and price policies bore the earmarks of much hesitation and conflicting views after the liberation; today divergent concepts still lead to conflicts among different government services. It is equally true that an administrative structure dating back to the Consulate of the first Napoleon operates expensively: in 1952 government expenditures for civilian goods and services were about ten percent higher than in Great Britain for instance. But businessmen commonly exaggerate the significance of these factors. A poll revealed that in their opinion the salaries of civil servants amounted to fifty or sixty percent of total government expenditures while actually the share is not higher than fifteen percent. In the opinion of one observer, "such errors are intentionally maintained by a systematic propaganda, subsidized by large business firms."[45]

Their simplifying views hide from the businessmen their own responsibility for monetary instability and the extent to which they, like almost everybody else, have installed themselves, more or less comfortably, in the environment of an inflationary economy. No sooner had the CNPF been created than it insisted, in spite of continuing scarcities, on rapidly abandoning all economic and price controls. In the fall of 1946 when M. Ricard expressed his agreement with the resolve of the Monnet plan to sustain prolonged austerity for the sake of massive investments, his organization had already concluded agreements which led to sharp inflationary price rises and thereby endangered the objectives of the plan.

At the so-called Palais-Royal conferences, the organizations of business, labor, and agriculture had agreed on supporting their mutual requests for substantial wage and price increases. The employers in particular were willing to grant wage increases so as to strengthen their demands for the lifting of price controls. The government, torn by internal dissensions, had abdicated its role as an arbiter and left the responsibility for their decisions to

---

[45] Sauvy, "La situation économique," *Droit Social*, xviii, 1955, pp. 279-80. For a comparison of administrative expenditures in selected countries see *U.N. Report 1954, op.cit.* (n. vi-36), p. 176.

the interest groups. As a consequence the inflationary spiral began to function again.[46] Worse yet, a precedent was set, and for the ensuing two years vacillating government policies and the pressure of interest groups combined to aggravate the process of inflation. Capital and labor agreed also on other policies which by hampering production widened the gap between supply and demand. Although practically full employment has prevailed in post-war France, M. Ricard stated in the Economic Council that the CNPF shared the views of the communist trade union leader who had warned against increasing the flow of immigrant labor.[47]

When the employers' movement backed the "Pinay experiment" in 1952, it expressed its agreement with the premier's intention to use moral persuasion and a slump in world prices for price stabilization. Pinay's somewhat surprising popularity seemed to indicate that for the first time since the war businessmen and wage earners alike were willing to abandon immediate advantages for the sake of monetary stability. But also Pinay was caught in the dilemma of French post-war economy: his price and investment policies led, in spite of the continuing armament boom, to a painful recession in many fields. Only an expanding production could have dispelled permanently the still threatening atmosphere of inflation.[48] Two years later when Mendès-France sought to escape the dilemma by practicing a policy of "priorities" and by proposing to eliminate the dead weight of unproductive economic protectionism, he was opposed by most of organized business.[49]

There is little doubt that in present-day France "the tasks of

[46] Excellent on the significance of the Palais Royal agreements (to be discussed for their impact on industrial relations below Chapter IX), Gérard Dehove, "Le Mouvement Ouvrier et la Politique Syndicale," *Revue d'Economie Politique*, LVIII, 1948, p. 1249; Delouvrier, *op.cit.* (n. II-52), pp. 331-32, and especially Georges Boris, "Monnaie, Progrès, Stagnation, Décadence," *La Nef*, Nouvelle Serie x, June 1953, p. 184. For the early requests of the CNPF to lift price controls, see *Bulletin*, No. 2, December 15, 1946, p. 3.

[47] See *Bulletin du Conseil Economique*, July 31, 1948, p. 1025. On the manpower and immigration needs of the French economy, see *U.N. Report 1954, op.cit.* (n. VI-36), esp. pp. 193-94.

[48] Interesting on the temptations which the inflationist mentality held out to businessmen also under the Pinay government, is Maurice Duverger, "La Nostalgie de l'Inflation," *Le Monde*, December 20, 1952.

[49] When Mendès-France explained his position to an audience of the *Jeune Patron* movement he won however the admiration of the group's leadership. See "La Monnaie et l'Economie," *Jeune Patron*, VI, July-August 1952, pp. 15-20.

the state are too heavy, too numerous, and too costly."[50] But an analysis of budgetary figures shows that the state, accused from many quarters of too much *dirigisme* actually directs far less than it protects. Long-term economic planning might actually be less costly than the haphazard practice of economic subsidies and other economic and social transfers. It is altogether impossible to evaluate the total cost of such operations, listed as they are under many different treasury accounts. An influential member of the CNPF, president of its Tax Committee, put the amount of governmental subsidies to private enterprise for 1954 at 500 billion francs, without indicating how he had arrived at that figure.[51] Even a full discussion of all traceable economic subsidies would still not reveal how many other civil and military expenditures of the state have the effect of an indirect subsidy. But most French businessmen who complain about the size of the public budget have only the haziest of notions about the incidence of government expenditure for their own firms.[52]

The considerable governmental *dirigisme* which has survived war-time controls in matters of price and investment policies not only operates frequently for the benefit of private enterprise but also in close conjunction with the latter's defense organizations. Here public and private *dirigisme* complement rather than oppose each other. In the words of the Commission of National Accounts, "the proliferation of administrative rulings, of admitted or occult protections leads to a situation where the price of each commodity has nothing to do any more with economic laws. It can be justified only by a monographic description which takes into account not only the technical structure of the branch but also the number of producers, *their political influence, their sociological solidarity.*"[53]

[50] See the declaration by Premier Edgar Faure in *Le Monde*, October 6, 1953.
[51] See *Bulletin*, VIII, No. 114, February 5, 1954, p. 9. For a realistic discussion of the question whether and which public expenses could be reduced, see Jeanneney, *op.cit.* (n. IV-26), pp. 231 f.
[52] In the specialized employers' press speaking for big business such insights are not lacking. See e.g., the remarks in *L'Usine Nouvelle*, February 26, 1953: "Our economy depends more and more on public credits. . . . One understands therefore with how much vigilant attention—not free from anxiety—the business world is watching governmental decisions concerning such credits."
[53] *Mendès-France Report 1953, op.cit.* (n. IV-4), p. 55 (emphasis supplied). Excellent on these points also is Jarrier, *op.cit.* (n. V-69), pp. 898-901.

At which points do "political influence" and "sociological solidarity" enter the price picture?

In present-day France there are still specifically government-fixed prices, prices which are in the category of "controlled freedom," and free prices.[54] Where prices are fixed by the government, the authorities rely on the trade associations for selecting three "representative" firms (large, medium, and small) and for submitting data used in determining the "average" production costs of these firms. For the long list of industrial prices and services which are still under the regime of "controlled freedom," the trade associations submit their proposals for maximum prices directly to the Ministry of National Economy, and the role of the government is reduced to the rare exercise of a veto right. Whenever prices were "freed," the trade associations were unhampered in their own price-fixing and attempted to enforce the prices stipulated in cartel and similar agreements, at least until the Pinay and Laniel governments took their decrees against private price-fixing.[55]

The importance which trade associations have in the determination of all prices was explicitly acknowledged when Premiers Pinay and Laniel, both active businessmen, relied heavily in their campaigns for price reduction on the business organizations. The psychological significance of such collaboration between government and organized business seems to have been greater than the decline of prices, which remained insignificant. At the very time when legislation was introduced to limit the price-fixing activities of the trade associations and of their cartels, the role which the government assigned to them in obtaining lowered prices reinforced the apparatus and the cohesion of the same associations.[56]

The government has at times been vigorously criticized for having placed in its price policies so much reliance on the employers' movement. The remarkable report in which the Economic Council analyzed in 1948 the reasons for the continuing

[54] For a fairly recent description of price regulations, see Ministère de Finance, "La Réglementation Actuelle des Prix," *Statistiques et Etudes Financières*, No. 74, February 1955, pp. 113-22.

[55] For a full discussion of the cartels and effectiveness of governmental control action see below Chapter VIII.

[56] For a pertinent remark on this point, see Sauvy, "La Situation Economique," *Le Droit Social*, VII, 1952, p. 452.

inflation called upon the government to muster the necessary "courage" and to eliminate the trade associations from all price-fixing. Once this residue of the Vichy legislation on the CO was liquidated, the report went on to say, there was hope that the employers' movement would be freed for such needed tasks as lowering the costs of production and distribution. In their comment, the employers' representatives on the Council did not deny the influence of organized business on the government in matters of price formation but argued that it was highly beneficial.

Still five years later the director of price controls in the Ministry of National Economy described the unchanged practices of price-fixing as sheer corporatism rather than as state intervention. According to him the maximum prices (and most prices will invariably conform to the maximum) are set so that they "correspond to the average necessary for all enterprises to live." That means that either by explicit agreement or, more frequently, by unconscious adaptation to the social milieu, the best-equipped and productive firms sell at prices permitting marginal firms a precarious survival, and efficient units large margins for self-financing (or capital export).[57]

"The insufficiency of our productivity," Premier Pleven, a conservative and once a businessman himself, declared in the National Assembly, "the entirely too high price level of some manufactured goods results sometimes from the practices inspired by the worst of *dirigisme* which allows inefficient producers to survive without seeking progress, and others to make excessive profits, all to the detriment of the community. . . . The price of liberty is competition."[58]

After relative monetary stability had been established in 1952 and inflationary pressures had subsided, the discussion centered mostly on the discrepancy between French and world market prices. In spite of multiple efforts, the former continue to be on the average about ten to fifteen percent higher than the latter. Succeeding governments or competing ministries have entrusted to one committee after another a study of the reasons for the

[57] See Louis R. Franck, "Planisme français et démocratie," *Revue Economique*, IV, 1953, pp. 210, 211, 218.

[58] *J.O. Débats Ass. Nationale*, August 9, 1951, p. 6252. The report of the debates notes at this point: "applause from the left, the center and the right."

disparity in prices. The employers' movement has praised or criticized the often contradictory conclusions of the committees, depending on whether or not they were in agreement with the views which business held on price developments.

In the interminable discussion, two series of factors are generally put forward to explain the high price level: cost elements whose incidence is not determined by business, such as tax structure, interest rates, and the so-called "social charges" of the wage payrolls; and costs which result from the structure of French industry, trade, and agriculture.[59]

The CNPF has consistently taken the view that the "external" factors in combination with the devastating legacy of the inflation were alone to blame. The data which the employers' movement collected to prove its point did not lack cogency and pointed up some of the existing discrepancies.[60] But other studies, especially those by the Office of Price Controls and by the Nathan Committee (a special governmental committee), have attached in their explanations of the French price level equal if not greater importance to "Malthusian" practices, of which the artificial survival of marginal producers and the methods of price-fixing are important but not the only expressions. Since M. Nathan himself is a business leader who takes a prominent part in the activities of the CNPF, it was particularly painful for the employers' movement that his report highlighted those factors which organized business refuses to recognize as a valid explanation of the French plight.[61]

Similarly, René Mayer, another premier with close business connections, explained before parliament the price disparity by

[59] For an incisive general view on the discussion about the price controversy, see Louis Rosenstock-Franck, the director of price controls in the ministry of Economic Affairs, in a speech made before an audience of progressive businessmen, *Pourquoi nos prix sont-ils trop chers?* Paris, 1953, esp. pp. 7 ff.

[60] For the most complete and very able statement of the employers' position formulated by a committee under the chairmanship of M. Fayol, manager of the Boussac interests, see "Les causes de la disparité des prix français et étrangers, Supplement to the *Bulletin*, No. 88, November 20, 1952, pp. 1-11.

[61] See "Le Rapport de la Commission Nathan," *Bulletin*, VIII, No. 118, April 1954, pp. 35-36 and Georges Villiers, "Le Déséquilibre Réel de l'Economie Française appelle des réformes urgentes," *ibid.*, No. 120, June 1954, p. 2. For a critical evaluation of the Nathan report and of employers' attitudes, see Jean Constant, "Le Rapport de la Commission Nathan," *Le Monde*, March 31 and April 2, 1954. For the official text of the Nathan Report, see *Rapport général de la Commission créée pour l'Etude des Disparités entre les Prix Français et Etrangers*, Paris, 1954.

structural rather than extraneous factors: "The essential cause—
I say it with moderation, but with conviction—of our high prices
is the system of protectionism, that growing protectionism of
which we cannot rid ourselves, the survival of unproductive enterprises, the private cartelization which one day legislation . . .
must definitely destroy . . . I add that when industrialists pursue
another and progressive policy, that of initiative and discipline,
they are capable of exporting."[62]

To answer such criticism the CNPF has pointed out, and with
some justification, that the existing economic knowledge is insufficient to measure the gap which might exist between the
production costs of the efficient and the marginal firms. The
CNPF admits, however, that, since France is "an old country
where numerous enterprises have survived the historical reasons
which created them," the desire to keep such firms afloat has
weakened the spirit of competition.[63]

Twenty years earlier, M. Duchemin in one of his yearly addresses to the CGPF had almost proudly declared that production
costs in France would always be higher than in other industrial
countries since in matters of modernization and competition
Frenchmen would always show "that moderation which corresponds to the genius of the race."[64] His successors while given
to less flowery language are not less defensive in their argumenta-
tion. On the one hand they equate efficiency with a cruel
industrial concentration which would unavoidably lead to unemployment and other social upheavals. On the other hand they
point out that the businessmen are not the only Frenchmen who
prefer protection and security to competition and progress. If
the entire society is infected by the disease of timidity, the employers could not be expected to remain immune. To the possible
objection that the business community, which claims elite status

---

[62] *J. O. Débats Ass. Nationale*, May 20, 1953, p. 2793. Also his remarks were
frequently interrupted by vivid applause from "the left, the center and various
benches on the extreme right."

[63] "Les causes de la disparité entre les prix français et les prix étrangers,"
*Bulletin*, VII, No. 97, April 20, 1953, pp. 3-5. This is an editorial different from the
report mentioned above in n. 60. Some two years later another editorial by President Villiers seemed to indicate that the thinking of the CNPF leadership has
undergone some modifications in regard to the survival of marginal firms: see
below at n. VI-106.

[64] Duchemin, *op.cit.* (n. I-17), p. 169.

as protagonist of the capitalistic system, cannot evade responsibility for economic progress, the answer is made beforehand that the atmosphere of class struggle is not conducive to developing the spirit of competition.

For M. Gingembre, the professional spokesman of the unproductive enterprises, the situation is considerably simpler. In his opinion no problems of "marginal firms" exist, since in comparison with its foreign competitors, all of French business has become marginal by the heavy burden imposed on it by fiscal and social legislation.[65]

\*            \*            \*

The constant and strident complaints of the employers' movement about the difficulties which arise for French business from high interest rates and from the all but total disappearance of a capital market are well substantiated by the facts. But in their search for the factors that are responsible for such developments the employers are once more content with blunt accusations against a voracious public budget, against inflation, and against a highly developed social security system for having caused the discouragement of savings. The historical record tends to show that the decline of investment in private enterprise has other, and possibly more weighty, reasons as well. In the absence of the guarantees which an expanding internal market offers, potential investors have for a long time turned to public funds or have transferred their capital abroad, if they have not preferred outright hoarding.

With one short exception the French capital market has constantly contracted since the First World War; in 1936 it reached a catastrophic low from which it has not recovered since the liberation. Already before 1939 investments decided upon by the mechanisms of a classical free market economy had shrunk to 39 percent of total investments, the remainder being provided principally by public funds and self-financing. By 1951, 92 percent of the investments came from sources other than the capital market.[66]

[65] See a passage from one of M. Gingembre's articles quoted (without indication of source) by Lavau, op.cit. (n. IV-21), p. 381.

[66] See to this point U.N. Report 1954, op.cit. (n. VI-36), p. 176. On developments

The attitude of organized business toward public investments has been uncertain at best. After the initial enthusiasm of the CNPF had vanished for the objectives of the Monnet plan, the employers' movement has on several occasions encouraged the natural inclination of parliament to improve the budgetary position by cutting back productive investments. In 1950 the CNPF admonished the authorities to examine with the greatest of care the "profitability of the planned investments" and to use "wisdom and moderation."[67] A similar attitude prevailed during most of the Pinay experiment. The arguments used by the CNPF against the possibly inflationary effects of a bold investment program showed the traditional distrust of the small and medium-sized firms against any expansion as long as there was no certainty of an increased demand. If large groups of the French population seem to be imbued with an inflationist mentality, the same people reason in a way which shows them to be almost constitutionally averse to the fundamentals of Keynesian economics.[68]

Since Pinay's demise, and with the shifting emphasis of the Second Modernization Plan, the CNPF and some of the important trade associations have become more favorably disposed toward investments out of public funds. Such a change undoubtedly also reflects the generally diminished weight of small business in the employers' movement as a whole.

More than 36 percent of investments in the private sector of the economy is contributed by public funds; about 45 percent is obtained by income retention. While this method of financing is widely practiced everywhere, the limitations of the French capital market have steadily altered the proportion of reinvested and distributed profits in favor of the first, until the present when

during the inter-war period see Charles Bettelheim, "Principaux aspects de l'évolution de l'économie française," in *La Crise*, . . . *op.cit.* (n. 11-52), pp. 48 ff. For a complete view of the investment picture between 1938 and 1951, see *Mendès-France Report 1953, op.cit.* (n. IV-4), pp. 84-91.

[67] See "Le Patronat et les Investissements," *Bulletin*, IV, No. 42, January 1950, p. 1 and *ibid.*, No. 44, February 5, 1950, p. 3.

[68] The majority of those business leaders who have any notion of Keynes' ideas consider them outright socialistic. For a contrasting picture in the United States cf. the observation by Gailbraith, *op.cit.* (n. IV-24), p. 84: "With time there has been some explicit and a great deal of implicit acceptance of Keynesian formula by American businessmen."

about 80 percent of all profits is plowed back.[69] The CNPF admits that this rate is high, but does not judge it excessive.[70] The employers' movement as such has never considered the incidence of self-financing in its discussion of the French price level. Only a few business publications and some ranking civil servants have warned that the amount and the current practices of income retention seriously add to the economic disorder.[71] "The freedom of self-financing without guidance," the report of the Commission of National Accounts has stated, "coupled with government control of prices without economic perspective has favored investments which profit futile activities and which operate to the detriment of important branches of the national economy."[72]

For the United States the point has been made that the removal of the market place as ultimate arbiter of capital application has probably enhanced and certainly not diminished the rate of industrial progress.[73] What seems to be decisive for the net effect of modes of self-financing in various countries is less the extent to which they are practiced than the specific economic environment in which they are taking place. Where French prices are

[69] See *Mendès-France Report, 1953, op.cit.* (n. IV-4), pp. 84, 90 f., and for a comparison between French and U.S. practices see Marcel Malissen, *Autofinancement en France et aux Etats-Unis*, Paris, 1953, esp. pp. 109 ff. Comparisons between different countries are extremely difficult. Even if the statistics were more reliable than they are, they are necessarily based on different samples of enterprises. But vaguely comparable data seem to indicate that in the United States the relationship between distributed and undistributed profits is on the order of about 65:35.

[70] In an interesting note prepared for me by the economic services of the CNPF. The report of the Commissariat Général etc. *Cinq ans etc., op.cit.* (n. VI-11), pp. 325-27 also holds that the present share of self-financing is not excessive. In its first report, *Rapport Général etc., op.cit.* (n. VI-11), the Commissariat had been far less lenient and concluded, p. 91, that "prices should include allowance only for sums necessary for normal renewal of the existing material, and for interest and amortization on loans, for expansion and modernization." Everybody agrees that at present self-financing goes far beyond that.

[71] See e.g. the series of articles on self-financing in *Bulletin Acadi*, No. 67-69, March 1953, pp. 73-90, 155-59, 179-98; and in *Jeune Patron*, VII, September-October 1953, pp. 36-40. In part these articles are devoted to favorable editorial comment on the richly documented and very critical paper on the self-financing practices in France by Hubert Brochier, "Autofinancement des entreprises et théorie économique," *Revue Economique*, III, 1952, pp. 609-35. Some of the harshest criticism of self-financing was uttered in addresses made to audiences of businessmen: see Mendès-France, *op.cit.* (n. VI-49), esp. pp. 17-18; and Louis Rosenstock-Franck, *op.cit.* (n. VI-59), pp. 10 ff. The latter stated that if the Office of Price Controls could "act freely," it would like to see self-financing in all industries reduced as much as possible.

[72] *Mendès-France Report 1953, op.cit.* (n. IV-4), p. 102.

[73] See Adolf A. Berle, Jr., *The 20th Century Capitalist Revolution*, New York, 1954, p. 41.

still controlled, the present-day mechanism of price-fixing by the authorities and the trade associations combined permits in most cases the self-financing *a priori*, i.e., prices are set beforehand so as to permit the desired margin for reinvestment. While originally the administration granted such a margin only for the ends of modernization and desirable expansion, of late such limitations have in fact been discarded. Moreover, the practice of pegging prices high enough to let the least efficient firms survive provides an additional margin for self-financing. As far as the "free sector" is concerned, the government has abandoned supervision of prices generally in those domains which are of less importance to the economy as a whole. Hence it is possible for firms in the least essential sectors to accumulate profits with even greater ease than elsewhere and to obtain thereby considerable means for reinvestment. Over-investments in luxury goods industries and some "hoarding" of ultramodern machinery which remains idle in essential branches of industry are the not infrequent results.[74] Here lies the explanation for the many signs of conspicuous, and socially dangerous, consumption, such as luxury housing for the upper income groups and office palaces in the midst of a continuing housing shortage.

The existing data do not permit an exact determination of the incidence of self-financing on the price level. But there is no doubt that the low degree of competition which prevails makes it possible to thrust on the consumer the role which previously was held by the investor. In that sense the presumably nonexistent "cost" of self-financing has the effect of another indirect tax. Hence the conjunction of a high amount of corporation financing by income retention and of other market conditions tends to aggravate and perpetuate maladjustments which the employers' movement, in its discussion of the country's unfavorable economic position, regularly attributes to external factors.

## 4. Taxation

M. Villiers himself has once described accurately the difficulties which surround every change in the French tax system. On the eve of what should have been an important tax reform,

---

[74] See, reporting on the results of an inquiry of the Ministry of National Economy, Jean Fourastié, *La Productivité*, Paris, 1952, p. 100, and, particularly sharp, *Mendès-France Report 1953*, *op.cit.* (n. IV-4), pp. 102-103.

he wrote of the multiple requests coming from a variety of economic interests all asking that either a particular measure be included or another be eliminated.[75] That in France questions of fiscal policies give rise even more than elsewhere to stubborn struggles which pin one interest group against the other is easily explained by the heavy tax burden, made still more onerous by its unequal distribution.

Although estimates vary greatly, it is generally assumed that in 1952 the total tax yield amounted to about 30 percent of the gross national product or more than 40 percent of the net national income. Such burden is slightly lighter than that in Great Britain and Germany but appreciably larger than in the United States and Italy. Compared with 1938, the share of taxes in the national product has increased by more than 50 percent.[76]

The high level of taxation and a monstrously complicated tax code leave the majority of taxpaying groups uncertain not only about their obligations but also about their relative position in the total tax structure. While there is universal agreement on the need for drastic change, any concrete reform proposal must involve a transfer of the burden, and such transfer will be rejected by every group as unbearable, since it believes more or less sincerely that it is already the most heavily taxed of all. Under pressure from organized interests, even the more ambitious reforms that have been tried soon lose sight of the general principles which they had sought to enact. Patchwork is added onto patchwork. The Ministry of Finance seems to have an unlimited reserve of minor and uncoordinated proposals to replace those sources of revenue which dry out under parliamentary opposition. The frequent fiscal tinkering has in itself the bad effect that few taxes acquire the advantage of familiarity which might lessen the initial unpopularity of new measures. At other times the only way out of the dilemma is a progressive increase of the rates for

[75] Georges Villiers, "La Réforme Fiscale," *Bulletin*, vi, No. 86, October 5-20, 1952, pp. 1-2.

[76] These are the figures communicated by the under-secretary of the budget to the National Assembly, *J.O. Débats Ass. Nationale*, March 24, 1954, p. 1185. Estimates vary greatly, see the different figures coming from various sources, mentioned by Williams, *op.cit.* (n. v-42), pp. 256-57, n. 8, 9. In M. Villiers' opinion the share of all taxes in the national income has reached 48 percent (see *Le Monde*, March 27, 1953).

already established taxes, without due consideration for its economic and psychological effect.

Since all reform proposals affect different groups of the business community in a different way, the CNPF, after a few valiant efforts at establishing a common doctrine of the employers' movement in tax matters, has resigned itself to an outwardly more passive role: it will expound to government and parliament the "principles of a sound fiscal reform" but will ostensibly avoid all interventions on the many questions about which its affiliates are in disagreement.[77] A common basis of departure for the various sectors of the employers' movement, and more particularly for the CNPF Tax Committee and M. Gingembre's CGPME, is their criticism of the high level of public expenditure. But even at that point the agreement appears to be superficial. As the spokesman for small business, M. Gingembre insists in classical fashion that tax receipts pay solely for normal government operations and that funds used for investment purposes should be raised by loans. To him the use of taxation for the distribution of wealth or for similar purposes of "social engineering" is altogether improper.[78] The CNPF is far less sanguine about the possibility of eliminating suddenly all investment expenses from the ordinary budget.

In its general opposition to capital taxes, the employers' movement knows that it has the backing of public opinion. Though such taxes are among the oldest elements of the French system, their share in total tax receipts has constantly fallen in the past forty years. Unpopularity of the taxes has resulted in much fraud and evasion. M. Gingembre asks today for the formal elimination of all capital transfer taxes while the CNPF would like to see at least the disappearance of the tax on all wealth transferred in a direct line between husband and wife or between parents and their children.

[77] See "La Récente Réforme Fiscale," *Bulletin*, No. 121, July 1954, p. 33, and No. 133, June 1955, p. 34. The article by M. Villiers, quoted above (n. vi-75) tried to be more specific. Since that attempt was badly received by the CNPF's affiliates, it was not repeated.

[78] The attitude of M. Gingembre and of M. Labarre, writing respectively for the CGPME and the Tax Committee of the CNPF are fully expounded in their contributions to a special issue on tax questions of the *Nouvelle Revue de l'Economie Contemporaine*, No. 33-34 (no date; but obviously published in 1952), pp. 24-25, and 19-23.

In France, unlike the situation prevailing in other countries
of advanced economic development, direct taxes have never
yielded much more than one-fourth of total budgetary receipts.
That a tax system based so prominently on indirect taxation
furthers inflationary trends is rarely acknowledged by the business community in its criticism of public finances. From the time
individual and corporate income taxes were introduced their
share has remained inferior to the expectations of their early
promoters, such as Caillaux. Since the war their importance has
further dwindled. The CGPME considers this development
sufficiently significant to justify its request for a progressive sub-
stitution of all direct by indirect taxes. Once more M. Gingembre
formulates the secret desires of most small businessmen: since
excise taxes reduce the contact between taxpayer and tax-collector to the minimum, and since the entire painful process of
contributing to the expenses of government becomes less conspicuous, the ultimate objective is to see all income taxes
disappear.

Those speaking for the CNPF as a whole do not think that it
will be possible to dispense with income taxes altogether and
therefore make a series of reform proposals directed primarily at
avoiding double imposition and the stiff progressiveness of a
surtax. Here the chairman of the CNPF's Tax Committee stresses
the well-known fact that attempts at evading the progressive
income tax communicate fraudulent practices to the field of
excise taxes; in order to conceal profits that would be subject to
the surtax, businessmen make entire transactions which should
yield excise taxes vanish from the records. If on the whole the
criticism of the CNPF against taxes on business profits remains
moderate, this is probably due to the fact that much of the tax
on the earnings of both corporations and unincorporated firms is
passed on through higher prices.

Generally speaking, the CNPF is a fervent advocate of
equality of tax treatment. Since an equitable tax system is economically profitable and psychologically desirable, and since the
existing inequitable distribution of the tax burden provides a
costly shield for those who hamper the development of the
country's resources, the CNPF can claim here with more justification than in many other fields to defend the general interest. But

since it is also true that the present tax legislation favors exorbitantly the marginal firms in industry and commerce, the CNPF by pleading for equal treatment defends here in fact the interests of the large and more efficient producers.

When the CNPF characterizes as "inadmissible" a situation where the tax rates on business profits vary between 10 and 34 percent, it has in mind the conspicuous advantages of the artisans (whose number has trebled since 1939), of the unincorporated firms, and of most of the commercial sector in general.[79] Both technical and political factors have constantly increased the privileges of the least efficient firms. While assessment and enforcement methods have markedly improved in regard to the larger enterprises, the small manufacturers, shopkeepers, and farmers are assessed for a lump sum, a system which especially in a period of rising prices is highly unsatisfactory. Even after relative price stability has been established, the average receipts from taxpayers assessed for a lump sum are so low that the amounts evoke hilarity.

For the benefit of modern accounting methods the large firm had to sacrifice at least part of the French passion for secrecy. But the inefficient producer and shopkeeper are rightly blamed by the CNPF for the hundreds of invisible transactions and unrecorded sales in which they engage at various stages of the production or distribution cycle. It is generally acknowledged that one of the major excise taxes is not only evaded in a proportion as high as 40 percent, but it also serves to keep afloat many an unproductive firm which collects the tax from the customer without turning it over to the collector.[80] Many of these practices are so widely known and admitted that, unlike other French statistics, those calculating the incidence of fraud are

[79] For a very critical view of the advantages granted to the unproductive units and especially to the artisans, see M. Lauré, *La Taxe sur la Valeur Ajoutée*, Paris, 1952, pp. 70 ff. On the general issue of taxation and productivity see the report of a special committee set up to study these questions in Ministère des Finances, *Statistiques et Etudes Financières*, No. 42, June 1952, pp. 529 ff.

[80] See James L. Houghteling, Jr. in his excellent study "The Income Tax in France," *Public Policy*, v, 1954, p. 342, and Georges Boissière, "De la fraude à l'incivisme fiscal," *Esprit*, xvii, January 1949, pp. 24-32. The second article contains something of a catalogue of tax evasions in which different firms and groups indulge depending on their juridical form and character of operations. For a brief but telling discussion of the "paralyzing" features of the fiscal system, see also Jeanneney, *op.cit.* (n. iv-26), pp. 236-37.

considered remarkably reliable. They assume that, taken as a whole, industry is paying 80 percent of taxes due, commerce and services only 72 percent, with much lower figures for certain branches. The greatest difference prevails between small and large firms: fraud is found to be three or four times as extensive among the concerns with a turnover of less than seven million francs, as among those with a turnover of more than 200 million.[81] Poincaré still spoke amusedly about his country as a land of excessive taxation, tempered by fraud. Today the annual loss of tax income through fraud amounts to about 500 to 600 billion francs, or 20 to 25 percent of total tax receipts. Obviously such a drain narrows down considerably the alternatives to present tax policies.

If the CNPF protests against privileges and fraud as thoroughly falsifying competition, it can also justifiedly complain that the public treasury will compensate for its losses by imposing ever stiffer rates on those firms which can neither escape nor evade. Among the commercial establishments for instance the integrated concerns which are often able and sometimes willing to sell at lower prices find themselves not only subject to the higher rate of the new transaction tax, but they are also unable to engage in unrecorded sales.

Here as so often in modern France the cause of economic and technical progress clashes with the desire for social stability. The small firm, however inefficient, enjoys the sympathy of politicians and public as the advertised symbol of social harmony and the shield of the individual against the tyrannical tax collector. The streamlined corporation leaves the public cold and is suspect for the company its managers keep. But the popularity of the small firm will continue to subsidize the wheelbarrow out of the tax income which is furnished by the humming of modern machines.[82]

Quite understandably, the CNPF has paid most attention to the production tax which provides today about one-third of total tax receipts. Since indirect taxes continue to yield as much

---

[81] See *Mendès-France Report 1953, op.cit.* (n. IV-4), pp. 61-64 and "Réforme fiscale," *Réalités*, November 1950, pp. 57-58; 115-16.

[82] See the very pertinent remarks on that point by Alfred Sauvy, "La Situation Economique," *Droit Social*, XVI, 1953, p. 16.

as three-fourths of tax income (which with the exception of Italy is by far the highest ratio in any western country),[83] most reform proposals must necessarily center on the excise taxes.

Although the rates of the production tax have trebled since it was transformed in 1936 from an ill-defined turnover tax into a tax on the processing of goods and the furnishing of services, organized business has resisted the consecutive increases without any vigor. Here at least was a tax whose built-in safeguards against evasion satisfied the need for equal treatment, and whose costs could most easily and inconspicuously be passed on to the consumer,[84] though inflationary price rises were thereby encouraged.

Before it was altered in 1951, the production tax had imposed most heavily on all capital-intensive industries and had in fact penalized certain uses of energy. There was little incentive for labor-saving devices and other forms of mechanization, but certain advantages were offered to those concerns which economized on materials.

Pressed into action by the integrated and modernized steel and chemical industries, the CNPF voiced its support for proposals to transform the production tax into a true tax on value added. Since the high bureaucracy in the Ministry of Finance had long favored such a change, the chances seemed favorable to include it with M. Pinay's long heralded fiscal reform.[85]

As it turned out, the issue was explosive enough to weaken the position of the Pinay government and to rock the unity of the CNPF. In the Gingembre confederation the commercial sector was most vociferous in denouncing a proposal which might lead to the replacement of the popular, because evaded, sales tax by

[83] Here again estimates vary. In the report which Ramadier submitted in the spring of 1956 to parliament indirect taxes were described as footing more than 77 percent of the tax bill; see *Le Monde*, Sélection hebdomadaire, April 12-18, 1956.

[84] The Nathan Report attributed part of the disparity between French and world market prices to the fact that incorporation of indirect taxes into prices is much heavier in France than elsewhere, see *op.cit.* (n. VI-60), pp. 16-18. For an unorthodox view on the question of transferability of taxes under French conditions, see Maurice Duverger, "Chacun sa part," *Le Monde*, February 5, 1952.

[85] The book that has done much to clarify the issues involved was written by an official of the Ministry of Finance, M. Lauré; see *op.cit.* (n. VI-79). See also *ibid.*, the interesting preface by Prof. Laufenburger. For very similar proposals made by a group of Catholic trade unionists, see "Lignes directrices d'une Réforme Fiscale," *Bulletin des Groupes Reconstruction*, supplement to No. 39, June 1951, esp. p. 27.

a more easily enforceable device. But also the wholesale trade opposed certain aspects of the proposed reform. More significant and eventually fatal was the opposition that came from one of the most influential industrial federations. The textile industries took it upon themselves to defend all trades which employ a large labor force and did not wish to lose the advantage bestowed on them by the old production tax. Nor were they inclined to see their more highly mechanized brethren favored by an increased consideration for investments. That "Boussac and his cotton empire had killed the Pinay tax reform" was the general conviction of many business leaders in the fall of 1952.[86]

The outburst of parliamentary criticism against the tax bills proposed by Pinay was to a large extent inspired by the lobbying activities of M. Boussac and the CGPME, who formed a united front with agricultural interests equally fearful of some of the proposed measures. For the CNPF the episode meant a forced retreat to more cautious tactics in all tax matters.

However when the Laniel government had obtained decree power, it took in April 1954 some effective steps to reform the production tax. Most of the discriminations against investment goods and other intermediate operating expenses were lifted and the rates of the tax were once more increased. This move was all the more interesting since Premier Laniel himself owns a textile firm and had formerly been an officer of the Textile Trade Association which had opposed all such proposals.

It may be assumed that politicians of the stature of Joseph Laniel or René Mayer, though both close to organized business, cannot stay in office long without becoming convinced that, given the economic and financial situation of the country, it is impossible to satisfy at all times the appetite of the interest groups. The CGPME and its allies in parliament protested against the new measures as vigorously as they had against the earlier attempt of Pinay.[87] But for once their influence had undoubtedly diminished in the meantime. Moreover, just because

[86] See Manuel Salte, "Les Intérêts professionnels en face de la Réforme fiscale," *Le Monde*, November 19, 1952 and *ibid.*, December 5, 1952. Interesting also is the almost violent letter which M. Roy, then president of the National Textile Union, addressed to M. Villiers protesting against the Pinay tax reform; see *Le Mois Textile*, No. 59, November 1952, pp. 59-60.

[87] See *Le Monde*, October 29, 1953 and November 20, 1953.

Pinay had so openly invited the support of the same business groups which disapproved of his projected tax reforms, he was more vulnerable to their attacks than Laniel who had known how to assert his independence. Furthermore, some of the opposition was appeased by the traditional half-way measures: the new tax was "for the time being" not applied to the commercial sector; artisan enterprises continued to be favored; the tax on services and the frequently evaded transaction tax were "not immediately" merged with the tax on value added.

Eighteen months after the enactment of the new law only a few additional steps had been taken to make the new measure into a uniform and single tax applicable to all steps of production and distribution. The CNPF Tax Committee has stated frankly that as long as the commercial sector was exempted from the new legislation, the question of an effective and equitable contribution to the tax load by all business remained partially unsolved.[88]

The almost insurmountable difficulties which the employers' movement faces when it seeks to take a stand on critical issues of tax policy are also well illustrated by the discussions on the so-called parafiscal taxes. Parafiscal taxes have long been known in France but have multiplied in number and importance over the last decades. They are contributions determined by public law which, instead of flowing to the public treasury, benefit private organizations, and among them many trade associations. The funds so collected are usually destined to further economic development in a specific field. The contributions by business to the sales organizations in the steel and aluminum industries are imposed by law; a number of research laboratories are financed by parafiscal taxes; in other cases such contributions seem merely to subsidize anemic branches of industry. A recent official inquiry revealed that there exist more than 140 such taxes, collected sometimes by the government, sometimes directly by private organizations with the force of law behind them; it

[88] For the general views of the CNPF on the tax reforms of the Laniel and Faure cabinets see *Bulletin*, No. 121, July 1954, pp. 33-35; No. 122, August 1954, p. 14; No. 132, May 1955, pp. 42-45. The president of the CNPF Tax Committee had explained the divergent views of industry and commerce with great clarity in his article, *op.cit.* (n. vi-78), pp. 22-23.

is considered impossible to figure even approximately their total yield.[89]

The entire system has been under attack from many sides. It has been blamed as being a violation of sound and democratic fiscal practice since parliament has practically no influence over either size or use of these contributions. Sometimes parafiscal taxes are considered as an instrument of *dirigisme* by which the government is able to distribute favors in accordance with its over-all economic designs. To others they are a flagrant case of costly, if hidden, subsidies to private business. Almost everybody agrees that their effect is that of yet another excise tax paid eventually by the consumer.

The CNPF has occasionally found strong words in criticism of the parafiscal taxes. Its Tax Committee has characterized them as an example of internal "protectionism" which permits the survival of all too many producers who should long have been eliminated if a climate of healthy competition had prevailed. When the entire system of parafiscality was made the subject of scorching criticism by a senator, the CNPF published the report in its *Bulletin*, but then praised those parafiscal taxes which serve the ends of better organization and higher productivity.[90] It is obvious that some of the weighty affiliates of the peak association are unwilling to abandon the privileges which the existing system offers to them.

On one issue of tax policies the CNPF has taken a definite stand: it has constantly rejected all single tax proposals and especially the proposition to replace existing taxes by a levy on the sources of energy, such as coal, electricity, or oil. In view of the obvious weakness of the scheme, it might be astonishing that so much effort had to be spent to refute the arguments of those favoring the tax on energy. But actually the most ardent

[89] For an excellent general discussion of the problems and techniques involved, see Paul Nollet, "La Parafiscalité," *Droit Social*, XVI, 1953, pp. 65-74.

[90] For M. Labarre's criticism, see especially *Bulletin*, VIII No. 114, February 5, 1954, pp. 12-13. Very comprehensive on the attitude of the CNPF is the article, "La Parafiscalité de caractère économique," *ibid.*, No. 134, July 1955, pp. 40-43. For an attack against the system coming from another sector of the employers' movement, see Comité d'Etudes pour le Redressement etc., *Notre Production va-t-elle être plus longtemps paralysée par les taxes parafiscales? Un cas typique: Le Bois*, Paris, n.d. If the case is described accurately the parafiscal taxes are indeed a striking example of "economic Malthusianism."

and vociferous advocate of the tax is a well-known industrialist, M. Schueller, of the Mon-Savon and Oréal soap and perfume concern, who represents his trade association in the councils of the CNPF.[91] His campaign for the tax is not his first reform proposal: the voice of this self-made industrialist, who started as a manual worker, has often been heard—and with particular stridency during the years of the German occupation—in favor of flamboyant schemes for the transformation of capitalist enterprise. Also the grass-roots membership of the CGPME and many small businessmen outside of the Confederation thoroughly approve of such an assessment, so that this issue has remained one of the few questions which still give rise to debate in the otherwise dull sessions of the CNPF's General Assembly.[92]

The popularity of the proposed tax is easily explained. A tax levied at the "source" would enable the French businessman to sever completely his relations with the tax-collector. As it is, "fiscal anesthesia" is one of the principles already consciously applied by the government when it selects among alternative tax reforms usually those that are most unobtrusive. Here the principle would be driven to its logical conclusion: the citizen would have nothing to declare and would be left with the soothing impression of not paying anything.[93]

So far, none of the proposed or enacted tax reforms has removed the causes of the economic and financial dilemma. It has correctly been said that the gravity of the French financial situation is to be found less in the size of the budgetary deficit, than in the inability of the government to ever reduce that deficit submitting as it does to competing demands.[94] An excessive

[91] For M. Schueller's proposals, see his *L'Impôt sur l'énergie*, Paris, 1952, and his *Réfutations au rapport de la Commission de réforme fiscale sur la taxation de l'énergie*, Paris, 1952. For one of several rebuttals of the proposal by the CNPF, see "La Taxe sur l'Energie," *Bulletin*, No. 128, February 1955, pp. 23-26.

[92] For the espousal of the proposals for a tax on energy see the resolution of the Tax Committee of the *Etats Généraux des PME*, held in June 1952, p. c.f.2, and also the general tenor of the General Assembly of the CGPME held in October of the same year, as reported in *La Croix*, October 16, 1952. At this point even M. Gingembre and with him other leaders of the CGPME are unwilling to give in to the wishes of their membership.

[93] Very good on this point is René Sédillot, "Why Frenchmen Don't Pay Taxes," *New York Times Magazine*, September 6, 1953, p. 42. The term "fiscal anesthesia" was coined by Louis Trotabas, *Les Finances Publiques et les Impôts de la France*, Paris, 1953, p. 153.

[94] See Jeanneney, *op.cit.*, (n. IV-26), p. 232.

amount of government expenditures is implicitly desired by the business community and by almost everybody else, but can hardly be met by further tax increases. Ever since the rise in prices has stopped and since policies leading to a possible resumption of inflation are regarded as a political liability, it has become increasingly difficult to shift the entire tax burden to the consumer. Internal and external markets are limited by high prices which could be reduced only by measures considered undesirable by the same who in fact are opposed to a reduction of public expenses.

There seem to be no lasting remedies for the deficiencies of the economy outside of fundamental changes in its structure.[95] Will the employers' movement committed as it has been in the past to the defense of that structure, be able to strive energetically for the necessary solutions?

## 5. Summary: A Divided Economy

For all their contradictions, economic and fiscal policies of the post-war period have had one effect in common: by insuring the survival of the unfit they have preserved the "pointillist" character of the economic picture. After the liberation the already large number of small enterprises increased drastically. Neither the inflation nor the shift from rigid governmental controls to a manipulated market economy has eliminated a significant number of these firms.[96]

Comparisons between the inflation in Germany and in France seem to suggest that a rapid and catastrophic depreciation of the currency such as occurred in the Weimar Republic might easily wipe out a host of small and medium-sized establishments, while the slow and steady deterioration of the French franc encouraged their continued existence. In France the prolongation of the inflationary process over decades gave to people in all walks of life the feeling of being eternally deceived by their governments. It encouraged and even gave respectability to those forms of asocial behavior for which after the liberation the term *incivisme*

[95] Changes the need for which is admirably described in their general context by the *U.N. Report 1954, op.cit.* (n. vi-36), pp. 187-96.

[96] For some tentative statistical data on the present-day business structure see Appendix, Table IV.

was coined.[97] Since operation of the small firm was made difficult, but not impossible as in a runaway inflation, almost all means for avoiding ruin by shirking responsibilities seemed permitted. But the mere survival of the marginal enterprises does not insure their productive vitality; in general their owners eke out a drab and comfortless existence. Because the majority of these firms are less and less able to catch up with technological progress, they impose on the economy a burden which has been estimated by a business magazine as amounting to a yearly "hidden tax" of a billion francs.[98]

On the other side of the scale post-war price and investment policies have also favored business concentration, most frequently by the merger of already large firms. At least in some branches and mostly through the initially vigorous public investment program, the traditional bias which had held back development of large-scale industry has been broken. The best equipped firms, though unwilling to use their dominant position for the elimination of their weaker brethren, have constantly improved their equipment and in many cases their productivity. Hence the gap between the modern and the unproductive sectors of the economy has steadily widened. In the words of another business magazine, the economic make-up of the country in both industry and agriculture resembles more and more a harlequin costume made of multicolored and unequal cloth.[99] The division between a modern and a backward France is further deepened by great contrasts among different regions, in part the consequence of demographic developments. The net effect is that today numerous French departments resemble southern rather than northern and central Europe.[100]

[97] An entire issue of the magazine *Esprit* was devoted to a discussion of that phenomenon; see *Esprit*, xvii, January 1949. Especially the articles by Boissière, *op.cit.* (n. vi-80), and by Fabrice Marpier, "Epargne forcée, impôt voluntaire et solidarité nationale," *ibid.*, pp. 23 ff. deal with the *incivisme* of what is now called "Gingembre's France."

[98] "Le Coût des Entreprises Marginales," *Entreprise*, No. 34, August 15, 1954, p. 31 f. Pierre Drouin arrives at similar conclusions in "L'essoufflement de l'économie française. Une poussière de petites entreprises," *Le Monde*, September 16, 1953.

[99] L'Usine Nouvelle, *op.cit.* (n. vi-28), p. 3.

[100] The important demographic factors and maldistribution of resources between various regions cannot be dealt with here, but is very comprehensively and excellently discussed in *U.N. Report 1954, op.cit.* (n. vi-36), pp. 178-87. Recently also the CNPF has given increasing attention to such uneven developments; see the

The coexistence of the "two Frances" could not long continue in the mid-twentieth century if there prevailed what the Economic Council, investigating the causes of the French inflation, called the "harsh laws of a liberal market economy." Under such hypothetical circumstances, torrents coming from the dynamic and progressive sectors of the economy would soon destroy the fields cultivated by the laggards. But to forestall such effects protective devices have been built to serve as locks between the different levels on which the economy operates. Hope is sometimes expressed that competition from the outside would promote greater efficiency of French industry.[101] It can however be argued that at least initially competition must not necessarily come from the outside. If the modern concerns were willing to force the inefficient enterprises to gird themselves for sterner market competition, much could be accomplished to enlarge the industrial potential and thereby prepare for the wider opening of the borders.[102]

Admittedly the economic policies of the post-war period have done little to prepare for that day. But they have been the faithful expression of a common mentality to which "measures of protection come to look more attractive than measures of modernization, and measures of modernization less repelling than measures of expansion."[103] Objective observers admit that, if there is an intimate connection between the prevailing mentality and the economic structure of the country, such a state of mind is not that of business alone: "the outlook of individuals, the activities of organized business, the attitudes of the banks, the intervention of the public authorities, everything in this country gives priority to the search for security, to the preservation of acquired positions, and contributes thereby to a sclerosis of the structures. That phenomenon necessarily hinders the adaptation of the enterprises and of the general economic mechanism to the progress of production techniques and to the development of consumption

---

well documented though inconclusive article, "L'Evolution de la richesse relative des Départements Français de 1946 à 1953." *Bulletin*, VIII, No. 121, July 1954, pp. 38-50.

[101] For details see below Chapter VIII.

[102] This is the view expressed by the *U.N. Report 1954, op.cit.* (n. VI-36), p. 190.

[103] *Ibid.*, p. 189.

needs. . . . Profit is no longer obtained by competition on the market, but is defended in spite of it. It has become a fixed rent, which one seeks to conserve not to increase."[104]

In one of its widely quoted reports, the French Economic Council drew up a yet more incisive bill of particulars against the employers: "Does French industry still have today the men who measure up to its ambitions? Or did the painful consequences of two successive wars, the depressing influence of governmental regulations, the willingness to count on the intervention of the public authorities for obtaining help which they should provide for themselves, the refusal to dare for fear of losing, did all these factors take away from all too many industrialists those qualities that are the virtues of a leader? Less virtuous, hence less certain of themselves, they hesitate to exercise leadership. . . ."[105]

French industry can rightfully answer that there are in its midst many who have not lost their stamina and who do not have to fear comparison with the foremost leaders of the business elite in other countries. But because of the structure of the employers' movement, the trade associations can give little room to the views of the brave and must instead continuously represent and reproduce the structural rigidities which enable a majority of their constituents to survive. Organized business also has to tolerate, if it does not encourage, the mentality so generally deplored as "economic Malthusianism."

There are occasional outcries by the leaders of the CNPF proving that they recognize the incongruity of their policies. In terms never before equalled for their sharpness and urgency, M. Villiers used one of his customary editorials in the *Bulletin* to ask for a "clean-up" of business: "The expansion of the economy postulates that a healthy competition rewards the efforts and penalizes the errors of everybody; it favors the development of the most efficient and best equipped enterprises, but imposes the

---

[104] Alain Berger, "Sortir du Malthusianisme Economique," *Esprit*, XXII 1954, p. 24. The entire article makes an excellent contribution to the question here discussed. See also on the same subject the enlightening series of articles by Jean Constant, "Saurons-nous rénover notre économie?" *Le Monde*, March 4, 5, 10, 11, 1954, and Maurice Duverger, "Le Poumon d'Acier," *La Nef*, x, June 1953, pp. 165-72.

[105] *Bulletin du Conseil Economique*, July 31, 1948, p. 1052.

elimination of the least productive firms."[106] In his criticism of
the existing bankruptcy legislation, the president of the CNPF
warned that more business failures were a necessity.

Another unprecedented step was taken when the CNPF organized, under the chairmanship of the former inspector of finance
who has become the executive of the Trade Association of the
Cotton Industry, a committee to study changes in the "structures"
of the economy. While in part the committee was set up as a
defense reaction against reproaches of "immobilism," its first
report hailed business concentration and the elimination of unproductive firms in a language entirely new in the employers'
movement, though somewhat remindful of the philosophy of a
Bichelonne.[107]

It remains to be seen whether such declarations will be followed by an actual change in orientation and policies. Given the
long-range character of the policies which are involved, the
changes could be slow and gradual provided that the determination to effect them does not slacken.

[106] Georges Villiers, "L'assainissement des Professions," *Bulletin*, No. 134, July
1955, pp. 1-2.
[107] See *ibid.*, No. 150, August 1956, pp. 17-22.

# CHAPTER VII

# Economic Issues: II

## *1. Productivity*

"The French industrialist has many general ideas but
never applies them. He works very hard. For since he pays
his collaborators badly, they are mediocre. . . . He lives in
the present with the past. He asks nothing from the future."

Detoeuf, *Propos de O. L. Barenton*

"Intensification of national production" was among the foremost reform proposals formulated in the program of the National
Council of Resistance.[1] The fact that technical progress in France
had lagged for decades behind other industrial countries was
generally admitted, though not always exactly documented.[2]
Although the country has been rich in great inventors, and has
also excelled at all times in the technical application of such
inventions, comparative statistics seem to confirm that French
industry had often failed to exploit fully the material and human
resources at its disposal.[3]

French and outside observers agree that in many cases the
reasons for unsatisfactory productivity were to be found in a
mentality rather than in specific methods. A French historian
has warned: "Buy machines? Organize production? No. I mean
to say: let us not reverse the order of things. We shall buy
machines, beautiful machines, once we have espoused, high and
low, a mechanical mentality. We shall effectively organize production once we have rid ourselves of a certain mentality which
is that of the *petit bourgeois* of Louis-Philippe's time. First
think. Then act. Or rather organize to act. . . ."[4]

---

[1] See Michel and Mirkine-Guetzevitch, *op.cit.* (n. II-68), p. 216.

[2] For interesting discussions of the rate of industrial progress in pre-war France,
see Pierre Naville, "Le Progrès Technique en France depuis Cent ans," in *La
crise, op.cit.* (n. II-52), pp. 213-29, and Ministère des finances et des affaires économiques, *op.cit.* (n. II-53), p. 89 f. The most respected French work on the
statistical and general problems of measuring progress is A. A. Vincent, *Le
Progrès Technique en France depuis Cent ans*, Paris, 1944.

[3] Further to this point see the balanced observations by Gignoux, *op.cit.* (n. I-31),
pp. 12-13, and the desperate outcry of André Gide in his *Journal 1889-1939*, Paris,
1951, p. 654: "The enraging thought, that France is the country of inventors!
One comes always back to the same: We do not know how to profit from our
resources. . . ."

[4] Lucien Febvre, preface to Morazé, *op.cit.* (n. IV-5), pp. VIII-IX.

Frenchmen have often pondered the fact that their country, which has produced the father of rationalism, has not formed the vanguard of the movement for industrial rationalization. The query and the playing on terms on which it is based are significant enough. Some industrialists find consolation in the thought that their compatriots, as worthy sons of Descartes, engage in rationalization without knowing it, like Jourdain who had unwittingly spoken prose all his life.[5] Others are less certain of the benefits of the Cartesian method and of the excessive training the young Frenchman receives in it. Does not, they ask, the solid grounding in logical and mathematical methods strengthen a rigidity of mind which moves at will in realms of general abstraction, but is incapable of grasping the infinite and often contradictory variety of business life? If, as a consequence, there is little interpenetration between philosophy and daily practice, the latter is left without the impulse coming from a general orientation.[6]

It has been said that the intense preoccupation of the educated Frenchman with his country's history makes him doubt whether institutions and techniques which are much younger than the great revolution really deserve the attention of civilized mankind.[7] Such retrospective propensity frequently crowds out an understanding of the present. Admiration for the past glories of their own nation leads many Frenchmen to a cultural ethnocentricity which easily discards the advice or the example of foreigners. "Other nations play an altogether effaced role in his life," wrote Detoeuf about the outlook of the French industrialist.[8]

But the same French businessman who prides himself on thinking in broad and historical terms is in the daily conduct of his enterprise burdened with a mass of details and routine which,

[5] See the curious remark by Duchemin, op.cit. (n. I-17), p. 39.

[6] When M. Villiers introduced the newly founded CNPF Center of Research and Study he found it necessary to engage in a curious discourse about the advantages and inconvenience of the Cartesian method. See his "Présentation du Centre de Recherches et d'Etudes des Chefs d'Entreprise," Bulletin, VII, No. 109, November 20, 1953, pp. 1-3.

[7] See Morazé, op.cit. (n. IV-5), p. 206.

[8] Detoeuf, op.cit. (n. I-75), p. 76. The two pages Detoeuf devoted to a characterization of his French colleagues in contrast to the German, American, and British industrialists belong to the most candid if unflattering descriptions ever written of the mentality of the French businessman.

as he will frequently complain, prevent him altogether from reflecting. He will blame the red tape of multiple government regulations and the complication of the tax and social security system for a harassment which proves a serious handicap for productivity.

Since a majority of enterprises suffer from an understaffing on the management level, the French executive must supervise personally many more activities than his American counterpart.[9] While he might professedly regret a shortage of people who are capable of filling managerial positions, many businessmen do not truly wish for talented assistants and do little to attract talent by sufficient pay. The deep-seated distrust which many businessmen harbor for their collaborators extends easily to members of their own family. Here the diffidence of a peasant race, convinced that one is never as well served as by oneself, is compounded by the pride of the petty bourgeois who fears that a division of responsibility might lead to a weakening of prestige. Under the pretext that he wishes to remain "master in his own house," the industrialist jealously keeps to himself what he often foolishly considers a manufacturing secret.[10]

The low degree of vertical and horizontal mobility adds a further obstacle to technological development. The engineers who, instead of graduating from the *grandes écoles*, have had practical training, and the middle management ranks are in general educationally set off sharply from the managerial elite which in turn lacks on-the-job experience. This leads to insufficient communication among the various levels of the managerial hierarchy, even where such hierarchies are well-defined.[11] The advice of engineers and foremen on the improvement of production methods is often ignored and suggestions by workers are

[9] On this and the following see the perceptive paper by F. H. Harbison and Eugene W. Burgess, "Modern Management in Western Europe," *Journal of Sociology*, IX, 1954, p. 16 and passim.

[10] Dieterlen, *op.cit.* (n. III-32), p. 377. See also *Bulletin du Conseil Economique*, July 31, 1948, which makes the businessman's lack of self-confidence responsible for his unwillingness to decentralize managerial functions.

[11] On this point see the revealing psychological details of the testimony of a man who has entered industry from outside the circle of top management, Pucheu, *op.cit.* (n. II-21), pp. 306-07. For an interesting attempt to evaluate sociological causes and consequences of the limited social mobility, see Edmond Goblot, *La barrière et le niveau: Etude sociologique sur la bourgeoisie française moderne*, Paris, 1925.

seldom sought and consequently not offered. In the eyes of the average employer even the skilled worker has an entirely passive role.[12]

The limited horizontal mobility expresses itself in a general reluctance of top management to change jobs, and consequently hampers the spread of new ideas among various enterprises. But even mutual plant visits or the exchanges of technical or managerial information are frequently frowned upon. With a few significant exceptions this holds true even for large concerns, and the small businessmen will frequently regard all offers of technical assistance, even when they come from research centers or professional consultants, as mere pretexts for spying.[13]

Also inimical to productivity-mindedness is the foremost concern for security rather than for growth and expansion. "What is essential and comes before all other things is stability," wrote the steel magnate, Eugène Schneider, years before the depression had reached his country. "If we had to choose between exceptionally favorable but unstable general conditions and others less brilliant but assured of great stability, we would not hesitate to choose the latter."[14] For the businessman the impossibility or even unwillingness to visualize a "brilliant" future for his firm was, at least until the recent more drastic inflation, reflected in hopes for an early and honorable retirement from business life. And even while still active, the employer like everybody else is not averse to exchanging higher incomes for the enjoyment of leisure.[15]

Before the war the employers' movement gave perfect expression to a mentality so widespread among its constituents. At the

[12] See Laroque, op.cit. (n. 1-5), p. 319. See below Chapter IX for the consequences of such mentality for the workings of the post-war legislation on plant committees.

[13] On these aspects of the employers' practices American and French observers agree : see e.g., the report and the oral remarks by James Silbermann of the United States Department of Labor, reproduced by the French Foundry Association under the title, La Faiblesse de la Productivité Française vue par les Américains, Paris, 1952, pp. 2-5, and Commissariat Général du Plan, Commission Interministérielle de la Productivité, Recueil de Documents relatifs à la Productivité, Paris, 1949, esp. pp. 16 ff.

[14] Quoted from Dautry, Notice sur la vie et les travaux de M. Eugène Schneider, Paris, 1948, p. 6.

[15] For more details on this point see Louis Salleron, Les Catholiques et le Capitalisme, Paris, 1951, p. 154, and Shepard B. Clough, "Retardative Factors in French Economic Development," Journal of Economic History, Supplement VI, 1946, esp. p. 102.

turn of the century, Paul-Boncour spoke about the hostility of the trade associations toward modernization.[16] The president of the pre-war CGPF constantly praised the "prudence" of the French industrialist in matters of rationalization. Not to have adopted suddenly measures of standardization or mass production was considered by him a virtue, worthy of a country which has always honored the *juste milieu*, but also a tribute to nature, for *natura saltus non fecit*. The high level of French prices was to be regarded as the "ransom" for the meritorious modesty of modernization efforts. When the depression had hit the United States, M. Duchemin felt justified in his warnings against rationalization and a policy of high wages: immoderation had led to catastrophes which the French sense of balance would be able to avoid.[17] Those industrialists who before the war favored more rapid mechanization had therefore to move in a milieu which was generally hostile to their objectives. The official inquiry investigating shortly before the war the reasons for unsatisfactory productivity concluded that, together with the sluggishness of machines, "certain attitudes and a certain intransigence" of both capital and labor were harmful to output and the rate of technological advance.[18]

For all these reasons a report by the National Committee on Productivity was quite justified when it stated in 1953 that "until quite recently we were hardly concerned with seeking the cause of our weak productivity, nor did we make any efforts to remedy the situation or even to envisage the results that might be expected from such efforts."[19]

Here the situation has drastically and sometimes dramatically changed in post-war France. M. Monnet's formula, "modernization or decadence," the importance of mechanical superiority demonstrated by the victory of American arms, the emphasis which the economic assistance programs have placed almost from the beginning on factors of productivity, the rubbing of shoulders

---

[16] Paul-Boncour, *op.cit.* (n. 1-20), p. 419: "The machines have sometimes no more resolute enemies than the groups representing the industry which employs them."
[17] See Duchemin, *op.cit.* (n. 1-4), pp. 64, 82-84, 87, 99, 169.
[18] *J.O.*, December 16, 1937, pp. 13,738 ff.
[19] Comité National de la Productivité, *Actions et Problèmes de Productivité. Premier Rapport 1950-1953*, Paris, 1953, p. 423. Significantly enough, even the term "productivity" was hardly known in pre-war France.

with other industrialized nations of Europe in the OEEC and elsewhere—from all sides the need for increased productivity has been urged upon Frenchmen. Sometimes one might feel that the previous lack of interest has been replaced by an obsession: a skeptical official of the CNPF likened the productivity drive to a "collective hysteria."

Among the various external impulses to the productivity consciousness of French business, the American example plays undoubtedly a role of the first order. Until the end of 1952 a total of almost 400 French employers and more than 700 engineers had participated in various "productivity missions" to the United States, studying conditions in their respective industries and trades. After that date other missions of the same kind have been organized, although the number of participating industrialists has dwindled since the missions have become more exclusively technical in character and also since the costs are now borne by the participating firms rather than by United States grants. Simultaneously several dozens of American experts have served in a variety of fields as advisers on both general and technical aspects of productivity methods.[20] The employers' movement as such was involved most directly in the "mission" organized on the occasion of the First International Conference of Manufacturers in New York in December 1951. The impressions then gathered by leading French businessmen and pressure group officials were incorporated into an extremely interesting and revealing, though not entirely candid, report "on the causes of the high productivity in the United States."[21]

The "missionaries" and businessmen who are in touch with Americans visiting and advising in France have rendered usually lengthy accounts to their trade associations and other business audiences. But the American "model" penetrated much farther.

[20] The data on productivity missions, etc. are taken from *ibid.*, pp. 55-67.

[21] See supplement to the *Bulletin*, VI, No. 80, April 1952. The report is presented as a synthesis of impressions received by the various members of the employers' delegation. It makes an effort at toning down some of the more violently negative reactions and bears the imprint of M. Ricard's style and thinking. Interesting conclusions presenting a somewhat different point of view were added by M. Perrin. An intelligent comment on the various types of reaction by French businessmen to the USA is provided by Robert Weinmann, "Les Chefs d'Entreprises devant les réussites de l'industrie Américaine," *Jeune Patron*, V, No. 48, September-October 1951, pp. 25-26.

Frequent discussions in the press, simplified statistics comparing the number of working hours needed for the purchase of goods in France and the United States, the emphasis given to the economic achievements of the United States in American propaganda media, and educational exchanges of various kinds have spread the lessons of American "efficiency" so widely that, in the opinion of many industrialists, a saturation point for such information has been reached.[22]

The reports, drawn up by the "missionaries" on the basis of technical observations gathered in American factories, have usually shown a fairly wide agreement among the management and labor members of the delegation who were optimistic about the possibilities of applying in France what had been learned abroad. But in many cases engineers, skilled workers, or trade union officials became discouraged sometime after their return. Then the usual complaint was that either outright hostility of both management and labor or general slackness defeated the purposes of the missionaries who soon felt isolated and cut off from the refreshing interchange of impressions and views which their trip had afforded them.[23] In other cases, where initial success on the technical level was apparent, some observers have taken the critical view that later disappointments have set in and have discredited all "American methods" since a mere mechanical imitation could not infuse the new mentality which was needed.

Several prominent figures of the employers' movement have attempted to gain an understanding of American production methods by seeing them against a broader cultural and economic background. The executive of the Textile Association, M. René Catin, gave on his return from the United States a report to his constituents which, together with technical suggestions, amounted to a careful and lucid analysis of American industrial society. With remarkable and quite unique detachment M. Catin drew

[22] A French writer of international fame and a substantial knowledge of the American scene reports that frequently French business audiences would urge him: "Be sure not to talk to us about American productivity."

[23] Compare some of the testimonies in Comité National de la Productivité, *Sondage par questionnaires des participants aux Missions de Productivité*, Paris, 1952, esp. pp. 80 ff. with certain optimistic reports of technical missions, frequently published by the trade associations.

comparisons between the two countries. Having laid bare the roots of American productivity methods and having reduced the much discussed underlying "mentality" to its simple elements, the executive of the Textile Association left it to his audience to decide on the applicability of the related experiences. He made it clear however that in his opinion reforms of French production methods, though involving far more than a mere adaptation of techniques, could well take their inspiration from across the ocean.[24]

Such an opinion is not entirely exceptional among leaders of the employers' movement. M. d'Halluin, now one of the CNPF's vice-presidents, and others active in the various vanguard groups have returned from the United States, deeply impressed with the "climate of human relations." Members of the vanguard groups have become convinced by their closer contact with American reality that French industry could look for guidance to the United States, while previously they had considered the American business civilization and the Soviet order equally alien and meaningless for their country.

On the other extreme there are numerous spokesmen of the employers' movement who still believe that France has no lessons to accept from the Babel of modern materialism and senseless standardization. To them (and there are prominent members of the CNPF Social Committee among them), there is not much new in the American experience and whatever might be new is without significance for the smaller European market. The high standard of living in the United States is admitted as a fact, but little of it is attributed to managerial policies or to production techniques. The relationship between American employers and their workers is ridiculed for its superficial cordiality and contrasted with the callousness that consists in laying off thousands of workers from one day to the next. The "enthusiasm" of the worker on the job is dismissed as one of many over-advertised features of American society. The entire preoccupation of French business with things American is regarded as a "fashion that will

[24] See Roger Catin, "Exposé sur les bases de la productivité américaine," *Le Mois Textile*, supplément No. 1, January 1952, pp. 23-35. There is a marked difference between that report and the one presented by the CNPF delegation, mentioned above (n. VII-21).

blow over," as soon as American publicity devices will have spent themselves.

Also others who do not dismiss so lightly the present and future impact of the United States on European economic developments will frequently discuss the American scene in critical terms. They return the reproach of "economic Malthusianism" made against French businessmen by pointing to American immigration and tariff policies. In their eyes the idea of productivity has become in the United States a "mystical dogma" relying on techniques well-known if not always correctly applied in France. They note with mixed feelings the great mobility prevailing on many levels of American management and society. For, they will ask, is the American system still capitalistic? Will not an educational *aurea mediocritas*, the levelling of wealth through taxation and the great political influence of the trade unions, combine to create a society which, before a decade is over, will have all the earmarks of socialism or communism, hardly tempered by formal democratic institutions? Are not the European business elites justified when they cling to their older traditions instead of imitating practices or espousing a philosophy which, under the guise of neo-capitalism, might lead straight to a new form of totalitarianism?

Much of this reasoning is obviously defensive. If in France "free enterprise" has admittedly been less efficient and less productive of economic and social satisfaction than in the United States, this is explained by the difficulties which must necessarily beset capitalism everywhere. American business would know the same handicaps had it not in fact abandoned capitalism and set its sails on an uncharted and dangerous sea. Whatever its psychological motivation, such an appraisal will obviously limit the validity of the American experience for French business.

The president of the CNPF has generally sided with those leaders of the employers' movement who favor the productivity drive. M. Villiers has also taken a more hopeful attitude than many of his colleagues in regard to the lessons that can be learned from the American example. His emphasis on the need for establishing a new "human climate" if lasting progress is to be achieved, has led M. Villiers to consider earnestly the question of how the personnel could share in the results of increased productivity.[25]

It was quite typical that long before certain sectors of French industry had adopted productivity policies heated debates were already under way as to who was to benefit from as yet unknown advantages. In his official statements M. Villiers proposed that the consumer in the form of lowered prices, the workers in the form of wage incentives, and business by increased profits should all be given a stake in the campaign for higher productivity. In practice, the CNPF has constantly warned against "isolating" any of the factors or favoring any one of the three groups over the other. It has therefore opposed any contractual agreements by which the workers were assured in advance of individual or collective premium payments. In line with such reasoning, the CNPF has expressed its hardly concealed displeasure with a widely circulated report by the governmental National Committee on Productivity, which dealt comprehensively with desirable methods of letting the personnel share in the results of productivity. Because of the energy of its chairman, M. Migeon, an industrialist who in his concern is practicing what he preaches, a subcommittee completed its report on "Productivity and Co-operation of the Personnel" well ahead of all others. In a commentary the CNPF warned strongly against "drawing definite conclusions from necessarily fragmentary studies covering only one part of a problem whose larger aspects remain to be determined."[26] At the same time the CNPF, especially upon the urging of its Social Committee, intimated that too liberal a productivity bonus would lead to hidden wage increases and might set the inflationary spiral into motion.

Since then the employers' peak association and many of its principal affiliates have strenuously criticized all legislation

[25] The principal thoughts of M. Villiers on productivity were developed in two articles which since then have been quoted many times: "Un climat humain de productivité," *Bulletin*, v, No. 68, June 20-July 5, 1951, pp. 1-2, and "Les exigences de la productivité," *ibid.*, vi, No. 87, November 5, 1952, pp. 1-2. In 1954 the CNPF Committee on Productivity was directly attached to the office of M. Villiers, presumably in order to eliminate interference from less friendly quarters such as the Social Committee.

[26] *Ibid.*, vi, No. 84, July 20-August 5, 1952, p. 45. For the report of the Migeon Committee, see "Premier Rapport sur les Travaux de la Commission: Productivité et Coopération du Personnel des Entreprises," *Les Cahiers de la Productivité*, No. 11, June 1, 1952, pp. 1-48.

granting tax and credit privileges to firms which give their personnel an assured share in the results of increased productivity.[27] On the whole, the CNPF has been successful in its efforts to hold the line against any direct agreements between employers and their workers concerning the benefits to be derived from new working methods. Individual employers, as well as some of the vanguard groups, have criticized such negativism and have frequently insisted on the need for giving priority to the problem of remuneration in all firms planning a productivity drive. But presently it is at best uncertain whether the agreements which have been concluded in firms of the private sector, or the plans which have been adopted can be considered as more than isolated instances and whether they have yielded any appreciable results.

Behind the frequently sterile debate on appropriate ways of interesting workers in a productivity drive another more fundamental problem is hidden. Many employers are afraid lest productivity policies be used to obtain an objectionable degree of "co-determination" of their personnel in the management of enterprise. With the encouragement of their associations numerous businessmen are willing to reward their personnel who have participated in a productivity drive with a bonus commensurate with the increase in profits. But they are reluctant to make the size or the distribution of the bonus a subject of consultation with their personnel or with the unions represented in the shop. They are even less inclined to discuss beforehand their plans for an increase in production with their workers or the trade unions. The free unions, although they do not reject like the CGT all productivity policies from the outset, consider the attitudes of management proof that the employers are not ready to do their part in the improvement of the industrial "climate."[28]

*   *   *

Such fundamental and as yet unresolved divergencies furnish at least a partial explanation for the rather spectacular failure

[27] On these points see the periodic reports of the CNPF Productivity Committee to the General Assembly and the minutes of its meetings, especially in *Bulletin*, No. 122, August 1954, pp. 74-79, and No. 134, July 1955, pp. 5-7.

[28] The free trade unions have founded an Inter-Union Center for Productivity Studies (CIERP) which enjoys a modicum of benevolent support from the em-

in which some of the more widely advertised experiments in productivity have ended. The so-called foundry experience in particular illustrates well the impediments which arise for productivity policies both from within and without the employers' movement.[29]

Under the leadership of M. Ricard the trade association for the foundry industry had utilized the facilities offered by the Vichy regime for the establishment of a Technical Center which continued its activities after the end of the war. Supported by a parafiscal tax, it served as a model clearinghouse for technical information dispensed by a validly organized trade association to its members. M. Christa, a collaborator of M. Ricard, returned from one of the early productivity missions to the United States deeply impressed with what he had seen. The trip had also brought him into close personal contact with the representatives of the non-communist unions who had been members of the same mission. From the observations he made after his return, M. Christa became convinced that, without a psychological shock, it would be impossible to overcome the distrust of employers, engineers, and workers against any idea suggested to them from the outside.[30]

In order to create the shock effect, it was decided to engage in 1951-52 upon a pilot project in which finally only nine medium-sized foundry establishments participated, after having been rather haphazardly chosen from a total of 2,400 firms. The project was far from receiving the approval of the entire indus-

ployers' movement. A good general view of the hopes (rather than the achievements) of the CIERP is provided by its report, *op.cit.* (n. vi-21). The same report contains on pp. 101 ff. a number of interesting "testimonials" from industrialists in regard to productivity. Behind the cautious wording a great variety of viewpoints can be detected.

[29] For a description of the foundry experiment by those who instigated it, see Roger Christa and Pierre Ricard, "L'expérience de la fonderie," in *Expériences Productivité*, Paris, 1952, pp. 15-19. At length also in Comité National etc., *Actions etc., op.cit.* (n. vii-19), pp. 253-59. Since the existing descriptions dwell on the initial successes but do not describe the eventual demise of the experiment, more attention is paid here to the latter.

[30] For an interesting description of the mentality which every productivity program will face in France, see Roger Christa, "L'Opération Productivité dans la Fonderie," *Productivité Française*, No. 5, May 1952, pp. 7-9. The first rather courageous act of the Foundry Association was to confront French industry with an unfavorable picture of its own behavior and methods by publishing the report of M. Silbermann's, *op.cit.* (n. vii-13).

try. Leading personalities in the employers' movement predicted that those participating in the experiment were probably preparing their own bankruptcy. However, since the project was entirely financed by American and French government funds, the courage shown by the nine firms might be judged to have been somewhat short of heroic.

The project itself was designed according to an elaborate and interesting, if typically French, formula: employers, engineers, and workers, and at a somewhat later stage American efficiency experts, were brought together in a secluded location for training sessions of various lengths; the trade association circulated at regular intervals a "bulletin of liaison" among all participants, mixing technical information with homely pep talk; at regular intervals the progress made was to be tested by elaborate methods. What the technical results of these efforts have been has never been exactly determined. M. Christa and his staff had warned from the outset that a project involving only nine firms could not be more conclusive than any laboratory exploration; that another project comprising a hundred foundries was to follow immediately; that from there on the entire industry and, it was hopefully added, other industries as well might be fired by an infectious enthusiasm for productivity methods.

Actually the experiment never went beyond the laboratory stage. After the "program of the nine" had come to an end, the entire project was abandoned under mutual recriminations involving personalities in the employers' movement and the free trade unions, as well as various offices of the United States Mutual Security Administration. In retrospect one of the main reasons for the failure seemed to have been the vagueness of the agreements among the parties which engaged in the pilot project. While industry had promised to refrain from any dismissal of personnel as a direct consequence of increased productivity, it was difficult to decide what kind of lay-off fell under the agreement. While there had been consultation between management and labor, the free trade unions were dissatisfied with its extent and sought to obtain contractual regularization of their status through the American labor representatives in MSA. Such demands, industry demurred, were in no way justified by the strength of either the Christian or the FO unions in the foundry industry; moreover, the interference by the American authorities was considered improper.[31]

Such vagueness as had prevailed was at least in part intended since it corresponded to the equally vague status of the promoters of the experiment in their respective organizations. M. Christa and the union officials collaborating with him had hoped that the success of their endeavor would break down the resistance of the milieu for which they were acting. But the success could not be outstanding, if only because of the voluntary limitation of the first project, and because no preparations had been made to find a market for the possibly increased production. When it became clear that the follow-up would entail material sacrifices for the participating firms and, worse, would involve principles of labor-management collaboration to which the employers' movement was unwilling to consent, the traditionalists on both sides saw fit to call a halt to the vastly over-advertised experiment. The position of those who had predicted failure, seemed inassailable when the walls failed to give in to the publicity trumpets.

The outcome of the foundry experiment was undoubtedly quite symptomatic for the chances of reform action in present-day France. Whenever the atmosphere of general inaction becomes too stifling, individuals are found who seek to ignore or circumvent the institutionalized obstacles to all change. Their initial success is often due to a general dissatisfaction with immobilism. But as soon as their efforts lose momentum, the more solidly organized interests are able to put an end to experiments which frequently and naturally have a certain amateurishness. But—and here might be found the most important single difference from similar situations elsewhere—in France the conservative forces will in general not incorporate any part of the reformatory designs into their program of action, but will consider their own triumph as a justification for yet more stubborn immobilism if not for revenge.

In the employers' movement the collapse of the foundry project led to a considerable weakening of the position of those, mostly of the younger generation, who had hoped to develop the campaign for increased productivity beyond the strict limitations

[31] After the shipwrecking of the foundry experiment officials of the ACADI group made an attempt to bring the labor and industry representatives together, only to find out that the gap was unbridgeable.

which their organizations had prescribed for the collaboration between management and personnel. As a symbol for their victory the most conservative forces in the CNPF succeeded in having the new president of the Foundry Association, an aged industrialist who had already played a considerable role in the pre-war employers' movement and who had never concealed his fundamental opposition to the productivity experiment, elected to the executive of the peak association.

Since that time a number of other similar attempts have met with varying success. American advisers have reported that as long as they were working with individual firms results were highly satisfactory, but that the interference from the trade associations was generally detrimental to their efforts. One of these experts spoke of an "anti-productivity conspiracy" existing in many trade associations and was merely told by the embarrassed French government official in charge of productivity matters that he should not "generalize."[32]

Officially the trade associations have encouraged the pursuit of productivity programs undertaken with various intensity both on a national and regional scale in a number of industries, but all promoted solely by business without the participation of labor organizations; other trade associations have at least set up a working group concerned with matters of modernization.[33] An old-established organization, such as the *Commission Générale d'Organisation Scientifique* (CEGOS), continues to document its members, individual firms or trade associations, about rationalization methods and seeks to further a greater open-mindedness of industry by encouraging the interchange of information and factory visits. Before the war CEGOS was directly affiliated with the CGPF; now it functions independently but still as an adjunct to the employers' movement.[34]

[32] For excerpts from a letter of protest which Mr. Mark T. Shaw addressed to the United States Embassy in France, see *New York Times*, July 8, 1955; for the reply by M. Ardant, see *ibid.*, July 15, 1955. It is interesting to compare the comments of Mr. Shaw with an early over-optimistic description of his successes by Edmund Taylor, "The Plane, the Blast Furnace, and the Shoemaker," *The Reporter*, XI, November 18, 1954, pp. 24-27.

[33] For a listing of such undertakings, see *Bulletin*, No. 122, August 1954, pp. 77-78. While the list is fairly long, some of these endeavours are said to exist merely on paper.

[34] For its activities and membership, see CEGOS, *Annuaire des adhérents, 1951-1952*, Paris, 1952.

Some other business organizations and trade associations have been willing to give labor a voice in productivity matters and have concluded agreements of which the CNPF disapproves in principle. The national collective agreement which the Textile Association entered in the summer of 1953 with the free trade unions contained a clause according to which the workers were to "benefit effectively from the results of an improved productivity." Similar promises are contained in contracts concluded in the printing trade and in the shoemaking industry.

Another effort to bring about union-management cooperation in productivity matters is made by the *Comité National de l'Organisation Française* (CNOF), especially since M. Baruzy has assumed its presidency.[35] The functions and activities of this management organization, resembling somewhat the American Management Council, are similar to those of CEGOS except that it emphasizes the training of technical and lower management personnel in formal courses. On its board a number of trade union delegates have joined with some outstanding industrialists, so that the meetings and study sessions of the organization still provide a forum for the exchange of experiences and opinions.[36]

*        *        *

Governmental administration of productivity policies has frequently shifted over the last years. There have been long intervals during which the transfer of responsibilities from one board to the other, or a vast reorganization effort all but paralyzed official activities. The attempt at solving weighty problems of economic policy by consultative boards which seldom reach the required unanimity was once again frustrated by the basic divergencies dividing the main interest groups involved.[37]

The attitudes of the employers' movement toward the official organizations which coexisted or succeeded each other were, as in

[35] On Count Baruzy's general outlook, see above Chapter IV.
[36] Several of the personalities active in CNOF have founded together with M. Migeon and M. Buron, a MRP Deputy, *the Comité d'Action Sociale pour la Productivité*, an organization devoted particularly to the encouragement of all experiments which share the benefits of heightened productivity with the personnel. See *L'Usine Nouvelle*, No. 52, December 25, 1952, p. 23. On a similar organization, CADIPPE, see above Chapter IV.
[37] For a history of the official organisms concerned with productivity questions, see *Bulletin*, VIII, No. 122, August 1954, pp. 74-77.

other fields, conditioned by the desire to be closely associated with the processes of decision making, to insure to its members access to available funds, and to prevent a strengthening of economic controls by the government. The CNPF has constantly insisted that considerations of productivity should not bring into the purview of the governmental National Committee on Productivity too broad a range of economic and social problems. If productivity were to become an overriding economic principle to which individual enterprises had to submit, it would in the eyes of the CNPF contain the germs of a new *dirigisme*, not less objectionable than that of the immediate post-war years.[38]

On the whole the employers' movement was in favor of seeing in 1953 the shapeless National Committee transformed into a General Commissariat, headed by an eminent inspector of finance. Confident as it was, that, because of its generally excellent relations with the administration, its own influence would not be diminished, the CNPF was satisfied to see the veto rights of labor and other groups which were represented on the earlier Committee curtailed.[39] The CNPF continues to send to the various advisory boards of the commissariat ranking officers of its own study committee on productivity questions, and especially M. Norguet whose distinguished career has shown him to be a firm believer in technical progress.[40]

The employers' movement still wishes to forestall as far as possible all legislative action in productivity matters, since it believes that regulation by statute would introduce too much rigidity where flexibility should prevail. If the CNPF makes the point that also in the United States the legislator does not concern himself with the efficiency of business, it can be answered that governmental interference is less likely where output and economic growth are satisfactory, and that it might be expected where economic protectionism is as developed as it is in France.

[38] See the very critical observations in a report by the CNPF Committee on Productivity in *Bulletin*, vi, No. 84, July 20-August 5, 1952, p. 40.

[39] The newly appointed Commissioner, M. Gabriel Ardant, is the author of a book widely noted for its originality, *Techniques de l'Etat*, Paris, 1953. His economic views, showing him as an unrepentant Keynesian, are brilliantly expounded in two articles, "Le Grand Tournant," *Le Monde* (weekly edition), July 14-20, 21-27, 1955. See also the book he co-authored with M. Mendès-France, *op.cit.* (n. VI-10).

[40] For a description of his career, see above Chapter VI.

In regard to the disbursement of funds for the purposes of modernization and heightened productivity, the CNPF is generally opposed to seeing administrative agencies entitled to award or refuse grants or loans, since this would enable the bureaucracy to decide on the survival or the ruin of a given firm. But inasmuch as the money is derived from American aid which France received under the Moody amendment, specifically for the purpose of helping productivity programs, the sums are awarded under certain conditions stipulated by United States legislation and by the terms of the Franco-American treaty. Not to accept those conditions would be tantamount to refusing all grants from American and French sources, and this industry and its representatives cannot well afford.[41]

Henceforth the strategy of organized business has been to insist with the authorities that the trade associations should be the principal, if not the sole, agents of all productivity efforts so that "one day it becomes impossible to disassociate the term productivity and that of *organisation professionnelle*."[42] This will be of little comfort to those French and foreign observers who have found trade associations to be more inimical to policies and practices of productivity than individual businessmen. Certain elements within the employers' movement are quite aware of the fact that it might be incongruous to entrust the cause of dynamic progress to the same organizations which are eager to insure security for all through price-fixing, cartels, and similar arrangements. Even a group that is as much imbued with the idea of *organisation professionnelle* as the *Jeune Patron* has warned that many of the trade associations as they are presently constituted might act more as a brake than as a motor.[43]

---

[41] The CNPF informs its membership in detail about the available credits without taking any position in regard to the policies involved; see *Bulletin*, VII, No. 100, June 5, 1953, pp. 26-29, on the Moody funds, No. 130, March 1955, pp. 31-34, and No. 134, July 1955, pp. 44-45.

[42] See *ibid.*, V, No. 70, September 5, 1951, p. 10, and in a similar vein more recently, *ibid.*, No. 127, December 1954-January 1955, p. 6.

[43] See Weinmann, *op.cit.* (n. VII-21), and, by the same author, "La Productivité," reprint from *Jeune Patron*, No. 49, November 1951. Most interesting is the very crucial article on the attitude of trade associations in productivity matters by Maurice Duverger, "Les fonctionnaires du capitalisme," *Le Monde*, September 2-3, 1951. See also *ibid.*, September 19, 1951, for an account of the interesting correspondence which the author received in reply to his article from many businessmen who agreed with his conclusions.

It is as yet impossible to pass judgment on the over-all progress of productivity efforts. The dearth of statistical data, and especially the impossibility of valid comparisons with the pre-war period, make it hardly possible to measure what has been achieved. In its discussion of productivity the report of the achievements of the first Monnet plan departs from its general optimism to admit that in 1951 over-all productivity had just reached the low pre-war level and that therefore the situation in France compares unfavorably with developments in other European countries, not to speak of the United States.[44] Slightly more optimistic are the conclusions arrived at by the first report of the National Committee on Productivity which estimated that the pre-war level had already been equalled in 1949 and that for the ensuing three years the average progress was of an order of three percent, but not more than two percent in 1953.[45]

From the obtainable information it is evident that national averages are even less meaningful in France than elsewhere. So far modernization policies have been highly successful in certain branches, in certain regions of the country, and in certain large concerns, but they seem to have further widened the gap which exists between the developed and backward sectors. There is general agreement among government officials and business leaders that in the long run progress will depend not so much on the dissemination of technical know-how or on devices for improving human relations, as on general economic developments affecting the climate in which business enterprise operates.

Undoubtedly the long drawn-out inflation, rendering economic calculation both on the plant level and on a larger scale extremely difficult, was as little propitious for any productivity drive as the recession that set in during 1952-53. Since then the steady improvement of the economic situation and new tax and credit policies have improved the chances for the kind of long-range general economic policies which alone promise lasting progress. There is no indication as yet that even under favorable

---

[44] See Commissariat, etc., *Cinq ans etc., op.cit.* (n. VI-11), pp. 356-57, and *Mendès-France Report 1953, op.cit.* (n. IV-4), p. 52. An interesting comparison between the development of productivity in France and the United States showing France steadily falling behind and ranking just above Italy, was given publicity by the CNPF in *Bulletin,* VIII, No. 117, March 20, 1954, p. 23.

[45] See Comité National de la Productivité, *op.cit* (n. VII-19), pp. 434-35.

conditions the majority of French employers and their associations are willing to abandon slow rationalization in favor of a policy of massive investments by which modernization and the necessary regional development could be achieved.[46]

For good or evil, the trade associations will continue to play a major role in the promotion or the retarding of productivity policies. Already at present the great differences which exist in the pursuit of such policies reflect the different outlook of the leadership of employers' organizations. If one compares the mentality of certain personalities in the present employers' movement with the pronouncements of the pre-war CGPF on productivity matters, it is quite obvious that important changes have indeed occurred. As yet those who are willing to encourage productivity policies with all their implications are neither sufficiently numerous nor strong enough to insure what some have optimistically described as the final "breakthrough" of the cause of progress in the employers' movement. Much will depend on whether or not the productivity conscious leaders of organized business, in conjunction with like-minded personalities in the administration, and aided by at least a modicum of prosperity, will wield increasing influence. Their success alone would still not be sufficient to overcome the many handicaps which stand in the way of heightened productivity, but it could be a factor in bringing to France what Jean Fourastié in his enthusiastic language has called "the great hope of the twentieth century."[47]

## 2. Nationalizations

At a dinner organized by ACADI in the fall of 1951 and attended by a galaxy of businessmen, managers, and civil servants, the war axe between nationalized and private enterprise

[46] The *U.N. Report, op.cit.* (n. vi-36), concludes however, pp. 194-95, that "both from the point of view of French interest and from a wider international standpoint, there are strong reasons for the second, more ambitious, program rather than the first."

[47] See Jean Fourastié, *Le grand espoir du XXᵉsiècle (progrès technique, progrès économique, progrès social)*, Paris, 1949, 1950, 1952, and also the same author's "Productivity and Economics," *Political Science Quarterly*, LXVI, 1951, pp. 216-25. Men like Fourastié who are closely associated with present-day productivity efforts seem to be as sharp in their criticism of the general French mentality as they are over-optimistic in regard to all efforts which try to combat the prevailing attitudes. A case in point is Fourastié's description of the foundry experiment and other recent activities in the concluding chapter of his *op.cit.* (n. vi-72), pp. 105-11.

was officially buried. Speaking for the CNPF, Messrs. Ricard and Lafond announced that the quarrel between the two sectors of the economy was over, and that the post-war nationalizations were an accepted fact. Their declarations were all the more remarkable as they were made in answer to an aggressive speech by the director of the nationalized railroads, M. Louis Armand. Making himself the spokesman of all nationalized industries, M. Armand without mincing words had appealed to the representatives of private business to cease a campaign whose inanity he denounced in strong and concrete terms.[48]

Directing his criticism mostly against certain unnamed but clearly identifiable members of parliament—the same who are considered the spokesmen of organized business in the National Assembly and the Council of the Republic—as well as against such pressure groups as the truckers' association, M. Armand accused their propaganda of indulging in falsehoods and libel. With a great deal of moral conviction he defended the much-maligned personnel of the railroads and maintained that any attempt to split the economic life of the nation into two opposite camps was detrimental to the badly needed increase of productivity in both sectors. He dwelled lengthily on the problem of the control of nationalized enterprises and on what he called the "abuses of control," showing why in his opinion most of the proposed reform legislation in the field contained amateurish suggestions made by incompetent demagogues. He called it an outright illusion to believe that the economy could be freed from the tutelage of the state, and insisted therefore more specifically on a close collaboration between the administration and the representatives of organized business. While recognizing explicitly the important place of the employers' movement in a system of a mixed economy, he tried to differentiate among the leaders of the general movement and those organizations which were devoted to the narrow defense of special interests.

It might be hazardous to conjecture that by applauding M.

[48] L. Armand, "Entreprises nationalisées et entreprises privées. Vers un climat de meilleure compréhension et de meilleure productivité," *Bulletin Acadi*, No. 53, December 1951, pp. 415-37. M. Pierre Uri, chief economist of the Monnet plan office had spoken earlier of the polemics concerning the nationalizations as irrational manifestations of a religious war. See his interesting article, "La Querelle des Nationalisations," *Les Temps Modernes*, v, 1949, pp. 165-70.

Armand's speech even such men as Ricard and Lafond under-wrote the philosophy to which the speech had given expression. They did however testify, as many of their colleagues have done since then, to a new and realistic appraisal of the nationalizations which the organizations of private industry had come to consider no longer as a threat, but as an asset.

According to available estimates, the number of personnel employed by the state has increased during the decade 1938-48 from 1.8 million to approximately 3 million, or one-fourth of all those gainfully employed (outside of agriculture). The industrial concerns controlled by the state employ 13 percent of the personnel covered by the French production index and account for 14 percent of the total production. In such fields as energy, transport, and credit, the government has established and maintained a preponderant position.[49] If nevertheless private industry no longer feels alarmed by such preponderance, this is in large part due to the well-founded belief that nationalizations will not spread further and that at present the state does not dominate the national economy to the extent earlier advocates of nationalization had foreseen.

The point could be made that those who proceeded after the liberation with the long awaited "structural reforms" had insufficient knowledge of the very structure they set out to reform and were therefore unable to forecast correctly the effect of the enacted measures.[50] In matters of credit control for instance, it has been said correctly that, although the nationalized banks transact more than half of French banking activities, their nationalization "has not in any tangible manner modified the habits and structure of the French banking system."[51] The fact

[49] These calculations, probably of somewhat dubious exactness, were furnished by the National Institute of Statistics; see Ministry of Finance, etc., op.cit. (n. 11-52). The Annexe, No. 4794 to the J.O. Ass. Natle. Doc. Parl., July 7, 1953, contains on pp. 2770-811 a complete list of the more than hundred enterprises in which the government holds title.

[50] See on this point the thoughtful article by Jean L'homme, "Le Profit et les Structures Sociales," Revue Economique, III, 1952, p. 413. For a somewhat similar and earlier discussion by which the then executive of the National Steel Association gave his conditioned approval to the first nationalizations, see Louis Charvet, "Nationalisations," Politique, XX, Nouvelle Serie, II, 1946, pp. 428 ff. But at that time the author spoke as a member of the Executive of the MRP rather than in the name of the trade associations.

[51] Pierre Dieterlen and Charles Rist, The Monetary Problem of France, New

that the managers of the nationalized banks are in outlook and training particularly close to the leading figures in private business might be far more significant than the existence of a board such as the National Credit Council. Moreover, the extent to which business engages in self-financing makes any of the existing banking and credit controls of dubious efficiency. While businessmen might still complain about deficiencies of the credit system, they are not in any serious manner hampered by the nationalizations as such. If the promoters of the post-liberation legislation had hoped to manipulate a large sector of the private economy through the "nationalization of credit," such hopes have been frustrated.

Equally reassuring for business was the fact that already in the summer of 1946 a virtual stoppage of nationalizations occurred, although only about half of the program endorsed by the resistance movement had been carried through at that time.[52] With the exception of a statute nationalizing the Parisian passenger transportation, all bills demanding further nationalizations were easily defeated in parliament. Enthusiasm had been waning so completely that during the election campaign of 1951 not a single party, and this includes the socialists and communists, even raised the issue of nationalization.

The reasons why disappointment with the results of a transfer of ownership had set in so early and became so general need not be discussed here.[53] As far as industry was concerned, its accom-

---

York, 1948, p. 17. The same conclusion is reached by J. M. Fourier, "Bilan de la nationalisation des banques," *Le Droit Social*, xv, September-October 1952, pp. 515-18, in an article that contains interesting information on the collaboration between the nationalized banks and private business. For a general survey of the problems involved in the French mixed banking system, see also Margaret G. Myers, "The Nationalization of Banks in France," *Political Science Quarterly*, LXIV, 1949, pp. 189-210.

[52] See David H. Pinkney, "The French Experiment in Nationalization 1944-1950," in *Modern France, op.cit.* (n. III-50), p. 355. Excellent on the history of French nationalizations is also Mario Einaudi et al., *Nationalization in France and Italy*, Ithaca, 1955.

[53] The most critical appraisals of the nationalizations are to be found in the bitter writings of disillusioned ex-socialists; see Laurat et Pommera, *op.cit.* (n. III-6), pp. 70 ff., 140 ff., and Lefranc, *op.cit.* (n. 1-56), pp. 294-306. Far more balanced but also accounting for the disappointment of the working class are the two articles by Adolf Sturmthal, "The Structure of Nationalized Enterprises in France," *Political Science Quarterly*, LXVII, 1952, pp. 357-77, and "Nationalization and Workers Control in Britain and France," *Journal of Political Economy*, LXI, 1953, esp. pp. 59-67.

modation to a system of mixed economy became possible when it felt assured that no additional nationalization measures were threatening.

From the very beginning, the economic loss which the postwar nationalizations inflicted on private business had been resented far less than the intentionally punitive character of the first legislative measures. As early as 1942, General de Gaulle had declared in a widely heralded speech that "disaster and betrayal have disqualified most of the owners and men of privilege," and that it would therefore be "unacceptable to leave intact a social and moral order which had worked against the nation."[54] During the extremely short parliamentary debates on the nationalizations, expressions of political distrust of private enterprise were at least as strong as anti-capitalist feelings. The "trustophobia" which had developed during the period of the Popular Front had waxed stronger during the occupation. At least the nationalizations of the major banks and insurance companies were to a large extent motivated by a desire to curtail in the future what had long been described as the "maneuvering funds" of private business.[55]

For a time the mystical belief in the beneficial effect of nationalizations was so infectious that in the first Constituent Assembly hardly more than sixty deputies voted against the legislation. At that time public opinion polls showed that certain nationalizations were overwhelmingly approved by the public at large and that even a majority of managerial personnel and of the liberal professions favored them.[56]

In the nationalized enterprises themselves the partly chastising character of the operation was highlighted by the enforced personnel changes among top management. It is true that in that respect differences existed among the various concerns. In the mining industries business resented what it considered, in the words of an official of the employers' movement, the "brutal

[54] Quoted from Marcel Ventenat, L'Expérience des Nationalisations, Paris, 1947, pp. 110-11.

[55] For an excellent discussion of the motivations for the nationalizations, see Georges Vedel, "La technique des nationalisations," Droit Social, IX, 1946, pp. 49-57 and 93-99, and Lefranc, op.cit. (n. 1-56), pp. 290-94.

[56] See Institut Français d'Opinion Publique, L'Opinion du Monde du Travail sur les conditions de vie économique et sociale, Paris, 1946, p. 52.

elimination . . . of an entire intellectual and technical elite."[57] Elsewhere, as in the Renault works and the railroads, personalities who had been active in the resistance movement, such as Messrs. Lefaucheux and Armand, were chosen to head the former staff from which only "collaborators" with an all too objectionable record were dismissed. Everywhere however there was an influx of political appointees to positions of influence, and the political convictions of the *homines novi* were overwhelmingly unfriendly to private business.

But if the mythical and psychological, rather than the economic, significance of the nationalizations had been resented most, then the dispelling of the myth and the rapid disappointment with the results were apt to heal the wounds which had been inflicted on the self-esteem of private business. The intended loss of prestige was soon repaired after it turned out that no truly new managerial elite emerged and that the bourgeoisie was able to effect a comeback in public and political life. From then on the continued existence of a large public sector of the economy held less and less terror. On the managerial level a slow but steady amalgamation between several groups took place over the years. The successive shifts were not the same in all nationalized enterprises, but they have resulted eventually everywhere in a fairly homogeneous leadership. Engineers, trained at the *Ecole Polytechnique* or at the *Ecole Centrale* are still prominent, though slightly less so than after the liberation. Members of the high bureaucracy, usually rather technicians of administration than experts in engineering, have joined them. Finally top-flight managers with a career in private business have been given an increasing share in the administration of nationalized enterprises, especially of the banks.

In some cases the personalities so employed have made in their careers a full circle: from high positions in public administration they have joined private industry, to find themselves once more in public service as administrators of a nationalized enterprise. Inasmuch as some of them have not abandoned their private business connections, they may now cumulate positions

[57] See Robert Fabre, "Réflexions sur les Nationalisations," reprinted from *Revue des Deux Mondes*, March 15, 1951, p. 10. Before the war the author had been the executive of the trade association of the private mining industry. See below n. VII-64 for the general significance of his article.

in the employers' movement with their functions in nationalized enterprises.[58] The number of outstanding business leaders who also hold posts in the nationalized sector was extremely high even before a series of decrees created additional places for them on the boards of the foremost nationalized companies.[59]

At first many civil servants, and especially the members of the *grands corps*, had looked askance at the nationalizations because of their political motivation. They spoke of the nationalized enterprises and of their early managers in the same terms as conservative members of parliament, dreading the emergence of a new "feudalism" to which the state might become subservient.[60] Since then it has been recognized that managerial positions in the nationalized enterprises offer a desirable outlet and a channel of additional influence for the bureaucracy. Inasmuch as the traditional bureaucracy considers the progressive osmosis of the two sectors desirable, they welcome the fact that in the day-by-day activities of the nationalized enterprises public administrators and business leaders brush shoulders constantly.[61]

The ranking engineers who still occupy leading positions in the management of some nationalized enterprises seem to have acquired a somewhat modified outlook. Their experiences have mitigated their technocratic mentality and have made them

[58] The following names might be mentioned as examples of many others: Guillaume de Tarde, Henry Davezac, Henri Lafond, Jean Faye, Olivier Moreau-Néret.

[59] See the decrees Nos. 53-416 to 53-420 of May 11, 1953, *J.O.* May 12, pp. 4332-34 creating new seats on the boards for "persons designated because of their competence in industrial and financial matters." Because of the protest from the trade unions these decrees had in part to be modified. On the significance of the decrees see the incisive comments by Einaudi, *op.cit.* (n. VII-52), pp. 29 f. The catalogue presented by the *J.O.* on July 7, 1953 (see above, n. VII-49), which is usually cited as evidence of the extensiveness of governmental influence in the economy, also offers, by publishing the names and affiliations of all full-time and part-time administrators, most valuable documentation on the interpenetration of the personnel of the private and the public sector.

[60] For the clearest exposition of the views of a conservative *fonctionnaire* on the nationalizations, see Albin Chaladon, "Le problème des entreprises nationalisées," *Revue Politique et Parlementaire*, LI, Tome CXCVIII, April-June 1949, pp. 223-35. The author is a young inspector of finance who in the meantime has entered private banking.

[61] For the present-day outlook of many civil servants on the nationalizations, see Uri, *op.cit.* (n. VII-48), p. 167; and Brindillac, *op.cit.* (n. II-44), p. 875. On this as on so many other questions the bureaucracy is divided, making any generalization difficult. But, again as in other fields, existing differences of opinion actually facilitate the operations of private business.

aware of political and economic intricacies as well as of the problems raised by industrial relations in a troubled period.[62] On the other hand, those who have come to public enterprise from private business and the bureaucracy belonged usually to the most productivity-minded elements of their milieu.

Out of the amalgamation here described there has emerged a common managerial spirit which is no longer essentially different from that of the directors of large private concerns. But what has been said earlier about the mentality of the managers in private enterprise holds also true of the administrators of nationalized concerns: they too are sometimes imbued with the spirit of the French bourgeoisie and of the patrimonial employers.[63] Yet as soon as it became evident that the outlook of management in both public and private enterprise had by and large become identical, there was no longer any reason for hostility or even cautious reserve. The colloquy between the two sectors which ACADI had instigated after the liberation as an isolated and originally rather bold venture became general. Leading personalities of the employers' movement paid open tribute to the "business-like" efficiency first of individual concerns, such as the mining companies, the *Electricité de France*, or the nationalized railroads. But soon the entire public sector was included in such praise. The reform proposals which business organizations still made never questioned the principle of nationalization as such. Since in the words of a prominent staff member of the CNPF, "the separation of the nationalized enterprises from the rest of the nation was a disservice to their own cause as well as to the general interest," all suggestions submitted by the employers' movement had the sole intention "of reincorporating them into the national economy."[64]

---

[62] It is interesting to compare statements made at various times by the late M. Pierre Lefaucheux; see his speech to the Renault workers in November 1944, (published in *Droit Social*, VII, 1944) pp. 305-8 and his address to ACADI "La Régie Nationale des Usines Renault," *Bulletin Acadi*, No. 27, May 1949, pp. 194-212, as well as his remarks before a CNPF Committee, reported in *Bulletin*, VI, July 20-August 5, 1952, p. 16.

[63] See above Chapter III.

[64] See Fabre, *op.cit.* (n. VII-57), p. 15. At the time of his writing the author was the permanent secretary of the CNPF's Economic Secretariat. His article was widely noted for its objective treatment and conciliatory tone. It is interesting to compare it with an earlier pamphlet by the same writer, Robert Fabre, *Silhouette de l'Industrie Houillère Française*, Paris, 1945.

The more rational view on nationalizations which organized business acquired opened a fuller understanding for the material advantages which the existence of the public sector held out for private enterprise. Even though publicly the deficits of some of the nationalized concerns were still criticized, the trade associations knew that their membership profited from a price policy which was to a large extent responsible for the deficits. With the sole exception of coal, the prices of products and services provided by the nationalized railroads and the electrical and gas companies remained far below the general price level for the first five years of the experiment; at a time when the wholesale and retail price index showed approximately a twentyfold increase over pre-war prices, gas, electricity, and railroad freight rates had risen only about twelve times.[65] Such a policy has resulted in deficits or at least in a drastic reduction of the funds available for the self-financing of the public concerns. Yet parliamentary debates and administrative regulations showed that such a policy was actually wanted by business not less than by the general public. Here was the counterpart of the all-pervading inflationist mentality which has been described earlier. Just as for a long time inflationary price rises were formally protested but actually desired because they avoided immediate catastrophies and the painful opting for priorities, low prices for public utilities were popular because they mitigated the effects of inflation without arousing organized resistance.

Attacks against the nationalizations have continued in some of the information media published by specialized groups of the employers' movement; in parliament they are still carried on by those who are often considered the most trustworthy spokesmen of business organizations. Especially Senators Armengaud and Pellenc have relented little in their criticism. By their important committee positions, both senators have an excellent opportunity to scrutinize the economic activities of the public sector. They incorporate their findings in speeches made from the floor of the Council of the Republic, in lengthy introductions to reform legislation which they periodically propose, or in pamphlets

[65] See for the situation between 1945 and 1951, *Mendès-France Report 1953*, *op.cit.* (n. IV-4), pp. 48-49. The report makes the point that in comparison with international prices also the price for French coal was kept low.

which they prepare for the benefit of certain business organizations.[66] All too often however the facts which they present have proven fictitious and their campaigns more noteworthy for partisan passion than for patent truth. Senator Pellenc still develops almost point by point the very arguments which the director of the nationalized railroads, applauded by members of the CNPF's executive, denounced as ludicrous and dangerous. But also the *Comité d'Action et d'Expansion Economique*, of which Messrs. Villiers, Ricard, and Mayolle are council members, was found to have falsified, as late as 1951, the text of a speech by M. Lefaucheux concerned with the financing of the Renault works.[67] The mixture of bad faith and of unreliability of which their foes have often been convicted has actually strengthened the case of the nationalized enterprises.

Such propagandistic efforts are no longer officially endorsed by the CNPF but they might still appeal to the feelings of many of the small businessmen and particularly to the clientele of the CGPME. But by and large the entire issue of nationalization has lost its political significance and urgency.

Among the study groups of the CNPF the Committee on Private Enterprise had originally been given the principal assignment to build a dam against what Léon Blum had called in 1946 the "expansive force and contagious virtue of the nationalizations."[68] Since nationalizations stopped spreading even before the group began its work, the study committee was able to devote its efforts to the detailed examination of legislation concerned with the public sector of the economy, outside of occasional protests against proposed further nationalizations.

The reports of the committee become vehement only where affiliates of the CNPF seek to defend themselves against operations of one or the other of the public enterprises, as when the

[66] For one of Senator Armengaud's comprehensive reform bills and its interesting *Exposé des Motifs*, see *J.O. Cons. Rép. Doc. Parl. Annexe* No. 11403, 1950, pp. 2034-40. The most vehement statements of Senator Pellenc's are to be found in his pamphlets, *op.cit.* (n. v-22).

[67] See Régie Nationale des Usines Renault, *Rapport Annuel de Gestion ... pour l'Exercice 1951*, Paris, 1952, p. 48. It is true that the Régie Renault is generally resented by business more than other nationalized enterprises because of the competition its manufacturing units and the steel work connected with it offer to private concerns. On this point see Einaudi et al., *op.cit.* (n. vii-52), p. 172.

[68] See CNPF, *Assemblée Générale, op.cit.* (n. iii-17) (mimeographed, no pagination).

road carriers wish to take over certain profitable lines from the railroads, or when manufacturers protest the fabrication of small ammunition by the government monopoly.[69] Otherwise the committee scrutinizes with cool detachment the bills which are proposed for the reform of nationalized enterprises; the impatient suggestions made by Senator Armengaud are now given rarely the seal of approval. Without saying so explicitly, the CNPF seems to feel that proposals aiming at more rigid controls or a more uniform structure for the various enterprises are likely to create unnecessary disturbances.[70]

In the dispute over the nationalizations organized business has clearly settled for the *status quo*.

### 3. Reform of Capitalist Enterprise

"The idea means little: the will is everything. Ideas? One finds as many as one wants, more than one wants. In France everybody creates, transports, offers them to those who need them and to those who don't. . . .

Detoeuf, *Propos de O. L. Barenton*

Impassioned discussions, legislative proposals, and practical experiments, all centering around the problem of how to reform capitalist enterprise, are not a novel phenomenon in modern France. But if the interest in this kind of reforms has markedly increased since the war, it was prompted not only by theoretical search or moral uneasiness, but also by eminently practical considerations. Many industrialists and intellectuals judged that the needed increase in production and productivity would be difficult to obtain if the majority of workers remained estranged from their jobs because they felt excluded from any social and economic progress. Such reforms as had been conceived by the resistance movement and had been enacted during the early post-liberation period had done little to integrate the working class into the nation and its industrial life. The nationalizations had been "stolen by the trusts"; the productivity drive was a "fraud perpetrated by the employers"; the plant committees a "sop" deprived of real significance—such feelings were widespread even without the communists exploiting them skillfully.

[69] See e.g., *Bulletin*, No. 129, February 1955, p. 34.
[70] See *ibid.*, VIII, No. 114, February 5, 1954, p. 26 and No. 129, p. 35.

If therefore the frustration of the workers continued unabated and was actually aggravated by the general economic situation, and especially by the shortage of housing, the solution of the problem was to be sought elsewhere.

The often noted lack of confidence of the French worker in the competence of his employer, and the bourgeois rather than industrial mentality of the businessmen, suspected of giving their personal status and well-being priority over the success of their firm, have frequently been the starting point for reformatory zeal. But even where capitalist enterprise was considered a technical success, the human frustrations it involved were unpalatable to both the Christian and the libertarian strands in French social thought.[71] Should technical shortcomings and psychological frustrations not be overcome by associating workers and employers in a novel way with the enterprise and hence with each other? Were not the *Code Napoléon*, product of an age of incipient industrialism, and its property concept responsible for keeping apart those who ought to be partners?

French thinking on social organization and on capitalist enterprise as one of its foremost cells has been characterized for more than a century by a number of traits, which are still influential in present-day experimentation and debate. That the discussion was largely inaugurated by jurists and still revolves around the desirability of fundamental changes in the civil law is in itself a tribute to the legalism which is under attack. Most significant is the fact that the concept of "institution" was first developed in a country where the relationship between individual and general prosperity has at all times been tenuous and disputed. In the largely identical terms of the two jurists who claim its paternity, the institution is that organism, or that "system of power equilibrium" which serves the common good, becoming "a consortium *invicem membra.*"[72] Considered as an institution, the plant is divorced from the owner of the plant, the enterprise

---

[71] A monumental and richly documented work is that by Pierre Lassuège, *La Réforme de l'Entreprise*, Paris, 1948; interesting also is the study, published under the auspices of Professor Perroux (who has a certain influence among business leaders), *La Participation des Salariés aux Responsabilités de l'Entrepreneur*, Paris, 1947.

[72] See Maurice Hauriou, *Principes de Droit Public*, Second ed., Paris, 1916, pp. 108-73; and Georges Renard, *L'Institution, Fondement d'une Rénovation de l'Ordre social*, Paris, 1931.

from the entrepreneur. Instead the plant is transformed into a social community; property changes from a bundle of subjective rights belonging to a legal or natural person into an institution integrating management and personnel. Property, no longer a private matter, becomes socially relevant, the distinction between public and private law is erased, the Civil Code presumably exploded.

In France as well as in the countries to which the concept has spread, institutionalist ideas have found their way into progressive as well as traditionalist, and even authoritarian and fascist labor theories; the European democratic labor movement, neo-Thomism and nazism alike have fed on the anti-capitalist and anti-liberal notions of the institutionalists.[73] All of the present advocates of a reform of capitalist enterprise in France are convinced institutionalists, whether they hold out for a "communitarian," an "associative," or a corporatist solution, whether they wish to strengthen or to eliminate sooner or later independent trade unions.[74]

Another particularity of the French reform discussion pertains to the size of the firms for which a transformation is envisaged. In other countries, but particularly in the United States and Germany, traditional economic and legal concepts have been found unsuited for a realistic appraisal and the necessary reforms of the large modern corporation.[75] In France not less than

[73] See the brilliant remarks on this and the general problem of institutionalism in Franz Neumann, *Behemoth. The Structure and Practice of National Socialism*, New York, 1942, pp. 449-51. These pages represent the summary of the same author's more comprehensive and particularly enlightening discussion in "Der Funktionswandel des Gesetzes im Recht der buergerlichen Gesellschaft," *Zeitschrift fuer Sozialforschung*, VI, 1937, esp. pp. 585-95.

[74] For an almost classical expression of contrary attitudes see the discussion of two eminent law professors, in Georges Ripert, *Aspects Juridiques du Capitalisme Moderne*, Paris, 1946, esp. pp. 296-303 and Paul Durand, "Droit Moderne et incorporation du personnel dans l'entreprise," *Bulletin Acadi*, No. 71, July-August 1953, esp. pp. 258-60; and Durand's review of Ripert's book, "Les Aspects juridiques du capitalisme moderne. A propos d'un livre récent," *Droit Social*, X, 1947, pp. 7-11.

[75] We refer, of course, to the treatise by Adolf A. Berle, Jr. and Gardiner C. Means, *The Modern Corporation and Private Property*, New York, 1932. Almost equally remarkable is the short essay by Walter Rathenau, *Vom Aktienwesen*, Berlin, 1918. See also the more recent examinations of the same problems by Sigmund Timberg, "Corporate Fictions. Logical, Social and International Implications," *Columbia Law Review*, XLVI, 1946, pp. 533-80. and Peter Drucker, *Concept of the Corporation*, New York, 1946.

elsewhere corporate management gives rise to serious strains; it is acknowledged that the problem of workers' morale is particularly acute in the large concerns. But in spite of occasional affirmations to the contrary, all reform proposals refer clearly to the small or at best the medium-sized firm and to the relationship between the patrimonial employer and his personnel. Hardly any of the reforms which have been tried out in practice have ever touched the important joint stock companies; truly crucial situations have not been tackled. This gives to the discussions from the very outset a somewhat phalansterian character.

It is true that the Vichy regime inaugurated a reform of the corporation law, inspired largely by a nazi model, yet possibly opening the way for changes that could have led in other, more desirable, directions.[76] But here again the principles of the legislation have been discarded because they seemed connected with ideas and personalities of a better-to-be-forgotten period of French history.

When the employers' delegation to the Economic Council was faced in 1950 with a report summarizing current reform proposals and making suggestions for an effective participation of the personnel "in the property of the means of production and in the running of the enterprise," it rejected the report without any qualification.[77] It might be considered doubtful whether the *rapporteur*, M. Lasserre, a professor of political economy close to the Christian Socialists, had ever hoped to obtain the approval of the employers' group in the Economic Council. The tenor of the report is clearly socialistic—though in no way Marxist—inasmuch as all schemes of profit participation are considered to fall short of desirable goals. Attacks on the "sovereignty" of the employers are bolstered by vague threats that French capitalism ought to accept reforms before another "economic Fourth of August" might impose them, and that the employers would incur a grave responsibility if they opposed peaceful change. The author's lack of concern for the technical problems of production

[76] See the laws of September 18 and November 14, 1940, *J.O.E.F.* September 19 and November 26, 1940, pp. 5059, 5828-29. For an analysis of the legislation see Jean Michel, *Les lois des 18 septembre et le 16 novembre 1940 sur l'administration des Sociétés Anonymes,* Paris, 1941.

[77] See Conseil Economique, Etudes et Travaux, No. 11. *La Réforme de l'Entreprise,* Paris, 1950.

and administration is fairly manifest throughout the report; as an intellectual he also underrates the interest which the worker has in better pay and better working conditions, short of a reform of the legal structure. That the report takes all of its encouragement from minuscule firms and contains only vague allusions to the large concerns shows it to be faithful to the traditions of French reform thought.

It took only one meeting of the Economic Council to turn down the report with the combined votes of the communist CGT and the employers' delegation. The representatives of the CNPF greeted its reading with a probably deliberate and at any rate officially recorded sneer.[78] In a taunting speech, M. Paul Bernard, today a member of the CNPF's Executive, ridiculed the report in a way which its author could only characterize as a gross misrepresentation of his thoughts. The employers' delegation read into the record a declaration in which it praised for once the benefits of capitalism in a rather imprudent language rarely considered suitable to the public mood: workers' promotion to managerial posts was described as being open to those who had the "qualities of initiative and the taste for risk"; the system of free enterprise was characterized as one that "never asks for assistance nor help from anyone."

Afterwards the attitude of the employers' delegation was criticized sharply by some individual businessmen, especially those belonging to the vanguard groups and other fringe movements. M. Lasserre received letters from many employers expressing regret about the mentality which the delegation had shown. The point was made that, even though the report was highly vulnerable to rightful criticism, it should not be the pretext for further immobilism and insensitivity to reform on the part of the employers' movement.[79] But other proposals submitted

[78] For the debate see *Bulletin du Conseil Economique*, March 23, 1950, pp. 162-65. The employers' declaration is reprinted in Conseil Economique, *op.cit.* (n. VII-77), pp. 88-89.

[79] See e.g., "Suggestions pour des Etudes sur la Réforme de l'Entreprise," *Bulletin Acadi*, No. 51, October 1951, pp. 365-72, making *inter alias* the point that to criticize proposals as the work of impractical intellectuals made it particularly imperative for business to come forward with positive contributions to the debate. Even more friendly towards the report was the UCE.ACT. as expressed in its pamphlet, *Structures Humaines, etc., op.cit.* (n. IV-71), p. 19.

directly to parliament made it equally easy for organized business to react with a categorical "no."

\*　　\*　　\*

The history of French legislation introducing a partnership between employers and their workers is full of interesting and unhappy episodes. The earliest of such attempts seemed to have ended in a series of unsavory ventures: when the National Assembly of 1848 decreed the allotment of several million francs to firms which would form an association between workers and employers, many firms applied which hoped to save themselves from bankruptcy but did little for the common prosperity of the "associates."[80] A law enacted during the First World War encouraged the acquisition of shares by the personnel of joint stock companies granting a measure of managerial control to the worker-shareholders. But the law remained a dead letter. A number of reform bills submitted since the liberation never found parliamentary approval.

De Gaulle's projects concerning an "Association of Capital and Labor" caused, at least for a time, more of a stir than preceding bills. The ideas underlying the proposed reforms had first been formulated by de Gaulle in his widely discussed speech at St. Etienne; they were incorporated into a bill soon after the elections of 1951 together with a lengthy *exposé* explaining its philosophy. The Labor Committee of the National Assembly rejected the proposal by a strong majority; outside of the RPF only a few members voted for it.[81]

In its original form the bill proposed to abolish class struggle, collective bargaining, and the existing plant committees in favor of an "association" constituted on the plant level. A production council, on which management and the different groups of employees would be represented, was to distribute net profits be-

[80] See Edouard Dolléans, *L'Histoire du Mouvement Ouvrier*, Vol. I, Paris, 1950, pp. 242, 245. For various other laws and bills, see Conseil Economique, *op.cit.* (n. VII-77), pp. 35, 99 ff.

[81] For the text of de Gaulle's speech in St. Etienne, see *Année Politique 1948*, Paris, 1949, pp. 324-25. For the first version of the bill "aiming at the establishment of contracts of association between capital and labor," see *J.O. Ass. Nationale Doc. Parl. Annexe*, No. 135, Séance July 17, 1951, pp. 1426-27, and for the detailed criticism by the Labor Committee, *ibid.*, *Annexe*, No. 4134, Séance July 11, 1952, pp. 1755-58.

tween capital and labor in accordance with the stipulation of the association contract. While it was explicitly stated that management would have full authority in the running of the enterprise, the production council was to be kept fully informed about the general financial situation and production developments. For the time being the associative scheme was offered on a voluntary basis to all employers who felt inclined to avail themselves of this means to establish a "true community" and to reap the substantial tax advantages which the bill promised. Only for the major nationalized enterprises the "association" was to become compulsory immediately.

The parties of the left and the foremost students of labor law were not alone in finding the bill "disquieting by its ideology and disappointing in its content . . . unnecessary and dangerous."[82] Vivid criticism came also from those sectors of the employers' movement that were most interested in a reform of capitalist enterprise, such as the UCE. ACT.[83]

When in December 1952 the RPF presented a revised version of its proposal, it intended clearly to appease its critics of the moderate left. All features smacking of outright authoritarianism were eliminated; unions and plant committees were permitted to survive, and their contribution to the cause of productivity invited; the nationalizations were left alone.[84] Nevertheless also the new bill was killed in committee.

The CNP was adamantly opposed to the RPF projects in all their forms though it maneuvered adroitly at times not to provoke opposition from its affiliates or from individual employers who might have favored either de Gaulle's or other more liberal proposals. After the 1951 election a RPF deputy had come before the General Assembly of the CNPF to solicit a benevolent attitude toward the "capital-labor" bill; he pointed out that,

[82] These are the conclusions of an excellent critical article by Paul Durand, "L'association capital-travail," *Droit Social*, xiv, 1951, pp. 604-09. A good short criticism is also given by Robert G. Neumann, "Formation and Transformation of Gaullism in France," *Western Political Quarterly*, vi, 1953, pp. 259-61.

[83] See for instance the article by Alexandre Dubois (written on the basis of de Gaulle's speech and the explanations in the Gaullist press), "L'Association capital-travail est-elle un leurre?" *Economie et Humanisme. Diagnostic Economique et Social*, viii, February 1949, pp. 63-68.

[84] For the new proposal, see *J.O. Doc. Parl. Ass. Nationale*, Annexe No. 4916, Séance December 2, 1952, pp. 3050-52.

due to his own efforts, the *exposé* of the bill was paying allegiance to the principle of free initiative and condemned state intervention in economic life.[85] His plea remained unheeded, and the pleader seized the first opportunity to leave de Gaulle's party.

Since 1948 M. Villiers' presidential addresses and the reports of the CNPF's Committee on the "Legal Status of Enterprise" have developed a consistent line in regard to all schemes associating capital and labor through a novel structure of the enterprise. If an employer wanted to install a plan of benefit-sharing in his plant, he was free to do so on his own, but his colleagues were warned not to generalize from the very small number of experiments which had been undertaken. All legislation connecting special forms of remuneration with rights of the personnel to be informed and consulted was rejected as leading to the ruin of managerial authority, and measures promising tax or credit privileges to the employers who would grant such rights were criticized as compounded evil. The superimposed threats of "codetermination" and tax inequality were in the opinion of the CNPF "spelling dangerous consequences for the French economy."[86]

In this respect, as in some others, the attitude of the CNPF has considerably stiffened over the years. At the first General Assembly, M. Villiers still expressed the willingness of the employers' movement to study sympathetically all proposals which might give the personnel a stake in the enterprise.[87] Louis Charvet, then the executive of the National Steel Association and a leading member of the MRP, spoke without inhibition about the possibility that various experiments in enterprise reform might form the prototypes for new solutions just as there had been such prototypes before the legislation on joint stock companies was enacted in 1867.[88] Since then the stubborn opposition of

[85] The information on this incident is provided in Durand, *op.cit.* (n. VII-82), p. 605.

[86] See *Bulletin*, VII, No. 103, July 20, 1953, p. 14; for earlier statements to this question, see *ibid.*, IV, No. 25, January 1, 1949, p. 3; *ibid.*, IV, No. 54, July 20-August 5, 1950, p. 3; *ibid.*, VI, No. 78, February 20, 1952, p. 8.

[87] See CNPF, Assemblée Générale, *op.cit.* (n. III-17).

[88] See the quotation from a speech of M. Charvet's in Pragma, Publications de l'Institut de Science Economique Appliquée, *La participation des salariés aux responsibilités de l'entrepreneur*, Paris, 1947, p. 78, and the same author's rather vague article "Réforme et Evolution de l'Entreprise," in *Bulletin Acadi*, No. 2, January 1947, pp. 1-14.

M. Meunier, vice-president of the CNPF and chairman of its Social Committee, has induced the organization to steer clear of all commitments to specific reform legislation or ideologies. There was little reason to interfere with the practical experiments that have been tried out here and there, since none of them proved contagious.

Endeavors to bestow on labor a partnership in the enterprise have taken many and varied forms. In some firms the privileges of the personnel are restricted to more or less regularized bonus shares; elsewhere labor is invited to participate in the exercise of certain managerial functions; in other cases the transformation of the firm into a cooperative or "community" has gone as far as to establish a non-capitalist production unit.

Mere benefit-sharing plans, giving to labor a partnership in profits but denying all other participation, were practiced at the end of the 19th century in a little over one hundred firms; but since then their number has dwindled. A new technique of profit-sharing which still enjoys a certain vogue was introduced during the last war by Eugène Schueller.[89] The "proportional salary" formula which M. Schueller has propagated with the sense of publicity in which he is a past master has the advantage over older schemes that the workers' share is not calculated on the basis of annual profits, but of monthly turnover; therefore less controversial factors are used for the computation and the interest of the personnel in production might be more permanent.

M. Schueller's inclination to transpose the technical solutions of which he is fond to a general plane has led him to conceive of his bonus system as a milestone to a "proportional economy" of which he wishes to become the revered apostle. To such ends he has established a consulting firm assisting concerns which wish to experiment with his formula.[90]

According to a survey organized by the Ministry of Labor in 1950, there were then 71 firms practicing the "proportional

[89] For the industrial connections of M. Schueller and his quixotic tax proposals, see above Chapter VI.

[90] For an explication of the principle and the application of the proportional salary see M. Montaudoin, *La Part Du Travail*, Paris, 1951, and E. Schueller, *Introduction au Salaire Proportionnel*, Paris, 1952. For a sympathetic portrait of M. Schueller's achievements and philosophy in a publication subsidized by the CNPF, see Merry Bromberger, "Eugène Schueller," *Essor*, No. 1, May 1953, pp. 11-24.

salary" in a wide variety of industrial and commercial fields. The majority were small concerns, but about one-fourth of them employed a personnel of between 200 and 1,000, and 5 were larger firms.[91] The promoters of the Schueller formula admit that since then the "movement" has not spread and might already be retrogressive. The proportional salary has elicited little interest among industrialists seeking an overall increase in productivity. Given the present industrial climate, an arrangement which grants the personnel no voice in determining the modes of payment or in the management of the enterprise seems to have proven insufficient to bring about the improvement of labor-management relations necessary for greater productivity. It is true that in many concerns the workers have come to regard M. Schueller's scheme, as well as other participation schemes, as a generally welcome increase in salary. Those who expected labor to have only scorn for material advantages granted unilaterally by management seem to have been as wrong as those who hoped that modes of remuneration held the key to the reform of capitalist enterprise. But industrial relations in the concerns that engage in such practices seem to have been little affected by the methods of payment alone.

Under prevailing circumstances employers who wish to combine benefit-sharing plans with a participation of the personnel in the actual running of the business must usually enter into special agreements with their workers to organize such an "association." It is characteristic for the mentality of these employer-reformers, and for the environment in which they operate, that every practical experiment is presented by its sponsors as having a claim to general validity. In their anxiety to overcome social and economic conservatism, the innovators want to believe that isolated instances will easily spread, if they are sufficiently discussed and given general, indeed philosophical, meaning. The established employers' organizations need only point to the small number of firms and workers involved to deflate and implicitly ridicule the averments of the system builders. Moreover, those who are opposed to reforms have no difficulty in arousing sus-

---

[91] See "Enquête sur les modalités de participation ouvrière aux benéfices, à la gestion ou à la propriété des entreprises," *Revue Française du Travail*, v, January-March 1950, pp. 13-32.

picion against the reforms, since all proposals which go beyond the mere granting of a production bonus must invade that domain of managerial "sovereignty" which is particularly sacrosanct—that of privacy and secrecy. For evidently the community of interest which the bolder schemes seek to establish cannot become real when one part of the "community" possesses all the facts and the other has only guesses, and usually suspicions, to go on.[92]

Wherever an individual firm has been successful in establishing more developed forms of partnership between management and labor, organized business will explain such experiments in terms of particularly favorable and unique circumstances, rather than as a solution inviting imitation.

In more than one respect the case of the *Compagnie Télémécanique Electrique*, a manufacturing concern for circuit-breakers and similar equipment in the Paris region, is illustrative. From one side the "philosophy" and "novel structure" of this successful company are extolled as the cure-all for the social and industrial problems of the country, although in fact all reforms were introduced empirically and without any change in the legal set-up of a traditional corporation. From the other side the *Télémécanique* is described as a monopoly profiting from special market conditions, though actually the concern has been commercially successful in a competitive domestic and foreign market by a combination of technical skill, inventiveness, and specialization, careful surveillance of the cost element, and aggressive sales methods.[93]

The management of the firm prides itself upon the fact that the reforms it has introduced in the field of industrial and human relations are largely conditioned by the commercial success of a firm which nevertheless has had its ups and downs. The bonus system practiced here consists in a combination of a collective production premium and a sliding wage scale, adding from 33 to 65 percent to base salaries. No individual piece work exists, but

[92] See G. S. Walpole, *Management and Men*, London, 1944, p. 37.

[93] Fairly extensive material on the Télémécanique is to be found in "La Télémécanique Electrique," *L'Economie*, supplement to No. 345, April 10, 1952, pp. 1-8, *Bulletin Acadi* No. 37, April 1950, pp. 129-35 and No. 51, October 1951, pp. 368 ff. For a succinct description, see also Harbison and Burgess, *op.cit.* (n. vii-9), p. 22.

the differences in pay manifest a preference for a strong hierarchization of positions. The monthly bonus which distributes 50 percent of net earnings is discussed in a meeting of the "bonus committee," composed of representatives of management and the elected members of the plant committee constituted in accordance with the post-war legislation. In these meetings a great amount of business information is divulged and often more answers are volunteered than questions asked. The bonus committee is therefore regarded as the focus of the "association," which according to the views of management has transformed in fact, though not displaced in law, the existing individual and collective labor contracts. In addition about 15 percent of the capital is owned, in forms of regular shares, by the personnel; it seems that this opportunity is offered more as an educational device than as an indispensable element of the associative idea.

Social services of all kinds are unusually well developed and are run entirely by the plant committee. Here, as in other respects, special and constant care is taken that none of the opportunities is offered on a compulsory basis, and that every resemblance to the practices of a company union is avoided. The great transparency of operations and of industrial relations at every level provides a striking contrast to the majority of French enterprises. The success in that field can be measured by the complete absence of strikes since the founding of the firm; all trade unions, including the CGT, are represented among the personnel, but none has a numerous membership. For a concern employing less than 2,000 workers, there are said to be about 16,000 job applications on file, almost exclusively from workers employed elsewhere; however the turnover of labor has been nil.

It is impossible to decide which specific factors have made the industrial climate and the productivity of this concern comparable to the very best in the United States. It is likely that the combination of all circumstances, but not alone the pay scheme or joint consultation, are responsible. Hence the *Télémécanique*, though it certainly deserves the emulation by other enterprises, hardly offers convincing proof that any particular structural reform holds out the guarantee of success.

The fact that the experiences of the firm are as widely discussed as they are, is partly due to the missionary zeal and philosophical bent of its eminently practical director general, M. Henri Migeon. Having intentionally kept aloof from the established employers' movement and even its opinion groups, he has criticized the CNPF in his writings for practicing a "Marxism in reverse" and therefore being unable to offer constructive solutions. M. Migeon's concepts too are essentially institutionalist (and in other respects personalist) : since he expects the individual enterprise to provide the basis for a reform of society, he foresees the gradual disappearance of all industry-wide workers' and employers' organizations.[94] For the present, he argues, it would be dangerous to offend the workers' feelings and their dignity by proposing the elimination of trade unions. But he believes that, once a broad application of an associative plant organization has deprived unionism of its *raison d'être*, labor unions would quickly wither away.

The methods operative in the *Télémécanique* stand halfway between a successful profit-sharing plan and the more advanced associative forms such as advocated and practiced by the members of the UCE. ACT.[95] The latter admit that they still have not come to grips with the problems which are central to their way of thinking and to their future action: How to combine the distribution of managerial authority between employer and personnel with a structure that does not give up the distinction between them? How to spread the experiences made on an extremely small scale since, if they remain isolated, the reforms may be psychologically and commercially condemned? In fact, the firms whose owners belong to the UCE. ACT. seem to evolve in either of two directions. Some have abandoned complicated schemes of benefit-sharing without industrial relations taking a turn for the worse, where joint consultation and similar methods have been maintained. Others have gradually evolved towards cooperatives of production, losing all capitalist aspects.

Although discussions on the desirability of enterprise reform are not likely to abate, there is little chance to find here the solution to problems which neither the nationalizations, nor the

[94] See Henri Migeon, *Le Monde après 150 Ans de Technique*, Paris, 1952, pp. 44-46. The entire work is extremely interesting for the author's general outlook. On pp. 39-40 there is a good schematization of all enterprise reforms presently undertaken or advocated.

[95] For details, see above **Chapter IV.**

post-war social legislation, nor the productivity drive were able to attack successfully. The integration of the working class in industrial society might everywhere have other prerequisites than the mere work satisfaction which is expected from the proposed reforms. If its critics accuse the employers' movement for being especially sterile in this field, they themselves are open to the reproach that illusions have never yet effectively changed society.

# CHAPTER VIII

# Economic Issues: III

## *1. Competition and Cartels*

"Competition is an alkaloid; in moderate doses it is a
stimulant, in massive doses a poison."

Detoeuf, *Propos de O. L. Barenton*

When he submitted to the first National Assembly one of the
numerous abortive bills designed to insure "fair and free competition," M. Henri Teitgen, a moderate deputy and illustrious
lawyer, prefaced his proposition with a description of the place
and role of French cartels: "Without status and without law, in
a sort of vagabondage, they wander through society as outcasts;
they hide behind a more or less opaque secrecy and are more
tempted by the evil to which one seems to consign them than by
the good nobody considers them capable of."[1]

The desire to dilute or conceal the character of an often highly
formalized institution is perceptible in the very name which was
given to the French cartels: the word *entente* is designed to
convey the impression of a friendly and entirely voluntary understanding. Because business concentration in France has been notoriously slower than in other countries, and because it has
seldom led to complete amalgamation and has left intact a
myriad of independent producers, the *entente* which was presumably a "milder" cartel was regarded as particularly suited
to the needs of French business organization.

The promoter of one of the earliest cartels, Robert Pinot, comparing the French creation to the American trust and the German
*Interessengemeinschaft*, concluded enthusiastically that "here
once more our Latin genius has found the correct middle way
and knows how to harmonize its constructions."[2] Such praise for
the *entente* as a happy breed of the "French race" was echoed
frequently in the annual addresses of M. Duchemin to the CGPF
and recurs today whenever organized business wishes to defend

[1] Quoted in Conseil Economique, Etudes et Travaux, *Contrôle des Ententes
Professionnelles*, Paris, 1950, p. 73.
[2] See Pinot, *op.cit.* (n. 1-24), p. 14.

its practices against apprehensions expressed from across the Atlantic.

Before the First World War only a few cartels existed, the most important among them being the aluminum cartel and the *Comptoir de Longwy*; before the turn of the century the latter established for the pig-iron and steel industries the pattern of organization which was to become current in France.[3] In form the *comptoirs* were mere selling syndicates; industry stressed constantly the fact that through economies in staff and in transportation these organizations reduced operating costs. Actually they were regarded from the very beginning by the business leaders who sponsored them as desirable agencies for controlling the market. "One cannot stop technical progress," Eugène Schneider remarked, "but one should make efforts to stabilize the market . . . It is not impossible to regularize orders, to space them by the establishment of convenient *ententes* between producers and large consumers . . ."[4]

The First World War gave great impetus to the vertical integration of industry which proceeded mostly through non-proprietary arrangements such as the rapidly expanding exclusive buying and selling agreements. But only a few years after they had lived their "finest hour," the major cartels disbanded. The temporary extinction of the consortiums formed during the war and of the pre-war iron and steel cartels was in no way enforced by the authorities or by a hostile reaction of public opinion. It was rather the immediate consequence of the economic recession which followed the war, and of competition from industries in the newly recovered Lorraine and the Saar. Under such pressure the cartels lost the market controls which they had hoped to be permanent. With their characteristically French penchant for

---

[3] A good recent summary of cartel developments is given by Robert Goetz-Girey, "Monopoly and Competition in France," in Edward H. Chamberlin, ed., *Monopoly and Competition and Their Regulation*, London, 1954, pp. 21-42. A classical, very richly documented but largely legalistic treatment is that by J. Tchernoff, *Ententes Economiques et Financières*, Paris, 1933 and supplement, 1937. Excellent for developments during the depression is André Piettré, *L'Evolution des Ententes Industrielles en France depuis la Crise*, Paris, 1936. Most alive to the political issues involved is the thesis by Elizabeth Dussauze, *L'Etat et les Ententes Industrielles*, Paris, 1939.

[4] Quoted in *Le Monde des affaires*, etc., *op.cit.* (n. 1-37), p. 108. For cartel agreements limiting the volume of metallurgical production as early as 1887, see Bézard-Falgas, *op.cit.* (n. 1-19), pp. 162 ff.

historical memories, business leaders have not forgotten the lesson of the twenties. They have taken it to mean that stronger forms of organizational discipline are needed to prevent economic fluctuations or foreign competition from destroying years of patient cartel building efforts. Such considerations had much to do with the tenacity which business showed after the Second World War in defense of the organizational legacy of the Vichy regime and, a few years later, with the attacks which the Steel Association and its allies directed against the anti-cartel provisions of the Schuman plan.

The revival of cartel operations during the interwar period followed in the wake of international cartels which French industry was invited to join and was in part due to the depression. At that time the French *comptoirs* and *ententes* became frequently akin in functions and powers to the German cartels: their activities now centered around price-fixing and the determination of production quotas for member firms. On the eve of the war the number of valid cartel agreements was variously estimated to be between 1,000 and 3,000. How large a sector of the economy was regulated by them is difficult to determine. In most industries where agreements existed, the volume of production represented by outsiders rarely exceeded fifteen to twenty percent.[5]

It has been mentioned earlier[6] that with the approach of the depression the CGPF and its president emphasized increasingly the beneficial effects of the *ententes* which should be as broad as possible without, however, becoming compulsory. Yet once more the voluntary disciplines in which M. Duchemin had put his faith proved too weak in the face of growing difficulties: outsiders threatened the existing cartels, and several of the industries already bound by cartel agreements showed little eagerness to see the relative stability which they enjoyed extended to other fields. In that situation the CGPF reluctantly suggested that legislation be introduced to make existing cartel agreements compulsory for an entire industry provided that a qualified majority of the producers favored such a measure. In the Chamber of

[5] See the lengthy exposé of pre-war cartel practices in *Centre d'Informations Interprofessionnelles, Journée d'Etudes et de l'Organisation Professionnelle Economique,* Séances de Travail, 7-9 Juin, 1943, Paris, 1944, pp. 204-18 and passim, and Langele, *op.cit.* (n. 1-76), pp. 187-94.

[6] See above, Chapter I.

Deputies the Flandin-Marchandeau bill incorporating these suggestions was accepted by a large majority; its *rapporteur* happened to be M. René Coty, who twenty years later was to become the second President of the Fourth Republic. The bill permitted enforcing industry-wide agreements dealing with the "adaptation of production to the situation of the interior and exterior market, especially by a restriction of the means of production," or concerned with "discipline in the market" and with a wide array of other activities through which the cartels were actually regulating competition. The bill never became law, since it was killed in the Senate, always a more reliable supporter of economic liberalism. Almost violent opposition to the compulsory features of the proposed legislation had come from agricultural and certain business interests such as the textile industry.[7]

Since the CGPF had identified itself with the bill, it too suffered defeat, once more because of disunity in its own ranks. Subsequent attempts to make cartel agreements binding through administrative decree remained similarly unsuccessful. On the whole the ambivalence of French business toward questions of economic organization continued unabated. The existing cartels functioned without official blessing or assistance but also without supervision by the government. In many cases the *comptoirs* and *ententes* exercised already before the war more rigorous market controls than those proposed by the advocates of corporatism, a system so strenuously opposed on the verbal level by such business leaders as Duchemin and by the mouthpiece of the steel industry, *Le Temps*.[8]

At present cartel agreements have further increased their effectiveness and extend to a far wider range of business activities than before the war. But the available information is spotty and, as it were, accidental; systematic investigations are still lacking. The details which become known frequently concern fringe activities, while business decisions of general significance remain in the dark. How much of total industry is affected by

---

[7] For the interesting history of the Flandin bill, see Tchernoff, *op.cit.* (n. VIII-3), supplement, pp. 44-72, and François Chappellu, *Les Expériences Françaises d'Organisation Professionnelle*, Lyon, 1941, pp. 41-59. The Chamber of Commerce of Paris had also voiced its opposition against the bill, see *Le Temps*, June 5, 1935.

[8] See above, Chapter I at n. 45.

cartels has become a matter of wild guesses rather than of exact calculation. When the first vice-president of the CNPF stated before an international business audience in the United States that "less than five percent of industrial activities are subject to private cartel agreements,"[9] informed observers considered such an estimate little short of hilarious and therefore not apt to disarm the critics of French business behavior. In the opinion of high functionaries in the statistical services of the government, at least thirty percent of economic activities are bound by cartel agreements, although it is admitted that these calculations are also far from reliable.

For the cartels as they exist at present it is characteristic that there is a yet closer and more regularized integration between them and the trade associations than before the war. To a large extent this is the direct legacy of the Vichy years when the CO were the vehicles for activities of both trade associations and cartels, and when many of the practices of the latter were given official sanction. After the liberation the gradual transformation of the Committees shifted important market functions, like the sub-distribution of raw materials and advice on price-fixing, to the trade associations; but by then the relations between associations and cartels had once more grown close. Even with the progressive elimination of economic controls, some of the rules issued by the CO have not lost their validity and are often administered by the trade associations and the cartels connected with them.[10]

Today most of the top administrators in the technical offices of the Ministry of Industrial Production take on the whole a sympathetic attitude toward the cartel activities which come under their purview. Here again accusations against *dirigisme* in its various forms become confusing. Business complains about an oppressive governmental *dirigisme*; labor and other groups request that the government fight the *dirigisme* of business as practiced by the trade associations and the cartels.[11] Actually there are many instances where both controls converge or merge with

[9] See *Proceedings of the First, etc., op.cit.* (n. iii-61), p. 395.

[10] See the interesting details in an article by P. Bollet, "Que subsiste-t-il des décisions réglementaires des anciens comités d'organisation?" *Droit Social,* xviii, June, 1955, pp. 345-49.

[11] See e.g., the resolution submitted by the Christian Trade Union delegates to the Economic Council, in Conseil Economique, *op.cit.* (n. viii-1), p. 5.

the effect of denying to the individual entrepreneur the freedom of decision and of further reducing the scope of competition.

As might be expected, the relationship between trade associations and cartels, while everywhere fairly close, takes on different forms in different industries. Businessmen have reported that the periodic meetings of the employers' organization to which they belong serve no other purpose than to obtain from the membership acquiescence to proposed minimum prices which "insure continuing profits to those firms whose costs are particularly high because of bad organization."[12] Other employers are genuinely unaware that there exists a cartel in their branch since the trade association shields from their view whatever cartel activities might directly or indirectly affect their business.

But in general prominent leaders of the employers' movement have openly advocated the actual integration of trade associations and cartels. As early as 1947, Henry Davezac, in a widely noted pamphlet published under the auspices of the *Jeune Patron*, laid down the principle that a "resolute policy of industrial *ententes*" could give to the employers' movement the strength it was still badly lacking at the time. "Only the employers' organization," M. Davezac continued to explain, "can effectively initiate and promote the *entente* because it alone expresses validly the wishes of the entire branch. It alone has the indispensable moral authority to obtain adherence [to the cartel] and to reduce opposition."[13] Since then M. Davezac's advice has become the accepted doctrine of most of the employers' movement. In all industries where strong cartels are known to exist, such as steel, cement, chemicals, petroleum, electrical equipment, glassware, paper, packing material, bicycle, hardware, cast iron, and steel tubes, they sometimes share offices with the corresponding trade association, frequently they share some of the ranking officers, and always provisions for common decision making.

Semantically speaking, the concept of an *organisation professionnelle* has proven particularly suited for providing the desired amalgamation. Since the term does not indicate for what ends the *profession*, the trade, is organized, there is room under

[12] See the remarks made by M. Paul Poitté in *Jeune Patron*, VI, No. 58, September-October, 1952, p. 71.

[13] See Henry Davezac, "L'Organisation Professionnelle," *op.cit.* (n. II-38), especially pp. 24-26.

this roof for all activities of business organizations, the defense of the employer's interest in the labor market, as well as his protection against economic competition. By a wave of the hand, the cartel and even the *entente* have disappeared. When M. Ricard submitted his report on the policies of competition to the NAM sponsored conference in New York, he spent considerable time explaining the constructive activities of the French *organisation professionnelle* which in his words was "roughly analogous to the American 'trade association.' " What must have been the neatest *petitio principii* of the meeting was his conclusion that "by its very nature the *organisation professionnelle* cannot bring about any restrictive practice and, therefore, cannot in any way harm the interests of the consumer."[14]

Even the very incomplete data that have been gathered during the last years permit an insight into some of the actual cartel practices. Most agreements acknowledge their goal of establishing "reasonable minimum prices" enforceable on all producers. It is often stipulated explicitly that only the *entente* or the association, as the case might be, is entitled to fix prices. In order to forestall "unfair competition," the cartel provides for periodic control by its inspectors (and they might be numerous) of all invoices, bills, and "other useful documents" to be submitted by the member firms.[15] In other cases more supple arrangements, such as the circulation of price lists by leading firms, will often be sufficient to obtain the desired uniformity. To guard against violation, specific sanctions and penalty clauses are frequently provided for in the contract; blank checks or posted bonds are used to insure the payment of fines which go into a common

---

[14] See *Proceedings of the First, etc., op.cit.* (n. III-61), p. 394. For the United States, the Temporary National Economic Committee *Trade Association Survey*, Washington, 1941, concluded that "mutual restraints of competition . . . are found among the activities of a large proportion of national and regional trade associations." (p. 346).

[15] The description of present-day cartel practices is largely gathered from Conseil Economique, *op.cit.* (n. VIII-1), esp. pp. 30-45; from the well documented articles by Camille Anbert, "Autour des projets antitrusts," *Le Monde*, March 22, 23, and 24, 1950, and from the particularly revealing article by Jean Mazard, "Prix imposés et prix d'entente," *Droit Social*, XVI, 1953, pp. 129-34. (The author is a public prosecutor in Paris.) The various parliamentary debates which took place whenever a bill on the control of cartels was discussed, also unearthed a mass of interesting details which it is, however, usually difficult to verify. Of greatest interest is the report by M. Poimboeuf, a MRP deputy in *J.O. Documents Parl. Ass. Nationale*, February 25, 1951.

operating fund. The uses to which such funds are put becomes clear from the wording of some agreements: "The cartel will fight all competition. Prices sufficiently low will be quoted . . . so as to take business away from competitors. The difference between the price charged and the normal price will be borne by the cartel." More serious than fines can be the ultimate penalty of removing a firm from the association, since such a step is usually combined with a boycott by suppliers or customers.

For the large purchasing programs of the administrative services and of the nationalized enterprises it is generally impossible to obtain bids which are not prearranged in regard to prices and conditions of delivery; in this way it is made certain that the orders go to firms selected in advance by the cartel. Frequently not more than one offer is received. A mammoth concern, such as the SNCF, the nationalized railroads, is frequently unable to obtain even price quotations from other than its customary suppliers. "My client is the automobile industry," a substantial firm would answer when asked why it never submitted offers to the railroads on nonspecialized equipment—as if such a division of the markets was immutable and permanent. In a hearing before the Economic Council a SNCF official estimated that eighty percent of the purchases of the railroads encounter either cartel agreements or *de facto* monopolies.[16] Whether it is noticed, as in the cases here mentioned, or not, the cartels form a screen between sellers and buyers and frequently eliminate all free discussion or bargaining between them.

The distribution of orders among the members of the cartel is obviously connected with the widespread practice of setting production and sales quotas for the member firms. Transgressions of the quota are also sanctioned by fines. The rigidity of such quotas, usually established on the basis of past performance but occasionally also under pressure from an influential concern, varies in different industries. Conflicts which arise over these or similar questions are usually settled by an arbitrator chosen from within the cartel; his decisions must be accepted beforehand by all members as final.

[16] See the testimony of M. Gros, chief engineer in charge of supply for the national railways, in Conseil Economique, *op.cit.* (n. VIII-1), pp. 37-38, and the observations by other railroad officials in "Les Ententes Professionnelles devant la Loi," *Documentation Française. Notes et Etudes Documentaires*, No. 1736, May 5, 1953, p. 11.

The extent to which the cartels' insistence on regulating the market can take on the characteristics of a power struggle has been observed occasionally when a buying agency of the government or a nationalized enterprise decided to obtain more favorable conditions from foreign suppliers. In a number of cases they were able to do so. But more often, and especially whenever the trade association affected by the transaction enjoyed excellent relations with the high administration, business beat back these attempts to circumvent cartel controls. Import licenses were denied, protest actions were organized inside and outside parliament, and occasionally the communist inspired plant committees joined in the chorus by conjuring up the ghost of unemployment. While in these and similar instances the trade associations multiplied their efforts, the cartels could keep in the background.

One of the most successful cartels, the *Comptoir Sidérurgique* serving the steel and pig-iron industries, has remained the prototype for many other similar agencies.[17] Until 1952 the National Steel Association and its *Comptoir* established detailed production programs for the 130 concerns which exist in the steel industry and which all have adhered "voluntarily" to the association. Raw materials were allocated in accordance with the production program; all orders for steel products were to be placed with the *Comptoir*, which had the monopoly for distributing them among member firms. Absolutely binding minimum prices for all products were fixed by the *Comptoir*, generally without consultation of the membership. Where a firm quoted a price above the minimum, its conditions would often prevail, since the *Comptoir* was empowered to allocate the incoming order to such a firm, whether or not its higher prices resulted from inefficiency.

The *Comptoir* functioned as a direct selling agency only for part of the transactions, leaving in general its member firms "free" to deal directly with their buyers—at rigorously established conditions. But in order to control all commercial operations, the *Comptoir* alone established bills, received payment, and credited the accounts of its members.

[17] The structure and activities of the *Comptoir* are described in Conseil Economique, *op.cit.* (n. VIII-1), pp. 33-35. See also J. J. Lederer, "La Sidérurgie Européenne et les Cartels avant le Plan Schuman," *Politique Etrangère*, XVI, 1951, pp. 397-412.

In the summer of 1952 the *Comptoir* relinquished its monopoly of receiving and distributing orders.[18] Whether this was
a consequence of the ratification of the Coal and Steel Treaty
and its anti-cartel provisions or was motivated by the desire not
to run afoul of the Pinay law against price discrimination is
controversial, just as it is still a matter of dispute how far the
actual effects of the widely advertised changes have reached. The
possibility for customers of the industry to get directly in touch
with their suppliers seems to have resulted in a greater flexibility
of market conditions and some decline in prices. But the residual
powers of the *Comptoir* are considerable; it is entitled to receive
carbon copies of all bills and functions as a sort of credit bureau
centralizing all customer payments. Obviously these activities
alone permit a continued supervision of prices and of sales conditions, though the officers of the Steel Association have given
their "word of honor" that they do not try to influence possible
price fluctuations. Much would depend here on the effectiveness
with which the recent legislation against private price-fixing is
being enforced.

The cartel in the electrical equipment industry has been only
slightly less effective than the steel *Comptoir*. In an industry
where a few leading concerns exist simultaneously with a great
number of more modest enterprises, and where conditions are
therefore almost classically those of "monopolistic competition,"
the *entente* boasts of controlling better than eighty percent of
the production and ninety percent of all firms in the industry.[19]
The *entente* of M. Davezac has always been proud of its excellent statistical services, which in fact have hardly their equal in
other French industries. The wealth of available information
greatly facilitates price-fixing and enforcement. The cartel,
housed in the same building as the trade association, employs a
large number of inspectors to control compliance with its rules
and to decide on the appropriate sanctions in case of violation.
Orders are centralized and distributed by methods which differ
slightly from those practiced by the steel *Comptoir*, but also

[18] For a description of the changes which took place, see "Le Comptoir des
Produits Sidérurgiques vient de se réformer," *Le Monde*, September 17, 1952. For
a discussion of the Pinay law see below.

[19] The cartel of the electrical engineering industry is accurately described,
though not mentioned by name, in the article by Anbert, *op.cit.* (n. VIII-15).

here the prospective buyer will finally find only a single valid offer, which has been selected by the *entente*. Much to the regret of M. Davezac and his collaborators, more recent agreements, concluded since 1952, have resulted in a certain loosening of controls. Like the steel interests, the electrical equipment industry also claims that such changes as have occurred have nothing to do with legislative measures. In their opinion, the activities of the *entente* have furthered specialization and the lowering of production costs so substantially that no law against the misuse of economic power could ever affect them.

Even critics admit that the *comptoirs* and similar cartel agencies are completely staffed. In view of the frequently lamented shortage of managerial personnel, the question might be raised whether it would not be more rational to employ in industry those who are manning the offices of cartels and trade associations today. French business will answer that the shortage of management is one of the reasons which makes a strong *organisation professionnelle* indispensable. By handling centrally such problems as pricing, marketing, labor relations, and even financing, the cartels and trade associations relieve the overburdened industrialist and his insufficient staff of many tasks which they are presently unable to handle.[20]

Because of the unevenness of available information, it is extremely hazardous to generalize on the over-all economic effects of the described agreements. Much depends on the market conditions for a particular product or branch. When the representative of the Office of Price Control appeared before the Economic Council, he did not hesitate to give a fairly candid description of the practices which the Ministry observed in its daily contacts with organized business. But he reserved judgment as to the consequences of cartelization. In his opinion the latter could lead to a desirable "equilibrium," just as it could bring about the "systematic exploitation of the consumer." These, he concluded, are "questions of fact which must be appraised differently

[20] These explanations are endorsed by Peter F. Drucker in "Europe's Invisible Brick Wall," *Harper's Magazine*, ccvii, 1953, p. 51. The author concludes: "If, as Americans have long claimed, European expansion is not possible without abandonment of the cartel system, then European expansion is not possible without a tremendous increase in the supply of management people."

in each individual case."[21] To dismiss such caution merely as another instance of the "collusion" between business and high administration is not a sufficient explanation, although it is quite true that a fairly large number of former civil servants have changed over to leading staff positions in the cartel organizations. But also the most independent members of the high bureaucracy are not prepared to recommend the disbanding of all cartels.

If, because of the present narrowness of the French and the European markets in general, economic planning is unavoidable, the prevailing cartel agreements are instrumentalities of such planning, even though the French businessman still abhors the term.[22] Given the notorious lack of statistical information and the lack of specialization in French industry, the best organized *ententes* and *comptoirs* have notably improved the existing situation, thus creating some of the conditions necessary to strengthen the industrial potential and to increase productivity.

But in addition to the contradictions from which no cartelized industry anywhere can extricate itself, specific French conditions have still aggravated the effects of market regulation by business. In the description which a minister of economic affairs gave from the tribune of the Council of the Republic: "The mechanism of all too many *ententes* is based on the following practice: He who has the greatest difficulties cries, 'Help me to protect myself.' He furnishes his cost elements and sees to it that the price fixed by the *entente* will at least cover his costs. He who could have the advantage of eliminating others by the mechanism of competition prefers to settle for a 'rent of rarefaction.' He limits his production, but at the same time enjoys a larger profit margin."[23]

It is true everywhere that maximum profit does not necessarily coincide with the maximum expansion of production. But if the cartels are setting their conditions so that all can at least vegetate, profits accruing to the efficient units may lose all relation to the needs of investment and technical progress. Considered as an industrial planning system, European cartels have the advantages and dangers inherent in any planning system.[24] But under the

[21] See Conseil Economique, *op.cit.* (n. VIII-1), p. 32.

[22] See the excellent discussion of European cartels in Berle, *op.cit.* (n. VI-73), pp. 126-29.

[23] Robert Buron in *J.O. Débats, Cons. Répubt.*, February 21, 1953, pp. 748-49.

[24] See Berle, *op.cit.* (n. VI-73), p. 127.

conditions prevailing in France the possibly beneficial effects of cartels are diminished and their dangers maximized. Specialization programs, even where attempted, have often not been carried out. Before the Schuman plan came into force, the policies of the *Comptoir Sidérurgique* in the field of specialization or generally in regard to innovation had been over-cautious. Its investment practices were insufficiently vigorous; its pricing practices had often the effect of granting a premium to the non-specialized firms. In some cases the *Comptoir* was instrumental in reopening the most marginal of firms which had already been compelled to shut down. If such was the record of a powerful cartel in an industry where there exist a little over 100 firms, it is understandable why elsewhere the presumed efforts of the cartels to gird French industry for more energetic competition have fallen far short of announced goals.

The narrowness of the market enables even the weaker cartels to exercise a control which the most moderate observers consider oppressive to the long-range general interests of the French economy.[25] The high level of prices which the cartels maintain in the name of stability creates domestic and especially international difficulties for the sale of French goods. The *ententes* have therefore contributed to the anemia of the economy and have sometimes caused the economic fluctuations which they were designed to eliminate. For all these reasons legislative measures have been designed time and again to insure a stricter supervision of the cartels and a greater degree of competition.

\*     \*     \*

For little less than a century and a half, monopolistic practices and all other forms of restraint of trade have been regulated in France mainly by the celebrated article 419 of Napoleon's Penal Code whose wording was insignificantly altered in 1926. An outgrowth of the bad souvenirs of the *ancien régime*, the provision penalizes fraudulent acts and conspiracies which have the object of raising or lowering prices "artificially" or of obtaining a gain beyond that resulting "from the normal effects of supply and demand." The application of this vague patina-covered text

[25] See e.g., the excellent article by Gilles Pasqualaggi, "Les Ententes en France. Leurs principaux aspects. Les problèmes que posent leur contrôle," *Revue Economique*, III, 1952, pp. 63-82.

has been difficult at all times. Altogether only a few dozen judgments have been rendered during 140 years, punishing here an innkeeper, there the village bakeries, the fishmongers, or the agents of the market-halls of Paris. Monopolies were altogether out of reach for a law which had been conceived in the days of an infant industrialism. As to cartels, the courts attempted without much success to penetrate into the affairs of the earliest steel *comptoir* at the turn of the century; only a few other cases have been prosecuted since then. Recently a highly placed official of the Ministry of Justice explained that a modern *entente* would have to show an unusual amount of ineptness to invite judicial action against it.[26]

Invited by the wording of the law, criminal and civil courts have developed over the decades a distinction between good and bad cartel agreements, without being able to take effective sanctions against the latter. The only lasting impact of the Napoleonic law seems to have been the additional impulse which it gave to the business community for hiding its operations from the public eye. The courts found it all the more difficult to penetrate to the intricacies of economic life, and the notoriously formalistic training of the French jurists added to the perplexities of judges and prosecutors.

The general wrath against governmental controls which swept most social milieus and political movements so soon after the liberation was not favorable to a regulation of competition or monopoly. While the communist party and its trade union movement were still accusing the "trusts" of all evils under the sun, they disclaimed any interest in anti-cartel legislation since only total victory over capitalism would free the consumer.

The earlier protests of small business against the "money wall" and the tyranny of big business have long since lost their verve. Fearful of granting to the administration or the judiciary the means that would be necessary to control economic power,

26 There are innumerable descriptions of the meager application which article 419 has found since the early nineteenth century. See, e.g., Jacques Lapergue, *Les syndicats des producteurs en France*, Paris, 1925, pp. 67-126. By far the best critical analysis is to be found in Paul Reuter, "A propos des ententes industrielles et commerciales," *Droit Social*, xvi, 1953, esp. pp. 3-12. For the general problem of regulation of cartel activities see also the equally remarkable previous installments of the same article, *ibid.*, xv, 1952, pp. 442-50 and 508-15.

the small and inefficient firms have also found that the cartels sheltered them from death, though not always from servitude. To gauge consumer attitudes toward cartels is difficult, if only because they are not structured. But it seems to be true that in general the French consumer feels protected rather than slighted by the practice of established (and often published) minimum prices for household goods and similar wares.[27]

If during the last years an unusual amount of critical attention has been paid to the influence which business organizations have on the market and on economic development, such criticism has usually come from intellectuals and politicians in the middle of the political spectrum. Outside of the parliamentary chambers and the columns of little read magazines or journals, their discussions and suggestions have hardly any echo. They operate in a vacuum created by public indifference so that organized business can oppose successfully all proposals for effective regulation.

Before the Pinay experiment of 1952 the employers' movement criticized every one of the half-dozen bills introduced to insure "fair competition." The ACADI group, most vigorous in its defense of cartels, complained at one point of the "wave of anti-trust legislation" following the "wave of nationalizations."[28] Spokesmen for the trade associations directed their attacks against the weakest points of the reform legislation which had to grapple with the same difficulties as all measures attempting to control the concentration of economic power.[29] Explicitly or not, most proposals sought to distinguish between "good" and "bad" cartels, making here the "general interest," there an enumeration of reprehensible practices the dividing line between what was approved and what should be condemned. The difficulties arising here are not dissimilar to those which American courts have to face in anti-trust cases.[30] But in France the opponents of the

---

[27] This opinion was expressed during a discussion of cartel practices in the Economic Council. See *Bulletin du Conseil Economique*, June 22, 1950, pp. 234-37.

[28] See the interesting article, vividly critical of all proposed anti-cartel legislation, published in the group's bulletin, *op.cit.* (n. IV-63).

[29] A good survey of the various proposals and their fate in the legislature is provided by the introduction to Philippe Souleau's article, "La réglementation des ententes professionnelles dans le décret-loi du 9 août 1953," *Droit Social*, XVI, 1953, pp. 577-84. The bill submitted in 1950 by the government as well as some earlier proposals are discussed fully in Conseil Economique, *op.cit.* (n. VIII-1), pp. 66-81.

[30] It is well known that also American courts, in spite of occasional sweeping dicta that Congress "did not condone 'good' trusts and condemn 'bad' ones" (see

proposed regulations could capitalize on the fact that the vagueness of criteria is far more repulsive to a civil law system than to the common law. The spokesmen for organized business in the Council of the Republic did not hesitate to characterize such lack of precision as remindful of the worst nazi legislation, which was tactically more adroit than to compare the bills to the Sherman and Clayton Acts.[31]

Because of the need for effective enforcement, the various bills submitted to parliament proposed the creation of special organs of fact-finding, all the more indispensable since in France there is still so little known about existing business agreements. A bill adopted by the National Assembly but rejected by the upper house in 1952 came closest to paralleling in its "Superior Commission of *Ententes*" the Federal Trade Commission—the bill's sponsor, Mme. Poinso-Chapuis, a MRP deputy, had drafted her text after returning from a study mission to the United States. In addition, most of the proposals created a special tribunal called upon either to dissolve cartels contrary to the "general interest," or to take other sanctions against those involved. The demand for an economic jurisdiction—controlled however in the Poinso-Chapuis bill by the highest French court, the *Cour de Cassation*—was a reaction to the disappointing experiences which had been incurred when the regular courts tried to apply article 419. It was hoped that judges of a special tribunal with more than the traditional legal training would be able to develop the criteria of application which no statute could lay down with sufficient precision.

To the opponents of the proposed legislation the idea of special cartel courts was unacceptable and gave them an opportunity to denounce violently the entire statute for denying to business equality before the law. "Article 419 is still a useful instrument of sanction," the CNPF stated, "no serious criticism has ever been offered against it."[32] The most that might be necessary would be another modernization of the article's wording.

---

Judge Learned Hand in *U.S. vs. Aluminun Co. of America*, 148 F. 2d, pp. 416, 427) frequently make distinctions similar to those attempted in France.

[31] Such and similar arguments were brought out interestingly in the discussions in *J.O. Débats, Cons. Rep.*, February 21, 1953, pp. 738-61, and February 27, 1953, pp. 781-804.

[32] See *Bulletin*, VI, No. 82, June 5, 1952, pp. 15-16, in a comment on a recent

As in matters of productivity the hostility of organized business against all proposed cartel legislation is embittered because French industry feels unjustly attacked by the United States. But while many business leaders are willing to concede that France might have to learn much in order to increase the efficiency of its plants and of its commercial distribution, the American prodding in favor of anti-cartel legislation is almost universally resented. Trade association officials complain bitterly that Americans not only suspect everywhere the existence of restraints of trade but that they also recommend with a simpleness of purpose bordering on naïveté the export of the United States anti-trust legislation to Europe.

In their defense the French develop different lines of reasoning which are partly contradictory, partly well founded. They point to recent American criticism of the anti-trust policy such as can be found in the writings of David Lilienthal. They ask skeptically just how realistic the over-zealous descriptions are which try to accredit a picture of American big business engaging in a competitive free-for-all. But even the "imperfect competition" of the American market is deemed entirely unsuited for the conditions of the narrower European markets; exported to Europe it would lead to grave dislocations and hence an increase of political radicalism. Should it not be acknowledged, ask French businessmen, who then voluntarily confound the issues of bigness and of competition, that single American enterprises which remain unmolested by the courts often have a greater productive capacity than entire industries in several European countries combined? If their American colleagues were truly interested in the modernization of the French economy, they should understand that only the conscious efforts of the *ententes* can achieve the desired objective. Why not admit that cartels are freely entered contractual, and hence "democratic," agreements among businessmen, while a government attempting to regulate competition

decision by the criminal courts sentencing the president of an association of coal dealers for having denied supplies to a member firm which had underbid the prices laid down by the association. For the CNPF's criticism of the proposed cartel legislation in general, see *ibid.*, IV, No. 44, February 5, 1950, pp. 2-3 and VI, No. 84, July 20-August 5, 1952, p. 15. For an ironical remark of M. Villiers about the American attitude on European cartel practices, see *ibid.*, V, No. 69, August, 1951, p. 2.

will easily take on the powers of an economic, if not political, dictatorship? Not a few business leaders have concluded from their personal observations in the United States that the acknowledged superior performance of American industry could be equalled only by generalizing rather than by restricting cartel practices.

After his return from such a visit to the United States where policies of competition had been a foremost subject of discussion, a French industrialist and president of several trade associations noted, evidently unconvinced by what had been "preached" to him: "I know well that there are nefarious and unfortunate *ententes*. But I can also say that all those I have known during a long and varied industrial career had the sole result of preventing the collapse of business concerns, especially of small ones. They have also maintained the democratization of business, in other words contributed to the social stability of the country." Though French business leaders are often right when they question the validity of optimistic generalizations about the effectiveness of the Sherman Act, they voluntarily ignore the fact that the threat of an anti-trust prosecution remains somewhat of a nightmare for the head of a large American corporation.[33]

Almost rabidly in favor of cartels was a resolution adopted in 1952 by the old established and respected Society for the Encouragement of National Industry recruiting among the notables of the business world. The resolution had been prepared on the basis of a memorandum addressed to the Society by M. Duchemin, former president of the CGPF. The memorandum, and in abbreviated form the resolution, described the *ententes* as bringing nothing but advantages to producers, workers, and consumers alike, since they insured stability of prices and employment and since they served technological progress. M. Duchemin considered it unnecessary—though that part of his reasoning disappeared from the resolution as adopted—to distinguish between good and bad cartels. "To us, it appears naïve to think that it is possible to develop the former and prosecute the latter." Also M. Duchemin's memorandum contained the usual remarks about the inanity of proposals to introduce the American anti-trust legislation to Europe. Did one forget that there were no

[33] See Galbraith, *op.cit.* (n. IV-24), p. 65.

trusts in France and that the American economy was protected by tariff walls? Where national agreements were "completed" by international cartels, their advantages would be enhanced further. As to control measures, the resolution stated explicitly that the "free functioning" of the cartels should continue and that the consumer who had "really been hurt" would find protection through the classical provisions of the Criminal Code, possibly after a change of its wording.[34]

The tactics of the business lobby, which so far had struck down all suggestions for cartel control, changed temporarily when in the summer of 1952 the Pinay government, then at the height of its popularity, decided to rely in its campaign for price reduction on other means than mere persuasion. Advised by officials in the Ministry of National Economy, the premier submitted to parliament a short text outlawing all operations which resulted in the fixing of minimum prices by cartels or other agreements. Pinay hoped to use the support which business had tendered to his government for breaching the price wall by a relatively simple measure which, if effective would insure to his policies the further backing of public opinion.[35]

Even before the bill was submitted to parliament, the CNPF insisted successfully that all established prices for household goods and similar brands be excepted from the regulation; the direst consequences were predicted if strict uniformity was not permitted to prevail in this field.[36] During the discussion of the law by the National Assembly a number of deputies, sensing that here an escape clause for numerous products might be created, tried in vain to have the exception stricken from the

[34] See *Le Cent Cinquantième Anniversaire de la Société d'Encouragement pour L'Industrie Nationale et Les Problèmes Actuels de l'Economie Française*, Paris, 1952, pp. 221-22. Very similar, though more moderate in tone, is the resolution adopted by the International Chamber of Commerce and drafted by M. Giscard d'Estaing, then a member of the CNPF's Executive Committee; see *Bulletin*, VI, No. 88, November 20, 1952, pp. 18-19. All European delegates had voted for the resolution. Characteristic is the remark by Van Zeeland, Belgian statesman and business leader, as reported by Berle, *op.cit.* (n. VI-73), p. 190: "For us, the question is not whether there should be cartels; it is whether they are so operated that their results are good."

[35] See the interesting remarks by M. Pinay in a dinner speech before the ACADI group in *Bulletin Acadi*, No. 68, April, 1953, p. 145 ff., esp. p. 153.

[36] For a frank description of the steps undertaken by the CNPF to forestall action by the government in regard to prices for such goods, see the article "Prix Imposés," *Bulletin*, VI, No. 82, June 5, 1952, pp. 12-14.

statute. But when Senator Armengaud attempted to defend the undiluted and classical views of the employers' movement in the Council of the Republic, he had to beat a hasty retreat.[37] Since the National Assembly had passed the law unanimously, there was little the Council could do to change the text.

Except for little publicized protests by the ACADI group, the CNPF and the major trade associations kept silent about a law which was made into a test of popularity by the cabinet they had pledged to support.[38] The over-all effect of the Pinay law was somewhat controversial. A socialist deputy repeatedly called the law a toy pistol which could not do great harm to powerful cartels. The director of the Office of Price Control, on the other hand, considered the provisions of the statute sufficient to effect a considerable liberalization of the price structure, provided that the administrative services when trying to enforce the law were given a strong backing by the government.[39] It seems that, as soon as the Pinay cabinet was replaced by that of M. René Mayer less than six months after the enactment of the statute, enforcement became notoriously lax.

Before his overthrow, M. Pinay in a declaration to parliament rather proudly established the record of what he called his government's opposition to a "private *dirigisme*, replacing for the sake of its own profit governmental *dirigisme*."[40] He maintained that under the impact of his law, which undoubtedly had had a certain surprise effect, twenty-one cartels, "and not insignificant ones," had dissolved. In addition forty-six cases had been submitted to the services of the ministry for investigation. The premier had to admit that the penal sanctions of the law had never been put to practice and that it was unknown whether

[37] For the interesting debates in the Assembly and the Council see *J.O. Débats, Ass. Natle.,* June 21, 1952, pp. 3077-87, and *ibid., Débats, Conseil Rép.,* July 8, 1952, pp. 1566-75. For the text of the law, *J.O.* July 19, 1952, p. 7227.

[38] M. Morizot in his article, "La politique de concurrence, etc." *op.cit.* (n. IV-63), complained, p. 45, that the Pinay law had spectacularly victimized the cartels only to find that in the recession which followed it might be in need of their support.

[39] See M. Rosenstock-Franck's optimistic statement in "Planisme français et démocratie," *Revue Economique,* IV, 1953, p. 214; and in "Pourquoi nos prix . . ." *op.cit.* (n. VI-59), pp. 18-19. A well balanced picture of the possibilities and limitations of the 1952 law is provided by Pierre Drouin, "Trois mois de lutte contre les pratiques des ententes industrielles," *Le Monde,* November 13, 1952.

[40] See *J.O. Débats, Ass. Nationale,* December 10, 1952, pp. 6062-63.

after the formal dissolution of a cartel its policies were revived in other forms.

The Pinay law of 1952 owed its large parliamentary support in part to the empirical approach it had taken toward the question of a broader anti-cartel legislation. By merely stating that its provision would stay in force until "a general law concerning industrial *ententes*" would be enacted, the statute was able to neutralize the deputies who hoped to avoid such legislation by agreeing to the more limited text sponsored by the government. When the National Assembly turned, a few days after the discussion of the shorter law, to a consideration of the broad anti-cartel statute sponsored by Mme. Poinso-Chapuis, only the socialists and the MRP deputies seemed truly interested in seeing it enacted. Very little was said during the parliamentary debate against the principles involved in the bill. The business lobby operated wholly by what one of the deputies called "subterranean maneuvers." But in the final vote most of the deputies from the parties which are usually close to the employers' movement voted against the law—among them all of M. Pinay's party friends and two future and past premiers, Joseph Laniel and Edgar Faure. Due only to the abstention of deputies from the extreme right and left, the law was adopted by a weak majority of seventy votes.[41]

Under these conditions the stage was set for one of the rare occurrences when in the Fourth Republic, even before the constitutional amendments of 1953, the weak upper chamber could demolish legislation adopted by the National Assembly. An absolute majority of the senators "amended" the Poinso-Chapuis bill by public ballot in so drastic a fashion that its principles and structure were altered beyond recognition. According to article 20 of the Constitution, the National Assembly could have rescued its text only if there had been an absolute majority of the deputies backing it—which was not the case. Hence the legislation lost out, and another attempt to enact effective anti-cartel measures had come to naught.[42]

[41] See *ibid.*, July 11, 1952, p. 3867.

[42] For the discussions in the upper house, see *ibid.*, *Débats, Cons. Rep.*, February 21 and 27, 1953, pp. 738-61, 781-804. For the counterproposal of the Council as it emerged from these debates, see *ibid.*, *Documents Parl. Ass. Nationale Annexe* No. 5704, session of February 26, 1953, pp. 433-34.

Before parliament had an opportunity to try its hand at a revised cartel bill, Premier Laniel used the powers granted to him by the Assembly and issued in August 1953 a decree concerned with "the maintenance or the re-establishment of free competition in industry and commerce."[43] In many respects the new decree forbidding all agreements on minimum prices read like an extension of the Pinay law which it abrogated specifically. It retained from the senatorial counterproposals to the earlier bill a description of undesirable cartel practices; agreements to engage in them would be null and void. But all cartels for which it could be demonstrated that they "result in an amelioration of production and in an extension of sales or lead to the development of economic progress through rationalization and specialization" were specifically exempted from the sanctions of the law.

A Technical Committee, composed of eminent jurists, representatives of the trade associations, and members of the National Committee on Productivity, has the function of sorting the "good" from the "bad" cartels and of investigating all possible violations of the statute. Either upon the committee's advice or on its own initiative, the Ministry of National Economy may transmit cases that have attracted suspicion to the regular criminal courts, sole judges in the matter. For the courts the opinions expressed by the Technical Committee are in no way legally binding, and have at best the character of expert advice. Any conviction of the owner or manager of an enterprise for violation of the statute excludes his firm automatically from government contracts, unless the ministry decides otherwise. To forestall any further "surprise" effect, the new decree stipulated explicitly that it would apply only to cartel agreements in force after December 31, 1953, presumably to give to the existing *comptoirs* and *ententes* sufficient time to adapt themselves to the conditions created by the law. The extremely confused text, which subsequent ordinances have rendered only more contradictory, presented an amalgam of the technique followed by the Pinay law and of the proposal adopted in 1952 by the Council of the Republic. It is especially noteworthy that all de-

[43] For the text of the Laniel decree and its *exposé des motifs*, see *ibid.*, August 10, 1953, pp. 7045-47.

vices by which previous bills had wished to give publicity to condemned cartel practices are now eliminated.[44]

Organized business has accepted the decree without protest. In fact, the statute is hardly different from proposals which have been formulated by the economic services of the CNPF. Only the most fervent advocate of "productive" cartels, M. Perrin, president of ACADI, has warned that the law might discourage French firms from pooling their research resources and entice them to seek refuge in yet more pronounced individualism. Other representatives of industry have protested in the Economic Council that one could not call on the trade associations for support of the Second Modernization Plan and at the same time treat them with as much suspicion as the Laniel decree supposedly showed.[45]

But on the whole the decree seemed to have been understood as a useful gesture of appeasement for the sake of those persistent critics who see in the cartels one of the major reasons for the high price level and for economic stagnation. Where the Pinay law still spoke of the forthcoming anti-cartel legislation, the Laniel decree suggested that it had satisfied the need for such regulation. Whether this is actually the case only the future can tell.

Writing in 1954, a prominent jurist suggested that "some spectacular convictions during the next months would undoubtedly be more effective than the dead letter of the law."[46] Since then nobody has been convicted; the Technical Committee has considered only a few cases, and apparently without reaching a decision.[47] If the Committee had any activities at all, it has worked with the expected discreetness. Foes and friends of cartels agree that the decree of 1953 will have no more power to insure

[44] A full analysis and a generally favorable critique of the law is contained in Souleau, op.cit. (n. VIII-29).

[45] See R. Perrin, op.cit. (n. IV-63), pp. 273-77. For the remarks by the employers in the Economic Council, see J.O. Conseil Economique. Avis et Rapports, August 3, 1954, pp. 700 ff. For a general commentary on the "quietist" attitude of organized business towards the decree, see Sauvy, "La Situation Economique," Droit Social, XVI, 1953, p. 467.

[46] See R. Houin, "Le droit commercial et les décrets de 1953," ibid., XVII, 1954, p. 265.

[47] Best known among the committee members are M. Fabre, for years in charge of the CNPF's Economic Services, but also M. Gros who, in his work for the nationalized railroads has won many insights into cartel activities.

"free competition" than its illustrious predecessor, the often quoted and little applied article of Napoleon's Criminal Code.

\*     \*     \*

There are, to be sure, also other reasons for the flabbiness of competition in France than the activities of trade associations and cartels. Since these reasons lie deeper and in many cases antedate the emergence of the modern cartels, legal enforcement alone would hardly provide the solution to a stubborn problem of long standing.[48] In the United States too businessmen want "not a perpetual struggle, but a steady job—the job of producing goods at a roughly predictable cost under roughly predictable conditions, so that goods can be sold in the market at a roughly predictable price."[49] But in France behaviour patterns simultaneously protecting the marginal firm and proving profitable to the efficient low-cost producer were general long before the trade associations acquired enough strength to formalize them into specific agreements.[50]

Today, in the words of the Commission on National Accounts: "the sclerosis of competition goes far beyond the framework of these open or closed cartel agreements among some power groups. It results from a complex of practices which themselves are the product of a general mentality."[51] The respect for status and tradition finds its counterpart in an aversion to the consequences which technology and competition might have under conditions of a less strictly controlled market. The solidarity within the group outweighs competitive urges, not so much because the competitor is loved, but because any bankruptcy is regarded as a blight on the status defended by every member of the group. Alfred Sauvy might be right when he stated that lively competition implies either a definite interest in the public welfare or a somewhat primitive mentality.[52] The French businessman will

[48] Compare for the situation in the United States, the remark by Earl Latham, *The Group Basis of Politics*, New York, 1952, p. 26: "The Sherman Act had undoubtedly much to do with the noncoercive character of the trade associations."

[49] Berle, *op.cit.* (n. VI-73), pp. 51-52.

[50] See, also for the following, the very pertinent remarks by Sawyer, *op.cit.* (n. V-9), pp. 17-18.

[51] Mendès-France Report, *op.cit.* (n. IV-4), p. 57. Louis Salleron in CIERP, *op.cit.* (n. VI-21), p. 150, speaks about a "spontaneous cartel" among businessmen.

[52] "La Situation Economique," *Droit Social*, XV, 1952, p. 521.

easily claim that his "sophistication" distinguishes him sharply from his colleagues in other lands, and especially in the United States. The growing strength of business organizations has solidified the group solidarity to the point where it is no longer understood that the elimination or the transformation of unproductive units could in the long run serve the common good.

Effectively enforced legislation breaking the rigid price leadership and the production control exercised by business organizations would certainly have important economic and political effects. As so often in modern France the issue is one of redistributing power between the state and organized interests so that the government would be freer than it is at present to arbitrate between conflicting claims. But whether under present conditions cartel legislation as such would substantially contribute to an improvement of economic performance might well be doubted.

## 2. Foreign Trade

"Peasant nations have an inheritance of diffidence which makes them less suited for adaptation to modern life. This is probably the reason why Frenchmen are hampered in international economic competition."

Detoeuf, *Propos de O. L. Barenton*

In the field of foreign trade policies the contradictions between the announced objectives and the practices of organized business are so pronounced that the resulting attitudes are little short of schizophrenic. Addresses by M. Villiers and the reports of the CNPF's Committee on Trade Liberalization, headed by M. Roger Nathan, blame French firms as acridly for their inability to export as the persistent critics of the employers' movement. Where a Jean Monnet likes to characterize the French economy as a "hothouse economy," some spokesmen of the CNPF predict in similar terms that, if it continues to be sheltered from the outside, French economic life will remain stagnant. M. Nathan has described the French import quotas as the principal mechanism in the "protective apparatus" with which the economy has surrounded itself for more than two decades, and has admitted that the "economic cloistering" has developed "practices and policies which could not fail to have consequences for the cost

structure" of national production.[53] "As partisans of free enterprise we must be sincere liberals and accept the consequences of
trade liberalization," the president of the CNPF has warned and
added that if the French economy were not able to live up to
the liberalization goals set by the OEEC, either successive failures or permanent isolation would be the consequence, both
leading to economic regression and national decadence.[54]

In this domain the economic analysis offered by the CNPF
joins in every detail the unfavorable conclusions which international organizations have reached when discussing the development of the French economy. In one of his addresses, M. Villiers
warned the General Assembly of the CNPF that in reality the
foreign trade picture was far more unfavorable than over-all
statistics indicated. If exports to the French overseas territories,
particularly swollen as long as fighting continued in Indochina,
were deducted, the trade balance was already negative; and in
1954-55 a decrease of investments in overseas territories was
showing its effects in substantially reduced exports to the members of the French Union. The CNPF expressed particular
alarm over the fact that quantitatively the country's exports in
manufactured goods—in M. Villiers' words, "the sign of wealth
for modern nations"—had declined by more than 30 percent
since 1929. In terms of machinery alone, and again when overseas territories are excluded, France appears to be a net importer
and to have only a negligible export balance in transport equipment. French exports of manufactured goods to foreign countries
amounted to only 62 percent of total exports in 1953, while for
Western Germany and the United Kingdom the relationship was
in the order of about 80 percent. Since then the situation has
worsened further. But an export structure, weighted too heavily
in favor of basic food and raw materials, is exposing France to
critical price fluctuations and other uncertainties. And if the
difficulties for French trade were particularly great with hard
currency areas, M. Villiers concluded, France could ill afford to
irritate by its continued trade restrictions the continental countries participating in OEEC and in EPU.[55]

[53] See the Nathan Report, op.cit. (n. VI-61), pp. 3-4.
[54] See "La libération des échanges inquiète le CNPF," Entreprise, August 15,
1954, p. 14, and the general tenor of the reports of the CNPF Committee on
Trade Liberalization over the last years.
[55] See especially the addresses by M. Villiers in Bulletin, No. 122, August, 1954,

But after the correct analysis of a serious situation, the spokesmen for organized business have little to offer in the way of a solution. They voice the perennial complaints about the burden inflicted by taxes and by the costs of the social legislation on French prices. But in fact, exporting firms receive a special compensation, designed to equalize such special burdens as may exist. Moreover it has already explained that if French prices are too high, this is not due solely to the factors which the employers' movement likes to stress.[56]

Except for a few industries and some individual personalities of the business world, the employers' movement is opposed to another devaluation as a stimulus to exports. In that respect the CNPF expresses the now fairly general reluctance to tamper anew with monetary stability. Since past experiences have shown that depreciation of the French currency is always followed by a disproportionate rise in domestic prices, and since a new spiral movement of prices and income is dreaded, a devaluation seems to have become politically inadvisable, whatever its technical advantages might be.

Once more a mentality rather than specific handicaps seems to be primarily responsible for the universally acknowledged lag in export activities.[57] All too often the French businessman considers sales abroad as little more than a supplement filling his order books as long as the domestic market cannot absorb all of his products. Since his impulses to seek exports *per se* are weakly

---

pp. 1-2; and *ibid.*, No. 135, August, 1955, pp. 1-2, as well as his articles, "L'Economie Française devant des écheances inéluctables," and "Les impératifs de la libération des échanges," *ibid.*, VIII, No. 119, May 1954, pp. 1-2 and No. 130, March, 1955, pp. 1-2. For general remarks on French export developments, confirming M. Villiers' analysis, see *UN Report, 1953, op.cit.* (n. VI-36), pp. 20-22; and *UN Report 1954, op.cit.* (n. VI-36), pp. 187 ff.

[56] See the discussion above, Chapter VI. In regard to the relationship between prices, exports and foreign trade problems in general, see also *J.O. Conseil Economique, Avis et Rapports*, February 14, 1953, pp. 185-94.

[57] In 1954 French exports amounted to $101 per inhabitant while in Great Britain and Belgium corresponding figures were $152 and $253. Almost identical discrepancies exist for imports; see Jeanneney, *op.cit.* (n. IV-26), p. 129. For an excellent description of mentality and practices harmful to exports, see Pierre Drouin, "Désaffection pour les marchés extérieurs, ou trop bonnes 'affaires,'" *Le Monde (Sel. hebd.)*, September 25 to October 1, 1953, and a comment on the relatively favorable trade balance for the year 1954, "Globules rouges et béquilles," *ibid.*, August 18 to 24, 1955.

developed, any expansion of his sales at home will satisfy him to the extent of losing interest in foreign trade. One of the most vigorous of France's large concerns, the Pechiney Company, explained once a radical decline in the percentage of its production devoted to exports by an increase of domestic demands without considering the possibility of satisfying both by an expansion of production.[58] The fact that the overseas territories are (or were) able to absorb an important share of exports has further diminished the businessmen's eagerness to develop foreign sales.

Just as the trade associations did not create the habits determining the competitive behavior on the domestic market, they were not historically responsible for the protectionism to which French tariff policies shifted shortly after the birth of the Third Republic. Whatever might have been the relations between certain lobbying organizations and Jules Méline, father of the tariff bill of 1892, the trade associations of the period were far too weak to have created the strong current in favor of high tariffs. If parliament voted predominantly for protectionism, it merely expressed a widespread mood which until today has lost little of its pervasiveness.[59] Actually the tariff policies were one of the reasons why the French employers' movement remained so weak for so many decades. As long as business enjoyed sufficient protection by widely approved tariff laws, there was little reason for the individualistic French businessman to organize and to make financial contributions to the defense of interests that seemed well sheltered from intemperate winds.

The pre-war CGPF became actively protectionist only with the approach of the depression. Then it did much to further the introduction of the quota system and insisted on abandoning all

[58] See Sauvy, "La Situation Economique," *Droit Social*, XVIII, 1955, p. 214. For substantiated complaints in a business publication about the lax export policy of the steel industry, see Comité d'Etudes pour le Redressement Economique et Financier, *La Politique d'Exportation du Comptoir Français des Produits Sidérurgiques*, Paris, n.d. It is true that some regions, such as the North, are more "export-minded" than the rest of the country.

[59] See Frank Arnold Haight, *A History of French Commercial Policies*, New York, 1941, p. 51. The entire volume provides excellent background material for the problems here discussed, as does Clough, *op.cit.* (n. IV-12), especially in its Chapter IX.

commercial treaties which still contained the most-favored-nation clause.[60] From then on the collaboration of the trade associations for setting and adjusting the import quotas became indispensable to the authorities. Increasingly, connected tariff questions were also submitted for decision while the government's role as moderator and arbitrator was steadily reduced. Moreover the decrees establishing the quotas were generally preceded by negotiations between French manufacturers and their competitors in other countries, especially in Germany.[61]

This close connection of international cartels with French foreign trade regulation reached the point where M. Duchemin could optimistically forecast that the quota system might lead to the establishment of a European Customs Union. In some ways Hitler's New Order fulfilled such expectations, especially in the field of chemicals where M. Duchemin's own firm, the Kuhlman concern, resumed its "quota" negotiations with I. G. Farben shortly after the armistice.[62]

Since the war the extensive administrative tasks incumbent on the trade associations in the field of foreign trade have been broadened and regularized. Several months before the CNPF was founded, a national federation grouping all import and export associations had seen the light. At present under the presidency of one of the country's most active younger businessmen, the federation comprises hundreds of associations which are organized both regionally and according to the goods in which their members specialize.[63] Though usually working in close contact with the trade associations in their field, they have a vigorous life of their own, being sometimes more influential in administrative circles than the general associations, and frequently more affluent. Their income is derived from the fees

[60] See Duchemin, op.cit. (n. 1-17), esp. his address in 1932, pp. 103 ff., and his article, "La Crise Mondiale et la Politique Douanière et Contractuelle de la France," *Revue de Paris*, XL, 1933, pp. 3-28.

[61] See Haight, op.cit. (n. VIII-59), pp. 162-79 and 199-207. The author concludes (p. 204) that because of this arrangement corporatism had triumphed already before the war and that "the tariff has ceased to be a product of democratic government."

[62] See M. Duchemin's own account in *Histoire d'une Négotiation*, Paris, 1942. For an interesting memorandum on European unity which M. Duchemin had circulated in the 1920's, see Tchernoff, op.cit. (n. VIII-3), pp. 637-38.

[63] For a list of the various associations and descriptions of their objectives as contained in their by-laws, see *Annuaire Général*, etc., op.cit. (n. III-38), pp. 815-28.

which they levy for their services and which usually have the net effect of another private tax inflating French prices.

The substantial power of these associations is founded in part on the assistance they lend the government in its administration of the import licensing program. Since France is the only major European country which for long years after the war found it impossible to set its foreign trade free, close control of imports has continued through most of the period. A heavy bureaucratic machinery involving several ministries relies for advice on general policies and for the actual granting of licenses on a number of Technical Committees. Two-thirds of the committee members represent the importing interests and are selected by the trade associations and the Chambers of Commerce.

It is generally admitted that the Technical Committees have prevented the import policy from being completely stifled by a maze of bureaucratic regulation. But given the great influence of business organizations on these committees, the licensing system has operated in favor of already established import firms; the industry representatives have also successfully kept away from the borders those goods which they did not wish to see imported.[64] The favors which the associations can distribute by their participation in the import licensing program are of considerable value to their membership. Because of the discrepancy between many French and foreign prices, an import license will often allow great profits to the importing firm. Moreover, whenever there existed in France a gray market for foreign currencies, the monies obtained for import purposes could be used for speculative ends, a frequent practice in the opinion of the Economic Council.

Given these conditions the Commission on National Accounts appears to have been correct when it described French imports as being channeled by "great semipublic or private monopolies," and when it concluded that as long as this system prevailed it was not even possible to evaluate objectively the extent to which

[64] A complete discussion of the beneficial and possibly harmful activities of the Technical Committees are to be found in the report by the Economic Council, op.cit. (n. VIII-56). An earlier report by the Economic Council, ibid., March 11, 1949, pp. 62-75, had been even more severe for the practices prevailing in regard to import licensing.

French tariffs were or were not justified.[65] Reform proposals have been made to change the composition of the Technical Committees, to give greater publicity to the licensing procedures, and to centralize them so that not only the narrowly conceived special, but also more general economic interests could find a hearing. But all suggestions were discarded after the trade associations protested against them.

In the field of exports the activities of business organizations are partly promotional, partly administrative. The CNPF, the CGPME, and several trade associations assist all firms desirous of exporting with useful information and seek by all conceivable means to create interest abroad for French goods. Within the CNPF the personnel of the *Comité Franc-Dollar* and the *Comité Franc-Sterling* insure a close relationship between the business organizations and the ministries concerned; these services are easily among the most progressive and most energetic of the peak association.

The subsidies granted to French exporters in order to compensate them for taxes and social charges, which presumably make French prices too high on the international market, are administered with the aid of the export associations and the general trade associations. There is no need to discuss here the usefulness of such measures which have the effect of a "selective devaluation" and which can always be countered by similar arrangements on the part of France's competitors. That the policy has not been too successful is shown by the still unsatisfactory volume of exports.[66]

There are yet other funds involved in export activities, and they too are administered by the trade associations in a way that strengthens their position *vis-à-vis* their membership and in the process of over-all economic planning. As an incentive to seek exports, ten percent of the foreign currency, and more in the case of dollar exports, may be retained by the exporting firms for a number of purposes defined in the law, and generally useful for

[65] See *Mendès-France Report 1953, op.cit.* (n. IV-4), p. 56. Still more critical of the import groups and their incidence on French prices is Bernard Chénot, *Organisation Economique de l'Etat*, Paris, 1951, pp. 272-73.

[66] Moreover, cases are known where exporters, after having received such compensation, do not always grant their foreign customers the price differential that is expected, endangering thereby the chances of French firms to compete successfully.

the national economy as well as for the individual firm. In fact, a substantial share of the funds seems to have been utilized for imports of nonessential commodities, if not for speculative purposes. In 1953 the government wished to abolish these privileges since they no longer corresponded to a true need and since grave abuses had come to light. But the CNPF, speaking for the exporters, did not hesitate to defend the entire institution to the last detail and protested with unusual vehemence against its suggested abolition. It succeeded in obtaining formal promises from the government that the legislation would remain intact, one of the numerous examples showing that in France every privilege, once granted, will be perennial even after the reasons justifying it have long vanished.[67]

The deep involvement of the employers' movement and of some of its best organized associations with export-import controls puts the "liberalism" of the CNPF to a hard test. When in 1951 the government decided to experiment with trade liberalization, and a few months later when an acute shortage of foreign currencies forced it to reintroduce a rigid quota system, the CNPF offered belabored comments recommending liberalization "in principle" but warning against any suddenness in altering existing quotas.[68] From time to time the organization compounds its inconsistencies by publicizing for the elevation and education of its membership sharply critical reports about the nature and dangers of French protectionism. One such report, issued by the OEEC, described how, especially after other European countries had abolished all or most quotas, the French trade and price policies sheltered certain sectors of the economy by providing at least a triple advantage: French firms could buy raw materials abroad at a low price, sell at favorable conditions on a domestic market protected from foreign competition, and then profit from the government subsidies paid to stimulate exports.[69]

[67] See *Bulletin*, No. 129, February, 1955, p. 55. The activities of the trade associations in the export field are fully and critically described in the report, *op.cit.* (n. VIII-56), see esp. pp. 203-15.

[68] Compare *Bulletin*, VI, n. 79, March 5-20, 1952, pp. 3-6, with the attitude of the employers' delegation in the Economic Council when the general question of intra-European trade was discussed in *Bulletin Conseil Economique*, January 12-13, 1950, pp. 12-13, 25.

[69] The OEEC report with its uncomplimentary warnings to French business was reprinted in full, *Bulletin*, VIII, No. 112, January 5, 1954, pp. 5-7. In similar

The progressive trade liberalization which France has undertaken once more since 1954 under the constant prodding of its European partners has been greeted with a somewhat shamefaced relief by the CNPF leadership and especially by its Committee on Trade Liberalization. The Committee acknowledged that the abandonment of quota restrictions—still far below the corresponding percentages of most other countries—had not resulted in any serious threat to the French economy. But the CNPF also admitted that so far liberalization has taken place mostly in regard to commodities "where the reactions of the producers were the least lively."[70] France and other European governments as well have freed trade chiefly in those commodities where imports had previously been large and where competition was not greatly feared. Moreover, since import duties remain even where import quotas have been removed, and since such duties have frequently been raised under the guise of "compensation taxes," it is doubtful whether such liberalization measures as France has taken have really broken the hard core of protectionism and restored conditions of international competition for industry. It remains to be seen whether and at which point accustomed protections for high cost enterprises would be seriously threatened and what will be the reactions of organized business, should such a situation occur.

As on other occasions, the CGPME has been franker than the general employers' movement in its protests against trade liberalization measures. It has called for continued protection by import quota without concern as to whether such demands could be reconciled with its economic philosophy. Its convention in 1954 urged the government to grant the compensation taxes to all enterprises affected by liberalization.[71]

The general ambivalence of organized business toward international competition is quite understandable. Given the over-all

---

fashion the UN concluded, *UN Report, 1953, op.cit.* (n. VI-36), p. 12: "The effect of import restrictions appears to have been not so much to reduce the total of French imports from Europe as to distort their commodity composition *so as to give special protection to certain branches of industry*" (italics mine).

[70] *Bulletin*, No. 129, February, 1955, pp. 59-60. The somewhat tenuous effect of trade liberalization on the restoration of international competition has been described by Raymond Aron, "Problems of European Integration," *Lloyds Bank Review*, No. 28, April, 1953, p. 3.

[71] For various interesting pronouncements by the CGPME on trade liberalization, see Lavau, *op.cit.* (n. IV-21), p. 381.

situation of French business, it is possible that any true and general liberalization of trade would prove dangerous to many branches of French industry which are badly in need of strengthening. The crux of the matter is, in the words of the Commission on National Accounts, that an economy which has become deformed and sclerotic by a long isolation from the outside world would be imperilled by too sudden an opening of the national borders. Reasoning similarly the report of the United Nations Economic Commission for Europe, in its searching analysis of possible remedies for the economic ills of France, concluded that the mere unleashing of foreign competition would carry the risk of provoking a fall in French production. In the Commission's opinion increased domestic stimuli to competition would permit the modernization of agriculture and industry and thereby in the long run create the conditions necessary for a more favorable structure of French foreign trade.[72]

## 3. European Integration

"France is a country of free trade: any industrialist will
tell you so. He is opposed to tariffs, except in one very
particular case, his own. Unfortunately the total of these
particular cases equals that of all industries."

Detoeuf, *Propos de O. L. Barenton*

"International gatherings among industrialists must be multiplied. The future of Europe depends upon the success of the efforts aiming at the economic and even the political unity of Europe." Such a brave European creed was voiced by the CNPF in the summer of 1948.[73] Around the same time M. Villiers, in the name of the French employers' movement, took the initiative for organizing the Council of Industrial Federations of Europe (CFIE). At first the Council did little else than to furnish to the OEEC materials on all questions in which employers' organizations of the sixteen Marshall plan countries were interested. But soon it became a fairly well integrated confederation concerning itself with a broader range of problems, whether or not directly connected with the activities of the OEEC and espe-

[72] See *Mendès-France Report, 1953, op.cit.* (n. IV-4), p. 57, and *UN Report, 1954, op.cit.* (n. VI-36), p. 190.
[73] *Bulletin,* II, No. 17, July, 1948, p. 6.

cially with plans for the economic integration of Western Europe.[74]

The CNPF was able to play a prominent role in the new international employers' organization. For the first five years of its existence M. Villiers himself assumed the presidency of the CFIE; most of its functions were performed by ranking staff members of the French peak association; on both its steering committee and its secretariat the French were represented more heavily than other nations. There is little doubt that questions of prestige were in part responsible for the great amount of energy which the French employers displayed in making the work of the CFIE more significant. When the Council was founded, the German economy had just started on the way to recovery, and British production was still in the slowest phase of its up-hill climb. Though the international position of French business deteriorated during the ensuing years, France continued to be well and ably represented in the CFIE, thereby making its voice effectively heard in the councils of European businessmen. In a great number of the specialized European trade associations the position which the French acquired is equally strong; there too the French employers' movement was in many cases better prepared than others to perform the necessary services of coordination and policy formulation.[75]

But beyond the search for prestige, the leadership of the CNPF was convinced that the satisfactory operation of the Marshall plan and the OEEC depended on a better coordination of European business. While Villiers' attachment to the cause of European unity was at times colored by the sentimentalism which is characteristic of him, men like Lafond, Ricard, and Davezac, the prominent founding fathers of the CNPF, had long been accustomed to think in terms of continental markets. For all of them, and for many of their colleagues, the solution of the Franco-German problem was to be sought in collaboration rather than in uncontrolled rivalry.

As soon as the planning for economic integration of Western Europe gained momentum, prominent leaders of the French

[74] Compare *ibid.*, v, No. 60, December 20, 1950-January 5, 1951, pp. 8-9, with *ibid.*, vi, No. 87, November 5, 1952, pp. 11-12.

[75] For a listing of international business organizations, showing the preponderance of French personnel, see *Annuaire, op.cit.* (n. iii-38), pp. 875-94.

employers' movement developed proposals as to how existing and future cartels should become the pivot of the movement for unification. Reports by the CNPF Committee on International Cartels, presided over by the administrator of the Pechiney Company and of the Aluminum Français, insisted that trade restrictions and tariffs should be eliminated, but only after freely functioning industry agreements had carefully prepared for an equalization of conditions.[76]

The most complete scheme for economic integration relying heavily on the organizations of industry had been submitted by M. Ricard to the Basic Industries Committee of the European Economic Conference, held in Westminster in April 1949. A resolution, adopted unanimously by the Committee, had proposed to "Europeanize" coal, iron and steel, electrical power, and transportation industries. For the administration of the common markets the following organs were to be created: (1) a governmental body; (2) a consultative body consisting of employers, employees, and representatives of the public interest; and (3) "one or more organizations of employers drawn from both publicly owned and privately owned undertakings, on whom would fall, among other duties, the task of carrying out the general directives and recommendations of the European governmental body."[77]

If such were the objectives of organized business, the two most noted proposals for the economic unification of Western Europe, fell short of what business expected. Therefore a broad sector of the employers' movement successfully opposed the enactment of the Franco-Italian Customs Union and fought vainly the ratification of the Coal and Steel Treaty.

For the French government the main advantage of a Franco-Italian Customs Union consisted in its symbolic value as a practical first step toward the integration of European economies. When in the internationalist mood of 1947 France had sent out invitations to most European countries to join a customs union, only Italy had reacted favorably. In March 1949 a treaty, de-

76 See *Bulletin*, IV, No. 54, July 20-August 5, 1950, pp. 24-26. The reports were entirely in line with thoughts expressed by M. Duchemin before the Second World War.

77 See European Movement, *European Economic Conference of Westminster, April 20th-25th, 1949: General Account and Resolutions*, pp. 17-18.

signed to abolish within a year all tariffs and trade obstacles between the two countries, was signed by Messrs. Robert Schuman
and Count Sforza. Within six years a unification of tax, financial,
social, and commercial legislation of the two countries was to
achieve their complete economic fusion. A Council of the Customs Union, an incipient common economic government, was to
prepare administratively for the elimination of customs and later
for the economic union.[78]

As soon as the terms of the treaty became known, friends and
foes of the proposed customs union confronted each other in a
meeting of the CNPF's Board of Directors which at that time
still published accounts of controversial debates.[79] Most of the
commercial interests were highly favorable to the proposed
union. M. Lacour-Gayet, who then represented commerce and
especially the department stores in the councils of the CNPF,
made the approval of the treaty the touchstone of economic
liberalism and of the victory for the European idea to which he
was committed.[80] It seems that a number of French department
stores were prepared to profit from the customs union by selling
the cheaper Italian goods. Also the engineering industries and the
paper industry, but above all the chemical interests, were outspokenly in favor of a somewhat modified treaty with Italy. They
seem to have been joined by the steel interests which feared that
without the customs union Italian competitors might be driven
into the arms of German heavy industry.

The center of all activities hostile to ratification were the
cotton interests and especially Boussac's *Comptoir de l'Industrie
Cotonnière*. M. Boussac himself and his *grand commis*, M.
Fayol, highly respected throughout the employers' movement,
spoke, wrote, cajoled, and campaigned against the customs union
in the many political and administrative milieus to which they
have access. The members of the Economic Council and of both
houses of parliament were besieged by delegations and deluged
with letters pointing to the presumably disastrous consequences
of the proposed customs and economic union. The spokesmen of
the cotton industry felt certain that the French market would

[78] For the text of the Treaty, see *Année Politique 1949*, Paris, 1950, pp. 352-55.
[79] See *Bulletin*, IV, No. 35, June 15, 1949, p. 4.
[80] See his speech in the Economic Council, *Bulletin du Conseil Economique*,
p. 208, and his book, *Propos d'un Libéral*, Paris, 1947, pp. 80-81.

be flooded with low-priced Italian products. Not only were Italian wages lower, but also the Italian cotton industry had benefited from Marshall plan aid for its modernization, while its French competitors had never obtained foreign aid. The great advantage which the fight against the treaty could put to use was the fact that it became the rallying point for a large number of marginal interests. The French cotton industry, itself long since in an unfavorable position and since 1929 in need of protectionist crutches, gathered the support of M. Gingembre's CGPME, of the rice producers of the Camargue, of the flower, fruit, and vegetable markets of the Côte d'Azur, of the canned food industry, and of the French spaghetti makers. In parliament such an amalgamation of business and agricultural interests, similar to the support which the alcohol lobby can gather, proved particularly valuable.

The main arguments used by this propaganda attempted to show that, since the economies of the two countries were analogous and competitive rather than complementary, the union would necessarily work against the higher priced system of the two. Hence the proposed customs union would forever discredit rather than further the principle of European economic integration. "The Franco-Italian Customs Union, in theory a generous and noble idea, will in practice result in a struggle between . . . a France still rich and an Italy, alas yet poor and compelled to feed a rapidly growing population. The problem can find its solution only in a European framework, if not on a world scale."[81]

When the Bidault government became aware that resistance against ratification gathered strength in the country and in parliament, and that the National Assembly hesitated to bring up the matter for plenary debate, it decided to hasten developments and, if possible, outmaneuver the opponents of the customs union. Using prerogatives which had been granted to the Executive in tariff matters shortly after the war, it signed in March 1950 with Italy a "protocol" (approximately the equiva-

[81] See Comité d'Etudes pour le Redressement Economique et Financier, *Pas d'Union Douanière Franco-Italienne Clandestine*, Paris, n.d. Another pamphlet by the same business group, *Menace pour notre industrie, notre agriculture, et notre main d'oeuvre: l'Union Douanière franco-italienne*, Paris, n.d., warned against the customs union in downright hysterical terms.

lent of an Executive Agreement in the United States), according to which all quota restrictions were to be abolished within a relatively short period. Although the government could point out that such a measure was entirely in line with the liberalization policies advocated for all of Western Europe by the OEEC, the protocol let loose a storm of protests in which the CNPF participated vigorously.[82]

Before the signing of the protocol the employers' peak association had avoided taking a stand on a question on which its membership was divided. In fact this meant, as it does on many occasions, that the marginal groups were given a free hand to develop their campaign. But the protocol raised an issue of principle which brought the CNPF over to the side of the opposition. The document had been the result of a mere agreement of the sovereign governments without any consultation with the "interests involved," namely the trade associations. Moreover, in its newly drafted version the treaty contained a clause empowering the governments to forestall, in the interest of the consumers, all agreements which tend to limit production. The vice-president of the CNPF understood this as an unfriendly gesture toward existing cartels and the Franco-Italian Industrial Committee which had been formed by the CNPF and by the General Confederation of Italian Industry in order to prepare for an "equalization of conditions" between the two economies. With his customary frankness, M. Ricard explained that the necessary industry agreements might well include provisions for the limitation of production.[83] These comments made it quite clear that even those business groups which were presumably in favor of the treaty would lend their support only at a price.

If there existed still a chance for the ratification of the treaty, the policy of "shock-imports" which the government began practicing during the winter of 1950-51 definitely gave the upper hand to the enemies of the customs union. The sharp price in-

---

[82] For the attitude of the CNPF towards the protocol of March 1950 and its influence on the administration, see especially *Bulletin*, IV, No. 50, May 5, 1950, pp. 10-11; No. 54, July 20-August 5, 1950, p. 24; and No. 55, September 5, 1950, pp. 4-5. For the interesting discussions and votes on the proposed customs union in the Economic Council see *Bulletin du Conseil Economique*, May 11, 1950, pp. 208-09.

[83] See *Bulletin*, V, No. 62, February 5, 1951, p. 21.

crease following the outbreak of the Korean War induced the government to open the tariff and quota gates for certain products of current consumption for which French prices seemed particularly high. In spite of its commitment to the principle of trade liberalization, the CNPF and its various committees protested in sharp tones against such measures. Since the policy especially favored Italian imports of textiles and foodstuffs, the foes of the Franco-Italian treaty claimed that the customs union was introduced by a side door and that parliament was once more by-passed.[84] They now convinced most of French business that an extension of the policy of shock imports might endanger its competitive position.

In the meantime the Bidault government had been overthrown, and on the eve of general election the new cabinet decided not to press for a discussion of the treaty in a plenary session of parliament. Ironically enough the proposed treaty against which Boussac had campaigned with all the means which his cotton empire puts at his disposal succumbed shortly after the elections of 1951 to the stiletto of a communist deputy. Upon his motion, and presumably to protect the interests of the "agricultural toilers" of the Mediterranean basin, the treaty was pigeonholed in an Assembly committee and all operations resulting from the various Franco-Italian agreements were immediately suspended—*ad calendas graecas*.[85]

The first attempt to enlarge French markets beyond the country's national borders had been frustrated by a broad politico-economic alliance over which business interests exercised an only slightly concealed leadership. By the time the Franco-Italian treaty was shelved in the summer of 1951, organized business had already turned its attention to another proposal for European integration where far weightier interests seemed to be at stake.

Only a few weeks after Robert Schuman had made, in May 1950, his startling proposal for a pooling of coal and steel, the representative organizations of French business voiced their

---

[84] For protests concerning the shock-imports from Italy, see *ibid.*, v, No. 69, August, 1951, p. 31.

[85] See *J.O. Doc. Parl. Ass. Nationale Annexe*, No. 181 (Séance July 17, 1951), pp. 1452-53. For a good summary of the events leading to the demise of the Franco-Italian Customs Union, see Pickles, *op.cit.* (n. v-95), p. 201.

opposition to the treaty which was then being drafted. The General Assembly of the CNPF endorsed unanimously the stern warnings of M. Villiers: "While the CNPF is favorable to its [the plan] envisaged aim, it expresses the greatest reservation in regard to the proposed means. It would indeed be very undesirable if the enactment of this treaty were to reinforce the intervention of government in economic matters."[86] In the polemics surrounding the draft treaty the true issues that were at stake did not fail to emerge soon with all desirable clarity: What role would the trade associations and the cartels play in the projected community? Who should assume the function of regulating the common market—an international administration or business? The criticism against the composition and the powers of the High Authority merged with the strenuous objection to the anti-trust and anti-cartel provisions of the treaty (articles 65-66). During the debates in the National Assembly the *rapporteur* for the ratification bill maintained, probably correctly, that if "articles 65 and 66 had not been incorporated, organized French industry would not have opposed the treaty."[87]

The debate was well-joined during the testimony of Louis Charvet, then the executive of the Steel Association, before the Economic Council. M. Charvet had pleaded that industry was in need of a "regulatory mechanism," especially in a period of crisis. One of the members of the Council understood this to mean that the Association preferred the cartel to the High Authority. To which M. Charvet replied: "One prefers what one has negotiated oneself to what is imposed from the outside. Why? Because we believe that one is never as well served as by oneself."[88]

The way in which business would have wanted to see the proposed common markets organized was described in the "amendments" which the employers' delegation submitted to the Economic Council. The suggested changes asked for greatly extended prerogatives of the trade associations in line with the

[86] See *Bulletin*, IV, No. 54, July 20-August 5, 1950, p. 22. A full account of the fight of the trade associations against the Schuman plan is given in Ehrmann, *op.cit.* (n. III-56). For reasons of space this chapter only summarizes the fuller discussion presented in the article.

[87] See *J.O. Débats, Ass. Nationale*, December 7, 1951, p. 8858.

[88] See *Bulletin du Conseil Economique*, November 29, 1951, p. 172.

"proposals formulated by the European Movement at Westminster." The High Authority of the Community was to be deprived of all jurisdiction in matters affecting investments, and part of its powers were to be shifted to the Court, the Consultative Committee, and the Ministerial Council of the Community. The *a priori* prohibition of cartels was to be replaced by an *a posteriori* censure only of those agreements that had proved harmful. The definite establishment of the Community was to be preceded by an experimental period of five years, after which a modification of the treaty would be possible. But even afterwards any nation which felt harmed by the Community should be permitted to reintroduce tariffs and quotas, to dispense government subsidies, and to resort to other practices which the treaty considered irreconcilable with the fundamental goals of the Community.[89]

In their campaign against the treaty the trade associations presented an amalgam of economic and nationalist arguments. Before various expert committees and in the trade press, they sought to prove with a great amount of technical data that, because of the natural advantages of the Ruhr Basin, and because of fiscal and social legislation, French industry would be at a disadvantage from the outset. Hence the establishment of a common market would inevitably result in unemployment when French steel mills and coal pits would have to close down. Moreover, under the proposed treaty Germany was presumably free to refuse the shipment of coking coal to France, while there was nothing to prevent a rapid depletion of French iron ore reserves.[90]

Before less technical audiences and whenever their factual data were contradicted, the associations fell back on strong expressions of Germanophobia. From the tribune of parliament M. Pierre André described the consequences of common markets with Germany in outright defeatist terms. By others the treaty

[89] For the text of the employers' group, see Conseil Economique, Etudes et Travaux. *Communauté Européenne du Charbon et de l'Acier*, Paris, n.d., pp. 150-61; 166-69.

[90] See Louis Lacoste, an official of the National Association of Non-ferrous Metals, "Notre Fer en Péril," *Nouvelle Revue de l'Economie Contemporaine*, Nos. 16-17, 1951, p. 49. The entire issue of this magazine, described above Chapter V, as one of the information media of the employers' movement, was devoted to ardent polemics against the Schuman plan.

was characterized as a belated victory of Hugo Stinnes, prominent German industrialist of the twenties. P. E. Flandin concluded "that after having conquered Germany, we are offering
her what she would have imposed on us, if she had won."[91]

Whether such nationalistic arguments were but a rationalization of a desire to defend the economic *status quo*, or whether the
fear of Germany was primordial, appears to be a moot question.[92]
Both motivations were real; only the emphasis changed with the
audience. If the latter was considered to be amenable to "neu-
tralist" arguments, insinuations against the United States were
used as supporting arguments against the Community. The entire
draft treaty and especially its anti-cartel features were characterized as American-inspired and hence of foreign origin. European "humanism" was contrasted with American "materialism,"
which naïvely believed in the establishment of large markets as
the panacea for economic ills. Hints were dropped that a collusion existed between the American High Commissioner and the
Bonn government, between Washington and M. Monnet.[93] As
the proof that also leading American industrialists were looking
with misgivings on the Coal and Steel Community, an article
critical of the Community by the president of Inland Steel,
Clarence B. Randall, was given wide circulation especially
among members of parliament.[94]

It has been described earlier how the intensive efforts which
the trade associations undertook to prevent the ratification of
the Schuman plan in its proposed form came to naught in both
houses of parliament.[95] A comparison between this failure and
the success which crowned the opposition to the Franco-Italian
Customs Union is suggestive. In both cases the campaign was all

[91] Pierre-Etienne Flandin, "Les Aspects Politiques du Plan," *ibid.*, p. 6. See also
Pierre André, "Le Pool Acier-Charbon: Une Synarchie Internationale Omnipo-
tente," *Tour d'Horizon*, No. 24, January, 1953, pp. 29-36.

[92] Georges Goriély, "L'Opinion Publique et le Plan Schuman," *Revue Française
de Science Politique*, III, 1953, concluded, p. 592, that ungenerated nationalism was
at the root of all opposition to the treaty. Raymond Aron, *op.cit.* (n. VIII-70),
p. 11, is of the opinion that the French opponents "feared above all else" stepped
up exports from other participating countries.

[93] See especially Flandin, *op.cit.* (n. VIII-91), p. 7; and A. Dauphin-Meunier,
"Réactions Anglaises et Américaines au Plan Schuman," *ibid.*, pp. 66-72.

[94] See Clarence B. Randall, "European Steel: Monopoly in the Making," *Atlantic Monthly*, CLXXXVIII, October, 1951, pp. 34-38.

[95] See above, Chapter V, and, with more details, Ehrmann, *op.cit.* (n. III-56),
pp. 453 ff.

but openly conducted by business interests and directed against the implementation of the European idea which enjoyed a general though not very alert sympathy in public opinion. But the two campaigns were nevertheless different. The cotton interests mobilized against the customs union a broad front of large and small producers in industry and agriculture; M. Boussac's "Marginals of France unite" was bound to have wide appeal. Although a Gingembre was not less ardently opposed to the Schuman plan than he had been to the customs union, and though almost the entire CNPF threw its weight against the Coal and Steel Community, here the fight nevertheless bore the stigma of being waged primarily by the *Comité des Forges*. Hence the advocates of ratification could turn the battle into one against the "anonymous forces of industry"—still a good propaganda plank in France. Agricultural interests were at least neutralized, if not actually favorable to the Community, which the then still powerful General Confederation of Agriculture considered a desirable prototype for the "green pool," the common market for agricultural products.

It is also true that during the struggle over the Schuman plan the trade associations had in M. Monnet and his staff extremely able opponents. The Commissariat succeeded in mobilizing for the treaty the support of nationalized industry and did not altogether fail in its attempts to differentiate steel consumers' from producers' interests.[96] While the Westminster formula of the employers crystallized against them a suspicion of "government by business," Monnet and Schuman were able to point out that the treaty left it open whether or not the objectives of the Community would be accomplished by the marketing process and whether the High Authority would be "liberal" or "interventionist."[97] Hence the extremists of either school were deprived of effective arguments against the treaty, and much of the sting was taken out of the employers' warnings against the dangers of a "superbureaucracy."

[96] For the role of the Chambers of Commerce in the Schuman plan debate see above, Chapter IV.

[97] See the statements by Schuman before the National Assembly and by M. Uri, one of Monnet's principal advisers, in Conseil Economique, *op.cit.* (n. VIII-89), p. 116. The significance of this point is particularly stressed by Horst Mendershausen, *op.cit.* (n. VI-12), p. 271.

The at times dramatic struggle over ratification had its repercussion for the structure and cohesion of the employers' movement. If the CNPF had not hesitated to take an outspokenly hostile position, this was not only due to the great influence which the steel industries still exercised in its midst, but also to the fear of many other industries that the treaty's anti-cartel provisions might provide the pattern for subsequent European "communities." Generally antagonistic wings of the employers' movement, such as ACADI and M. Gingembre's CGPME, were equally opposed to the treaty, if for different reasons.[98] The only serious opposition to the line adapted by the employers' movement was quickly liquidated by a series of drastic organizational maneuvers. Since the Coal and Steel Community was to affect prices and supply of steel products, producers and consumers might have been expected to take different sides on the issue. The secretary general of the Association of Engineering Industries, M. Jean Constant, had taken the frank defense of the Schuman plan as soon as its outlines had become known. M. Constant, one of the energetic and outspoken, if somewhat adventurous, younger men for whom the confusion of post-war days had opened the door to important positions in the employers' movement, had at all times been an ardent advocate of modernizing French industry and of integrating it into larger markets. He also belonged to the small group of pressure group officials who were outspoken critics of any *dirigisme* by organized business.[99]

To counteract such policies, M. Métral was elected president of the Association of Engineering Industries shortly after the Schuman plan had been launched; within a few months he eliminated from the leadership of the association all those who were friendly to the plan or generally critical of the steel industry. Métral himself assumed a prominent role in the fight against the treaty, predicting boldly that "this treaty, drafted as it is with the definite, though unavowed and hence shame-

[98] See the violently hostile article, taking the defense of national and international cartels, "Plan Schuman," *Bulletin Acadi*, No. 45, February, 1951, pp. 54-75.

[99] See especially M. Constant's articles, "Le Plan Schuman" in the Association's official bulletin, *Les Industries Mécaniques*, No. 64, July, 1950, pp. 1-4, and "Le Problème de l'Acier," *ibid.*, No. 70, February, 1951, pp. 1-4.

faced, intention of destroying the very principle of business representation, will be rejected by the French parliament. . . ."[100]

After the facts had rather cruelly belied such predictions, other sectors of the employers' movement became restive over the outright political tactics which the CNPF had seen fit to use inside and outside parliament. The interests which M. Davezac's Association of Electrical Industries represents are as cartel-minded as others, but they were less fearful of the competition which might develop if European integration were to proceed at greater speed. Moreover they considered that the disastrous outcome had fully justified their warnings against identifying the general employers' movement with the steel interests. A prolonged crisis developed within the CNPF which ended by giving to the forces of opposition greater representation on the Executive.[101]

In the first General Assembly held after the ratification of the Coal and Steel Treaty, the CNPF reversed its previous position and promised wholehearted collaboration with the High Authority, pledging that French industrialists would match the vigor of their German colleagues. In an obvious desire to repair the damage which the ratification debates had inflicted on its reputation, the Steel Association expressed the hope that it would have the support of "government and parliament, of the users of steel products, and of public opinion in general" for the "peaceful competitive struggle that lay ahead." In a press conference, M. Ricard, who in the meantime had moved from the headship of the Foundry Association to that of the Steel Association, eulogized the president of the Community, M. Monnet, and his French staff, largely recruited from the Commissariat of the Modernization Plan. Yet at the same time the speaker also complimented the views of Mendès-France, who was known to be more reserved towards European unity than Monnet and concluded that in the eyes of the steel industry the Schuman plan remained a "dangerous venture."[102]

[100] André Métral, "Le Plan Schuman Constitue un Saut dans l'Inconnu," Nouvelle Revue de l'Economie Contemporaine, Nos. 16-17, 1951, p. 41. On Métral's career in the employers' movement, see above, Chapter III.

[101] For details see above, Chapter III.

[102] For Messrs. Villiers' and Ricard's addresses, see Bulletin, VI, July 20-August 5, 1952, p. 27, and ibid., VI, January 5, 1953, pp. 15-19.

Among the organizations affiliated with the CNPF only the CGPME did not depart from outward hostility. With his usual sense of melodrama M. Gingembre berated the "Europe of the Trusts"; to him the first carload crossing the border after the opening of the common market had not only carried "European coke" but also the "corpse of French industry." In a letter addressed as late as April 1953 to all deputies he protested against "the most gigantic cartelization which had been tried so far by the trade associations."[103]

The steel interests were highly pleased when the Pinay government appointed (probably in violation of the wording of the treaty) an industrialist to serve as one of the nine members of the High Authority. M. Daum, heir of Raymond Poincaré, descendant of an old family of Lorraine industrialists and a graduate of the *Polytechnique*, was prior to his nomination director of several important steel companies, such as Sollac and Sidclor. Active in the employers' movement since before the war, he had also been one of the representatives of the Steel Association in the councils of the CNPF. Actually M. Daum has given proof of so much independence in the exercise of his new functions in Luxemburg that officials of the Steel Association have frequently expressed their "disappointment" with what they considered an insufficient regard for the French steel interests on the part of their former colleague.[104]

The attitude of organized business toward the European integration plans which have been aired since the establishment of the Coal and Steel Community was at all times conditioned by the experiences made during the Schuman plan. The employers' peak association did not merely give, as in the case of the Franco-Italian Customs Union, a free hand to its affiliates to act as they pleased, but declared rather emphatically that it did not behoove the employers' movement to take a position in regard to such military or political integration proposals as the

---

[103] *La Volonté du Commerce et de l'Industrie*, February, 1953, and *Informations Confédérales*, April 8, 1953. For a discussion of the reasons for the **CGPME's** hostility to all plans for European unity, see above, Chapter **IV**.

[104] The relationship between the trade associations and the Community during the first years of its functioning calls for extensive further study. Of interest is the predominantly legal work by Paul Reuter, *La Communauté Européenne du Charbon et de l'Acier*, Paris, 1953.

European Defense Community or the Political Community, put forward by the *ad hoc* assembly. At one point the CNPF gave to understand obliquely that a majority among its leadership favored the enactment of EDC "for political reasons."[105]

In fact, the advertised neutrality was designed to hide a wide divergence of views among organized business. At least between the establishment of the Coal and Steel Community, which had sensitized many business leaders to the issues involved in integration, and the final defeat of the EDC in the National Assembly, the employers' movement only mirrored general divergencies on the desirability and the forms of further European unity.

M. Ricard, still president of the CNPF Committee on International Questions, and speaking for heavy industry, found a way to express his opposition to the Defense Community. After stating that the CNPF did not have to take position, he quoted approvingly an article on these questions by the pre-war president of the CGPF, M. Gignoux. But that article contained one of the most violent diatribes against the Coal and Steel Community, the Defense Treaty, plans for political unity among the "Six," and against other possible commodity pools.[106] The business elements hostile to European integration found their most outspoken protagonist in M. Métral, also a member of the CNPF's Executive. In spite of his antagonism against the Coal and Steel Community he had become chairman of the Consultative Assembly in Luxemburg, a post he resigned only when the French government opened criminal proceedings against him.[107]

M. Métral's diatribes against the proposed EDC and the *ad hoc* treaty were little short of violent. Since, in contrast to the Community, EDC provided for central agencies in charge of distributing military supplies, M. Métral could present the Defense Community as a potential threat to the myriad of firms interested in defense production of one kind or another. "One has the impression," he stated, with an obvious thrust at M.

---

[105] See e.g., *Entreprise*, March 1, 1954. After the failure of EDC, the CNPF created a Committee on the Economic Problems of Western Defense, placed under the chairmanship of the director of the Peugeot auto works. See *Bulletin*, No. 129, February, 1955, p. 65.

[106] For M. Ricard's report, see *ibid.*, VIII, No. 114, February 15, 1954, p. 40. For the article he quoted approvingly, see C. J. Gignoux, "L'Engrenage Européen," *La Revue des Deux Mondes*, VII, 1954, pp. 171-79.

[107] See above, Chapter III.

Monnet, "that a true madness of integration has befallen us. Cleverly arranged by an invisible conductor, this campaign tries to organize a rescue operation for the [Coal and Steel] pool, since its promoters now fear that it will not last long if it is not supported by military, agricultural, and pharmaceutical pools—waiting for yet others to come. *Quos vult perdere Jupiter dementat.*" The economic provisions of the proposed political community were described as inviting the "sovietization of the economies of all Schumania."[108]

Because of the discreetness which the CNPF requested from its affiliates, it is difficult to ascertain whether those sectors of the employers' movement which sided with M. Métral brought much influence to bear on the members of parliament when the various treaties and proposals were under consideration. The influential trade association of the chemical industry made no secret of its hostility to all integration plans, since at least for a time the "white pool" of pharmaceutical products was seriously considered. A deputy like Pierre André, who has long been regarded as the defender of steel interests in parliament, became the center of opposition to EDC, and Senator Maroger fought the Political Community from within the committee appointed to draft the treaty. In 1953 Pierre André formed a "National Committee for the defense of the unity between France and its overseas territory," with the announced objective of preventing the ratification of EDC.[109] From the outset the campaign launched by the committee was designed to have the broadest possible appeal and thereby to avoid the mistakes that had contributed to the enactment of the Schuman plan. To determine whether and to what extent various trade associations have been involved in these activities is difficult. Certainly the ultimate demise of the EDC, however much certain business interests might have rejoiced in it, was due to other and broader political causes.

[108] See A. R. Métral, "La Mécanique Française en face des Problèmes Nationaux et Européens," supplement to the March-April, 1953, issue of *Les Industries Mécaniques*, p. 29. The entire address, lengthy and violent though it is, is one of the ablest statements of the anti-European position among French business leaders.

[109] See *Le Monde*, February 14 and 19, March 18, 1953. For a description of the economic interests mobilized against the treaty, see Jacques Vernant, "L'économie française devant la C.E.D." in Raymond Aron, *et al.*, *La Querelle de la C.E.D.*, Paris 1956, pp. 109-121. The author does not discuss the means employed by these interests to prevent ratification.

On the other side of the scale the efforts of business leaders who favored rapid progress of European economic integration have centered around the European League for Economic Cooperation. Founded by Paul Van Zeeland, the League had for a long time counted among its membership very lukewarm supporters of the European idea. But shortly after the Coal and Steel Community had come into existence, M. Giscard d'Estaing assumed a more active leadership of the League's French section. From then on the League came forward in strong support of the EDC and even of the Political Community. M. Giscard d'Estaing himself submitted an imaginative plan for economic collaboration among all OEEC nations which, if enacted, might lead to a fusion of monetary systems, and to the establishment of a "functional commonwealth" among most European countries.[110]

M. Edmond Giscard d'Estaing, descendant of one of the country's most illustrious families, a former inspector of finance, and today an administrator of industrial corporations in many fields and director of one of the foremost investment banking houses, is too prominent a personality not to command a considerable moral authority in the employers' movement. Though he is no longer a member of the CNPF's Board of Directors, he continues to serve as president of the French National Committee of the International Chamber of Commerce and as such wields great, if again moral rather than actual, influence. Partly upon his urging the Executive of the International Chamber of Commerce has come forward with almost radical proposals for trade liberalization, convertibility of currencies, and even a customs union among European nations.[111] Yet what might be called the "pro-European" faction of the employers' movement is composed of individuals rather than of entire sections or branches of industry.

[110] See *ibid.*, No. 36, March, 1954, p. 25, and especially M. d'Estaing's lucid book, *La France et l'Intégration Economique de l'Europe*, Paris, 1953. The CNPF reviewed the book politely without a word of approval or criticism. See *Bulletin*, VIII, No. 115, February 20, 1954, pp. 32-33. For reports on the activities of the League and the positions taken by it, see *Europe Today and Tomorrow. International Bulletin of the European Movement*, No. 25, April, 1953, p. 11; No. 33, December, 1953, pp. 18-19; No. 40, July-August, 1954, p. 22.

[111] For a forthright pro-European resolution by the Executive Council of the International Chamber of Commerce, see *ibid.*, No. 40, July-August, 1954, p. 23. The CNPF's report on the meeting of the Chamber significantly tuned down its pro-European sentiments, see *Bulletin*, VIII, No. 119, May 1954, pp. 65-67.

The CNPF has kept clear of commitment to either the outspoken anti-European or the pro-European wing of the employers' movement. It has attached much attention to the work of the "Union of the Industries of the Six Countries of the Community" which emerged within the larger CFIE soon after the enactment of the Schuman plan. Since its founding the Union has in many ways become more active than the Federation, partly because it has more definite, if more limited, objectives. Its announced goal is not only to keep a close watch on the operations of the Luxemburg Community, but also to prevent the spreading of further "authoritarian" integration projects.[112] According to all appearances, a complete unity of views has been achieved among the employers' peak associations of the six countries, especially since the demise of EDC.

If during the last years the CNPF has become more and more engrossed in European matters, and if an increasing share of its activities are devoted to discussion with its European partners, this seems to correspond to a sincerely felt anxiety on the part of many of its leaders, M. Villiers among them, not to let the country slip back into economic isolation. Their declarations in favor of a higher degree of economic collaboration and even integration are not sheer exercises in oratory. But the unification of Europe they envisage is very different from that conceived by Jean Monnet and initially practiced in Luxemburg. Theirs is once more the Westminster formula: the establishment of common markets, the equalization of production and market conditions, specialization and productivity should be the result of agreements concluded autonomously by industry and its organizations. During the last years the CNPF has established an increasing number of working groups consisting of French industrialists and their colleagues from the major European countries. As far as known, these committees are doing spadework for the conclusion of desirable ententes.[113, 114]

[112] See especially, *ibid.*, VIII, No. 114, February 15, 1954, pp. 39-40; *ibid.*, No. 125, October, 1954, p. 5; and *ibid.*, No. 135, August, 1955, p. 65.

[113] See e.g., the revealing report by M. Métral, president of the Franco-German Industry Committee, *ibid.*, No. 129, February, 1955, pp. 51-53. For a characteristic attempt at popularizing among American audiences this approach to economic integration, see "French Industry sees Economic Progress and Common European Market," *France Actuelle*, v, March 15, 1956, pp. 1-2.

[114] Since this was written, the CNPF has sent to me its thorough and thoughtful

Whatever might be their differences in scope, and sometimes in outlook, the numerous and often overlapping international business organizations have constantly protested and often fought against a common dread—measures to curb national or international cartel activities. The French members of these international bodies have usually been most outspoken in their warnings.[115] After the detour of Hitler's New Order and of the Schuman plan those pre-war proposals which recommended that the unification of European economies be effected through the cartels might yet become reality.

French business leaders who favor economic integration consider it a desirable means of bringing about in their country a sustained increase in the rate of economic growth.[116] Knowing that French investments are insufficient, they hope that the wider market opportunities and the addition to real income which an integrated Europe might offer will induce business to match higher savings with more investments. But can it be expected that the possible results of integration will materialize unless competition becomes more vigorous and more effective?

French business argues that only an economic integration based on carefully worked out industry agreements can avoid upheavals which the economies of the continent can ill afford. But given the past record of national and international cartels, is it likely that their action will embolden competition and thereby create the necessary conditions for accelerated economic development?

---

studies on the common European market which it circulated privately in the summer of 1956. These studies cannot be discussed here in detail. Their over-all tenor is favorable to further and even far-reaching integration provided it does not follow the pattern of the Coal and Steel Community. There also is a definite tendency to consider as valid only an economic integration which follows in the wake of political unification of Western Europe or at least of the six Schuman plan countries. The critics of organized business will argue that, since political unification is out of reach, the proclaimed sympathy for the common market and other integration schemes is theoretical if not hypocritical.

[115] As examples, see the protests by the Federation of European Industrialists, *Bulletin*, VIII, No. 118, April, 1954, p. 55; by the Union, *ibid.*, No. 122, August, 1954, p. 45. For the position of the International Chamber of Commerce, discussed earlier, see *ibid.*, VI, No. 88, November 20, 1952, pp. 18-19.

[116] See also the conclusions reached in the interesting article by Franz Gehrels and Bruce F. Johnson, "The Economic Gains of European Integration," *Journal of Political Economy*, LXIII, 1955, pp. 275-92.

# CHAPTER IX

# Industrial Relations

## 1. Attitudes towards Social Reforms and Trade Unions

"Don't say: One should not expect gratitude from a worker.
Say: One should not expect gratitude from anybody."
Detoeuf, *Propos de O. L. Barenton*

Shortly before the war the customary "scenario" of social reform legislation in France was described ironically in a Catholic magazine: "(1) The employers say that they will not give in; (2) The employers are afraid and finally do give in; (3) One notices that nothing has changed; the employers have found ways to get around the laws."[1] Essentially that sequence and the mentality reproducing it at fairly regular intervals have remained unchanged.

Historical memories and contemporary responses alike give to the employers as a class, though not necessarily as individuals, the feeling that social reforms are unsound at every given moment. Barricades will be erected to stop the onrush of demands. Only when the pressure becomes too strong, as in 1936 and 1945, are the defenses hastily abandoned for a headlong retreat until the situation permits closing the avenues once more to social progress by new and not less elaborate barriers. Such terminology, deliberately chosen from the configurations of civil war, is commonly used, not only by the trade union movement but by many employers themselves when they view, critically or approvingly, the tactics of their organizations.

After the liberation, as after Matignon, massive social reforms such as the overhauling of the social security system and the institution of the plant committees were accepted by the employers without resistance, but also without any conviction that the mores of industrial relations would have to be changed. Another battle had been lost. With the passing of time and the change in political fortunes, there was always hope that abandoned ground could be reconquered.

[1] See Regis, *op.cit.* (n. 1-60), p. 562.

The psychological effects of perpetual warring are telling for both sides. In the words of a perceptive analysis furnished by the ACADI group, the French bourgeoisie has developed a deep-rooted inferiority complex and the working class an obsessional fear of being isolated and impotent.[2] The systematic hostility by which the employers feel surrounded has deepened their resentment for many a decade. Before the turn of the century the socialist Jean Jaurès spoke of the "miseries of the employers," and appealed to the workers not to hate or to insult but to prepare for the "mutual pity which might be the prelude of justice."[3] Sixty years later feelings of justice are still little known and French industrialists, who are willing to discover in American labor-management relations more than an abject example of social levelling, are most impressed with the absence of mutual hatred in the United States even after bitter industrial strife.

Since employers consider social gains won by the workers as a form of punishment for their own lack of vigilance and staying power, they prefer to see reforms imposed rather than granted. After having protested that concessions would be disastrous, management finds it easier to bow to the law than to absorb new changes voluntarily. In this way the shame over having acted cowardly is at least not compounded by the reproach for having given foolishly.

Almost all of the major social reforms bestowed during the Third and Fourth Republics had their origin in a conjunction of broad currents in public opinion and of painstaking efforts by high government officials.[4] When, as at Matignon, reform legislation was at least in form preceded by an apparently impressive act of collective bargaining, the employers' movement refused almost immediately afterwards to renew such meetings, leaving it to the authorities to implement the new legislation. By waiting for ineluctable reforms to be imposed from the outside, the employers' movement has adopted an attitude of social immobility akin to the policies of economic immobilism discussed earlier. Since

[2] See "Existe-t-il en France une classe ouvrière séparée du reste du pays?" *Bulletin Acadi*, No. 51, October 1951, pp. 346-47.

[3] Jean Jaurès, "Les Misères du Patronat," *La Dépêche de Toulouse*, May 28, 1890.

[4] For the situation prevailing at the end of the nineteenth century, see the classical description in Halévy, *op.cit.* (n. v-139), pp. 92-94.

the drafting of every major reform bill is left to the authorities, the laws and ordinances are frequently rigid and bureaucratic, which gives to the employers additional reason for complaint. If of late the close collaboration between high bureaucracy and a well-organized employers' movement has resulted in greater flexibility, this is still not the result of direct bargaining between the partners of industrial relations.

In matters of social policies the CNPF has developed a more consistent "doctrine" than in most other fields. If the practices which it recommends have been followed faithfully by a majority of its affiliates, this is in part a tribute to the authority enjoyed by the organization's Social Committee. The committee presided over by M. Marcel Meunier[5] is ably staffed, sharing most of its top personnel with the services of the UIMM, the metal trades organization. M. Meunier himself would not object to being classified as a *patron de combat*, an employer of the old school convinced of the need for toughness in the unavoidable social strife. Though practically inclined and frowning on discussions of social philosophy, M. Meunier also accepts being classified as a "paternalist." In his opinion there was much validity in Pétain's concept of a *pater*, and if the employers were to accept it without prying into the private lives of their workers, both sides would gain much from such an orientation. On the other hand, he considers any form of government intervention in industrial relations as opening the gates to collectivism and anti-Western totalitarianism, especially if it results in abetting the demands of organized labor.

The prestige which M. Meunier personally and the work of his committee have acquired throughout the movement is based undoubtedly to a large extent on the fact that they represent the common cause of the employers as such rather than naturally diversified economic interests. If French organized business amalgamates the economic and social functions of an employers' and a trade association movement, a division of labor exists nevertheless within the organizations so that usually separate staffs handle economic problems and industrial relations. The usually strict division of functions finds its frequent counterpart in a pronounced difference in mentality. With some notable

[5] For his background and business connections, see above Chapter III.

exceptions the industrial relations sections of the associations are led and staffed by men who by inclination would identify themselves with the views of a Meunier, while their own colleagues in other sectors of the employers' movement might frown upon such views and regard them as oversimplified, if not dangerous.

Hence it has happened that the president of the CNPF's Social Committee has, especially in international gatherings, expounded opinions which are apt to make his own colleagues shudder. But before an audience of French employers and of the industrial relations staffs of their associations, M. Meunier will win wholehearted approval from most sides. His stubborn forcefulness and energy are given credit for having steered organized business back to strength and respectability at a time when, after the liberation, many members of the business community considered silence and discretion the better part of wisdom. By and large the attitude which the Social Committee has taken toward the general problem of social reform seems to correspond to the feelings of most French employers.

As Keynesianism is rejected in the field of economic policies, the basic concepts of the social welfare state are entirely alien to the individualistic French employer. Legislation enacted since 1936 has undoubtedly made the country not less of a welfare state than Great Britain, but its structures have been at best tolerated, and more often been resented by most of the business community.

M. Meunier's committee ascribes the existing density of social legislation to what it calls a "national mania to legislate" and also to the competition of political parties vying with each other in the "pursuit of progress." Whatever little freedom the overzealous legislator has left to business for determining working conditions is completely quashed when management and labor are compelled by law to add contractual agreements to the rules set by other laws. After this no room is left for genuinely voluntary accord.[6]

[6] A moderate version of this thesis is formulated by Pierre Waline, "Le Patronat Français et les Conventions Collectives," *La Revue Economique* II, 1951, pp. 25-34. The president of the CNPF's Social Committee, M. Meunier, has couched it in far more violent terms. For an early statement on this question contained in a report by the Social Committee, see *Bulletin*, No. 2, December 15, 1946, p. 5.

It cannot be denied that these complaints of the employers' movement have a basis in reality. The sheer bulk of legislation is so heavy that it seldom has the liberating effect moderate reform legislation can have. Whether or not legislation has really destroyed the basis for authentic agreement, it is true that in the private sector of the economy voluntary collective relations have scarcely been tried; no major social reform has ever been introduced by collective agreement.[7]

But having thus analyzed the existing situation, the employers' movement refuses to declare its preferences for a way out of the diagnosed dilemma. If there exists little hope for a fruitful dialogue between management and labor, as the leadership of the CNPF's Social Committee maintains, then legislative regulation seems to offer the only opportunity for modifying labor relations. If on the other hand, bureaucratic intervention by statute and administrative ruling is considered harmful, then comprehensive contractual agreements should be regarded as desirable. But actually both legislation and collective agreement are rejected as ways of social reform; they are at best endured. Negativism is made into a policy; the possibility of future defeats is constantly envisaged, but little is done to avoid them.

Forced back to an essentially defensive attitude and a mentality which considers industrial relations as being fought over as on a battlefield, the CNPF's Social Committee has developed commensurate tactics. As in battle, "pockets" by which the "enemy" might penetrate the defenses must be avoided at all times. Hence individual trade associations ought not to grant concessions even when the actual condition of their member firms would permit greater liberality. Appeals to discipline are issued far more frequently in the field of industrial relations than in regard to other activities of the employers' movement. If in a particular case the CNPF has been unable to prevent the granting of "unauthorized" concessions by an affiliated organization, the latter might be openly criticized. In order to prevent the deepening of the "breach," warnings are issued to other members not to overlook that only special conditions might have justified what should not be conceded elsewhere.[8]

[7] On this point see Lorwin, op.cit. (n. 1-3), pp. 190, 212. The present chapter owes much to Mr. Lorwin's magistral treatment of French industrial relations in the recent past.
[8] As examples of many appeals for discipline see *Bulletin*, IV, No. 44, February

The policies recommended by the Committee have met with criticism from within the employers' movement. Fears have been voiced lest the CNPF invite another social cataclysm, possibly a regenerated Popular Front. At a time when there was still room for discussion in the meetings of the CNPF, the officials of some of the affiliated organizations expressed regret over the Social Committee's immobilism and pressed for broader negotiations between management and labor than the CNPF had considered opportune.[9]

In the field of industrial relations such important organizations as the Textile Association have often made use of the autonomy to which they are entitled under the by-laws of the CNPF. The head of the French employers' delegation to the ILO, M. Waline, himself an executive of the UIMM, has at least for a time defended in Geneva policies which appeared to be substantially more liberal than those of his colleagues in Paris. With varying emphasis the four vanguard groups of the employers' movement have formulated proposals and directives at least implicitly critical of the attitude of the Social Committee. But if many of the critics inside and outside the employers' movement have made the point that during the years following the liberation the country would have found the way to more lasting reforms had the CNPF not existed, they actually pay tribute to the effectiveness of the strategy which M. Meunier and his collaborators have pursued.[10]

*     *     *

During its early days the newly-founded CNPF fully recognized the right to existence of the trade union movement. In the declaration which the leadership of the employers' peak associa-

---

5, 1950, p. 18, and *ibid.*, v, No. 69, August 1951, p. 34, where M. Villiers explains that certain concessions made by the metal trades industry in Paris should not be followed.

[9] See e.g., *ibid.*, No. 3, February 1947, p. 8, when M. Catin, the delegate of the Textile Association asked that the CNPF give more leeway for negotiations and *ibid.*, IV, No. 36, July-August 1949, p. 15, when M. Meunier answered his critics in characteristic fashion that "to drive backwards is sometimes the only way to get the car out of a dangerous spot in which an imprudent driver has been caught."

[10] Lorwin, *op.cit.* (n. 1-3), p. 193, reports correctly that the CNPF has been criticized from one side as too "soft" and from another as too static and rigid. But without analyzing the sources of such criticism it is hardly possible to conclude, as the author does, that the CNPF has in fact maintained a "delicate balance" in social policies.

tion submitted to the government in February 1946, it acknowledged the need for frank collaboration between management and organized labor.[11] A few months later delegates of the CNPF met for the first time with officials of the CGT, most of them communists, in the solemnly announced National Economic Conference on Prices and Wages, the so-called Palais-Royal Conference. In an impassioned if over-sentimental speech, M. Villiers praised the meeting as a possibly epoch-making event opening the way to the mutual understanding of capital and labor. Evoking days of common resistance to the nation's enemies where Frenchmen had become brothers, he dramatically extended "fraternal greetings" to the trade union delegates.[12]

At a time when the CGT alone claimed a membership of five and one-half million wage earners, and when the communists occupied most of the ministries concerned with economic and social matters in the Provisional Government, the incipient and as yet unsure employers' association could hardly afford hostility or even indifference toward organized labor. Moreover the new leadership which had emerged in the employers' movement prided itself on its sense of realism and flexibility; it proposed to eradicate old prejudices of business against organized labor. As late as the summer of 1947, at a time when the honeymoon between the communists and the Fourth Republic had already come to an end, the CNPF upon the urging of the Monnet office engaged once more in central though separate negotiations with the CGT and the Catholic CFTC. "Within the framework of the existing law," the declarations published as the result of these meetings concluded, "the CGT does not dispute the authority of the employer, nor does the CNPF dispute the exercise of trade union rights."[13]

But with the change of the political situation and the ensuing decline in union strength, the attitude of organized business toward the labor movement switched back rapidly to traditional ways. The extreme fluctuations in strength of workers' and employers' organizations, characteristic of French social history for

---

[11] For some of the wording of the declaration, see above Chapter III.
[12] See xxx, "Le Conseil National etc.," op.cit. (n. III-11), pp. 206-209.
[13] For the two declarations, see *Bulletin*, I, No. 9, October 1947, pp. 8-10, and *Syndicalisme*, July 24, 1947, and also International Labour Office, op.cit. (n. v-93), p. 224.

many decades, have at all times prevented an equilibrium of force and feeling. The lack of balance between the two sides has impeded the functioning of the pluralist social democracy attempted during the declining years of the Third Republic and solemnly consecrated in the constitution of the Fourth. The sequence of defeat-victory-revenge for either group at different times has forestalled cooperation at almost any time. Management and labor, supposedly partners of industrial relations, have remained hostile factions, maneuvering to exploit weaknesses of the opponent. Here the disbelief in the lasting value of social reforms, a skepticism shared by both sides, merges with the lack of mutual esteem. Since labor considers all reforms as concessions granted unwillingly under heavy pressure, and since in fact many employers look at them as a loss of prestige and of profits, a purely defensive attitude is natural for both. But defense reactions find their most complete satisfaction in denying to the opponent his right to organize which in turn precludes a willingness to engage in practices of cooperation, either on the plant level or around the collective bargaining table.[14]

Probably most employers had seen in the post-war recognition of the trade unions by the CNPF little more than a tactical maneuver. As soon as the danger of a left-wing insurrection and of additional drastic reform legislation seemed passed, the reaction of individual employers and their organizations to the new situation was that of an immense relief. The feeling of having been successful in holding the front against threatening assaults strengthened the belief in the practical value of stubborn defenses. The elation of having avoided the worst was so general that it has precluded constructive action in the field of industrial relations and a frank recognition of the *fait syndical*, organized labor's right to existence.

The bourgeois mentality of the French employers, large and small, is spontaneously inimical to the sharing of authority which is involved in all collaboration between the organizations of management and labor. In principle, the freedom of association is recognized by the CNPF and its affiliates, for they have accepted the formula which the ILO has proposed to protect the

---

[14] For an analysis of the psychological situation here described, see Weil, *op.cit.* (n. 1-11), pp. 216 ff and passim.

right to organize.[15] But the consequences which that right implies are still resented as intrusions on the employers' discretion and authority.

In the shop, union activities are considered objectionable by a majority of employers.[16] Even in the larger enterprises, shop stewards and union representatives will often be treated with a "cold intransigence" which is as much an expression of managerial impatience with union activities as it is a method of rendering such activities ineffective. Employer hostility to unionism in the plant, a recent observer has concluded, is both response to and cause for continued conflict.[17]

Outside the enterprise the labor union is regarded as impinging upon the freedom of the workers and as exploiting social and economic "envy."[18] A long-time official of the employers' movement, who at present tries to obtain the collaboration of trade associations and labor unions for an improvement of workers' housing, reckons that today more than half of his colleagues refuse to sit around a conference table with labor delegates because they are afraid to create a precedent for organized labor-management collaboration.

Some progressive employers do not object to union activities in the plant or even to practices approximating a closed union shop. But they still see little value in unionism beyond the plant level. Though they wish the unions to be completely independent from management and are averse to all paternalism, they have no understanding of the psychological satisfaction their workers might derive from membership in a labor movement representing them beyond the horizons of an individual firm. To those employers the pyramid of trade union organizations is little more

[15] See International Labour Conference, 31st Session, *Report* VII. San Francisco, 1948.

[16] See O(lga) Raffalovich, "La Conclusion des Conventions Collectives de travail," *Revue Française du Travail*, IV, 1949, p. 10. The author is a high official in the Ministry of Labor.

[17] See Lorwin, *op.cit.* (n. 1-3), p. 255. On the relationship between management and the shop stewards, see the report, *op.cit.* (n. IX-2), pp. 346-47. It should be stressed that by comparison industrial relations in the concern described seem to have been typical, unsatisfactory though they were. The characterization of employers' behaviour as "cold intransigence" was used by Pierre-Henri Teitgen, MRP deputy and minister in a broadcast of March 17, 1950.

[18] For some searching comments on the failure of communication between labor and management, see Pierre Laroque (the one-time director of the Social Security administration), *Réflexions sur le Problème Social*, Paris, 1953, pp. 126-27.

than an obsolete bureaucratic form. It is true that they would often have the same criticism against their own associations which in their eyes envenom industrial relations just as much as does the labor movement. At this point the most forward-looking management rejoins the concepts developed once in Pétain's entourage.

Trade association officials might take the opposite view: as long as the union keeps out of the plant, it can become an acceptable partner for negotiation with the corresponding employers' association. Such officials are of the opinion that the anti-unionist creed and practices of businessmen are out of step with the times and will diminish the prestige of the employers' movement in modern society. But for the time being the attitude of the Social Committee, which in fact repudiates the *fait syndical* both inside and outside the plant, still represents well the animosities and interests of a majority of French employers.[19]

Under present conditions the natural preference of employers for paternalistic practices and the dismal state in which the labor movement finds itself reinforce each other constantly.

The philosophy of industrial paternalism appears to be deeply rooted in the French social structure; it has long formed one of the foundations of conservative thought, for which solidarity among men is far more natural when based on protection and subordination than on a theoretical fraternity among equals. Here, as in so many other domains, the community is considered an extension of the family, in French Catholic and Protestant circles alike a non-egalitarian institution. The authority wielded by the father and the employer finds, as for the benevolent despot, its counterpart in a duty to provide for material and moral protection.[20]

The services which firms of all sizes and employers' associations have organized on their own initiative for the benefit of

---

[19] The situation in post-war Germany is significantly different. There the employers associations and the trade union movement accept to face each other as representatives of their classes at a high political level sanctioning thereby a "mild form of class war"; see the excellent remarks on this situation by Clark Kerr, "Collective Bargaining in Postwar Germany," *Industrial and Labor Relations Review*, v, 1952, p. 330.

[20] On the foundations of paternalism in the philosophy of French conservatism see Jean Labasse, *Hommes de droite, hommes de gauche*, Paris, 1949, p. 22. The clearest statement of the paternalistic position is to be found in the writings of Frédéric Le Play; see for instance, his *Réforme Sociale en France*, Paris, 1864.

employees are often impressive. A quarter of a century ago Robert Pinot described with pride the numerous institutions which the metal industry had established to enhance the well-being of its personnel.[21] Today a list of such achievements would be impressively long and varied in most industries and in many regions. Some of the features, now incorporated into the social security legislation such as family allowances, had first been instigated by employers who had voluntarily pooled resources to spread the financial burden among them. Also in the field of industrial hazards and occupational diseases many firms did not wait for laws which had to be enforced by an understaffed labor inspectorate, but devised instead their own methods of detection and protection. Such efforts cannot be dismissed as mere devices to increase output and profits without exaggerating the efficiency-mindedness of most French businessmen. In the majority of cases paternalistic policies are sincere inasmuch as the improvement of workers' welfare is considered to be an end in itself. However, the moral satisfaction which the employers derive from doing their "duty" toward their subordinates is singularly heightened by the feeling that what is given unilaterally does not encroach upon managerial authority. As long as the employer is dealing directly with his personnel and bestowing upon them the benefits of his choosing, trade union "interference" is eliminated and the discretion of the employer strengthened.

Not infrequently, French employers are aware of the fact that even substantial advantages granted in this way evoke little gratitude. For having increased the dependence and inferiority feeling of their workers rather than their dignity and freedom, they often find themselves surrounded with resentment instead of loyalty.[22] In the eyes of the businessmen such "ingratitude" is artificially implanted and maintained by the trade unions. Hence there is an additional incentive to persevere in paternalism so as to whittle down further trade union influence. If at long last their workers will have learned by experience that only those reforms that have been granted voluntarily by the employers bring lasting improvements while all others are washed away by the tides

[21] Robert Pinot, *Les Oeuvres Sociales des Industries Métallurgiques*, Paris, 1924.

[22] For a searching criticism of the results achieved by paternalistic policies, see Laroque, *op.cit.* (n. IX-18), p. 119.

of social conflict, there is hope that eventually healthier labor-management relations will prevail.

It is true that vanguard groups, such as the *Jeune Patron* and the UCE. ACT., have criticized paternalism for being superficial and shallow. The Catholic personalism which largely determines their thinking considers all betterment of human welfare which does not increase human dignity as vain, and all reforms which do not aim at more equality in the relationship between capital and labor as ephemeral. Other business leaders fear that the acceptance of unilaterally granted benefits might cultivate the mentality on which the communists and the CGT thrive: accustomed to passivity and convinced of the futility of collective negotiations, the workers view the prospect of an authoritarian welfare state with satisfaction rather than dread. Hence paternalistic practices, far from weakening the trade union movement, actually cement the hold which the communist unions still exercise over the working class.

To the critics of paternalism the Social Committee of the CNPF has the answer that with receding *dirigisme* "collective procedures" have lost much of their value and that the single firm has become quite naturally the focus of all efforts aimed at improving the living standard of the personnel. This, in the opinion of the CNPF, is an entirely desirable method of "bringing the head of the enterprise closer to his collaborators on the concrete level of their daily preoccupations." Individual employers and their trade associations are praised for having made remarkable strides in the improvement of management-labor relations in the enterprise, though the CNPF regrets that the public knows too little about such improvements. The Social Committee does not fail to recognize that what it welcomes as an upsurge of paternalism is intimately connected with what some of its reports call the "crisis of the labor movement."[23]

That crisis has engulfed both the communist and the free trade union movement. Ever since the CGT repudiated in 1947 its tactics of class collaboration and patriotic production drives, it has reverted fully to the belief in the virtues of a *politique du*

---

[23] See *Bulletin*, VII, No. 93, February 5, 1953, p. 38. Very similar and with renewed insistence that the enterprise should be the focus of contacts between the employer and the workers is a more recent report by the Committee, *ibid.*, No. 122, August 1954, p. 58.

*pire*, policies which consider economic catastrophes and social clash as stepping stones to ultimate victory. Whenever the CGT unions have found themselves enmeshed in "reformist" activities in their day-by-day practice, they were periodically forced to submit to searching "self-criticism" and to annul previously reached agreements. A trade union organization so committed cannot and does not need to be considered a partner in labor-management cooperation at any level. Hence the CNPF and its affiliates have, as far as the CGT is concerned, justifiedly complained that the absence of a valid partner renders ineffective all social legislation which is based on the cooperation of organized labor and capital. For the employers' movement the situation offers solace on two grounds: it can refuse recognition to the major trade union confederation; and it can point to the inanity of social reform legislation.

But most employers, and many of their associations, refuse to distinguish between the communist CGT, the vaguely socialist CGT-FO, and the Catholic CFTC and to treat them differently. As soon as any labor organization formulates any demands, it is easily accused of demagoguery, "anarchism," or "collectivism."[24] (And in the judgment of French trade association officials, "collectivism" was also spread by the American CIO, just as the closed shop is considered in all earnestness a means of "sovietizing" the American economy sooner or later.)

To all appearances the activities of the free trade unions inside and outside the plants are resented sometimes more than the revolutionary gymnastics of the CGT. It is relatively easy to invoke against the latter its communist affiliation and its announced disbelief in the value of social reforms and labor-management cooperation. But claims made by the FO or the CFTC have to be rejected on other and more tenuous grounds. In the opinion of the employers their demands are frequently motivated by the desire to manifest to the workers that the free trade unions are as combative as the CGT. While this might sometimes be the case, the tactical difficulties besetting the non-communist trade unions furnish to the employers the excuse to reject almost

[24] See Gérard Dehove, "La Situation Sociale," *Droit Social*, xii, 1949, p. 280, and for similar attitudes before the war, Sérampuy, *op.cit.* (n. 1-12), pp. 659, 662.

all their demands as spurious. This in turn has led the membership of both the FO and the CFTC to believe that the French employers' movement has "learned nothing and forgiven nothing," and that by its intransigence and conservatism the bourgeoisie has irrevocably compromised the system which it defends.[25]

The notorious numerical and organizational weakness of the free trade unions provides another reason to ignore them as a factor in industrial relations.[26] Instead of supporting the free trade unions disgruntled workers have joined what Frenchmen call the "largest organization of all, the unorganized." The dearth of members results in empty treasuries. When it becomes known that the free trade unions receive subsidies from American sources, the employers' movement scoffs at such intrusion into "domestic relations." When it is whispered that the FO has at least indirectly drawn on funds contributed by business, the scorn turns into contempt and increased unwillingness to consider the anti-communist labor movement as a valid partner.[27]

There are, however, notable exceptions to such an attitude. Employers in various industries and regions have sought to establish more satisfactory relations with the free trade union movement. Some trade associations, especially in the textile branches, are willing to go far in making concessions to the FO and Catholic unions so as to strengthen the position of the non-communist organizations. Some employers have sincerely complained that the increasing apathy of their personnel has paralyzed all labor organizations. Within the CNPF a constant confrontation of views has opposed those who, like M. Meunier, openly welcome the return to paternalism and those who see dangers in confounding all sectors of the labor movement to the same degree. Of late the more progressive elements have rallied around M. Villiers who, so they claim, has long been critical of

[25] See e.g., the debates at the 1955 convention of the CFTC, as reported in *Droit Social*, XVIII, 1955, p. 438.

[26] The CNPF customarily exaggerates that weakness. At a time when informed observers, discarding inflated membership statistics, concluded that all trade unions together had a combined membership of between two and three million, the CNPF's Social Committee estimated that it did not exceed 1.5 million, half of whom affiliated with the CGT. These figures have to be compared with a total of almost 12 million wage earners. On various estimates of present trade union membership, see Lorwin, *op.cit.* (n. 1-3), p. 177.

[27] For more details on this sad episode see above Chapter V.

some of the concepts developed by the Social Committee. In the summer of 1955 the president of the CNPF addressed an urgent appeal to the affiliates of the Council to maintain with the free trade unions not only "human contacts making it possible to arrive progressively at a better mutual understanding, but also [to engage] in normal and regular rather than occasional confrontations . . . An understanding appears to be more and more possible; the possibilities of collaboration are infinitely great."[28]

Never since 1946 had the employers' movement used such language. When M. Villiers wrote, it was feared that a new strike wave was in the making; at St. Nazaire industrial conflicts had erupted into violence and once more some industrialists had yielded to pressure. It remains to be seen how persistent such appeals will be and whether they will eventually result in a new employers' outlook on unionism.[29]

## 2. Wage Determination and Collective Bargaining

> "Don't say: the French worker limits voluntarily his output and his wages. Say: A worker who sees customarily his wages reduced the moment he exceeds a certain figure which the employer has established, renounces efforts which he knows are futile to secure higher wages."
>
> Detoeuf, *Propos de O. L. Barenton*

The first post-war attempt to revive collective bargaining procedures failed entirely; since prices and wages continued to be largely determined by government, the law of December 23, 1946, which had a number of built-in defects, never brought forth collective agreements of any importance.[30]

[28] George Villiers, "Importance des Contrats Collectifs," *Bulletin*, No. 136, August 1955, p. 3. M. Villiers' conciliatory statement was probably made in answer to an appeal made to him by the leader of the FO. See *Le Monde*, July 7, 1955.

[29] For an appreciation of the events at St. Nazaire in 1955 by an industrialist, see R. Perrin, "La Leçon de Saint-Nazaire," *Bulletin Acadi*, No. 94, September 1955, pp. 287-92. The author indicts the employers of the region for not having understood the material and moral condition of their workers and for not having taken the necessary initiatives in time.

[30] See *J.O.*, December 25, 1946, pp. 10932-33. For the employers' views on the abortive negotiations carried on for years under the 1946 law, see CNPF, *La Discussion des Conventions Collectives Nationales. Etat de la Question en Avril 1949*, and a number of subsequent brochures published the same year by the CNPF.

When parliament was ready to replace the unworkable law on collective bargaining by a new statute, the CNPF expressed its doubts whether the time had yet come to return to a free discussion of wages and working conditions.[31] Although it once more professed liberalism "in principle," and although many prices had theoretically been freed in the meantime, the employers' movement wanted to see collective bargaining postponed until "a complete equilibrium of the market [including exports] had been established,"—a situation which might never be reached. In fact, the CNPF had good reasons to consider the moment for the enactment of a new collective bargaining law tactically inopportune. The balance of strength between the organizations of labor and management was rapidly shifting in favor of the latter. But the parliament which was discussing the new law had been elected in 1946 when anti-business sentiments had run high, while there was reason for hope that the new Assembly to be elected latest in 1951 would be more conservative.

Unable to prevent the enactment of the new statute, the employers' organizations criticized from the outset what they considered the law's fundamental contradictions. And with the tenacity characteristic of its Social Committee, the CNPF for years traced all practical and political difficulties which have arisen over the fixing of wages and working conditions to the initial defects of the 1950 law.[32]

Undoubtedly the statute laid itself open to the customary complaint of the employers' movement that it added to the "imposing legislative edifice" of the labor code further "minimum requirements" on which agreement between the partners was prescribed. Since the employers regarded the numerous obligatory clauses which the law prescribed for full-fledged collective agreements as infringing upon their authority and as generally burdensome, they preferred for many years to conclude simple wage settlements. By the summer of 1953, only 160 collective agreements and 306 annexes, but 3,467 wage settlements, had

[31] See *Bulletin*, IV, No. 44, February 5, 1950, p. 17.

[32] See *ibid.*, V, No. 62, February 5, 1951, pp. 24 f. Cf. also the interesting report which M. Meunier rendered on "four years of experience" with the law of 1950 in *Bulletin*, VIII, No. 122, August 1954, pp. 58-59. At that time M. Meunier obviously felt that all his dire predictions had come true. For the text of the law of February 11, 1950, see *J.O.*, February 12, 1950, p. 1688-93.

been recorded,[33] the latter usually extremely loose and fixing merely minimum wage scales which frequently did not determine actual wages.

In the opinion of the employers and especially of their organizations, wage settlements were in fact all that interested the personnel. The more ambitious provisions which the law prescribed for collective agreements, such as guarantees of workers' freedom of opinion and trade union rights, conditions of hiring and firing, the financing of welfare activities undertaken by the plant committees, conciliation procedures, vocational training, and the like—all these were regarded as being the concern solely of ambitious trade union officials. Moreover, the employers held that such matters had already been regulated in more than sufficient detail by numerous statutes. That, especially in a period of still rising prices, the "bread and butter" questions were of primary importance to the wage earners was undoubtedly true. Hence to stall agreements on all problems other than mere wage settlements had the additional and desirable effect of further sapping trade union influence by widening the gap between the rank-and-file and the trade union leadership.

In regard to the determination of wages, the employers' movement had objected, as soon as the statute was enacted, to the way in which its article 31 had injected the government-fixed interprofessional minimum wage into collective bargaining. Because of the general significance of the national minimum wage in a country where wage levels are low and where collective bargaining is insufficiently developed, the CNPF had correctly foreseen that this provision of the law would give to governmental decision a large place in determining the general wage structure.

The government was accused of maintaining a "hidden system of tenacious controls" instead of freeing wages. Moreover, employers also argued, and on the whole correctly, that because of the prevailing wage structure any changes in the minimum rates would always result in upsetting the entire wage hierarchy and would have a tendency to exaggerate the intended increases.[34]

[33] These figures are based on information obtained in June 1953 from the Ministry of Labor and reported by Lorwin, op.cit. (n. 1-3), pp. 215-16.

[34] See Georges Villiers, "Salaire minimum garanti et conventions collectives,"

For organized business matters were made worse by the right of a National Commission on Collective Agreements to draw up a "standard budget" which was to serve the government in its determination of the minimum wage. On the Commission, which discussed the price picture periodically on the basis of notoriously insufficient statistical data, the employers were in a minority. Hence the final decision which frequently furnished the key element in future wage negotiations could be made, after an acrimonious and partisan discussion, over the employers' opposition. The CNPF insisted consistently that the determination of minimum needs should be left to the more scientific judgments of technicians rather than to a confrontation of interest groups. Finally, in December 1953, when the CNPF sensed that the Commission might be made the vehicle for another round of wage increases through a change of the standard budget and of minimum rates, the employers' delegation sent an angry letter of protest to the minister of labor and withdrew from the Commission.[35]

Since the employers' movement was generally opposed to any administrative measure which might possibly lead to a generalized wage increase, it might appear strange that "business' own government," the Pinay cabinet, insisted on the voting of a sliding scale law for wages, approved by the conservative right and center against the votes of the left.[36]

Traditionally, the principle of an automatic adjustment of wages to prices had been defended by the trade unions and their supporters in parliament. The spokesmen for business on the other hand had always attacked the principles involved in a sliding scale legislation as inflationary and dangerous to the

---

*Bulletin*, v, No. 65, March 20, 1951, p. 1; and *ibid.*, vi, No. 78, February 20, 1952, pp. 32-33.

[35] See *ibid.*, viii, No. 112, January 5, 1954, pp. 2-4. Previously almost all of the reports of the CNPF's Social Committee abounded with complaints about the activities of the Commission on Collective Bargaining. For a more objective view, see Claude Lapierre, "L'Elaboration du budget-type et la fixation du salaire minimum garanti," *Droit Social*, xiv, 1951, pp. 380-87.

[36] For the text of the law, see *J.O.*, July 19, 1952, p. 7226. For the highly interesting debates in the Assembly, see *ibid.*, *Débats Ass. Natle.*, May 30, 31, June 4, 1952, pp. 2546-59; 2584-90; 2605-10, 2613-15. See also the full account of the history of sliding scale legislation in A. Philbert, "Le Problème de l'échelle mobile des salaires," *Droit Social*, xv, 1952, pp. 592-99.

freedom of enterprise. As late as January 1952 the CNPF had issued stern warnings against any such law.[37]

The sudden change of mind which the employers' movement underwent was in part due to its espousal of Premier Pinay's policies. Recognizing explicitly that now the level of prices was of greater importance for the general tactics of organized business than that of wages, the sliding scale law was accepted as a deflationary rather than an inflationary measure.[38] Moreover, the technicalities of the law were correctly considered as being predominantly favorable to business. The method of establishing the price index had always been criticized by the labor unions since the reference point was pegged arbitrarily so high that the automatic increases would be long deferred, if they were ever to come into play. Finally a sub-committee was formed in order to deprive the Commission on Collective Agreements, to which the employers' movement had so strenuously objected, of its participation in determining the minimum wage rates.

Actually even the law, as accepted, was not entirely to the liking of the CNPF's Social Committee and the organization's top leadership. In its reports to the General Assembly, M. Meunier would at first ignore the law and even a year after its enactment cover it with irony.[39] When the Pinay government defended the sliding scale as forcefully as it did, it acted under pressure from M. Gingembre's confederation rather than in an effort to please big business. The interests organized in the CGPME wished to convince themselves that the cautious deflationary course upon which the government had engaged would never be reversed and consequently that increases under the sliding scale law would never occur. At that time a deflationary contraction of the economy appeared to these businessmen as more desirable than an expansion which might threaten their existence. On the other hand, business firms whose bargaining position was notoriously weak hoped to be shielded by the law from any demands for wage increases not justified under its

[37] *Bulletin*, vi, No. 78, February 20, 1952, p. 33.
[38] See *ibid.*, vi, No. 84, July 20-August 5, 1955, p. 54, and for general remarks on the economic effects of the sliding scale law of 1952, see A. Sauvy, "La Situation Economique," *Droit Social*, xv, 1952, p. 374.
[39] See *Bulletin*, vii, No. 103, July 20, 1953, p. 51.

provisions. Of course this too was undiluted *dirigisme*. But French business and especially small business has never rejected the protections afforded to it by sympathetic governments.

\* \* \*

The law of 1950 had abandoned the requirements of the earlier statute that in any given industry a national agreement should precede the conclusion of regional or local contracts. The employers' movement has been generally opposed to industry-wide bargaining, though over the years it has been unable to prevent the conclusion of a number of important industry-wide agreements, which, however, usually provided little more than the skeleton for area contracts. Area-wide bargaining has become the prevailing pattern, usually over the strenuous objections of the trade unions, especially of the CFTC and the FO, which are far stronger at the top of the organizational pyramid than at its base. But for being united, far better organized and equipped than the labor unions, the employers' associations had usually few difficulties in determining the bargaining units, coinciding in most cases with that of the primary employers' organization, be it local, departmental, or regional.[40]

The authority which the CNPF and the major industrial federations wield over the content of collective bargaining and of wage agreements is rather considerable. In part, this is due to the prestige which the CNPF's Social Committee and the specialized labor relations services of many employers' associations enjoy. But at least equally important is the practical help which regional and, if need be, local employers' groups can obtain from national headquarters in their negotiations. Such assistance extends to information about conditions elsewhere and to statistical documentation; frequently also able specialists delegated by the Paris office will be made available for local negotiations. The advantages which the employers' movement derives from centralizing most bargaining activities are obvious: none of the trade unions, not even the CGT, has a comparable staff or the means to assist its affiliates in similar fashion.

Where the wage level is not simply a function of the local minimum scales, the money wages laid down in collective agree-

[40] Extensively on these points, see Lorwin, *op.cit.* (n. 1-3), pp. 193-97.

ments are also minima corresponding generally to the rates which marginal firms are willing to grant. In this field too the trade associations claim that they have to align themselves on the most feeble among their members. In the opinion of many industrialists, the claims of the marginal firms that they are unable to pay higher wages are frequently unsubstantiated and sometimes proven wrong after a strike movement has forced increases which the small concerns are also able to absorb—or pass on—without difficulties.[41]

In practice, however, the rates set in collective agreements are not mere minima which individual firms feel entitled to exceed at will. Employers claim that their associations constantly attempt to dissuade them from paying higher wages than these "minima." The customary appeals of the CNPF for employers' discipline contain warnings against any policy of high wages. "The results achieved in regard to the purchasing power," a report of the Social Committee stated in 1954, "remain fragile in a threatened economy. . . . It is impossible to hide the fact that in certain sectors an audacious policy of wage increases has been developed only under the protection of a privileged economic position." And after somber forecasts for future developments the report concluded: "In this difficult period the true interests of the enterprises and their employees are strictly solidary. An increase in cost prices of whatever nature risks endangering the results of several years of efforts."[42]

The acrimony of controversies raging between management and labor about the prevailing wage level is considerably sharpened by uncertainties concerning total labor costs and the wage earners' share in national income. Not only the general insufficiencies of French statistics, but also differences of opinion as to what should properly be regarded as "social charges" leave both sides convinced, and often in good faith, that they are unduly burdened. In a comparison of the "social charges" which their member firms had to pay in 1952, the Paris region of the metal trade association has calculated that such payments now amount to forty-three percent of the wage bill as compared with fifteen

[41] For an angry comment on this situation by an industrialist of the managerial group, see R. Perrin, op.cit. (n. IX-29), p. 288.
[42] Bulletin, No. 122, August 1954, p. 59.

percent before the war.[43] In other industries and regions where companies engage in a number of voluntary welfare activities, the costs for these expenditures might still be added to the payments required by law. In the opinion of the trade unions the designation of certain items as social charges is facetious. What matters, they argue, are total wage costs, and in that respect international comparisons seem to show that the French employer is not burdened excessively, and at any rate not more than his colleague in other European countries.[44]

A frequently heard and apparently justified complaint of French businessmen is that the increased employee benefits, which are stipulated by law and hence removed from the realm of contractual relations, have done nothing to improve the climate of labor relations. This is taken by many as a proof that the redistribution of income has failed to produce desirable results, and that fundamental, not only technical, reforms of the social security system are indicated.[45]

In fact, the available data seem to indicate that social security in France has not actually redistributed income from other classes to the wage earning group. As the report by the Commission on National Accounts has pointed out, the total mass of wage income in terms of real value was about the same in 1951 as in 1938. Hence if the "social wages" or transfer payments have increased, this took place to the detriment of direct wage payments. During the same period the share of wage earnings in total national income also remained about the same, although working hours lengthened and the work force was by about ten percent larger than before the war.[46] The increased benefits which have undoubtedly accrued to certain groups of wage earners have essentially been the result of a redistribution of income within the working class. But if, in the words of one

[43] See the table reprinted in Lorwin, *op.cit.* (n. 1-3), p. 226.
[44] This is confirmed by the careful comparisons made in Jeanneney, *op.cit.* (n. IV-26), p. 194.
[45] See the periodic reports of the CNPF's sub-committee on Social Security questions, and also the over-all appraisal of the new system in Lefranc, *op.cit.* (n. 1-56), pp. 309-26.
[46] See *Mendès-France Report, op.cit.* (n. IV-4), p. 46; and Pierre Bauchet, "Evolution des salaires et structure économique," *Revue Economique*, III, 1952, pp. 312-13. Jeanneney, *op.cit.* (n. IV-26), concludes, p. 182, that in July 1955 the average hourly real wages were 7 percent lower than in 1937.

of the most clearsighted observers of the French social scene, not more has happened than that "the poor help out the poorer,"[47] there is understandable reason why the employers have expected in vain a notable amelioration of industrial relations as a consequence of their increased contribution to the social wage bill.

Quite to the contrary, the employers have been indicted, not only by the labor unions but by the highest ecclesiastical authorities, for contributing to a climate of class struggle. If the workers are convinced that they are the victims of a system of social injustice and that their purchasing power has diminished, an inquiry conducted by the cardinals and archbishops of France concluded that this is largely due to a willful lack of understanding on the part of the employers.[48] That the business community smarts under such attacks, especially when the reproaches come from the trustees of the faith to which most of them belong, is easy to understand. Many employers take this to mean that their cause has won little if any sympathy since the post-war days when they found themselves completely isolated from the national community. Yet, unlike the situation which prevailed after the liberation, they have won back the strength that comes from cohesion and from political influence. Since they have little hope of securing widespread public sympathies, many employers will settle for strength and power.

\* \* \*

Since 1953, when prices became stable, average real wages have, according to the periodic inquiries of the Ministry of Labor, risen steadily and somewhat faster than in other European countries.[49] To an extent impossible to measure statistically, this was due to raises granted by individual wage agreements. On the one hand, quite a number of productive firms have ignored the plea of the employers' associations to consider wage minima as maxima; consequently the escalation in individually negotiated wage scales has become quite extensive. On the other

[47] See Michel Collinet, *Lettre aux Militants*, No. 1, November 20, 1950, p. 2.
[48] See the abstracts from the report and the comments printed in *Le Figaro* and *Le Monde*, May 20, 1953.
[49] See INSEE, "Comparaison des salaires français et étrangers," *Etudes et Conjonctures*, May 1955, here quoted from *Bulletin Acadi*, No. 81, 1954, pp. 209-22.

hand, M. Villiers has repeatedly recommended that member firms raise, without waiting for administrative action, hourly earnings which were still "abnormally low," i.e., below a certain explicitly stated level. In doing so, the CNPF pointed out, the employers had the advantage of granting unilaterally what would sooner or later be imposed by the government; this method would also offer a better chance of limiting increases to the low wages rather than affect the entire wage hierarchy, as governmental decrees on minimum wages always had done. It is true that many observers have doubted the general effectiveness of these recommendations which were never binding.[50]

It is therefore likely that the noted rise of real wages was mostly the result of the slow forcing upward of the legal minimum wage scales and of special "premiums" granted by successive governments. At first, the attitude of the CNPF and other employers' associations towards these policies designed to raise substandard earnings was not entirely negative. Since the employers' movement was well aware of the fact that their earlier recommendations for voluntary increases had not been followed widely, they preferred once more to "bow to force" and submit to regulation where they had not been able to obtain voluntary compliance. But when Premier Mendès-France announced that the government would confront the possibilities of the economy and the needs of the wage earners in a series of periodic "rendezvous," the CNPF lodged strong protests both against the principle involved and against the increases decreed on these occasions. Shortly before the fall of the Mendès-France government, the CNPF announced that if governmental intervention in the wage sphere was to continue at regular intervals the complete collapse of contractual agreements would be the unavoidable consequence. Employers would lose, it was somewhat threateningly added, "the *goût* of contracts and the sense of responsibilities."[51]

[50] On the problem of low wages see "Recommendations du CNPF aux chefs d'entreprise," *Bulletin*, VII, No. 105, September 5-20, 1953, p. 2, and *ibid.*, No. 122, August 1954, pp. 57-58. For many data on this question and a lucid discussion, see also two articles by Raymond Lévy-Bruhl, "L'Evolution des Salaires," *Revue d'Economie Politique*, LXIV, 1954, pp. 815 ff., and "L'Etude Statistique des Bas Salaires en France," *Bulletin Acadi*, No. 81, 1954, pp. 200-08.

[51] *Bulletin*, No. 129, February 1955, p. 79.

Mendès-France's successor was congratulated when he announced, after one more increase, that the practice of periodic rendezvous was to be discontinued; at the same time Premier Faure was sternly reminded that for the time being French industry had gone to the limit of its ability to raise the wage bill. After having declared for years that lasting improvements of the wage earners' position would have to wait for an expansion of production, the CNPF now warned that global figures indicating increases in production concealed in fact great discrepancies which existed among different branches and different firms in the same branch. Hence, the CNPF concluded, the statistically recorded increases did not justify general wage raises.[52] This, of course, was an implicit admission of how strongly the rigidities of economic development and of social policy reacted upon each other.

A few days after these explanations had been furnished, the striking workers at St. Nazaire obtained from their employers wage increases which exceeded by far all that had been granted previously. Ironically enough, the industrialist who in another fit of panic had made the most far-reaching concessions was M. René Fould, the director of the Penhoet shipyards, a prominent member of the CNPF's Board of Directors, and the president of the trade association for shipbuilding.

The dire predictions that governmental wage-fixing would spell the ruin of collective bargaining did not prove any more true than the assertions that further wage increases were impossible. Actually by January 1955, the number of collective agreements, including the so-called annexes, had risen from 475 in June 1953 to 779; the number of wage agreements amounted to 4,000. Though many contracts were originally concluded only with the free trade unions, the CGT unions would not infrequently adhere to the agreement once it had been signed.

More significant than the mere numbers is the fact, somewhat grudgingly admitted by the CNPF, that quite a few agreements, and among them some concluded on a national level, contained increasingly more than minimum conditions. Frequently the earlier meagerness of the contracts was overcome and the relationship between management and workers, between the em-

[52] *Ibid.*, No. 135, August 1955, pp. 79-81.

ployers and the trade unions represented in the shop was spelled out in greater detail. Faced with a development it had not been able or seen fit to prevent, the CNPF merely warned that too much regulation by collective agreement among the organized bargaining partners could be just as harmful as governmental intervention. Only the individual enterprise could provide lasting social progress. Hence it is primarily at the plant level, the Social Committee still insists, that collaboration between management and labor should be sought and would prove fruitful.[53]

Having laid down these principles, the CNPF was in no position to criticize the agreements which a number of large firms concluded with their personnel during the winter of 1955-56 and which followed closely the pattern laid down by the contract signed earlier by the nationalized Renault works.[54] The spectacular Renault agreement, concluded before the strike wave which had originated in St. Nazaire hit the capital, granted to the workers substantial benefits such as paid vacation for three weeks, increased benefits in case of maternity, sickness, or death. It reaffirmed a previous guarantee of a cost-of-living adjustment of wages and assured a wage raise of at least 4 percent per year for the contract's running time. All of the benefits, however, were conditioned by the observance of a pledge to refrain from strikes. A rather sweeping declaration expressed the joint interest of management and labor in heightened productivity.

The "Renault-type" agreements concluded by private firms with the free trade unions—and in some cases also with the communist CGT—could well inaugurate a new era in collective bargaining, shifting the elaboration of contracts from the employers' associations to the individual firm and taking therefore its standards from the successful rather than from the marginal concerns. The CNPF has so far refrained from commenting on the possibilities which such developments might hold.[55]

[53] *Ibid.*, p. 81.
[54] For an analysis and the text of the Renault agreement, see R. Jaussaud, "L'accord Renault du 15 septembre 1955," *Droit Social*, XIX, 1956, pp. 16-24. For a comment on similar agreements concluded in private industry, see Pierre Lassegue, "La Situation Sociale," *ibid.*, p. 37.
[55] See e.g. the rapport by the Social Committee, in *Bulletin*, No. 150, August 1956, pp. 91-99. To take an outright hostile position would have been extremely difficult in view of the appeal for collective agreements which M. Villiers had launched previously (see n. IX-28).

## 3. Employers and the Plant Committees

"In order to command, one must know the people. In order to know the people, one must listen to them . . . One works badly in a factory where one does not see well, and to see well one must have good lighting and a good accounting system."

Detoeuf, *Propos de O. L. Barenton*

The institution of the *Comités d'Entreprise*, the plant committees, furnishes an excellent illustration of the general problems besetting labor-management relations on the plant level. The discrepancy between what was expected from those committees at the time of their creation and their ultimate insignificance also bares the roots of the disappointment in which much of the post-war reform legislation has ended.

The Ordinance of February 22, 1945,[56] by which the Provisional Government ordered the institution of committees in all enterprises with more than one hundred employees, had been directly inspired by the thinking and planning of the resistance movement, both inside and outside the country. The authoritative clandestine *Comité Général d'Etudes* had suggested measures closely resembling those laid down in the ordinance. Entrusted by the central underground organization with the task of drafting fundamental reform legislation, the study committee had endeavored to express the general ideas of the resistance movement, rather than the beliefs of any particular party or group. The group was made up of economists, lawyers, civil servants, and trade union leaders; also some of the businessmen who had joined the ranks of the resistance movement had participated in the committee's preparatory work.[57]

The institution of the plant committees and their philosophy, which a preamble to the ordinance expressed in rather monumental language, were typical of several strands of social thought which the various resistance movements had hoped to weave

---

[56] See Ordinance of February 22, 1945, *J.O.*, February 23, 1945, p. 954.

[57] For quotations from the report prepared by the CGE and showing great similarities to the subsequent legislation, see O. Sargey, "Comités d'entreprises," *Cahiers Politiques*, No. 7, February 1945, pp. 78 ff. On the work of the CGE see also Michel and Mirkine-Guetzevitch, *op.cit.* (n. II-68), pp. 71 and passim. For the resistance background of many of the ideas expressed in the preamble to the ordinance, see André Hauriou, *op.cit.* (n. III-19).

together.[58] "The great popular movement which has freed France from the enemy," was described "not only as a movement of national liberation but also of social liberation." The new institution was conceived as a step toward "associating the wage earners with the direction of the national economy and with the management of enterprise." To overcome class antagonism was considered the noblest aim of the committees, "symbol of the fruitful unity among all productive elements [determined] to give back to France her prosperity and her grandeur."

During the months preceding the ordinance there had emerged in many parts of the country work councils or management committees which in a mixed mood of indignation and enthusiasm prepared to take over the running of concerns whose owners had fled or had been jailed as alleged collaborators. Undoubtedly the haste with which the Provisional Government instituted the plant committees was partly caused by the desire to stop the spreading of what might have led to a spontaneous "sovietization" of private industry.[59] Unlike these experiments, the plant committees, chaired by the employer but otherwise composed of elected representatives of the personnel, were given only consultative powers in economic matters. For, as the preamble stated: "It has seemed indispensable to leave to the head of the enterprise, who bears before the nation the responsibility for the concern which he directs, the authority commensurate with that responsibility."

The Provisional Government had submitted the proposed text of the ordinance to the Consultative Assembly as one of the first statutes to be considered by that body. Little opposition was voiced to the institution as such. Only M. Denais, frequent spokesman for business in the parliaments of the Third Republic, expressed the opinion that it might be better to wait for a regularly elected parliament before deciding on such a substantial piece of reform legislation. Strenuous opposition came rather

[58] For a similar observation concerning the post-war codetermination legislation in Germany, see Clark Kerr, "The Trade Union Movement and the Redistribution of Power in Post-War Germany," *Quarterly Journal of Economics*, LXVIII, 1954, esp. pp. 553-54.

[59] For a short description of these experiments, see International Labour Office, *op.cit.* (n. v-93), pp. 163-65. Interesting though overenthusiastic are the reports contained in Suzanne Charpy and Pierre Bernard, *Prendrons-nous les Usines?* Paris, 1946, pp. 25 ff.

from another direction: led by the socialist Gazier, most speakers criticized the ordinance as being too timid and putting insufficient trust in the managerial abilities of the workers. By a series of amendments a majority of the Assembly proposed to extend the scope and coverage of the committees. But the Provisional Government, using its prerogatives, disregarded such proposals and enacted the statute in its original form. One of the "fathers" of the reform, M. Parodi, then minister of labor, explained that it was deemed preferable to permit first the emergence of a working-class elite and to let the new institution penetrate into the mores before endowing the committees with broader powers.[60]

It was to be expected that the First Constituent Assembly, no longer limited in its powers, would seek its "revenge" all the more as the three parties forming its majority were vying with each other for trade union support and as the Ministries of Labor and of Industrial Production had passed into communist hands. After a superficial debate lasting twenty minutes during a poorly attended night session, the earlier ordinance was amended to become the law of May 16, 1946, expected to form one of the cornerstones of economic and social reform in the emerging republic.[61]

When the impatient Constituent Assembly requested that plant committees be established in all private enterprises employing more than 50 wage earners, it added by one stroke more than 11,000 firms to those touched by the first ordinance. But at that time even the committees initiated by the earlier law had not yet been organized in all concerns employing more than 100 workers. Also in its revised version the statute distinguished between the domain of social welfare and that of economic decisions. In regard to the former, the committees had extensive managerial responsibilities; in the economic field their functions remained advisory. But several new or reworded provisions seemed all designed to broaden the privileges of the committee members in matters traditionally reserved to the sole discretion of management. The committee had now to be "consulted" by

[60] For the important debate on the Plant Committees in the Consultative Assembly see *J.O. Débats, Ass. Consult.*, December 13, 1944, pp. 487 ff.
[61] For the text of the law of May 16, see *J.O.*, May 17, 1946, p. 4251. For the short debate see *ibid., Débats, Ass. Natle. Constituante*, April 25, 1946, pp. 2221-25. For an ironic description of the session, see *Combat*, April 25, 1946.

management on all questions concerning the organization and the operation of the enterprise, while the ordinance had prescribed merely "information." A legal obligation which the earlier text had established only for joint stock and very large companies was now imposed on all firms where committees were to be established: even the family concern with more than 50 employees was from now on legally compelled to communicate to its personnel how much profits it had made; committee members could offer suggestions concerning the use of the earnings. To make matters worse, the new text limited the professional secrecy by which the committee members were bound only to "methods of manufacture," while the ordinance had spoken of "all information of confidential character." Would in the future the French businessman share with his employers information which he customarily withheld from the tax collector?

In joint stock companies the committees were to enjoy particular privileges. Already the ordinance of 1945 had hoped that more extensive rights of the plant committees in such concerns would draw labor and management closer together. Given the greater economic importance of most corporations, membership in their committees also promised to provide training in the skills of corporate management. Once more the new law went farther than the earlier statute: in order to keep thoroughly informed about the economic and financial situation of the concern, the committee could appoint its own accountant to examine the books and all documents submitted to the stockholder meetings. Moreover, two representatives of the committee were to attend all meetings of the board of directors and could make suggestions concerning the running of the firm.

Since hardly any of the functions which the law had newly attributed to the committees became practical, the point could be made that a statute which did not effectively change the situation created by the earlier ordinance cannot be responsible for the ultimate over-all failure of the plant committees. But the non-observance of the new provisions discredited the institution as such. Instead of permitting the slow growth of labor-management collaboration for which the promoters of the original text had hoped, the bolder version of the law froze the partners in their traditional attitudes of antagonism and suspicion.

For the CGT, and perhaps for its reformist members more than for the communists, the plant committees became now a possible instrument for "workers' control" of industry. Ever since the end of the First World War that concept had taken the place of the more grandiose but entirely vague myth of the general strike. In 1947 even a skeptic such as Jouhaux regarded the plant committees as a means through which the working class might accede to a full-fledged managerial role in industry.[62]

For business the enactment of the new law was reason enough to become critical of the institution. Early in 1945 when the plant committees had been created, there existed no unified and self-reliant employers' representation to take a conclusive stand on the questions raised by the ordinance. The employers' delegation, appointed by the head of government, expressed its agreement "in principle." Though it asked for more mature reflection on the part of government and for its consultation of business, it was unable to compel either.[63]

At a time when the vast majority of businessmen sought refuge from attacks and insinuations in silence and anonymity, a few progressive employers came out in emphatic support of the new institution. For Detoeuf the plant committees would become a means of combatting the exaggerated secretiveness of the French businessman, and if they were to create and maintain a new mentality, possibly the "decisive factor of our recovery."[64] The *Centre des Jeunes Patrons*, in one of the most forceful statements it has issued before or since, sought to disarm the critics of the plant committees and addressed to both management and labor the urgent advice to make the institution work. The CJP was convinced of the inherent value of the committees to such a degree that it proposed to create them immediately also in enterprises with less than 100 employees. To use the committees as a means of furthering the emergence of a working class elite

[62] See Lefranc, *op.cit.* (n. 1-56), p. 353. At that time the non-communists had not yet left the CGT. For a good description of the significance of the "mythical" role of workers' control see Gérard Dehove, *Le Contrôle Ouvrier en France*, Paris, 1937, pp. 319 ff.

[63] See Philippe Bayart, *Comités d'entreprises*, 2nd edition, Paris, 1947, pp. 250-52.

[64] Detoeuf, *op.cit.* (n. v-10).

was to the *Jeune Patron* a welcome idea. In more moderate terms also the Catholic Employers Confederation applauded the ordinance inasmuch as it seemed to open vistas into a reform of the wage system.[65]

When the newly formed CNPF took violent exception to the law of 1946, it never failed to remind the public and the government that the employers' movement had been in favor of the earlier ordinance. Occasionally the employers' council had to warn its own constituents that it would be politically unwise to confound the two legislative texts in common opprobrium. Actually it appears doubtful whether many employers were as favorably inclined toward the act issued by the Provisional Government as their peak association later told them they should have been.[66]

Against the new statute the CNPF protested immediately, first in a letter addressed to the government, then in a motion adopted by its General Assembly. In the opinion of the employers' movement the legislature had destroyed the spirit of collaboration which had inspired the earlier text and had replaced it by an improper desire for inquisitive controls. Although the CNPF ominously remarked "the law cannot create authority and cannot destroy it," it expressed fears nevertheless that the new statute would facilitate outside attempts to interfere with the orderly running of all enterprises. One would have to wait for a new political situation before parliament would reestablish a more equitable balance between the social forces. In the meantime, the CNPF admonished its constituents to utilize the uncertainties of the law for a restrictive interpretation so as to leave intact the authority of the employers.[67]

Hardly enacted, the new institution, originally conceived to initiate a new era in labor-management relations in the plants,

[65] See Bayart, *op.cit.* (n. IX-63), pp. 252-56.

[66] For a discussion of the ordinance in the General Assembly of the CNPF, see *Bulletin*, I, No. 3, February 1947, p. 10. M. Constant, executive of the Trade Association for the Metal and Engineering Industries sharply criticized the ordinance instituting the plant committees as early as the winter of 1945. See Jean Constant, *op.cit.* (n. III-5), pp. 11-16. Also the Paris Chamber of Commerce had voiced criticism against the plant committees before the enactment of the new statute, see *Correspondance Économique, Technique et Professionnelle*, April 4, 1946.

[67] See *Bulletin*, I, No. 2, December 15, 1946, p. 6.

had already run aground on the shoals on which so many French social reforms have been stranded: the exaggerated combativeness of both sides falsified from the outset any experimentation with the novel plant committees.

By giving frequent and detailed directives concerning the election and the functioning of the committees, the as yet young CNPF established its usefulness and authority. In turn, it insisted on being kept informed whenever a plant committee sought to abuse its position. Only two years later the CNPF could report with a sigh of relief that the tactics it had recommended had borne fruit: according to the employers' movement an institution which the law of 1946 had forged as a tool of social revolution had been rendered harmless by the wisdom of the employers.[68]

From then on the CNPF could content itself with mere protests against attempts to tamper again with the legislation. A bill introduced by a socialist deputy and designed to lend more precision to the law, not to extend the functions of the committees, was resisted with almost ferocious violence. Its consequences were described as the certain doom of private enterprise. Such opposition, which was ultimately successful, was understandable since the employers' movement had utilized to the utmost the uncertainties of the 1946 law. Simultaneously the CNPF and its affiliates also advised against including provisions concerning plant committees in collective agreements.[69]

*     *     *

Obviously the activities of the plant committee would bring into the foreground of discussion the thorny question of union activities in the shop. Since the plant committee members were to be elected from lists presented by the "most representative" trade union organizations, they could, as management recognized and labor openly requested, become another "long arm of the

---

[68] See *ibid.*, IV, No. 25, January 1, 1949, p. 14. For examples of interesting directives concerning the committees given by the CNPF, see *ibid.*, II, No. 12, February 1948, p. 11 and No. 17, July, 1948, p. 24.

[69] Particularly revealing in these respects are two brochures published by the CNPF, *Comités d'entreprise. En Allant de l'Ordonnance du 22 Février 1945 à la Proposition de Loi No. 6611 de M. Gazier*, and *L'Action Contre l'Entreprise dans le Cadre de la Discussion des Conventions Collectives et des Travaux Parlementaires*, Paris, 1949.

trade union movement" in the enterprise. To this the employers' movement was fundamentally opposed. The elected delegates of the personnel, be they shop stewards or plant committee members, should under no circumstances represent trade union interests or act under directives from the unions.[70]

It is true that the legislation which proposed to rescue the workers from the employers' tutelage by giving to their delegates a solid organizational link with the trade unions established another, frequently not less "tyrannical" guardianship—that of the communist CGT. As long as the communists had been fighting the "battle of production" the plant committees were assigned their role in that battle; they exhorted workers in certain plants to perform exhausting deeds of Stakhanovism. But with the change of party line the former minister of labor and prominent CGT leader, M. Croizat, who in the eyes of the employers had been mainly responsible for the 1946 law, announced that the plant committees must be regarded as organs of the class struggle and of the fight against imperialist warmongers. The committees voted fiery resolutions that had nothing to do with the tasks assigned to them in the enterprise. Plant libraries were cleansed of "bourgeois trash," i.e., non-Stalinist literature, and welfare funds were used to send young workers on their pilgrimage to the itinerant shrines of peace congresses.[71]

Such intensive politicization of the plant committees could rightly be brandished by the employers as an unwarranted interference by outside forces in company affairs. But when the law had changed election procedures so as to permit several unions to compete for the designation of plant committee members, the resulting "pluralism" of trade unions offered to management another opportunity to condemn all union activities in the plant. By firing the most active members of labor organizations, including the plant committee members, insufficiently protected by the

[70] The employers' philosophy on union representation in the plant is most clearly expressed in CNPF, op.cit. (n. IX-30); see also the pamphlets cited in the preceding footnote.

[71] See the excellent treatment of the question in Michel Collinet, "Les Comités d'Entreprise," Lettre aux Militants, July 20, 1951; Lorwin, op.cit. (n. I-3), pp. 267 ff., and the factual description of the committees' functioning in Pierre Chambelland, Les Comités d'Entreprise. Fonctionnment et Résultats Pratiques, Paris, 1949.

law, the employers whether intentionally or not further discredited the entire institution in the eyes of their workers.[72]

As to the provisions by which the law sought to enforce greater publicity for plant operations, the unwillingness of most businessmen to communicate to the plant committees what they considered their private domain was stubborn enough to defeat the purposes of the legislation even without urging from the employers' associations. At a time when enforcement of the law was still feared, family concerns were known to have split up into different firms employing less than fifty workers, and hence no longer under an obligation to suffer interference from a committee. Joint stock companies escaped into other juridical forms where plant committee members would have less inquisitive power. When it turned out that the rights of the plant committee members in all economic matters amounted to little if anything, such drastic steps to avoid the commands of the law were no longer needed. But hopes that the institution of the plant committees would bring more light into the conduct and behavior of French firms were once more frustrated.

Also in this respect, it is true, the communist unions did all to furnish to the employers a pretext, if pretext was needed, for being chary with information. Figures and data communicated to plant committee members would frequently appear in the communist press and be used for propagandistic purposes. Certain appeals made by the CGT suggested almost openly that the communist plant committee members should consider their positions as an opportunity to spy on defense production and on manufacturing generally.[73]

Detailed investigations on the status and development of the committees, conducted either by such employers' groups as ACADI or by a scholarly journal such as *Droit Social*, seem to agree that all generalizations are hazardous, that results achieved or failures acknowledged seem to have little to do with either the size of the concern, a specific business activity, or the locality. Under almost identical conditions some committees have worked

---

[72] See CNPF, *op.cit.* (n. IX-30), p. 9. Lorwin, *op.cit.* (n. I-3), pp. 261 f., 274 f., discusses comprehensively and concretely the dismissals of trade union activists.

[73] See Collinet, *op.cit.* (n. IX-71). The official party line on plant committee activities can be gauged from the *Revue des Comités d'entreprises* which the CGT published since 1948.

satisfactorily, others floundered.[74] It seems to be true that the institution has hardly taken any hold in the small firms to which the legislation was extended in 1946 nor in very large concerns. But what kind of medium-sized enterprises proved favorable to the functioning of the committees cannot be stated in general terms. While on a nationwide scale a definite decline of fruitful activities has been noted since 1947—the time of the change in the communist party line—not a few employers report that in their firms committees have proven more valuable during the last years.[75]

Perhaps the great discrepancies in outcome suggest that the actual influence of the committees on plant relations has been negligible. Where such relations had been unsatisfactory, the committees were either unable to alter them or might still have aggravated existing tensions. Where the atmosphere had been better, the plant committees were usually welcome as an additional channel of communication between labor and management. But had they not been instituted by law, similar organs might have emerged in these concerns by formal or informal agreement.

It is universally admitted that the plant committees have been least successful in the economic domain and this in spite of the hopes of the moderate trade union elements. Even the committees which function fairly well in other fields are generally not consulted by management on any questions involving over-all business decisions; books and accounts are not examined; the participation of committee members in board of directors' meetings has become either a farce or a nuisance. While in general the employers feel relieved about such negative results, the situation cannot be ascribed solely to their unwillingness to admit the workers to the kind of partnership which the law had envisaged.

[74] The most comprehensive reports on the functioning of the plant committees in addition to the excellent work by Chambelland, op.cit. (n. IX-71), are contained in "Journées des Comités d'Entreprise," *Bulletin Acadi*, No. 48, 1951, pp. 159-251; and in "L'expérience des comités d'entreprises. Bilan d'une enquête," *Droit Social*, XV, 1952, pp. 14-32, 92-103, 163-78. The CNPF refused to contribute material to the inquiry organized by *Droit Social* because it objected to the journal's "social philosophy."

[75] Great uncertainties prevail also in regard to the number of existing committees. In 1948 the Ministry of Labor had been notified of the constitution of committees in little over half of the concerns falling under the 1946 law. In 1951 a careful observer estimated that committees functioned in not more than 2,000 firms. See ILO, op.cit. (n. v-93), pp. 171, 223, and Collinet, op.cit. (n. IX-71).

The committee members themselves and their constituents, the employees of the concern, show extremely little interest in all questions of this nature; they complain that the figures which might be communicated to them are meaningless and their activities altogether futile. Where the free trade unions, sometimes with the support of progressive employers, have tried to remedy the situation by offering training courses in accountancy and similar subjects, the results have been almost universally disappointing. The difficulties were not capable of solution on a merely technical level.

Since in general the French worker has little respect for the creative ability of his employer,[76] his unwillingness to share responsibilities for management will seldom be based on a feeling that it would be wrong to interfere with a job well done by business. But, given the present climate of labor-management relations, the workers fear, even when they are not influenced by communist directives, that the suggestions they offer may ultimately increase profits but never improve their own situation. The role of the committees in helping productivity has generally been negligible, although the law provided for activities in that field. Where the committees have assisted in the setting-up of collective premium payments, they have been criticized for doing the "boss' job."

There might be more profound reasons for such failure to interest the workers in the economic functions of the committees. Experiences elsewhere seem to suggest that what the French post-war legislation wanted to bring about, namely the participation of labor in the "plant community," will hardly be realized by giving to the employees managerial responsibilities. Even where industrial relations are more satisfactory than in most French concerns, workers regard such participation as meaningless.[77] It has been found to be generally true that democratic plant government is successful where it assists in overcoming the possible dichotomy between the worker's loyalty to the enterprise and to his union. Hence the existing aversion of French management to give to any labor union a place in the plant has

[76] In this respect the feelings to which Griffuelhes gave expression half a century ago, see op.cit. (n. v-12), have hardly changed.
[77] See the interesting though controversial remarks on this problem in Drucker, op.cit. (n. iii-50), pp. 286-91.

contributed much to the failure of an experiment whose objectives in this respect were never clearly stated.

It is generally agreed that the committees which still function have been most satisfactory in the "social" domain where the law has assigned to them powers of direct administration or of supervision. In many concerns of various sizes the committees run (or have run) cafeterias and cooperative stores, plant libraries, vacation camps for workers or their families, sports clubs, day nurseries, or other similar institutions. They have taken over the operation of already established housing projects or participate in the construction of new workers' housing. Committees are also concerned with safety and industrial hygiene, with apprenticeship and vocational training in the plant.

In numerous concerns employers and plant committees alike have, out of a common desire to win the sympathies of the workers, shown a preference for spectacular and impressive welfare activities. Though the communists now frown on all committee activities in the economic domain, the CGT is entirely willing to become the champion of the workers' welfare in the shop. The communist unions know full well that, because of the low living standard of the French working class, many of the committees' welfare activities are likely to arouse intense feelings. They have been extremely adroit in seizing upon this opportunity to strengthen their hold on the workers. As usual they have not hesitated to use the influence thus gained for political ends and for discrimination against their opponents. In the opinion of anti-communist labor leaders, the employers who seek to increase their own popularity by furthering the showy welfare activities of their plant committees are at least indirectly responsible for reinforcing communist influence.

According to some observers, there is now little that distinguishes the committees, divested as they are of their economic functions, from the Social Committees of the Vichy regime.[78] But if the committees are nothing else than a new version of paternalism in a new cloth, they will do as little as old-style paternalism for eliminating workers' resentment and diffidence

[78] For very bitter remarks to that effect by the former president of the CGPF, who, for his all too open participation in the policies of the Vichy regime, was eliminated from leadership in the employers' movement, see C. J. Gignoux, *Feu la Liberté*, Paris, 1948, p. 37.

against management. Hence it is not astonishing that in many firms the employees also regard plant committee activities in the social domain with indifference. Shop stewards and union delegates are usually held in higher esteem than the plant committee members who, in the opinion of their fellow workers, are either totally useless or have become the tools of the employers.

Other experiences have led a number of industrialists and trade unionists to conclude that their committees have done much and can do more to replace company paternalism by fruitful democratic methods. To manage welfare activities has given to many committee members enough training and experience to render unnecessary the interference or even the constant advice from the employer. Some plant committees have acquired a competence which commands the respect of employers and employees alike. The habits of cooperation that have been built up in this way have sometimes been extended to an exchange of ideas in other matters and have, in the most favorable cases, permitted the committees to make suggestions in matters of production and productivity. Then a general improvement of the climate of industrial relations in the plant has been noticed.

The attitude of individual employers toward the committees has been as varied as the committees' achievements. There are many concerns where the employers persist in what a progressive industrialist has termed a "scandalous do-nothing" attitude. After having at first dreaded the meetings of the committee for being an infringement of their authority, they have soon found out that there was nothing to fear if they showed enough intransigence toward the committees. Such employers have done all they could to irritate or discourage the committee members until it became frequently impossible to find candidates for the post and half of the employees abstained from voting.[79] In the opinion of some of their colleagues, employers who have contributed to the demise of the institution have passed up an opportunity of improving the climate of industrial relations.

But the workers' indifference is not confined to firms where employers may have done their part in sabotaging the legislation.

---

[79] For sharp criticism directed against the attitude of many employers see Chambellan, op.cit. (n. IX-71), Perrin in *Journées etc.*, op.cit. (n. IX-74), and *L'expérience etc.*, op.cit. (n. IX-74), pp. 93-95.

In a number of firms progressive industrialists have exhorted their workers by posters and handbills to vote in the committee elections; elsewhere the labor inspectorate has insisted that the committees be made to work in accordance with the legislation whether or not management and labor were interested. A general lassitude has stood in the way of such efforts. The decline of civic spirit, aggravated by the ravages of communist demagoguery, has driven many classes and groups in France toward the self-centered "privatization" which discounts the advantages of all organizational efforts.[80]

In view of such negative experiences, even those businessmen who see the need for a greater amount of industrial democracy and who in principle do not deny to the trade union its place in the plant have frequently abandoned the hope that the committees can be made to work satisfactorily. In their opinion practices of cooperation must be developed outside of the discredited committees, either through collective bargaining or other contractual means but not through reform legislation which has once more shown its inability to transform mores and mentality.

The decline in importance of the committees might be gauged by the sparse attention which the CNPF and the principal trade associations are now paying to the institution. The topic is no longer mentioned in the biennial detailed reports which the CNPF's Social Committee submits to the General Assembly. For a moment, the spokesmen for organized business feared that the codetermination legislation enacted by the German Federal Republic in 1951 and 1952 might once more kindle the interest in labor-management committees in France. Taking a highly exaggerated view of the real meaning of the German laws,[81] the CNPF accused the American labor movement and implicitly the United States government for having let loose by its support of the German trade union demands another round of dangerous reform proposals. But it turned out that there was no danger.

Measured by the objectives of their original promoters, the plant committees have undoubtedly fallen far short of the tasks assigned to them. Inasmuch as they were designed to redistribute

---

[80] For the effect which communist policies have had on the functioning of the Committees, see the important statement by the director of the Renault works, the late Pierre Lefaucheux in *ibid.*, p. 101.

[81] For a realistic appraisal see Kerr, *op.cit.* (n. IX-58), passim.

power in the economy and in society they have failed even more completely than have similar institutions in other lands. Their activities have not overcome labor's frustration, and one might doubt whether any works council legislation is able to strike at the roots of such feelings. The committees have also hardly altered managerial concepts of authority, prestige, and reticence. For having been unable to exorcise general skepticism and mutual diffidence, the committees have modified the basic pattern of industrial relations only in a few exceptional cases; in general a desire for cooperation is still considered by both management and labor as a sign of weakness. The employers feel that, while they might have as individuals the esteem of their workers, they continue to be distrusted and despised as a class. But under such circumstances the cycle of useless victories and painful defeats remains unbroken.

### 4. "Human Relations"—A Solution?

> "Man does not live by bread alone; one must give to those whom one employs a wage and an ideal. But man lives first of all by bread; one should not forget the wage under the pretext that one furnishes an ideal."
>
> Detoeuf, *Propos de O. L. Barenton*

During the study session which the ACADI group had organized to explore the record of the plant committees, an industrialist reported to a receptive audience how much he had been impressed by the remark of one of his women workers: "You will not be able to do anything as long as you do not overcome the fear and the diffidence of the workers."[82] None of the postwar reforms has been able to transform the human atmosphere in the enterprise, whether private or nationalized. From many sides and for many reasons, a variety of remedies have been suggested which all place emphasis on the importance of human relations for the solution of a stubborn problem.

If post-war reforms have been disappointing, it is argued, this is not primarily due to the imperfections of legislative texts but to a lack of understanding for the roots of frustration and to an unwillingness to remedy the alienation of the working

---

[82] See *Bulletin Acadi, op.cit.* (n. IX-74), p. 224.

class from the industrial and national community.[83] The evil must be attacked where supposedly the frustration arises—in the enterprise; and in order to free the workers of their fear and suspicion the attack must be directed to the human mind.

The human relations approach espoused by many progressive French employers and developed by a number of their vanguard organizations is partly rooted in the philosophical orientation of this milieu. Based on a belief in the primary importance of human perfectionment, on impatience with reforms aimed merely at the improvement of material well-being, and on the distrust of bureaucratic organizations, such creed takes its cue simultaneously from social Catholicism, though not paternalism; from a revolutionary syndicalist turned mystic, such as Simone Weil; and also from some free-thinkers who have outgrown their affiliations with the French left.[84] Their personal experience as employers or managers, sometimes also the accounts of young bourgeois who have temporarily sought a working class existence, have convinced these businessmen that capitalist enterprise even when a technical success has been a failure in human terms. If it is true that the worker has to accept orders, he should nevertheless understand the orders that are given. There are, in the words of an industrialist speaking to the *Jeune Patron*, two remunerations which management owes the worker: besides his salary "that of the spirit. It is that second remuneration which we do not give him. And since the worker does not know, cannot know, how it can be given to him, it is up to the employers to find the means."[85] What has to be done is to rid the worker of his prole-

---

[83] See the remarkable letter by xxx, "A propos de l'enquête sur les Comités d'entreprises," *Droit Social*, xv, 1952, pp. 179-80.

[84] In many respects, one of the collaborators of Albert Thomas, Hyacinthe Dubreuil, has had a profound influence on those who favor the human relations approach in France. Among his prolific writings *La République industrielle*, Paris, 1924, and *A chacun sa chance. L'Organisation du travail fondée sur la liberté*, Paris, 1935, are the most interesting. The best survey of present-day thinking on the problems of human relations in industry and society is to be found in the special issue of the review *Fédération*, December 1952, with many statements and contributions by industrialists, union leaders and intellectuals. The magazine is known to live on employers' subsidies. For an excellent critical review of the theoretical foundations and the realizations of the "human relationists" in the United States and in France, see "Relations Humaines," suppl. No. 5, *Cahiers des Groupes Reconstruction*, June-July 1956, pp. i-xvi.

[85] See *Fédération, op.cit.* (n. ix-84) pp. 813-14.

tarian mentality by giving him a new outlook on his work and his place in the enterprise.

If naturally every human relations approach to industrial problems puts action on the plant level into the foreground, the stronghold which institutionalist concepts have always had on reform thought in France makes French employers particularly receptive to concentrate attention on the enterprise.[86] According to them the enterprise is an autonomous institution, in an industrial society, in which the place of the state and political power is to an increasing extent occupied by the social group. Only through the enterprise and through the "plant community," which is its part, can the worker obtain his right to status and to that "second remuneration" about which progressive employers in France like to speak. Starting from such premises they conclude not only that the single concern must be made the center of all economic and social reform proposals, but also that there is hope to cure the ills of French industrial society by an improvement of human relations within the plant.[87]

Institutional concepts have an honored French ancestry. Indeed the particular difficulties which the country has experienced when it had to adapt itself to the needs of an industrial civilization might have led to the vigorous growth of institutional thinking in France. But since the Second World War a new impetus for developing such traditions has come from the study of human and public relations in the United States.

Alexander Dubois, undoubtedly one of the most sincere and in many ways most "radical" of the employers active in the vanguard groups, has stated emphatically: "The Americans have rediscovered the importance of the human factor . . . Immersed in the sea of authentic human relations, man loses his harshness, his diffidence, his egoism. . . . It is true," Dubois adds, "that all this *might* lead only to a more sophisticated exploitation of man by man."[88] Without any reservations Count Baruzy, speaking about American industrial experiences, exclaims: "It is not exaggerated to say that the 'public relations' [in English in

[86] See above Chapter VII.

[87] On these problems, see again the interesting and parallel remarks in Drucker, *op.cit.* (n. III-50), pp. 281 ff.

[88] See *Fédération, op.cit.* (n. IX-84), pp. 774-75.

the text] are one of the important means offered today for defending a civilization which we want to be based on the respect of the personality and individual liberty . . .'"[89] And in the columns of the *Figaro*, André Siegfried, often critical of the United States, praises before his conservative audience the lessons to be learned from the American emphasis on human relations in industry.[90]

The human relations approach is developed in practice and theory by various wings of management which do not necessarily see eye to eye on other questions. Firms which are regarded by many industrialists with suspicion because of their reformatory zeal, such as the nationalized Renault works or the privately owned *Télémécanique*, have done much to propagate methods employed in their concerns. But also companies run along more traditional lines, such as the Simca automotive concern, various firms belonging to the Boussac combine, Ugine, Alsthom, part of the Pechiney concern and factories in the industrial North, traditional fief of paternalism, pride themselves on having discovered in human relations a promising way of changed personnel practices.[91] The techniques that have been developed are similar to those applied also in the United States and are recommended as likely to prove more effective in changing the climate of labor-management relations than productivity drives or legal reforms of enterprise structure.

Foremost among the groups formed within the employers' movement with the explicit purpose of furthering the improvement of human relations is the CARHEC. In the words of its founder and sponsor, Henri Migeon, the committee proposes to ameliorate human relations "in the enterprise, among organized business, in the *Cité* [the national community]. The committee's

[89] Count Baruzy, *Aspects d'Ensemble de la Question Sociale, op.cit.* (n. IV-74), p. 11.
[90] A. Siegfried, "Une Collaboration Nécessaire," *Le Figaro*, March 31, 1952, and, commenting on the national bargaining agreement in the textile industry as an application of the human relations approach, "Un Exemple à suivre," *ibid.*, February 1, 1954.
[91] For some interesting remarks by Boussac, see John McDonald, "Marcel Boussac: Tycoon," *Fortune*, September 1952, pp. 193 ff. For a statement by a textile industrialist from the North, see Louis Mulliez, "Les relations humaines à l'intérieur des entreprises," *Fédération, op.cit.* (n. IX-84), pp. 792-96.

field of action extends to the totality of the economic and social domain."[92] As early as 1948 ACADI had formed a study group on the employer-employee relationship in the enterprise; under the chairmanship of a steel industrialist, active in the National Steel Association, the committee came forward with a number of concrete suggestions, all of them designed to achieve greater identification of the workers with the enterprise.[93]

In 1952, at the height of the honeymoon between the Pinay cabinet and business, but also at a moment when deflationary governmental policies had resulted in a slowdown of production, the four vanguard groups published with considerable fanfare a "Common Declaration."[94] The general press and especially Catholic newspapers greeted the declaration with enthusiasm as the most constructive statement to come from organized business since the war, and as evidence that at least part of the employers' movement was aware of its moral obligations. There were those who expected that the declaration would mark an important date in the history of France.

The text discussed the functions of management in terms which corresponded to the last detail to institutionalist notions: from the enterprise economic well-being and social harmony should spread to society at large. By proclaiming the indissoluble unity of economic and social questions, the authors of the declaration evidently wished to distinguish their outlook from that of the paternalists who have always separated social services about which the employees might have their say from economic performance which should remain the sole prerogative of management. Some of the economic postulates put forward by the declaration amounted to a straightforward condemnation of all "Malthusian" practices. By discussing the implications of an expanding economy for social progress, the authors criticized at least implicitly certain policies of organized business.

By its general tone and in its conclusions the text clearly announced that the solution to most of the problems it raised

[92] See *ibid.*, p. 777 and the articles quoted above (n. IV-73). For more details, see above Chapter IV.

[93] See *Bulletin Acadi*, No. 20, October 1948, p. 6.

[94] See *ibid.*, No. 59, 1952, pp. 203-11 for the text of the declaration and *ibid.*, No. 61, 1952, pp. 303-06 for interesting excerpts from the press commenting on the declaration.

were to be found in the "humanization of relations in the enterprise." The trade unions were mentioned only once, and then in an oblique manner. Instead those methods were hopefully described which belong everywhere to the arsenal of "human relations": "efforts in the field of training and of promotion; a search for elevating the intellectual level and the human value of all; sincerity in the plant committees; the desire to understand and to make oneself understood; willingness to accept the free reactions of those we have the honor of commanding and all suggestions made in a constructive spirit and in conformity with the general interest. In one word, the realization within the enterprise of a team spirit which has nothing in common with egoistic particularism but develops, on the basis of collaboration, large views on the outside world . . ."

The reaction of the free trade unions to the declaration was generally cool.[95] Even if the text was to be taken at its face value, a newspaper expressing the views of both FO and CFTC unions remarked, it could not claim to express a truly progressive employers' mentality. At best the thoughts were characteristic of an enlightened managerial despotism. Its generous intentions, born out of a tormented guilt consciousness, became vague when future action was outlined and presented little more than the lowest common denominator of reformatory intentions of certain managerial circles. The test of such intentions would be a positive attitude toward proposals for meaningful economic code-termination; of that however there was no trace in the declaration. If, the free trade unions argued, the would-be progressive wing wished to engage in serious and sincere criticism of the employers' movement, why did the signatories of the text fail to attack the reactionary leaders of the CNPF with the same sharpness with which the free trade unions customarily exposed a Frachon or other communist leaders of the CGT?

Such and similar criticism appeared to be partly vindicated by the fact that the declaration as such had hardly any immediate effect on the general policies of organized business or on industrial relations. But if the authors of the declaration had

---

[95] For a fairly representative criticism of the declaration by a spokesman for the free trade unions, see "Y a-t-il en France un 'Patronat Progressiste'?" *L'Echo du Spectacle*, No. 8, August 25, 1952 (published jointly by FO, CFTC and autonomous unions).

conceived of their initiative not as an instrument of differentiating the employers' movement but as seeking a common ground with as many of their colleagues as possible, then the approach they had chosen proved fruitful. Inasmuch as human relations policies put the individual enterprise into the foreground and dissolved the labor-management relationship into a bundle of "cooperations" between the "head of the enterprise" and his "collaborators," they were acceptable to many leaders of organized business.

It has already been mentioned that the CNPF's Social Committee, through the reports of its chairman, M. Meunier, has frequently stressed the importance of the individual enterprise for more satisfactory industrial relations. In these reports it becomes quite clear how thin a dividing line separates outright paternalism and human relations policies. The Employers' Center of Research and Studies, personally promoted by the CNPF's president, is undoubtedly seeking a more modern approach than classical paternalism.[96] Its sessions, however, lay similar emphasis on the study and implementation of public and human relations. In the most reflective parts of his addresses to the General Assembly M. Villiers frequently reverts to the responsibilities of the employers' movement in this field.[97]

Also individual trade associations pay increasing attention to the new techniques. The executive of the Textile Union, M. Catin, one of the most dynamic leaders in the employers' movement, is personally convinced that a functioning plant community between employers and employees must be made the starting point for improved industrial relations. According to him and to those who think like him, the workers' share in plant government can be large as long as it does not impinge on managerial functions; strikes are considered as virile expressions of differences among partners in a common enterprise as long as the notion of an existing partnership and of a permanent community is not disputed. The nation-wide collective agreement which the Textile Association concluded in 1953 with the noncommunist

[96] For details see above Chapter III.

[97] See esp. *Bulletin*, VII, No. 109, November 20, 1953, pp. 1-5, and *ibid.*, No. 135, August 1955, p. 5.

trade unions reflected such views. In a language hitherto seldom heard in France the free unions, in return for important concessions which were designed to strengthen their position in the industry, expressed their belief in the intrinsic value of the free enterprise system.[98]

\* \* \*

It is undoubtedly possible to formulate against the French apostles of the human relations creed, be they businessmen or not, the same criticism which has been voiced against their American prototypes.[99] The basic orientations, perspectives, and concrete suggestions of an Elton Mayo and of those who believe they have discovered in better human relations a solution for France's ills are largely identical, although the writings of the Mayo school and the Hawthorne studies are generally unknown in France. The value system underlying the thinking of the "human relationists" in France and the United States is the same and can be criticized for the same reasons. If nevertheless the conclusions which have been reached by them in both countries deserve to be viewed in a somewhat different light, this is solely due to a difference in social and political conditions.

It is well known that in Mayo's social thinking the functions of trade unions in society and in the plant are hardly given any place at all; in other writings of the same school unions might be recognized but mainly as a tool for implementing enterprise policy.[100] Similarly, however much progressive French employers may talk about labor's spiritual needs, they almost never consider the trade unions as a means by which the worker could fulfill his longing for human dignity. In a company such as the *Télémécanique* the administration of modern and satisfactory personnel policies and the smooth functioning of the plant com-

[98] Industrie Textile, *Convention Collective Nationale et Annexes*, Paris, 1953.

[99] I follow here in many points the arguments in the excellent study by Reinhard Bendix and Lloyd H. Fisher, "The Perspectives of Elton Mayo," *Review of Economics and Statistics*, XXXI, 1949, pp. 312-19. Among the writings of Elton Mayo the most important of his works in the present context is *The Human Problems of an Industrial Civilization*, 1933, new edn., 1946.

[100] See Solomon Barkin, "A Pattern for the Study of Human Relations in Industry," *Industrial and Labor Relations Review*, IX, October 1955, pp. 95 ff; and Bendix and Fisher, *op.cit.* (n. IX-99), p. 316.

mittee take place without any of the established trade unions having a foothold in the firm.

But it must also be admitted that at present neither the communist nor the free trade union movement are able to fulfill the necessary functions of organized labor in a democracy. The politicization and demagoguery of the one, the weakness and divisions of the other account for much in the difficulties that have arisen in labor-management relations. One does not need to be imbued with a systematic hostility to a democratic labor movement to conclude that present-day French unionism should be reformed in so many respects that one hesitates to propose whence the changes could come.[101] And the employers desiring to transform the prevailing mores of industrial relations are convinced that they cannot wait until the day when perhaps a new unionism may arise.

Progressive elements among French management are often bitterly critical of the bureaucratic methods of the employers' organizations, their tendency to align themselves with the "laggards" of the business community, and their ways of keeping alive the spirit of class antagonism. They maintain that many employers would gladly flout the often intolerable discipline imposed by their associations, if only the workers were willing to ignore directives coming from their unions, and in fact often from a political party.[102]

Such ideas lead in France as well as in the United States to a frankly elitist thinking. If the interest groups would leave industrial life alone, it is argued, the best elements among management and labor would find a new basis for understanding. In the opinion of some dynamic French businessmen, all that is needed to transform the general atmosphere are "a few thousand industrialists" setting an example.[103] Some of the groups which consider themselves the most advanced elements in the general employers' movement philosophize at length about the leadership role which the individual businessman rather than his organization should

[101] See the conclusions by Lorwin, op.cit. (n. 1-3), pp. 304-07, and of Collinet, op.cit. (n. 1-5), pp. 213-29.

[102] See the interesting remark in Bulletin Acadi, No. 20, October 1948, p. 31. I have heard similar opinions expressed frequently by a variety of employers.

[103] See ibid., No. 48, May-June 1951, p. 225.

play in the political life of the nation. But again it is true that in present-day France the corporate organization of interests has reached a point where it becomes a threat to the cohesion of government and constantly impedes economic growth and social progress. Hence protests against the overbearing influence of the pressure groups cannot simply be discarded as a lack of understanding for the workings of a pluralist democracy.

Those who in France advocate the human relations approach harbor very often a fundamental distrust of all conflict, an attitude also characteristic of the Mayo school in the United States. The philosophy of a Migeon concentrates on the "profound unity" among those working in the modern enterprise and living in modern society. The degree of cooperation and harmony is made into a yardstick of "social health," dear to Elton Mayo; the preoccupation with "divisive" politics is considered a breach in the wall of cooperation.

Such thinking is not far removed from the philosophy of those who see in the corporate state the fulfillment of their hopes for a complete integration of the workers into the plant community and of conflicting interests into a nebulous and ill-defined general interest. But once more it must be considered that in present-day France the wrath over prevailing political methods is not confined to authoritarian critics of democracy; the divisions rending apart French society in many directions have long given deep concern to others than the social romanticists.[104]

Finally the concern of progressive French businessmen with changes in education for management is partially based on the notion that social problems can be solved by reconstructing the individual entrepreneur's make-up. Not unlike Mayo, they believe that the educational process should lay far less stress on technical competence than on making the future businessman familiar with social situations and with the problems of organization he will encounter as an employer.

But the voices raised in favor of such educational reforms do not only come from businessmen wishing for a more sophisticated manipulation of their personnel. The deficiencies of French secondary and higher education in many fields outside the logical,

[104] See some of the thoughtful contributions in *Crise . . . etc., op.cit.* (n. v-37).

legal, mathematical, and technical training are widely recognized. And some of the new programs in the field of business training belong undoubtedly to the more encouraging facts of the management picture in France.[105]

Hence it might be at least premature to reject the human relations policies, which some elements in the French employers' movement have adopted fairly recently, as a wholly erroneous orientation bound to lead to new disasters. As in the United States, many of the manifestations of the "new spirit" are incredibly wordy and need to be cleansed of what might well turn out to be unnecessary metaphysics.[106] In other cases, and this is often acknowledged, "human relations" have been infected by "public relations" to an extent that the sermons pronounced in the name of the new faith have become indistinguishable from empty advertising slogans. More important yet would be a recognition of the fact that the proposed policies have at best a limited usefulness, and are by themselves unable to bring about the desired social transformation.

As institutionalist thinkers and practitioners everywhere, the French businessmen believe that they have penetrated closer to reality than other schools of legal and political thought. But by isolating the modern enterprise from its environment, they have actually barred themselves from a realistic understanding of the processes with which they deal.[107] Whether French employers approve or dislike the political and social milieu in which they have to operate they cannot ignore the factors which shape the attitudes of their workers outside the plant. An artificial unity within the enterprise will not long withstand the pressures from a divided society. The "proletarian" mentality cannot permanently be chased from the workshop if it is constantly reproduced by the civilization beyond the factory gates.

The conversion of the worker from a proletarian into a citizen might well be one of the foremost problems of French democ-

---

[105] On this point, see Harbison and Burgess, *op.cit.* (n. VII-9), p. 23.

[106] Similarly, Barkin, *op.cit.* (n. IX-100), investigating the question whether it is possible to "cut the umbilical cord" between the human relations approach and the writings of Elton Mayo.

[107] On this point, see Neumann, "Funktionswandel," *op.cit.* (n. VII-73), pp. 592-93.

racy, and without an improvement of industrial relations democracy cannot be made a living reality in the daily existence of the working class. In order to overcome some of the disastrous divisions of French politics and society, it is indeed necessary to extend the agreement on democratic values to the economic and social spheres.[108] But such an agreement can never be lastingly reached on the plant level alone. To achieve their objectives the advocates of human relations must set their sights higher and farther.

[108] See the important remarks, by Goguel, *op.cit.* (n. v-56), pp. 170-71.

# PART FOUR
Conclusion

## CHAPTER X

# Organized Business and the Future of French Democracy

Political stability is related everywhere to the ability of groups active in the society to compose their differences. The attitude of the groups will in turn depend largely on the degree of consensus which it obtains in the community. In France social and political values, aspirations and ideologies have been so divisive for so long, that there has rarely existed substantial agreement on the "rules of the game" determining the administration of the *res publica*. A political vacuum has resulted into which the interest groups have extended their activities and their intransigence, while the machinery of the state has veered uneasily between collaboration with and submission to the groups.

During the period covered by this study governments have vacillated back and forth in their cooperation with capital and with labor, thus accrediting the belief that reform and counterreform are the prizes of a ceaseless struggle. Resentments are exacerbated and the habits of compromise not learned, since the groups are never convinced that the interests they represent are in the long run best defended by the approximation of an equilibrium. The managers of British pressure groups have been described to be moderate in action, either by temperament or because in England moderation is a good way to get what you want.[1] Questions of temperament aside, in France the interaction between government and pressure groups invites immoderation.

Today the feelings of social injustice and frustration, widespread among many groups and classes, must be overcome before a better integration of French society can be achieved, and that measure of agreement be established without which no government can function both democratically and efficiently. But the past decades have shown that a redistribution of wealth never had a lasting effect, if wealth itself was not increased. The

[1] W. J. M. Mackenzie, "Pressure Groups in British Government," *British Journal of Sociology*, VI, 1955, p. 146.

insufficiency of economic growth was one of the main reasons why antagonistic groups successively won and lost access to the sources of authoritative decisions and why internal strains have constantly taxed the political process. Today the business lobby has succeeded, against considerable initial odds and after a sustained organizational effort, in reaching a position where it influences and frequently originates those public policies which can further or hamper economic growth. Moreover, the present weakness and confusion of the forces opposed to capitalism have singularly increased the opportunities for initiatives coming from the business elite and its organizations.

But, in the present economic and political configuration of the country, what are the chances to see the business groups exert themselves for economic and social change? And assuming that such efforts were made, what would be their foreseeable political effect?

Even when the economic weather vanes of France indicate favorable winds, serious observers of the country's economy are generally unwilling to be swayed by facile optimism or to hide their misgivings. Like Letitia Bonaparte who watched her son's career with a dryly skeptical *"pourvou que cela doure,"* commentators have usually explained encouraging production figures and other indices of increased wealth as the result of happy circumstances which might well be temporary.

Although the gross national product has risen in 1954 and 1955 by over 5 per cent each year and industrial production by 9 per cent, such progress is as yet considered insufficient to shake France out of its position of an "underdeveloped country." The modernization of the French economy still lags behind results achieved elsewhere. Between 1929 and 1955 the national product has increased only by about 22 per cent as against 114 per cent in the United States. Comparisons with French production of the lean pre-war years seem to point to a substantial improvement of the situation. But over the last twenty-five years the index of production goods indicates a rise of merely 5 per cent, that of consumption goods one of 22 per cent. Recent developments have not yet significantly altered the explosive fact that for the first time in two centuries the gross national product has remained almost stationary from one generation to the next.[2]

The nation is rightly warned that as long as productive investments remain inadequate and nearly two-thirds of the increased output is absorbed by private consumption neither production figures nor the standard of living will necessarily rise further.[3] High prices prevent a healthier export-import structure and impede a sincere liberalization of foreign trade. In view of the severe housing shortage and of recent demographic trends the volume of dwelling construction continues to be unsatisfactory; productivity is still low in all too many branches of industry, to say nothing about the techniques of distribution. For once the recent expansion of industrial production has not let loose inflationary pressures, in part because it has been facilitated by the progressive employment of idle capacity. But inflation could again threaten when such possibilities are exhausted; the relatively favorable balance of payments could once more take a turn for the worse when extraordinary dollar resources will diminish. If for whatever reason the steep rate of economic growth should not keep up, the gap between France and other countries would widen further. If government and interest groups are afraid that the French economy would be outdistanced by her neighbours, and especially by Germany, they are likely to oppose further European integration and thereby hinder developments on which the long-range stability not only of France but of Western Europe depends.

Economic forecasts must be guarded because the same structures which for over a century have made urban and industrial progress in France unsteady have not been altered sufficiently. The manifold obstacles which impede until today a more intensive development of the country's material and human resources have been described throughout this volume. They have been

[2] Sauvy, "La Situation Economique," *Droit Social*, xvi, 1953, p. 591. In spite of recent progress, the author's estimates based on long-range developments are still substantially correct. National averages, it is true, hide the significant fact that some regions are getting wealthier and others poorer.

[3] See OEEC, *Economic Conditions in France, 1955*, Paris, 1955, pp. 7 ff. The data on post-1953 developments as given in the text are mostly based on the annual OEEC reports and on the study by Jeanneney, *op.cit.* (n. IV-26), esp. pp. 75-76, 214 and passim.

found to be psychological no less than material, social no less than economic and, above all, political. The Fourth Republic had proposed to join finally economic and political democracy and to endow both with a hitherto unknown efficiency. The thinking of the most reflective groups in the resistance movement, the debates of the two Constituent Assemblies, and the text of the constitutional drafts all gave expression to pluralistic concepts as a means to achieve the announced goal. But the decisive problem of the relationship between groups and the state was never clearly faced, and even the question "pluralism for what?" received a vague answer in the Constitution and early legislation.

The Vichy experience had led to an abhorrence of corporatist schemes although, generally, pluralist doctrine and practices have travelled on the continent in corporatist clothes. A pluralism which was lopsided in favor of labor and its allies appeared natural at the time of the liberation, and since labor was directly represented in the predominant parties of the new republic there seemed to be little need for determining the precise place of organized interests in the state. Only a form of "administrative pluralism" was invited when such bodies as the Economic Council were given constitutional standing and when tripartite boards were encouraged in many fields. There seemed to be the vague hope that by multiplying the "advisory" capacities of interest groups one might be able to neutralize their power.

The confusions of the historical moment increased the uncertainties which French liberalism had at all times derived from the legacy of Rousseau's thought and from the individualism of 1789. Rousseau's fear that economic interests were dangerous to social and political unity, and that little societies should be ignored rather than organized, has lived on in the suspicion that even modern-styled screens between the individual and the government might pose not less a threat to individual liberty than the intermediary *corps* of pre-revolutionary days.

Just a century before the Matignon agreement Tocqueville had told his countrymen: "In democratic countries the science of association is the mother of science; the progress of all the rest depends upon the progress it has made."[4] But the liberal tradition in France did little to develop that science and went hardly

---

[4] Alexis de Tocqueville, *Democracy in America*, New York, 1945, Vol. II, p. 110.

beyond an empirical toleration of the multiple associations which came into existence. The country whose *Code civil* had permitted the greatest refinement of contractual notions remained largely unaware of the shift that has led modern society back from contract to status, making "man socially important only as a holder of standard qualifications and as a member of authorized groups."[5]

Generally speaking only Social Catholics, the institutionalists, and other yet more conservative French thinkers had wrestled with the problem of the intermediary groups. With a few exceptions no member of these schools took part in the drafting of the new Constitution. The writings of the resistance movement indicated, it is true, that the "new men" had understood to what extent the structures of modern industrialism had grown up outside the formal institutions of the bourgeois state.[6] They were determined to fill the gap which had developed between the constitutional texts of the liberal Third Republic and political reality. Nonetheless, also the Constitution and other fundamental legislation left all but open the question whether and how organized interests were to participate in the ultimate determination of economic and social policies.

During the first decade of its existence the Fourth Republic has been at least as happy a hunting-ground for organized interests as the Third Republic. Indeed, the complaints that the state has been invaded and infested by groups to the point of losing its freedom of action and the ability to decide between conflicting claims, are more strident than before the war. Now the Social Catholics are inclined to believe that Le Chapelier's hostility to the corporations might have been justified. Pius XII himself, in a remarkable message, has admitted that recent French experiences made it imperative to correct the optimistic beliefs of *Rerum Novarum* in regard to the beneficial activities of the intermediary groups.[7]

Disquieting comparisons are drawn between the Fourth Re-

---

[5] Mackenzie, *op.cit.* (n. x-1), p. 146.

[6] See generally on this point John E. Sawyer, "Strains in the Social Structure of Modern France," in Earle, ed., *op.cit.* (n. III-50), p. 311.

[7] See esp. Jean Rivero, "Corps intermédiaires et groupes d'intérêts," in Cinquantenaire etc., *op.cit.* (n. v-37), pp. 317 f. For the "Lettre de S. S. Pie XII à M. Charles Flory," see *ibid.*, pp. v-x.

public and the pluralist stagnation which led to the ruin of democracy in pre-Hitler Germany. In the judgment of French public opinion large grants of power to private groups have remained suspect. In reality organized interests are no longer merely "represented" in the various branches of government, but, posing as defenders of a nebulous "general interest" tend to substitute their activities for those of the government. The boundary line between state and society frequently disappears.[8]

In such a situation governmental instability and the violence of demands of pressure groups easily reinforce each other. Prodded by their own clients the leadership of the groups will incessantly attack a government that has refused their demands, since the next cabinet may prove to be less adamant. And the new government which has usually started out by making concessions will sooner or later find that it cannot continuously give in to ever increasing demands. At that point it has outlived its usefulness, and the lobbies will scheme for its replacement.[9]

It cannot be denied, Tocqueville had warned, "that the unrestrained liberty of association for political purposes is the privilege which a people is longest in learning how to exercise. If it does not throw the nation into anarchy, it perpetually augments the chances of that calamity."[10] That the "calamity" is particularly grave in the field of economic policies is obvious. As in other democracies the French government has long been compelled to transgress the boundaries of classical Keynesianism: it can no longer be content to merely set the pattern and create the climate for decisions by individual entrepreneurs and the consumers, but has to intervene directly in the process of decision making. The long-term effect of most of the decisions that are involved here makes the conditions of political instability only more harassing. In the twenty cabinets which have succeeded each other during the last eleven years, there were only five different foreign ministers, but fifteen different ministers of finance and twelve ministers of economic affairs.

[8] The recent work by Kaiser, op.cit. (n. 1-20), has discussed interestingly and critically the problems and the terminology here involved. On p. 310 the author reviews briefly the French literature concerned with the question of "interest representation."

[9] For an elaboration of this point, see Delouvrier, op.cit. (n. v-37), p. 87.

[10] op.cit. (n. x-4), Vol. I, p. 195.

During the first troubled years of the Fourth Republic Raymond Aron predicted that the future of pluralistic democracy in France would depend mainly on three factors: "the restoration of government authority capable of settling the disputes between groups and enforcing the decisions necessary in the community's joint interest even when they are unpopular; an efficient economic administration or, more generally, the elaboration of an intermediate system, which will not result in making the economy static or paralyzing it, but will preserve mobility, revive incentives, and encourage workers and entrepreneurs to work harder and better; lastly the limitation of the influence of those who do not want to promote reconstruction in the present framework of society."[11] All this still holds true. But if the chances for seeing these conditions fulfilled have not run out completely, they have seriously diminished with the lapse of time.

The critical significance of the employers' movement at this juncture arises from the fact that its membership can generally be counted among the most solid supporters of the institutions which prove a hindrance to progress, but that it also comprises many elements who believe that the task of modernizing the country's economy rests squarely on the shoulders of business organizations.

The cramps from which industrialism in France has suffered can only in part be explained by inadequate natural resources such as coal. A persistent handicap for industrial development has arisen from the mentality of producers and of businessmen in general. Some four decades ago French intellectuals, traditionally contemptuous of a capitalist system lacking in dynamism, coined for such attitudes the curious term "economic Malthusianism." Admittedly complex in origin and not always described with great precision, Malthusianism is still made responsible for many and not only the economic manifestations of the French crisis.

As long as economic security and social equilibrium are most highly valued, property will remain more attractive as a promise of enjoyment and consumption than as a medium for expanding

[11] "Social Structures and the Ruling Classes," *British Journal of Sociology*, I, 1950, p. 140.

production and for economic development. The artisan shop and other marginal enterprises are defended not so much out of sympathy with the less fortunate, but because of a vague belief that economic success is suspect. "Why has one succeeded where so many others have failed? Has he not profited from illicit favors awarded by the state?"[12] While the government is criticized for heavy-handed intervention in business it is also asked to preserve and protect, if possible forever, the economic and social hierarchy established during the last century under the system of economic liberalism. The ensuing lack of social and geographic mobility, whether enforced or voluntary, affects all groups and constantly reproduces the conflict between traditionalist patterns and the prerequisites of an expanding industrial order.[13] Even the needed changes in fiscal policies would not permanently remedy the chronical under-investment in capitalist enterprise as long as the psychological roots of the investors' hesitations are not removed.

This study has suggested, either expressly or implicitly, some striking parallels between the behaviour pattern of organized business in France and in the United States. But the prevalent attitudes towards reform and progress have remained significantly different. Because the community sets great store by progress, and because technical progress is an important source of business prestige, the American environment is unfavorable to any systematic restraint on technological innovation and mobility.[14] In France the "Malthusian party" (as some have called it) thrives in an environment which has never overcome its fundamental skepticism towards urbanization and technological development.

[12] See Charles Morazé, *Les Français et la République*, Paris, 1956, p. 73. The entire book as well as the author's earlier work, *op.cit.* (n. IV-5), offer excellent and mature considerations of the impact which the Malthusian mentality of the French bourgeoisie has had on social and economic developments.

[13] The question of mobility has been discussed recently with many interesting details and in a significant political perspective by Drexel Godfrey, Jr., "The Communist Presence in France," *American Political Science Review*, L, 1956, esp. pp. 336-38 on the general problems involved here. See also Sawyer, *op.cit.* (n. X-6), esp. p. 301.

[14] See on this point Galbraith, *op.cit.* (n. IV-24), p. 95. Reinhard Bendix, *Work and Authority in Industry*, New York, 1956, discusses in Chapter V American attitudes with a greater amount of sophistication and introduces a number of needed modifications.

The cult of the *droits acquis*, of established positions, is accompanied, and often made possible, by the businessmen's ignorance of economic realities, such ignorance being commonly excused as a counterpart to the national gift for abstract reasoning. But often impeccable logic is applied to hasty and incomplete premises; the passion for theory and intemperate eloquence are then a thin disguise for an indolent fatalism and a near phobia of patient and empirical, yet imaginative reform action.[15] If economic immobilism and passion for theory dwell together in the minds of the French bourgeois the penchant for civic disobedience is akin to both. *Incivisme* rests on the belief, classically expressed by Alain, that distrust of authority is a virtue. It also thrives on the suspicion of the citizen that not the hard facts of economic development but the interference of government and political parties destroy a chimerical equilibrium of forces.

Such quixotic attitudes are bound to affect the tactics of pressure politics. Most interest groups everywhere will verbalize and thus harden the state of mind of their members. But they might hesitate to merely express the mentality of a special group when they must fear to offend thereby other influential strata, or the community in general. Moreover, where it is recognized that the values cherished by the membership could be harmful to the permanent interests of the group, responsible leadership may use its authority to modify the outlook of its constituents.

In France organized business derives its apparent strength from the fact that the peculiar predisposition of the employers is widely spread throughout society and forms one of its dominant ideologies. Writing in 1930 André Siegfried found the bourgeois spirit "latent everywhere."[16] After the defeat of 1940 Marc Bloch inquired: "Could anything have been more *kleinbuergerlich*, more *petit bourgeois*, than the attitude adopted in the last few years . . . by most of the big unions?"[17] Another observer reflecting on the social structures of the Third Republic com-

[15] For very critical remarks on this vice of his compatriots by the one-time inspector of finance and Vichy minister, Bouthillier, see his *op.cit.* (n. II-9), p. 485. In a similar vein, also Jeanneney, *op.cit.* (n. IV-26), p. 269.

[16] See André Siegfried, *France: A Study in Nationality*, New Haven, 1930, p. 6. A very complete and useful analysis of the bourgeois mentality is given by John B. Christopher, "The Dessication of the Bourgeois Spirit," in Earle, ed., *op.cit.* (n. III-50), pp. 44-57.

[17] *Strange Defeat*, London, New York, 1949, pp. 138-39.

mented: "The outlook of the whole population was that of an heir rather than a pioneer, thinking far more of enjoying life than of handing to their descendants improved means for the production of wealth. That may be," the French writer melancholically added, "a sensible attitude, but it is certainly not propitious for economic development."[18] The storms of the last twenty years have hardly modified the private and public behaviour of the French bourgeois, and a variety of widely recognized and respected groups have taken their defense.

Not only the organizations of Messrs. Gingembre and Poujade, but also the various agricultural lobbies, educational associations, the unions of civil servants and of professional workers, the lawyers' and doctors' guilds—they are all devotees of the same cult. Economic conservatism is not the monopoly of the conservatives. As a tribute to the strength of such traditions the communist party furnishes, without blushing, in its farm and trade union propaganda some choice samples of economic Malthusianism.[19]

Ever since the rebirth of a unified employers' movement the leadership of the CNPF and of the major trade associations has wrestled with the problems which have arisen from a mentality detrimental to a vigorous economic development. However wide the ramification of the Malthusian party may be, not all of France is Malthusian. Similarly, some of the most dynamic elements in the employers' movement admit that if organized business will always bow to the wishes of its constituents it will be unable to perform its role as the country's "productive elite."

The personalities of those who criticize the habitual outlook of their colleagues mirror the contradictions of the movement which they lead. It has been described how strongly the bourgeois outlook influences not only patrimonial employers but corporation managers and pressure group officials as well. In many

[18] Raymond Aron, op.cit. (n. x-11), p. 13.

[19] See Henry W. Ehrmann, "The French Peasant and Communism," *American Political Science Review*, XLVI, 1952, pp. 19-43. The general secretary of the CGT remarked recently: "The modernization of the economy can only accentuate the enrichment of the rich and the impoverishment of the poor." (Quoted by Godfrey, op.cit. [n. x-14], p. 333.) See also for enlightening remarks on the general phenomenon of economic conservatism, Georges Vedel, "L'Etat débordé: le conflit du politique et de l'économique," in Cinquantenaire, etc., op.cit. (n. v-37), p. 109.

of them, however, also other traditions are frequently alive. Whether or not they are conscious disciples of Saint Simon, they fully subscribe to the Saint-Simonist concept of the nation being essentially a vast industrial society in which organization *per se* and scientific thought are expected to insure success. Like Saint Simon they express a contempt for outdated privileges and are critical of classical property notions. Most of them would subscribe to the fundamentally anti-bourgeois precept of the master: "True economy consists not in spending little but in spending well."[20] Many of these business leaders also share the illiberal beliefs of Saint Simon, his discounting of individual freedom as a positive social force, his penchant for "social leadership," and for a benevolent despotism to be managed preferably by the captains of industry. If criticized they will argue that in France a liberal regime will never be able to open the way to resolute progress because it will not dare to attack the marginal.

Other employers are opposed to the restrictive practices of French industry and trade without any doctrinaire attachment to a particular philosophy. They simply wish to reap the benefits of technological development, and realize that their interests are slighted by the collective comportment of the business community.[21]

The dilemma of the employers' movement is obvious: Should the leadership, out of deference to democratic respectability, continue to put above all other considerations the unity of an employers' movement representing all of business? Should such a movement be content to express views which are accepted by the bulk of the community, and succeed thereby in submerging pressure group activities in the maelstrom of dominant beliefs?

Or should the major trade associations and an active minority in the CNPF refuse to be the hostages of business "unity" and rather use the high degree of organizational completeness and authority to engage in a strenuous campaign of educating their own membership? Should they, without waiting for the somewhat doubtful results of such long-range campaign, declare themselves everywhere, but especially in their contacts with

[20] Quoted by Roger Soltau, *French Political Thought in the Nineteenth Century*, New Haven, 1931, p. 141.
[21] See the observations by Berger, *op.cit.* (n. VI-104), p. 26.

parliament and administration, in favor of policies which combat Malthusianism and benefit economic expansion?

Many business leaders recognize that such an alternative faces them. Although they may have to strive in practice for a solution compromising the extremes, the issue remains nevertheless one of sanctioning or resisting ideals of the French bourgeoisie. At present the ambivalent position in which the leadership of organized business is caught, explains the often noted contradictions in its behaviour. Frequently a gap between announced principles and day-to-day activities exposes the movement to ridicule. Individual firms or their associations are taken to task by other sectors of the employers' movement or by the CNPF for their sluggishness, but when general economic conditions are considered unsatisfactory, business still blames, as it always has, labor, rival nations, and governmental policies for all and every difficulty.[22] The statistical habits which certain trade associations seek to cultivate among their membership, and their national and international market research are designed to give a greater sense of reality to businessmen who heretofore had little understanding of the world outside the narrow confines of their firm. But the same associations will sponsor cartel agreements which shelter even the weakest unit from the "reality" that has first been described.

Until now the prevailing ambivalence has also prevented the employers' movement from exploring the philosophical premises under which it operates. "They must consider," A. A. Berle stated when speaking about American business leaders, "the kind of community in which they have faith, and which they will serve, and which they intend to help to construct and maintain. In a word, they must consider at least in its more elementary phases the ancient problem of the 'good life,' and how their operations in the community can be adapted to affording or fostering it."[23] It might well be that in France similar considerations if they were effectively communicated to the milieu of businessmen would combat the plague of *incivisme*, just as they could also help to overcome the lack of mobility. So far only

[22] Morazé, *op.cit.* (n. x-12), shows (p. 46, and passim) that this has been the attitude of French businessmen for more than a century.
[23] Berle, *op.cit.* (n. vi-73), p. 166-67.

some of the small vanguard groups of the employers' movement have ventured into such directions. But even if more influential circles of organized business were to assume the task of developing a public philosophy, they should know that little would be won, if once more the customary hiatus between high-sounding declarations and practices were to develop.

One of the reasons for the reluctance of prominent French business leaders to state their premises may be the fact that many of their beliefs (and that applies to the most progressive sector of the employers' movement as well) bear much resemblance to principles which are officially discredited since the days of Vichy. Corporatism lives on in the minds of business leaders who still prefer to speak about "organizing" production and markets rather than about expanding both. Inasmuch as the social theory of corporatism tries to justify, in the name of an "organic" concept of society, the survival of every existing firm, it becomes a paralyzing doctrine.[24] When corporative organizations offer to their constituents the degree of protection which can be obtained only by assaulting the state with exorbitant claims, they cumulate economic and political dangers. Since many business leaders are not fully aware of the corporatist strands in their thinking, they are unable to recognize the particular threat which corporatism holds in a country whose economic development has to overcome a series of retardative factors. They will dispute the thought that there is an alternative between "organization" and "expansion" and will affirm that they organize in order to expand. They will defend the need for producers' discipline by pointing to the traditional anarchical behaviour of the French businessman and citizen. They will explain their lukewarm sympathies for parliamentary democracy by the governmental instability which leaves no room for long-range economic policies except through close collaboration between administration and interest groups. In short, if they were to admit corporatist beliefs, they would show them to be in harmony with the corporatist pattern into which much of the public life of the Fourth Republic has fallen.

The working contact which exists at present between the leaders of organized business and the high bureaucracy does not

---

[24] On this point see Jeanneney, *op.cit.* (n. IV-26), p. 260.

simply carry on the practices of the Vichy "synarchy." Situations where French capitalism bogged hopelessly down in defeatism and inaction, and had to be extracted from its unfavorable position by technicians, have occurred periodically also before 1940.[25] Today the old-new alliance between the executives of private and public administration is praised for fulfilling equally salutary functions. The fact that since the war managers and technicians rather than employers have risen to important leadership and staff positions in the business organizations has naturally furthered the solidarity between the two groups; the successful nationalizations had a similar effect. While the personalities making up the two groups are far from having an identical outlook and loyalty, most of them are convinced that they alone are able to provide the efficiency which to them is the justification of government, and to strike at the immobilism which perpetuates social injustice and political disorder.

In the eyes of the small businessmen and of numerous politicians who consider themselves the paladins of the urban and rural middle-classes a regime shaped by the concepts of these groups smacks of technocracy and of the government-backed rule of the "trusts." In fact, as this study has shown, the high administration deals now mostly with representatives of big business interests, and the institutions of administrative pluralism in which the masses of small and medium-sized producers had been given a voice have lost much of their influence. It is equally true that in a number of important fields French business has long since achieved monopolistic or near monopolistic positions.

After looking critically at the American economy and at some familiar liberal assumptions John K. Galbraith has written. "The net of all this is that there must be some element of monopoly in an industry if it is to be progressive."[26] Does such an evaluation also apply to France?

Business concentration alone is not the answer to the urgent French problem of an optimum utilization of resources. But the clinging to established pattern, common to smaller producers, suggests that in many domains large enterprises, whether private or public, are better prepared to bring about technological inno-

[25] See Morazé, *op.cit.* (n. X-12), p. 97.
[26] Galbraith, *op.cit.* (n. IV-24), p. 93.

vations, high productivity, and lower production costs, all needed for a lasting improvement of living standards. In merely economic terms large scale capitalism of monopolistic and progressive bent can be of advantage to the country, and it is that kind of capitalism which the CNPF and some of its principal affiliates increasingly represent. The danger inherent in such development is not economic but political. How can this form of capitalism and the groups organized to uphold it be prevented from becoming "despotic"?[27] Will not the blurring of the dividing line between two important elite groups, the public bureaucrats and the businessmen, be detrimental to the processes of political democracy?

Everywhere the behaviour of a particular pressure group or of a coalition of groups may lead to an eclipse of representative government. A peril of a particular kind arises when an interest group does not merely exercise its influence from without but settles in a compartment of government, substituting its decisions for those of the state without submitting to the established constitutional controls.[28] If the collaboration between high bureaucracy and organized big business holds out some promise for the solution of the country's most pressing problems, its inherent dangers would be diminished if there existed a "countervailing power"[29] acting as a check on big business and on its supporters.

In other democracies, and the United States among them, such power is usually held by any or all of three forces: a dynamic, though usually not radical labor movement; large retail buying organizations, be they traditional capitalistic or, as in a few countries, cooperative concerns; and the bundle of unorganized interests which are as yet vaguely ascertained as "public opinion" but which are potentially able to assert their claims in organized forms whenever necessary.

In present-day France none of these forces are strong enough to provide, separately or together, the needed balance. Organ-

[27] The expression is that of Jeanneney, op.cit. (n. IV-26), who furnishes on pp. 261-62 a brief but excellent discussion of the dangers and opportunities of "bigness" in present-day France.

[28] For important remarks about the political consequences of such a situation, see Carl Schmitt, *Der Leviathan in der Staatslehre des Thomas Hobbes*, Hamburg, 1938, esp. p. 117 f., here quoted from Kaiser, op.cit. (n. I-20), p. 283.

[29] The term was, of course, coined and commented upon by Galbraith, op.cit. (n. IV-24).

ized labor has long ceased to hold the position assigned to it during the heady post-liberation days. If at times the working class movement was feared as a revolutionary force, and if at others it has advanced its cause through the support of friendly governments, it is seldom respected by the employers as a partner in decision making, or considered as a force to be reckoned with.

The weakness and backwardness of much of French commercial organization are notorious. Although some concentration has taken place lately, the number of small distribution points, far too large before the war, has substantially increased. But even the department and chain stores are generally unwilling and unable to use their buying power in a way that would represent consumer interests in better and cheaper products. (It is true that in an inflationary situation such as France has known for so long, the "countervailing power" of labor and of trade will always be considerably reduced.)

In the United States, it has been said, the corporation understands that it has a "constituency" to deal with, and that public opinion, especially because of its practical and non-doctrinaire character balances corporate power to a certain degree.[30] In France the distrust of big business is so deep that corporate capitalism has abandoned all appeals to its "constituents." But that distrust is entirely negative. There is an absence of shared beliefs which could correct the excesses of the "technocrats" and still leave intact the fruitful results of a collaboration between bureaucracy and organized big business.

The widespread skepticism which has settled on French public life draws strength from the suspected evils of pressure group activities. Although experiences with legislative regulation of lobbying have not been too encouraging elsewhere, in the French climate of universal distrust, systematic attempts to bring more light into the relationship between groups, parties and administration, would help to alleviate the suspicions and fears on which cynicism feeds. However, even the most adroitly designed technical devices will hardly be able to penetrate to the roots of the crisis.

Historical experiences within their lifetime have left French-

[30] Berle, op.cit. (n. VI-73), p. 56.

men convinced that there is no virtue in great upheavals. The World Wars had to be paid for in human and economic losses impossible to repair, so that the country emerged from them not as a victor but as a martyr. In 1936 and then again in 1944 almost bloodless revolutions aroused high hopes only to end in painful frustration, so that by now all groups, and the working class as much as any of them, have lost their revolutionary elan. But instead of inducing a search for other methods of social change, such loss has led to indifference towards all public policy. In present-day France a-political moods abound: technicians, veterans, intellectuals, shopkeepers, taxpayers, and many others see the reasons for their discontent in "politics."[31] It is well known that such attitudes can be used by demagogues for political ends; in the raw they hamper the emergence of any consensus in the community.

"In a relatively vigorous political system," David Truman has written, ". . . unorganized interests are dominant with sufficient frequency in the behaviour of enough important segments of the society so that, despite ambiguity and other restrictions, both the activity and the methods of organized interest groups are kept within broad limits."[32] Though today most Frenchmen belong to one or several organizations defending outdated privileges of one kind or another,[33] general skepticism prevents unorganized interests from ever becoming dominant.

Since the would-be insurrectional strikes which the communists attempted to launch in 1947 the only movement to sweep the country and pull thousands of Frenchmen out of social atomization has been the protest movement of Pierre Poujade who fought for the salvation of the most unproductive branches and the least developed regions of static France. But during the same period an inspector of finance, a member of the "technocratic

[31] See the pertinent remarks in Touchard, op.cit. (n. IV-34), p. 41.

[32] op.cit. (n. I-27), p. 515.

[33] On this point see Maurice Byé, "Les Pouvoirs publics devant les antagonismes économiques," op.cit. (n. V-37), p. 294. For the United States the point has often been made, especially by Truman, op.cit. (n. I-27), p. 157 ff., that overlapping membership by weakening group cohesion has the over-all effect of strengthening the unorganized or even the public interest. Additional investigations will be necessary to determine why the same phenomenon of overlapping membership has rarely the same effect in France.

camarilla" and prime-mover for a more sensible tax system, called for—revolution as France's last chance.[34]

In a world of permanent international conflict and crumbling empires the country will hardly be in a position to keep pace with its competitors if it does not adjust the political process to the demands of economic growth. While the need for change is widely recognized there is lack of agreement on what such adjustments should be, and how they might be effected. Which of the presently practiced rules of the game must be discarded? Which cannot be abandoned without endangering democratic liberties? Should it prove impossible to settle these questions by consent, either immobilism might continuously reproduce injustice, social cleavage and alienation from the community, or the unchecked impatience of the elite might produce some form of despotism.

Less drastic solutions are available at least for a time. In the recent past organized big business has sometimes shown restraint without being compelled to such behaviour by outside forces. Much will depend on whether it can maintain such an attitude in the face of contrary pressures from its membership. If a moderate prosperity were to continue without new jolts, caused by inflation, recession, international or colonial conflicts, diminished feelings of insecurity may result in a lessening of Malthusian practices by individuals or even some pressure groups. The population growth of the last decade has already provided a noticeable psychological uplift. Remarkable industrial achievements of the last years and an increase of productivity in both industry and agriculture prove encouraging to those Frenchmen who believe that also in their country economic progress and liberty are compatible. The borderlines between static and dynamic France have become more fluid, and in many fields the dynamic sectors are pushing the lines outward. Since the international situation weighs on every hope and act certain sectors

[34] See Maurice Lauré, *Révolution, dernière chance de la France*, Paris, 1954. The author, while in office, had set up the more stringent tax controls which brought the Poujade movement to the fore. After having become the bête noire of the small businessmen he was removed from his position. It is all the more significant that in an unprecedented move, the bulletin of the CNPF presented a lengthy summary of a recent treatise by M. Lauré on the tax system to its readers without comment "for purposes of information." See *Bulletin*, supplement to No. 154, December 1956, pp. 1-8.

of business seem to gird themselves for the more strenuous competition which a higher degree of European economic integration may bring about.

All this, however, will not be enough to free the government from the ordeal of being too weak to arbitrate and of being frequently paralyzed when the need for decisions arises. Succeeding cabinets have looked in vain to an informed public for the support of progressive policies. Without a new public spirit most institutional and economic reforms may prove as futile as many of them have in the past. The welfare state which France has long since become, cannot function properly as long as a large number of Frenchmen in all social categories deny its philosophy and flout its rules. To bring about widespread acceptance of the general premises on which state and society are to operate is everywhere a long and complicated process. In France prognostics of success or failure in solving a crisis situation have at all times been particularly hazardous because of the contradictions and surprising reversals of public and private attitudes.

In a celebrated passage of *Democracy in America* Alexis de Tocqueville rejected the idea that nations obey unchangeable laws fashioned from anterior events, from their race, or from the soil and climate of their country. However, as a historian of the *Ancien régime* he described the circle which seems to be traced around the French community in terms still true in our days:[35]

> "When I consider this nation in itself, I find it more extraordinary than any events in its history. Has there ever appeared in the world any nation so full of contrasts and so extreme in all its actions, more led by sentiment less by principles; always acting worse or better than expected . . . a people so unalterable in its primary instincts that it is recognizable in its portraits drawn 2,000 or 3,000 years ago, and at the same time so changeable in its daily thoughts and in its tastes, that it remains, as astonished as foreigners, at what it has just done. . . . Indocile by temperament, always adapting itself more easily to the arbitrary and even the violent rule of a prince than to the free and regular government of the chief citizens; today the declared enemy of all obedience, tomorrow employ-

[35] Alexis de Tocqueville, *L'Ancien Régime*, Oxford, 1949, pp. 220-21.

ing in servitude a sort of passion which the nations with the greatest gift for servitude cannot attain, led by a mere thread as long as no one resists; ungovernable as soon as the example of resistance is anywhere given; always thus deceiving its masters who fear it either too much or too little . . . more capable of heroism than of virtue, of genius than of good sense; more ready to conceive great designs than to carry through great enterprises; the most brilliant and the most dangerous of the nations of Europe and the best adapted to become by turn an object of admiration, of hatred, of pity, of terror, but never of indifference."

Who then would dare to predict the future of democracy in France?

## TABLE I

Illustrating the network of employers organizations with which a small concern is connected through its affiliation with a primary trade association

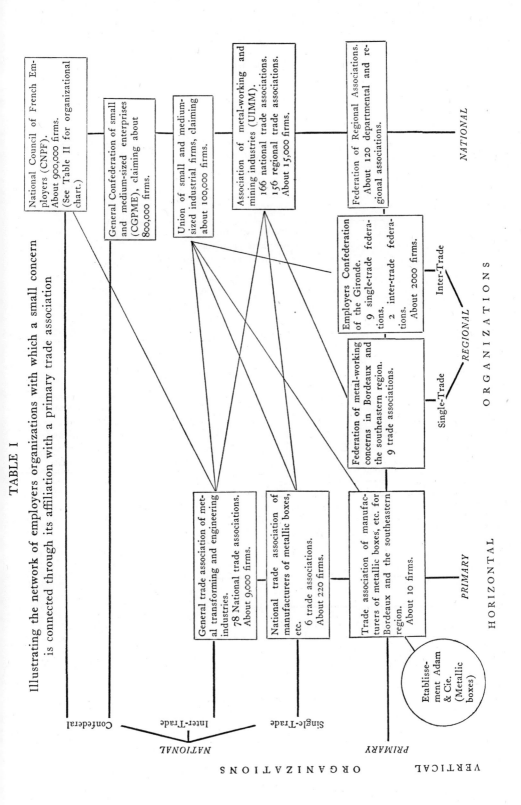

## TABLE II

### Organization Chart of the National Council of French Employers (CNPF)*

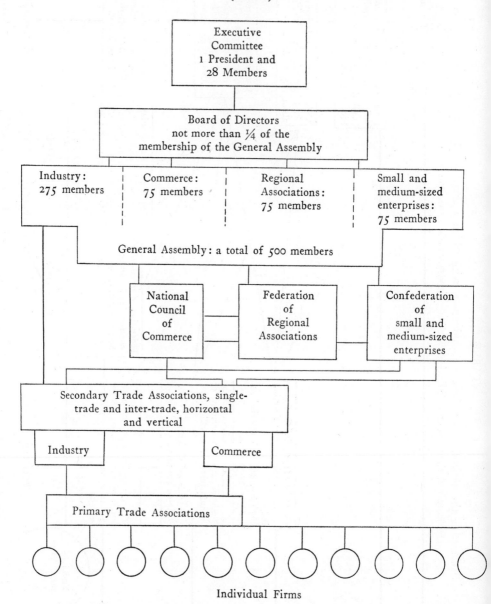

Individual Firms

\* Adapted from *Annuaire Général du Patronat Français, Années 1951-1952*, Paris, 1952.

## TABLE III

Number of secondary organizations in the French employers' movement.*

(Since the nomenclature of organizations often varies from one branch to the other this listing is not entirely uniform. It shows however the elaborate structuring of most branches of the employers' movement.)

I N D U S T R Y

| BRANCHES | UNIONS OR CONFEDERATIONS | FEDERATIONS | GROUPS | TRADE ASSOCIATIONS National | Regional |
|---|---|---|---|---|---|
| Furniture | | 1 | | 11 | 79 |
| Outfitters of ships | | 1 | | | |
| Art and creation (jewelry, furs, perfumes, *haute couture*, etc.) | | 8 | 10 | 36 | 115 |
| Insurance | | 2 | | | |
| Banks | | 1 | | | |
| Building and public works | | 3 | 2 | 26 | 213 |
| Wood | | 4 | 8 | 50 | 196 |
| Leather and hides | | 5 | 5 | 34 | 70 |
| Health & medical services | | 7 | | 11 | 118 |
| Agricultural and food industries | 2 | 40 | 44 | 54 | 431 |
| Chemical and allied industries | 2 | 5 | 7 | 111 | 135 |
| Printing | | 3 | | 39 | 117 |
| Hotel industry | 1 | 3 | | | 110 |
| Textiles | 1 | 11 | 11 | 101 | 171 |
| Building materials | | 3 | 3 | 40 | 43 |
| Metal industries | 1 | 21 | 11 | 158 | 206 |
| Non-nationalized coal mines | | 1 | | | |
| Non-nationalized public utilities | | 1 | | | |
| Salterns | | 1 | | 1 | 3 |
| Paper and allied products | 1 | 3 | 3 | 22 | 28 |
| Photography | | 2 | | 9 | |
| Amusement | | 1 | 4 | 7 | 21 |
| Transport and storage | 1 | 18 | 17 | 8 | 208 |
| Glass | | 1 | 1 | 4 | 4 |
| Clothing | 1 | 5 | 5 | 15 | 148 |
| Various industries | | 10 | | 8 | 54 |
| TOTAL INDUSTRY | 10 | 161 | 131 | 745 | 2,470 |

(continued on following page)

* Compiled from *Annuaire Général du Patronat Français, 1955*, Paris, 1955.

## TABLE III (continued)

### COMMERCE

| BRANCHES | UNIONS OR CONFEDER- ATIONS | FEDER- ATIONS | GROUPS | TRADE ASSOCIATIONS National | Regional |
|---|---|---|---|---|---|
| *Trade in foodstuffs* | 1 | | | | |
| Wholesale trade | | 19 | 23 | 19 | 911 |
| Retail trade | 1 | 16 | 1 | 6 | 354 |
| Food chain stores | | | | 2 | |
| *Trade in other than foodstuffs* | | | | | |
| Wholesale trade | | | 10 | 39 | 190 |
| Retail trade | | | 11 | 32 | 469 |
| Trade in coal and other fuels | 1 | 3 | 2 | 1 | 108 |
| Chain stores | | | | 2 | |
| Department stores | | 1 | | 5 | 21 |
| Brokerage, etc. | | 4 | | | |
| TOTAL COMMERCE | 3 | 43 | 47 | 106 | 2,053 |
| TOTAL INDUSTRY | 10 | 161 | 131 | 745 | 2,470 |
| TOTAL INDUSTRY AND COMMERCE | 13 | 204 | 178 | 851 | 4,523 |

# TABLE IV

Manufacturing and commercial establishments (exclusive of nationalized concerns) classified according to the number of wage earners: 1950*

| BRANCHES | TOTAL NUMBER OF ESTABLISHMENTS | NUMBER OF ESTABLISHMENTS EMPLOYING: | | | | | | | | |
|---|---|---|---|---|---|---|---|---|---|---|
| | | 0 to 5 | 6 to 10 | 11 to 20 | 21 to 50 | 51 to 100 | 101 to 200 | 201 to 500 | Over 500 | Not declared |
| **I N D U S T R Y** | | | | | | | | | | |
| Metal mining | 320 | 109 | 23 | 21 | 31 | 22 | 22 | 41 | 20 | 31 |
| Blast furnaces, steel works and rolling mills | 1,407 | 505 | 131 | 146 | 169 | 91 | 83 | 100 | 112 | 70 |
| Foundry, heavy machinery | 14,881 | 9,046 | 1,372 | 1,278 | 1,391 | 518 | 357 | 215 | 123 | 581 |
| Engineering and manufacturing of metallic articles | 93,319 | 83,883 | 2,426 | 1,923 | 1,476 | 479 | 247 | 150 | 58 | 2,677 |
| Shipbuilding | 1,727 | 984 | 166 | 142 | 152 | 76 | 44 | 24 | 29 | 110 |
| Automobiles and bicycles | 59,762 | 52,678 | 2,566 | 1,469 | 859 | 228 | 73 | 44 | 46 | 1,799 |
| Aircraft | 346 | 112 | 36 | 31 | 33 | 26 | 22 | 30 | 39 | 17 |
| Electric machinery, appliances | 14,459 | 11,605 | 663 | 602 | 532 | 230 | 104 | 87 | 62 | 574 |
| Precision and optical instruments; watchmaking | 18,182 | 15,888 | 562 | 452 | 344 | 138 | 59 | 38 | 14 | 687 |
| Jewelry, goldsmiths, etc. | 4,586 | 3,681 | 291 | 255 | 153 | 58 | 14 | 5 | – | 129 |
| Glass and glass products | 2,002 | 1,261 | 235 | 187 | 115 | 52 | 47 | 31 | 20 | 54 |
| Building materials | 8,183 | 5,578 | 949 | 635 | 424 | 120 | 40 | 18 | 7 | 412 |
| Ceramics and preparation of building materials | 11,097 | 7,731 | 944 | 748 | 659 | 213 | 162 | 75 | 15 | 550 |
| Building and public works | 228,675 | 193,568 | 10,458 | 7,594 | 6,166 | 2,145 | 901 | 423 | 90 | 7,330 |
| Various extracting industries | 486 | 187 | 73 | 79 | 60 | 29 | 11 | 6 | 9 | 32 |
| Chemicals and allied products | 10,951 | 6,215 | 1,167 | 1,002 | 914 | 384 | 239 | 146 | 82 | 802 |
| Rubber and rubber products | 2,794 | 2,137 | 194 | 144 | 111 | 33 | 30 | 23 | 18 | 104 |
| Bakeries | 61,969 | 58,827 | 1,130 | 394 | 166 | 63 | 22 | 13 | 4 | 1,350 |
| Other food industries | 36,090 | 27,384 | 2,529 | 1,807 | 1,460 | 506 | 267 | 125 | 27 | 1,985 |
| Textiles and allied industries | 32,125 | 21,416 | 2,149 | 2,106 | 2,435 | 1,047 | 766 | 533 | 208 | 1,465 |

(continued on following page)

## TABLE IV (continued)

| BRANCHES | TOTAL NUMBER OF ESTABLISHMENTS | NUMBER OF ESTABLISHMENTS EMPLOYING: | | | | | | | | |
|---|---|---|---|---|---|---|---|---|---|---|
| | | 0 to 5 | 6 to 10 | 11 to 20 | 21 to 50 | 51 to 100 | 101 to 200 | 201 to 500 | Over 500 | Not declared |
| **INDUSTRY** | | | | | | | | | | |
| Apparel and other finished products from fabrics | 109,576 | 96,754 | 3,913 | 2,891 | 1,997 | 658 | 249 | 108 | 16 | 2,990 |
| Leather and hides | 79,151 | 71,392 | 1,854 | 1,498 | 1,309 | 471 | 201 | 71 | 19 | 2,336 |
| Wood and furniture | 60,019 | 49,776 | 3,293 | 2,314 | 1,622 | 379 | 109 | 32 | 4 | 2,490 |
| Paper and allied products | 3,200 | 1,540 | 367 | 362 | 440 | 166 | 131 | 85 | 18 | 91 |
| Printing, press, publishing | 20,553 | 16,287 | 1,316 | 1,059 | 716 | 263 | 114 | 61 | 29 | 708 |
| Trucking | 54,891 | 46,601 | 1,690 | 1,251 | 766 | 300 | 67 | 26 | 8 | 4,182 |
| Other industries | 15,293 | 11,726 | 1,059 | 877 | 617 | 169 | 64 | 26 | 4 | 751 |
| TOTAL INDUSTRIES | 946,044 | 796,871 | 41,556 | 31,267 | 25,117 | 8,864 | 4,445 | 2,536 | 1,081 | 34,307 |
| **COMMERCE** | | | | | | | | | | |
| Food, agricultural products | 355,079 | 326,432 | 5,732 | 2,950 | 1,414 | 487 | 102 | 62 | 24 | 17,876 |
| Textile, clothing and leather | 105,133 | 95,636 | 2,911 | 1,542 | 723 | 265 | 21 | 7 | 1 | 4,027 |
| Ambulant trade | 99,207 | 93,418 | 285 | 824 | 412 | 406 | 2 | – | – | 3,860 |
| Other commerce | 156,212 | 136,280 | 6,274 | 3,703 | 2,063 | 719 | 127 | 54 | 21 | 6,971 |
| Hotels† and tobacco | 315,023 | 297,573 | 3,182 | 1,844 | 888 | 403 | 50 | 22 | 2 | 11,059 |
| Banks and insurance | 10,307 | 5,734 | 1,468 | 961 | 679 | 338 | 146 | 78 | 32 | 871 |
| Entertainment and movies | 7,677 | 5,026 | 1,007 | 626 | 267 | 59 | 29 | 12 | 4 | 647 |
| Health and medical services | 77,229 | 72,512 | 1,230 | 799 | 372 | 169 | 47 | 19 | 4 | 2,077 |
| TOTAL COMMERCE | 1,125,867 | 1,032,611 | 22,089 | 13,249 | 6,818 | 2,846 | 524 | 254 | 88 | 47,388 |
| TOTAL COMMERCE AND INDUSTRY | 2,071,911 | 1,829,482 | 63,645 | 44,516 | 31,935 | 11,710 | 4,969 | 2,790 | 1,169 | 81,695 |

* Source: Institut National de la Statistique et des Etudes Economiques, *Bulletin Mensuel de Statistique*, Supplement April-June 1952, pp. 40 ff.
† Including restaurants and taverns.

# GLOSSARY OF ABBREVIATIONS

ACADI. Association de Cadres Dirigeants de l'Industrie pour le Progrès Social et Economique

ARS. Groupe Indépendant d'Action Républicaine et Sociale

CADIPPE. Comité d'Action pour le Développement de l'Intéressement du Personnel et de la Productivité des Entreprises

CARHEC. Comité pour l'Amélioration des Relations Humaines dans l'Economie

CCOP. Comité Central de l'Organisation Professionnelle

CEGOS. Commission Générale d'Organisation Scientifique

CEPEC. Centre d'Etudes Politiques et Civiques

CFIE. Conseil des Fédérations Industrielles d'Europe

CFP. Confédération Française des Profession. *Also* Centre Français du Patronat Chrétien

CFTC. Confédération des Travailleurs Chrétiens

CGPF. Confédération de la Production Française. *Also* Confédération du Patronat Français

CGPME. Confédération Générale des Petites et Moyennes Entreprises

CGT. Confédération Générale du Travail

CGT-FO. Confédération Générale du Travail-Force Ouvrière

CIO. Congress of Industrial Organisations

CJP. Centre des Jeunes Patrons

CNC. Conseil National du Commerce

CNOF. Comité National de l'Organisation Française

CNPF. Conseil National du Patronat Français

ECA. European Cooperation Administration

EDC. European Defense Community

EPU. European Payments Union

ILO. International Labour Office

JP. Jeunes Patrons

MRP. Mouvement Républicain Populaire

MSA. Mutual Security Administration

NAM. National Association of Manufacturers

OCM. Organisation Civile et Militaire

OEEC. Organization for European Economic Cooperation

PPF. Parti Populaire Français

RGR. Rassemblement des Gauches Républicaines (Radical-Socialists)

RPF. Rassemblement du Peuple Français

SEDEIS. Société d'Etudes et de Documentation Economiques, Industrielles et Sociales

SFIO. Section Française de l'Internationale Ouvrière (Socialists)

SNCF. Société Nationale des Chemins-de-fer Français

UCE.ACT. Union des Chefs d'Entreprise pour l'Association du Capital et du Travail. *Also* Union des Chefs d'Entreprise. Action pour des Structures Humaines

UIMM. Union des Industries Métallurgiques et Minières

X. Ecole Polytechnique

# INDEX